Looking at the
Doctrine & Covenants
Again for the Very First Time

Looking at the
Doctrine & Covenants
Again for the Very First Time

A Study Guide for Families, Organized by Location

Second Edition

James W. McConkie II

TEMPLE HILL BOOKS

Interspersed throughout the text of this book are QR codes, small squares with a black and white matrix pattern. Pointing a smartphone with a QRC app at the square will take the reader to a short YouTube video of the author commenting on and explaining parts of this book. Install the free *QRC Reader and Barcode Scanner* app on the phone, open it, point the phone's camera lens at the square in the book, and the phone will automatically load the video.

Deseret Book has published this book as an e-book with the same videos explaining some of the important aspects of the Doctrine and Covenants. It is available through Deseret Book, Kindle, and others.

All photographs in this book are used courtesy of Trevor K. DeVore and Greg R. DeVore Jr.

Copyright © 2010, 2017 by James W. McConkie II. All rights reserved.

Printed in the United States of America.

ISBN 978-1-4341-0409-0

The views expressed in this book are the responsibility of the author and do not necessarily represent the position of the publisher. The reader alone is responsible for the use of any ideas or information provided by this book.

Published by Temple Hill Books, an imprint of The Editorium

Temple Hill Books™, the Temple Hill Books logo, and The Editorium™ are trademarks of The Editorium, LLC

The Editorium, LLC
West Valley City, UT 84128-3917
templehillbooks.com
templehillbooks@editorium.com

Contents

Page Location of Section Commentary	ix
Acknowledgments	xiii
A Resource for the Family	xv

1 Introduction — 1

1	How to Use This Study Guide	3
2	Anchor Sections	8
3	Chronology and Summary by Location	10
4	Chronological by Time	33

2 The Big Picture — 37

5	The Importance of Context	39
6	The Doctrine and Covenants As a Reflection of Mormon History	44
7	"The Kingdom of God or Nothing"	54
8	The Doctrine and Covenants and Systemic Injustice	60
9	A Book of Revelations	66
10	The Doctrine and Covenants: The Mormon Metanarrative	76

3 The Manchester, New York, Period — 83

11 Beginnings: Manchester, New York, Period, 1823–1830 — 85

12 The Big Questions: Manchester, New York, Period — 89

13 The Sacred Grove — 93

14 The Smith Home — 105

4 The Harmony, Pennsylvania, Period — 123

15 The Book of Mormon: Harmony, Pennsylvania, December 1827–August 1830 — 125

16 The Big Questions: Harmony, Pennsylvania — 127

17 Joseph Smith Jr. Home — 130

18 Susquehanna River: Harmony, Pennsylvania — 178

5 The Fayette, New York, Period — 183

19 Organization of the Church: Fayette, New York, July 1829–January 1831 — 185

20 The Big Questions: Fayette, New York — 189

21 Whitmer Home — 191

6 The Kirtland, Ohio, Period — 239

22 Building a Church Organization: Kirtland, Ohio, 1831–1837 — 241

23 The Big Questions: Kirtland, Ohio — 244

24 Whitney Home: Kirtland, Ohio, February 1831–December 1831 — 249

25 Morley Farm: Kirtland, Ohio, March 1831–September 1831 — 276

26 Whitney Store: Kirtland, Ohio, September 1832–December 1833 — 324

27 Joseph Smith Home: Kirtland, Ohio, February 1834-December 1835 — 413

28	Printing House: Kirtland, Ohio, March 1835–August 1835	430
29	Kirtland Temple: Kirtland, Ohio, March 1836–July 1837	446
30	John Johnson Home: Hiram, Ohio, October 1831–August 1832	468

7 The Missouri Period — 529

31	The Establishment of Zion: The Prophet Joseph's Trip to the Promised Land	531
32	The Big Questions: Independence, Jackson County, Missouri	534
33	Joshua Lewis Home: Jackson County, Missouri, July–August 1831	537
34	Setting Zion in Order: Jackson County (Independence), Missouri, April 1832	558
35	Zion's Camp: Summer 1834	567
36	The Saints Forced Farther Away from Zion to Far West: March–July 1838	574
37	Lessons Learned about the Nature of God in Missouri: Joseph Smith Incarcerated, Liberty Jail, Missouri, March 1839	618

8 The Nauvoo Period — 633

38	At the Point of a Gun: Nauvoo, Illinois, January 1841–June 1844	635
39	The Big Question: Nauvoo, Illinois	637
40	Nauvoo, Illinois: January 19, 1841–July 12, 1843	640
41	Among Friends at Ramus: Ramus, Illinois, April and May 1843	692

9 Winter Quarters and Beyond — 713

42	The Big Question: Winter Quarters and Salt Lake City, Utah	715
43	Winter Quarters: January 14, 1847	719
44	Salt Lake City, Utah: October 6, 1890–June 1978	724

Conclusion	739
Bibliography	742
Index	750

Page Location of Section Commentary

Section	Page	Section	Page
Section 1	470	Section 36	229
Section 2	105	Section 37	232
Section 3	130	Section 38	233
Section 4	134	Section 39	236
Section 5	135	Section 40	236
Section 6	137	Section 41	249
Section 7	140	Section 42	254
Section 8	142	Section 43	267
Section 9	152	Section 44	271
Section 10	156	Section 45	276
Section 11	161	Section 46	282
Section 12	163	Section 47	289
Section 13	178	Section 48	290
Section 14	192	Section 49	292
Section 15	192	Section 50	295
Section 16	192	Section 51	464
Section 17	193	Section 52	300
Section 18	196	Section 53	305
Section 19	110	Section 54	307
Section 20	200	Section 55	309
Section 21	210	Section 56	310
Section 22	117	Section 57	537
Section 23	120	Section 58	539
Section 24	164	Section 59	547
Section 25	168	Section 60	551
Section 26	173	Section 61	552
Section 27	174	Section 62	555
Section 28	213	Section 63	313
Section 29	217	Section 64	317
Section 30	219	Section 65	475
Section 31	219	Section 66	477
Section 32	222	Section 67	481
Section 33	226	Section 68	486
Section 34	228	Section 69	489
Section 35	229	Section 70	272

Page Location of Section Commentary

Section 71	490	Section 106	425
Section 72	273	Section 107	430
Section 73	492	Section 108	427
Section 74	493	Section 109	446
Section 75	523	Section 110	454
Section 76	495	Section 111	605
Section 77	505	Section 112	459
Section 78	508	Section 113	578
Section 79	513	Section 114	581
Section 80	515	Section 115	583
Section 81	517	Section 116	599
Section 82	560	Section 117	588
Section 83	564	Section 118	592
Section 84	324	Section 119	595
Section 85	339	Section 120	598
Section 86	343	Section 121	621
Section 87	345	Section 122	627
Section 88	349	Section 123	629
Section 89	362	Section 124	640
Section 90	367	Section 125	660
Section 91	372	Section 126	663
Section 92	374	Section 127	667
Section 93	375	Section 128	667
Section 94	387	Section 129	674
Section 95	390	Section 130	693
Section 96	393	Section 131	702
Section 97	395	Section 132	678
Section 98	398	Section 133	522
Section 99	520	Section 134	440
Section 100	525	Section 135	707
Section 101	406	Section 136	719
Section 102	413	Section 137	462
Section 103	416	Section 138	726
Section 104	422	Declaration 1	708
Section 105	568	Declaration 2	714

"Our children will rise up and call us blessed; and generations yet unborn will dwell with peculiar delight upon the scenes that we have passed through, the privations that we have endured; the untiring zeal that we have manifested; the all but insurmountable difficulties that we have overcome in laying the foundation of a work that brought about the glory and blessing which they will realize . . . to bring about the destruction of the powers of darkness, the renovation of the earth, the glory of God, and the salvation of the human family."—Joseph Smith (*Teachings*, 232.)

Acknowledgments

Over the years I have been blessed with many good friends who have been an inspiration and support to me and have expanded my understanding and commitment to the gospel of Jesus Christ. First and foremost among them, of course, is my gifted wife and companion, Judith. Among my other dear friends who have been of real help to me in compiling these materials are some of my confidants—Richard Lambert, Brent Ward, and Bob Stephenson—and my law partner of over thirty-five years, Brad Parker. At this point in my life I have lost track of the number of times I have broken bread with them over lunch discussing Mormonism and its applications. Their encouragement has been a consummate blessing in my life. Finally, I am also indebted to Jay Parry, who carefully edited this text and offered many salient suggestions that greatly strengthened my modest efforts to put pen to paper and find expression for the ideas herein.

The real impetus for writing this text are my mother, our children, and their spouses; I am indebted to all of them for the many keen insights they have shared with me over the years during study sessions, meals, and on family outings. They are faithful and true adults who will continue to pass on to their descendants knowledge and devotion centered in the Lord Jesus Christ.

Given the nature and scope of this commentary on the Doctrine and Covenants, I have not been able to treat many complex issues in depth but instead have provided some preliminary observations to prompt further analysis and thinking. Sometimes there are different points of view on some issues. I try to present some of the alternative interpretations as well as my own for the reader's consideration. I believe that we all benefit from seeking information from a wide variety of sources in our search for truth and understanding.

A Resource for the Family

When we were raising our family years ago my wife and I decided to study the gospel with each of our children one-on-one. We came to this conclusion for a number of reasons. First, we noticed that differences in our children's ages made it difficult in a family home evening setting to study the gospel in depth with the older children and still entertain the younger ones. Second, during various stages of family life, parental attempts to formally teach our children the gospel were resisted by some members of the family, which sometimes turned family home evening into family home argument. Therefore, a more tailor-made approach suited to the individual interests and needs of each of our children seemed reasonable.

Our approach was to invite each of our children, beginning at age twelve, to meet with me for an hour or so once each week to study the gospel. I gave each child a leather-bound edition of the standard works with his or her name inscribed in gold on the front cover. The first year we studied the Doctrine and Covenants, the second year the Book of Mormon, the third year the New Testament, the fourth year the Old Testament, and the fifth year we returned to the Doctrine and Covenants. Each year Mormon history books were assigned, along with other enrichment materials designed to provide context for scripture study. In one instance we studied anti-Mormon literature with our oldest son because he was on his high school debate team and wanted to understand what our detractors claimed.

We felt like the Doctrine and Covenants was a good place to begin and end our course of study because, unlike the other standard works, the Doctrine and Covenants can easily be structured topically, and therefore it provided a road map for gospel study. Many of the sections were given in answer to specific questions and addressed specific topics. For this reason, it was easy to identify key sections that addressed basic gospel subjects such as the Godhead (section 130), faith (section 20), repentance (section 19), and baptism (section 20). Other essential gospel subjects were also addressed, such as life after death (section 76 and section 138), Sabbath day observance (section 59), and marriage (section 131 and 132). We asked each of our children to memorize the section number associated with some of the more important subjects found in the Doctrine and Covenants. Every once in a while we would have a pop quiz around the dinner table. I would call out a section number, and one of our children would identify what gospel subject was covered there. The winner was rewarded with a five dollar bill.

This approach helped our children identify *anchor sections* associated with key gospel doctrines. It also became a simple cross-referencing method. Sites for similar themes found in the other standard works were noted in the margins of the appropriate anchor sections. In this way the Doctrine and Covenants functioned as a way to systematically arrange gospel knowledge around modern revelation.

Because the quality of education is bound to vary in a lay institution such as the Church, we felt it was helpful for us to become personally involved in our children's spiritual education. You never know what your children are learning at Church unless you ask them. Also, the scriptures themselves make it clear that "parents [who] have children in Zion" are to teach them the basic doctrines of "repentance, faith in Christ the Son of the living God, and of baptism and the gift of the Holy Ghost." (D&C 68:25.) Finally, it became away of initiating conversations with our children about values, important ideas and different points of view.

It was with these thoughts in mind that we have put together this study guide. It is intended for our children to use with our grandchildren. But, perhaps others will also find it a useful tool for studying the gospel with their children or as part of their own personal study of the gospel.

In retrospect, studying the gospel with our children has had other obvious benefits. It has stimulated an interest in education generally and helped our children develop their analytical skills. It has made searching for truth and exploring ideas on a wide variety of fronts a natural part of family life. It has facilitated family conversations that have and will continue to increase our awareness and appreciation for life. It has given our children the opportunity to know what we believe and to hear our testimonies and know of our struggles in the context of a "household of faith." Most importantly, it has helped our children realize that learning the gospel is essential in order to live the gospel, an idea peculiarly associated with the teachings of Joseph Smith. He said,

> A man is saved no faster than he gets knowledge.... Knowledge saves a man; and in the world of spirits no man can be exalted but by knowledge ... so long as a man will not give heed to the commandments he must abide without salvation. If a man has knowledge he can be saved; although he has

A Resource for the Family

been guilty of great sins, he will be punished for them. But when he consents to obey the Gospel, whether here or in the world of spirits, he is saved.[1]

In our view, knowledge about the gospel reinforces and motivates our children to live the gospel. Gospel study facilitates the spirit of revelation, which increases testimony and enlightens the mind. (See D&C 93:25.) This reinforcing relationship between knowledge and obedience is a principle of the gospel that leads to a sure conviction of its truthfulness.

It should be clearly understood that in writing this study guide I do not consider myself a scholar but rather a reporter. Of necessity I have relied on secondhand sources and the opinions of others. In tracking some of the history, I have paraphrased what other capable historians have said. When I do this I have tried to indicate where the material comes from and give credit where credit is due. Both Judith and I hope, however, that this volume may benefit our grandchildren and others who are making an effort to understand the Doctrine and Covenants and its implications. Finally, the contents of this study guide have been written as a resource for adults. Therefore, it will be necessary for parents to pick and choose what parts of this study guide are useful and appropriate when teaching their children. This will, of course, depend upon the age, interest, and maturity of the child.

In retrospect, we do have some regrets about the way in which we went about teaching our children the gospel. We grew up in a world where men's and women's roles were more carefully defined, a world in which men's roles were dominant and women's roles diminished. It was not until some time later that we realized gender equality was an important issue in family life. Consequently, many years ago, when we began this study process, it seemed natural that I should be the instructor and almost exclusively conduct our study sessions. This has been a great disservice to our children, who missed the opportunity to study with their mother, who has a remarkable knowledge, understanding, and testimony of the gospel. If we had it to do over again, we would change all of this and jointly teach our children the gospel. The irony of this was that, as part of a ward program, Judith studied the gospel with other children in the ward, one-on-one—but more occasionally with her own children.

Although I have taken the laboring oar in putting pen to paper, the overall organization, the "big questions," and many of the insights and ideas come directly from my best friend and companion, Judith. She and I have taught Doctrine and Covenants courses together and separately in the Church Institute system and in the Church Education System for

---

1. Minutes of General Conference, April 1844.

over a decade. She is a master teacher and has the ability and talent to organize materials in meaningful ways for students. I am the beneficiary of her unique gifts and abilities. We have also had the opportunity to be teachers on a number of Church history tours. All of this has facilitated so much discussion and interaction between us that most of the ideas in this study guide are not mine or hers but ours. Although she insists that her name not be cited as author, it well could be. Her encouragement and thoughts on the Doctrine and Covenants have been invaluable. I simply could not have done it without her.

Part 1

Introduction

Chapter 1

How to Use This Study Guide

Purpose of This Study Guide

The purpose of this study guide is fivefold:
1. To put forward a suggested method for parents to teach their children the gospel;
2. To provide an easy way to organize gospel knowledge;
3. To make available contextual materials to enrich understanding and appreciation for the Doctrine and Covenants;
4. To provide some thoughts on how particular verses of scripture in the Doctrine and Covenants may be interpreted; and
5. To act as a travel guide for those who venture out on a Church history tour.

How This Study Guide Is Organized

This study guide is organized by geographic location, places where revelations in the Doctrine and Covenants were received.[1] For instance, in chapter 2, "The Manchester, New York, Period," the reader will find all of the revelations Joseph Smith received in the log cabin home on the Smith family farm—section 2 (Moroni on the fulness of priesthood), section 19 (atonement), section 22 (baptism), and section 23 (advice to new members of the Church). This approach makes it easier to talk about the context for each of the sections by studying some of the events that took place

---

1. The idea of organizing this study guide by location developed for two reasons. First, my wife, Judith, and I lead Church history tours focused on where each of the revelations in the Doctrine and Covenants was received. Second, we were impressed with a web site authored by Steve Mortensen that organized the sections of the Doctrine and Covenants by place. See www.dcsites.com.

there. There are some excellent maps and pictures of historic sites located at the back of the Doctrine and Covenants.

The study guide is further organized around some of the major issues that confronted the Church at particular times in its history. These issues, expressed here in the form of questions, are referred to as the *big questions*. They are:

1. Manchester, New York, Period: Does God hear me? What makes a credible witness? Who can be a worthy vessel?

2. Harmony, Pennsylvania, Period: What is revelation? How does a person receive revelation? What is translation? Why John the Baptist?

3. Fayette, New York, Period: Why a Church? What is the structure of the Church?

4. Kirtland, Ohio, Period: How do we live together and build a community now that we have gathered? What is the structure of the Church?

5. Independence, Missouri, Period: What and where is Zion? How do we deal with disappointment and unrealized promises?

6. Nauvoo, Illinois, Period: How shall we be saved?

7. Winter Quarters and Beyond: How shall we survive?

Finally, the Doctrine and Covenants discusses all of the key doctrines of the restored gospel. We have attempted to identify the most important doctrinal sections and refer to them as *anchor sections*. The motivated student is encouraged to memorize the *anchor section* reference. In this way, the student can conveniently organize his or her gospel knowledge around the revelations in the Doctrine and Covenants.

For example, try to remember where in the scriptures you read something on the topic of the atonement. If you cannot remember several places where you have read about the atonement, can you recall one? If you cannot remember one, do you know where you could possibly go to find out what the scriptures have to say on the topic of the atonement?

What next?

All that searching may be easier, or at least more meaningful, if you had an organizational structure for your own study.

1. Realize that Joseph Smith received the revelations in the Doctrine and Covenants according to his and other's requests for knowledge from the Lord about doctrinal concepts or practical problems confronting the early Saints. Therefore, the Doctrine and Covenants is unique in its organization by major topics.

2. Therefore, if you memorize where a particular gospel topic is discussed in the Doctrine and Covenants, whenever you read something applicable to that topic or principle, you can note that topic in the margins

of the page where the particular section begins. With that approach, you need to recall only one section number to locate what the scriptures have to say about any given subject.

To illustrate, if you need to remember something about the Aaronic Priesthood, just remember that section 13 records the receipt of this priesthood by Joseph and Oliver Cowdery on May 1829 and sets forth the powers and purposes associated with it. In the margins write additional references you come across that remind you of other information contained in the scriptures about this topic. Rather than trying to remember everything and every place you have read about the Aaronic Priesthood, now you need to remember only section 13. In other words, use the doctrinal *anchor sections* in the Doctrine and Covenants to cross-reference your gospel understanding.

The Study Method Recommended

Parent preparation. This book is a study guide written for parents who intend to study the gospel with their children. For that reason, it is anticipated that parents will familiarize themselves with the material and adapt it to the age and maturity level of their children.

Start your course of study no later than age twelve. It is recommended that parents begin this course of study no later than their child's twelfth birthday. Twelve is a natural transition point for LDS children. Girls enter the Young Women's program and boys receive the priesthood. If you wait even a year longer, you will find that your children will resist studying the gospel in favor of being with their peer group. If you start early, then gospel study will be a natural part of family life. Your children will be less likely to question the approach and more likely to look forward to gospel study.

Begin and end each study session with prayer. Parents should begin and end each session with prayer. Invite the Spirit into your discussions. Prayer places you and your children in a more receptive mood for studying the gospel.

Study one-on-one. Parents should study with one child at a time. From a pedagogical perspective, the smaller the student-teacher ratio, the more the student learns. Therefore, one-on-one affords the best opportunity for your child to become a student of the gospel. In larger families, however, this may not be possible.

This is not the time and place for parents to deliver a monologue on their understanding of the scriptures. Use the Socratic method. Ask questions so that you can gauge whether or not your child understands the material. Analyze the text together, paying particular attention to detail and the meaning of words. Establish context. Interpret the scriptures precisely and accurately. Developing such analytical ability with your child will not only facilitate better gospel study, but it will also have a carry-over effect in school.

Study sessions should last about an hour. Each session should last about an hour. The first half hour should be devoted to one of the *anchor sections* of the Doctrine and Covenants. The second half hour should be devoted to a discussion of a reading assignment from a Church history text[1] or a basic gospel text like *The Articles of Faith*, by James E. Talmage.

Study on a weekly basis at the same time. Parents should study with their children weekly. Consistency is important. Set aside a particular time each week when gospel study can be planned for and anticipated. This way, gospel study becomes part of the family routine.

Give reading assignments. At the conclusion of each study period, assign the next *anchor section* and your child's supplemental reading assignment. Some of the *anchor sections* are too long for one session and should be divided and discussed over a longer period of time. The amount assigned depends upon the maturity and capability of each of your children.

Test your children on the anchor sections. At some time during the study session, test your children on the *anchor sections* previously studied; you can ask them in what section a particular doctrine or principle is taught or you can call out an *anchor section* number and ask them to tell you the doctrines or principles that are discussed therein. Pop quizzes at the dinner table during the week can also be fun if they are done in the right spirit.

Both parents should teach and study with their children. We suggest that both parents teach the materials. The father may teach the materials for one year and the mother the next. Or you may wish to teach together. A team approach will help sons and daughters recognize that both parents believe it is essential to know and study the gospel.

Future courses of study. After you and your children have concluded your study of the Doctrine and Covenants, it is recommended that you study the Book of Mormon the second year, the New Testament the third year, and the Old Testament and Pearl of Great Price the fourth year. During the fifth year, return to a study the Doctrine and Covenants. Help your children read as widely and comprehensively as possible.[2]

Be flexible. The foregoing are suggestions only. Parents know what works

---

1. See the bibliography for a list of suggestions that may be appropriate depending on the age and maturity of your child.

2. During this course of study, you can delve into more than just the *anchor sections*. One possibility is to have your children read the *History of The Church of Jesus Christ of Latter-day Saints* (6 volumes) or *Comprehensive History of the Church* (6 volumes). Or very good alternative sources are Richard Bushman's *Joseph Smith: Rough Stone Rolling* or *Church*

How to Use This Study Guide

best for their children. Adjust and redesign until you get it right for your own family. Modify the curriculum to the level of your children.

History in the Fulness of Times, which can be read in place of the multivolume official histories of the Church.

Chapter 2

Anchor Sections

As mentioned in the previous chapter, "How to Use This Study Guide," most of the key doctrines of the restored gospel are addressed in various sections in the Doctrine and Covenants. We have attempted to identify the most important doctrinal sections and refer to them as *anchor sections*. The motivated student is encouraged to memorize the list of *anchor sections*. In this way, the student can conveniently organize his or her gospel knowledge around the revelations in the Doctrine and Covenants by cross referencing in the margins of the anchor sections other scriptures on the same topic.

THE ANCHOR SECTIONS

- 1   Preface
- 8   Revelation defined
- 9   How to get revelation
- 13 Restoration of the Aaronic Priesthood
- 19 Atonement (Alma 42)
- 20 Church organization
- 27 Restoration of the Melchizedek Priesthood
- 42 Commandments/Law of Consecration
- 43 Revelation for the Church comes through constituted authorities
- 45 Second Coming
- 46 Gifts of the Spirit
- 50 False revelation/Teach by the Spirit
- 56 Poor and rich/God may revoke a commandment
- 58 Be anxiously engaged in good causes
- 59 Sabbath day

Anchor Sections

64	Forgive others
67	Rend the veil
68	Parents should teach their children
76	Three degrees of glory
78	Be equal in temporal things
84	Oath and covenant of the priesthood
88	Calling and election/Light of Christ/Resurrection/Learn doctrine/School of the prophets
89	Word of Wisdom
93	All may see Jesus/Men and women can become like God/Truth/Teach your children
98	Renounce war and proclaim peace
102	High council
104	Rich and poor
107	Melchizedek Priesthood
109	Kirtland Temple dedicatory prayer
110	Restoration of priesthood keys
119	Tithing
121	Use of priesthood power
122	Tribulation
124	Temple endowment
128	Baptism for the dead
129	Discerning spirits
130	God has a body
131	Marriage
132	Marriage
134	On government
138	Spirit world

Chapter 3

Chronology and Summary by Location

PART ONE: THE MANCHESTER, NEW YORK, PERIOD

The Beginning (1823–1830)

The Big Questions

Does God hear me?
What makes a credible witness?
Who can be a "worthy vessel"?

Sacred Grove (Spring 1820)

First Vision   God, Jesus Christ, and angels personally appear to the Prophet Joseph. He comes to know that God lives and answers prayers.
   Does God hear me? Yes. God, Jesus Christ, and angels personally appear to the Prophet Joseph.

Eight Witnesses   Joseph Smith shows the Book of Mormon gold plates to eight witnesses.
   What makes a credible witness? Eyewitnesses—eight trustworthy people who see, touch and handle the Book of Mormon gold plates in broad daylight.

Chronology and Summary by Location

Smith Log Home (September 1823 and Spring 1830)

Section 2   The angel Moroni promises Joseph Smith that at some future time God will restore again the *fulness of the priesthood* or *endowment*. (See sections 110 and 124.)

Does God hear me? Yes. The angel Moroni appears to Joseph Smith.

Section 19: Atonement   Christ made atonement for all that men and women might not suffer if they repent.

Who can be a worthy vessel? Imperfect and ordinary people, provided they repent. Martin Harris rebuked for his serious transgressions. The Lord assures him that he may continue in his Church callings provided he repents. Christ made atonement for all that they might not suffer if they repent.

Section 22   Authoritative baptism into The Church of Jesus Christ of Latter-day Saints is required for a person to be saved.

Does God hear me? Yes. God answers Joseph inquiry about baptism.

Section 23   Early disciples are called to preach, exhort, and strengthen the Church. Hyrum Smith, Samuel H. Smith, and Joseph Knight Sr. are called to the work.

Who can be a worthy vessel? Ordinary people are called to preach, exhort, and strengthen the Church.

PART TWO: THE HARMONY, PENNSYLVANIA, PERIOD

THE BOOK OF MORMON

The Big Questions

What is revelation?
How does a person receive revelation?
What is translation?
Why John the Baptist?

Introduction

Smith Log Cabin, Harmony, Pennsylvania (July 1828–August 1830)

Section 3   Joseph Smith rebuked for the part he played in losing the first 116 pages of the translation of the Book of Mormon.
Who can be a worthy vessel? Imperfect people.

Section 4   Joseph Smith receives a revelation on behalf of his father informing him that a marvelous work and a wonder is about to begin.

Section 5   Martin Harris, in spite of his past sins, is promised that if he is humble and remains faithful he will be given the privilege to become one of three witnesses to the gold plates.
Who can be a worthy vessel? Imperfect people. Martin Harris, in spite of his past sins, is promised that if he is humble and remains faithful he will be given the privilege to become one of three witnesses to the gold plates.

Section 6   Oliver Cowdery appointed to be the Book of Mormon scribe to take down the words as Joseph translated from the gold plates.
What is revelation? When the Spirit speaks peace to the mind. Oliver Cowdery reassured that he received a revelation when the Spirit "spoke peace to his mind."

Section 7   Joseph Smith translates a parchment that contains the writings of the Apostle John. John will tarry in the flesh until Jesus comes in glory.
What is translation? A revelation from God making known the same meaning in English of an ancient text.

Section 8: Revelation Defined   Revelation is a communication from God directly to the mind and heart.
What is revelation? A message from God directly to the mind and heart.
What is translation? A revelation from God that makes known the meaning of an ancient text in a modern language. In the case of the Book of Mormon, the translation was at first accomplished with the aid of physical objects such as the Urim and Thummim and seer stone.
How does a person receive revelation? In the mind and heart and, under some circumstances, through the medium of a physical object.

Section 9: How to Receive Revelation   Oliver Cowdery's failed attempt to translate the Book of Mormon.
How does a person receive a revelation? Oliver Cowdery is told why he could not translate the Book of Mormon. As a general rule, revelation comes after a person has studied an issue out his or her own mind, come to a conclusion, and then asked God if the conclusion was correct.

Chronology and Summary by Location

Section 10 Joseph Smith is given permission to translate the Book of Mormon once more after he lost the privilege for a season on account of his sins.

Who can be a worthy vessel? Imperfect people. The Lord describes Martin Harris as a wicked man for his part in the loss of the 116 pages. Joseph Smith repents of the part he played in the episode and is given permission to translate the Book of Mormon once more.

Section 11 Counsel to Hyrum Smith to keep the commandments, study the word of the Lord, and trust in and deny not the spirit of revelation and prophecy.

What is a revelation? The spirit of revelation encourages a person to "do good," "to do justly, to walk humbly, to judge righteously . . . [and] shall enlighten your mind, which shall fill your soul with joy."

How does a person receive revelation? Ask and you will receive.

Section 12 Joseph Knight called to work in the Church and is promised answers to his prayers.

How does a person receive revelation? Be fully engaged in the "cause of Zion."

Section 24 A revelation of encouragement to Joseph and his scribe Oliver as they continue to translate the Book of Mormon. Told not to require miracles.

Who can be a worthy vessel? Joseph Smith, because he has been "delivered from the powers of Satan" and is willing to repent of his sins, magnify his office, continually call upon God, write down his revelations, expound the scriptures, devote all his service to God, be patient in afflictions, and seek not after the wealth of the world. Oliver Cowdery, if he glory not in himself and declares the gospel at "all times, and in all places."

Section 25 Emma Smith is an "elect lady." She is commanded to "make a selection of sacred hymns," and to exhort and expound scripture.

Who can be a worthy vessel? Emma Smith, provided she repents of her sins, is faithful, walks in the paths of virtue, murmurs not, shuns pride, and keeps the commandments.

Section 26 The law of common consent reiterated.

Section 27 Joseph entertains an angel who warns him that enemies of the Church are attempting to poison the wine used for the sacrament. Restoration of the Melchizedek Priesthood confirmed.

How does a person receive a revelation? When there is a particular need for the Lord to communicate in a very direct and plain manner.

Introduction

Susquehanna River (May 1829)

Section 13: Aaronic Priesthood   The idea of authority and the need for saving ordinances introduced. John the Baptist visited Joseph Smith and Oliver Cowdery and restored the Aaronic Priesthood, empowering men to baptize, entertain angels, and administer the gospel of repentance.

Why John the Baptist? To restore the authority necessary to perform baptisms, entertain angels, and administer the gospel of repentance.

PART THREE: THE FAYETTE, NEW YORK, PERIOD

Organization of the Church

The Big Questions

Why a church?
What is the structure of the Church?

Whitmer Home/Fayette (June 1829–January 1831)

Sections 14, 15, 16   Revelation to David Whitmer, John Whitmer, and Peter Whitmer.
Why a church? To preach the gospel.

Section 17   Oliver Cowdery, David Whitmer, and Martin Harris are promised that they would see the gold plates, breastplate, sword of Laban, the Urim and Thummim, and directors or Liahona.

Section 18   Church to be organized around twelve disciples to be chosen by Oliver Cowdery and David Whitmer.
What is the structure of the Church? Church to be organized around twelve disciples to be chosen by Oliver Cowdery and David Whitmer.

Section 20: Organization of the Church/Aaronic Priesthood In the beginning the Church to be organized around apostles, elders, priests, and teachers who are to help the Saints perfect themselves. (This section is a Church handbook of instructions.)

Why a church? The Church organization is established to encourage and provide opportunities for people to have faith, repent of their sins, be baptized, pattern their lives after Jesus, and become like him.

What is the structure of the Church? Elders, priests, and teachers were charged with special responsibilities to assist in the work of the Church. Elders were to meet in quarterly conferences "to do church business whatsoever is necessary." Section 20 reflects the status of the organization at its inception. Over the next few years the Lord would continue to reveal his will concerning the organization of his Church. By 1835 the basic structure of the Church would be in place, as set forth in section 107, which describes all of the governing quorums of the Church and explains their basic functions and relationships to each other.

Section 21 Leaders of the new Church appointed.

What is the structure of the Church? Joseph Smith is to head the Church as the "First Elder" and Oliver Cowdery is to be the "Second Elder."

Section 28 Hiram Page received revelations through his seer stone, which he falsely claimed should govern the Church.

What is the structure of the Church? Only Joseph (the "First Elder") may receive revelations for the entire Church.

Section 29 A revelation on the signs that will precede the Second Coming and a discussion of various doctrinal matters—the resurrection and final judgment, all things spiritual to the Lord, premortal life of God's children, the fall and atonement, and little children are innocent and redeemed through the atonement.

Why a church? To prepare a people for the Second Coming of Jesus Christ.

Sections 30–31 David Whitmer, Peter Whitmer Jr., and John Whitmer called to preach to the Lamanites.

Who is a worthy vessel? David Whitmer, although he was chastened by the Lord for his failure to serve diligently. (See verses 5–8.)

Why a church? To preach the gospel.

Section 32 Parley P. Pratt, Oliver Cowdery, Peter Whitmer Jr., and Ziba Peterson called to preach to the Lamanites.

Why a church? To preach the gospel.

Section 33 Ezra Thayre and Northrop Sweet called as missionaries.
Why a church? To preach the gospel in preparation for the Second Coming.

Section 34 Orson Pratt baptized and called as a missionary.
Why a church? To preach the gospel in preparation for the Second Coming.

Kingdom (Waterloo), New York (December 1830)

Sections 35–36 Sidney Rigdon called to assist Joseph Smith as his scribe as Joseph continued his revisions of the King James Bible. Rigdon and Edward Partridge called to do missionary work.
Why a church? To preach the gospel, baptize, and confer the gift of the Holy Ghost.

Section 37 Members of the Church are called to gather in Ohio.
What is the structure of the Church? A united group of believers who congregate together in close proximity in "gathering places."

Whitmer Home/Fayette (December 1830)

Section 38 Conference of the Church in preparation for the gathering to Ohio.
Why a church? To prepare for the Second Coming and to organize a Zion-like people with no poor among them.

Sections 39–40 James Covel invited to join the Church but disaffiliates himself shortly thereafter.

PART FOUR: THE KIRTLAND, OHIO PERIOD

The Big Questions

How do we live together and build a community now that we have gathered?
What is the structure of the Church?

Chronology and Summary by Location

KIRTLAND, OHIO

Newel K. Whitney Home (February 1831–December 1831)

Section 41 Members of the Church living in communal orders and sharing wealth equally experience ill will between the participants. The Lord condones the practice of communal orders and promises to reveal more about the principles of consecration. The first bishop, Edward Partridge, appointed.

How do we live together and build a community now that we have gathered? Live together in communal orders in which wealth is shared equally.

What is the structure of the Church? Bishops should be appointed to help administer the temporal affairs of the Church.

Section 42: The Laws of God and Consecration and Stewardship Principles of communal living expounded and the law of consecration introduced. Important ethical teachings mentioned in the Ten Commandments and elsewhere are reiterated to God's people in a modern day. The Saints instructed to care for each other temporally and to heal and nurture the sick.

How do we live together and build a community now that we have gathered? Establish communal living orders where wealth is shared equally, live by the ethical standards in the Ten Commandments and elsewhere, and care for each other.

Section 43 Only Joseph Smith receives revelations that are binding on the entire Church. Missionaries are sent out to warn of the impending Millennium.

What is the structure of the Church? Joseph Smith (First Elder) is the recognized leader and revelator for the Church

Section 44 Saints told to prepare to implement the law of consecration and to send out missionaries to grow the Church.

How do we live together and build a community now that we have gathered? Implement the law of consecration and send out missionaries to grow the Church.

Section 70 Saints told to prepare to implement the law of consecration and to send out missionaries to grow the Church.

How do we live together and build a community now that we have gathered? Implement the law of consecration and send out missionaries to grow the Church.

Make Church publications available to the members.

Section 72   Bishops called to administer the law of consecration.

What is the structure of the Church? Bishops called to administer the law of consecration in Kirtland, Ohio, as well as in Zion—Independence, Missouri.

Isaac Morley Farm (March 1831–September 1831)

Section 45: Second Coming   Signs of the Second Coming set forth and the desolation of the earth described. The Saints are commanded to gather and build the New Jerusalem in Jackson County, Missouri. As part the events of his Second Coming, Jesus will visit the New Jerusalem.

How do we live together and build a community now that we have gathered? Prepare for the Second Coming. Build the New Jerusalem in Jackson County, Missouri.

Section 46: Gifts of the Spirit   Gifts of the Spirit enumerated.

How do we live together and build a community now that we have gathered? Encourage members to seek after the best spiritual gifts to bless and edify each other.

What is the structure of the Church? Church services are open to the public. A bishop's responsibility is to discern which gifts of the Spirit are from God and which are not.

Section 47   John Whitmer appointed Church Historian.

What is the structure of the Church? A Church historian should be appointed to chronicle the history of the Church.

Section 48   Share what you have with the Saints migrating to Kirtland, Ohio, from the East. Prepare financially to purchase land at the location of the New Jerusalem.

How do we live together and build a community now that we have gathered? Share what you have with the Saints migrating to Kirtland from the East.

Section 49   Missionaries are sent to the Shaker community and are rejected.

What is the structure of the Church? Send missionaries into the world to grow the Church.

Section 50   False spiritual manifestations abroad in the Church at Kirtland.

How do we live together and build a community now that we have gathered? By carefully discerning which spiritual gifts are from God and which are not.

Section 52   The ordination of men to the "high priesthood." The general location of Zion revealed.
What is the structure of the Church? Men ordained to the "high priesthood."

Section 53   Sidney Gilbert ordained an elder and called to travel to Independence, Missouri, and serve as a bishop's agent.
What is the structure of the Church? Agents appointed to assist the bishop.

Section 54   The Colesville Saints are commanded to leave Kirtland, Ohio, and travel to Missouri (Zion) to establish the law of consecration.
How do we live together and build a community now that we have gathered? Establish the law of consecration and share temporal blessings equally.

Section 55   William W. Phelps called to be the printer for the Church.
What is the structure of the Church? The Church should establish a publishing house to print Church materials.

Section 56   Ezra Thayre criticized for his pride and selfishness as it pertained to his participation in a communal order. He puts off a mission call.
How do we live together and build a community now that we have gathered? Live the law of consecration. Encourage the rich to give their property to the poor. Encourage the poor to be satisfied with what they have and to labor diligently.

Section 63   Some of the Saints commanded to go to Zion in Jackson County, Missouri. Members of the Church are warned against seeking after signs.
How do we live together and build a community now that we have gathered? Continue to assemble and build up Zion in Jackson County, Missouri. Do not seek after miraculous signs.

Section 64: Forgiveness   Joseph prepares to move from the Morley Farm to live on the Johnson Farm, also just outside of Kirtland.
How do we live together and build a community now that we have gathered? Forgive each other unconditionally.

Newel K. Whitney Store (September 1832–December 1833)
Section 78 (See Hiram, Ohio)[1]

Section 84: Oath and Covenant of the Priesthood   Elders had begun to return from their missions in the eastern states and to make reports of

---

1. There is a question as to whether section 78 was received in the Newel K. Whitney store or in Hiram, Ohio.

their labors. Instructions on missionary work. The higher or Melchizedek Priesthood is associated with the power of godliness and brings men and women into the presence of God.

What is the structure of the Church? Members should preach the gospel and fund missionary work.

Section 85   The Saints should divide their inheritance in Zion, Jackson County, Missouri. "One mighty and strong" predicted.

How do we live together and build a community now that we have gathered? By dividing inheritances and willingly entering into the law of consecration.

Section 86   Joseph Smith continues to make inspired changes and additions to the New Testament. He reinterprets the parable of the wheat and the tares in the context of the restoration.

Section 87   Prophecy on the American Civil War and other wars that will follow.

Section 88: Calling and Election; Light of Christ; Resurrection; Learn Doctrine; Eternal Law; School of the Prophets   Concerns about the Second Coming addressed. The School of the Prophets established.

What is the structure of the Church? Schools must be built to educate the Saints in temporal and spiritual matters.

Section 89: Word of Wisdom   Health code revealed for the physical well-being of members of the Church.

Section 90   First Presidency organized.

What is the structure of the Church? A First Presidency should be organized to lead the Church. Each member of the presidency holds the keys of the kingdom.

Section 91   Reading the Apocrypha is of particular benefit to those enlightened by the Spirit.

Section 92   United Orders established as part of the law of consecration.

What is the structure of the Church? Establish united orders, economic units organized to carry out specialized economic objectives within the law of consecration.

Chronology and Summary by Location

Section 93: All May See Jesus; Deification; Definition of Truth; Intelligences; Teach Your Children   The Mormon metanarrative, deification, eternality of matter, intelligences, spirits, premortal life, mortal life, the purpose of worship, and the resurrection.

How do we live together and build a community now that we have gathered? Parents should teach their children the concepts contained in this section.

Section 94   The Saints instructed to build Zion after the pattern of ancient Israel. Administrative offices and a printing house initiated.

What is the structure of the Church? A Church administration building should be constructed for use by the First Presidency, as well as a printing house to publish Church literature.

Section 95   Start building the Kirtland Temple.

How do we live together and build a community now that we have gathered? Build temples so that the Saints may be endowed with power from on high, be taught, and prepared to preach the gospel.

Section 96   Lands purchased for the construction of a Church administration building and temple.

What is the structure of the Church? United Orders should be established in conjunction with the law of consecration to accomplish various specific economic objectives of the Church.

Section 97   The Saints living in Zion, Jackson County, Missouri, warned that if they do not live the commandments they will not be protected.

How do we live together and build a community now that we have gathered? Repent!

Section 98: Renounce War and Proclaim Peace   Counsel to the Saints on violence, the constitutional law of the land, elected officials, and church and civil authority.

How do we live together and build a community now that we have gathered? Love your enemies, support constitutional principles, elect good and wise people to public office.

Section 101   The Lord explains why the Saints were forced out of Zion, Jackson County, Missouri, and addresses the issue of when the Saints will be able to return and redeem the land of Zion.

How do we deal with disappointment and unrealized promises? Live the commandments.

Introduction

Joseph Smith Jr. Home (February 1834–December 1835)

Section 102   First high council established.
What is the structure of the Church? Establish formal church councils.

Section 103   Joseph raises an army (Zion's Camp) to save the Saints in Missouri from destruction and to redeem Zion.
How do we deal with disappointment and unrealized promises? Live the commandments.

Section 104   God reproves the saints for not living law of consecration. United orders or firms based upon the law of common consent. Underlying principles of the law of consecration explained. Property belongs to the Lord and therefore it is not for man to decide how the resources of the world are to be used.
What is the structure of the Church? Organize united orders or firms based upon the law of common consent.

Section 106   Predictions about the Second Coming—it will not overtake faithful Saints like a thief in the night.

Section 108   Lyman Sherman to be one of the "first of mine elders" to be spiritually endowed in the Kirtland Temple. He is to "strengthen" others in all his "conversation, . . . prayers . . . exhortations, and . . . doings.
How do we live together and build a community now that we have gathered? Be spiritually endowed with power from on high and set a good example.

Printing Office Site (March 1835–August 1835)

Section 107: Melchizedek Priesthood   Church government, presiding quorums, and offices of the Aaronic and Melchizedek Priesthoods described.
What is the structure of the Church? Church will be administered by presiding priesthood quorums through priesthood offices that govern upon the principle of unanimity.

Section 134: Civil Governments   A declaration of belief on the role of governments.
How do we live together and build a community now that we have gathered? Seek to prevent government interference in the affairs kingdom of God.

Chronology and Summary by Location

Kirtland Temple (January 1836–July 1837)

Section 109: Kirtland Temple Dedication *How do we live together and build a community now that we have gathered?* Build a temple or sacred place to endow the Saints with spiritual power.

Section 110: Visitation of Jesus, Moses, Elias, and Elijah Jesus, Moses, Elias, and Elijah appear to Joseph Smith and Oliver Cowdery in the Kirtland Temple and restore the keys and authority to perform temple vicarious ordinances for the living and the dead.

What is the structure of the Church? Keys and authorities must be restored for the salvation of the human family.

Section 112 Thomas B. Marsh, the president of the Quorum of the Twelve, calls a meeting of his quorum.
What is the structure of the Church? The Quorum of the Twelve should take counsel from the First Presidency.

Section 137 All who have died without a knowledge of this gospel, who would have received it if they had been permitted to tarry, shall be heirs of the celestial kingdom of God.

THOMPSON, OHIO

Leman Copley Farm (May 1831)

Section 51 The Lord commands the Colesville Saints arriving in Kirtland, Ohio, to live the law of consecration.
How do we live together and build a community now that we have gathered? Enter into and live the law of consecration.

HIRAM, OHIO

John Johnson Farm (October 1831–August 1832)

Section 1 Preface to the Doctrine and Covenants.
How do we live together and build a community now that we have gathered? Canonize and act upon the revelations of Joseph Smith.

Section 65 A prayer that God's kingdom might be established on the earth—a stone cut out of the mountain.

Section 66 (See also Orange, Ohio)[1] A revelation to William E. McLellin—five personal questions answered.

Section 67 Conference held to discuss the publication of Joseph's revelations. Some critical of his revelations challenged to do better. William E. McLellin makes the attempt.

How do we live together and build a community now that we have gathered? Canonize and act upon the revelations of Joseph Smith. Also, seek the face of the Lord.

Section 68: Parents to Teach Their Children the Gospel Revelation addressed to certain members who attended the conference to discuss the publication of some of Joseph's revelations.

How do we live together and build a community now that we have gathered? Seek the spirit of inspiration, live the law of consecration with a generous heart, and parents teach their children the gospel.

Section 69 Oliver Cowdery assigned to carry the manuscript containing Joseph's revelations to Independence, Missouri, to be published.

How do we live together and build a community now that we have gathered? Compile and make available to the Saints the revelations of Joseph Smith.

Section 71 Joseph and Sidney Rigdon directed to stop work on their inspired revisions of the Bible and defend the Church against its critics.

How do we live together and build a community now that we have gathered? Defend the faith when the Church is criticized by detractors.

Section 73 Joseph and Sidney Rigdon commanded to start revising the Bible once again after a hiatus during which they devoted their energies to a public defense of the Church.

Section 74 Joseph Smith continues work on the inspired version of the Bible (1 Corinthians 7:14). Paul's views on marriage explained.

Section 76: Three Degrees of Glory Joseph Smith continues work on the inspired version of the Bible (John 5:4). Joseph and Sidney Rigdon's vision of the three degrees of glory.

Section 77 Joseph Smith continues work on the inspired version of the Bible. Interpretation of the book of Revelation.

---

1. There is a question as to whether section 66 was received in Hiram, Ohio, or in Orange, Ohio.

Section 78: Be Equal in Temporal Things   Plans made for a storehouse in Kirtland, Ohio, and Independence, Missouri.
How do we live together and build a community now that we have gathered? Establish united orders and be equal in temporal things.

Section 79   Jared Carter called to do missionary work.
What is the structure of the Church? Missionaries are called to preach the gospel.

Section 80   Stephen Burnett and John Murdock called to preach the gospel and teach what they have "heard ... believe ... and know to be true."
What is the structure of the Church? Missionaries are called to preach the gospel.

Section 81   Presidency of the High Priesthood organized.
What is the structure of the Church? The Presidency of the High Priesthood is organized and given the "keys of the kingdom" or right to direct the affairs of the Church.

Section 99   John Murdock called as a missionary.
What is the structure of the Church? Missionaries are appointed to make converts.

Section 133   Information included in the appendix of the 1833 edition of the Doctrine and Covenants. Building up Zion in preparation for Second Coming of Jesus.

Orange, Ohio

Serenes Burnett Home Site (October 1831)

Section 66 (See Hiram, Ohio)[1]

Amherst

Simeon Carter Home (January 1832)

Section 75   Joseph Smith sustained and ordained President of the High Priesthood. Twenty missionaries called.
What is the structure of the Church? At its head there should be a President of the High Priesthood. Send out missionaries.

---

[1]. There is a question as to whether section 66 was received in Hiram, Ohio, or in Orange, Ohio.

Introduction

Perrysburg (South Dayton), New York

Freeman Nickerson Home (December 1833)

Section 100 Joseph and Sidney Rigdon, while on a mission to Perrysburg, New York, are assured that their families are well. Rigdon to be a spokesman and Joseph a revelator.

PART FIVE: THE MISSOURI PERIOD

The Big Questions

What and where is Zion?
How do we deal with disappointment and unrealized promises?

Zion, Jackson County (Kansas City), Missouri

Joshua Lewis Home (July and August 1831)

Section 57 Where the temple in Zion will be built.
What and where is Zion? Zion should be built in Independence, Jackson County, Missouri. A temple will be built there. The Saints are to enter into the law of consecration.

Section 58: Zion God commands some of the Saints to gather in Zion. Instructions are given on how Zion should proceed forward and be organized.
What and where is Zion? Zion is compared to a feast where all sup without rank or social distinction. Zion is a place that is dedicated to the Lord where the Saints are to gather to be protected from the travails of the last days and to await the Second Coming of Jesus.

Section 59: Sabbath Day The law of the Sabbath reiterated in a modern day.
What and where is Zion? Zion is a place where the people are holy, sanctified, and observe the Sabbath day.

Section 60 Missionaries are to preach the gospel. It is not necessary to ask the Lord for revelations on the inconsequential aspects of everyday life.

Chronology and Summary by Location

By Missouri River (near Miami, Missouri)

McIlwaine's Bend (August 1831)

Section 61   The power of destroyer on the waters made manifest as Joseph and his brethren return from a short visit to Zion, Jackson County, Missouri.

By Missouri River (near Cazzell, Missouri)

Site of the Town of Chariton (August 1831)

Section 62   Revelation given to bless and encourage the prophet's brother Hyrum and friends Joseph had met on his way back from Missouri to Kirtland. The Lord forgives them of their sins. In the mundane affairs of life it often does not matter to the Lord what men and women do.

Jackson County (Independence), Missouri

Setting Zion in Order

Edward Partridge Home and Schoolhouse (April 1832)

Section 82   Saints in Missouri called upon to repent and establish Zion. The Lord is bound when the Saints obey the commandments.
  What and where is Zion? Zion is a place where the Saints are "to be equal," taking into account "wants and . . . needs."

Section 83   If a husband dies or is killed, his survivors (widow and children) may remain on the family inheritance (land) and the Church must provide for them.
  What and where is Zion? Zion is a place where widows and orphans are cared for.

Fishing River (Lawson), Missouri

Zion's Camp

East Fork, Fishing River (June 1834)

Section 105   Zion's camp disbanded and hopes to redeem Zion put on hold.
  How do we deal with disappointment and unrealized promises? Repent of sin and be patient!

Far West (Caldwell County), Missouri

The Saints Flee from Zion to Far West

Joseph Smith Jr. Home Site (March 1838–July 1838)

Section 113 An interpretation of Isaiah 11 and 52.

Section 114 David W. Patten, a member of the Twelve, told to prepare for a mission in the spring. Prior to his mission he was killed in the Battle of Crooked River.

Section 115 The Saints in Kirtland commanded to resettle in Far West. The official name of the Church revealed. Brigham Young and his associates lay the cornerstone under trying circumstances.
  What and where is Zion? Zion is a place where the Saints gather and build a temple.
  How do we deal with disappointment and unrealized promises? Do all that is humanly possible to follow the commands of the Lord.

Section 117 The Lord's perspective on property. William Marks and Newel K. Whitney told to close their financial interests in Kirtland and immediately go to Far West.
  What and where is Zion? Zion is a place where the Saints should not be focused on personal wealth and in any way take advantage of their neighbors.

Section 118 The Twelve rebuked. Some dropped from the quorum. Specific instructions given on how to reconstitute the quorum. Certain members of the Twelve to be called on missions and leave for Great Britain.
  How do we deal with disappointment and unrealized promises? Follow the instructions of the Lord to the best of your ability under the circumstances.

Section 119: Tithing The law of tithing introduced.

Section 120 A council headed by the First Presidency organized to decide how tithing funds should be disposed of.

Spring Hill (Daviess County), Missouri

Spring Hill, Adam-Ondi-Ahman (May 1838)

Section 116 A place where Adam dwelt identified.

Chronology and Summary by Location

LIBERTY (CLAY COUNTY), MISSOURI

Joseph Smith Incarcerated

Liberty Jail (March 1839)

Section 121: Proper Use of Priesthood Authority Priesthood power can be exercised only upon the principles of righteousness - no hypocrisy, no self-aggrandizement, no coercion no deception.
What and where is Zion? Zion is a place where power and authority are based on gentle persuasion.

Section 122 The importance of gaining experience in this life.
How do we deal with disappointment and unrealized promises? Understand that disappointment, sorrow, and unrealized promises are experiences that may be consecrated for our good and self-development.

Section 123 Petition the government for the redress of wrongs perpetrated on the Mormons in Missouri.
How do we deal with disappointment and unrealized promises? Make an effort to change the situation.

Salem, Massachusetts, Site of a Boarding House on Union Street (August 1836)

Section 111 Instructions on finding buried treasure and the accuracy of prophetic utterances.

PART SIX: THE NAUVOO PERIOD

The Big Question

How shall we be saved?

Doctrinal Developments

Eternal matter
Anthropomorphism
Eternal marriage

Vicarious work for the dead
Endowment
Calling and election
Apotheosis
Plurality of gods

Brigham Young Log Home (July 1841)

Section 126   Brigham Young instructed that it was no longer necessary for him to be called away from his family to serve missions.
   How shall we be saved? Nurture family relationships.

Joseph Smith Homestead (January 1841–September 1842)

Section 124: Fulness of the Priesthood/Temple Endowment   The fulness of the priesthood and the temple endowment.
   How shall we be saved? By entering into temple covenants.

Section 125   The Saints who have immigrated to the Iowa side of the Mississippi should remain there.
   How shall we be saved? Gather to various geographical areas and build up Zion.

Red Brick Store (September 1842–July 1843)

Section 129   Keys are given whereby messengers from beyond the veil may be identified.
   How shall we be saved? Learn to detect false from true revelation.

Section 132: Eternal Marriage/Holy Spirit of Promise   Covenants must be performed by the properly authorized priesthood and be ratified by the Holy Ghost in order to be valid. Plural marriages explained.
   How shall we be saved? Live worthily so that saving ordinances are ratified by the Holy Ghost (sealed by the Holy Spirit of Promise). Enter into the new and everlasting covenant of marriage.

Site of Edward Hunter Home (September 1842)

Sections 127–128: Baptisms for the Dead   *How shall we be saved?* Perform vicarious temple ordinances for the dead.
   General instructions on baptisms for the dead and vicarious work for the dead.

Ramus (Webster), Illinois

Joseph's Visit to Ramus—More Doctrine

Site of the Town of Ramus (April and May 1843)

Section 130: God the Father and the Son Have Bodies of Flesh and Bone Joseph visits Ramus, not far from Nauvoo. The Father and the Son have bodies of flesh and bones. The Holy Ghost is a personage of spirit. The time of the Second Coming withheld. Intelligence gained in this life rises with us in the resurrection. All blessings are predicated upon obedience to law.

Section 131: Marriage Is an Order of the Priesthood Joseph's second visit to Ramus, not far from Nauvoo. Celestial marriage qualifies men and women to enter the highest degree of the celestial kingdom. Calling and election explained. Spirits are composed of refined matter.

Nauvoo

John Taylor Home Site (Summer 1844)

Section 135 Eulogy to Joseph Smith, the martyr.

PART SEVEN: WINTER QUARTERS AND BEYOND

The Big Question

How shall the Church survive?

Winter Quarters (Florence), Nebraska

Site of Brigham Young and Heber C. Kimball Homes (January 1847)

Section 136 *How shall we survive?* Organize and cooperate.
Instruction on how to organize for the exodus to the Great Basin Kingdom.

Introduction

Salt Lake City, Utah

Wilford Woodruff Home and Office (October 1890)

Declaration 1   President Wilford Woodruff announces the cessation of the practice of plural marriage or polygamy.
  How shall we survive? Cease the practice of polygamy.

Beehive House, Where Joseph F. Smith Lived (October 1918)

Section 138: The Spirit World   Joseph F. Smith's vision of the spirit world.

Salt Lake Temple (June 1978)

Declaration 2   Authorization for all worthy males to hold the priesthood.
  How shall we survive? Give the priesthood to all worthy males on an equal basis.

Chapter 4

Chronological by Time

The following is drawn from the introductory material to the Doctrine and Covenants. (* = At or near place specified.)

Year	Time	Place	Sections
1823	September	Manchester, New York	2
1828	July	Harmony, Pennsylvania	3
	Summer	Harmony, Pennsylvania	10
1829	February	Harmony, Pennsylvania	4
	March	Harmony, Pennsylvania	5
	April	Harmony, Pennsylvania	6, 7, 8, 9
	May	Harmony, Pennsylvania	11, 12, 13
	June	Fayette, New York	14, 15, 16, 17, 18
1830	March	Manchester, New York	19
	April	Fayette, New York	20*, 21
	April	Manchester, New York	22, 23
	July	Harmony, Pennsylvania	24, 25, 26
	August	Harmony, Pennsylvania	27
	September	Fayette, New York	28, 29, 30, 31
	October	Fayette, New York	32*, 33
	November	Fayette, New York	34
	December	Fayette, New York	35, 36, 37
1831	January	Fayette, New York	38, 39, 40
	February	Kirtland, Ohio	41, 42, 43, 44
	March	Kirtland, Ohio	45, 46, 47, 48, 49
	May	Kirtland, Ohio	50
	May	Thompson, Ohio	51
	June	Kirtland, Ohio	52, 53, 54, 55, 56
	July	Zion, Jackson County, Missouri	57

33

Introduction

	August	Zion, Jackson County, Missouri	58, 59, 60
	August	By Missouri River, Missouri	61, 62
	August	Kirtland, Ohio	63
	September	Kirtland, Ohio	64
	October	Hiram, Ohio	65
	October	Orange, Ohio	66
	November	Hiram, Ohio	1, 67, 68, 69, 133
	November	Kirtland, Ohio	70
	December	Hiram, Ohio	71
	December	Kirtland, Ohio	72
1832	January	Hiram, Ohio	73, 74
	January	Amherst, Ohio	75
	February	Hiram, Ohio	76
	March	Hiram, Ohio	77, 78, 79, 80, 81
	April	Jackson County, Missouri	82, 83
	April	Independence, Missouri	83
	August	Hiram, Ohio	99
	September	Kirtland, Ohio	84
	November	Kirtland, Ohio	85
	December	Kirtland, Ohio	86, 87*, 88
1833	February	Kirtland, Ohio	89
	March	Kirtland, Ohio	90, 91, 92
	May	Kirtland, Ohio	93, 94
	June	Kirtland, Ohio	95, 96
	August	Kirtland, Ohio	97, 98
	October	Perrysburg, New York	100
	December	Kirtland, Ohio	101
1834	February	Kirtland, Ohio	102, 103
	April	Kirtland, Ohio	104*
	June	Fishing River, Missouri	105
	November	Kirtland, Ohio	106
1835	March	Kirtland, Ohio	107
	August	Kirtland, Ohio	134
	December	Kirtland, Ohio	108
1836	January	Kirtland, Ohio	137
	March	Kirtland, Ohio	109
	April	Kirtland, Ohio	110
	August	Salem, Massachusetts	111
1837	July	Kirtland, Ohio	112

Chronological by Time

1838	March	Far West, Missouri	113*
	April	Far West, Missouri	114, 115
	May	Spring Hill, Daviess County, Missouri	116
	July	Far West, Missouri	117, 118, 119, 120
1839	March	Liberty Jail, Clay County, Missouri	121, 122, 123
1841	January	Nauvoo, Illinois	124
	March	Nauvoo, Illinois	125
	July	Nauvoo, Illinois	126
1842	September	Nauvoo, Illinois	127, 128
1843	February	Nauvoo, Illinois	129
	April	Ramus, Illinois	130
	May	Ramus, Illinois	131
	July	Nauvoo, Illinois	132
1844	June	Nauvoo, Illinois	135
1847	January	Winter Quarters (now Nebraska)	136
1890	October	Salt Lake City, Utah	Official Declaration—1
1918	October	Salt Lake City, Utah	138
1978	June	Salt Lake City, Utah	Official Declaration—2

Part 2

The Big Picture

Chapter 5

The Importance of Context

The title of this book, *Reading the Doctrine and Covenants Again for the First Time*, is borrowed from Marcus Borg, a well-known Christian scholar. He titled his book *Reading the Bible Again for the First Time* and said that the key word in the title was *Again*. His point was that as time passes, the way we read a book is conditioned by our culture and way of life. As Borg put it, "How we see affects how we read."[1] The idea of Borg's book, however, is somewhat different from my own. Borg hoped to help his readers see or interpret the Bible in its historical context, with an emphasis on what parts of the Bible can best be understood metaphorically. My concern is not so much how figuratively or literally we read the Doctrine and Covenants but rather whether or not we understand its message in the context in which it was written - understand the text like first generations Mormons did. The point is that if a person reads the Doctrine and Covenants through a modern lens, he or she may miss the true intent of the message and in some cases even misapprehend what is being said.

The approach advocated involves a study of the Doctrine and Covenants by placing it in its historical setting. As Borg points out, reading in context "enables us to see meanings ... that would otherwise be hidden from our sight. It unearths meanings that otherwise would remain buried in the past. Moreover, it allows us to hear the strangeness of these texts that come to us from worlds strange to us. Thus, it helps a person avoid reading ... simply with our current agendas in mind and frees the [text] to speak for itself."[2] To sum up, reading something in context unfolds and clarifies the original intent and meaning.

Brigham Young in 1856 also spoke about need for contextualization when he commented on a revelation in the Doctrine and Covenants given some 25 years before. "These revelations," he said, "after a lapse of years,

---

1. See Borg, *Reading the Bible Again for the First Time*, 3.
2. See Borg, *Reading the Bible Again for the First Time*, 39.

become mystified to those who were not personally acquainted with the circumstances at the time they were given."[1] He went on to express his apprehension that the scripture upon which the Church was founded may become "as mysterious to our children ... as the revelations contained in the Old and New Testaments are to this generation" and obscure their intended meaning.[2]

With that purpose in mind, this study guide is designed to help you and your children *study* rather than just *read* the scriptures—two very different tasks. Reading the scriptures is a way to familiarize oneself with what is there. Studying the scriptures implies much more.[3] It involves placing each section in its original setting in an effort to uncover how the section was understood at the time it was written. This is not always easy and requires at least two things. First, understanding what was going on at the time the section was written, and second, knowing how words were defined and used at the time the section was given. This means, among other things, apprehending why each section was given, knowing something about the individuals involved, and, most importantly, understanding the cultural and social perspective of the time. All of this information breathes life into the text. It helps the student grasp the importance, significance, meaning, and power of the book. Finally, for Latter-day Saints, studying the scriptures means to meditate, ponder, and pray over the sections studied and to ask God for greater understanding.

To further illustrate the importance of understanding context, consider the different ways the word *course* can be used. What does it mean if you hear someone say, "Wow, that was a good course!" At face value, and without more information, this statement is entirely ambiguous. Placed in context, the usage becomes clear. Assume, for example, that this statement was made when two people exited a college classroom. In this situation the word "course" refers to an excellent course of study at school. On the other hand, assume that this statement was made when two people came off a golf course. In this circumstance, the reference is to a game of golf. Yet again, assume that the statement was made when two people walked out of a fine restaurant. In this situation the words describe an exceptionally good meal. Context is meaning!

An example of the importance of understanding historical context can

---

1. Mark Lyman Staker, *Hearken, O Ye People: The Historical Setting of Joseph Smith's Ohio Revelations*, Kindle location, 761.
2. Ibid 768.
3. The word *study* comes from a Latin word meaning "to busy oneself about a thing." When we literally busy ourselves with the scriptures, by implication we ponder them, compare them to other things we know, learn more things we do not know about them, and pray over our efforts.

be found in Doctrine and Covenants 8. In Joseph Smith's day it was commonly for people to use physical objects through which they believed God revealed his will. This is not a new notion for Mormons who are familiar with the Urim and Thummim of the Old Testament and the Liahona described in the Book of Mormon. In section 8, verse 6, the "gift of Aaron" is mentioned and then in verse 8 we are informed that the "gift of Aaron" is something that can be held in our hands. The meaning of theses passages becomes clearer when we understand that Oliver Cowdery had asked the Prophet Joseph to inquire about the use of Oliver's divining rod (forked stick) that he *held in his hands* and through which Oliver received revelations from God. With this added understanding, the meaning of section 8 is illuminated. It is a discussion about the propriety of using physical objects as aids to receive revelations from God.

Section 8 is remarkable and describes a God who is sensitive to the cultural assumptions that people made during Joseph Smith's time—namely, that God can reveal his will through the use of physical objects. While the Lord explains in this section that it is not necessary to receive revelation through physical objects, because inspiration may come directly from him into our minds and hearts (verses 2–3), he will condescend to communicate with his children through objects they are familiar with and use for this purpose. However, whether revelation comes directly to the mind or through some object (rod, seer stone, Urim and Thummim), God reminds his children to "remember that without faith you can do nothing; therefore ask in faith" (verse 10).

Another interesting example of the importance of understanding historical context involves a discussion about the recommended size of families in Doctrine and Covenants 90:25. The Lord says, "Let your families be small . . . as pertaining to those who do not belong to your families." Taken at face value, the words either seem confusing or, taken literally, seem to suggest that members of the Church limit the size of their families. In context, however, the actual meaning becomes clear. In Joseph's day it was a common practice for guests to be invited to live with families over an extended period of time. With this piece of information, it becomes obvious that the Lord is not making a comment about the number of offspring but rather the advisability of inviting unrelated outsiders to become part one's family.

An example of the importance of understanding the original definition of the words is found in the way in which the term "light-minded" is used in Doctrine and Covenants 88:121. In modern usage it means frivolous, not serious, or given to laughter. Nevertheless, in 1832, when this section was received, it meant something entirely different. Webster's 1832 dictionary defines "light-minded" as unsettled, unsteady, volatile, or not considerate.

Therefore, when we come across this expression, we should not assume that the Lord is advising the Saints to avoid good humor. Rather, God is recommending that his children be steadfast in the gospel.[1] In passing, it is interesting to note that in the Topical Guide located in the Latter-day Saint editions of the Bible, "light-minded" is cross-referenced with the word "levity" and in this instance points the student of the scriptures in the wrong direction.

Joseph Smith understood the importance of context. When asked how he studied the scriptures he said the "key" was to "enquire what was the question which drew out the answer or caused Jesus to utter the parable."[2] Explaining further, he said "we must dig up the root" or get to the bottom of what is going on—establish background. As illustrated above, this was the approach necessary in order to more fully understand section 8. Once the reader knows that Oliver Cowdery is asking Joseph Smith about the use of his divining rod, the fog is lifted.

Joseph's method of study is apparent in the way he approached the parable of the lost sheep. First, he described the setting. He noted that Jesus was addressing the "Pharisees and scribes" who "murmured" and complained that Jesus ate with sinners. Based on this finding he suggested that the ninety-nine sheep represented the Pharisees and the Sadducees to whom Jesus spoke. These were the ones who considered themselves the "Great I" and other people the "little you."[3] He said that teaching the gospel to such people was like "rain off from a gooses back."[4] He concluded his analysis by pointing out that God rejoiced more over the one lost sheep than the ninety-and-nine because the ninety-and-nine were so self-righteous that they would "be damned anyhow; you cannot save them."[5]

If the student avoids the hard work of contextualization, "digging at the root," as the Prophet Joseph recommended, he or she is more likely to misapprehend what it really being said. The student will superimpose a modern understanding on a historical document that was written in another place and time. To do so makes it more likely that the scriptures will be misunderstood and used to support one's own individual biases and prejudices. If this is the case, the scriptures fail to serve their intended purpose, which is to help us see things from God's viewpoint and to help

---

1. It is a good idea to have the *American Dictionary of the English Language: Noah Webster*, 1828 edition, nearby when you study the Doctrine and Covenants to check your understanding of how words are used.
2. See Smith, *Teachings of the Prophet Joseph Smith*, 276–77.
3. See Ehat and Cook, *Words of Joseph Smith*, 161.
4. See Ehat and Cook, *Words of Joseph Smith*, 161.
5. Joseph used this same reasoning to conclude that the "Eldest son" in the parable of the prodigal son represented "pharisees & sadducees murmuring & complaining." (Ehat and Cook, *Words of Joseph Smith*, 162; see also Smith, *Teachings of the Prophet Joseph Smith*, 278.)

all men and women cast aside cultural assumptions and predispositions in favor of a gospel perspective. Students of the gospel must first understand what is actually being said before they can "liken" the scriptures to their own situation. (See 1 Nephi 19:23.)

Chapter 6

The Doctrine and Covenants As a Reflection of Mormon History

The Doctrine and Covenants, for the most part, is a collection of revelations given by God to the Prophet Joseph Smith. Through these revelations, Joseph's earliest followers came to understand the unique beliefs of Mormonism and learned how to organize a church. Most of Joseph's revelations came in answer to specific questions Joseph or others had about doctrinal, organizational, or social issues. In a number of instances, some members simply wanted to know what their standing was before God and, more specifically, what God required of them. The first revelation Joseph received was the appearance of the Father and Son in the spring of 1820; it is not recorded in the Doctrine and Covenants but rather in the Pearl of Great Price.

To define the Doctrine and Covenants as a collection of Joseph's revelations, however, is incomplete. It is also a reflection of Mormon history and therefore expresses the viewpoints and aspirations of the first Mormons. This observation is especially important because 19th-century Mormonism is markedly different from 21st-century Mormonism. Mormonism's founding fathers understood Mormonism differently and emphasized different parts of it. For them the gospel was all about building a holy city—Zion, or the New Jerusalem—in preparation for the Second Coming of Jesus. To accomplish this objective, it was necessary that they gather together in one location and build a holy city. This city was to be built on principles of economic and social equality like the communities described in the early chapters of Acts and in the latter part of Book of Mormon—societies where "they had all things common among them" (3 Nephi 26:19; 4 Nephi 1:3). These objectives required radical social, economic, and political change that challenged mainstream society. Conflict was inevitable given the radical nature of the Church's teachings. For Mormonism to survive, it would temper its ambitions over the years and do what was necessary to fit more comfortably into the surrounding culture.

The evolving nature of Mormonism is a well-recognized phenomenon and has been studied and written about by a number of professional historians. One of the best books on the subject is by Thomas G. Alexander and is called *Mormonism in Transition: A History of the Latter-day Saints in 1890–1930*. It covers a time of rapid change in the Church, when Mormonism was emerging from its violent and turbulent nineteenth-century roots and becoming the more staid and "elaborate twentieth-century organization we now know."[1] But what was involved was more than "modernization." Outside forces had compelled Mormonism to modify some of its most fundamental and distinguishing beliefs—chief among them were communal orders, millennialism, and polygamy. Hence, understanding these often less-talked-about aspects of the faith is critically important if one is to understand the Doctrine and Covenants.

Social and historical pressures, however, do not alone account for Mormonism's changing landscape. Prophetic utterance, inspiration, and revelation have always been a chief consideration. Without it, for example, Wilford Woodruff never would have stepped away from polygamy, and he publically said so. At each step along the way, Church leaders have sought and received divine guidance. Sometimes the Lord has required the Church to stay the course, as he did in the case of completing the Nauvoo Temple and, as it turned out, in turbulent and difficult times: " . . . and if you do not these things . . . ye shall be rejected as a church." (D&C 124:32.) Yet, in other times and circumstances, the Lord excused the Saints from arduous responsibilities: "When I give a commandment to any of the sons of men to do a work unto my name, and those sons of men go with all their might and with all they have to perform that work, . . . and their enemies come upon them and hinder them from performing that work, behold, it behooveth me to require that work no more at the hands of those sons of men, but to accept of their offering." (D&C 124:49.) This tug of war between what the times require and what the Lord allows has always been the primary consideration of Church leaders.

The Mormon path to peaceful co-existence over the course of the twentieth century has made the selection of materials for this study guide somewhat problematic. Sometimes Church leaders and members alike began to feel that certain topics that might be challenging to nonmembers were off limits. Normalization meant change, and change meant that some of the more controversial aspects of the faith would be less and less talked about and understood. Official Church publications and lesson manuals

---

1. Richard Bushman, dust jacket.

avoided such topics as plural marriage, communalism, and discussions about the translation process Joseph Smith employed to produce the Book of Mormon.[1] Over time, members in general have lost touch with some of the themes that are at the heart of much of what is in the Doctrine and Covenants. The Church is now trying to reverse this trend by publishing essays on its website to inform members and non-members alike about its past.

While a certain amount of adaption was essential if Mormonism was to survive and remain vibrant as it grew into the twentieth century, at least two concerns have arisen as a result of what some have described as a "hands over eyes" approach. First, lack of knowledge about certain subjects related to Mormonism—such as seer stones, divining rods, communalism, millennialism, and plural marriage—make it difficult for Latter-day Saint readers of the Doctrine and Covenants to appreciate and comprehend some of the passages of Joseph's revelations. Second, members are sometimes blindsided and feel misled by the Church when they read for the first time about Joseph's use of seer stones and divining rods in the mainstream media and are "shaken" because they lack information about the historical context. A case in point was an article that appeared in the *New York Times Magazine* that freely discussed such issues.[2]

In recognition of this problem, the Church began in 2014 to publish essays on its website that transparently discussed many, if not most, of these topics. In the past there had been an effort to put forward a sanitized history of the Church that was simplified and carefully choreographed to attract converts and inspire members of the Church. More problematic subjects, such as the multiple accounts of the First Vision, race issues and priesthood, plural marriage in Nauvoo and in Utah, the "translation" of the Book of Mormon, the historicity of the Book of Abraham, and the Mountain Meadows Massacre are now officially available on line. These difficult issues have been addressed with careful regard for the facts and the most recent scholarship. These essays, along with the Joseph Smith Papers—the collection and publication of all the manuscripts and documents created by or under the direction of the Prophet—have made

---

1. When Joseph translated the Book of Mormon, he placed "a small seer stone into his hat and then, placing his face in the hat to block the light, would dictate the Book of Mormon aloud while various scribes wrote down his words. This process was open and observable by all in the household because it did not require Joseph to directly consult the plates, which at times were wrapped in linen on the table or even hidden elsewhere." (See Hardy, *The Book of Mormon: A Reader's Edition*, xiii.) Although the use of seer stones was common in Joseph's time and part of his culture, since the practice seemed off-putting today, Mormon writers tended to ignore it.

2. See Feldman, "What Is It About Mormonism?" 34.

the origins of Mormonism readily accessible to scholars and anyone else interested in the subject.

The next hurdle is introducing these materials into general Church publications, lesson manuals, and curricula of the Church Educational System. Reeducating the membership will require a delicate balance because some members of the Church do not know about these issues; and some of those who do know about them are disturbed by them. Reassuring those who know about these issues, while at the same time speaking to those who do not know about them, will be one of the challenges the Church will face in coming years. The Church's effort to make a more complete account of Mormon history widely available will increase understanding of the Doctrine and Covenants.

With these thoughts in mind it seemed important to explain the Doctrine and Covenants on it own terms without a modern gloss by placing all the facts on the table for consideration and exploration. And the thought of our children and grandchildren learning about these issues for the first time from outsiders was far less palatable than discussing them openly and honestly in a more faithful family environment. After all, Mormonism is not any less defensible than any other religious tradition that emphasizes the miraculous, except for the fact that it is younger. As Feldman explained, "There is nothing inherently less plausible about God's revealing himself to an upstate New York farmer in the early years of the Republic than to the pharaoh's changeling grandson in ancient Egypt. But what is driving the tendency to discount Joseph Smith's revelation is not that they seem less reasonable than those of Moses; it is that the book containing them is so new. When it comes to prophecy, antiquity breeds authenticity. Events in the distant past, we tend to think, occurred in sacred, mythic time. Not so with revelations received during the presidencies of James Monroe or Andrew Jackson."[1]

Finally, this strategy of minimizing discussion about some things that were typical of Mormonism when it came onto the scene, for the purpose of avoiding criticism, has meant that each succeeding generation of Mormons has known less and less about some of the original doctrines that fueled the faith. This lack of knowledge, to some extent, has led to a greater acceptance on the part of some members of the Church of a more Protestant or Catholic understanding of their own faith. For example, it is not uncommon to hear members of the Church refer to Jesus as their "personal Savior," terminology that has it roots in the evangelical wing of Protestantism. (See section 19 on the atonement for a more complete discussion.) Hopefully, this study guide will help Latter-day Saints con-

---

1. See Feldman, "What Is It About Mormonism?" 36.

sider how Mormonism's founding fathers understood the faith and why it is important to preserve that understanding.

In this regard, Richard Bushman captured the historical context of nineteenth-century Mormonism as it is reflected in the Doctrine and Covenants. His keen understanding of the Prophet Joseph Smith and his interest in Joseph's ideas are reflected in his landmark biography of the prophet, *Joseph Smith: Rough Stone Rolling*. It is with this in mind that we quote, almost verbatim, a brief sketch of the history of early Mormonism given by Bushman at the Pew Forum on Religion and Public Life on May 14, 2007, in Key West, Florida, before the national press corps. His description is useful because he identifies the spirit of Mormonism at the time the Doctrine and Covenants was written. In doing so, Bushman acknowledges the difference between nineteenth-century Mormonism and what followed, what he refers to as Mormonism's "split image." I have taken the liberty to cross-reference his discussion to the relevant sections in the Doctrine and Covenants.

> That split image applies also to Mormonism's history, which also divides right down the middle. We think of the 19th century as a time when Mormonism was radical in about every dimension you can imagine, while in the 20th and 21st centuries Mormons are considered conservative in about every dimension you can imagine.... The interesting thing is that this switch from radicalism to conservatism occurred in such a short period of time, from about 1890, when polygamy ended, to about 1910, after the Reed Smoot hearings, which I'll talk about a little more later on.
>
> Let me talk first about 19th century radical Mormonism and point out some aspects of it that don't always get emphasized in histories of Mormonism but were absolutely critical to its original impetus.
>
> The radicalism, of course, is basically theological. You have to say, at the very least, that Joseph Smith, Mormonism's founding prophet, was daring and bold; perhaps you could say he was extravagant and rash. He seemed to be willing to challenge virtually everything in American culture. Beginning with the theological: he claimed to write new Scripture. His Book of Mormon and Doctrine and Covenants broke the monopoly of the Bible on the word of God. [See D&C 1:37; 20:1–16; 70; 73; 1 Nephi 13:26–29; 2 Nephi 29.] He even claimed he could revise the Bible, the most sacrosanct text in the Western world, through his own inspiration. [See D&C 24; 35; 36.] He added new passages and corrected the language where he chose, which was, by any measure, a heaven-daring act for a Christian to undertake in the 19th century. [See D&C 74; 77; 113; and Moses in the Pearl of Great Price.]
>
> In the social sphere, he breached Victorian moral conventions with the introduction of plural marriage, which nearly cost him his wife and nearly brought the church down. A lot of church members were horrified. In all of those ways, he was clearly radical. [See D&C 131 and 132.]
>
> But let me get a little closer to politics by talking about his daring in the

re-envisioning of society. What is not recognized about Joseph Smith is that there is a very deep strain of what I am calling "civic idealism" in him, by which I mean the construction of a new kind of urban society that would embody Christian principles more thoroughly.

The Mormon Church was organized in April of 1830. Within six months, Joseph Smith added to the church organization a civic organization, which he called the City of Zion. He attached it to the Book of Revelation's reference to the New Jerusalem. In 1831, a site for the city was chosen in Independence, Missouri. It was to be a place where the saints were to gather. It was a "city at the end of time" in that it was to function primarily as a place of refuge in the calamities that were certain to accompany the return of Christ in the last day. [See D&C 42:30; 44; 45; 51; 54; 57; 58; 63; 78; 82; 83; 85; 92; 96; 104.]

He planned that city, laid out a plat for it and instructed his people to gather there—not in a rush but in good order and in due time. From that point on, the creation of a City of Zion was at the very heart of Joseph Smith's work. In fact, he called it "The Work." By those words, he meant gathering people from out of the world into the city, instructing them in the ways of God, building a temple [see D&C 95; 109; 110; 115] and then sending out missionaries [See D&C 14; 15; 16; 35; 36; 44; 49; 60; 75; 79; 80; 84; 99] again to gather more. When one of these cities reached its capacity, which he estimated at 15,000 to 20,000 people, they were to build another city and, as he said, "so fill up the world in these last days."

His commitment to this city over against congregational worship is dramatized by the fact that never in his life did Joseph Smith build a chapel. When the population of Kirtland, Ohio, grew large enough—there were hundreds of Mormons in the town—that members came to him and suggested they ought to put up a little meeting place, he said, "No; I have another plan," and proposed the Kirtland Temple. Its two chapels stacked on top of another served as a meetinghouse, but it bore the name "temple" and served purposes that went far beyond a simple meetinghouse. From then on, wherever he built a city, he built temples—and never a chapel.

In Nauvoo, Illinois, the 5,000 to 10,000 people in town met outside in groves of trees or, in cold weather, in houses or other buildings. They were very casual about Sunday worship. Someone was selected as the moderator and he called people out of the congregation on the spot to preach. There was no pastor for many of these congregations. The organization at this level was thought of as temporary. The little branches of the church were really holding pens in preparation for the time when Mormons would all move to one of the gathering cities.

The city was meant to be not just a gathering place but an ideal society. One Scripture describes it this way: "And the Lord called his people Zion, because they were of one heart and one mind, and dwelt in righteousness; and there was no poor among them." [See Moses 7:18.] It was to be a unified, egalitarian, righteous society. Everyone was to live there. Farmers were to live in its bounds, their farms outside the city and their houses inside. A population of 15,000 to 20,000 seems small to us, but it wasn't small against the scale of cities in that time. St. Louis had 10,000; Cincinnati, the largest city in the West except for New Orleans, had 30,000 in 1830. So 15,000 or 20,000 is genuine urbanization; it's not a little village, but a city. [See D&C 42:30; 44; 45; 51; 54; 57; 58; 63; 78; 82; 83; 85; 92; 96; 104.]

To deal with the poor, everyone who came to the city was to consecrate everything—all of their property—to the bishop of the church, who in return would deed back to them properties sufficient for their needs. It was an equalization program. In fact, the word "equal" has a fairly strong place in Joseph Smith's revelations. For example: "That you may be equal in the bonds of heavenly things, yea, and earthly things also, for the obtaining of heavenly things. For if you are not equal in earthly things ye cannot be equal in obtaining heavenly things." [See D&C 78:5.] At another point, he made the drastic statement that inequality was a sign that the whole world lay in sin. [See D&C 49:20.] These Cities of Zion were to create unified, egalitarian societies and eventually fill up the world. [See D&C 42:30; 44; 45; 51; 54; 57; 58; 63; 78; 82; 83; 85; 92; 96; 104.]

Joseph Smith's thought evolved as he went through life. Initially, the city was just a place for Mormons, a "come-ye-out-of-Babylon-into-Zion" gathering place. But by the time he got to Nauvoo, Joseph Smith saw the city as more open. One of the first ordinances passed by the Nauvoo council was a toleration act specifying that all faiths were welcome in the city and listing a number of them: Presbyterians, Baptists, Methodists, Latter-day Saints, Catholics, Jews and "Mohammedans," as Muslims were called. There was probably not a Mohammedan within a thousand miles, but it was a gesture of openness to every religion.

Nauvoo, then, was to be a diverse city, indicating that Joseph Smith's civic idealism went beyond his own people to envision a much more cosmopolitan society. Nauvoo didn't develop that way; it came to an end too soon, but that is what he projected. Up to this point, Joseph Smith's reformist impulses were restricted mainly to the church and its program. But during the Nauvoo period—a seven-year window from Nauvoo's founding in 1839 to the Mormons leaving there in 1846—he expanded the city's scope.

Smith also got more involved in politics. Initially, he was disdainful of politics the way all millenarians are, taking the attitude that the nations of the earth are going to crumble and the kingdom of the Christ, as a Messiah, would arise. Smith was forced into politics by the abuse that the Mormons received. As soon as they were driven out of their first city site in Independence, Mo., he turned to the government for redress. [See 101:76; 105:25; D&C 134:11.] He never obtained it. No level of government, from local justices of the peace to governors to the president of the United States—to whom he constantly appealed—ever came to the defense of the Saints. But Joseph Smith became a great devotee of constitutional rights because they seemed like his only hope. [See D&C 98:5–6; 101:77, 80; 109:54.] He said some very extravagant things about the Constitution being God-given because of those rights and became quite conversant in constitutional matters. He even visited the president of the United States, Martin Van Buren, in the White House in 1839.

Gradually, then, Joseph Smith backed into American politics. In the fall of 1843, as the 1844 campaign began to take shape, the authorities of the church wrote to all of the known political candidates asking them about their views of the Mormons, and none returned a satisfactory answer from the Mormon point of view. The Mormons wanted a pledge that these candidates would protect them if they were attacked again, and they couldn't get it.

Joseph Smith was nominated as a protest candidate in February of 1844. Like other protest candidates, he began to warm to his work and got quite excited about it. He may have dreamed for a moment that through some strange concatenation of events, he would get elected. Every candidate has to dream such things.

His involvement in politics was manifested in a political platform of which he was very proud. He would bring it out whenever he had visitors and read from it. It is an interesting document because it represents a man whose world had been his own people, whose own project had been to create a kingdom of God, and who now had to turn his mind to politics.

He began by citing the Declaration of Independence, the famous passages about all men being equal and endowed by their creator with inalienable rights, which of course could be a lead-in to religious rights. But he didn't use it that way. Instead, in the very next sentence, he talked about the obvious contradiction: "Some two or three million people are held as slaves for life because the spirit in them is covered with a darker skin than ours." His platform called for the elimination of slavery, proposing that the funds from the sale of Western lands, a major source of revenue along with the tariff in those days, be devoted to purchasing slaves from their masters in order to avoid the conflict that would otherwise ensue. [See D&C 134:12[1] and D&C 101:79.]

Josiah Quincy, soon to be mayor of Boston, visited Joseph Smith in the spring of 1844 when this platform was in circulation. Much later, Quincy wrote about that visit, saying that Joseph Smith's proposal for ending slavery resembled one that Emerson made 11 years later in 1855. [See D&C 101:79.]

As Quincy put it, writing retrospectively in the 1880s, "We, who can look back upon the terrible cost of the fratricidal war which put an end to slavery, now say that such a solution of the difficulty"—Joseph Smith's and Emerson's—"would have been worthy a Christian statesman. But if the retired scholar was in advance of his time when he advocated this disposition of the public property in 1855, what shall I say of the political and religious leader who had committed himself, in print, as well as in conversation, to the same course in 1844?"

I cite this example to illustrate the radical tone of Joseph Smith's political thought, which seemed to carry over from his religious radicalism. It extended to prison reform and better treatment of seamen, big issues in the 1840s and 1850s. Smith seemed to identify with all of the underdogs in society. I think that was why he thought he might get elected—because the little people, the beat-up people, would rise and select him.

---

1. The sentiment in D&C 134:12 was more of a public relations statement than a statement of heartfelt belief. (See commentary to section 134.) The statement in section 101 that "it is not right that any man should be in bondage one to another" more accurately reflected Mormon thinking on this question.

This part of his platform accords perfectly with what modern people like us would have liked a candidate in 1844 to say. But Smith went beyond our sense of political propriety in other parts of his platform: he blended his role as candidate with his role as prophet. He was already mayor of Nauvoo and lieutenant general of the Nauvoo Legion when he ran for the presidency. He seemingly had no sense that church and state should be separated. He gave no hint that he was going to give up his religious offices if he were to become president of the United States.

In the closing peroration of his platform, Joseph Smith indirectly, but I think clearly, offered himself to be the priest of the people, as well as the president. "I would, as the universal friend of man, open the prisons, open the eyes, open the ears, and open the hearts of all people to behold and enjoy freedom, unadulterated freedom; and God, who once cleansed the violence of the earth with flood, whose Son laid down his life for the salvation of all his father gave him out of the world, and who has promised that he will come and purify the world again with fire in the last days, should be supplicated by me for the good of all the people." He would be the intercessor as priest as well as prophet.

Of course, that is the point at which moderns part company with Joseph Smith. We don't want a prophet with his authoritative words from God governing the nation. That seems to lead to the exclusion of unbelievers and the repression of naysayers. All the alarm bells go off when we see these roles merging.

But I would appeal to you, before you turn away completely from that idea, to pay heed to the underlying theme of that platform and that proposal. I think it can be argued that Joseph Smith actually felt he was fulfilling one of America's dreams. We think of the American dream as the promise of ascent for the wretched refuse of the teeming shores—the promise that in America, everyone has a chance to prosper and to achieve respectability. That is a dream for the individual.

But there also is a corporate dream, whether we like it or not, and that is of a righteous America, a people who are blessed of God—an America not too far from Joseph Smith's Zion, where the people are of one heart and one mind and dwell in righteousness and there are no poor among them. There is an American dream of a goodly society. Joseph Smith's word for his own political philosophy was "theo-democracy": God and the people.

This corporate American dream includes a virtuous political leadership with the unselfish purpose of seeking, without regard for personal good, the public good—not just to manage the varying interests of society but to bless people. This is the way Joseph Smith put it: "The wisdom which ought to characterize the freest, wisest and most noble nation of the 19th century should, like the sun in its meridian splendor, warm every object beneath its rays. And the main efforts of her officers, who are nothing more nor less than the servants of the people, ought to be directed to ameliorate the condition of all, black or white, bond or free."

I think you are aware of the aspiration of the Puritans for a "city on a hill" notable for its goodness more than its wealth. The dream of a goodly society lies behind famous pictures like "The Apotheosis of George Washington," which depicts Washington ascending to heaven accompanied by angels, just like Mary, turning him into a secular saint, almost. It is evident in the post-Civil War rhetoric describing Abraham Lincoln as the savior of the people, one who sacrificed his life for the nation's freedom. What I'm suggesting is that the image of goodness is in our collective imagination; it's present in our national culture.

Although Bushman does not mention all of the themes that were at the heart of early Mormonism in the nineteenth-century, such as the imminent expectation of the Second Coming, Millennialism, the rejection of original sin and some of Joseph's radical doctrines (the materiality of God, and the deification of men and women), his description of a religion centered on literally building a city called Zion, the ideal of economic equality, new scripture, controversial marriage practices, missionary activity, and changing the political and social structure of society, describes the setting in which the Doctrine and Covenants was written and many of the important issues that this study guide addresses. Since some of these themes are not emphasized and even marginalized by the Church today, readers of the Doctrine and Covenants may have a tendency to gloss over them and miss the message. By doing so a person fails to see the appeal of early Mormonism and the far-reaching and revolutionary ideas that attracted and energized its first converts. The Doctrine and Covenants is a far more sweeping book of scripture than is first realized by a modern reader and advocates comprehensive religious, social, economic, and political change. It is an early Mormon Manifesto.

Chapter 7

"The Kingdom of God or Nothing"

John Taylor was the third president of the Church. He followed his parents to Canada in 1832, where he met the Mormons and embraced the gospel in 1836. In 1837 he moved to Far West to join the main body of the Saints. He was ordained an apostle on December 19, 1838, and was one of the Prophet Joseph's closest associates. He was with the Prophet and the Prophet's brother Hyrum in Carthage when they were killed and was severely wounded himself. His eulogy to the Prophet Joseph was later canonized as Doctrine and Covenants 135.[1] No one understood better the original aims and aspirations of Mormonism than John Taylor. Over his lifetime, as opposition to the Church mounted, he fought valiantly to maintain his vision of what Joseph's kingdom of God was to become. He exhausted himself in the effort and died on July 25, 1887.

His successor, Wilford Woodruff, would reluctantly reassess the level of the opposition to some of Joseph's ideas and begin the process of changing Mormonism so that it could coexist with the government and the society at large. After spiritually agonizing over the need for change, Wilford Woodruff, one of the most visionary and inspired men of this  dispensation aside from Joseph Smith, received the revelations necessary to begin the process. (See commentary on Declaration 1.) As part of this transformation, the Church would begin a process of downplaying its more radical elements—communalism and polygamy. Based on these adjustments, Mormonism would be more fully accepted and assimilated into mainstream America, a process that haltingly continues even to this day.

Taylor's struggle to maintain Mormonism and build up the kingdom of God along the lines outlined by Joseph's revelations in the Doctrine and Covenants were impressive and can be summed up in his motto,

---

1. See *Encyclopedia of Mormonism*, 4:1438–41.

"The Kingdom of God or Nothing." The words themselves signified that the Saints had no interest in pledging allegiance to any government or organization that would to any degree diminish the religious and social vision of the Saints as a community where the most vulnerable were cared for and protected. For example, his commitment to the needs of the community and the poor was illustrated on April 6, 1880, when he proclaimed a jubilee year as observed in the Old Testament. He said that "it occurred to me that we ought to do something, as they did in former times, to relieve those that are oppressed with debt, to assist those that are needy . . . and to make it a time of general rejoicing."[1] He excused half the debt owed to the Perpetual Emigrating Fund, a fund set up to loan money to those who wished to migrate to the Great Basin. In addition, one thousand cows and five thousand sheep were given to the poor.[2]

The conflict to uphold the entirety of Joseph's vision for society after the Saints moved to the West was ferocious. Once settled in Utah, persecution under President Taylor's administration intensified. Missionaries were killed in the southern states. The U.S. Secretary of State tried to prevent Mormon immigrants from entering the country, stating that they were lawbreakers for belonging to an organization that sanctioned polygamy. The Edmunds Act was passed in 1882, which made polygamy a felony and prohibited Mormons from voting, holding public office, or serving on juries. Hundreds of Mormons, men and women, were arrested and put in prison. President Taylor established places of refuge in Mexico and Canada, and he and his counselors withdrew from public view to live on the run from federal marshals. By 1887 the Congress had passed the Edmunds-Tucker Act that "abolished women's suffrage [among Mormons], forced wives to testify against their husbands, disincorporated the Church, and escheated much of its property to the United States."[3] During these troubled times, President Taylor continued to preside over the Church in exile.

Ultimately the struggle to uphold some of Mormonism's original revelations would be lost, and those that followed would make the necessary changes so that the kingdom of God could survive in part, if not in whole. By the end of John Taylor's administration it was clear that the kingdom of God could not coexist with the kingdoms of the world. Within months after John Taylor's death, the Church would donate Arsenal Hill, the munitions arsenal for the transplanted Nauvoo Legion, to the Territory of Utah for property to build a capital. It was about this time that East Temple was changed to Main Street and Second East was renamed State Street. These

---

1. *Encyclopedia of Mormonism*, 4:1439.
2. See *Encyclopedia of Mormonism*, 4:1439.
3. *Encyclopedia of Mormonism*, 4:1439.

kinds of changes, though symbolic, corresponded to a more far-reaching transformation that was inevitable if Mormonism was to carry on and endure. At each step along the way, Mormon leaders sought and received inspiration and revelation to find out what God expected of them and what changes were necessary.

The conflict was not just about marriage practices; it also involved the Mormons' unwillingness to integrate into the mainstream American economy. As historian Leonard Arrington explained, polygamy was only one of the issues that plagued the Church. "As part of the 'deal'" for the territory to become a state, the Church would not only give up polygamy but also "discontinue its alleged fight against Gentile business and relax its own [communal] economic efforts."[1] Therefore, it was about this time that the First Presidency, after much prayer and thoughtful consideration, began to tone down its appraisal of what they described in 1877 as the "growing spirit of acquisitiveness and individualism" in the world and to emphasize "a more saintly selflessness and devotions to the building of the Kingdom."[2] Not long thereafter, the Church began to discontinue its various communal economic orders, which had emphasized equality of wealth and centralization of capital in Church hands for the good of the community rather than leaving resources in individual hands for selfish consumption. Arrington put it succinctly, saying that along with polygamy, "The temporal Kingdom, for all practical purposes was dead—slain by the dragon of Edmunds-Tucker."[3]

Joseph Smith's vision of the "ideal society" would be put on hold and in large part has been lost to modern Latter-day Saints who do not have an interest in Mormon history and assume that the Mormonism of the twenty-first century has not changed much from its origins. In the beginning, the Mormon kingdom was a society patterned after Enoch's ideal society and the one that Jesus established in the Americas after the resurrected Lord visited the American continent. At base, these societies were organized around the principle of equality of wealth and opportunity, a state of being in which the world was transformed into a place of plenty, with no slave or tyrant. The scope of the transformation is summed up in a passage that reflects the economic idealism of first generation Christians found in Sibylline Oracles 2, as cited by John Dominic Crossen in *The Apocalyptic Jesus: A Debate:*[4] "The earth will belong equally to all, undivided by walls or fences. . . . Lives will be in common and wealth will have no division.

---

1. Arrington, *Great Basin Kingdom*, 379.
2. Arrington, *Great Basin Kingdom*, 338.
3. Arrington, *Great Basin Kingdom*, 379.
4. Crossen, in *The Apocalyptic Jesus: A Debate* (Santa Rosa, CA: Polebridge, 2001), 58–59. See also Borg, *Jesus*, 187.

For there will be no poor man there, no rich, and no tyrant, no slave. Further, no one will be either great or small anymore. No kings, no leaders. All will be on a par together." Like their spiritual forebears, this was the same society that the early Latter-day Saints were striving for.

Both the Book of Mormon and the Doctrine and Covenants talk about God's kingdom in similar ways. In describing the antithesis of what God envisioned for his sons and daughters, the Book of Mormon warns that societies have a tendency to be "lifted up unto pride and boastings because of their exceedingly great riches." (3 Nephi 6:10.) Further, this unacceptable state of affairs comes about because societies distinguish "by ranks, according to their riches and their chances for learning; yea, some were ignorant because off their poverty, and others did receive great learning because of their riches." (3 Nephi 6:12.) "And thus there became a great inequality in all the land." (3 Nephi 6:14.) This depraved condition was reversed when the Savior appeared on the American continent, the high point in the Book of Mormon. He launched the kingdom of God on earth, a society where the people had "all things common among them; therefore there were not rich and poor, bond and free, but they were all made free and partakers of the heavenly gift." (4 Nephi 1:3.) Consequently, the gifts of the Spirit were generally present, and there was no strife. The overall assessment was that "there could not be a happier people among all the people who had been created by the hand of God." (4 Nephi 1:16, 5, 7, 13, 17.)

The kingdom of God established by Jesus in the Americas just after his death and resurrection was the kind of society that Joseph Smith was trying to establish in Jackson County, Missouri. "And behold, thou wilt remember the poor, and consecrate of thy properties for their support." (D&C 42:30.) "Every man" was to be "equal according to his family, according to his circumstances and his wants and needs." (D&C 51:3.) "Nevertheless, in your temporal things you shall be equal, and this not grudgingly." (D&C 70:14.) The reason it was so important to reinstitute this economic vision was because of its social consequences—all, not just some, of God's children could be nurtured, and cared for. If this were the case, then each of God's sons and daughters would progress and have the opportunity to advance and improve and grow to be increasingly like their Heavenly Parents. (See D&C 76:50–70.) As God revealed to Joseph, "That you may be equal in the bonds of heavenly things, yea, and earthly things also, for the obtaining of heavenly things. For if ye are not equal in earthly things ye cannot be equal in obtaining heavenly things." (D&C 78:5–6.)

Kingdom building along the lines that Jesus and his prophet Joseph envisioned almost always comes into sharp disagreement with the mores and way of life in the existing social order. Jesus' kingdom provoked bloodshed before and after his death. The revelations to Joseph patterned after Jesus' model would meet similar resistance.

It is with these thoughts in mind that when reading the Doctrine and Covenants, it is important for us to recognize that the revelations Joseph received were radical and far-reaching. Beginning with the move west, the implications of what Joseph had in mind were subdued, and after fierce persecution by the society at large the idea that it was the kingdom of God or nothing gave way to a more pressing question: How can we survive?

The first two casualties that gave way to outside pressure were polygamy and economic idealism, the main points of contention between the Mormons and the outside world. These two practices alone made it impossible for Mormons and non-Mormons to live next to each other peacefully. In addition, other ideas and doctrines contributed to outsiders' skepticism that fueled the firestorm of anti-Mormon resentments. The suggestion of God's anthropomorphism, the doctrine of three distinct and separate members of the Godhead instead of the traditional Trinity, the deification of worthy men and women, the plurality of gods, the errancy of the Bible, the introduction of secret rites and rituals, Mormon anti-slavery sentiment, the belief that the Indians were a favored people (a branch of the house of Israel), and the Saints' insistence that Jackson County, Missouri, was Zion, a place that Jesus would visit at his Second Coming, all contributed to the basic antipathy of those outside the fold. Add to this the insult to non-Mormons when some Mormons erroneously claimed they had a divine right of ownership to the land in Jackson County, Missouri and that non-Mormons were disqualified from living there, and one begins to understand why Mormonism was unwelcome.

With the exception of the last mentioned, each of the concepts spoken about in the preceding paragraph was openly and unswervingly attested to in the revelations of Joseph Smith. There was no way around it. For example, as early as February 1832 Joseph Smith revealed that men and women could become gods and goddesses. (See D&C 76:58–60.) In reference to God having a body and the concept of the trinity, the revelations held that "the Father has a body of flesh and bones as tangible as man's; the Son also; but the Holy Ghost has not a body of flesh and bones, but is a personage of Spirit." (D&C 130:22.) And, in reference to the third member of the Godhead, Joseph clarified that the Holy Ghost was a "personage," by which he meant that the Holy Ghost was composed of "refined matter."[1] (See D&C 131:7–8.) This direct attack on the almost universally accepted ideas about the Godhead and the three-in-one Trinity was more

---

1. Smith, *History of the Church*, 4:575.

than enough to earn Joseph Smith a bad reputation among traditional Christianity.

Chapter 8

The Doctrine and Covenants and Systemic Injustice

Systemic injustice is defined as an excessive inequality of wealth and station in a society that comes about as a consequence of the way in which the prevailing social order or establishment is structured. It is a configuration that devalues the contributions made by some of its members and allows the ruling elite to prosper at the expense of others. It inevitably includes a disparity in wealth and social status and oftentimes results in the violation of basic human rights. In a religious context, systemic injustice is a moral issue because it involves the mistreatment of God's children.

Marcus Borg, a well-known Christian scholar, suggests several questions that can reasonably be asked in connection with this idea. To what extent does a society benefit at the expense of the many or serve all equally? Does the society produce a large impoverished class or result in a more equitable distribution of resources? Does the society produce conflict or peace? Does the society destroy or nourish the future?[1]

A primary example of systemic injustice is slave labor prior to the American civil war period. The economy of the South depended on a subservient class exploited by the ruling class to produce the wealth necessary for the ruling class to live luxuriously and enjoy social and political influence. Southern hospitality played favorites, and there was a  vast difference between the privileged white Americans and black African slaves, who were denied equal social, political, educational, and economic prospects.

To a lesser or greater degree, depending upon the social and political order, the very same dynamic is at work in the world today. Ruling elites,

---

1. See Borg, *Reading the Bible Again for the First Time*, 139.

disproportionate wealth, unequal educational opportunities, differences in access to medical care, the incongruent treatment of LGBTs, the disparate treatment of women, racial discrimination around the globe, and the exploitation of a servant class abound. Such behavioral patterns are ubiquitous and without exception are condemned in the canon of scripture. For example, just prior to the coming of Jesus to the Americas, the prophets condemned Nephite civilization for its inequality. "And the people began to be distinguished by ranks, according to their riches and their chances for learning; yea, some were ignorant because of their poverty, and others did receive great learning because of their riches." (3 Nephi 6:12.) The Book of Mormon says that the "cause of this iniquity" was Satan, who "had great power, unto the stirring up of the people to do all manner of iniquity, and to the puffing them up with pride, tempting them to seek for power, and authority and riches, and the vain things of the world." (3 Nephi 6:15.) Such conduct was described as a "willful" rebellion against God.

Social injustice and its converse, the recognition that members of societies have a collective obligation to care for each other, are important considerations when approaching the Doctrine and Covenants. Like the Book of Mormon, the Pearl of Great Price, and the Bible, the Doctrine and Covenants is filled with unease about the misuse of power and wealth. "For if ye are not equal in earthly things ye cannot be equal in obtaining heavenly things." (D&C 78:6.) "We have learned by sad experience that it is the nature and disposition of almost all men, as soon as they get a little authority, . . . they will immediately begin to exercise unrighteous dominion." (D&C 121:39.) In fact, nearly a third of the sections in the Doctrine and Covenants are in some way connected with the building of Zion, a society where all things were held in common and all were on the same standing with God and each other. This classless, communitarian society is held up as the ideal and was a chief concern for Joseph and first-generation Mormons.

To place this idea of systemic injustice in perspective, it is useful to examine its roots in the Old and New Testament, where it is assumed that societies as well as individuals sin. In fact, this idea was so engrained in Jewish culture that not only did individuals seek forgiveness of sin but separate blood offerings were made for the society at large (the blood and sins of a generation). Each year on the Day of Atonement, the high priest would "present the bull as a sin offering to make atonement for himself and his family," just as others did for themselves and their families. Then the high priest would bring two goats to the door of the Tabernacle to atone for the collective sins of God's people. One was sacrificed and the other sent out into the wilderness as a "scapegoat" after the high priest had laid "both of his hands on the goat's head and confess[ed] over it all the sins and rebellion of the Israelites." (NLT Leviticus 16:6–23.) In this way the high priest figuratively transferred the sins of the society onto the head of the goat and sent the collective sins of the Israelites into the desert.

Jewish law did more than simply ask for forgiveness for the sins of society at large. The Torah proactively promoted social justice by implementing practices that resulted in greater parity. It is common knowledge that the Pentateuch required that land could not be bought or sold in perpetuity because it belonged to God. "And remember, the land must never be sold on a permanent basis because it really belongs to me." (NLT Leviticus 25:23.) The idea was to make sure that every family would be able to keep its land or redeem it if it were lost through debt. Every seventh year, all debts were forgiven and all indentured slaves were set fee. Thus a permanent servant class was discouraged. Finally, in the jubilee year (every fiftieth year), all rural land was returned, without payment, to the original family of ownership. This regulation acknowledged that a family might lose its land through foreclosure on debt, but absolutely mandated its eventual return. The idea prevented the growth of a landless class and the concentration of wealth by a few.[1] Everyone would have a plot of land to farm so that all would have the basic necessities of life.

The significance of Jewish social policy is demonstrated when compared to the "common form of society in the time from the emergence of early agrarian empires in 3000 B.C. through the Middle Ages of the current era."[2] The society had two primary social classes, the urban ruling elites—"elites holding the reins of power, wealth, and status—[which] consisted of the traditional aristocracy, the monarchy at its center. With their extended families, these elites comprised about one to two percent of the population."[3] The other class, which made up over 90 percent of the population, was composed of rural peasants (agricultural workers) as well as fisherman and artisans.[4] The primary economic fact was that about two-thirds of the annual production of wealth ended up in the hands of the ruling elites. This was accomplished by taxation on agricultural production and direct ownership of land, with peasants working as share-croppers, day-laborers, or slaves.[5] Marcus Borg said that you could describe such societies in three phrases. "They were marked by economic exploitation, political oppression (ordinary people had no voice in the structuring of society), and religious legitimation (the religion of the elites affirmed that the structures of society

---

1. See Borg, *Jesus*, 100.
2. Borg, *Reading the Bible Again for the Very First Time*, 103–4.
3. Borg, *Reading the Bible Again for the Very First Time*, 104.
4. See Borg, *Reading the Bible Again for the Very First Time*, 104.
5. See Borg, *Reading the Bible Again for the Very First Time*, 104.

were ordained by God)."[1] This was the world that Moses wanted to escape and what the radical economic legislation of the Pentateuch was designed to secure—one with universal land ownership and no monarchy.[2] *

Of all the Old Testament prophets, Amos leveled some of the most searing criticism at the social injustice that existed during his day when the collective community turned a blind eye and deaf ear to the cries of the less fortunate. "You trample the poor and steal what little they have through taxes and unfair rent." (NLT Amos 6:10–13.) Therefore, "How terrible it will be for you who lounge in luxury and think you are secure." (NLT Amos 6:1–7.) "This is what he, the Lord God Almighty, says: I despise the pride and false glory of Israel, and I hate their beautiful homes. I will give this city and everything in it to their enemies." (NLT Amos 6:8.) In the same tradition Isaiah spoke out against those who "beat my people to pieces, and grind the faces of the poor." (KJV Isaiah 3:15.)

The New Testament Jesus is equally critical of a social system that is unconcerned with economic and social disparity. The story of the rich man who was splendidly clothed and who lived each day in luxury illustrates the point. At his door lay a diseased beggar named Lazarus, who lay there longing for scraps from the rich man's table as the dogs licked his open sores. Both died, and the rich man found his soul in hell and Lazarus in heaven. "The rich man shouted . . . have some pity! Send Lazarus over here to dip the tip of his finger in water and cool my tongue, because I am in anguish in these flames." In the story, God ignores the rich man's cries as the rich man had ignored Lazarus' pleas. (NLT Luke 16:19–31.)

Jesus addressed such lack of correspondence by requiring his followers a Kingdom of God in which all shared what they had with each other. When another rich man approached Jesus, a man who had lived all of the commandments since his youth, Jesus commanded, "Go and sell all you have and give the money to the poor" and then "come, follow me." (NLT Matthew 19:16–30.) The rich man declined Jesus' invitation because "he had many possessions." (NLT Matthew 19:21.) Later, Peter and the apostles established an order where "all were of one heart and mind, and they felt that what they owned was not their own; they shared everything they had." (NLT Acts 4:32.) In the words of the King James translation, "[The Saints] had all things in common." (KJV Acts 4:32.)[3]

---

1. Borg, *Reading the Bible Again for the Very First Time*, 104.
2. See Borg, *Reading the Bible Again for the Very First Time*, 104.
3. Jesus' concern for systemic injustice may also be seen in his warning to the rich. "Woe to you who are rich, for you have received your consolation. Woe to you who are full now, for you will be hungry. Woe to you who are laughing now, for you will mourn and weep. Woe to you when all speak well of you, for that is what their ancestors did to the false prophets." (Matthew 6:24–26.) Of particular concern to the Sadducees and Pharisees was that Jesus

The Jesus of the Doctrine and Covenants is entirely consistent with the God and Jesus of the Old and New Testaments on this issue of systemic injustice. The rule of economic equality or law of consecration is presented as the order of things in heaven that must also be established on earth. (See D&C 88:5.) It is a financial arrangement that cares for the poor and uses the excess capital in the community for the benefit of the group instead of the individual. "But it is not given that one man should possess that which is above another, wherefore the world lieth in sin." (D&C 49:20. 6.) "Wo unto you rich men, that will not give your substance to the poor, for your riches will canker your souls; and this shall be your lamentation in the day of visitation, and of judgment, and of indignation: The harvest is past, the summer is ended, and my soul is not saved!" (D&C 56:16.) Like the early Christians, the Doctrine and Covenants directs that the Saints live so that "in your temporal things you shall be equal, and this not grudgingly." (D&C 70:14.) "And you are to be equal, or in other words, you are to have equal claims on the properties, for the benefit of managing the concerns of your stewardships, every man according to his wants and his needs, inasmuch as his wants are just." (D&C 82:17.) Indeed, the accord between the Old and New Testaments and the Doctrine and Covenants on the issue of systemic injustice and caring for the poor and for each other is evidence of Mormonism's divine origins. Had Joseph Smith left this out of the restoration it would be difficult for him to claim that he restored the Kingdom of God as the early Christians knew it.

Finally, both the Jesus of the New Testament and the Jesus of the Doctrine and Covenants seem to draw a distinction between his revulsion for systemic injustice and his compassion for individual weakness. In the four Gospels, Jesus' passion is aroused when He talks about the rich and powerful binding "heavy burdens" on people's shoulders and of the ruling elite devouring "widows' houses." He referred to these people as "serpents" and "sons of vipers" who were "clean on the outside" but "filthy" and "full of greed and self indulgence! . . . filled on the inside with dead people's bones and all sorts of impurity." (KJV and NLT Matthew 23.) It was to these that he queried, "How will you escape the judgments of hell?" (Matthew 23:33.) It is of those who give offense to the weak that he said that it would have been better that a millstone be tied around their neck and they be drowned.

By way of difference, Jesus unerringly responded to people's sins with sympathy. To the woman caught in adultery he spoke softly and respect-

---

intended to do something about the disparity between the rich and the poor. He publicly prayed that the kingdoms of the earth would give way to the kingdom of God. "May your kingdom come soon. May your will be done here on earth, just as it is in heaven." (NLT Matthew 6:10.)

fully. He did not accuse her as the Pharisees had done but told her that there was time to change. (See John 8:11.) Jesus was equally as kind to the Samaritan woman who lived in sin because she had cohabited with five husbands and was not even married to the man she was presently living with. (See John 4:16–18.)

Likewise, the Jesus of the Doctrine and Covenants severely condemns those in a position to exploit others, while showing compassion to the individual sinner. "Behold, I say unto you, were it not for the transgressions of my people, speaking concerning the church and not individuals, they might have been redeemed even now. But behold, they . . . are full of all manner of evil, and do not impart of their substance . . . to the poor and afflicted among them." (D&C 105:2–3.) On a personal level the Lord reassures, "Notwithstanding their sins, my bowels are filled with compassion towards them. I will not utterly cast them off; and in the day of wrath I will remember mercy." (D&C 101:9.)

For Mormons in the twenty-first century, who practice their religion with an eye on personal righteousness and are less concerned than their forefathers about bringing about social justice, the Doctrine and Covenants is yet another reminder that personal goodness, although essential, is just half of the equation. The other half acknowledges that salvation also requires that people live in cities, towns, and nations that are focused on "love of neighbor" and thought and care for the very "least" person.[1] The ideal of Zion involves community, living in a society in which people "dwell" together in "righteousness" as "one," with "no poor among them." (Moses 7:18.)

---

1. This idea is summed up in the parable of the sheep and goats. "But when the Son comes in his glory, and all the angels with him, then he will sit upon his glorious throne. All the nations will be gathered in his presence, and he will separate them as a shepherd separates the sheep from the goats. He will place the sheep at his right hand and the goats at his left. Then the King will say to those on the right, 'Come, you who are blessed by my Father, inherit the Kingdom prepared for you from the foundation of the world. For I was hungry and you fed me. I was thirsty, and you gave me a drink. I was a stranger, and you invited me into your home. I was naked, and you have given me clothing. I was sick, and you cared for me. I was in prison and you visited me.' I assure you, when you did it to one of the least of these my brothers and sisters, you were doing it to me!" (NLT Matthew 25:31–36.)

Chapter 9

A Book of Revelations

"That every man might speak in the name of the Lord."
Doctrine and Covenants 1:20

THE CONCEPT OF UNIVERSAL REVELATION AND CONFLICT WITHIN THE CHURCH

From the very beginning Joseph taught his followers that revelations from God were not restricted to the Prophet alone but were available to everyone who believed. He said that "God has not revealed anything to Joseph but what He will make known unto the Twelve, and even the least Saint may know all things as fast as he [or she] is able to bear them."[1] Thus, the kingdom of God would not have only one prophet but many prophets and prophetesses.[2] It would be a fulfillment of Moses' plea: "Would God that all the Lord's people were prophets, and that the Lord would put his spirit upon them!" (Numbers 11:26–29.) As far as Joseph was concerned, when it came to revelation it was not necessary to have priest intercessories.

---

1. Smith, *Teachings of the Prophet Joseph Smith*, 149. The idea of universal revelation is found in the preamble to the Doctrine and Covenants. As part of the restoration of the gospel, it was intended that "every man might speak in the name of God the Lord, even the Savior of the world." (D&C 1:20.) Also, "This is an ensample unto [all people], that they shall speak as they are moved upon by the Holy Ghost, and whatsoever they shall speak when moved upon by the Holy Ghost shall be scripture, shall be the will of the Lord, shall be the mind of the Lord, shall be the word of the Lord, shall be the voice of the Lord, and the power of God unto salvation." (D&C 68:2–4.)

2. Joseph Smith also taught that women could and should enjoy the same spiritual privileges that men did. (See D&C 93:1.)

The idea that all members of the Church could receive revelations sometimes created tension among the Prophet Joseph, other leaders of the Church, and the members. If all could speak in the name of the Lord, who should have the final say? These issues were sorted out during the Kirtland period and specifically addressed in the Doctrine and  Covenants. Suffice it to say that authoritative revelations for the entire Church were at first restricted to Joseph Smith and, after the Church was more fully organized, to the First Presidency. However, this did not prohibit other Church leaders from receiving divine guidance as they carried out their own Church assignments in areas where they had been given personal jurisdiction, as long as it did not conflict with higher authority. Revelation on a personal level was never restricted, but Joseph cautioned that all revelations were not of God and therefore it was important to learn how to discern the difference between false and true communications from the unseen world.[1]

Methods the Lord Used to Communicate with Joseph Smith

The revelations which the Prophet Joseph received and which were included in the Doctrine and Covenants were communicated in a number of different ways:

1. Declarations and polices that were not considered revelations. (DC 134)

2. Inspired letters or written statements. (See D&C 85; 121; 122; 127; 128; 129.)

3. Inspired interpretations of scripture. (See D&C 7; 74; 77; 113.)
4. Audible voice from heaven. (See D&C 130:12–13.)
5. Open visions. (See D&C 76; 137; 138.)
6. Angelic appearances. (See D&C 13 [John the Baptist]; 27 [angel]; 110 [Moses, Elias, Elijah].)
7. Appearances of God the Father and Jesus Christ. (See D&C 76 [God the Father and Jesus Christ]; 110 [Jesus].)

---

1. Joseph Smith said, "The Church of Jesus Christ of Latter-day Saints has also had its false spirits; and as it is made up of all those different sects professing every variety of opinion, and having been under the influence of so many kinds of spirits, it is not to be wondered at if there should be found among us false spirits." (Smith, *Teachings of the Prophet Joseph Smith*, 213.)

On many occasions, Joseph's revelations were received during or after he had called a group of followers together to solve problems in an impromptu "conference" of twenty or so individuals who would "sit in council" with Joseph. Those present were free to speak, make suggestions, and ask questions about matters of importance. On other occasions, a revelation might grow out of a conversation Joseph had with one or more individuals on a given subject. Parley P. Pratt described how a revelation was received in a situation where Joseph, John Murdock, and others had been talking about discerning the difference between true and false spirits. Joseph had the brethren join in prayer in the translating room in the Whitney store located in Kirtland, Ohio. Pratt said:

> Each sentence was uttered slowly and very distinctly; and with a pause between each, sufficiently long for it to be recorded, by an ordinary writer, in long hand.
>
> This was the manner in which all his written revelations were dictated and written. There was never any hesitation, reviewing, or reading back, in order to keep the run of the subject; neither did any of these communications undergo revisions, interlinings, or corrections. As he dictated them so they stood, so far as I have witnessed.[1]

Once recorded, members considered the statements authoritative and would sometimes ask to make copies of what was said. Handwritten copies were sometimes referred to as "pocket revelations" because they could be carried around and quoted. Ultimately, it was decided that it would be better to simply publish a book of Joseph's revelations.

Continuing Nature of Revelation

Since revelation was considered ongoing, new revelations were added as time went on. The first book of Joseph's revelations, known as The Book of Commandments, contained 65 revelations, while the second (1835) edition had 103. Two items in the 1835 edition contained policy statements, one on marriage[2] (then D&C 101) and another on the role of government (D&C 102; now D&C 134).[3] After Joseph's death, regular additions to the Doctrine and Covenants were discontinued. However, additions were made as recently as the 1981 edition, which included Joseph F. Smith's vision of the spirit world and one new declaration discontinuing a policy

---

1. Pratt, Autobiography, 65–66.
2. D&C 101 on marriage did not reflect an understanding of "celestial" marriage and was therefore taken out later and eventually replaced by D&C 132.
3. Oliver Cowdery possibly wrote D&C 134.

that did not allow persons of African lineage to hold the priesthood or participate in temple rituals.

THE DOCTRINE AND COVENANTS AND INERRANCY

Joseph Smith never considered his revelation—or for that matter any book of scripture[1]—a perfect reflection of what God intended. Scripture was given to men and women "in their weakness, after the manner of their language, that they might come to understanding." (D&C 1:24.) It was expected that God's word was limited by man's ability to express it. Therefore, spelling and grammatical errors, as well as mistakes in content, were to be expected. The part that men and women played in expressing God's will meant that there was no such thing as inerrancy.

Understanding that revelations from God were not faultless, Joseph organized a committee to correct as many errors as could be found in his revelations before they were published in the second edition of the Doctrine and Covenants (1835). Spelling and grammatical errors were corrected and language and meaning clarified. Some revelations received additional language to reflect ideas that had been revealed more recently. (See D&C 20.) Some sections were combined with others for convenience' sake. Most of the changes made were minor.[2]

Some members who believed that revelations from God should be faultless criticized Joseph Smith.[3] When the decision was being made to publish the revelations at a Church conference, William E. McLellin objected because he felt some of the revelatory language was substandard and inferior. He thought he could do better. He was invited to do so but failed in his attempt. (See D&C 67.) Sidney Rigdon also raised concerns about errors and mistakes in the revelations. The decision was made to request "Brother Joseph Jr. [to] correct those errors or mistakes which are in [the] commandments and revelations which he may discover by the

---

1. Even the Book of Mormon warns, "Whoso receiveth this record, and shall not condemn it because of the imperfections which are in it, the same shall know of greater things." (Mormon 8:12, 17.)

2. An exception to this general rule is D&C 8 on the "rod of Aaron."

3. Jonathan B. Turner adversely reacted to changes in the revelations. He said, "It would have been well for the world if Smith's divinity, instead of giving him a pair of stone spectacles, had given him a divine printer, and a divine press, and such types that he might have been enabled to fix the meaning of his inspired revelations, so that it would be possible to let them stand, at least two years, without abstracting, interpolating, altering, or garbling, to suit the times. But the ways of Smith's providence are indeed mysterious. We will not pretend to judge." (Turner, *Mormonism in All Ages*, 226.)

Holy Spirit while reviewing the revelations and commandments and also the fullness of the scriptures."[1]

Richard Bushman addresses the issue of Joseph Smith and language limitations in his book of essays, *Believing History*. He referred to a letter dated November 1832, written by Joseph Smith and sent to W.W. Phelps, who, at that time, was the editor of the Church newspaper in Missouri. In this letter Joseph expressed his fervent desire that at last he might be delivered "from the little, narrow prison" of language which he described as "almost . . . total darkness of paper, pen and ink; and a crooked, broken, scattered and imperfect language."[2] As Bushman points out, the words suggest that Joseph envisioned more than he could express. Gazing into heaven was one thing. Writing it down was another.

The idea that revelation was continuous meant that clarifications could always be made in what had come before. Therefore, "the flow of revelations prevented him [Joseph Smith] from ever saying the work was finished."[3] By its very nature, revelation was an ongoing process. Coming to a perfect understanding was a step-by-step process, "line upon line, precept upon precept." Therefore, Joseph Smith never intended that his revelations, once received, could not be changed, or that they represented the "totality of belief."[4] The idea that revelation was an unfinished product also influenced Joseph's thinking about religious creeds that locked down a particular understanding of doctrine. He said, "The creeds set up stakes, and say hitherto shalt thou come, and not further—which I can not subscribe to."[5]

Pocket Revelations and the Publication of a Book

At first, when Joseph received revelations, converts and later members of the Church were anxious to read and refer to them. Joseph allowed some members to copy them. People would literally fold handwritten copies and put them in their pockets for future reference. As mentioned, copied revelations were referred to as "pocket revelations."[6] Since there were no copy machines, the scraps of paper containing important revelations were riddled with errors made by the copyist.

As for making the revelations generally available the early revelations

---

1. Cannon and Cook, *Far West Record*, 29.
2. Bushman, *Believing History*, 249–50.
3. Bushman, *Joseph Smith*, 285.
4. Bushman, *Joseph Smith*, 285.
5. Bushman, *Joseph Smith*, 285.
6. Robin Scott Jensen, Richard Turley Jr. Riley M. Lorimer, *The Joseph Smith Papers: Revelations and Translations*, Vol. 2, xxiv.

"cautioned leaders against sharing the texts widely."[1] A revelation in March 1830 warned "she not these things neither speak these things unto the World." (D&C 19:21) However, by November of 1831 the Lord commanded that certain revelations were now "to go forth unto all flesh and this according to the mind and the will of the Lord." (D&C 133:60-61)

It was under these circumstances that Joseph spoke with W. W. Phelps about publishing a book of revelations. (See D&C 55:4.) Phelps was a printer and newspaper editor by trade and therefore was particularly well qualified. He was commanded to establish a print shop in Independence, Missouri. (See D&C 57:11–12.) Phelps had purchased a printing press in Cincinnati in September 1831 and transported it to Independence, where he had started to publish a monthly newspaper called *The Evening and Morning Star.* Some of the earliest revelations of Joseph Smith were published in this paper.

The formal decision to publish revelations in book form was made at a conference of the Church in Hiram, Ohio, in early November 1831. By that time Joseph had received and written down about 70 revelations. At first it was decided to publish 10,000 copies, but this idea was scaled back to 3,000. A Literary Firm was organized in Independence, Missouri, as the publishing arm of the Church. The Lord authorized Joseph Smith, Oliver Cowdery, Sidney Rigdon, John Whitmer, and Martin Harris to be compensated for their work on this project. (See D&C 72:20–21.) In addition to the Doctrine and Covenants, it was anticipated that the firm would also publish Joseph's inspired version of the Bible, children's literature, an almanac, a newspaper, and a hymnal.

By December 1832 Phelps had undertaken publication of Joseph's revelations. He sent proofs to Kirtland for the Prophet's approval. Unfortunately, tensions developed between the incoming Mormons and the local Missourians, which centered around religious, political, and social concerns. An anti-Mormon mob was organized on July 20, 1833, and destroyed the printing press and most of the copies of the Book of Commandments (the name for the first Doctrine and Covenants). The name Book of Commandments came about because members of the Church commonly referred to Joseph's revelations as "commandments." (D&C 1:6.) The destruction of the press in Independence, Missouri, necessitated moving this function to Kirtland, Ohio, which in 1835 printed the second compilation of Joseph's revelations now named the Doctrine and Covenants.[2]

Since the Book of Commandments "did not succeed in making the reve-

---

1. Ibid, xxiii.
2. The destruction of the earliest editions of the Book of Commandments makes it one of the most difficult books for Mormon collectors to acquire. A copy of the original 1833 edition can be found in the New York Public Library, New York City, New York.

lations widely available, printed versions of some revelations had become publicly available as early as 1832" when the Church started the first official newspaper called *The Evening and Morning Star*.[1] Eventually, 26 full of partial revelatory texts appeared between June 1832 and June 1833.[2]

The second (1835) edition of The Book of Commandments was re-named the Doctrine and Covenants of the Church of Latter Day Saints. At a general conference in August 1835, it was accepted as the word of the Lord by a vote of the Church. The name of the book was changed from the Book of Commandments because Joseph decided to include in it a series of seven theological essays known as *The Lectures on Faith*. The lectures were placed in a separate section titled, *On the Doctrine of the Church of the Latter Day Saints*. The part of the book containing the revelations of Joseph Smith was titled *Part Second, Covenants and Commandments*. This part of the book contained all that Joseph had intended to include in the original 1833 edition, plus other revelations the prophet had received since then. Therefore, the word "doctrine" in the title of the 1835 edition referred to *The Lectures on Faith*. The word "covenants" sometimes used interchangeably with the word "commandments" denoted Joseph's revelations.

Other Major Editions of the Doctrine and Covenants

In 1844, shortly after the death of the Prophet Joseph, a third edition appeared. Eight new revelations were added (D&C 103; 105; 112; 119; 124; 127; 128; and 135). In 1876, Orson Pratt, a member of the Quorum of the Twelve, headed up publication of another edition. Twenty-six new sections were added (D&C 2; 13; 77; 85; 108–11; 113–18; 120–23; 125–26; 129–32; and 136). Elder Pratt divided each revelation into verses. It was in this edition that the sections on "eternal marriage" were added (D&C 131–32). In 1921 President Heber J. Grant authorized another edition. *The Lectures on Faith* were removed from the book at this time; however, the title of the book did not reflect this and remained the same. The footnotes were revised, and the pages were divided into double columns. Later, a declaration ending the practice of polygamy, Joseph F. Smith's vision of the spirit world, and a declaration ending a policy that banned those of African lineage from holding the priesthood were added.

---

1. Robin Scott Jensen, Richard E. Turley, Riley M. Lorimer, *The Joseph Smith Papers: Revelations and Translations*, Vol. 2, xxvii.
2. Ibid.

THE OVERALL STRUCTURE AND TONE OF THE DOCTRINE AND COVENANTS

The Doctrine and Covenants tracks the history of the Church. Therefore, it is convenient to group its revelations based on the particular time period and place the revelations were received. Sections 2 to 19 were received in New York and Harmony, Pennsylvania, prior to the organization of the Church. Sections 20 to 40 concern issues that arose in Harmony, Pennsylvania, and in Fayette, New York. Sections 41 to 123 deal with the Ohio and Missouri periods. Sections 124 to 135 concern the Nauvoo period and the closing days of the Prophet Joseph's ministry. The remaining sections (136 to 138) move the Saints from Winter Quarters to the Great Basin.

The Doctrine and Covenants quotes liberally from the King James Bible and contains more than 2,000 parallels to biblical passages.[i] The sections range from "forms as transcendent as visions (sections 3, 76, 110), angelic annunciations (sections 2, 13, 27), and prophecies (sections 87, 121); through such ecclesiastical proclamations as prayers (sections 109, 121), epistles (sections 127, 128), scriptural explanations (sections 74, 77, 86), commandments (section 19), and official declarations; to down-to-earth instructions (sections 130, 131) and minutes of meetings (section 102)."[ii]

Most important, the tone and tenor of the book reveal a direct connection and close proximity with God. God is portrayed as a "friend" capable of responding to human need (see 84:63, 77; 94:1; 98:1; 100:1; 104:1). The book, therefore, "speaks with biblical power to the immediate conditions of modern life . . . and lifts [the] readers' eyes above mortal disappointments toward eternal hopes."[iii]

THE PORTRAYAL OF CHURCH LEADERS IN THE DOCTRINE AND COVENANTS

For some it may be disquieting to read in the Doctrine and Covenants about the weaknesses of Joseph Smith and some of his colleagues. For example, God severely rebuked Joseph Smith for his sins and weaknesses when Martin Harris lost the first 116 pages of the Book of Mormon. (See D&C 3:4–15.) Joseph was also criticized by the Lord for not teaching his family the doctrines of the Church, a point that should not be overlooked in a study guide designed to facilitate family study of the Doctrine and Covenants. (See D&C 93:47.) Such scriptural candor does not diminish Joseph's credibility and in fact enhances it. Had Joseph been the author of his own revelations it is unlikely that he would have rebuked himself and held himself up to justifiable criticism by the general membership of his fledgling Church.

Leonard Arrington, a respected Mormon historian, raised the issue of Joseph's critical self-disclosures and suggested that people may take comfort in the fact that religious leaders have faults and foibles. He approaches the subject by noting that "Biblical writers had an insistent tendency to avoid hiding or concealing the sins and misdeeds of the persons they wrote about, whether they were the chosen people of Israel or individual prophets, patriarchs, and apostles. Moses, the greatest character in the Old Testament, and Peter, the apostle of Jesus, are three-dimensional persons, capable of both error and wondrous uprightness."[1] It is fair to add that this same observation holds true for the Book of Mormon as well. By way of proof, one need go no further than the prophet Alma the Younger, whom, we are told, "murdered the souls of men." Arrington builds on this observation and concludes by saying that if the scriptures are so candid about religious leaders, the approach "suggests that salvation comes from the Lord, not from divinely appointed leaders, and that the thousands of 'little people' who have personal burdens have reason to be reassured. If [Church leaders] have struggled to overcome weaknesses, their triumphs may inspire the rest of us."[2]

In light of the fact that both the Bible and the Book of Mormon are candid about its leaders and peoples, it should not be surprising to find the same unveiling of human weakness in the Doctrine and Covenants as well. The point is, "The same censure and encouragement were given early members and officers of the LDS Church in the Doctrine and Covenants."[3] In fact, if the Doctrine and Covenants were not candid about early Church leaders' foibles, it would be inconsistent with the way prophet-leaders are treated in the canon of scripture generally and raise questions about the authentic nature of the Doctrine and Covenants itself. As Paul expressed it, this precious gospel treasure is given to imperfect people ("earthen vessels") so that all might know that when God's glory shines forth it is of God. (See KJV and NLT 2 Corinthians 4:7.)

Joseph's sins and weaknesses were not hidden. In spite of it all, his accomplishments are nothing short of incredible. Those who knew him best were willing to take him as he really was—a mortal man with a prophetic calling. Perfection is something we do not meet in men and women in this life, with the exception of the Son of God. All fall short, as the Apostle Paul taught. Consider Lorenzo Snow's feelings; he said that he saw Joseph do some things that he would not have done. "Yet . . . I thanked God that He would put upon a man who had these imperfections the power

---

1. Arrington, *Adventures of a Church Historian*, 6–7.
2. Arrington, *Adventures of a Church Historian*, 6–7.
3. Arrington, *Adventures of a Church Historian*, 6–7.

and authority which He placed upon him [Joseph]. . . . For I knew I myself had weaknesses and I thought there was a chance for me."[1] Close up and personal did not lessen Snow's regard for the Prophet Joseph Smith.

THE VOICE OF JESUS IN THE DOCTRINE AND COVENANTS

When reading the Doctrine and Covenants, we are confronted in most sections with the voice of Jesus. As Richard Bushman points out, most writers try to persuade us that they are speaking with authority. Not so in the revelations of Joseph Smith. Jesus simply speaks, and we are left to accept or reject the message. The voice rarely gives reasons at all but is declarative in tone. "Authority comes almost entirely from the force of the words themselves."[2] "The Lord speaks and demands that people listen. They must decide for themselves to believe or not, without reference to any outside authority—science, common sense, tradition, or the opinions of the educated elite. Within the rhetorical space of the revelation, the hearer is left alone, facing the person behind the pure voice, with the choice to hearken or turn away."[3]

Jesus' self-authenticating approach in the Doctrine and Covenants is entirely consistent with the way that he is presented in the Four Gospels. Consider the Sermon on the Mount, where Jesus refers to the scripture but then overrules it. "It has been said . . ." but "I say unto you." Such a stance was the antithesis of that used by the scribes and Pharisees, who liberally referred to the Pentateuch and the law to give force and authority to their statements. They reasoned from the scriptures—but not Jesus. He relied upon His own authority as the Son of God.[4] Some believed and others did not. But, it was not necessary then, nor is it necessary now, for the Son of Righteousness to justify himself. On almost every page of the Doctrine and Covenants we are simply confronted with the proposition, "Verily, thus saith the Lord!" (D&C 93:1.)

---

1. Arrington, *Adventures of a Church Historian*, 4.
2. Bushman, *Believing History*, 258.
3. Bushman, *Believing History*, 258.
4. Take, for example, the following from the Sermon on the Mount: "*Ye have heard that it hath been said*, Thou shalt love thy neighbor and hate thine enemy. *But I say unto you*, love your enemies, bless them that curse you, do good to them that hate you, and pray for them that despitefully use you and persecute you." (KJV Matthew 5:43–44; emphasis added.)

Chapter 10

The Doctrine and Covenants: The Mormon Metanarrative

The term *metanarrative* literally means the big or comprehensive (meta) story (narrative). Generally, it is used as a synonym for a worldview as expressed in a storyline. Metanarratives incorporate the most basic and fundamental assumptions about a religion, society, or culture. As N. T. Wright observed, "Worldviews are thus the basic stuff of human existence, the lens through which the world is seen, the blueprint for how one should live in it, and above all the sense of identity and place which enables human beings to be what they are. To ignore world views, either our own or those of the culture we are studying, would result in extraordinary shallowness."[1] In sum, the big picture is the grid according to which humans organize reality, not the bits of reality that offer themselves for organization.[2] It is the story that ties all other stories together.

It is by recognizing and being familiar with these big stories that one can discover how a particular culture answers the basic questions about existence: who are we, where did we come from, where are we, why are we here, what is wrong, what is the solution, and where are we going? "All cultures cherish deep-rooted beliefs which can in principle be called up to answer these questions. All cultures . . . have a sense of identity, or environment, or a problem with the way the world is, and of a way forward—redemptive eschatology, to be more precise—which will, or may lead out of that problem."[3] It is by identifying this fundamental storyline or account that an outsider can truly begin to understand how a particular society makes sense out of existence and gauge how a particular society might respond to information that may challenge its way of being.[4]

---

1. Wright, *The New Testament and the People of God*, 124.
2. See Wright, *The New Testament and the People of God*, 125.
3. Wright, *The New Testament and the People of God*, 123.
4. N. T. Wright explained that "some worldviews become progressively harder and harder

Although metanarratives are always present, like the foundations of a house, metanarratives are vital but invisible. "They are not usually called up to consciousness or discussion unless they are challenged or flouted fairly explicitly, and when this happens it is usually felt to be an event of worryingly large significance."[1] Without explicit reference to them, they function as social or cultural boundary-markers. Those who observe them are insiders, and those who do not are outsiders. Such things are generally too deep to be spoken about in casual conversation. "They determine how, from day to day, human beings will view the whole of reality. They determine what will, and what will not, be intelligible or assimilable within a particular culture."[2] It is because this controlling story is often imperceptible to an outsider that it must be uncovered and exposed if one is to begin to understand the most basic motivations of a particular society.

This said, the Mormon metanarrative as presented in the Doctrine and Covenants is almost identical to the Judeo-Christian worldview, but with a few differences that are highly significant. The Judeo-Christian story begins with the propositions that God is the creator and that human beings are made in God's image. God's children are situated on earth and given certain purposes to fulfill. Ultimately God's children (house of Israel) rebel and discount God's counsel, which results in dissonance between God and his children, making it impossible for God's children to come back into his presence after death. To rescue his children, God sends prophets and inspired messengers to invite his children to repent and enter into a covenant to be obedient to God's laws. However, since all men and women sin, all fall short and are therefore excluded from God's presence. The climactic event in the history occurs when God's son, Jesus, intervenes, institutes a new covenant, spills his blood for mankind (atones), is resurrected, and frees God's creation from its ensuing plight.

The story continues with the Creator acting through his own Spirit within the world to redeem God's family (house of Israel) and all others who are baptized into the new covenant, a covenant that is all inclusive without regard to race, gender, social class, geography, or location. In this way God deals with the weight of evil set up by human rebellion.[3] This done, Jesus foretells his own Second Coming when he will arrive to vanquish all evil and take personal charge of this world. Just prior to

---

to retain, needing more and more conspiracy theories in order to stay in place, until they (sometimes) collapse under their own weight." He cites as an example the Flat Earth society, which is "progressively undermined by each round-the-world sailing, each photograph from space." (Wright, *The New Testament and the People of God*, 117.)

1. Wright, *Jesus*, 125.
2. Wright, *Jesus*, 124.
3. See Wright, *The New Testament and the People of God*, 132.

that event, God will set up the New Jerusalem (Zion), where the pure in heart will be gathered together just before a millennial era in the earth's history is launched, during which the world will be at peace and God will comfort all of his children.

As stated, the Mormon metanarrative adopts the Judeo-Christian story but adjusts it in momentous ways through the revelations of Joseph Smith as found in the Doctrine and Covenants. First and foremost, the Mormons are the new house of Israel charged with the duty to bring about the latter-day New Jerusalem in preparation for Jesus' Millennial Second Coming. Second, the Judeo-Christian metanarrative is strengthened by adding into the story the idea that all of God's children lived with their heavenly parents in a premortal existence and were the literal spiritual offspring of heavenly parents. Once God's children were located on earth, their duty was not only to bring about God's purposes in history, but also to gain experience, develop their capacities, understand better the difference between good and evil, and become more and more like their heavenly parents, ultimately to become gods and goddesses in their own right. This paradigm assumes that their divine parents have eternal bodies, just like Jesus' resurrected body, that they reside in time and place, and that they enjoy social relationships and discourse. Such a view altogether rejects the more traditional Trinitarian conception of Deity.

Based on the Mormon metanarrative, Mormons would answer life's questions much as most Christians do, but again with some very meaningful differences. The similarities and dissimilarities are briefly mentioned here.

Who Are We?

Like most Christians, Mormons conceive of themselves as sons and daughters of God, but in a far more literalistic sense. For Latter-day Saints, each person is co-eternal with God and, like God, has always existed. (See D&C 93:23, 29.) Since Mormons see God as part of the universe and not apart from it, God is made out of a material substance (resurrected body). (See D&C 130:22.) In this scheme of things, men and woman first existed as "intelligences." (See D&C 93:23.) Although not much is known about man's early origins, "intelligences" are egos, conscious of themselves and separate and distinct from each other.[1] As a conscious entity, an

---

1. Orson Pratt, one of Mormonism's founding fathers, disagreed. He believed in what Doug Parker, a law professor at BYU, called the "soup" theory of intelligence. This theory holds that all intelligence was one body, like soup in a pot, and that at some point in time God took soup spoons full of intelligence out of the pot, as it were, and fashioned them into individuals.

"intelligence" has a memory and can process information, make decisions, exercise judgment and enlarge its capacities. (See D&C 93:30–31.)

At some point in time, God the Eternal Father and Mother clothed intelligences with a spirit (refined matter not visible to the naked eye). (See D&C 131:7; 138; Abraham 3:21–28.) When this occurred the intelligence and spirit became one, a child of God. It was this step (unalterably connecting intelligence and spirit together) that made it possible for intelligences to advance further and in all respects become like their heavenly parents. (D&C 76:58–62; 93:20.)

Where Did We Come From?

Men and women come from a pre-mortal existence where they lived with their heavenly parents and spirit brothers and sisters in a family-like environment. (See Hebrews 12:9.) In this place they developed their talents and capacities, enjoyed social discourse, associated together, and were free to make choices either to obey or disobey their heavenly parents. (See D&C 93:29–32.)

In order for God's children to continue to advance and become gods, God the Father proposed a plan that required his children to leave his presence, come to an earth, clothe themselves in an earthly body, and learn to live independently, without prior knowledge of their previous existence. This plan, which was espoused by Jehovah (Jesus), the First-born spirit Son of God, was opposed by another of God's spirit children, a Son of the Morning later known as Lucifer, Perdition, or Satan. A war ensued and Satan and all his followers, a full third of God's sons and daughters, were cast out of heaven and not allowed to receive earthly bodies, and continue to progress (a condition referred to as damnation). (See D&C 29:36–37; 121:32; Revelation 12:7–13.)

Where Are We?

God's children find themselves on an earth created by God the Father and his Son, Jesus Christ, and others. (See Abraham 4.) Matter has always existed in some form. (See D&C 131:7; Abraham 4.) God created the earth by organizing matter into a world that sustains life. There is no such thing as an ex-nihilo creation. (See Abraham 4.)

Since the earth was created by God it is good. (See Moses 3:9; Genesis 1:4, 10, 12, 18, 21, 25, 31.) There are innumerable earths like this one, populated with God's spirit children. Such worlds are continually being created. (See Moses 1:33, 38.)

Why Are We Here?

Men and women are placed on the earth to receive earthly bodies, to learn for themselves the difference between and the consequences associated with pleasure and pain, sickness and health, good and evil, and life and death—and to gain knowledge and learn to make wise personal choices. This process causes God's children to change and mature, increase their capacities, and become more like God. (See D&C 93:1–40.) These lessons can be learned only in an earthlike environment when God's children are separated from him. (See D&C 122:7.) There is no other way. (See D&C 88:34–42; 130:20–21; Abraham 3:26–28.)

However, men and women may advance only if they are morally upright and love God and neighbor. The progress of men and women may not come at the expense of others, and each of God's children must learn to emulate the Son of God, the great Exemplar—Jesus. (See 2 Nephi 31:16; Mormon 7:10; John 13:15; 1 Peter 2:21.)

What Is Wrong?

Since men and women on earth cannot remember their premortal life and are free to act and to be acted upon, they often make unwise choices and thwart God's plan for them. God's purposes are often thwarted. (See D&C 93:27–32.) God's children sin and intentionally and unintentionally harm each other. While this is necessary for them to gain experience, breaking God's laws makes it impossible for them to advance and come back into the presence of God for the reason that no unclean—or sinful—thing may dwell there. (See D&C 88:32–34; 122:9; Moses 7.)

What Is the Solution?

Even as matter is eternal, so are the physical laws that govern it. (See section 130.) Since God is material, he and all other material beings are governed by the laws that control the material world which include scientific, physical, moral, and social laws of cause and effect. God is God because he applies these laws to control his environment and to make it possible for others to become like him. (See Alma 42.) Men and women have estranged themselves from their heavenly parents by breaking these laws. To put things right, God relies on another invariable law of existence—the law of vicarious sacrifice. For reasons only partially understood, God's children may come back into his presence upon the condition of repentance, baptism and other ordinances, provided a sinless person (Jesus) voluntarily sacrifices his life to atone for their sins. (See D&C 19; Alma 42.) This having been done, all mankind may return to their heavenly parents and continue to advance and become like them. (See 2 Nephi 31:16; Mormon 7:10; John 13:15; 1 Peter 2:21.)

WHERE ARE WE GOING?

After death, the spirits of men and women go to the spirit world, where they are once again given the opportunity to make choices, repent, obey God's laws, and advance further. (See D&C 128; 138:32–34, 58–59; 1 Corinthians 15:29.) At some point in the future, like Jesus, the spirit and the body are inseparably reunited in the resurrection allowing God's children to experience the utmost physical powers, pleasures, and joys. (See D&C 93:33–34.) Like God's body, this new corporeal creation is not subject to disease and death.

God's plan is designed to be successful, and the vast majority of God's children will enjoy some degree of happiness and continue to advance and progress in the hereafter. A handful of the most incorrigible (sons of perdition) are damned and sent to rule over Satan and the third of the hosts of heaven who rebelled against God in the premortal life. (See D&C 76.) While all of God's children live together, enjoy sociality, and continue to make progress, those most advanced (worthy and knowledgeable[1]) begin to participate more and more in the work of the God the Father and Jesus Christ as gods and goddesses in their own right. (See D&C 130:2, 19–23.) Their prime directive, like that of their heavenly parents and Elder Brother Jesus, is to continue to expand God's righteous family, allowing all to advance and become like their heavenly parents. (See D&C 132:18–26.) "For behold, this is my work and my glory—to bring to pass the immortality and eternal life of man." (Moses 1:39.)

---

1. In Joseph Smith's theology, righteousness and knowledge are needed in order to be exalted or "saved." (See "One is saved no faster than he gets knowledge" in Smith, *Teachings of the Prophet Joseph Smith*, 217.) "Knowledge through our Lord and Savior Jesus Christ is the grand key that unlocks the glory and mysteries of the kingdom of heaven." (Smith, *Teachings of the Prophet Joseph Smith*, 298.) "God hath not revealed anything to Joseph, but what He will make known unto the Twelve, and even the least Saint may know all things as fast as he is able to bear them." (Smith, *Teachings of the Prophet Joseph Smith*, 149.)

Part 3

The Manchester, New York, Period

Chapter 11

Beginnings: Manchester, New York, Period, 1823–1830

The Smith family moved to Palmyra, New York, in 1816 in hopes of settling down and making a good living. Even though the Prophet's father, Joseph Smith Sr., was an industrious man, he found it difficult to comfortably provide for his family. Just after Joseph Sr. married Lucy Mack on January 24, 1796, they settled on a farm in Tunbridge, Vermont, where Joseph Sr. and his father, Asael, planned to work the land in halves. While living in Tunbridge, Joseph and Lucy had their first three of six children, and with each ensuing year Joseph Sr. realized that his efforts to care for his growing family would be thwarted by the stony and unproductive farmland he had purchased. Accordingly, Joseph and his family pulled up stakes and made arrangements to rent farmland in Randolph, Vermont.

Upon Joseph Sr.'s arrival in Randolph, he was encouraged by the thought that he might find quick financial success by investing in ginseng, a plant that grew wild in the area and was in great demand in China to cure impotence and various maladies. Unfortunately, he was persuaded to invest a large sum of money in the ginseng venture and ended  up being cheated out of all of it. This financial setback convinced him to sell what he had and move to Royalton, Vermont, for a few months and then to Sharon, Vermont, where he rented a farm. He and his wife continued to have children, and Joseph Smith Jr. was born on December 23, 1805. But once again the land was unproductive, and plans were made to search for better opportunities.

For several years the Smith family moved from place to place, trying to find a suitable area to farm. They moved to Norwich, Vermont, perhaps as squatters. Their crops failed, and the family sustained themselves by selling fruit from the trees on the land. The next year the crop failed a second time when unusually cold weather swept the area, causing a famine. Dejected and weary, the Smiths moved to the Palmyra, New York, area in 1816. Joseph Sr. left Norwich and headed to Palmyra ahead of his wife, who later made her way to join her husband. But first she had to satisfy creditors, who demanded $150 to settle old debts. Once they were paid, she hitched up the wagon and left.

For a year and a half after their arrival in Manchester, New York, the Smiths were unable to purchase a farm. They lived just down the road in a town called Palmyra. Each member of the family labored to keep food on the table. Lucy contributed by making and selling painted oilcloth table coverings. The family sold refreshments from a small shop and peddled goods from a cart. Joseph Smith Sr. and his sons worked at odd jobs in the area, such as harvesting hay, gardening, and digging wells.

Palmyra was located near the Erie Canal, which brought an influx of people into the area. The economy boomed, and higher wages made it possible for the Smith family to purchase a wooded area about two miles from downtown Palmyra. The Smiths set about clearing the land for farming. They sold cordwood, made maple sugar, and raised wheat. They also made small items for sale, such as black-ash baskets and birch brooms, and continued to make cakes, sugar, and molasses to sell to their neighbors. The Smith children continued to do occasional odd jobs around town to bring in extra money.

Finally the Smiths saved enough money to build a small dwelling on their newly acquired land. At first they lived in a log cabin, but later they were able to build a more luxurious home with wood siding. The move to more spacious quarters was particularly satisfying to Joseph Smith's mother, Lucy, who complained from time to time that the women in downtown Palmyra had insulted her because of her family's modest living situation. The move proved problematic, however, when lack of funds made it impossible for the Smiths to pay their mortgage, and they were forced to return to their log cabin. The Smiths simply could not seem to avoid living life on the financial edge, a difficulty that would be a life-long concern.

Joseph Smith Jr., like the other Smith children, lived and worked on the family farm. It was during this time that he took an interest in and pondered religious matters. At about age 14 his spiritual strivings prompted him to pray earnestly in a grove directly behind the family log cabin, where he was visited by the Father and the Son. A few years later he would be informed by an angel of the location of gold plates that contained a secular and religious record of peoples who had migrated from the eastern to the western hemisphere well before the time of Christ. Joseph obtained the plates and was informed that God intended for him to make known their contents, which included a visitation of the Lord Jesus Christ to the Americas just after His death and resurrection in the Old World.

When people in the neighborhood heard that Joseph had valuable metal plates, some plotted to steal them. In an effort to preserve them, Joseph moved the record from place to place, sometimes just moments before treasure-seeking mobs arrived. Once he hid them under the hearthstone of the fireplace of the Smith frame home. Another time, he hid the chest with the plates in them under the wooden floor of the cooper's shop just across the road from the frame home; then he was prompted to move them and hide them in the flax in the loft. That night a mob, which apparently had been tipped off about their probable location, tore up the floor of the cooper's shop and, much to their consternation, found nothing.

Joseph Smith had first seen and spoken with the angel Moroni about the existence of what later became known as the Book of Mormon plates on September 21, 1823. Moroni told him that the plates were hidden in the Hill Cumorah, not far from the Smith farm. He made an attempt to take possession of them but was told by the angel that the time was not right. Between 1824 and 1827 Joseph made annual visits to the Hill Cumorah to be instructed by the angel, who apparently revealed to Joseph some of the contents of the ancient plates.[1] Joseph's mother, Lucy, recalled that during this time period Joseph would occasionally speak about the things he had discussed with the angel Moroni. "He would describe the ancient inhabitants of this continent, their dress, mode of traveling, and the animals upon which they rode; their cities, their buildings, with every particular; their mode of warfare; and also their religious worship. This he would do with as much ease, seemingly, as if he had spent his whole life among them."[2]

Economic pressures continued to bear down on the Smith family. By October 1825 it was necessary for Joseph to find work in the South Bainbridge, New York, area. He secured a job working for Josiah Stowell, who hired him to look for buried treasure. Treasure hunting was a common activity at the time because many people believed that the Spaniards had once lived in the area and had left behind buried treasures. While looking for valuable booty, Joseph and his associates boarded nearby with Isaac Hale in nearby Harmony, Pennsylvania. Hale lived near a mine site where Josiah Stowell expected to find valuable treasure. It was during this time that Joseph met Isaac Hale's daughter, Emma. Joseph was smitten, but Emma's father made it known that he did not particularly like this young suitor, and Joseph

---

1. It was during this period that persons in the Book of Mormon appeared to and tutored Joseph Smith. Joseph reports meetings with Nephi, Alma, and others who instructed him.
2. *Church History in the Fulness of Times*, 41.

was unable to obtain permission to marry her. The couple decided to elope and were married by a justice of the peace on January 18, 1827, in nearby South Bainbridge, New York. Joseph and Emma then returned to Harmony, where they lived with Emma's parents for a short and difficult time before the couple returned to live with the Smiths in Palmyra.

On September 22, 1827, the angel Moroni entrusted Joseph with the gold plates. Those who believed in buried treasures had little difficulty believing that Joseph had stumbled upon something of real value, and he lived in fear that someone might find and steal the ancient record. Efforts to pilfer the plates intensified. Some in the mob had been Joseph's partners during his money-digging days and felt that on that basis they also deserved to profit from the gold plates. Once a mob gathered in front of the Smith home but dispersed when Joseph and his brothers faked a counterattack by running out the front door threatening them as if a whole body of armed men were inside ready to resist the rabble.

In need of help, Joseph contacted Martin Harris, a friend of the Prophet. Harris, by the standards of his day, was a prosperous second-generation member of the community and had frequently hired Joseph Smith as a farm hand. Harris came to the Smith residence, and Joseph told him about the gold plates. In an effort to convince Harris that he was telling the truth, he allowed Harris to heft a box containing the record. Harris was impressed, went home, prayed, and was convinced that Joseph was being truthful. He later provided funds ($50.00) for Joseph and Emma to move from Palmyra to an area where Joseph was less known and the plates would be safer.

Joseph wrote Alva Hale, Emma's brother, asking him to drive up from Harmony, Pennsylvania, with a wagon to take Joseph and Emma back to Harmony. With Harris's funds, Joseph paid off a few debts and arranged to leave. Joseph heard rumors that his detractors were aware of his pending move and planned to tar and feather him before he could get out of town. To deceive them, he announced his departure date publicly and then left for Harmony two days early. He hid the plates in a barrel that he placed in a wagon along with Emma and their scant worldly possessions.[1]

---

1. See *Church History in the Fulness of Times*, 45. The move was not easy for Emma, who was pregnant at the time.

Chapter 12

The Big Questions: Manchester, New York, Period

Does God Hear Me?

Joseph's interest in religion and whether or not God exists was undoubtedly encouraged by his religious upbringing. His mother, Lucy, was engrossed by religion and said that her "mind was much agitated" about the various ideas and doctrines taught during her day.[1] Her religiosity is illustrated by an experience she had in 1803 when she caught a cold and then a fever and became deathly ill. Bushman describes the situation well. "At the height of her illness, when her husband despaired of her life, she pleaded with the Lord to spare her that she might bring up her children and comfort her husband."[2] Lucy said during the night she "made a solemn covenant with God, that, if he would let me live, I would endeavor to serve him according to the best of my abilities. Shortly after this, I heard a voice say to me, 'Seek, and ye shall find; knock and it shall be opened unto you. Let your heart be comforted; ye believe in God, believe also in me.'"[3]

Lucy's fervor for religion spilled over into her family life. She joined the Western Presbyterian Church in Palmyra and convinced some of her children, Hyrum, Sophronia, and Samuel, to go with her. However, Lucy's other children were influenced more by their father, who chose not to go to church. He was more skeptical about religion in general. In fact, as Bushman points out, "Lucy's only explicit reservation about her husband was his diffidence about religions. After his brief flirtation with Universalism in 1797, Joseph Sr. hovered on the margins of the churches."[4] More

---

1. See Bushman, *Joseph Smith: Rough Stone Rolling*, 24.
2. Bushman, *Joseph Smith: Rough Stone Rolling*, 24.
3. Bushman, *Joseph Smith: Rough Stone Rolling*, 24.
4. Bushman, *Joseph Smith: Rough Stone Rolling*, 23.

influenced by their father, Alvin, William, and Joseph Jr., also decided not to attend church.[1]

Lucy was not alone in her interest in religion. Joseph and his family lived at a time when many were intensely anxious about religion. Spiritual revivals resulted in large gatherings and were common occurrences in the Palmyra area where Joseph and his family lived. Itinerant preachers stirred up religious feelings and divisions as they competed with one another for followers by teaching a variety of inconsistent doctrines.[2] Young Joseph attended many of these so-called "camp meetings" where various ministers vociferously preached the gospel.

The religious environment caused him to contemplate whether or not there was a God and, if so, which of all the churches was correct. Oliver Cowdery recalled that Joseph wondered for a time whether a supreme being actually existed. Bushman suggests that Joseph's interest at getting to the bottom of religion "was to satisfy his family's religious want and, above all, to meet the need of his oft-defeated, unmoored father."[3] In any case, Joseph's intense interest in religious matters led to his well-known theophany. Once having seen the Father and the Son, he would never again doubt their existence or the importance of religion.

What Makes a Credible Witness?

Joseph Smith realized that some of the claims he made about religions and his religious experiences seemed incredible. He understood why others had difficulty believing his story and said on April 7, 1844, just months before he was gunned down, "I don't blame you for not believing my history, had I not experienced it [I] could not believe it."[4] From the first to the last, his credibility was always at issue. This helps explain why Joseph was so relieved when others experienced for themselves some of the very same spiritual manifestations that he had received. Joseph expressed joy when Martin Harris, David Whitmer, Oliver Cowdery, and the Eight Witnesses were given permission by the Lord to see the Book of Mormon gold plates for themselves. Their testimonies were a great relief to him. When he told his mother about the witnesses, she said Joseph threw himself down beside her and said, "The Lord has now caused the plates to be shown to more besides myself. . . . They will have to bear witness to the truth of what I have said, for now they know for themselves, that I do not

---

1. See Bushman, *Joseph Smith: Rough Stone Rolling*, 37.
2. See Bushman, *Joseph Smith: Rough Stone Rolling*, 37.
3. Bushman, *Joseph Smith: Rough Stone Rolling*, 27.
4. Bushman, *Joseph Smith: Rough Stone Rolling*, 551.

go about to deceive the people.... I feel as if I was relieved of a burden which was almost too heavy for me to bear, and it rejoices my soul, that I am not any longer to be entirely alone in the world."[1]

The witnesses chosen to see the gold plates for themselves were credible witnesses—ordinary men not given to exaggeration and with a reputation for truthfulness. The first three saw the plates as they were presented to them by the angel Moroni, who assured them that the plates were translated by the gift and power of God. The eight saw the plates under natural circumstances in broad daylight and were allowed to touch, heft, and examine the ancient-looking writings etched on the thin metal pages. Although some of them came to believe at a later time that Joseph had become a fallen prophet, they never denied what they had seen and heard.

Who Can Be a "Worthy Vessel"?

From the very beginning Joseph was worried about his sins. When he wrote down his first account of the First Vision, his own doubts about personal worthiness were an important part of the experience.[2] The visitation of the Father and Son also brought with it God's assurance that Joseph was forgiven of his sins. He felt redeemed and said that his "soul was filled with love and for many days I could rejoice with great joy and the Lord was with me."[3] As time progressed, he realized that being forgiven was one thing and remaining obedient was another. On numerous occasions in the Doctrine and Covenants thereafter Joseph is rebuked for his weaknesses, as are others. (See D&C 3:4-6; D&C 5:21; 93:47–48.) He referred to himself as a "rough stone rolling" and was "but a man... a plain, untutored

---

1. Bushman, *Joseph Smith: Rough Stone Rolling*, 79.
2. Joseph Smith's concern for his sins was originally described in the *Times and Seasons* but toned down in the History of the Church. In the *Times and Seasons* Joseph said, "I was left to all kinds of temptations, and mingling with all kinds of society. I frequently fell into many foolish errors and displayed the weaknesses of youth and the corruption of human nature, which I am sorry to say led me into divers temptations, to the gratification of my appetites offensive in the sight of God. In consequence of these things I often felt condemned for my weakness..." See *Times and Seasons* 3:749. In the History of the Church it was changed to "... I was left to all kinds of temptations; and mingling with all kinds of society, I frequently fell into many foolish errors, and displayed the weakness of youth, and the foibles of human nature; Which I am sorry to say, led me into divers temptations, offensive in the site of God." See History of the Church 1:9. The history also adds, "In making this confession, no one need suppose me guilty of any great or malignant sins. A disposition to commit such was never in my nature. But I was guilty of levity, and sometimes associated with jovial companions... not consistent with that character which ought to be maintained by one who was called of God as I had been. But this will not seem very strange to anyone who recollects my youth, and is acquainted with my native cheery temperament. In consequence of this, I often felt condemned for my weakness..." See History of the Church, 1:9.
3. Bushman, *Joseph Smith: Rough Stone Rolling*, 39.

man; seeking what he should do to be saved."[1] As the Church began to be organized, sections 19 and 23 confirm that God is willing to work through less than perfect servants, provided they are willing to continue to strive for forgiveness and moral excellence.

---

1. Bushman, *Joseph Smith: Rough Stone Rolling*, 527, 561.

Chapter 13

The Sacred Grove

THE FIRST VISION: SACRED GROVE, MANCHESTER, NEW YORK, SPRING OF 1820

Heading

God, Jesus Christ, and angels personally appear to the Prophet Joseph. He comes to know that God lives and answers prayers.

The big question

Question: Does God hear me?
Answer: Yes! God answers the prayer of Joseph Smith.

Historical background

As a young man, Joseph Smith prayed and asked God which church he should join. In what is now referred to as the "First Vision," God the Father and Jesus Christ personally appeared to Joseph and instructed him that he should not join any of the established churches of his day. Although the First Vision is not recorded in the Doctrine and Covenants, it bears examination for at least two reasons as we begin our study of the book. First, it made a lasting impression on Joseph Smith and shaped his understanding of the Godhead.[1] Second, although the First Vision was not widely acclaimed during the opening years after the Church was organized, it plays a far more central role today and is often referred to.

---

1. Joseph Smith saw two personages, the Father and the Son, and he understood that they were not one in the same person. We should not assume, however, that he also understood that God had a body. *[but did he not behold the bodies standing above him in the air? Maybe add the word "fully" before "understood" or say, "fully understood the nature of God's body"]* This concept developed later and was revealed explicitly in D&C 130:22.

There are varying accounts, but it was most likely in early 1820 that Joseph decided to approach God. He said it was the first time he had prayed vocally—aloud. The Smiths lived in a small log cabin on their farm in Manchester. The home had two small rooms on the main floor and a little space in an upstairs attic. With no hope of privacy at home, he walked out the back door and straight into a grove of trees not far from the house, where he could be alone. It was in this wooded area that he had his remarkable experience.

The First Vision was not a mystical experience in the sense that it came as a fleeting dream or apparition. Joseph Smith saw God the Father, Jesus Christ, and angels in broad daylight, when he was fully cognizant. Rather than experiencing a trance or vision, Joseph understood it to be an actual appearance of two personages. He was able to have a conversation with them, ask questions, and receive instruction over a prolonged period of time. It was Joseph's conversion experience, and it forever put to rest in his mind the question of whether there was a God. The vision informed Joseph that God spoke for himself and sent heavenly messengers to converse with men and women. It was the first of a series of revelations, many of which are recorded in the Doctrine and Covenants.

Prior to the First Vision, Joseph had at least four concerns. First, does God exist? Second, if God does exist, will he speak to me? Third, what is my standing with God? And fourth, which church truly represents God?

On the first issue, of whether God exists, after Joseph had experienced his theophany, he was fully convinced of the existence of God, Jesus, and angels.[1] Although later he wondered on occasion why God would not reveal certain things to him and deigned not to bring about certain events, Joseph knew of God's reality as surely as we know that a person exists whom we have personally met. On the second issue, regarding God's communication with men and women, Joseph never doubted again that God would speak to him. On the third issue, concerning Joseph's standing with God, he was reassured that his sins were forgiven and that he was acceptable to God. Finally, concerning which of the churches was correct, he was told to "join none of them, for they were all wrong" (JS–H 1:19). Jesus explained that "all their creeds were an abomination in his sight; that those professors were all corrupt; that: 'they draw near to me with their lips, but their hearts are far from me, they teach for doctrines the commandments of men, having a form of godliness, but they deny the power thereof'" (JS–H 1:19).

---

1. Young Joseph had said that he thought the creation of the earth and of the men and women who populate it was evidence that there must be an intelligent Supreme Being; otherwise, how did it all come to be? However, he told Oliver Cowdery that prior to the First Vision he had on occasion wondered whether God existed.

Today the First Vision is usually cited by members of the Church for two primary reasons: first, to show that Joseph Smith is a prophet of God; second, to prove that the existing churches in Joseph's day were false, thus making it necessary for him to start a new one. On the first proposition, the fact that Joseph Smith saw God certainly is consistent with his prophetic mission. The second assertion that Joseph's vision commissioned him to start a new church is probably not correct. It is doubtful whether Joseph understood at the time of the First Vision that this would be the case. At the time he just wanted to know whether he should join any of the existing churches of his day. This concern was no doubt cultivated by the number of competing sects in the area, the general religious excitement in and around his home, and the fact that his family did not all belong to the same denomination.[1]

Various accounts of the First Vision

There are a number of different accounts of the First Vision—eight to ten versions in all depending on how you count them. Three of these, with minor revisions, are duplications of a previous one. The first of these accounts (1832) – the only one written in Joseph's own hand – was produced twelve years after the event. In the accounts that followed, either a scribe or private individual was responsible for writing it down. Different aspects of the experience were emphasized in different reports. The 1835 and 1838 versions were far more personal than some of the later accounts. Different concerns and questions drew out different aspects of the vision. Undoubtedly, his experiences since the time of the First Vision influenced his way of interpreting the event as well. Once he had established a Church, aspects pertaining to this part of his vision were emphasized. It is apparent that the later accounts were written for a wider and more public audience in support of a fledgling religion.

Joseph Smith's critics attack the historicity of the First Vision for three primary reasons. First and as stated, it was not written down until 12 years after the event, implying that it was a figment of Joseph's own imagination. Second, there are some significant differences and apparent contradictions between some of the accounts (1832 vs. 1842) that also implied that Joseph Smith was simply making the experience up. Third, the only reason Joseph claimed to have had a conversion experience like this was because others during his lifetime claimed to have had similar experiences.

---

1. Four churches met within a few miles of the Smith home. The Presbyterians were the largest in Palmyra and in 1820 had the only meetinghouse in the center of town. Within a short period of time, however, others would spring up.

On the issue of not writing the account down for 12 years, Mike Quinn, a well respected and prominent Mormon historian points out that visitations of God and Jesus were common at the time. Others who claimed the Father and the Son appeared to them, like Joseph, failed to write it down until 5, 10, and fifteen years after the event. He also points out that in Joseph Smith's case, he was uncomfortable writing in the first place. There are very few letters in his own hand and most of those were written to his own family. When he did write he preferred dictating to a scribe or a clerk because he was self-conscious about his poor grammar and spelling.[1] Furthermore, references to Joseph Smith's First Vision was well enough known that it was referred to in various newspaper accounts as early as 1827, usually derisively.[2] Finally, when Joseph Smith did write down the vision in 1832 it was the first time in his life that he attempted to keep a diary, a short-lived experiment.

On the issue of contradictions between the accounts, Quinn points out that when people experience overwhelming spiritual events they do describe them in different ways at different times in their lives depending upon the audience and the occasion. For example the 1832 account is far more intimate and personal. It emphasizes Joseph's desire to be forgiven of his sins. The 1842 account was written for public dissemination and leaves out this personal reference and includes information about whether or not he should join a particular faith or not.[3]

The most prominent omission between accounts is the apparent lack of any reference to God the Father in the 1832 account and his inclusion in the 1842 account. There are two responses. First, Quinn takes the position that it is not improbable that Joseph did not mention the Father in the 1832 account because God's role was minor. Even in the 1842 account God only speaks seven words by way of introduction, "This is My Beloved Son. Hear Him!" The rest of the rather prolonged encounter is between Joseph and Jesus who answered Joseph's questions. (JS 1:17) Second, for those who read the 1832 account very carefully, Joseph may very well have referred to two personages in his 1832 account, the Father and Son. The account begins by stating that "the Lord opened the heavens" and thereafter states "I saw the Lord, and he spoke unto me saying ... " An inspection of the original handwritten manuscript indicates that Joseph went back in and by way of a caret inserted the first reference to the "Lord" by which he may have been making reference to God the Father in addition to the Son. If only one deity was present it seems to make

---

1. Personal interview with the author on videotape in the possession of the author produced during the fall of 2015.
2. Ibid
3. Ibid

more sense to simply say something like, "The Lord opened the heavens and spoke to me." Therefore, based on the insertion of the first "Lord" it may be concluded that Joseph was speaking about two deities being present – Lord (God the Father) who "opened the heavens" and a second Lord (Jesus Christ) who conversed with him. If this is the case, the 1832 account, although brief, agrees in all principle respects with the more complete accounts that followed.

The point that others saw God and Jesus and therefore it is less likely that Joseph Smith did is nonsensical. Quinn takes just the opposite position. The fact that others were claiming similar happenings only strengthens Joseph claim that he also had a heavenly vision. Certainly God is not selfish. Mormons have never claimed that they are the only people to whom God ministers on earth.

Excerpts from various accounts

1832 "[F]rom the age of twelve years to fifteen I pondered many things in my heart concerning the situation of the world . . . the wickedness and abominations and the darkness which pervaded the minds of mankind. . . . [M]y mind became exceedingly distressed for I become convicted of my sins. . . . I felt to mourn for my own sins and for the sins of the world. . . . I cried unto the Lord for mercy, . . . and the Lord heard my cry. . . . [W]hile in the attitude of calling upon the Lord in the 16th year[1] of my age a pillar of light above the brightness of the sun at noon day come down. . . . I was filled with the spirit, . . . and the Lord opened the heavens. . . . I saw the Lord, and he spake to me saying, Joseph, my son, thy sins are forgiven thee."[2]

November 9, 1835 "[A] pillar of fire appeared above my head. . . . [A] personage appeared in the midst of this . . . flame, which was spread all around . . . [A]nother personage soon appeared like unto the first. . . . [H]e said unto me thy sins are forgiven thee. . . . I saw many angels. . . . I was about 14 years old."[3]

---

1. Critics have pointed out that there is a discrepancy between the written accounts regarding how old Joseph was when he saw the Father and the Son. In Joseph's earliest written account (1832) he stated that he was in his sixteenth year (fifteen years old). In his later account (1835) Joseph said that he was "about 14 years old." John W. Welch points out that "in light of Joseph's background it is not surprising that the boy Joseph did not record his experiences that spring morning in 1820 after returning from the grove." (Welch, *Opening the Heavens*, xiii.) The fact that Joseph did not have a contemporaneous record of the experience undoubtedly explains his inability to recall precisely whether the visitation occurred when he was fourteen or fifteen years old.

2. Welch, *Opening the Heavens*, 5, 7; spelling and punctuation modernized.

3. Welch, *Opening the Heavens*, 8; spelling and punctuation modernized.

1838 "I saw two Personages. . . . One of them spake unto me, calling me by name and said, pointing to the other—*This is My Beloved Son. Hear Him!* . . . My object in going to inquire of the Lord was to know which of all the sects was right. . . . I was answered that I must join none of them, for they were all wrong." (JS–H 1:17–19.)

The tenor of the times as context for the First Vision

It was not uncommon for people in Joseph Smith's day to claim that they had seen a vision of Jesus and or God the Father. D. Michael Quinn notes, "Devout claims of seeing God, particularly by adolescents, were quite common in Smith's time."[1] Benjamin Putman wrote about an experience when he was fourteen. "I instantly had a view as I thought, of the Lord Jesus Christ with his arms extended in an inviting posture."[2] Billy Hubbard of Berkshire County, Massachusetts, age eleven, wrote, "When I came to the place of prayer, had kneeled down, and closed my eyes, with my hands uplifted toward the heavens, I saw Jesus Christ on the right hand of God, looking down upon me, and God the Father looking upon him."[3]

Joseph's vision of Jesus and God the Father, however, seems to be qualitatively different from those of his contemporaries for a number of reasons. First, and as mentioned earlier, his "vision" was not a fleeting transitory experience. Joseph describes an extended conversation with Deity that covered a number of different topics. Accounts of others' personal experiences generally describe more fleeting visionary occurrences. Sometimes the person viewing the vision was commissioned to preach the gospel. But in the main, these experiences were momentary. Unlike Joseph's experience, the emphasis of these experiences was on being reassured of the reality of God and Jesus. These experiences were not meant to be informative about a number of different subjects.

Second, his experience, although ecstatic, rejected the extreme religious enthusiasm he had observed as a young man visiting camp meetings where various ministers preached hellfire and brimstone, spoke in tongues, and experienced the outpouring of what Joseph considered strange manifestations of the Holy Spirit. For example, the shouting Methodists and other "religious enthusiasts expected that 'the power,' meaning the power of God or the Holy Spirit, would come as they prayed, causing them to fall to the ground, binding their tongues, making it impossible to speak, and sometimes accompanying these manifestations with jerks and trembling."[4]

---

1. Quinn, *Early Mormonism and the Magic World View*, 13.
2. Ibid., 12.
3. Ibid., 13.
4. Staker, *Hearken O Ye People*, Kindle locations 4665–68.

It is true that when Joseph began his prayer just prior to the First Vision, he, like the shouting Methodists, felt that his tongue was bound and that he could not speak. But Joseph attributed these effects to the devil, not God. Joseph recounted, "I . . . retired to a place to pray. . . . I kneeled down and began to offer [a prayer]. . . . I was seized upon by some power which entirely overcame me, and had such an astonishing influence over me as to *bind my tongue* so that I could not speak" (Joseph Smith—History 1:15; emphasis added). He said he had to exert all of his power to overcome this "enemy which had seized" him and that he had begun to sink into "despair and abandon" himself "to destruction" when his vision of the Father and the Son burst upon him and saved him from this unseen power that afflicted him.

Mark Lyman Staker points out that Joseph's rejection of "binding of the tongue" type manifestations (that so many others prayed fervently to have) set him apart. It was at the point when Joseph rejected the religious enthusiasm others experienced that he recalled, "My mouth was opened and my tong liberated."[1] Joseph's disquiet and apprehension of "tongue binding and ecstatic religion separated him from shouting Methodists."[2] On the other hand, the fact that he had a vision at all separated him from the Campbellites and from the "more rationally oriented Methodist ministers of most other congregations."[3] Joseph's experience made him unique in a sea of religious fervor and passion juxtaposed against the ever-growing rationalism of the more educated elites. Years later he would institute rules for judging spiritual experiences in general that charted a middle course between the two extremes (see section 46 and section 50:1–4).

EIGHT WITNESSES: SACRED GROVE, MANCHESTER, NEW YORK, SUMMER OF 1829

Heading

Joseph Smith shows the Book of Mormon gold plates to eight witnesses.

The big question

Question: What makes a credible witness?
Answer: Eight trustworthy individuals who see, touch, and handle the Book of Mormon gold plates in broad daylight.

---

1. "Joseph Smith, History, 1834–1836," in Jessee, *Personal Writings of Joseph Smith*, 104.
2. Staker, Kindle locations 4677–85.
3. Ibid., 4685–86.

Depiction of the Sacred Grove, where Joseph Smith saw the Father, the Son, and other heavenly beings (angels). We do not know the exact location where the vision occurred in the grove. The grove is located west of the log cabin home on the Smith farm in Manchester, New York. At the time, the Smith family was clearing the area for farming. Some of the trees in the area were being used to harvest maple syrup.

The Sacred Grove

Historical background

In the summer of 1829, Joseph Smith was living in Fayette, New York, in the Whitmer home. He was translating the small plates to replace the 116 pages that were previously lost by Martin Harris. (See D&C 10:43–45.) While translating, he was made aware of the need for witnesses to confirm the authenticity of the Book of Mormon translation and the existence of gold plates. (See 2 Nephi 27:12–14.) There were a number of different people who actually saw the gold plates. Ultimately, eleven witnesses would be chosen to sign statements confirming the existence of the plates. These statements would be placed at the end of the Book of Mormon. Three stated that the plates were shown them by an angel, and eight said that Joseph Smith showed them plates and allowed them to examine them.

The Three Witnesses (Oliver Cowdery, Martin Harris, and David Whitmer) most probably saw the plates in early July 1829, after they retired to the woods to pray, asking God to show them the plates. The angel Moroni appeared and showed them the plates, confirming their existence. In addition, the Lord corroborated that Joseph Smith had translated the plates "by the gift and power of God." All of the Three Witnesses were dependable and trustworthy men in their communities. Oliver Cowdery was a schoolteacher and early convert to Mormonism. Before he became one of the official testators of the Book of Mormon, he had already had at least one other very important angelic visitation when John the Baptist appeared to him and Joseph Smith and conferred on them the Aaronic Priesthood. Martin Harris was a respected farmer in the Palmyra area. He had a reputation for being a visionary man but was also esteemed as an honest man. David Whitmer and his family were among the earliest adherents to Mormonism. He was a businessman and farmer. None of the three ever denied his testimony.

A few days after the angel Moroni showed the plates to the Three Witnesses, eight additional witnesses were chosen to see and handle the plates. Joseph Smith took them as a group into the Sacred Grove on the Smith farm directly behind the Smith log cabin home. All eight were well acquainted with the Prophet.

The Eight Witnesses were:

1. *Joseph Smith Sr.*, the prophet's father. He was *57* when he saw the plates. Joseph Sr. was a *farmer*. He died in the faith in September 1840 in Nauvoo, Illinois.

2. *Hyrum Smith*, the prophet's older brother. He was *29* when he saw the plates. Hyrum was a *farmer*. He was martyred in June 1844 with the Prophet Joseph in Carthage, Illinois.

3. *Samuel Smith*, the prophet's younger brother. He was *21* when he saw

the plates. Samuel was a *farmer*. He died in the faith in Nauvoo, Illinois, in July 1844, shortly after his brothers, Joseph and Hyrum, were killed.

4. *Christian Whitmer*, a son of Peter Whitmer Sr., who had invited Joseph Smith to live in his home in Fayette while Joseph finished the translation of the Book of Mormon. He was *31* when he saw the plates. Christian was a *shoemaker*. He died in the faith in Clay County, Missouri, in November 1835.

5. *Jacob Whitmer*, a son of Peter Whitmer Sr. He was *29* when he saw the plates. Jacob was a *shoemaker*. He died in Richmond, Missouri, in April 1856. He was *disaffected* from the Church at the time of his death.

6. *Peter Whitmer Jr.*, a son of Peter Whitmer Sr. He was *19* when he saw the plates. Peter was a *tailor and farmer*. He died in the faith in Liberty, Missouri, in September 1836.

7. *John Whitmer*, a son of Peter Whitmer Sr. He was *26* when he saw the plates. John was a *farmer*. He died in Far West, Missouri, in July 1878. He was *disaffected* from the Church at the time of his death.

8. *Hiram Page*, a brother-in-law to the Whitmers. He was *29* when he saw the plates. Hiram was a *physician and a farmer*. He died in Excelsior Springs, Missouri, in August 1852. He was *disaffected* from the Church at the time of his death.

The Eight Witnesses confirmed that:

1. each saw the plates;
2. the plates had the appearance of gold;
3. each saw the engravings on the plates;
4. the engravings were of "curious workmanship";
5. the engravings had the appearance of "ancient workmanship";
6. each handled the individual leaves from which the prophet Joseph had translated; and
7. each hefted the plates.

The testimony of the Eight Witnesses was distinctly different from the testimony given by the Three Witnesses. The Three Witnesses' experience was based on a supernatural appearance of the angel Moroni, who showed them the plates and testified that the translation of the ancient record was accurate. The three were not allowed to touch them for themselves. The Eight Witnesses' experience was based upon the natural senses. They saw, felt, and hefted the plates. They could testify that gold plates existed, but based upon this experience alone they could not testify to the accuracy of the translation, as the Three Witnesses did.

The sworn testimony of the Three and Eight Witnesses confirms that Joseph had gold plates and received them from an angel. It is the kind of sworn testimony often heard in the courtroom, where witnesses commonly describe their firsthand experiences—what they saw and heard. It is the kind of evidence that a juror either believes or disbelieves. Acceptance of the evidence means that the juror believes that the events described actually occurred. Rejection means that the juror has concluded that the witness is either mistaken or was lying. The fact that there are eleven witnesses who agreed on the points set out in their sworn statements make it difficult to convincingly argue that they were mistaken or somehow deceived. Therefore, the only reasonable ground upon which their testimony may be rejected is that all eleven were in a conspiracy with Joseph Smith to lie about these extraordinary experiences in order to attract followers or for some other nefarious reason. This explanation fails because none of the eleven witnesses, including the six who left the faith, ever suggested that they gave perjured testimony.

The credibility of the Three and the Eight Witnesses is reinforced by the fact that each had a reputation for telling the truth and that they stood by what they said even when challenged. For example, David Whitmer, one of the Three Witnesses, reported that in 1833 in the public square in Independence, Missouri, some 500 armed men demanded at the point of a gun that he repudiate his testimony of the Book of Mormon. The event so impressed John P. Green, a new convert to the Church, that he recorded the following in his diary.

> [W]hen the mob again assembled they went to the houses of several of the leading Mormons. And taking Isaac Morley, David Whitmer, and others, they told them to bid their families farewell, for they would never see them again. Then driving them at the point of the bayonet to the public square, they stripped and tarred and feathered them, amidst menaces ordering them to cock their guns and present them at the prisoners' breasts, and to be ready to fire when he gave the word, he addressed the prisoners, threatening them with instant death unless they denied the Book of Mormon and confessed it to be a fraud; at the same time adding that if they did so, they might enjoy the privileges of citizens. David Whitmer, hereupon, lifted his hand and bore witness that the Book of Mormon was the word of God. The mob let them go.[1]

David Whitmer simply would not deny what he had heard and seen, in part because he knew that if he did, he would be accountable to God.

David Whitmer later left the Church, claiming that the Book of Mormon was true but adding that since its publication Joseph Smith had sinned and had become a fallen prophet. Just prior to his death he was visited by Angus Cannon. Bedridden and "as helpless as a child," the octogenarian entertained his visitor, who wanted to hear his testimony of the Book of Mormon. After a lifetime of reiteration David said: "My friend, if God ever

---

1. Anderson, *Investigating the Book of Mormon Witnesses*, 83–84.

uttered a truth, the testimony I now bear is true. I did see the angel of God, and I beheld the glory of the Lord, and he declared the record true."[1]

---

1. Anderson, *Investigating the Book of Mormon Witnesses*, 90.

Chapter 14

The Smith Home

Section 2: Smith Log Home, Manchester, New York, September 21, 1823

Heading

The angel Moroni promises Joseph Smith that at some future time God will restore again the *fulness of the priesthood* or *endowment*. (See D&C 110 and 124.)

The big question

Question: Does God hear me(n)?
Answer: Yes. The angel Moroni appears to Joseph Smith.

Introduction

An extract from the words of the angel Moroni to Joseph Smith the Prophet, while in the log house of the Prophet's father at Manchester, New York, on the evening of September 21, 1823.[1] Moroni was the last of a long line of historians who had made the record that is now called the Book of Mormon. On this occasion the angel Moroni informed Joseph that "there was a book deposited, written upon gold plates, giving an account of the former inhabitants of this continent." (JS–H 1:34.)

---

1. See Smith, *History of the Church*, 1:12. The "Introduction" was taken almost verbatim from the section headings in the Doctrine and Covenants, as have all such "Introductions" throughout this study guide. Occasionally, however, thoughts have been added or the wording changed.

Historical background

On September 21, 1823, Joseph Smith was visited for the first time by the angel Moroni. Moroni was surrounded by brilliant light and appeared to Joseph in his upstairs bedroom in his family's log cabin home on the Smith farm, in Manchester, New York. The cabin was located a short distance from the grove where Joseph visited with the Father and the Son in the spring 1820.

Moroni informed Joseph that at some future time he would be entrusted with an ancient record engraved on gold plates, from which the Book of Mormon would be translated. He was also instructed that this record was buried in the Hill Cumorah, just down the road from the Smith farm. Moroni said that Satan would try to tempt him because of his family's indigent circumstances. Joseph was cautioned that he should not try to obtain the plates for the "purpose of getting rich." His motives must be pure, or otherwise he would not be permitted to secure this treasure. (See JS–H 1:46.)

Following the directives of the angel, Joseph located the plates on the west side of the Hill Cumorah, not far from the top, in a box of considerable size. He made an attempt to take the plates out of the box but was forbidden. He was told that he must wait before he would be given this privilege. In the meantime, he was instructed to come to the spot where the plates were buried in exactly one year. At that time he was promised that the angel Moroni would visit him again. He was told that he should continue to follow this pattern until he was allowed to remove the plates from the stone box. Between 1824 and 1827, he made three annual visits to the Hill Cumorah. On each occasion he was visited by the angel and given instructions.

Section 2 is a brief extract based upon what Moroni told Joseph Smith on his first encounter with him in September 1823. The three short verses in this revelation foreshadow the future restoration of the *fulness of the priesthood*, or the *temple endowment*. (See D&C 110; 124.) This section was first included in the Doctrine and Covenants in the 1876 edition by Orson Pratt, with the approval of the First Presidency.

In 1836 Elijah appeared to Joseph Smith and Oliver Cowdery and bestowed the keys necessary to perform the endowment as it was practiced in the Nauvoo Temple. Two years later in 1838 Joseph dictated the official history and "for the first time revealed what the angel Mormoni had told him about Elijah in 1823"[1]: "Behold I will reveal unto you the Priesthood, by the hand of Elijah the prophet, before the coming of the great and

---

1. Michael D. Quinn, Origins of Power, 35.

The Smith Home

Joseph Smith log cabin home on the Smith Farm in Manchester, New York. The angel Moroni appeared to the Prophet in his bedroom on the second floor.

Hill Cumorah, also known as Mormon Hill, Gold Bible Hill, and Inspiration Point, in Manchester, New York, where Joseph Smith found the Book of Mormon plates.

dreadful day of the Lord." (D&C 2:1) In January 1841, Joseph received Section 124 on the endowment and in May of 1842, Joseph performed the first temple endowments involving only 9 men. About a year later 9 women were invited to join with their husband in the endowment. It was not until the Nauvoo Temple was completed in May of 1846 that the endowment was introduced to the members of the Church generally. Prior to that time it was limited to those few who belonged to what was called "The Quorum of the Anointed."

The content of section 2

In section 2, Moroni gives a variation of the words in Malachi as they are recorded in the King James Bible. (See Malachi 4:5–6; JS–H 1:38–39.) These same verses are also quoted in Doctrine and Covenants 110:14–15; 128:17; 3 Nephi 25:5–6; and Joseph Smith's Inspired Version of the Bible. However, all the latter agree with the wording found in the King James Bible rather than with the rendition given by Moroni. Robinson and Garrett suggest that "this clearly indicates that we are dealing here not with 'correct' and 'incorrect' versions of the biblical passage but rather with different shades or levels of meaning reflected in the different versions."[1]

The angel's departure from the wording in the King James Bible is the first indication Joseph had that it is appropriate to rephrase passages of scripture to elucidate meaning. After Joseph finished his translation of the Book of Mormon, he would be instructed to follow Moroni's example and begin to rework, correct, and even add various passages to the Bible. Although Joseph referred to this process as "translating," it should be clearly understood that he never claimed to be translating the Bible from any ancient texts but rather was making changes in the text based on the spirit of revelation. (See the Joseph Smith Translation [JST] or Inspired Version [IV] of the Bible.)

The fulness of the priesthood

At the inception of the Church in 1830, Joseph Smith spoke about priesthood in connection with the various offices that authorized men to perform an assortment of duties and rituals in the Church. (See D&C 20.) As time progressed, Joseph's view of priesthood broadened. For example, when Joseph Smith first ordained men to the office of high priest in June 1831,[2] he explained that the priesthood was the power by which individuals could come into presence of God. By September 1832 he added that this process was or would be linked to various "ordinances" of the priesthood. (See D&C 84:21.) "And without the ordinances [of the priesthood] . . . the power of godliness is not manifest unto men in the flesh; for without this no man can see the face of God, even the Father and live." (D&C 84:21–22.)

Priesthood as a vehicle for bringing people into the presence of God would be further elaborated on in 1842 when the rituals of the endowment were revealed. Within the walls of the temple, men and women would figuratively be ushered into God's presence and given to understand that, if

---

1. Robinson and Garrett, *A Commentary on the Doctrine and Covenants*, 1:31.
2. The first high priests in this generation were ordained in the log school house located on the Morley farm just outside of Kirtland in June 1831.

worthy, they could also literally come into God's presence. In a later revelation given to Joseph Smith in 1833, he explained that "every soul [without respect to gender] who forsaketh his sins and cometh unto me, and calleth on my name, and obeyeth my voice, and keepeth my commandments, shall see my face and know that I am." (D&C 93:1; see also D&C 88:68.)

Ultimately, Joseph would associate priesthood with the temple endowment and refer to this part of the priesthood as the "fulness of the priesthood," the same expression used by the Moroni in section 2. (See D&C 124:27–48.) This part of the priesthood includes the sealing powers that bind families together eternally, all of which, Joseph said, are part of the ancient covenant God made with Abraham (Abrahamic Covenant). Whereas offices of the priesthood were bestowed by the laying on of hands, the "fulness of the priesthood" was conferred "by the ordinance of my holy house" as part of the temple endowment. (D&C 124:39.)[1]

Section 19: Smith Log Home, Manchester, New York, Summer 1829[2]

Heading

Christ made atonement for all, that men and women might not suffer if they repent.

The big question

Question: Who is a worthy vessel?
Answer: Martin Harris, in spite of his weakness, serious sins, and imperfections, provided he repents.

Introduction

Revelation given through Joseph Smith, at Manchester, New York, March 1830.[3] In his history, the Prophet introduced it as "a commandment of God and not of man, to Martin Harris, given by him who is Eternal." The revelation commands Harris to finance the Book of Mormon, repent of his sins, and preach the gospel.

---

1. See Smith, *Doctrines of Salvation*, 2:131–34.
2. See Michael Hubbard MacKay and Gerrit J. Dirkmaat, *From Darkness unto Light: Joseph Smith's Translation and Publication of the Book of* Mormon, 192.
3. See Smith, *History of the Church*, 1:72–74.

The Smith Home

Smith family farm in Manchester, New York.

Anchor section

Memorize: Atonement

Historical background

The translation of the Book of Mormon was finished in the summer of 1829. In search of a publisher, Joseph Smith approached Egbert B. Grandin, the owner of the Grandin Press located near his childhood home in Palmyra, New York. Grandin refused because he doubted the book would sell. Joseph and Martin Harris contacted other printers but to no avail. With no other viable options available, Joseph made a last appeal to Grandin. Although some of Grandin's friends urged him not to go forward with the project, Grandin said he would if Joseph could assure him that he would be paid. Joseph agreed and convinced Martin Harris to help provide the necessary collateral—some farmland.[1] Thereafter, Grandin agreed to print 5,000 copies.[2]

The financial risk Martin Harris was being ask to make was substantial. Three thousand dollars was required to typeset, print and bind 5,000 copies, nearly the value of Harris' entire farm.[3] In *From Darkness into Light: Joseph Smith's Translation and Publication of the Book of Mormon*, authors Michael MacKay and Gerrit Dirkmaat put the cost in perspective. "Joseph had purchased his fourteen-acre, already cultivated farm with accompanying house, in Harmony for only $200. The Book of Mormon cost, by comparison, was fifteen times that of his home and farm. Day laborers in New York often worked for a dollar per day, making the cost of the Book of Mormon printing at least ten times the amount Joseph Smith could have made digging wells for an entire year."[4]

Concerns that the book would not be financially viable increased as the time for publication approached. Joseph's claim that the Book of Mormon was scripture offended fellow Christians, and some organized public meetings to persuade people to boycott the book. Even the church that Joseph's mother and two brothers attended[5] raised objections. Deacon George Beckwith approached them (Lucy, Hyrum, and Samuel) to discuss the matter. When the family refused to denounce the Book of Mormon, the church censured them and suspended them from partaking of communion.

It was under these circumstances that Martin Harris was wavering back and forth as to whether of not he should collateralize the printing of the Book of Mormon. Harris went to Joseph and asked the Prophet to inquire of the Lord. Joseph was reluctant at first, but Harris was insistent. Joseph submitted the matter to the Lord and received Doctrine and Covenants 19. In it Harris was commanded to do what was necessary to convince Grandin to undertake the publication of the book.

---

1. "The proceeds from the book were intended to help defray the costs of establishing a new church, but by January, Martin Harris wanted to guarantee he received a portion of the sales. On 16 January 1830, Smith signed an agreement with Harris allowing Harris 'equal privilege' to sell copies of the Book of Mormon until he had been reimbursed for the value of his property." See Michael Hubbard MacKay and Gerrit J. Dirkmaat, *From Darkness into Light: Joseph Smith's Translation and Publication of the Book of Mormon*, 213.

2. After the Book of Mormon was off the press, Grandin's concern that it would not be a money maker came true. In February 1831 Harris was forced to sell off 151 acres of his 240-acre farm for $3,000 and give the money to Grandin to make up the shortfall. Harris' willingness to help finance the printing of the Book of Mormon was one of a number of issues that created distrust and conflict in Harris's marriage, which ultimately resulted in a divorce.

3. Michael Hubbard MacKay and Gerrit Dirkmaat, *From Darkness into Light: Joseph Smith's Translation and Publication of the Book of Mormon*, 165.

4. Ibid.

5. Lucy, Hyrum, and Samuel attended the Western Presbyterian Church in Palmyra, New York.

God works with and through imperfect vessels

During the translation of the Book of Mormon, both Martin Harris and Joseph Smith were severely chastised by the Lord for losing the first 116 pages of the translation, an event that will be taken up in detail in our discussion of section 3.[1] In section 19 the Lord once again rebuked Martin Harris for his personal transgressions.

It is worth noting that Harris's offenses were serious and cumulative. In addition to the 116-page debacle, he fell short because he wanted to have sexual relations with his neighbor's wife, had thoughts about killing his neighbor, was not praying consistently, refused to declare the gospel to others, and would not impart of his property for the publication of the Book of Mormon. (See D&C 19:25–32.) Yet, despite all of this, the Lord continued to strive with him. Martin Harris repented of his sins and parted with his money to insure the publication of the Book of Mormon. Ultimately, Harris found favor with God and was blessed by the visitation of the angel Moroni, who showed him the gold plates and assured him that the Book of Mormon was an accurate translation of an ancient record. Surely, God works with and through imperfect vessels.

God's punishments are limited in duration

Section 19 addresses four concepts: the severity of God's punishments for sin, the length of punishments for sin, the mitigating effects of the atonement on punishments, and repentance. On the issue of the severity of punishments, section 19 is unequivocal. Chastisement for sin is dreadful, "which suffering caused myself, even God, the greatest of all, to tremble because of pain, and to bleed at every pore, and to suffer both body and spirit—and would that I might not drink the bitter cup, and shrink." (D&C 19:18.)

On the issue of the duration of punishment, God's retribution is finite. (See D&C 19:8–12.) Since punishments in the scriptures are often described as "everlasting," "endless," and "eternal,"[2] section 19 explains that this is not actually the case. Rather, words that appear to be adjectives—"everlasting," "endless," and "eternal"—should be read as nouns or names for Deity. Thus, "Endless [noun] is my name. Wherefore—Eternal

---

1. Undoubtedly, Harris continued to feel troubled over his part in this affair. Later, when it became time for Joseph to identify three witnesses to testify to the reality of the gold plates and the correctness of the translation, Harris was concerned that he would not be chosen because he was unworthy.

2. See Matthew 25:46, "And these shall go away into everlasting punishment: but the righteous into life eternal."

[noun] punishment is God's punishment. Endless [noun] punishment is God's punishment."[1] (D&C 19:10–12.)

On the issue of repentance, men and women are promised that they may escape punishment for sin if they repent. And on the issue of the mitigating effects of the Atonement, section 19 explains that Jesus takes upon himself the consequences of our sins. "For behold, I, God, have suffered these things [punishments] for all, that they might not suffer if they would repent" (D&C 19:16).

Finally, it should be noted that section 19, by correcting the notion that God's punishments are eternal in duration, introduces the idea that prophets in prior dispensations do not always fully understand the intents and purposes of God. Based on the text, few if any of God's children in the Old Testament understood much about the afterlife and certainly not anything about graded kingdoms of glories, although the idea is hinted at in the New Testament and in the writings of Paul (section 76; John 14:2; 1 Corinthians 12:2–4; 15:35–44). The idea that there is always more to know and that some of what we assume to be correct is outdated is expressed in the Articles of Faith: "We believe all that God has revealed, all that He does now reveal, and we believe that He will yet reveal many great and important things pertaining to the Kingdom of God" (1:9). Prophetic utterance, continued heavenly guidance, and increased understandings is a given in Mormonism.

Eternal punishment and how Joseph viewed the scriptures

Joseph's revelation that God's punishments are not everlasting directly contradicted *Book of Mormon* teachings on the subject and illustrated Joseph's view of scripture. The fact that Mosiah taught that sinners "drinketh damnation to his own soul; for he receiveth for his wages an everlasting punishment, having transgressed the law of God" evidently did not trouble him. It was part of his understanding that the scriptures were an ongoing project requiring emendations based on further light and knowledge from God. Scripture therefore was a mixture of ideas of the contemporary culture of the authors and a more pure understanding revealed from God. Building on this idea, Joseph's successor, Brigham Young commented:

I cannot say what a minister once said to me. I asked him if he believed

---

1. Section 19 explains that God did not correct what the scriptures seemed to teach taken at face value, namely, that punishments were eternal, because it "worked upon the hearts of the children of men, altogether for my name's glory." (Verse 7.) In other words, if the idea that God's punishments for sin lasted forever encouraged people to live *God's commandments, so much the better.*

[all] the Bible and he replied, "Yes, every word of it." ... "Well" said I, "you can beat me at believing that's certain. As I read the Bible it contains the words of the Father and Son, angels, good and bad, Lucifer, the devil of wicked men and of good men, and some are lying and some ... are telling the truth; and if you believe it all to be the word of God you can go beyond me."[1]

For Joseph ongoing revelation was the paramount concern.

Limited punishments, good works and Original Sin

The idea in Section 19 that God's punishments were limited in duration and that every person would be judged "according to his works and the deeds which he hath done" (D&C 19:4) was a radical departure from the sin drenched theology of Joseph's day. The doctrine of Original Sin and cries for repentance from the revivalists holding camp meeting in and around Palmyra were infused with Calvinist ideas about Adam's Sin. Original Sin or what was sometimes called "ancestral sin" described humanity's state stemming from the fall of Adam as one of total depravity and guilt for all humans. Augustine developed the idea and it was popular among Protestant reformers (Martin Luther, John Calvin).

In Palmyra, there were four churches that dominated the city' center intersection, the Methodists, Presbyterian of America, Baptists and Episcopalians. Each of them believed in a variation of Original Sin and equated it to one degree or another with concupiscence resulting in what Augustine had described as *massa damnata* (mass of perdition, condemned crowd) that limited freedom of will. Undoubtedly Joseph's sense of sinfulness and his desire to be forgiven of his sins in his youth was influenced his Presbyterian mother and siblings. Martin Harris' despair centered on the fact that he felt he could never be one of the Three Witnesses because of his corrupt nature. Both were colored by such dark Calvinist doctrines.

Section 19, therefore, signals a break with the mainstream Christianity of Joseph's day, a change of direction that would be reinforced in revelations yet to be announced. Instead of humankind being tainted by Adam's sin, Joseph would express his views on the subject in the Articles of Faith, a document meant to summarize Mormon teachings on this subject. "We believe that men will be punished for their own sins and not for Adam's transgression." (Article of Faith 2) Infants need no longer be baptized to either free them from or reduce the effect of Adam's transgression on the human family. Consequently, Mormons would baptized their children after

---

1. Philip L. Barlow, Mormons and the Bible, 33. See also Mormon 8:12 and Mormon 9:30-31.

the eighth birthday because they "cannot sin" before the age eight when they became more accountable before God. (D&C 49:46-47) Instead of men being born evil their natural inclination was to do good. Just a few years after this revelation in May of 1833 Joseph would teach that "[e]very spirit of man was innocent in the beginning; and God having redeemed man from the fall, men became again, in their infant state, innocent before God." (D&C 93:38) This idea was ultimately reinforced by Joseph's teaching that all of us are the literal offspring of God and capable of becoming like God.

Alma's explanation of the atonement

In nearly all cases, the most complete theological statements on any given gospel subject are found in the Doctrine and Covenants. However, the doctrine of the atonement is an exception to this general rule. The most comprehensive statement on this subject is found in Alma 42. Hence, in organizing one's gospel knowledge, section 19 should be considered in conjunction with Alma 42.

In context, Alma's discussion on the atonement begins in Alma 39. We are informed that Alma's son Corianton was serving a full-time mission in a distant place. During his ministry Isabel, an exceptionally alluring prostitute, seduced him. We know this because Alma tells us that "she [Isabel] did steal away the hearts of many." In any case, Corianton was unable to resist her charms. (See Alma 39.)

Convicted of his sins, Corianton returned home to confess his misdeeds to his father, who was also the head of the Church. Alma's response was to condemn the sin, require his son to repent, and teach his son the doctrine of the atonement. Thereafter, Corianton repented and returned to his missionary labors.

Alma's conversation with his son Corianton on the atonement is found in Alma 42. In it Alma explains that because all mankind has fallen (sinned) they may not come back into the presence of God unless they repent *and* an *atonement* be made for their sins. Alma explains that repentance is not possible unless "God himself atoneth for the sins of the world, to bring about the plan of mercy, to appease the demands of justice, that God might be a perfect, just God, and a merciful God also." (Alma 42:15.) A complete discussion on the reasons why repentance without atonement does not allow for forgiveness of sin is beyond the scope of section 19. However, suffice it to say that the rationale revolves around the governance of law. Law reigns in the universe. Everyone and everything is under the dominion of law—even God himself. The eternal laws require atonement, and therefore it is the law, not God, that necessitates the shedding of Jesus' blood to bring about forgiveness of sin.[1]

The atonement spoken about by Alma in the Book of Mormon differs from the Protestant approach on the subject. In the Protestant tradition it is assumed that men and women are fallen creatures and are not capable of perfection. Therefore, the purpose of the atonement is to make it possible for imperfect individuals to come into and live in the presence of God. Individuals are *saved in their sins*. In Mormonism it is assumed that men and women are capable of perfection—becoming gods and goddesses. Therefore, the purpose of the atonement is to make complete restitution for past mistakes, thereby making it possible for individuals to be fully forgiven of their sins and to reach a state of moral excellence and godlike perfection. It is this process of becoming like God that qualifies a person to dwell in God's presence.[2] Individuals are *saved from their sins*.

Section 22: Smith Log Cabin, Manchester, New York, April 1830

Heading

Authoritative baptism into The Church of Jesus Christ of Latter-day Saints is required for a person to be saved.

---

1. For more information on the atonement see, Roberts, *The Seventies Course in Theology, Fourth Year, The Atonement*, and Roberts, *The Truth, the Way, the Life*. Andrew C. Skinner in the introduction to *The Truth, the Way, the Life* explains: "Roberts's primary emphasis in his atonement chapters is the consistency, immutability, and overarching governance of law.... The law guarantees regularity. That regularity, however, makes atonement absolutely necessary. Each violation of the law brings a penalty which must be exacted. Hence, atonement 'is but the vindication of the law.' ... Roberts's concept of the universal reign of law dictates his views about the attributes of God. Because law is absolute and unchangeable, for example, God does not have to be immutable. He can, in Robert's view, progress even in knowledge: 'new thoughts and new vistas may appear.' God's other attributes depend upon law as well. God is limited in power, might, dominion, and knowledge by the reign of law. Thus, one can only believe in the traditional 'omni's' attributed to God if those 'omni's' are qualified...." (Page cxlv.) (See D&C 88:42; 2 Nephi 9:20.)

2. This difference in outlook on the atonement is also reflected in the Book of Mormon when the prophet Amulek contended with the false teacher Zeezrom. Like the Protestants, Zeezrom put forward the idea that God allows people who are "unclean" or imperfect to come into his presence—God *saves his people in sin*. (See Alma 11:34.) Alma, on the other hand, countered that this notion was false. "I say unto you ... that he [God] cannot *save them in their sins*." (Alma 11:37; emphasis added.) Why? Because "no unclean thing can inherit the kingdom of heaven." (Alma 11:37.)

The big question

Question: Does God hear me?
Answer: God answers Joseph's inquiry on the need for baptism to qualify for salvation.

Introduction

Revelation given April 16, 1830[1] through Joseph Smith the Prophet in the Smith cabin on the family farm located in Manchester, New York.[2] At this time Joseph was staying with his family while he made final arrangements for the publication of the Book of Mormon. This revelation was given to the Church when some who had previously been baptized into another church desired to unite with the restored church without rebaptism.

In the Book of Commandments, section 22 appeared just prior to section 20. This may suggest that it was given prior to section 20, which marks the organization of the Church. Section 22 was first published in *The Evening and Morning Star* in June 1832 as the concluding verses of section 20. Both sections 20 and 22 were referred to as the Articles and Covenants of the Church.

Historical background

Just after the organization of the Church on April 6, 1830, some new converts who had been baptized into other denominations wondered if it was necessary for them to be rebaptized into the new faith. In addition, some others who had been previously baptized by Joseph or Oliver Cowdery wondered if they needed to be rebaptized.[3] On the issue of whether or not a baptism into another church qualified one for membership, Doctrine and Covenants 22 makes it plain that although a person "should be baptized an hundred times [into another church] it availeth him nothing." (D&C 22:2.) On the issue of whether or not those baptized by Joseph Smith and Oliver Cowdery should be rebaptized, it was declared that they ought to be because "all old covenants have I caused to be done away in this thing; and this is a new and an everlasting covenant, even that which was from the beginning." (D&C 22:1.)[4]

---

1. Robin Scott Jensen, Richard E. Turley Jr., Riley M. Lorimer, *The Joseph Smith Papers: Revelations and Translations*, Vol. 2, 59.
2. See Smith, *History of the Church*, 1:79–80.
3. Between May and the organization of the "Church of Christ" on April 6, 1830, as it was first known, dozens of new converts had been baptized into a community of believers. (See Quinn, *Origins of Power*, 6.)
4. Woodford, *The Historical Development of the Doctrine and Covenants*, 360.

The formal organization of the Church and the application of the principles found in section 22 signify a change in the basic nature of Joseph's group of followers. Prior to this time, from about 1828 to May 1829, "my church" was an unorganized body of "my people" with no ordinances for membership or priestly authority. However, after baptism was introduced by the angelic messenger by John the Baptist in May 1829, things began to change.[1] Baptism was introduced along with the authority to perform this ritual. (See D&C 13.) As time progressed the Church would continue to grow, and other ordinances and authorities would be introduced incrementally until such time as the Melchizedek Priesthood, with all of its rights, authorities, offices, and rituals, had been fully established. (See D&C 88; 107; 124.)[2]

Years later, in the afternoon of November 2, 1873, Orson Pratt spoke to the Saints about section 22 in the Thirteenth Ward Meeting House in Salt Lake City. His subject was how a person could know whether or not a man had divine authority from God. He explained that in the early days of the Church, some belonged to denominations that also believed in baptism by immersion. He described them as "very moral and no doubt as good people as you could find anywhere."[3] He said that they believed in the Book of Mormon but had been baptized into the Baptist church and therefore felt that they didn't need to be baptized Mormons.[4] Pratt explained that "no man can ... officiate in [Church] ordinances acceptably, unless he is called of God as was Aaron" and stated that this was "the reason why the Lord commanded ... the Latter-day Saints—to re-baptize all persons who [came] to them professing to have been baptized before."[5]

New and Everlasting Covenant

The new and everlasting covenant referred to in section 22 is new only in the sense that it has been restored again in this dispensation of the gospel.

---

1. See Quinn, *Origins of Power*, 6.
2. David Whitmer and some others felt uncomfortable with the developing structure and introduction of authorities and rituals. He wanted the Church to remain a spiritual community of believers. Some of the earlier revelations seemed to support his position. A revelation received in 1828 (D&C 10) stated, "Behold, this is my doctrine—whosoever repenteth and cometh unto me, the same is my church. Whosoever declareth more or less than this, the same is not of me, but is against me; therefore he is not of my church." (D&C 10:67–69; see also Quinn, *Origins of Power*, 6–7.) As the Church continued to grow and mature and established governing quorums and complex rituals, Whitmer ultimately became disaffected and longed for what he called the simple doctrines taught in the Book of Mormon.
3. *Journal of Discourses*, 16:293.
4. *Journal of Discourses*, 16:293–94.
5. *Journal of Discourses*, 16:293.

Joseph Smith taught that baptism was an ancient practice beginning with Adam. Two months later he received a revelation known as the Book of Moses, which is not contained in the Doctrine and Covenants but rather is part of the Pearl of Great Price. The Book of Moses contains a description of Adam being baptized and receiving the gift of the Holy Ghost. (See Moses 6:51–53.) Years later, in September 1842, the Prophet spoke about the early origins of baptism, as well as other principles of the gospel: "Now taking it for granted that the scriptures say what they mean, and mean what they say, we have sufficient grounds to go on and prove from the Bible that the gospel has always been the same; the ordinances to fulfill its requirements, the same; and the officers to officiate, the same; and the signs and fruits resulting from the promises, the same."[1]

SECTION 23: SMITH LOG HOME, MANCHESTER, NEW YORK, APRIL 1830[2]

Heading

Early disciples are called to preach, exhort, and strengthen the Church.

The big question

Question: Who can be a worthy vessel?

Answer: Ordinary people are called to preach, exhort, and strengthen the Church.

Introduction

Revelation given in April 1830 through Joseph Smith the Prophet, in his log cabin home located on the Smith farm in Manchester, New York.

---

1. Smith, *Teachings of the Prophet Joseph Smith,* 264. See also D&C 20:25–26.

2. This section is a composite of five revelations first printed in the Book of Commandments. In that book, they were dated April 6, 1830. This date was not duplicated in subsequent printings. It is "important that we now know that April 6 could not have been the date of reception, and what was printed in the Book of Commandments was in error. This removes part of the basis for the argument used by some that the location of the organization of the Church was in Manchester, not Fayette, New York." (Woodford, "Discoveries from the Joseph Smith Papers Project," 29.)

The Smith Home

Historical background

Shortly after the organization of the Church on April 6, 1830, Joseph Smith moved back to his childhood home on the Smith farm in Manchester, New York. After the Book of Mormon was published in 1830, four recently baptized converts came to the prophet and asked him what the Lord expected of them. Joseph received a revelation on their behalf. In the 1833 Book of Commandments the revelations to each of these individuals were included as separate revelations. Today they are combined and comprise section 23.[1]

Oliver Cowdery was admonished to beware of pride, "lest thou shouldst enter into temptation." (D&C 23:1.) This counsel was particularly important in Oliver's case, since he was designated the Second Elder in the Church and was destined to become a prominent Church leader. (See D&C 21:10–11.)

Hyrum Smith, the Prophet's brother, was told to teach the gospel and "strengthen the Church continually." (D&C 23:3.) Earlier, in May 1829, he had been advised to study but not "declare" the word of the Lord. (See D&C 11:21–22.) Now it was time to speak out.

Samuel Smith, the Prophet's brother, was advised that he should preach the gospel and strengthen the Church. He was one of the Eight Witnesses to the Book of Mormon. Later, at age twenty-two, he would become the first Mormon missionary. (See D&C 23:4.)

Joseph Smith Sr. was counseled to exhort and strengthen the Church throughout all of his life. He would go on to become the patriarch to the Church and thereafter comfort, advise, and admonish members of the Church while giving inspired blessings. (See D&C 23:5.)

Joseph Knight, a close friend of the Prophet Joseph, was told to preach the gospel and strengthen the Church. He was admonished to "pray vocally before the world as well as in secret, and in your family, and among your friends, and in all places." Finally, Knight was invited to be baptized—to "unite with the true church." At the time he was still officially a member of the Universalist faith. Knight followed the counsel he received in this revelation to him and was baptized two months later on June 9, 1830. (See D&C 23:6–7.)

---

1. Robin Scott Jensen, Richard E. Turley Jr., Riley M. Lorimer, *The Joseph Smith Papers: Revelations and Translations*, Vol. 2, 55–57.

Part 4

The Harmony, Pennsylvania, Period

Chapter 15

The Book of Mormon: Harmony, Pennsylvania, December 1827–August 1830

As people in Palmyra and the surrounding community became more and more aware of what Joseph Smith claimed to have experienced, the Smiths felt marginalized by their friends and neighbors. As time progressed, outright persecution ensued and physical threats were made against Joseph. On one occasion he was attacked by marauders who wanted to steal the gold plates, and mobs ransacked the Smith home looking for them. Joseph began to fear for his life, and he and Emma decided it would be best to move so that Joseph could find the peace and tranquility he needed to translate the Book of Mormon record.

With little by way of worldly wealth, it seemed reasonable to move to Harmony, Pennsylvania, where Emma had previously lived with her parents and family. With the help of Martin Harris,[1] a friend and previous employer of the Prophet, Joseph and Emma climbed into a wagon that accommodated all their earthly belongings and headed southeast in  December 1827. When they arrived, Joseph and Emma lived temporarily with Emma's parents until he was able to purchase a house from Emma's eldest brother, Jesse, a stone's throw away from Emma's parent's home.

In Harmony, Joseph was able to settle down and continue his efforts to translate the Book of Mormon. At first, Emma acted as Joseph's scribe and wrote down the paragraphs that he dictated from the ancient record. This became more and more impracticable as Emma's household duties conflicted. Consequently, Joseph sought the help of Oliver Cowdery, a schoolteacher who had been living with Joseph's parents on the Smith farm in Manchester, New York. Oliver moved to Harmony in 1829 and

---

1. Martin Harris gave Joseph and Emma $50.00 to facilitate the move.

from that point forward the Book of Mormon translation continued at a faster pace.[1]

However, once again, the oft-repeated pattern of discontent with Joseph's claims stirred skepticism and resentment among his neighbors. In June 1829, Joseph and Emma thought it would be best if they moved to Fayette, New York, just over one hundred miles northwest of Harmony, to complete the Book of Mormon project. When they arrived, they accepted an invitation to stay at the Whitmer home, new friends who had expressed interest in what Joseph was doing. It was in Fayette that Joseph would complete the translation; he then returned to Palmyra for a short time to arrange for the publication of the Book of Mormon.

---

1. It was also during this time that Joseph Smith and Oliver Cowdery were baptized. (See D&C 13.)

Chapter 16

The Big Questions: Harmony, Pennsylvania

What Is Revelation?

Revelation is a communication from God, and Joseph's theophany in the spring of 1820 convinced him that God could and did communicate with individuals. The First Vision, as it is called, was so defining that from that moment forward revelation would be a fundamental operating principle of Mormonism. Therefore, it is not surprising that some of Joseph's early revelations talked about, defined, and described what revelation was and how a person could receive communications from God.

Implicit in a study of the Doctrine and Covenants is the realization that revelation is multifaceted and that God communicates with mankind in a number of different ways, some of which are more direct and certain than others. At least six different modes of revelation are found in the Doctrine and Covenants. They are:

1. Inspired letters or written statements. (See D&C 85; 121; 122; 127; 128; 129.)

2. Inspired interpretations of scripture. (See D&C 7; 74; 77; 113.)

3. Audible voice from heaven. (See D&C 130:12–13.)

4. Open visions. (See D&C 76; 137; 138.)

5. Angelic appearances. (See D&C 13 [John the Baptist]; 27 [angel]; 110 [(Moses, Elias, Elijah]).

6. Appearances of God the Father and Jesus Christ. (See D&C 76 [God the Father and Jesus Christ]; 110 [Jesus].)

Of these six, actual appearances of God the Father, Jesus Christ, angels, and spirits are the most certain and direct. Generally speaking, such appearances are reserved for situations where absolute certainty about the message is required. The other modes of communication—inspiration, voices, dreams, and visions are more subjective in nature. Taking this into consideration, it is not surprising that a number of Joseph's early revelations discuss how a person may identify and interpret a communication from God.

Because there is always the possibility that a person may mistake an angel of darkness for an angel of light, learning to distinguish the difference is important; and the subject of how to distinguish true from false revelation was a matter of concern throughout Joseph's lifetime. Communications on how to discern whether a seemingly heavenly messenger was of God or the devil was still being discussed as late as February 1843. (See D&C 129.)

The most common way God communicates with his children is through the Spirit of the Holy Ghost. This is described as a communication to the "mind" and the "heart" and is discussed in some detail in section 8. Finally, material objects that were used to facilitate revelations from God are discussed. The notion that God uses stones, rods, and other instruments to make known his mind and will is foreign to our culture and way of thinking. However, at the time of Joseph Smith, in biblical times, Book of Mormon times, and in other cultures, such instruments were common. Section 8, therefore, not only addresses God speaking to individuals directly but also communications from God that come through revelatory objects.

What Is Translation?

What Joseph Smith meant when he said he translated the Book of Mormon, Bible, or Book of Abraham is commonly misunderstood because Joseph used the word *translate* in a peculiar way. By it, he did not mean changing words from one language into another. Rather, "translation" in a Mormon context means receiving a revelation that discloses the meaning of an ancient text. (See D&C 7; 8.)

How Does a Person Receive Revelation?

As a general rule, people receive revelations when searching for answers.[1] It is well known that prayer and thought precede a communication from God. Casual interest in something is rarely enough to precipitate a heavenly communication. To receive a revelation, it generally helps to reason something out to a logical conclusion and then ask God if it be right. If it is, God will cause a person's "bosom to burn." This term of

---

1. There are certainly other occasions when God simply interjects himself without any thought on the part of the recipient. Alma the Younger and Paul, while in serious sin, were visited by an angel and called to repentance. However, there are not many such examples in scripture, and, therefore, these two instances should be taken as exceptions to the general rule.

art and method of understanding whether a conclusion is true or false is discussed in detail in section 9.

Why John the Baptist?

Although the early Church was focused on receiving revelation, the importance of "authority" from God became a key consideration when Joseph and Oliver Cowdery were told that they were not authorized to perform baptisms because they lacked the authority from God to do so. The idea that a person must have the right to act for God was first introduced when John the Baptist restored the Aaronic Priesthood, which authorized Joseph and Oliver to ordain each other priests and thereafter baptize one another. (See D&C 13.)

Chapter 17

Joseph Smith Jr. Home

Section 3: Smith Log Home, Harmony, Pennsylvania, July 16, 1828

Heading

Joseph Smith rebuked for the part he played in losing first 116 pages of the translation of the Book of Mormon.

The big question

Question: Who is a worthy vessel?
Answer: Joseph and Martin Harris, who fail to follow the instructions given them by the Lord. Both repent and once again regain God's favor.

Introduction

Revelation given to the Prophet Joseph Smith in his log home in Harmony, Pennsylvania, July 1828, relating to the loss of the 116 pages of manuscript translated from the first part of the Book of Mormon, which was called the "Book of Lehi." The prophet had reluctantly allowed these pages to pass from his custody to that of Martin Harris, who had served for a brief period as scribe in the translation of the Book of Mormon. The revelation was given through the "Urim and Thummim," which in this instance probably refers to Joseph's seer stone.[1] (See also Doctrine and Covenants 5 and 10 relating to this incident.) Joseph Smith is rebuked for his part in the 116-page debacle. He is told that even though he may have had many revelations and had power to do mighty works, if he boasts of his own strength and does not take seriously the counsels of God, the

---

1. Smith, *History of the Church*, 1:21–23.

Lord will forsake him. The gold plates and the Urim and Thummim are taken from him, and he loses the privilege of translating the gold plates for a period of time.

Section 3 received through instrumentality of the seer stone, referred to in this context as the Urim and Thummim

Section 3 is believed to be Joseph Smith's first recorded revelation. Although the heading in Doctrine and Covenants states that it was received through the Urim and Thummim, it may have been received through the instrumentality of the seer stone.[1] This is a reasonable assumption for at least two reasons. First, we know that when Joseph "lost" the privilege to translate, the angel took back the gold plates and the Urim and Thummim. Second, sometimes the words "Urim and Thummim" were used interchangeably with the words "seer stone" or "interpreters." (For a discussion on seer stones and other objects used to receive revelations, see section 8.) However, some Mormon historians disagree. Dennis L. Largey, for example, makes the case that Moroni returned the Urim and Thummim to Joseph long enough for him to receive section 3 and then once again took the instrument into his custody.[2]

Joseph and Martin Harris lose the first 116 pages of the Book of Mormon

Joseph moved to Harmony to escape persecution and work on the translation of the Book of Mormon undisturbed. The first part of the Book of Mormon contained the record of Lehi and was referred to as the Book of Lehi. At first, Emma acted as scribe. However, as time went on Emma's household duties slowed down the translation process. Therefore, Joseph was relieved when in the spring of 1828 Martin Harris agreed to act as scribe. Harris was a well-to-do farmer from the Palmyra, New York, area and became interested in Joseph Smith and the Book of Mormon when Joseph lived there.[3] Harris assisted in the translation process from April 12, 1828, through June 14, 1828.

---

1. Joseph used a stone through which he received revelations. This subject is taken up in more detail in Doctrine and Covenants 8.
2. See Largey, *Book of Mormon Reference Companion*, 774.
3. Martin Harris was born in 1783 and had moved to Palmyra when he was nine years old. He became a prosperous farmer. In the fall of 1827 he heard of Joseph for the first time. Joseph occasionally worked for Martin on his farm, where he picked corn; we also have record that Joseph wrestled on the farm and that Joseph and Martin enjoyed each other's company. Martin gave Joseph the $50 necessary to move himself and his family to Harmony, Pennsylvania.

Harris' willingness to move from his home in Palmyra, New York, and go to Harmony, Pennsylvania, was spurred on by a visionary experience he had in which it was affirmed that Joseph was a prophet of God. Nevertheless, Martin's wife, Lucy, was skeptical of Joseph Smith's claims and pressured Martin for physical evidence that Joseph was not a fraud.[1] As a result, Martin asked Joseph if he could borrow the first 116 pages of the book to show her. Twice Joseph was told through the Urim and Thummim that Martin should not be allowed to take possession of the manuscript. Martin continued to persist and Joseph approached God a third time and was told that Martin could take the manuscript but only under certain strict conditions.[2] Martin was told that he could show the manuscript only to a restricted group of people—his wife; his father and mother; his brother, Preserved Harris; and his wife's sister, Mrs. Cobb. Manuscript in hand, he went back to his home in Manchester, New York, to assure doubters that Joseph really was producing a text about an ancient American civilization.

Meanwhile, Emma was about to give birth to their first child. The soon-to-be parents were deeply distressed when their little baby son died shortly after birth on June 15. By this time Harris had been gone with the manuscript for about three weeks, and Joseph had heard nothing. Although very ill and in mourning, Emma encouraged Joseph to go by stagecoach to Palmyra and find out why Harris had not returned with the manuscript.

Joseph arrived in Palmyra and walked the last few miles at night until he arrived at the home of his parents in Manchester, New York. He sent word for Harris to meet him at breakfast the next morning. Breakfast was prepared and Joseph and members of his family waited. "Several hours passed before Martin finally plodded up the walk with his head hung down. He climbed on the fence and sat there with his hat down

---

1. Lucy Harris was known to have had an "irascible temper." She accused her husband of beating her about the head and also of adultery with a Mrs. Haggart." See Dan Vogel, *Early Mormon Documents*, 2:34–36 (1999).

2. It is not surprising that Joseph felt pressured to give Harris the manuscript. Harris was Joseph's senior by more than twenty years and a wealthy and prominent member of the community in the Palmyra area. Joseph had worked for him as a day laborer and was beholden to Harris for giving him $50 to move from Palmyra to Harmony so that he could translate the Book of Mormon without interruption. It was also not surprising the Harris was pressuring Joseph to give him evidence that he was not engaged in a fraud. "After Mr. Harris left again for Pennsylvania, his wife went from place to place, and from house to house, telling her grievances to everyone she met, but particularly bewailing that the deception which Joe Smith was practicing upon people was about to strip her of all that she possessed. 'But' said the woman, 'I know how to take care of my property, and I'll let them see that pretty shortly.' So she carried away her furniture, linen and bedding, and other movable articles, till she well-nigh divested the premises of everything which could conduce to comfort or convenience. These things she deposited with her friends in whom she reposed sufficient confidence to assure her of the safety of her property." (See Smith, *History of Joseph Smith by His Mother* [1996 ed.], 157–58.) *Church History in the Fulness of Times*, 48.

over his eyes. Finally he came in and sat down at the breakfast table, but he could not eat."

Lucy Mack Smith, the prophet's mother, recorded what happened next.

> He took up his knife and fork as if he were going to use them, but immediately dropped them. Hyrum, observing this, said "Martin, why do you not eat? Are you sick?" Upon which Mr. Harris pressed his hands upon his temples and cried out in a tone of deep anguish, "Oh, I have lost my soul!"
>
> Joseph, who had not expressed his fears till now, sprang from the table, exclaiming, "Martin, have you lost that manuscript? Have you broken your oath, and brought down condemnation upon my head as well as your own?"
>
> "Yes; it is gone," replied Martin, "and I know not where."
>
> [Joseph cried out in anguish,] "All is lost! All is lost! What shall I do? I have sinned—it is I who tempted the wrath of God. I should have been satisfied with the first answer which I received from the Lord; for he told me that it was not safe to let the writing go out of my possession." He wept and groaned, and walked the floor continually.
>
> At length he told Martin to go back and search again.
>
> "No," said Martin, "it is all in vain; for I have ripped open beds and pillows [looking for the manuscript]; and I know it is not there."
>
> "Then must I," said Joseph, "return with such a tale as this? I dare not do it. And how shall I appear before the Lord? Of what rebuke am I not worthy from the angel of the Most High?"[1]

Joseph returned home to Harmony heavy hearted and empty handed. He fervently prayed to the Lord for forgiveness. Shortly thereafter, Moroni appeared and required Joseph to return the plates and the Urim and Thummim. Section 3 chastised Joseph for "[setting] at naught the counsels of God" but held out hope that if he repented he would at some time in the future be allowed to translate again.

The imperfections of men

Joseph's and Harris' imperfections are spoken about in Doctrine and Covenants 3 in some detail. Joseph had boasted of his own strength and "set at naught the counsels of God, and follow[ed] after the dictates of his own will and carnal desires." (Verse 4.) In addition Joseph had transgressed the commandments of God by being pressured by others. (See verse 8.) As a result of his sins, he was warned that "if thou art not aware thou wilt fall." (Verse 9.) Harris is described as a "wicked man, who has set at naught

---

1. Church History in the Fulness of Times, 48.

the counsels of God, and broken the most sacred promises which were made before God, and depended upon his own judgment and boasted in his own wisdom." (Verses 12–13.)

Hope was held out, but only upon the condition of these two men's repentance. "But remember, God is merciful; therefore, repent of that which thou hast done." (Verse 10.) For Joseph, repentance was an arduous process. "I commenced humbling myself in mighty prayer before the Lord, and as I poured out my soul in supplication to him, that if possible I might obtain mercy at his hands and be forgiven of all that I had done which was contrary to his will."[1] No doubt Joseph's experience of relying upon his own judgment and will and then failing, only to have Moroni appear and take back the Book of Mormon plates and the Urim and Thummim for a time, was one of the most distressing and formative experiences of Joseph's life. Both men regained their spiritual standing. Moroni returned the plates and Joseph completed the translation. Martin Harris saw the angel Moroni for himself and became one of the Three Witnesses to the Book of Mormon.

Section 4: Smith Log Home, Harmony, Pennsylvania, February 1829

Heading

Joseph Smith receives a revelation on behalf of his father informing him that a marvelous work and a wonder is about to begin.

Introduction

Revelation given through the Prophet Joseph to his father, Joseph Smith Sr. in his log cabin home located in Harmony, Pennsylvania, February 1829. Joseph's father had come to visit his son to inquire after his welfare. A marvelous work and a wonder is about to come forth. A Christian character qualifies a person for the work.

Joseph's parents concerned for their son's well-being

For Joseph's part in the loss of the 116 pages, the angel Moroni had taken the gold plates and the Urim and Thummim from Joseph in July 1828. Consequently, he focused on supporting his family and worked on his thirteen-acre farm in Harmony, Pennsylvania, which he had purchased

---

1. Smith, *History of Joseph Smith by His Mother* (1996 ed.), 173–74.

from his father-in-law, Isaac Hale. After Joseph's heartfelt repentance, the plates were returned to him late that same summer or early in the fall. (See D&C 10.) Although Joseph wanted to immediately begin translating once again, work on the farm and the need to support his family prevented him from doing so. The situation was not helped by the fact that even though Emma's father and mother lived close by, they refused to lend assistance because they harbored bad feelings against Joseph, who appeared to be a person of little education and meager financial resources. In addition, Joseph and Emma got off to a bad start when they married, contrary to the wishes of Emma's parents, and eloped.

Joseph Knight Sr., a friend of the Smith family who lived a few miles away in Coleville, New York, described the situation during the winter of 1828–29.

> Now, he [Joseph] could not translate but little, being poor and [having] nobody to write for him but his wife, and she could not do much and take care of her house, and he being poor [having] no means to live but work. . . . I let him have some little provisions and . . . a pair of shoes and three dollars in money to help him a little.[1]

Understandably, this was a difficult time for Joseph and Emma.

Under these circumstances, it was not surprising that Joseph's parents were anxious to make contact with their son to offer love and encouragement.[2] Father Smith made the journey from Manchester, New York, to Harmony to be with Joseph and Emma. It was during this stopover that Father Smith sought a revelation from his son. Section 4 acknowledged that "a marvelous work is about to come forth among the children of men." (Verse 1.) Responding to Father Smith's desire to be associated with that work, he was counseled to prepare himself to participate by seeking after and developing the character traits of a follower of Jesus—"faith, hope, charity and love, with an eye single to the glory of God." (Verse 5.)

---

1. Robinson and Garrett, Doctrine and Covenants Commentary, 1:41–42.
2. The last time that Joseph's parents had seen their son was when he was in agony over the loss of the 116 pages.

Section 5: Smith Log Home, Harmony, Pennsylvania, March 1829

Heading

Martin Harris, in spite of his past sins, is promised that if he is humble and remains faithful he will be given the privilege to become one of three witnesses to the gold plates.

The big question[1]

Question: Who is a worthy vessel?
Answer: Imperfect people, such as Martin Harris, a man who had disobeyed the Lord and as a consequence lost the first 116 pages of the Book of Mormon. The Lord promised him that if he would humble himself and have faith he would be one of three witnesses who would be shown the gold plates.

Introduction

Revelation given through the Prophet Joseph Smith in the log cabin located in Harmony, Pennsylvania, in March 1829 at the request of Martin Harris. Harris was promised that he would be given the privilege of seeing the gold plates for himself if he would not be prideful and humble himself. (See verse 24.) Two other witnesses would also be called and afforded the same privilege.

Harris concerned about his standing before God

About seven months had passed since Martin Harris lost the 116-page Book of Mormon manuscript.[2] During the interim, Joseph had been reprimanded by the Lord and the gold plates taken from him in July 1828. Joseph repented for the part he played in this debacle, and the plates were returned to him at the end of the summer.

Undoubtedly, Harris was concerned about his standing before God and whether or not he would ever be fully trusted by the Lord again. Harris deeply regretted his behavior and decided to travel from his home in Palmyra, New York, to visit with the Prophet in Harmony, Pennsylvania.

---

1. The focus of Doctrine and Covenants 5 is on the sins of Martin Harris. However, it is worth noting that Joseph Smith is also commanded to "repent and walk more uprightly before me, and to yield to the persuasions of men no more." (See verse 21.)
2. The 116 pages consisted of what Joseph called the Book of Lehi.

Foremost in his mind was whether or not the gold plates had been returned to Joseph so that the Prophet could continue translating.

When Harris arrived in Harmony, he was welcomed by the Prophet and informed that the translating process was going forward with Emma as scribe. Of course, Harris was anxious to know what role, if any, he would play in the coming forth of the Book of Mormon. In answer to that question, Joseph received Doctrine and Covenants 5. Harris was relieved to know that he had been forgiven of his past sins and would be allowed to become one of the Three Witnesses, provided he was humble and remained faithful. (See 2 Nephi 27:12–14.)

Joseph Smith commanded to stop translating the Book of Mormon for a season

Harris was not invited to be Joseph's scribe again. Emma's family duties and responsibilities made it difficult for her to continue in this role. Consequently, the Lord informed Joseph that he could rest for a season and that at some point in the future he would be provided with the "means whereby thou mayest accomplish the things which I have commanded thee." (D&C 5:34.) Not long thereafter, Oliver Cowdery came to Harmony to meet the Prophet and was commissioned to write down what Joseph translated.

Section 6: Smith Log Cabin, Harmony, Pennsylvania, April 1829

Heading

Oliver Cowdery appointed to be the Book of Mormon scribe to take down the words as Joseph translated from the gold plates.

The big questions

Question: How does a person receive revelation?
Answer: Revelation comes in answer to prayer.
Question: What is revelation?
Answer: A reassuring message from God that brings peace to the mind.

Introduction

Revelation given to the Prophet Joseph Smith and Oliver Cowdery in Joseph's log cabin located in Harmony, Pennsylvania, in April 1829.[1] Oliver Cowdery began his labors as scribe in the translation of the Book of Mormon, April 7, 1829. He had already received a divine manifestation of the truth of the Prophet's testimony respecting the Book of Mormon. The Prophet inquired of the Lord through the seer stone and received this response.

Oliver Cowdery visits the Prophet Joseph in Harmony, Pennsylvania

In 1829 Oliver Cowdery was an itinerate school teacher boarding with the Joseph Smith Sr. family in Manchester, New York. While there he taught the Smith children and in conversations with the family became acquainted with the story about Joseph and the gold plates. Cowdery was curious, approached the Lord about the matter, and became convinced that Joseph's claims were true. Anxious to meet the Prophet, Cowdery went with Joseph's younger brother Samuel to meet him. They waited until school was in recess at the beginning of April to make their journey.[2]

Lucy Mack Smith, the prophet's mother, recalled that Cowdery told Joseph Smith Sr. that he had been praying in his bedroom and was deeply impressed by what he had heard about the Prophet Joseph. He said that he had been in serious study upon the subject all day, and that "it was impressed upon his mind, that he should yet have the privilege to write . . . for Joseph."[3] Oliver said that his sense of assurance that he would at some future time write for the Prophet was accompanied by a feeling of "peace." (See D&C 6:23.)

As soon as school was over, Samuel Smith and Oliver Cowdery started for Harmony in late March or early April 1829, just three days after Joseph had asked the Lord in prayer to provide another scribe so that he could resume translating the Book of Mormon.[4] Almost immediately, Joseph asked Cowdery to be his scribe and received Doctrine and Covenants 6.

Cowdery had *not* told the Prophet Joseph about the confirming spiritual experience he had had while praying one night in his bedroom at Joseph Smith Sr.'s home. For this reason, it was added confirmation to Cowdery that Joseph was indeed a prophet of God when Joseph referred to his

---

1. Smith, *History of the Church*, 1:32–35.
2. It is about 125 miles from Manchester, New York, to Harmony, Pennsylvania.
3. Smith, *History of Joseph Smith by His Mother* (1958 ed.), 139, 141.
4. Emma had tried to be Joseph's scribe but her household duties made it impractical. Therefore, the Lord told Joseph that he could rest for a season. (See commentary on D&C 5.)

experience in section 6. "Cast your mind upon the night that you cried unto me in your heart, that you might know concerning the truth of these things." (D&C 6:22.)[1]

Oliver told to admonish the Prophet Joseph in his faults

Oliver was told that he should "admonish [Joseph] in his faults, and also receive admonition of [Joseph]." (D&C 6:19.) Although it may seem somewhat presumptuous for the Lord to direct Oliver to "admonish" Joseph "in his faults," all men and women, regardless of their rank or station, benefit from frank and honest counsel. Such candor is even more important as a person is given more power and authority because the natural tendency is that leaders become isolated and out of touch. The more power a person has, the less likely it is that those around him or her will offer critical assessments for fear of reprisals. Such isolation leads to errors in judgment. Therefore, leaders must make an effort to reach out beyond the confines of their high station in life. The Lord's advice to Oliver and to Joseph helps guard against this tendency.

As the Church became more fully organized, this principle of candor between individuals was embodied in its governing quorums. By 1835 the decision-making process required equals to come to unanimity before a decision was reached, making it more likely that competing points of view would be considered. (D&C 107:27–31.)

Oliver told that he would be allowed to translate ancient records

Cowdery was promised that he would be able to translate ancient records even as the Prophet Joseph had. "I grant unto you a gift, if you desire of me, to translate, even as my servant Joseph." (Verse 25.) In context, the promise that Oliver would be allowed to translate could have referred to records, other than the Book of Mormon, "which contain much of my gospel, which have been kept back because of the wickedness of the people."[2] (See verse 26.) If this is the case, then this prophecy was fulfilled in section 7, where both Joseph and Cowdery translated a record authored by the Apostle John, which he had made on a parchment. "Revelation given to Joseph Smith . . . *and Oliver Cowdery* . . . when *they* inquired through the Urim and Thummim. . . . The revelation is a translated version of

---

1. See Smith, *History of the Church*, 1:32–35.
2. Oliver Cowdery did try to translate the Book of Mormon plates but failed. See commentary on D&C 9.

the record made on parchment by John and hidden up by himself." (See heading to D&C 7; emphasis added.)

Another possible fulfillment of the promise that author/historian Oliver Cowdery would "translate, even as my servant Joseph" has been suggested by Royal Skousen. He pointed out that in the original Book of Mormon manuscript there is evidence Joseph took over as scribe for just 28 words in Alma 45:22 where the text is in Joseph's hand rather than Oliver's. This may represent his only and unsuccessful attempt at translation.

Note that when Joseph and Cowdery used the word *translate*, they did not mean looking at an ancient language and interpreting the words and phrases into English. Rather, the word *translate* is used to mean making known the message of an ancient text by the spirit of revelation. Therefore, having the text or the record physically present is incidental to the process. For example, when Joseph translated the plates he did not look at the words on the plates during the process. Rather, he used the interpreters to discern the message of what was contained in the ancient record. We know this because those who saw Joseph translate the Book of Mormon plates said that the actual record was closed and sitting on the table near Joseph when he received by revelation the meaning of its contents and dictated the words to his various scribes. (See commentary to D&C 9.) Likewise, when Joseph and Oliver translated the parchment of John, the actual parchment was not present. The books of Moses and most probably Abraham, which are contained in the Pearl of Great Price, were received in this same manner.

Other records held back because of the wickedness of the people

Section 6 speaks about many "records which contain much of my gospel, which have been kept back because of the wickedness of the people." (Verse 26.) The Book of Mormon also speaks about books containing gospel truths becoming available in the last days. "I beheld other books, which came forth by the power of the Lamb, from the Gentiles unto them, unto the convincing of the Gentiles and the remnant of the seed of my brethren, and also the Jews . . . that the records of the prophets and of the twelve apostles of the Lamb are true." (1 Nephi 13:39.) Since the time of Joseph Smith, many ancient books containing information about God's dealings with other cultures have been discovered. The Dead Sea Scroll, Pseudepigrapha, Forty Day Documents, and Nag Hammadi collection are but a few. Each of these collections contains valuable information that helps place the restored gospel in a broader context.

Section 7: Smith Log Home, Harmony, Pennsylvania, April 1829

Heading

Joseph Smith translates a parchment that contains the writings of the Apostle John. John will tarry in the flesh until Jesus comes in glory.

The big question

Question: What is translation?
Answer: A revelation from God making known the same meaning in English of an ancient text. (See also section 8.)

Introduction

A revelation to the Prophet Joseph and Oliver Cowdery received in Joseph's home in Harmony, Pennsylvania, in April 1829. During the course of the translation of the Book of Mormon, questions arose about various gospel subjects. Section 7 is a revelation that reflects an inquiry made concerning whether or not the Apostle John will tarry in the flesh until Jesus comes for a second time.

Did the Apostle John tarry in the flesh?

As Joseph and Cowdery translated the gold plates, the ideas presented in the Book of Mormon initiated theological and religious conversations. A difference of opinion arose between them revolving around the account of John the apostle in John 21:21–23 as to whether John died or continued to live as a translated being to minister on the earth until the beginning of the Second Coming.[1]

Section 7 recounts how Joseph and Oliver saw in vision a parchment that had been authored by the Apostle himself. Joseph and Oliver translated the parchment, which clarified that the Apostle John will "tarry until I come in my glory." (Verse 3.) This promise given to John is reminiscent of a similar promise given the three Nephites at the close of Jesus' ministry in the Americas. (See 3 Nephi 28:1–12.)

The fact that Joseph and Oliver were shown an ancient text in vision does not mean that they were translating from an ancient language into English. Rather, the meaning of the text was made known to Joseph and

---

[1]. See Smith, *History of the Church*, 1:35–36.

Cowdery by the spirit of revelation and then written down. (See commentary on D&C 8.)

Based on this revelation, it is understood that John the Beloved will live on and minister on earth until Jesus comes a second time. In 1831 Joseph received a revelation that indicated part of John's mission involved a mission to the lost ten tribes of Israel. (See D&C 77:14.)

The reference that the Lord had promised to make John "as a flaming fire and ministering angel" is another way of stating that John was a "translated" being. Joseph Smith explained that a translated body is not subject to death allowing such a person to fulfill "future missions" on earth until the Second Coming occurs.[1] At some future day John will receive a resurrected celestial body; however, this transformation will not involve dying first. (See 3 Nephi 28:6–10.) Verses 6–7 were added in the 1835 edition of the Doctrine and Covenants.

Section 8: Smith Log Home, Harmony, Pennsylvania, April 1829

Heading

Revelation is a communication from God directly to the mind and heart.

The big questions

Question: What is revelation?
Answer: A message from God directly to the mind and heart.
Question: What is translation?
Answer: A revelation from God that makes known the meaning of an ancient text in a modern language.
Question: How does a person receive revelation?
Answer: In the mind and heart and sometimes with the aid of a physical object.

Anchor section

Memorize: Revelation defined

---

1. See Smith, *Teachings of the Prophet Joseph Smith*, 191.

Joseph Smith Jr. Home

Introduction

Revelation given through the Prophet Joseph Smith to Oliver Cowdery in his home in Harmony, Pennsylvania, in April 1829.[1] In the course of the translation of the Book of Mormon, Cowdery, who continued to serve as Joseph's scribe, desired to translate for himself. The Lord responded to his supplication by granting this revelation. Section 8 explains that a revelation from God comes to the mind and heart and that the process may be enhanced by the use of a physical object.

Revelation defined

Revelation is a message from God to the "mind" and the "heart." (See D&C 8:2.) The idea of a communication to the "mind" necessarily involves the notion that information or knowledge has been transmitted.[2] However, section 8 makes clear that a revelation is more than simply the transfer of intelligence from God to man. It also involves the "heart." This mention of the "heart" refers to a physical sensation from the Holy Ghost, which confirms or corroborates that the information received in any given revelation is from God—true and correct—and therefore may be relied upon.

This physical sensation, which substantiates that information is from God, is more than an emotional reaction. Sometimes it is a described as a "burning in the bosom" or a sense of warmth in the torso. (See D&C 9:8.) This sensation is generally accompanied by a transcendent feeling of joy, a sense of well-being, and a peaceful assurance that calms the soul. A clarity and purpose of mind is experienced, which makes one confident that a decision, course of action, or intellectual conclusion is right.[3]

Joseph said that learning to distinguish the feeling that comes from the Holy Ghost from counterfeit feelings is vitally important because if we

---

1. Smith, *History of the Church*, 1:36–37.
2. Joseph Smith taught that when the Holy Ghost is present, something is revealed or made known. (See Smith, *Teachings of the Prophet Joseph Smith*, 328.)
3. In Doctrine and Covenants 6:23 the Lord reminds Oliver Cowdery, "Did I not speak peace to your mind concerning the matter?" Doctrine and Covenants 85:6 described the physical sensation as "the still small voice, which whispereth through and pierceth all things, and often times it maketh my bones to quake while it maketh manifest." On February 23, 1847, Brigham Young related an experience he had at Winter Quarters when speaking to the Twelve. Brigham said he saw Joseph in the spirit. Joseph explained when the Holy Ghost is present he "will whisper peace and joy to their souls; it will take malice, hatred, strife and all evil from their hearts; and their whole desire will be to do good, bring forth righteousness and build up the kingdom of God." (See *Manuscript History of Brigham Young [1846–1847]*.) See also Doctrine and Covenants 11:13: "I will impart unto you of my Spirit which shall enlighten your mind which shall fill your soul with joy."

mistake emotion or some other feelings for spiritual confirmation we have no guarantee of trustworthiness and can easily be led off course. Joseph understood that it was possible for him and his followers to mistakenly believe an impression or even a visitation was from God. He taught that men and women must be cautious because "some revelations are of God; some revelations are of men; and some revelations are of the devil."[1] In reference to a false revelation, he cautioned that "nothing is a greater injury to the children of men than to be under the influence of a false spirit when they think they have the Spirit of God. Thousands have felt the influence of its terrible power and baneful effects."[2]

Joseph also recognized that study as well as revelation was a legitimate way to learn about God, religion, and, for that matter, any subject. (See D&C 88:77–79.) Later, in 1832, when Joseph established the school of the prophets, the Lord counseled the Saints to "seek learning" out of the "best books." (D&C 88:118.) However, he also encouraged them to exercise their faith in conjunction with their learning and taught that both can work together. "And as all have not faith, seek ye diligently and teach one another words of wisdom; yea, seek ye out of the best books words of wisdom; seek learning even by study and also by faith." (D&C 88:118; see also commentary to D&C 9.)

The Book of Mormon and the translation process

Joseph and others (including the Lord) said that he "translated" the Book of Mormon. However, implying that Joseph translated the Book of Mormon in the usual sense of the word is misleading. "Translate" generally means to render from one language into another. Of course, this assumes that the person doing the translating knows at least two languages. This was not the case with the Prophet. When he "translated," he meant that he received a revelation from God setting forth the message and content of an ancient record. The prophet publicly explained that the message of the book "was communicated to him, *direct from heaven*. . . . [H]e had penned it as dictated by God."[3] Consequently, it is inaccurate when thinking about the translation process to imagine Joseph Smith poring over the archaic

---

1. Roberts, *Comprehensive History of the Church*, 1:165–66, and commentary for D&C 111.
2. Smith, *Teachings of the Prophet Joseph Smith*, 205.
3. 2 Nephi 27:20 plainly states that the Lord would "give" the words of the translation to the Prophet. This idea is repeated in Doctrine and Covenants 10:42, where the Lord refers to the material in the 116 pages of the Book of Lehi as "my words." (See Brown, *Plates of Gold*, 162, 169. See also D&C 3:12; 6:28; 21:1; 107:92; 127:12; 135:3; Roberts, *Comprehensive History of the Church*, 4:79.)

words on the gold plates and thereafter rendering an English version based on his knowledge of ancient languages.

The evidence suggests that the revelation about the contents and message on the gold plates came about in at least three different ways. First, through the use of the Urim and Thummim; second, by the use of a seer stone; and third, by direct revelation.

The Urim and Thummim was in the stone box with the plates when Joseph took possession of them at the Hill Cumorah. The Urim and Thummim, or interpreters, as the Book of Mormon refers to them (Mosiah 8:13; 28:20; Alma 37:21; Ether 4:5), consisted of two transparent stones fastened together.[1] The seer stone was a chocolate-colored rock, which was round and about the size and shape of an egg. Such stones were commonly used in Joseph Smith's day for divination.[2] As Joseph reached the end of the Book of Mormon project, Orson Pratt reported that he translated portions of the Book of Mormon without the aid of an object.

Those who witnessed Joseph translate said that he would use the Urim and Thummim or seer stone in a hat to avoid light.[3] He would place his head face down in the hat and look at the physical object.[4] About twenty

---

1. Lucy Mack Smith described the Urim and Thummim as "consist[ing] of two smooth three-cornered diamonds set in glass, and the glasses were set in silver bows, which were connected with each other in much the same way as old fashioned spectacles." (See Largey, *Book of Mormon Reference Companion*, 773.) The "spectacles" were attached to a breastplate, according to William Smith, and "by [a] rod which was fastened at the outer shoulder edge of the breastplate. . . . This rod was just the right length so that when the Urim and Thummim was removed from before the eyes it would reach to a pocket on the left side of the breastplate where the instrument was kept when not in use." (See Largey, *Book of Mormon Reference Companion*, 773; spelling standardized.) William Smith went on to say that "a silver bow ran over one stone, under the other, around over [the] one and under the first in the shape of a horizontal figure 8 much like a pair of spectacles. . . . They were much too large for Joseph and he could only see through one at a time." (See Largey, *Book of Mormon Reference Companion*, 774; spelling standardized.)

2. See Quinn, *Early Mormonism and the Magic World View*, 37–41, 77, 145–48, 194, 195–204; see Largey, *Book of Mormon Reference Companion*, 712.

3. It is difficult to know for sure how Joseph used the Urim and Thummim. Some accounts suggest that he placed it in a hat, while others suggest that he looked through the stones. See Brown, *Plates of Gold*, 160–74, for statements on the translation process through the eyes of different observers. No doubt some of the confusion on this subject comes about as a result of the nomenclature. Sometimes a seer stone was referred to as a Urim and Thummim. For example, the following statement describes the Urim and Thummim in such a way that it leads one to the conclusion that in fact the author (William Smith, the Prophet's younger brother) is speaking about the seer stone. "The manner in which [the translation] was done was by looking into the Urim and Thummim, which was placed in a hat to exclude the light . . . and reading of the translation, which appeared in the stone by the power of God." (See Brown, *Plates of Gold*, 170.)

4. Most who have studied the subject believe that Joseph began the translation of the Book of Mormon using the Urim and Thummim (often referred to as interpreters) and then at some time thereafter switched over to a seer stone. The seer stone was described as a stone that was chocolate-colored and about the size of an egg." (See Brown, *Plates of Gold*, 164–65.)

to thirty words would appear on it, and Joseph would say aloud what was on the object and his scribe would write it all down.[1] The scribe would then repeat back to Joseph what he had written down to make sure it was correct. Punctuation and the spelling of most words were left up to the scribe. Joseph would spell out difficult names.[2]

What emerges from the facts is that when Joseph received the revelation making known what was on the golden plates, he did not look at the ancient text. The plates were incidental to the process and remained on the table next to him, covered with a cloth. It is apparent that Joseph was engaged in a process much like that which he employed when he produced the Book of Moses, but with the latter he had no ancient text nearby.[3]

Although Joseph's use of objects to receive revelations may seem odd to those who live in the twenty-first century, such objects were in common use in Joseph's day. D. Michael Quinn points out that white magic and the supernatural were widespread. "The majority of early Americans gave at least some attention to astrology in their daily lives, and evidence indicates that white magic influenced the folk medicine that was almost universal during the period."[4] The *Palmyra Reflector* is a good source for describing the environment. "Rods," "balls," and "peep stone" or pebbles taken from the brook or field were familiar and considered reliable guides.[5]

B. H. Roberts, a member of the Quorum of Seventy and Church historian at the turn of the twentieth century, has suggested that what Joseph saw with the Urim and Thummim and seer stone was a reflection of what the spirit of revelation placed in the Prophet's mind. Others have taken a more

---

1. See Brown, *Plates of Gold*, 169–71.
2. See Brown, *Plates of Gold*, 169–71.
3. This point of view is supported by Orson Pratt's statement that as Joseph became more and more proficient at translation, he did not need any instrument at all.
4. Quinn, *Early Mormonism and the Magic World View*, 20.
5. See Quinn, *Early Mormonism and the Magic World View*, 22. Such objects were commonly employed to find buried treasure believed buried by the Spaniards. Such treasure hunting was referred to as "money digging" and participated in by Joseph Smith during his teenage years. (See Quinn, *Early Mormonism and the Magic World View*, 23.) Several of Joseph's neighbors had seer stones. Sally Chase had a greenish-colored stone. John Stafford and Joshua Stafford had a "peepstone which looked like white marble and had a hole through the center." Both Chase and the Staffords used their stones to dig for treasure. It was a common idea that the Spanish had buried valuable objects in the earth in and around the New York area. (See Quinn, *Early Mormonism and the Magic World View*, 38.) Joseph first obtained a whitish, opaque stone in September 1819. Later he found a brown seer stone about the size of an egg, which he used in translating the Book of Mormon. He said that he found this stone when digging a well for the Chase family in Palmyra in about 1822. Joseph also used his stone, although unsuccessfully, to dig for treasure. (See Quinn, *Early Mormonism and the Magic World View*, 40–41.) Jan Shipps noted that Smith's experience as a treasure-seer was "an important indication of his early and continued interest in extra-rational phenomena, and that it played an important role in his spiritual development." (See Quinn, *Early Mormonism and the Magic World View*, 51.)

involuntary approach and suggested that Joseph was simply reading what was placed on the stone, much like reading words on a computer screen. Still others suggest a position somewhere in between.

One possible explanation for the process Joseph was engaged in is something called scrying or sometimes referred to as peeping or seeing. It is the practice of looking into a translucent ball, stone, or even water (hydromancy). By tuning out one's surroundings and staring at an object and thereby clearing the mind from outside distractions, divine information could be obtained from visions and revelations projected onto the object like a movie screen. In this manner it was believed that a scyre or seer could divine the past, present, and future. Various methods of scrying are common in many cultures. John Dee (circa 1527-1609) was one of the most learned and best-known scryers in England. An astronomer and mathematician, he became interested in white magic and turned to the supernatural for knowledge. He sought contact with spirits by scrying or crystal-gazing accompanied by prayer and fasting which he believed were intermediaries between himself and the divine.

Finally, those who worked with Joseph said that while translating he could stop the dictation in the middle of a paragraph, go to lunch, and return and pick up where he left off, without having the scribe read back any of the text. Firsthand accounts state that no other extraneous books or other writings were used when Joseph translated. This meant that the chapters of Isaiah and the entire Sermon on the Temple Mount were dictated while Joseph was looking in the hat. Occasionally, he would express surprise at what he was translating. Emma tells of an experience where Joseph said to her while dictating parts of Nephi, "I didn't know that Jerusalem had walls around it." Lastly, if Joseph was angry or had a disagreement with Emma, he could not translate until he repented of his untoward feelings.

Cowdery attempts to translate the gold plates

As Joseph's scribe, Oliver Cowdery observed the translation process starting in April 1829 and undoubtedly wanted to try it himself. He was encouraged by the fact that he had been given explicit permission from the Lord to do so. (See D&C 6:25.) It was just after Cowdery informed Joseph that he was ready to make the attempt that section 8 was received. In section 8 Cowdery was assured that if he would "ask" he would be able to "translate" the "ancient records." (Verse 11.)

Permission to translate was one thing—making it happen was another. There are no accounts of the precise method Cowdery intended to use. Perhaps he intended to try the seer stone as he had seen Joseph do. Or, he may have thought that he could use a divining rod that was known to be in his possession. Divining rods, like seer stones, were regarded as instruments of revelation. The rods in use were generally made out wood and shaped like a "Y." "Rodsmen," as they were called, would grasp the forked end of the rod and use it to answer specific questions or to locate water or other objects. In Oliver's case, he probably used it to receive "yes" and "no" answers. The method employed was to ask a question. If the rod dipped the answer to the inquiry was "yes," and if the rod remained motionless the answer was "no."[1]

The idea that Cowdery may have contemplated using a wooden rod to translate in some way is suggested by the language in the first edition of the Book of Commandments (Doctrine and Covenants) published in 1833, which makes specific reference to Cowdery's "rod."[2]

> Now this is not all, for you have another gift, which is the gift of working with the rod: behold it has told you things: behold there is no other power save God, that can cause this rod of nature, to work in your hands, for it is the word of God; and therefore whatsoever you shall ask me to tell you by that means, that will I grant unto you, that you shall know." (D&C 8:6; emphasis added.)

In the 1835 edition, reference to the word "rod" was omitted and the term "gift of Aaron" put in its place.[3]

Some Mormon historians have suggested that the rod mentioned in section 8 was not a forked-branch type but rather like the rod or staff associated with Aaron and Moses. Those who take this position claim that is why the term "rod of nature" was changed later to "gift of Aaron." The

---

1. See Quinn, *Early Mormonism and the Magic World View*, 30. Forked hazel rods were in use at the time of Joseph Smith. The rodsman's "course of procedure was to swear the rod . . . and looking reverently upwards, [he] administered in a solemn tone the usual form of an oath; directing it to tell him the truth to such questions as he should ask, in relation to these [ancient] monuments. He then inquired whether the French, the Spaniards, the English, the Dutch, the Romans, and several other nations, had erected them; to all which the rod remained immovable. Finally he asked if it was the Welsh, or the same people who had build the mounds. To this it gave a gentle nod, which the rodsman knew from former trials, meant yes." (An account of the use of a rod by a rodsman nicked-named "Commodore," in Quinn, *Early Mormonism and the Magic World View*, 30.)

2. The idea that Oliver Cowdery was using a "Y" shaped rod as part of his attempt to translate is supported in the original revelation itself. "O remember these words & keep my commandments remember this is thy gift now this is not all for thou hast another gift which is the gift of working with the *sprout*." A "sprout," of course, is a shoot of a plant and implies that the rod was a stick of some kind. (See *The Joseph Smith Papers*, facsimile edition, volume 2; emphasis added.)

3. I could find no indication why Doctrine and Covenants 8 omitted direct reference to the "rod." Since such objects were in common use at the time of Joseph Smith, I doubt it was to obfuscate what was really going on.

Mormon historian Richard L. Anderson takes this position.[1] However, Cowdery never compared his rod to Aaron's and never suggested that he was doing anything but using a forked branch rod that he had in possession. Such rods were used well into the twentieth century to look for water and for oil. In 1826, the *American Journal of Science and Art* described the situation nationally. "From north to south, from east to west, the divining rod has its advocates. Men . . . of the soundest judgment . . . and most exemplary lives, do not disown the art."[2]

Physical objects and revelation

The idea that God uses objects as mediums to reveal his will illustrates his condescension to his children and his willingness to labor with men and women within the context and cultural milieu of the times. Strictly speaking, Doctrine and Covenants 8 explains that a revelation comes from God directly to the "mind" and "heart." (See verses 2–3.) It follows, therefore, that revelatory intermediary physical objects are not required. That said, section 8 demonstrates how the Lord views contemporary practices and illustrates his willingness to employ seer stones and other revelatory objects to accomplish his purposes. However, those who use such are cautioned to "remember that without faith you can do nothing; therefore ask in faith." (Verse 10.) Faith is at the root of spiritual experience.

The Urim and Thummim Throughout religious history, various physical objects have had revelatory properties. One need only consider the Urim and Thummim, the casting of lots, and the Liahona, to name a few.

In the Bible a Urim and Thummim was used by the high priest to communicate the will of God to the people. (See Exodus 28:30; Deuteronomy 33:8; 20:18; 1 Samuel 14:3, 18; 23:9; 2 Samuel 21:1.) Urim literally means "light" or "revelation." The word Thummim means "truth." In other words this instrument was used to obtain "light and truth," a common scriptural phrase denoting revelation from God.

Like the Urim and Thummim in Joseph's possession, the Urim and Thummim of the Bible was attached to a breastplate. (See Exodus 25:7.) However, the breastplate was of embroidered cloth, not metal.[3] Both

---

1. See Quinn, *Early Mormonism and the Magic World View*, 32.
2. See Quinn, *Early Mormonism and the Magic World View*, 29–30.
3. The cloth breastplate of the Bible Urim and Thummim was set with four rows of precious stones, three in each row. On each stone was engraved the name of one of the twelve tribes. In size, the breastplate is about ten inches square. The two upper corners were fastened to the ephod (two pieces of linen which hung from the neck and covered both the back and front above the tunic and outer garment) by blue ribbons. It was not to be "loosed" from the ephod. (See Exodus 28:15–29; 39:8–21.)

breastplates had fastening devices. The Bible breastplate was fastened to the girdle (a sash worn around the waist) of the priest. The Book of Mormon breastplate was held on the chest by straps that fastened at the back. The Bible Urim and Thummim is described by Bible scholars as two small objects or images like teraphim (idols in human shape). The Urim and Thummim Joseph had involved two stones held together by some sort of wire. Both Urim and Thummim, when not in use, were stored in a small bag or pouch that was a part of or connected to the breastplate.[1]

---

1. The Urim and Thummim that Joseph had and used to translate the first 116 pages of the Book of Mormon is described by Joseph's mother, Lucy Mack Smith, in her history. She "found that it consisted of two smooth three-cornered diamonds set in glass, and the glasses were set in silver bows, which were connected with each other in much the same way as old fashioned spectacles." (See Anderson, *Lucy's Book*, 379.) Lucy Mack Smith felt it one afternoon and held it in her hands wrapped in a thin muslin handkerchief. She said it was "so thin that I could feel its proportions without any difficulty. It was concave on one side, and convex on the other, and extended from the neck downwards, as far as the center of the stomach of a man of extraordinary size. It had four straps of the same material, for the purpose of fastening it to the breast, two of which ran back to go over the shoulders, and the other two were designed to fasten to the hips. They were just the width of two of my fingers, (for I measured them,) and they had holes in the end of them, to be convenient in fastening. After I examined it, Joseph placed it in the chest with the Urim and Thummim." (See Roberts, *Comprehensive History of the Church*, 1:92–93.) Martin Harris, on the other hand, described the Urim and Thummim as "white, like polished marble, with a few gray streaks." (See Anderson, *Lucy's Book*, 379.) William Smith, the prophet's brother, added to the details when he said, "A pocket was prepared in the breastplate on the left side, immediately over the heart. When not in use the Urim and Thummim was placed in the pocket, the rod being of just the right length to allow it to be deposited. This instrument could, however, be detached from the breastplate when translating, as it permitted him to have both hands free to touch the plates." (See McConkie and Ostler, *Revelations of the Restoration*, 88.) The *Comprehensive History of the Church* adds that Joseph apparently detached it from a breast plate that was hidden under his own clothing. (See Roberts, *Comprehensive History of the Church*, 1:87.) The Urim and Thummim was used not only as a translating device but also to receive revelations of a more general nature. Lucy Mack Smith reports that "Joseph kept the Urim and Thummim constantly about his person, by the use of which he could in a moment tell whether the plates were in any danger." (See Anderson, *Lucy's Book*, 383.) When the angel Moroni appeared to the Prophet Joseph in September 1823, he used the Urim and Thummim to show Joseph "many things which he saw in vision." (See Anderson, *Lucy's Book*, 389.) In fact, the Urim and Thummim was "used . . . to direct the Prophet to write a letter to David Whitmer requesting him to come and provide transportation for himself and Oliver Cowdery to his residence because Joseph was concerned that there was a plot to take his life." (See Anderson, *Lucy's Book*, 446.) Latter-day scripture adds to our understanding of the Urim and Thummim. We know that this instrument was the special prerogative of a "seer," a person who is called upon to translate ancient languages. (See Mosiah 8:13–18; 28:13, 16.) Abraham used a Urim and Thummim. (See Abraham 3:1–4.) The prophets among the Nephites (Omni) used the Urim and Thummim. (See Omni 1:20; Ether 4:1–7.) Clearly, there is more than one Urim and Thummim. Joseph Smith used the brother of Jared's Urim and Thummim when he translated the first 116 pages of the Book of Mormon. (See Ether 3:22–28; D&C 10:1; 17:1; see also Easton, *Illustrated Bible Dictionary*, and McConkie and Ostler, *Revelations of the Restoration*, 88.)

Lots Casting of lots was also used to obtain the will of the Lord. In the New Testament, this method was used to replace a member of the Twelve—Matthias, who was then "numbered with the eleven." (See Acts 1:24–26.) The Hebrews also resorted to this process as a way to discern the divine will. (See Proverbs 16:33; Esther 3:7; Numbers 26:55; 34:13; Joshua 7:14, 18; 1 Samuel 10:20, 21; 1 Chronicles 24:3, 5, 19; Leviticus 16:8.) How lots were used is somewhat obscure, but we do know that small stones were involved. "We did throw the dice, but the Lord determines how they fall." (See NLT Proverbs 16:33; NLT Numbers 33:54; NLT Jonah 1:7.)

Liahona In the Book of Mormon the Liahona, compass, or director was used by God to inform the community. It was prepared by the hand of the Lord to help Lehi and his family find the New World. (See 2 Nephi 5:12.) It was described as a ball made of fine brass. It had two spindles, one of which pointed the direction Lehi and his family should travel. (See 1 Nephi 16:10.) Written messages sometimes appeared on the instrument with specific directions. (See 1 Nephi 16:26–29.) Like the comment the Lord made about Cowdery's rod, this instrument functioned by faith. (See 1 Nephi 16:28.) It was sometimes referred to as the "ball, or director." (See Alma 37:38.) This device was seen by the Three Witnesses when they viewed the Book of Mormon plates. (See D&C 17:1.)

A "seer"

As early as April 1830, when the Church was first organized, Joseph was referred to as "seer" and a "translator." (See D&C 21:1.) As Joseph undoubtedly understood from his translation of the Book of Mormon, "seer" and "translator" were related. Mosiah had "interpreters" just as Joseph did. Mosiah used his interpreters to "translate" the twenty-four gold plates of the Jaredites. Mosiah, like Joseph, was not a scholar, nor did he pretend to have knowledge of the Jaredites' language when he rendered his translation. Rather, Mosiah said, just as Joseph did, that by looking into the interpreters it was possible for him to make known what the Jaredites had written. This method of translating was unique, and prophets who could translate by the gift and power of God were called "seers."

Seers were considered greater than prophets because "a seer can know of things which are past, and also of things which are to come, and by them shall all things be revealed." Through a seer "shall secret things be made manifest, and hidden things shall come to light, and things which are not known shall be made known by them." (Mosiah 8:17.) Hence, "God has provided a means that man, through faith, might work mighty miracles; therefore he becometh a great benefit to his fellow beings." (Mosiah 8:18.)

As Richard Bushman notes, Joseph's ability to make known the meaning of ancient records distinguished him from other prophets. It was unique and an essential part of his mission, in addition to his prophetic calling. He was at his pinnacle when he exercised his gift of "translation" as he wrote page after page of the Book of Mormon. And his involvement with translation did not stop after he published the Book of Mormon. Within three months of the book's publication, in June 1830, the Lord instructed him to "translate" the Bible. Joseph immediately set about making inspired changes that in some cases underwent a number of reiterations. His biblical emendations included whole books, such as the Book of Moses, the writings of Enoch, and the Book of Abraham, some of the loftiest and most eloquent of all scripture. He was still exercising this gift until close to the end of his life in 1842. Joseph himself described what was meant by translation when he said, "By the power of God I translated the Book of Mormon from hieroglyphics; the knowledge of which was lost to the world: in which wonderful event I stood alone, an unlearned youth, to combat the worldly wisdom, and multiplied ignorance of eighteen centuries."[1]

Section 9: Smith Log Home, Harmony, Pennsylvania, April 1829

Heading

Oliver Cowdery's failed attempt to translate the Book of Mormon.

Introduction

Revelation given through the Prophet Joseph Smith to Oliver Cowdery in the Smith log home located in Harmony, Pennsylvania, April 1829.[2] In April 1829 Oliver Cowdery traveled to Harmony and offered his services as a scribe. Joseph Smith agreed and within a few days Cowdery began to record the translation of the Book of Mormon. Cowdery obtained a promise that he to could also translate. He made the attempt but failed. Section 9 explains why Cowdery was unable to translate.

Anchor section

Memorize: How to receive revelation

---

1. Bushman, *Believing History*, 245.
2. Smith, *History of the Church*, 1:37–38.

The big question

Question: How does a person receive revelation?

Answer: Study a subject out in your own mind. Come to a conclusion. Ask God if the conclusion is right. If the conclusion is right, God will confirm it by the power of the Holy Ghost—your bosom will burn. If the conclusion is wrong, you will experience a stupor of thought. If you receive a stupor of thought, start the process again.

The reasons Cowdery could not receive revelation to translate

As discussed in section 8, when Joseph and Cowdery used the term "to translate," they did not mean to render from one language into another based upon their understanding of an ancient language. Rather, translation meant receiving from God a revelation that makes known the meaning of an ancient text in modern language—a process that was sometimes accomplished though the use of a physical object or medium such as the Urim and Thummim or seer stone. It was with this understanding in mind that Cowdery petitioned the Lord to translate the Book of Mormon. (See commentary for D&C 8.)

One reason Cowdery's attempt failed was that he assumed that all he must to do was ask God and thereafter God would dispense a revelation. Section 9 informed him otherwise. Cowdery was instructed that greater mental effort was necessary on his part if he was to be given the privilege to translate. He must study it out in his own mind, come to a conclusion, and then ask God if his conclusion was correct.

> You have not understood; you have supposed that I would give it [translation] unto you, when you took no thought save it was to ask me.
> . . . you must study it out in your mind; then you must ask me if it [a conclusion] be right. (D&C 9:7–8.)

A second reason Cowdery's effort failed was because he was afraid—"But you feared." (D&C 9:11.) In other words, his faith failed him.

Once Cowdery formulated a conclusion, he was assured that his hypothesis would either be validated by the Holy Ghost (described as a burning sensation) or "you shall have no such feelings."[1] (D&C 9:9.) This idea of feeling that something is right was discussed in more detail in the commentary to section 8. The main point of section 9 is to describe the

---

1. The pattern for receiving a revelation found in Doctrine and Covenants 9 assumes that a conclusion may or may not verified. If the conclusion is not verified, then the process of mental effort continues until other conclusions are reached that may then be presented to the Lord for spiritual confirmation.

process that procures a revelation from God. As Robinson and Garrett described it, "Most often revelation is an active rather than a passive process. The receiver must think, must work to understand, must come up with a plan, a proposal, a theory—in short must do as much of the work as possible to bridge the gap between the known and the unknown."[1]

Cowdery's inability to translate must have been very discouraging to him. Yet the Lord did not forsake him. Just a few weeks later he would see his first angel when John the Baptist appeared to restore the Aaronic priesthood. Of that experience he would write in detail about how he marveled as he gazed upon a messenger sent from heaven.

Cowdery certainly learned from this experience that obtaining the mind and will of God is an arduous task. Yet, Joseph was confident that all of his followers could approach God and receive revelations, and he encouraged his followers to do so. He explained that people grow in the principle of revelation and that as a first step people should pay attention to the spiritual impressions that come to them from time to time.

> A person may profit by noticing the first intimation of the spirit of revelation; for instance, when you feel pure intelligence flowing into you, it may give you sudden strokes of ideas, so that by noticing it, you may find it fulfilled the same day or soon; those things that were presented unto your minds by the Spirit of God, will come to pass; and thus by learning the Spirit of God and understanding it, you may grow into the principle of revelation, until you become perfect in Christ Jesus.[2]

He promised that with persistence the day would come when anything that had been revealed to Joseph Smith would be made known to the "least" of the Saints as soon as they were able to bear it.[3]

"Study it out" in the context of translating the Book of Mormon

The idea that Joseph had to "study it out" in order to come up with a translation implies that the translation process required Joseph to "reformulate the Nephite record into his own words."[4] Therefore translating

---

1. Robinson and Garrett, *Doctrine and Covenants Commentary*, 1:68. Certainly a "burning in the bosom" is not the only way confirmations come or revelations are received. Oliver Cowdery had already experienced other variant manifestations of the Spirit. (See D&C 6 and 8.) The point of Doctrine and Covenants 9 is that unsolicited communications from the Lord are rare.
2. See Smith, Teachings of the Prophet Joseph Smith, 151.
3. See Smith, *Teachings of the Prophet Joseph Smith*, 151.
4. Hardy, *The Book of Mormon: A Reader's Edition*, xv; see also D&C 9:8.

was not entirely a mechanical process and more than simply reading off of the seer stone or interpreters what Joseph saw, although some observing the process assumed this was exactly what he did.

The fact that Joseph had a part to play in the translation is consistent with what we know about the original text and the use of the King James language in the text. First, as to the original language in the text. If the book were dictated to Joseph word for word by God, we would not expect to find hundreds of grammatical errors and spelling errors, along with no paragraphing and punctuation, which was left up to the publisher. These errors were weeded out over time, and it is important to note that most of the revisions involved a single word or an attempt to smooth out and regularize unfamiliar King James usages. Only a half dozen revisions affected doctrine or corrected the narrative. For example, in 1 Nephi 11:18, Joseph changed "the virgin which thou seest is the mother of God" to "the virgin whom thou seest is the mother of the Son of God." "While perhaps disturbing to those who hold fundamentalist views of scripture, Latter-day Saints regard these corrections as a prophet's prerogative to reformulate a revelation in the clearest language possible."[1]

It is also apparent that Joseph made no attempt to conceal the fact that he used passages in the King James Bible to reveal the meaning of the Book of Mormon text. About two dozen chapters are adaptations from the King James Bible, from such books as Isaiah, Malachi, and Matthew. But even more striking is "the constant use, transformation, and recontextualization of the King James phrases," which allows the Book of Mormon "to function as something of a commentary on the Bible. This can be seen, for example, at 1 Nephi 11:22, where Nephi interprets the tree that his father saw in a dream. Nephi draws a connection between the birth of Jesus and the tree and exclaims, 'Yea, it is the love of God, which sheddeth itself abroad in the hearts of the children of men.' The text here reflects the wording of Romans 5:5, 'the love of God is shed abroad in our hearts by the Holy Ghost which is given unto us.' For careful LDS readers, the connotations of Paul's 'love of God' will be expanded to include the incarnation as well as the work of the Holy Spirit."[2] However, it should be clearly understood that there is no evidence to suggest that Joseph during his translation of the Book of Mormon even paused to consult the Bible.

It is important to recognize, as Grant Hardy did, that:

---

1. Hardy, *The Book of Mormon: A Reader's Edition*, xiv.
2. See Hardy, *The Book of Mormon: A Reader's Edition*, xvi. See also Mormon 9:9, which adopts the language found in Hebrews 13:8, which itself is repeated seven times in the Book of Mormon.

Mormons have yet to work out a fully satisfying theory of inspired translation ... but such an account would have to allow for the influence of Joseph Smith—as evidenced in grammar and vocabulary—while still admitting the sophisticated literary forms and devices that seem to indicate ancient origins. Some Latter-day Saints claim to have discovered characteristic Hebraisms in the English text, while others report that close readings or statistical analyses make it possible to distinguish the different voices of various Nephite authors.... A few Mormons have argued that at least some of the infelicities may be the result of a too literal translation, one that, for example, somewhat mechanically rendered a presumed Nephite formulaic transition as the ubiquitous "and it came to pass."[1]

The point here, however is not to debate the various possibilities but to recognize that section 9 implies that Joseph, as part of the translation, had to "study it out" or bring his own intellectual powers to bear on the process.

The Lord does not condemn Cowdery for his failure to translate

Although Cowdery failed in his attempt to translate, the Lord did not chastise or condemn him. Rather, the Lord gave him encouragement. "It is not expedient that you should translate now." (Verse 10.) Be content as a scribe, "and you shall prosper. Be faithful, and yield to no temptation." (Verse 13.) "Be patient, my son, for it is wisdom in me, and it is not expedient that you should translate at this present time." (Verse 3.) The Lord assures him that there are "other records" that Cowdery may be able to translate at another time.[2] (See verse 2.) And finally, "Do not murmur, my son, for it is wisdom in me that I have dealt with you after this manner." (Verse 6.)

---

1. See Hardy, The Book of Mormon: A Reader's Edition, xvi.
2. "Other records" may refer to the book of Abraham, or his work on the Joseph Smith Translation of the Bible (JST or IV), both of which were "translated" by Joseph with the help of Oliver Cowdery.

Section 10: Smith Log Home, Harmony, Pennsylvania, Summer 1828[1]

Heading

Joseph Smith is given permission to translate the Book of Mormon once more, after he lost the privilege for a season on account of his sins.

The big question

Question: Who can be a worthy vessel?
Answer: Errant men like Martin Harris and Joseph Smith, who stood in need of repentance for the part they both played in the loss of the 116 pages. Both were forgiven and thereafter entrusted with many other sacred responsibilities.

Introduction

Revelation given to Joseph Smith at Harmony, Pennsylvania, in the Smith log cabin home in the summer of 1828.[2] Herein the Lord informs Joseph of alterations made by wicked men in the lost 116 pages from the translation of the "Book of Lehi"[3] in the Book of Mormon. These manuscript pages had been lost while in the possession of Martin Harris, to whom the sheets had been temporarily entrusted. (See heading to D&C 3.) The evil design was to await the expected retranslation of the matter covered by the stolen pages, and then to discredit the translator by showing discrepancies created by

---

1. "Although the two dates assigned to this revelation were May 1829 and then summer 1828, we now feel confident that if it is not a composite of more than one revelation combined later, the correct date is April 1829, shortly after the arrival of Oliver Cowdery on April 3. Even if a composite, April 1829 best fits the date when it was brought together to form the revelation as we know it today." (Woodford, "Discoveries from the Joseph Smith Papers Project," 28–29.)

2. There has not always been agreement on the date this section was received. The current editions of the Doctrine and Covenants place the date in the summer of 1828. However, editions prior to 1921 place the date as 1829. The confusion may have arisen over the fact that some additions to the revelation were made in 1829. In this regard, it is important to note that the Prophet Joseph Smith himself indicated that section 10 was received just after section 3, which came in July 1828. In 1921 B. H. Roberts and a committee preparing the publication of the 1921 edition discovered that section 10 had been misdated in previous additions. The numerical order of the revelations was not changed. Consequently, section 10 is presently out of chronological order. Were it in order, it would come directly after section 3. See Smith, *History of the Church*, 1:20–23.

3. Although the lost portion of the Book of Mormon is referred to as the Book of Lehi, the lost portion came from Mormon's abridgment of Nephi's large plates, which were then replaced for translation purposes by Nephi's small plates. The small plates covered the same period of time but were less secular and more doctrinal in orientation.

the alterations. The plot to alter was foreseen by the Lord even while Mormon, the ancient Nephite historian, was making his abridgment of the accumulated plates, as is shown in the Words of Mormon 1:3–7. Nephi also wrote in his account that he was commanded to make the small plates "for a wise purpose in him, which purpose I know not." (1 Nephi 9:5–6.)

Historical background

Sections 3 and 10 are companion revelations. Section 3 rebukes Martin Harris and Joseph for losing the first 116 pages of the translation and takes away the privilege to translate. Section 10 restores that privilege and speaks about Joseph's repentance and the return of the gold plates. According to Lucy Mack Smith, the Prophet's mother, Joseph took possession of the plates again on September 22, 1828, a short time after this revelation was given.

Martin Harris, a "wicked man," repented and later is entrusted with sacred responsibilities

It is apparent from the language of section 10 that Martin Harris's part in the loss of the 116 pages was more than simple negligence. Some of the language implies bad intent on Harris's part. "Even the man in whom you [Joseph] have trusted [Harris] has sought to destroy you [Joseph]." (Verse 6.) In keeping with this interpretation, Harris is referred to as a "wicked man" and is accused of allowing the 116-page manuscript to fall into the hands of conspiring and wicked men.[1] (See verses 7, 9.) All of this indicates that Harris failed to comply with the explicit instructions given him by Joseph that he could show the manuscript only to a limited number of individuals who had been approved in advance by Joseph.

Yet, regardless of Harris's sinful thoughts and actions, he repented, was forgiven by the Lord, and thereafter entrusted with many sacred responsibilities—chief among them, his call to be one of the Three Witnesses. His life, taken in a larger context than the loss of the 116 pages, reflects commitment to the Church and a good and generous heart. Over the objections of his wife he agreed to help Joseph translate and finance the Book of Mormon. He was present at the formal organization of the Church on April 6, 1830. In May 1831 when the Saints were called to gather in

---

1. Doctrine and Covenants 10 contains a description of the character of the individuals who plotted to prove Joseph was a fraud—they were condemned because "they will not ask of me." These close-minded individuals' "hearts are corrupt, and full of wickedness and abominations" because they "love darkness rather than light, because their deeds are evil." (See verse 21.)

Joseph Smith Jr. Home

Ohio, he led fifty converts from Palmyra to Kirtland. During the summer months of the same year he went with the Prophet to Missouri to dedicate the new Zion. Later he served a mission, baptizing about one hundred new converts at Chenago Point (now Binghamton), New York. His missionary duties continued, not without personal hardship. In January 1833 he was imprisoned because he refused to stop preaching the gospel. When the time came, he volunteered to march with Zion's Camp. Had it not been for a period of intense conflict in Kirtland between the leaders and members of the Church, he may have remained faithful. Clashes with Sidney Rigdon, Joseph's first counselor, and doctrinal differences with Joseph embittered Harris, and he wandered away from the Church and was excommunicated in December 1837. However, he never denied his testimony of the Book of Mormon, and he eventually came back into the Church.[1]

The return of the gold plates and the Urim and Thummim

As a result of the loss of the first 116 pages of manuscript, the gold plates and the Urim and Thummim were taken from Joseph and the translation process halted. After much consternation on Joseph's part, section 10 gave permission for the Prophet to begin translating again; the angel Moroni returned the gold plates to him shortly thereafter. However, various historians disagree about whether or not Joseph received back the Urim and Thummim at this time.

Emma Smith said, "Now the first that my husband translated, was translated by the use of the Urim and Thummim, and that was the part that Martin Harris lost, after that he [Joseph] used a small stone, not exactly black, but was rather a dark color."[2] This recollection is supported by the fact that those who observed the translation process said that after the 116 pages had been translated Joseph used his seer stone to effectuate the translation. David Whitmer confirmed this when he said, "By fervent prayer and by otherwise humbling himself, the prophet, however, again found favor, and was presented with a strange, oval shaped, chocolate-colored stone, about the size of an egg, only more flat, which, it was promised should serve the same purpose as the missing Urim and Thummim.... With this stone all of the present Book of Mormon was translated."[3]

On the other side of the equation, Lucy Mack Smith, the Prophet's mother, reported that Joseph had the Urim and Thummim after the gold plates were returned. She said that when she went to Harmony, Pennsyl-

---

1. See *Encyclopedia of Mormonism*, 2:576–77.
2. Emma Smith Bidamon to Emma S. Pilgrim, March 27, 1876, RLDS library-archives; published in Vogel, *Early Mormon Documents*, 1:532.
3. Quinn, *Early Mormonism and the Magic World View*, rev. ed., 172 and 480, footnote 309.

vania, to visit her son in the winter of 1829, Joseph indicated that he had the plates and the Urim and Thummim in a red morocco trunk lying on Emma's bureau.[1] Some of the confusion surrounding this question is that it was not uncommon for members of the Church to refer to a seer stone as a Urim and Thummim.

The end does not justify the means

Part of the plot regarding the loss of the 116 pages involved hoping that Joseph could not reproduce the manuscript. To thwart this scheme, the Lord warned Joseph that if he attempted to retranslate, his enemies would change the wording of the original. Joseph's enemies justified their tactics becuase they believed Joseph was a deceiver. In response the Lord said, "Verily, verily, I say unto you, wo be unto him that lieth to deceive because he supposeth that another lieth to deceive, for such are not exempt from the justice of God." (Verse 28.) The principle is clear: even if the cause is just, the end does not justify the means.

"Thou shalt not tempt the Lord thy God"

In section 10, the Lord warns that men should not tempt God, or put God to the test to prove that he exists. (See verses 15, 29.) In this context, to tempt the Lord specifically had reference to translating the 116 pages again. (See verse 15.) The idea was that doubters would believe if the Lord would show forth his power by inspiring Joseph to retranslate the Book of Lehi exactly as it had been translated in the first instance. And then, even if Joseph accomplished the feat, wicked men made plans to change the text so that they could prove the contrary.

To "test the Lord" is to require that God do something of our choosing so that we may pass judgment on him. This is strictly forbidden. It is "a presumptuous sin."[2] Satan tempted Jesus to test the Lord when he taunted, "If thou be the Son of God, cast thyself down: for it is written, He shall

---

1. "I continued my supplications to God, without cessation, and on the twenty-second of September [1828], I had the joy and satisfaction of again receiving the Urim and Thummim, with which I have again commenced translating, and Emma writes for me, but the angel said that the Lord would send me a scribe, and I trust that it will be so. The angel was rejoiced when he gave me back the Urim and Thummim, and he told me that the Lord was pleased with my faithfulness and humility, and loved me for my penitence and diligence in prayer, in the which I had performed my duty so well as to receive the Urim and Thummim and was able to enter upon the work of translation again." (See Smith, *History of Joseph Smith by His Mother* [1996], 176; see also Woodford, *Historical Development of the Doctrine and Covenants*, 143.)

2. See Robinson and Garrett, *Doctrine and Covenants Commentary*, 1:72.

give his angels charge concerning thee: and in their hands they shall bear thee up, lest at any time thou dash thy foot against a stone." (Matthew 4:6.) In response Jesus replied, "Thou shalt not tempt the Lord thy God." (Matthew 4:7.)

Testing God is a common error people make. Men and women take the position that they will believe if the Lord will simply do a specific act or answer a particular prayer. Such behavior is self-destructive and contrary to the will of God. Many Latter-day Saints have left the Church by putting God to an arbitrary test—by attempting to bind God to their own terms and conditions. Rather, people should prove the Lord by keeping his commandments and waiting upon him.[1]

Fear of the Lord

Section 10, like other sections in the Doctrine and Covenants, talks about "fearing" God and adopts the King James usage of this word. For example, in section 10 the revelation says, "But it is they who do not *fear me* ... that I will disturb, and cause to tremble and shake to the center." (Verse 56; emphasis added.) Robinson and Garret point out that the use of the word "fear" is one of the most "misunderstood phrases in scripture, a misunderstanding caused by unfortunate shifts in meaning for some English words since 1611 [when the King James Version of the Bible was published]." The word was used originally to mean a sense of awe, reverence, and respect, not a sense of terror.[2]

SECTION 11: SMITH HOME, HARMONY, PENNSYLVANIA, MAY 1829

Heading

Counsel to Hyrum Smith to keep the commandments, study the word of the Lord, and trust in and deny not the spirit of revelation and prophecy.

The big questions

Question: What is revelation?
Answer: The spirit of revelation encourages a person to "do good," "to do justly, to walk humbly, to judge righteously ... [and] shall enlighten your mind, which shall fill your soul with joy."[3] (Verses 12–13.)

---

1. See Robinson and Garrett, *Doctrine and Covenants Commentary*, 1:72.
2. See Robinson and Garrett, *Doctrine and Covenants Commentary*, 1:76.
3. Note the interplay between the "mind" and the "heart"—a feeling of joy. Revelation

Question: How does a person receive revelation?
Answer: Ask and you will receive. (See verse 5.)

Introduction

Revelation given through the Prophet Joseph Smith to his brother, Hyrum Smith, at the Joseph Smith home in Harmony, Pennsylvania, in May 1829. This revelation was received through the Urim and Thummim, or seer stone, in answer to Joseph's supplication and inquiry sometime after the restoration of the Aaronic Priesthood.[1] It gives guidance and direction to Hyrum Smith. He is told to keep the commandments, study the scriptures, and learn the gospel before he attempts to teach it, and he is counseled to trust in and deny not the spirit of revelation and prophecy.

Historical background

As previously mentioned, Joseph and Emma moved to Harmony, Pennsylvania, to escape persecution in the Manchester area so that Joseph could more comfortably attend to the translation of the Book of Mormon. Joseph's move precipitated visits from concerned family members.[2] Not too long after Joseph's arrival in Harmony, his brother Samuel visited. Shortly thereafter, Hyrum arrived. Like Martin Harris, Hyrum asked if he could make a handwritten copy of the translation of parts of the Book of Mormon for teaching purposes. His request was denied.[3] In the meantime, Hyrum was instructed to learn the gospel so that when the time came he could be an effective gospel teacher. "Seek not to declare my word, but

---

will "enlighten [his] mind" and "fill [his] soul with joy." Compare Doctrine and Covenants 8, wherein the Lord defines revelation as a communication from God to the "mind" and "heart." (D&C 8:2.) By this process Hyrum will gain understanding. (See D&C 11:11–14.) He is told that he should trust in the spirit of revelation. See also D&C 9:8 on confirming revelation by a feeling described as a "burning in the bosom."

1. A specific day is not mentioned. However, we know that this section was received after the Aaronic Priesthood was restored on May 15, 1829, because this revelation concerns Hyrum Smith, who arrived in Harmony just after his brother Samuel H. Smith had been baptized. Therefore, if this section were in chronological order it would follow Doctrine and Covenants 13, which marks the beginning of the practice of baptism.

2. Samuel H. Smith, the Prophet's brother, came to visit Joseph and Emma in Harmony, Pennsylvania, and inquired about Book of Mormon. When Samuel Smith arrived, Oliver Cowdery was hard at work as Joseph's scribe. Samuel engaged Oliver in religious discussions and approached the Lord in prayer and had a conversion experience. Thereafter, Samuel was baptized by Oliver Cowdery on May 25, 1829. Just after his baptism, the Prophet Joseph Smith recorded that Samuel went home "greatly glorifying and praising God, being filled with the Holy Spirit." (See Smith, *History of the Church*, 1:44; Woodford, *Historical Development of the Doctrine and Covenants*, 218.)

3. See Robinson and Garrett, *Doctrine and Covenants Commentary*, 1:80.

first seek to obtain my word, and then shall your tongue be loosed; then, if you desire, you shall have my Spirit and my word, yea, the power of God unto the convincing of men." (Verse 21.)

Seek not for riches

Like the Prophet Joseph and Oliver Cowdery, (see D&C 24:8–9; 6:7), Hyrum was informed that his mission was spiritual and that he should not seek after worldly wealth. "Seek not for riches but for wisdom; and, behold, the mysteries of God shall be unfolded unto you, and then shall you be made rich. Behold, he that hath eternal life is rich." (Verse 7.) Hyrum was promised that in this way he would be "the means of doing much good in this generation." (See verse 8.)

SECTION 12: SMITH HOME, HARMONY, PENNSYLVANIA, MAY 1829

Heading

Joseph Knight called to work in the Church and promised answers to his prayers.

The big question

Question: How does a person receive revelation?
Answer: Be fully engaged in the "cause of Zion"; then one may ask God and receive revelation.

Introduction

Revelation given through the Prophet Joseph Smith to Joseph Knight Sr. in the Smith home in Harmony, Pennsylvania, in May 1839.[1] Joseph Knight believed that Joseph had the gold plates in his possession and gave material assistance to Joseph and his scribe to help with the translation. At Joseph Knight's request, he received this revelation through the Prophet.

Historical background

In May of 1829 Joseph and Oliver Cowdery were in need of essential provisions for not only the Book of Mormon project but also for rather

---

1. Doctrine and Covenants 12 is out of chronological order and should come after section 13.

basic sustenance. Their days were virtually consumed by the translation of the plates and they "had been left with no time to earn money to buy more paper on which to record the translation."[1] Neither was there food for the two men and Emma. On previous occasions Joseph's friend, Joseph Knight Sr., had provided help. Knight had once given Joseph $50 to make the second payment on his newly purchased home.[2]

In an attempt to petition Knight once more, Joseph and Oliver left Harmony and journeyed to Colesville, about 20 miles away, to visit Knight at his home. When they arrived they discovered that Knight had left on business and they returned empty handed to Harmony. They began an unsuccessful search for employment.

Meanwhile, Joseph Knight returned to his home in Colesville. Upon learning of Joseph's visit and desperate petition for help days earlier, Knight set out for Harmony with provisions and groceries, as well as a quantity of writing paper. During his stay, he asked Joseph to seek a revelation on his behalf. What is now titled Section 12 followed.

Knight was told that a "marvelous work" was about to commence. (Verse 1.) He was invited to become fully engaged in Joseph's religious project. He was to "thrust in his sickle." (Verse 5.) He was told that in order to be effective in the "cause of Zion" (see verse 6), he must be "humble and full of love, having faith, hope, and charity, being temperate in all things."[3] (Verse 8.) He was "called" to the work (see verse 4) and promised that if he would ask God he, too, would receive revelation. (Verse 5.) Joseph, acting as voice for the Lord, dictated a revelation Michael MacKay and Gerrit Dirkman call "apocalyptic." Using a phrase that is virtually identical to one in revelations for other early supporters including Joseph's father, his brother Hyrum, Oliver, David Whitmer, Thomas B. Marsh, Ezra Thayre, and Northrup Sweet (see Sections 4:4, 11:3, 6:3, 14:3, 31:4, and 33:7), Knight was advised that the "field is white and already to harvest; therefore, whosoever desireth to reap, let him thrust in his sickle with his might, and reap *while the day lasts.*" (Section 12:3 *emphasis added*). The scope of their mission was breathtaking with eternal consequences to all mankind. It was one that, for these men of truly destitute circumstances, meant ultimately a comprehension of "the impending Second Coming of Christ".[4]

---

1. Michael Hubbard MacKay and Gerrit J. Dirkman, *From Darkness into Light: Joseph Smith's Translation and Publication of the Book of Mormon*, 141.
2. Ibid.
3. The idea that a person can assist in God's work only if they are "humble," "full of love, having faith, hope, and charity, being temperate in all things" is a theme more fully developed in Doctrine and Covenants 121:34–46.
4. Michael Hubbard MacKay and Gerrit J. Dirkman, *From Darkness into Light: Joseph Smith's Translation and Publication of the Book of Mormon*, 142.

Section 24: Smith Home, Harmony, Pennsylvania, July 1830

Heading

A revelation of encouragement to Joseph and his scribe, Oliver Cowdery, as they continue to translate the Book of Mormon.

The big question

Question: Who can be a worthy vessel?
Answer: Joseph Smith, because he has been "delivered from the powers of Satan," and is willing to repent of his sins, magnify his office, continually call upon God, write down his revelations, expound the scriptures, devote all his service to God, be patient in afflictions, and seek not after the wealth of the world (see verses 1–9). Oliver Cowdery, if he glories not in himself and if he declares the gospel at "all times, and in all places" (see verses 11–12).

Introduction

Revelation given to the Prophet Joseph and Oliver Cowdery in Joseph's home in Harmony, Pennsylvania, July 1830.[1] Though less than four months had elapsed since the Church was organized, persecution had become intense, and the leaders had to seek safety in partial seclusion. Sections 24, 25, and 26 were given at this time to strengthen, encourage, and instruct.

Historical background

Soon after the Church was organized in April 1830, Joseph visited his friend and past employer, Joseph Knight Sr., in Colesville, New York. While there, he held a number of religious meetings, many who heard the gospel were baptized, and a branch of the Church was organized. It was a time of intense spiritual manifestations. On that occasion, Joseph Knight's son Newel was possessed by an evil spirit. His visage was distorted, and his body was raised to the ceiling. Those present sought the assistance of Joseph, who arrived and cast the devil out. Newel immediately floated down from the ceiling, came to his senses, and saw a vision of eternity.[2]

---

1. See Smith, *History of the Church*, 1:101–3.
2. This incident is often referred to as the first miracle in the Church because it occurred shortly after the Church was organized. "One of the people who regularly attended the meetings [in Colesville] was Newel Knight.... Newel ... was afraid to pray vocally, but

The message and the power of God manifest caused the Church to continue to attract attention and grow, and by June 1830 Colesville had become a primary center for members of the Church.[1] On June 9, 1830, Joseph convened a general conference for members in Fayette, New York, the place where the Church had recently been organized. At the close of the meetings Joseph returned to his home in Harmony, Pennsylvania. However, Church duties quickly summoned him, his wife (Emma), Oliver Cowdery, John Whitmer, and David Whitmer to Colesville[2] once again.

When the group arrived in Colesville, the situation was tense. Enemies of the Church accused Joseph of disturbing the peace and had him arrested and taken to South Bainbridge in Chenago County for trial. Members of the Church testified in Joseph Smith's favor, and he was acquitted but immediately rearrested by a sheriff in another county for the same charge. Joseph was acquitted a second time and returned to Colesville with Oliver Cowdery, where they confirmed members of the Church who had been baptized. His presence infuriated anti-Mormons in the area, and Joseph and Oliver were forced to make a quick escape back to Harmony. It was at this time that section 24 was received.[3] In the context of these events, Joseph was told that he would experience many afflictions and therefore must learn to be patient in enduring tribulation. By way of comfort, the Lord promised that he would be with him. "Be patient in afflictions, for

---

he finally accepted the persuasive challenge of the Prophet to do so in the next meeting. When the moment arrived, Newel declined, promising that he would pray later in private. The next morning he went into the woods where he tried to pray, but he failed because he felt guilty for refusing to pray publicly. He began to feel uneasy and to grow ill, and he returned home, where his wife was alarmed by his appearance. Newel asked her to send for Joseph. When the prophet arrived, Newel was 'suffering very much in his mind, and his body acted upon in a very strange manner; his visage and limbs distorted and twisted in every shape and appearance possible to imagine; and finally he was caught up off the floor of the apartment, and tossed about most fearfully.' Neighbors and relative[s] gathered to witness the frightful scene. Joseph finally caught hold of Newel's hand. Newel said he knew he was possessed of the devil, and he also knew that Joseph had the power to cast him out. Acting on Newel's faith as well as his own, Joseph commanded the devil to depart in the name of Jesus Christ. Newel immediately declared that he saw the devil leave him and vanish. . . . Newel Knight's facial expression returned to normal, and the distortions of his body ceased. . . . The Spirit of the Lord came over Newel so that the visions of eternity were opened to him. In his weakened condition he was placed on his bed, but he said he felt himself 'attracted upward, and remained for some time enwrapt in contemplation, insomuch that I knew not what was going on in the room.' In this state his body was elevated until he felt the ceiling beams pressing against his shoulder and head." (See *Church History in the Fulness of Times*, 69–70.)

1. Other members of the Church also lived in and around Palmyra and Fayette, New York.
2. Colesville is about twenty miles north of Harmony.
3. It was also during this period that Joseph received a "vision of Moses" or what is now referred to as the Book of Moses in the Pearl of Great Price. The revelation came about as a result of Joseph's study of the Old Testament.

thou shalt have many; but endure them, for, lo I am with thee, even unto the end of thy days."[1] (Verse 8.)

The Lord informs Joseph Smith that he will not be blessed with temporal wealth

It was Oliver Cowdery's observation that money had always been a temptation for Joseph. After all, Joseph and his family had always been poor, and it was only natural that he sought to alleviate their situation. It was with this in mind that Cowdery recorded that when Joseph first saw the angel Moroni, he was cautioned that Satan would try to tempt him to get the plates for the purpose of getting rich. The angel strictly forbade Joseph, saying that "[he] must have no other object in view in getting the plates but to glorify God, and must not be influenced by any other motive than that of building his kingdom." (JS–H 1:46.)

Section 24 addresses the issue of money and affluence in Joseph's life and must have been a disappointment to him. The Lord said, "In temporal labors thou shalt not have strength, for this is not thy calling." (D&C 24:9.) Joseph was not meant for temporal riches but rather was called "to magnify thine office, and to expound all scriptures, and continue in laying on of the hands and confirming the churches."[2] (Verse 9.) In the meantime, he must, like other men and women, maintain himself and his family by the sweat of his brow. "Magnify thine office; and after thou hast sowed thy fields and secured them, go speedily unto the church which is in Colesville." (Verse 3.)

Require not miracles

The satanic possession of Newel Knight in the Church raised the issue of miracles, casting out devils, and healing the sick. Miracles are generally thought of as supernatural or unexplainable events, and section 24 instructs the Saints that they should not *require* miracles at the hands of the Lord unless commanded to do so.[3] (See verse 13.) *Requiring* miracles can be a way of testing the Lord, sometimes as a matter of proof that God exists.

---

1. The reference in verse 1 to "thou hast been delivered from all thine enemies" is also probably a reference to persecution in Colesville, New York.

2. "Confirming the churches" is probably a reference to the Prophet's recent activities in Colesville, where many were baptized and afterwards given the gift of the Holy Ghost and confirmed members of the Church.

3. An apparent exception to this general rule is illustrated by Elijah calling down fire from heaven to convince the pagans that the God of Israel was more powerful than the false gods. (See 1 Kings 18.)

Jesus faced this same issue when in the wilderness Satan tempted him to *test* the Lord by throwing himself off "a pinnacle of the temple." Jesus' response was, "Thou shalt not tempt the Lord thy God." (Matthew 4:5–7.)

Casting out devils, healing the sick, and asking the Lord to protect against the poisonous venom of serpents, however, were gifts that should be sought after. (Mark 16:15–18.) But they should be sought only when invited to do so by the person standing in need. (See verses 13–14.) Requiring a sick person to ask for a healing blessing is an indication that the ill person has faith enough to be healed in the first place. Jesus taught this same principle when rejected at Nazareth. "Because of their [the people of Nazareth's] unbelief, he [Jesus] couldn't do any mighty miracles among them except to place his hands on a few sick people and heal them. And he was amazed at their unbelief." (Mark 6:5.)

Without purse or scrip

The reference to "purse or scrip" occurs often in the Doctrine and Covenants and refers to preaching the gospel by relying upon the goodwill of the people to feed and clothe missionaries. The word "purse" refers to a wallet or coin pouch and "scrip" to a satchel or knapsack; scrip may also refer to paper money. In this way missionaries depended upon the Lord for their daily sustenance when preaching the gospel.

SECTION 25: SMITH HOME, HARMONY, PENNSYLVANIA, JULY 1830

Heading

Emma Smith is a worthy vessel and an elect lady. She is commanded to "make a selection of sacred hymns," and to exhort and expound scripture. (See verses 7 and 11.)

The big question

Question: Who can be a worthy vessel?
Answer: Emma Smith, provided she repents of her sins, is faithful, walks in the paths of virtue (see verse 2), murmurs not (see verse 4), shuns pride (see verse 14), and keeps the commandments (see verse 15).

Introduction

Revelation given through the Prophet Joseph Smith in his home at Harmony, Pennsylvania, July 1830.[1] Emma Smith is comforted by the Lord at a time when she had recently experienced religious persecution. She is admonished to comfort her husband, Joseph Smith, and put together a hymnal for the Church. She is given a special calling to exhort and expound scripture. (See verses 7 and 11.)

Historical background

Emma recently had been with the Prophet Joseph and Oliver in Colesville, where they were harassed and threatened with physical injury. (See commentary for D&C 24.) She witnessed the controversy that Mormonism attracted. She must have wondered if she could ever experience normal family life as long as Joseph was spearheading a new Church.

Emma commanded of the Lord to select hymns for the Church

Section 25 commands Emma to make a selection of hymns for the newly organized Church. She did not act upon this instruction, however, until five years later, after she and the Saints had moved to Ohio.[2] It was at this time that the Kirtland High Council, on September 14, 1835, resolved that she "proceed to make a selection of sacred hymns" in connection with W. W. Phelps's responsibility as printer for the Church.[3] The first edition of Emma's hymnal was published later that year and contained 90 songs. A second and more expanded edition was printed in 1841; it contained 340 hymns.

Emma's hymnal was titled *A Collection of Sacred Hymns for the Church of the Latter Day Saints*. Like most other hymnals in the early 1800s, the books were easily portable (pocket-size, usually around 2 ½ x 4 ½ inches), which accommodated a favorite evening pastime—gathering with family and friends to "sing the hymns of Zion."[4] It was also common in the early nineteenth century for people to read out loud the song lyrics that had been composed as poetry prior to the singing of the hymn.[5]

---

1. See Smith, *History of the Church*, 1:103–4.
2. In May 1832 it was intended that W. W. Phelps correct and print the hymns that had been selected by Emma Smith. The printing of the hymns, however, was forestalled because Phelps's press was destroyed by a mob (Poulter, "Doctrines of Faith and Hope Found in Emma Smith's 1835 Hymnbook," *BYU Studies* 37:2:34.)
3. See Woodford, "The Historical Development of the Doctrine and Covenants," 381–82.
4. Poulter, 37:2:33.
5. Ibid., 34.

Approximately a third of its ninety hymns were written by Latter-day Saints. The remaining hymns were either borrowed from other Christians without alterations or were adapted.[1] For example, the traditional Christmas hymn "Joy to the World" was modified to change "the spirit of the hymn from a celebration of the infant of Bethlehem to a hymn of joy in preparation for the Second Coming."[2] "Joy to the World; the Lord is come" became "Joy to the world! the Lord will come!" In some cases, uniquely Mormon verses were composed. "The Spirit of God," a Restoration hymn, celebrated the endowment as it was practiced in Kirtland and mentioned washings, anointings, and the washing of feet. "We'll wash, and be wash'd, and with oil be anointed Withal not omitting the washing of feet: For he that receiveth his PENNY appointed, Must surely be clean at the harvest of wheat." The word "PENNY" in upper case "suggests a symbolic meaning—perhaps gift or endowment."[3] It would be another fifty years, however, before Mormons would compose music for a hymn. As Givens points out, "In the early nineteenth century, it was still standard practice to print only lyrics, to be sung by congregations to any of a number of well-known tunes."[4] In this tradition, Emma's hymnal had words only, not music.

Even before Emma embarked upon her assignment to produce a hymnal, Mormon hymns began appearing in the *Evening and Morning Star* as early as February 1833 and dealt with subjects that reflected the aspirations of first-generation Mormons. One such hymn spoke about coming down from "mansions of glory" and announced that a record was hid in Cumorah, containing the "fullness of Jesus' gospel." Taken together, the hymns depict the faith and hopes of this new faith focused on Jesus, missionary work, the establishment of Zion, and the much-anticipated Second Coming.

As time went on, others would also add to the collection of uniquely Mormon hymns.[5] By the time the Kirtland Temple was dedicated, most of the hymns sung on this momentous occasion were of LDS origin, the words composed by such stalwarts as W. W. Phelps and Parley P. Pratt. Phelps's stirring hymn "The Spirit of God," which was composed for the Kirtland Temple dedication, is still sung at all temple dedications to this day.

Section 25 explains that singing hymns is prayerful worship of God. "For my soul delighteth in the song of the heart; yea, the song of the righteous is a prayer unto me and it shall be answered with a blessing upon their heads" (verse 12; see also 1 Chronicles 15:27; Job 38:4–7; Matthew 26:30;

---

1. Ibid., 39.
2. Ibid.
3. Ibid., 45.
4. Givens, *People of Paradox: A History of Mormon Culture*, 124.
5. See ibid., 118.

Mormon 7:7). From this modest beginning, Latter-day Saints eventually employed music and dance to worship and praise God. From a Latter-day Saint perspective, "everything that lives" should "sing praises to the Lord." God should be praised for his "unequaled greatness [by the] blast of the trumpet . . . the lyre and harp . . . tambourine and dancing . . . stringed instruments and flutes . . . [and the] clash of cymbals" (NLT Psalm 150 [verses?].) To this day the themes of the Restoration have been celebrated instrumentally and in song and dance. The Mormon Tabernacle Choir and the Orchestra at Temple Square are but two examples of the central place of music in Mormon worship.

Emma an "elect lady"

Emma was an "elect lady" in the sense that she was qualified and elected in the pre-earth life to receive the blessings of the gospel and chosen to perform a particular work.

Murmur not

Emma was cautioned that she should "murmur not because of the things which thou hast not seen, for they are withheld from thee and from the world, which is wisdom in me in a time to come." (Verse 4.) The reference to "things which thou hast not seen" probably referred to the fact that she had never been permitted to see the gold plates, although she handled them and observed their shape and size under a thin cloth that covered them.[1] Other frustrations that could have caused Emma to complain undoubtedly involved her stressful life as the wife of the Prophet. After three and a half years of marriage she had nearly died in childbirth in June 1828, been separated from her husband during the winter of 1830, seen Joseph arrested in Colesville for preaching and baptizing, and saw a mob threaten to tar and feather him. The fact that her own family did not view Joseph as a prophet only added to her stress.[2] In the face of oppression, the Lord comforted Emma and reassured her that "thou needest not fear, for thy husband shall support thee in the church." (Verse 9.)

---

1. Emma was a scribe for a short period of time when Joseph started translating the Book of Mormon. She said that "the plates often lay on the table without any attempt at concealment, wrapped in a small linen table cloth, which I have given him to fold them in. I once felt the plates, as they thus lay on the table, tracing out their outline and shape. They seemed to be pliable like thick paper, and would rustle with a metallic sound when the edges were moved by the thumb." (See Hardy, *The Book of Mormon: A Reader's Edition*, 641–42.)

2. See Preece, *Learning to Love the Doctrine and Covenants*, 48.

Emma to expound the scriptures

Emma was assured that she should not be a silent partner to her husband. "And thou shalt be ordained . . . to expound scripture, and to exhort the church, according as it shall be given thee by my Spirit." (Verse 7.) In this connection Joseph was commanded to "lay his hands upon" Emma and bless her with the Holy Ghost so that she could devote herself "to writing" and "learning much." (See verse 8.) The fact that Emma was afforded an opportunity to participate in the preaching and intellectual life of the Church in a New England environment was a signal that Mormonism had started to move beyond the restricting traditions placed on women by mainstream Christianity at this time in history. For example, in 1793 just one class in a Methodist school in Baltimore City was headed by a woman, and in 1800 all thirty classes were run by men.[1]

In March 1842 in Nauvoo, Joseph would organize the Female Relief Society. The women elected Emma Smith president, "and like presidents of priesthood quorums, she selected two counselors" and all were set apart by priesthood leaders.[2] By 1844 there would be 1,341 members. With the approval of Joseph, women healed the sick and bore heavy responsibilities to look after the wants of the poor and facilitate the building of the Nauvoo Temple. Emma became the first woman to receive her endowments and performed the temple ordinances for the women. During her later years she became disaffected from the Church over polygamy and withdrew from active participation.

Section 25 and the role of women in the nineteenth century

In the context of the early nineteenth century, section 25 liberally construed the role of women. In Joseph Smith's day, women were not allowed to enter universities. Any personal property a woman brought into a marriage reverted to the husband. If a married couple separated, the woman's husband maintained custody of the children and retained all the personal and real property of the union. A formal divorce was not an option and did not become available until the end of the century. Employment, especially in the professions, was closed to women, and a woman's wages belonged to her husband. Women could not represent themselves in court, sit on juries, or be elected to government office.[3]

In light of the culturally restricted roles of women at this time, the

---

1. See Andrews and Andrews, *The Methodists and Revolutionary America, 1760–1800*, 119.
2. See *Encyclopedia of Mormonism*, 3:1200.
3. See Frederickson, "D&C 25: Empowering Women in the Nineteenth Century in the Church of Jesus Christ of Latter-day Saints," n.p.

encouragement given them in section 25 to accept important Church assignments, to write, and to learn was far ahead of its time. (See verses 7–8, 11.) For example, it must be remembered that Harvard University excluded women from the student body until 1943. By way of contrast, Joseph's educational programs in Kirtland and in Nauvoo did not exclude women from participation, although it was understandably limited in light of the prevailing cultural attitudes about the role of women.

Section 26: Smith Log Home, Harmony, Pennsylvania, July 1830

Heading

The law of common consent reiterated. Let your time be devoted to studying of the scriptures and teaching.

Introduction

Revelation given to Joseph, Oliver Cowdery, and John Whitmer in his home at Harmony, Pennsylvania, July 1830.[1] They are instructed to study the scriptures and to preach the gospel. The law of common consent is given.

Historical background

The law of common consent is mentioned in Doctrine and Covenants 20:65: "No person is to be ordained to any office in this church, where there is a regularly organized branch of the same, without the vote of that church." Section 26 reiterated this principle just three months later. This practice may have been influenced by Book of Mormon and Bible precedents. (See Exodus 24:3; Numbers 27:19; Mosiah 29:25–26.)

From the very beginning Joseph sought advice and counsel. Even in the early days of the Church in New York, Joseph often called together a group of brethren in conferences or councils to discuss and make important decisions. As Bushman points out, these terms (conferences and councils) were used interchangeably.[2] Generally eight or so elders attended. The meetings were run by a moderator, with a clerk taking minutes. In one intense period between the end of August and the middle of November 1831, twelve conferences were convened in addition to the general Church

---

1. See Smith, *History of the Church*, 1:104.
2. See Bushman, *Joseph Smith: Rough Stone Rolling*, 251–52.

conference on October 25 and 26.[1] Later, this group decision-making model became operational for priesthood quorums, which required unanimity before a decision became effective.[2] (See D&C 107:27–31.) The idea that members must agree to be governed is a natural extension of seeking the consent of those directly affected by a decision. The principle of common consent has been repeatedly reconfirmed. (See D&C 38:34; 42:11; 102:9; 124:144.)

Although somewhat perfunctory today, the act of a Mormon congregation's agreeing to an appointment has not always been routine. In Nauvoo, Joseph found it more and more difficult to cooperate and work with his first counselor in the First Presidency, Sidney Rigdon. Although Sidney had made enormous contributions to the Church and defended and mentored Joseph, as Rigdon aged his behavior became more erratic. In all likelihood he was bi-polar, a condition that was exacerbated when he was living in Hiram and suffered a closed head injury on the night he was tarred and feathered. As time went on, Joseph began to question Rigdon's judgment and thought that he was plotting against him. Hyrum intervened and tried to convince Joseph to exercise patience. Unpersuaded, Joseph determined he wanted Rigdon out of the First Presidency and put it to a vote of the Church. On a motion seconded by Hyrum, the conference voted to retain Rigdon in the First Presidency over the objections of Joseph. Joseph abided by the decision even though it displeased him.[3]

Section 27: Harmony, Pennsylvania, August 1830[4]

Heading

Joseph entertains an angel, who warns him that enemies of the Church are attempting to poison the wine used for the sacrament. Restoration of the Melchizedek Priesthood confirmed.

---

1. See Bushman, *Joseph Smith: Rough Stone Rolling*, 251–52.
2. Unanimity is the ideal for all decisions made in the Church, where possible. "If ye are not one ye are not mine." (See D&C 38:27; 107:27–31.)
3. See Bushman, *Joseph Smith: Rough Stone Rolling*, 510–11.
4. This revelation is a composite of at least two separate revelations, and the various dates assigned to it have varied from July through September 1830. "We can say with certainty that the first part was received in the forepart of August 1830. There is no complete version extant, either manuscript or printed, before the version in the 1835 edition; however, evidence does point to September 1830 as the date for the second part. (See Woodford "Discoveries from the Joseph Smith Papers Project," 29.)

The big question

Question: How does a person receive a revelation?
Answer: When there is a particular need for the Lord to communicate in a very direct and plain manner.

Introduction

Revelation given through the Prophet Joseph Smith in Harmony, Pennsylvania, August 1830.[1] In preparation for a religious service in his home, at which the sacrament of bread and wine was to be administered, Joseph set out to procure wine for the occasion. He was met by a heavenly messenger and received this revelation, a portion of which was written at the time, and the remainder in the September following. In it, the Lord sanctioned the use of water as well as wine for the sacrament.[2]

Historical background

Joseph and Emma had recently been in Colesville, New York, where the Knight family lived. Joseph Knight had three sons and four daughters, all of whom joined the Church. He owned a farm, gristmill, and carding machine[3] and allowed Joseph to work for him as a young man starting in November 1826. Knight admired the prophet and, although Knight was quite a bit older, was a close friend. He lent the prophet his horse and wagon when the prophet courted Emma. Joseph borrowed Knight's horse and wagon on September 27, 1830, when he and Emma went to the Hill Cumorah to obtain the gold plates.

During the latter part of June 1830 the Prophet, Emma, John Whitmer, and David Whitmer visited the Knight family in Colesville. Joseph Knight

---

1. Smith, *History of the Church*, 1:106–8.
2. Doctrine and Covenants 27 was received in Harmony, Pennsylvania, in August 1830. Newel Knight, who was in Harmony at the time this revelation was received, reported that the first four verses were given to the Prophet in Harmony and the remaining verses given about a month later in September at Fayette, New York. This account, however, differs from the Prophet's, which suggests that the entire revelation was received in Harmony but that he wrote down only the first four verses and waited until September to write down the remaining part of the revelation. (See Woodford, *Historical Development of the Doctrine and Covenants*, 393–94.)
3. A carding machine was used to straighten or smooth raw fibers in a parallel fashion. The process was sometimes used to remove impurities in such products as cotton, wool, silk, and man-made staples. Carding produces a thin sheet of uniform thickness that is then condensed to form a thick, continuous, untwisted strand called a sliver. When very fine yarns are desired, carding is followed by combing, a process that removes short fibers, leaving a sliver composed entirely of long fibers, all laid parallel and smoother and more lustrous than uncombed types. Carded and combed sliver is then spun. (See http://www.answers.com/topic/carding.)

had read the Book of Mormon and was converted, as had been a number of others living in and around the area. All desired baptism. On Saturday, June 26, 1830, the brethren dammed a stream and made a pond deep enough for immersion. That night a mob demolished the dam. On Sunday, members of the Church gathered and proceeded with their planned meeting in spite of what had happened the night before. The mob attended and harassed those who attended.

Early the next day, on June 28, 1830, the brethren repaired the dam and held baptismal services. Thirteen people were baptized, including Emma Smith. Neighbors and onlookers mocked. After the services, the group went to Joseph Knight's home and then to Joseph Knight's son's home. Enemies followed, hurling insults along the way. The Saints had planned to hold a meeting that evening to confirm the new members, but before it began Joseph was arrested and taken to South Bainbridge and charged with being a disorderly person. Meanwhile, Emma headed for home. Joseph was acquitted, arrested a second time, again acquitted, and finally made it home with Oliver Cowdery in early August.

It was about this time that the Knights traveled to Harmony, Pennsylvania to visit the Smiths. Since Emma and Joseph Knight's wife, Polly, had been baptized but not confirmed, it was proposed that the ordinance be performed in Joseph and Emma's home in Harmony. Joseph suggested that as part of the services the group also partake of the sacrament. Joseph had bread but no wine and set out to procure some for the occasion. He said that "he had gone only a short distance when I was met by a heavenly messenger and received the following revelation," now section 27.[1] The heavenly messenger came to warn Joseph that it was not safe to buy wine from members of the local community, presumably because "enemies" of the Church had poisoned it. (See verses 3–4.)

Newel Knight's journal completes the story. "In obedience to this revelation we prepared some wine of our own make, and held our meeting."[2] The Knights and the Smiths and John Whitmer, who was also present, partook of the sacrament, and then Emma and Polly were confirmed.[3]

In this case the wine meant grape juice, because it was made and used on the same day. However, this was not generally the case. Some LDS congregations used fermented wine for the sacrament until just after the turn of the twentieth century. Since 1906 the official policy of the Church has been to use water. By then, the Word of Wisdom had undergone a number of interpretations, some lax and others more stringent. The Word

---

1. Woodford, *Historical Development of the Doctrine and Covenants*, 393.
2. Knight, "Labors in the Vineyard," in *Classic Experiences and Adventures*, 63.
3. See *A Commentary on the Doctrine and Covenants*, 178.

of Wisdom was not uniformly lived by Latter-day Saints until sometime in the early twentieth century. The reference to not buying "strong drink," and wine from Joseph's enemies, referred to hard liquor as distinguished from wine that contained less alcohol. (See verse 3.)

The sacrament at Adam-ondi-Ahman

Section 27 informed Joseph that "the hour cometh that I will drink of the fruit of the vine with you on earth," a reference to a future event when Jesus will break bread and drink wine with various prophets and others sometime prior to the Millennium at Adam-ondi-Ahman. (See verses 5–14; see also D&C 116.)[1]

Restoration of the Melchizedek Priesthood

There is no known written account of the restoration of the Melchizedek Priesthood that we know of. However, reference to it is mentioned in section 27. "And also with Peter, and James and John . . . unto whom I have committed the keys of my kingdom, and a dispensation of the gospel for the last times." (Verses 12–13.)

The stick of Ephraim

Section 27 references the "stick of Ephraim," or as this phrase is commonly interpreted, the Book of Mormon. (See verse 5.) It is an allusion to Ezekiel 37:15–19, "where the Hebrew word translated as *stick* actually means 'wood,' referring to the wooden writing tablets of the time. Technically, the two 'sticks' or 'wooden tablets' are symbolic of the descendants or 'houses' of Ephraim and Judah who had divided into two separate kingdoms and were in Ezekiel's time bitter enemies. [See Ezekiel 37:21–23.] Thus, Ezekiel's prophecy, on one level at least, is about the gathering and reconciling of the house of Ephraim and the house of Judah, the northern and the southern kingdoms, which together would comprise all of Israel, including the lost ten tribes, the Book of Mormon peoples, and the Jews. Hence, since the house of Ephraim is the 'stick,'" the Book of Mormon is correctly said to be the record of the house of Ephraim.[2]

---

1. See McConkie, *Millennial Messiah*, 578–79.
2. See Robinson and Garrett, *A Commentary on the Doctrine and Covenants*, 1:181.

Chapter 18

Susquehanna River: Harmony, Pennsylvania

SECTION 13: SUSQUEHANNA RIVER, HARMONY, PENNSYLVANIA, MAY 15, 1829

Heading

The idea of authority and need for saving ordinances introduced. John the Baptist visits Joseph Smith and Oliver Cowdery and restores the Aaronic priesthood empowering men to baptize, be ministered to by angels, and administer the gospel of repentance.

The big question

Question: Why John the Baptist?
Answer: To restore the authority necessary to perform baptisms, entertain angels, and administer the gospel of repentance.

Introduction

Ordination of Joseph Smith and Oliver Cowdery to the Aaronic Priesthood along the bank of the Susquehanna River in Harmony, Pennsylvania, on May 15, 1829.[1] The ordination was done by the hands of an angel, who announced himself as John, the same that is called John the Baptist in the New Testament. The same angel explained that he was acting under the direction of Peter, James, and John, the ancient apostles who held the keys of the higher priesthood, which was called the priesthood of Melchizedek. (See headnote to D&C 13 [1981 ed.].)

This revelation was not published until it was "lifted out of the history of the Prophet" and included in the 1876 edition of the Doctrine and

---

1. Smith, *History of the Church*, 1:39–42.

Covenants.[1] Later in his life, Joseph acknowledged that persecution forced him to keep secret the circumstances surrounding the restoration of the priesthood from heavenly messengers.[2] Therefore, revelations about the priesthood were not included in the Book of Commandments.

Anchor section

Memorize: Restoration of the Aaronic Priesthood

Why were Joseph and Oliver interested in baptism?

While translating the Book of Mormon, Joseph came upon passages concerning baptism. Oliver Cowdery reported that the particular passages were in connection with "the account given of the Savior's ministry." (JS–H, page 59.) Thereafter, Joseph and Oliver sought seclusion just a hundred yards or so behind Joseph's home on the banks of the Susquehanna River to prayerfully inquire about the need to perform this ordinance. John the Baptist appeared, placed his hands on each of their heads and conferred on them the Aaronic Priesthood. Joseph and Oliver Cowdery then, each in turn, placed hands on the other's head and ordained each other to the office of priest, one of the offices associated with the Aaronic Priesthood. Afterwards, each baptized the other.

Oliver Cowdery's description of John the Baptist

This was the first time that Oliver Cowdery had seen an angel—John the Baptist. He recorded the experience, and it was later published in the *Messenger and Advocate*, a Church-sponsored newspaper. In it he described in detail what he witnessed.

> The veil was parted and the angel of God came down clothed with glory. . . . What joy!, what wonder!, what amazement! . . . our eyes beheld, our ears heard. . . . Then his voice, though mild, pierced to the center, and his words, 'I am thy fellow-servant,' dispelled every fear. We listened, we gazed, we admired! . . . we rejoiced." (JS–H, page 59.)

Oliver said of John's visit that afterwards his faith about the reality of angels and the unseen world was supplanted by absolute knowledge. "Where was room for doubt? Nowhere; uncertainty had fled, doubt had sunk no more to rise." (JS–H, page 59.)

---

1. Woodford, "The Historical Development of the Doctrine and Covenants," 1:235.
2. Staker, *Hearken, O Ye People*, Kindle locations 5238–40.

The general powers and blessings associated with the Aaronic Priesthood

Conferral of the Aaronic Priesthood is not the same as receiving an office within that priesthood. When John gave Joseph and Oliver the Aaronic Priesthood, he bestowed upon them general powers and privileges. Thereafter, they ordained each other to the office of priest, which authorized each to use the powers of this priesthood in specific ways, namely to baptize.

The general powers associated with the Aaronic Priesthood are the keys of the ministering of angels, the gospel of repentance, and baptism by immersion. The ministering of angels is the highest privilege of this priesthood, and Joseph said that privilege should be understood literally. It is the promise that those who have this priesthood may be visited by angelic visitors.[1] By way of comparison, the highest privilege of the Melchizedek Priesthood is to see the face of God. (See D&C 107:19.)

The "offering to the Lord in righteousness"

John the Baptist concluded the conferral of the Aaronic Priesthood upon Joseph and Oliver by informing them that the Aaronic Priesthood would not be taken from the earth until the "sons of Levi do offer again an offering unto the Lord in righteousness."[2] What is this offering? Joseph Smith taught that prior to the Second Coming, the sons of Levi (holders of the Aaronic Priesthood or the literal descendants of Levi) would for a limited time reinstitute blood sacrifice in the temple to be built in Zion—Independence, Missouri.[3] Joseph explained that this practice was

---

1. See Smith, *Teachings of the Prophet Joseph Smith*, 180–81.
2. Oliver Cowdery remembered the phrase a little differently. "We received under his hand [John the Baptist's] the Holy Priesthood as he said, this authority, which shall remain upon the earth, *that* [instead of *until*] the Sons of Levi may yet offer an offering unto the Lord in righteousness." This difference does change the meaning. The official version in Doctrine and Covenants 13—"*until* the Sons of Levi do offer again an offering"—implies that after the last blood offering the Aaronic Priesthood will no longer function. Oliver's variation "*that* the Sons of Levi may yet offer" implies that the Aaronic Priesthood will continue.
3. On October 5, 1840, Robert B. Thompson recorded the following: "All the ordinances and duties that ever have been required by the Priesthood under the directions . . . of the Almighty in any of the dispensations, shall all be had in the last dispensation, therefore all things had under the authority of the Priesthood at any former period, shall be had again, bringing to pass the restoration spoken of by the mouth of all the Holy Prophets; then shall the sons of Levi offer an acceptable offering to the Lord. . . . The offerings and sacrifices are not all consumed upon the altar—but the blood is sprinkled, and the fat and certain other portions are consumed. . . . These sacrifices as well as every ordinance belonging to the Priesthood, will, when the Temple of the Lord shall be built, and the sons of Levi be purified be fully restored and attended to in all their powers, ramifications, and blessings. This ever did and ever will exist when the powers of the [Melchizedek] Priesthood are sufficiently manifest; else how can the restitution of all things spoken of by the holy Prophets be brought to pass? It is not to be understood that the law of Moses will be established again with all

Susquehanna River: Harmony, Pennsylvania

to be restored as part of the dispensation of the fulness of times, an epoch in which representative parts of the gospel from each period of the earth's history would be restored.[1] (D&C 84:3, 4, 31.)

Section 128 contrasts the sacrifice of the sons of Levi with a different kind of offering made in modern temples in which the old system of blood sacrifice is abolished and in its place the Saints are instructed to do vicarious work for the dead.

> Behold, the great day of the Lord is at hand; and who can abide the day of his coming, . . . and he shall purify the sons of Levi . . . that they may offer unto the Lord an offering in righteousness [blood sacrifice]. . . . Let us, therefore, as a church and a people, . . . offer unto the Lord an offering in righteousness [vicarious work for the dead]; and let us present in his holy temple, when it is finished, a book containing the records of our dead, which shall be worthy of all acceptation. (D&C 128:24.)

From the beginning, the first temples participated in blood sacrifice, a type that looked forward to the Son of God shedding his own blood to atone for the sins of mankind. Once Jesus shed his blood on the cross and the atonement was accomplished, it was no longer necessary for blood sacrifice to continue. It was at this point that temple worship switched from blood sacrifice to vicarious work for the dead, introduced by Jesus as part of his ministry. (See 1 Corinthians 15:29.) It is in this context that section 128 speaks about a record of ordinance work for the dead being documented in "a book containing the records of our dead, which shall be worthy of all acceptation." (D&C 128:24; see also D&C 84:31.)[2]

The idea of authority introduced

Prior to the restoration of the Aaronic Priesthood, the focus was primarily on the need for modern revelation, the gifts of the Spirit, and the coming forth of the Book of Mormon. After the appearance of John the Baptist, Joseph and Oliver understood that in addition to the foregoing, authorization to act in God's name and the performance of salvific ordinances were also a necessary component of God's work on earth. As time progressed, the idea of "authority" and additional saving ordinances would be introduced. The next step in this direction was the restoration of a higher, Melchizedek Priesthood by Peter, James, and John. By 1835 the

---

its rites and variety of ceremonies; this has never been spoken of by the Prophets; but those things which existed prior to Moses' day, namely, sacrifice, will be continued." (See Smith, *History of the Church*, 4:210–12.)

1. See Smith, *History of the Church*, 4:207–12.
2. Smith, *Teachings of the Prophet Joseph Smith*, 171–73.

bounds and limits of divine authority would be well defined in section 107, and by 1842 a series of saving ordinances known as the endowment would be revealed. (See D&C 128.)

The restoration of the authority to perform baptism prompted Joseph and Oliver to offer this ordinance to others. Sometime in May 1829 they baptized Joseph's brother Samuel in Harmony, Pennsylvania, and shortly thereafter they baptized others in Fayette, New York.[1] Baptizing others undoubtedly raised the issue of establishing a Church. In 1829, Oliver composed "The Articles of the Church of Christ," which explained that he had been given authority to baptize and which outlined the offices and duties of various positions in Christ's church.[2] "The Articles of the Church of Christ" were later modified and became section 20, which served as a handbook for the Church when it was organized on April 6, 1830.

---

1. Michael Hubbard MacKay and Gerrit J. Dirkmaat, *From Darkness unto Light: Joseph Smith's Translation and Publication of the Book of Mormon* (2015), 133.
2. Ibid.

Part 5

The Fayette, New York, Period

Chapter 19

Organization of the Church: Fayette, New York, July 1829–January 1831

Joseph and Emma Smith Move to Fayette, New York

Joseph's religious activities had not gone unnoticed in Harmony. Although he and Oliver Cowdery had been careful never to publicly say anything about the appearance of John Baptist, people generally knew that Joseph claimed to be translating ancient gold plates. Members of the community were suspicious, in part because Joseph was not willing to show the plates to anyone, even family members such as Joseph's father-in-law, Isaac Hale.[1] As the general populace became more aware of Joseph and his claims, controversy and misunderstanding increased, and the all-too-familiar pattern of persecution started all over again, leaving Joseph and Oliver feeling threatened.[2] As tensions grew, Joseph needed more uninterrupted time to complete the translation of the Book of Mormon.

As the situation in Harmony continued to deteriorate, Oliver decided to ask David Whitmer, a friend and associate of his, about the possibility of Joseph and Oliver moving to Fayette, New York, to board in David's

---

1. On one occasion Joseph did allow his father-in-law to heft a box in which the gold plates were contained.

2. At first Joseph and Emma enjoyed social acceptance in Harmony because Emma's extended family, the Hales, lived there. However, the protection the extended family provided dwindled, partially because Emma's father, Isaac, was unimpressed by Joseph's religious claims. According to Joseph's mother, the Lord instructed Joseph and Oliver by means of the Urim and Thummim to request to live with the Whitmers. "One morning as he applied it to his eyes to look upon the record, instead of the words of the book being given to him, he was commanded to write a letter to one David Whitmer, who lived in Waterloo. This man Joseph had never seen, but he was instructed to say to him that he must come with his team immediately, in order to convey Joseph and Oliver back to his house, that they might remain with him there until the translation should be completed, as an evil-designing people were seeking to take away Joseph's life in order to prevent the work of God from going forth among the world." (Smith, *History of Joseph Smith*, 1966, 192.)

parents' home. In response, David Whitmer's father, Peter Whitmer Sr.,[1] extended an invitation to Joseph and Emma to live with them in their log cabin home so that Joseph could find the solitude necessary for him to finish the Book of Mormon translation. David, who was living with his parents at the time, made arrangements to go to Harmony to help the Smiths move their belongings to Fayette.[2]

Before David could leave in early May, it was necessary for him to finish planting the family's crops in order to reap a fall harvest. David reported to his father one day that he had plowed twice as much as normal. His father remarked that "there must be an overruling hand in this, and I think you [should] go down to Pennsylvania as soon as your plaster of Paris is sown."[3] The next day, David went to the fields to sow the plaster and was surprised to find the work done. His sister who lived nearby said that her children reported that they had watched three strangers the day before spread the plaster with remarkable skill.[4]

David started on his three-day journey to Harmony, some 100 miles south. When he reached the outskirts of town, Joseph and Oliver met him. Prior to David's arrival, Joseph had miraculously seen the details of David's trip to Harmony and knew when he would approach. Some years later, Oliver informed David Whitmer that Joseph had revealed to him—in advance of his coming—the day David started from Fayette to Harmony, where he stopped the first night, and how he had read the sign on the tavern before retiring there. David's experience with planting his crops and Joseph's knowledge of the details of his trip to Harmony all served to convince him that Joseph was an authentic prophet.

When Joseph arrived in Fayette, the translation process began in earnest again. Joseph and a scribe sat in the second story of the Whitmer home on a landing just outside a bedroom. When Joseph started translating in 1827 he had started with the Book of Lehi, which Martin Harris lost. Thereafter,

---

1. Joseph was not unknown to Peter Whitmer and had met him on a prior occasion. Peter Whitmer was also acquainted with Joseph's parents, who had traveled by way of the Whitmer farm on their way to visit their son in February 1829. Oliver had also kept the Whitmers apprised of what Joseph was doing. Just after Oliver arrived in Harmony to act as Joseph's scribe, he wrote to David Whitmer and expressed his enthusiasm for what Joseph was accomplishing.

2. Emma did not go with Joseph Smith at this time but came to live with him a short time later.

3. See *Church History in the Fulness of Times*, 56. Plaster of Paris is "a white powdery substance made out of gypsum, a hydrated form of calcium sulfate that occurs naturally. Plaster of Paris is used chiefly for casts and molds in the form of a quick-setting paste with water." During Joseph Smith's day it was used as a fertilizer, a use considered questionable by today's standards. (http://www.google.com/search?hl=en&lr=&q=plaster+of+paris+definition.)

4. See *Church History in the Fulness of Times*, 57.

Organization of the Church: Fayette, New York, July 1829–January 1831

Joseph and Oliver started where they had left off at the beginning of Mosiah. By the time they left Harmony, they must have reached 3 Nephi because this was where Joseph and Oliver read about baptism, leading to the appearance of John the Baptist. Based upon these assumptions, it appears that Joseph finished translating the rest of the book through Moroni before going back to translate the small plates of Nephi containing 1 Nephi through the Words of Mormon.

Occasionally, circumstances interrupted the flow of translation. At times Joseph reported that he was "spiritually blind" and could not translate. He felt that this was because his mind dwelt too much on earthly things.[1] On one occasion he was at odds with Emma and attempted to translate but could not. Joseph went out into the orchard and prayed for about an hour. Afterwards, he came back, asked Emma's forgiveness, and was able to translate once again.

Once the translation was completed, Joseph's focus began to shift to missionary work and the establishment of a church. On April 6, 1830, interested individuals filled Peter Whitmer's small log cabin to overflowing, and the Church was formally established.[2] Up until this point in time Joseph had been viewed as a charismatic prophet, not an organizer.[3] He was only twenty-four years old and had no experience leading a group. As Bushman points out, Fayette marks the beginning of the formal organization of a religious society that would continue to grow until it filled the earth.[4] Without the spirit of prophecy no one could have predicted that the structure Joseph put in place would support a worldwide organization.

---

1. See Bushman, *Joseph Smith: Rough Stone Rolling*, 76.
2. At one time there was a controversy over whether or not the Church was organized in Fayette or in Manchester, New York. "In his 1838 history, Joseph said the organization took place at the Whitmer house in Fayette; in an 1842 letter to John Wentworth, a Chicago newspaperman, Joseph said Manchester. Although Fayette has been accepted traditionally as the place, the evidence for Manchester is not insubstantial. Historians have speculated that a Fayette meeting shortly after April 6 was confused with the Manchester organizational meeting." (Bushman, *Joseph Smith: Rough Stone Rolling*, 109.) However, the publication of the Joseph Smith Papers has convincingly established Fayette, New York, as the place where the Church was organized.
3. Bushman points out that the focus of converts was not on Joseph Smith but on revelation in general and its universal accessibility. Joseph rarely spoke about the First Vision or the appearances of the angel Moroni. (See Bushman, *Joseph Smith: Rough Stone Rolling*, 109–12.)
4. See Bushman, *Joseph Smith: Rough Stone Rolling*, 109–12.

Whitmer log home, in Fayette, New York, where the Church was formally organized on April 6, 1830, on the main floor. Joseph Smith and Oliver Cowdery finished translating the Book of Mormon on the second floor. The angel Moroni appeared to the Three Witnesses not far from the cabin.

Chapter 20

The Big Questions: Fayette, New York

WHY A CHURCH?

The Church was officially organized in Fayette, New York, on April 6, 1830. Its organization was modeled after the prototype of the primitive church as described in the four Gospels, with an emphasis on faith, repentance, baptism, revelation, prophecy, and the gifts of the Spirit. The Book of Mormon and its witnesses' accounts about the reality of gold plates and divine translation was tangible evidence that God was backing this new religious movement. Section 20 outlined the basic framework of the fledgling organization, governed by Joseph and Oliver Cowdery as the first among equals and assisted by a lay ministry based on John the Baptist's restoration of the Aaronic Priesthood. As section 20 explained, the Church was to help men and women walk "in holiness before the Lord." (Verse 69; see D&C 20 and 21.)

WHAT IS THE STRUCTURE OF THE CHURCH?

When the Church was organized, the members had only a glimpse of what the future organization of the Church would become. In the beginning, Church leadership centered in Joseph and his assistant, Oliver Cowdery, referred to respectively as the First and Second Elders. Although it was expected that all the members should experience personal revelation and the gift of prophecy, to avoid confusion, the Lord made it clear in section 28 that only Joseph could receive revelations for the entire Church. Lay elders, priests, and teachers were appointed to assist Joseph. Quarterly conferences were scheduled "to do church business" and whatever "is necessary." (See D&C 20:62.) The most notable aspect of Church association, however, was the expectation that virtually all of its members would be employed in the ministry. As Bushman observed, "Perhaps the most radical departure was the lack of provision for a professional clergy. Although never enunciated as a policy, the practice of ordaining every worthy male member quickly took effect."[1] While women were not utilized at first, by the time the Church organization came of age in Nauvoo, a women's Relief Society and a temple ritual that allowed females to administer ordinances would set the precedent that Church clerical positions were not strictly limited by gender.

By 1835 a higher priesthood had been introduced and additional offices and governing quorums defined. Based on Joseph's added understanding, when the Doctrine and Covenants was revised in 1835 section 20 was rewritten to reflect Melchizedek Priesthood authority. Also, the Aaronic office of deacon was included for the first time. References to the office of elder were already in Section 20 because it was originally considered to be part of the Aaronic Priesthood.[2]

---

1. Bushman, *Joseph Smith: Rough Stone Rolling*, 111. It should also be observed that the early organization of the Church was along the lines set out in the Book of Mormon, which specifically mentions the offices of elder, priest, and teacher, who were to "labor with their own hands for their support." (Mosiah 27:5; Alma 4:7, 16; 6:1; Moroni 3:1; 4:1; 6:1, 7.) The idea was that a "priest [did] not esteem himself above his hearers, . . . neither was the teacher any better than the learner; and thus they were all equal, and they did all labor, every man according to his strength." (Alma 1:26.) Although modern editions of section 20 mention an office not mentioned in the Book of Mormon, the office of deacon, this office was added to section 20 for the first time in the 1835 edition.

2. See Quinn, *The Mormon Hierarchy: Origins of Power*, 27–29.

Chapter 21

Whitmer Home

SECTIONS 14, 15, 16: WHITMER HOME, FAYETTE, NEW YORK, JUNE 1829

Heading

Revelation to David Whitmer, John Whitmer, and Peter Whitmer Jr.

Introduction

Sections 14, 15, and 16 were given to David Whitmer, John Whitmer, and Peter Whitmer Jr., respectively, in June 1829 in the Whitmer home located in Fayette, New York.[1] The Whitmer family had become greatly interested in the translation of the Book of Mormon. The Prophet established his residence at the home of Peter Whitmer Sr., where he lived until the book was finished and the copyright secured. The three Whitmers were convinced of Joseph's genuine prophetic calling and were anxious to know what God expected of them in connection with the restoration of the gospel. All three revelations came through the instrumentality of the Urim and Thummim or seer stone. (See headings to D&C 14, 15, 16.)

Whitmer family

Peter Whitmer Sr. was born in 1773 in Pennsylvania and died in 1854 at age eighty-one in Richmond, Missouri. He had five sons and three daughters. He and his wife were baptized on April 18, 1830, in Seneca Lake. Prior to his conversion to Mormonism he was a strong Presbyterian. One of his daughters, Nancy, died at age four months. His youngest daughter, Elizabeth Ann, married Oliver Cowdery. His sons Christian, Jacob, John,

---

1. Smith, *History of the Church*, 1:48–51.

and Peter Jr. were four of the Eight Witnesses of the Book of Mormon. His son David was one of the Three Witnesses. His oldest daughter, Catherine, married Hiram Page, another of the Eight Witnesses. Eventually his sons David and John became disaffected and were excommunicated from the Church.

Peter Whitmer Sr. purchased 100 acres and built a one-and-a-half-story log home about twenty-eight miles southeast of Palmyra, between the Seneca and Cayuga lakes. Joseph and Emma, along with Oliver Cowdery, lived with the Whitmers during the final stages of the Book of Mormon translation.[1]

On April 6, 1830, about fifty to sixty believers crowded inside the Whitmer home to witness the formal organization of the Church. Three general conferences of the Church were held in this home between June 1830 and January 1831. The home was sold in 1831 when the Whitmers went to Kirtland to be with the main body of the Saints. B. H. Roberts purchased it on behalf of the Church in 1926.[2]

Sections 14, 15, and 16

Section 14 speaks about a "great and marvelous work" that was about to come forth. The work referred to is surely the coming forth of the Book of Mormon. The phrase is used in the context of giving "heed to my word," along with a description of how powerful God's word is: "Behold, I am God; give heed to my word, which is quick and powerful, sharper than a two-edged sword." (Verses 1–2.) This verse and those that follow may also be read as an invitation to build the future kingdom of God.

Section 14 is very personal to David Whitmer, assuring him that if he will "thrust in his sickle and reap" he will be "called of God." (Verses 3–4.) He is further promised that if he prays, keeps God's commandments, and endures to the end[3] he will be blessed with "eternal life, which is the greatest of all the gifts of God." (See verses 4–7.) Finally, his calling as one of the Three Witnesses is foreshadowed. He will "stand as a witness of the things of which you shall both hear and see." (Verse 8.) Just a month or so later Moroni would visit him and show him the gold plates. Armed with this witness, he was to "declare repentance unto this generation." (Verse 8.) All of this was to help make known the "fulness of my gospel from the Gentiles unto the house of Israel." (Verse 10.)

---

1. It was about 100 yards directly out the front door in a wooded area that the Three Witnesses saw the gold plates in June 1829.
2. See Garr, Cannon, and Cowan, *Encyclopedia of Latter-day Saint History*, 1338.
3. Although he never repudiated his testimony, Whitmer was excommunicated from the Church in 1839, ten years later.

The mission of David Whitmer's brother, John Whitmer, is described in section 15. He was to "declare repentance unto this people." (Verse 6.) From Fayette, New York, to Kirtland, Ohio, John shared the message of the gospel. His missionary endeavors were commented on in the *Painesville Telegraph*. "A young man by the name of Whitmer arrived here last week . . . with a new batch of revelations from God, as he pretended, which have just been communicated to Joseph Smith."[1] Although section 15 is silent on the matter, John Whitmer would later become one of the Eight Witnesses to the Book of Mormon.

The mission of David Whitmer's brother, Peter Whitmer Jr., is commented on in section 16. His revelation mirrors his brother John's revelation and is identical except for their names in verse one and the word "unto" in verse 5 of section 16. In September 1830 Peter was called to preach the gospel with Oliver Cowdery: "Behold, I say unto you, Peter, that you shall take your journey with your brother Oliver; for the time has come that it is expedient in me that you shall open your mouth to declare my gospel . . . to build up my church among the Lamanites." (D&C 30:5–6.) Peter and others called to preach to the Lamanites, Edward Partridge, Parley P. Pratt, were among the most successful missionaries in the early Church. Although the Lamanites were not converted, many of the early stalwarts of the Church heard the gospel and were convinced that Joseph was a prophet—among them Sidney Rigdon, Edward Partridge, Parley P. Pratt, and others.

Section 17: Whitmer Home, Fayette, New York, June 1829

Heading

Oliver Cowdery, David Whitmer, and Martin Harris were promised that they would see the gold plates, the breastplate, the sword of Laban, the Urim and Thummim, and the directors or Liahona.

Introduction

This revelation was given through Joseph Smith the Prophet to Oliver Cowdery, David Whitmer, and Martin Harris, at Fayette, New York, in June 1829, prior to their viewing the engraved plates that contained the Book of Mormon record.[2] Joseph and his scribe, Oliver Cowdery, had learned during the translation of the Book of Mormon that three special witnesses would be designated. (See Ether 5:2–4; see also 2 Nephi 11:3; 27:12.) Oliver

---

1. Black, *Who's Who in the Doctrine and Covenants*, 332.
2. Smith, *History of the Church*, 1:52–57.

Cowdery, David Whitmer, and Martin Harris are here promised that they will be given the responsibility of viewing the plates and bearing record of them to the world as foreseen in the Book of Mormon. Section 17 was not included in the 1833 edition of the Book of Commandments but was first included in the 1835 edition of the Doctrine and Covenants. (See heading to D&C 17.)

Historical background

At about this time Joseph had sent word to his parents in Manchester that he had finished the Book of Mormon and wanted them to come to Fayette. Martin Harris, who was also very interested in what Joseph was doing, made the trip with them. Upon their arrival, Joseph, Martin Harris, Oliver Cowdery, and David Whitmer talked about how Nephi's account mentioned the need for witnesses. (See 2 Nephi 27:12–14.) This was not a new subject for these men. Because previous revelations had spoken about their role as witnesses, it had been on their minds for some time. (See D&C 5:11–13, 24–28; 6:25–28; 14:8.) Accordingly, the three asked Joseph to inquire of the Lord on the subject. Section 17 was the response.

One evening, Joseph and his guests looked through and read from the Book of Mormon manuscript. The next morning the group gathered as usual for prayer. Lucy Smith, the Prophet's mother, wrote: "Joseph arose from his knees, and approaching Martin Harris with a solemnity that thrills through my veins to this day, when it occurs to my recollection, said, 'Martin Harris, you have to humble yourself before God this day that you may obtain a forgiveness of your sins. If you do, it is the will of God that you should look upon the plates, in company with Oliver Cowdery and David Whitmer."[1]

This invitation must have been particularly heartwarming to Martin, who felt that after he had lost the first 116 pages of the Book of Mormon he no longer qualified for such a spiritual privilege.

Thereafter, the four retired to a wooded area about 100 yards or so straight from the front door of the Whitmer log cabin. After two unsuccessful attempts at asking for the divine messenger, Martin Harris felt that his presence hindered the process. He withdrew a distance and offered his own private prayers. The others stayed together seeking the promised witness. David Whitmer said that he, Oliver, and Joseph sat down and talked a while. The three then knelt in prayer. He said they got up and sat on a log conversing, when all at once a light came down from above that overshadowed and encircled the three men for some distance around

---

1. *Church History in the Fulness of Times*, 60.

them. It was not like the light of the sun or of fire but was more glorious and beautiful. The angel appeared in the midst of the light.

David said the angel stood just a few feet from him and was dressed in white and glorious in his appearance. Moroni addressed them and said, "Blessed is he that keepeth his commandments." The angel then showed David Whitmer, Oliver Cowdery, and Joseph Smith the gold plates, the directors or Liahona, the Urim and Thummim, and other records as well. David said that he saw the angel and the plates as plain as day and that he heard the voice of the Lord as distinctly as he had heard anything in his life, declaring that the Book of Mormon had been translated by the gift and power of God. David said that human language could not describe the heavenly things which they saw. In addition to what he saw, he said he felt a strange, entrancing influence that permeated his being so powerfully that he felt chained to the spot beside where Moroni was standing. He said it was a sensation of joy that was absolutely indescribable.[1]

Joseph said that after the angel appeared to him, David Whitmer, and Oliver Cowdery, he left them to find Martin Harris fervently engaged in prayer a considerable distance away. Martin said he had not yet received a witness and wanted Joseph to pray with him so that he could have the same privilege the others had experienced. Moroni then appeared for the second time that day, to Martin Harris and Joseph Smith. Martin was overcome.[2] He cried out "'Tis enough; 'tis enough; mine eyes have beheld; mine eyes have beheld."[3]

Of this event Joseph wrote that Moroni "turned over the leaves one by one, so that we could see them, and discern the engravings thereon distinctly.... We heard a voice from out of the bright light above us, saying, 'These plates have been revealed by the power of God, and they have been translated by the power of God. The translation of them which you have seen is correct, and I command you to bear record of what you now see and hear."[4] Joseph expressed relief to his mother, Lucy, that finally others had seen what he had and that he was no longer alone in bearing witness of these things.[5]

---

1. See Anderson, *Investigating the Book of Mormon Witnesses*, 79–90.
2. See Anderson, *Investigating the Book of Mormon Witnesses*, 79–90.
3. See *Church History in the Fulness of Times*, 60.
4. *Church History in the Fulness of Times*, 60.
5. In addition to the gold plates the witnesses also saw the breastplate, the sword of Laban, the Urim and Thummim, and the directors or Liahona. The breastplate was in the stone box that held the plates. See commentary on section 8 for a more complete description and discussion. The sword of Laban was described by Nephi: "The hilt thereof was of pure gold, and the workmanship thereof was exceedingly fine, and I saw that the blade thereof was of the most precious steel." (1 Nephi 4:9.) The Urim and Thummim could be attached to the breastplate and was used during the translation process. See Section 8 for a more complete

The Fayette, New York, Period

The power of eyewitness testimony

One of the most compelling evidences that Joseph was a genuine prophet is the fact that others saw and experienced what he did. He was not alone in bearing witness that he possessed gold plates, that angels visited with men and women, and that he had translated the Book of Mormon by the gift and power of God. The Three Witnesses would confirm all of these assertions by eyewitness testimony. Such proof is difficult to impeach and there is little middle ground for equivocation. The witnesses either saw an angel who showed them the gold plates stating that the record had been translated by the gift and power of God or they did not.

The certainty of such testimony is bolstered by the fact that at least three witnesses saw and heard the same angel in broad daylight at the same time and place. Consequently, it does not seem reasonable that they were both deluded, inasmuch as each reported that he saw exactly what the other did. Recognizing the boldness of their assertions, others who challenged Joseph's story looked elsewhere for an explanation of what happened and suggested that the Three Witnesses entered into a conspiracy with Joseph Smith to convince others of the divine credentials of the newly established Church. However, this assertion also falls short. None of the three had anything to gain financially and later even found themselves at odds with Joseph Smith, were excommunicated, and left the Church. Yet not one of them ever denied the actuality of this experience. The Three Witnesses, and later The Eight Witnesses, who also saw and hefted the gold plates, gave added evidence that what Joseph reported was factual. Joseph no longer stood alone. Other men of sound mind would "testify of them." (See verses 3–4.) All of this was to be accomplished so that "Joseph Smith, Jun., may not be destroyed, that I may bring about my righteous purposes unto the children of men in this work." (See verse 4.)

SECTION 18: WHITMER LOG HOME, FAYETTE, NEW YORK, JUNE 1829

Heading

The Church to be organized with twelve disciples to be chosen by Oliver Cowdery and David Whitmer.

---

description and discussion. The directors or Liahona gave instructions to the family of Lehi on the direction they should travel. (See 1 Nephi 16:10, 28; Alma 37:38–39.)

The big question

Question: What is the structure of the Church?
Answer: The structure of the Church requires the appointment of twelve disciples who are to evangelize and help govern and establish the Church.

Introduction

The revelation was given to Joseph Smith the Prophet, Oliver Cowdery, and David Whitmer, at the Peter Whitmer Sr. home in Fayette, New York, June 1829.[1] When the Aaronic Priesthood was conferred, the bestowal of the Melchizedek Priesthood was promised.[2] This section is given in response to a supplication for more knowledge on this matter. (See headnote to D&C 18; see also D&C 27:7, 8, 12.) The calling and mission of the twelve disciples is revealed. Oliver Cowdery and David Whitmer are commanded to search out this group of men. (Verse 37.)

Historical background

This revelation occurred just after Joseph Smith, Oliver Cowdery, and David Whitmer arrived at the Whitmer home on June 1, 1829, a few weeks after the restoration of the Aaronic Priesthood and before the restoration of the Melchizedek Priesthood. These brethren were gathered in prayer

when the word of the Lord came unto us in the chamber, commanding us that I should ordain Oliver Cowdery to be an Elder in the Church of Jesus Christ; and that he also should ordain me to the same office; and then to ordain others, as it should be made known unto us from time to time. We were, however, commanded to defer this our ordination until such times as it should be practicable to have our brethren, who had been and who should be baptized assembled together, when we must have their sanction to our thus proceeding to ordain each other, and have them decide by vote whether they were willing to accept us as spiritual teachers or not. . . . The following commandment will further illustrate the nature of our calling to this Priesthood, as well as that of others who were yet to be sought after.[3]

Joseph and Oliver were ordained elders eleven months later at the time of the organization of the Church on April 6, 1830. Joseph was sustained as the First Elder and Oliver as the Second Elder, the presiding offices in the new Church.[4]

---

1. Smith, *History of the Church*, 1:60–64.
2. See D&C 13, headnote.
3. See Smith, *History of the Church*, 1:60–62.
4. Joseph's brother William Smith wrote of this at the time of the 1831 conference: "Elders,

At this time the office of "elder" was associated with the Aaronic priesthood and later became an office in the Melchizedek Priesthood. When this occurred is a point where some Mormon historians differ, in part because there is no contemporaneous account of the restoration of the Melchizedek Priesthood. The more traditional and generally accepted understanding places the restoration of the Melchizedek Priesthood prior to the organization of the Church on April 6, 1830. For example, Joseph Fielding Smith, and Stephen E. Robinson and H. Dean Garrett, authors of *A Commentary on the Doctrine and Covenants*, take this position.[1] On the other side of the divide, Mormon historian Richard Bushman and others suggest that this may not be the case.

Bushman notes that before 1831 men were called to Church offices—elders, priests, and teachers—given authority, and licensed without reference to a bestowal of priesthood. In early June 1831, forty-four elders, four priests, and fifteen teachers met in a log schoolhouse on the Isaac Morley farm just outside of Kirtland. It was at this conference that the words *High Priesthood* were first used and priesthood was bestowed as if it were an addition to previous authority. The minutes record, for the first time in Church history, ordinations to "the High Priesthood" or Melchizedek Priesthood. Writing about this meeting years later, Joseph said that "the authority of the Melchizedek Priesthood was manifested and conferred for the first time upon several of the Elders."[2] Although Brigham Young came into the Church in 1832, he also believed that the Melchizedek Priesthood was restored after the organization of the Church.[3]

"Rely Upon the things that are written"

Section 18 commands Oliver Cowdery to "rely upon the things that are written ... for in them are all things ... for the foundation of my church." (Section 18:3-4) Therefore, Cowdery examined Book of Mormon passages that Joseph had recently translated as source material for Cowdery's "Articles of the Church of Christ" (later Doctrine and Covenants Section 20) and used it in his handbook of instructions for the new faith. The Articles set out the ritual of baptism, the sacrament prayers on the bread and the water

---

Priests, Teachers and Deacons received some general instructions from the Church concerning the Priesthood of Melchizedek, to which they had not as yet been ordained for they had not attained to all the power of their ministry." (See Quinn, *The Mormon Hierarchy*, 30.) It was not until 1832 that a revelation for the first time specified that "the offices of elder and bishop are necessary appendages belonging unto the high priesthood." (D&C 84:29.)

1. Smith, *Doctrines of Salvation*, 3:98; Robinson and Garrett, *A Commentary on the Doctrine and Covenants*, 1:103–4.
2. Bushman, *Joseph Smith: Rough Stone Rolling*, 158.
3. See Quinn, *The Mormon Hierarchy*, 26.

and several offices such as priest and teacher.[1] The sacrament prayers and baptismal ritual were copied verbatim from the Book of Mormon and included in Cowdery's original draft.

The fundamentals of Church governance

In Doctrine and Covenants 18 the Lord assured Oliver that the fundamentals of Church government are to be found in the revelations given through the Prophet Joseph. (See verse 2–5.) Oliver Cowdery was counseled to rely upon these written revelations as a guide in the establishment of the restored Church (see verse 4) and was reminded that on many previous occasions it had been given to him to know that these revelations were right. (See D&C 6:22–23; 13:1; 17:1.)

Oliver Cowdery and David Whitmer called as was Paul

Oliver Cowdery and David Whitmer were commissioned, as was Paul the Apostle, to preach the gospel abroad. The reference to "apostle" in this context probably does not refer to the priesthood office but rather to the commission to preach and baptize.[2] Like Paul on the road to Damascus (Acts 26:13–14) the Three Witnesses had seen a heavenly being and heard a voice. David Whitmer commented that "[d]uring 1829, several times we were told by Brother Joseph that an elder [not an apostle] was the highest office in the church."[3]

Missionary work

In preparation for the organization of the Church, missionary work was emphasized. "The worth of souls is great in the sight of God" (verse 10) because Jesus "suffered death . . . that all men might repent and come unto him." (Verse 11.) Missionaries will find "joy" by bringing souls into the Church. The emphasis was shifting from a focus on a divine book—the Book of Mormon—to the establishment of an organization.[4]

---

1. Hubbard and Gerrit, *From Darkness unto Light: Joseph Smith's Translation and Publication of the Book of Mormon*,147.

2. Robinson and Garrett disagree, based on their position that the Melchizedek Priesthood was restored prior to the establishment of the Church. "This verse further reflects the fact that apostolic authority had already been given to Joseph, Oliver, and David at this time. June 1829." See Robinson and Garrett, *A Commentary on the Doctrine and Covenants*, 1:105.

3. Quinn, *The Mormon Hierarchy*, 11.

4. See Bushman, *Joseph Smith: Rough Stone Rolling*, 109–12.

Oliver Cowdery and David Whitmer told to search out twelve disciples to help govern and establish Church

Oliver Cowdery and David Whitmer were given the charge to search out "the Twelve" (verse 37), who are referred to as disciples (verse 27), to evangelize and help govern and establish the Church. (See verse 37, 27–32.) Since the Twelve would become known as "especial witnesses" (D&C 27:12), it was appropriate for two of the Three Witnesses to the Book of Mormon to search out the Twelve.[1] It took six years to implement this directive. The Twelve were officially organized in February 1835.[2]

However, to understand section 18 in context it must also be pointed out that the earliest use of the term "apostle" (1829–1833) did not refer to the "Quorum of the Twelve" as we understand it today. Rather the designation "apostle" was used loosely to refer variously to an elder, a missionary, or a visionary man.[3] (See D&C 18:9; 20:2, 38; 21:1, 10.)[4] This understanding is corroborated at the first general conference of the newly established Church held on June 9, 1830. John Whitmer's written license referred to him as an "Apostle of Jesus Christ, an Elder of this Church."[5] Based on this and other historical documents D. Michael Quinn suggests that the Three Witnesses may have been involved in the appointment of these early leaders, also referred to as "apostles," and later (1835) the organization of a formal governing body known as the Quorum of the Twelve. Consequently, the Three Witnesses may have once again "fulfilled the 1829 revelation to select 'twelve disciples'—but within a transformed context."[6]

---

1. Martin Harris is not mentioned probably because at this point he was under condemnation for his part in the loss of the first 116 pages of the Book of Mormon. (See D&C 19:15, 20.)

2. The Three Witnesses gave each member of the first Quorum of Twelve a blessing emphasizing the role of the Twelve in missionary work. Oliver Cowdery told them to "bid a long farewell to Kirtland . . . even till the great day come . . . till your heads are silvered over with age." (Bushman, *Joseph Smith: Rough Stone Rolling*, 255.) This was entirely consistent with the Twelve's original calling, which was to preside in areas of the Church where stakes had not yet been organized. Their responsibilities were later broadened to include the regulation of stakes as well.

3. "Charismatic apostleship (without ordination) reemerged prominently in 1833. Smith's description of twenty-four temples to comprise the temple complex of Zion in Independence, Missouri, included three temples designated for the 'Sacred Apostolic repository.' A clue to what Smith meant is in a revelation that same June 1833 concerning the temple at Kirtland: 'And let the higher part of the inner court be dedicated unto me for the school of mine apostles, saith Son Ahman' (D&C 95:17)." (See Quinn, *The Mormon Hierarchy: Origins of Power*.)

4. See Quinn, *The Mormon Hierarchy: Origins of Power*, 7–14.
5. See Quinn, *The Mormon Hierarchy: Origins of Power*, 12.
6. See Quinn, *The Mormon Hierarchy: Origins of Power*, 7–14.

Section 20: Whitmer Home, Fayette, New York, April 1830[1]

Heading

In the beginning, the Church to be organized with apostles, elders, priests, and teachers, who are to help the Saints perfect themselves.

The big questions

Question: Why a church?
Answer: The Church organization is established to encourage and provide opportunities for people to have faith, repent of their sins, be baptized, pattern their lives after Jesus, and become like him. (See verse 68–73.)

Question: What is the structure of the Church?
Answer: Elders, priests, and teachers were charged with special responsibilities to assist in the work of the Church. Elders were to meet in quarterly conferences "to do church business . . . whatsoever is necessary." Section 20 reflects the state of the organization at its inception. Over the next few years the Lord would continue to reveal his will concerning the organization of his Church. By 1835 the basic structure of the Church would be in place as set forth in section 107, which describes all of the governing quorums of the Church and explains their basic functions and relationships to each other.

Introduction

This revelation on Church organization and government was given through Joseph Smith the Prophet at the Whitmer home in Fayette, New York, in April 1830.[2] Preceding his record of this revelation the Prophet wrote: "We obtained of him [Jesus Christ] the following, by the spirit of prophecy and revelation; which not only gave us much information, but also pointed out to us the precise day upon which, according to his will and commandment, we should proceed to organize his Church once more upon the earth." (See heading to D&C 20.)

Anchor section

Memorize: Church organization and Aaronic Priesthood offices

---

[1] "Although the essentials of section 20 were written over the span of almost a year, we now know that the version found in the current printing of the Doctrine and Covenants was written April 10, 1830." (Woodford, "Discoveries from the Joseph Smith Papers Project," 29.)
[2] Smith, *History of the Church*, 1:64–70.

Historical background

In the beginning Joseph Smith's visionary experience of the Father and the Son in 1820 answered personal concerns he had about God and religion. Joseph did not go into the grove to establish a new Church but to seek forgiveness of his sins and to find out which of all the churches was correct. On both counts he was satisfied. His sins were forgiven him, and he was told that he should not associate with any of the churches in his day because all of them based their faith on "creeds" that "were an abomination in his [God's] sight." (JS–H 1:19.) As far as we know, no mention of Joseph restoring the true church was spoken about in the First Vision.

A few years after the First Vision, on September 21, 1823, Joseph was visited by the angel Moroni, who told him that it was God's will that he translate the gold plates that contained a history of some ancient civilizations that lived in the Western hemisphere. Again, to our knowledge no mention of establishing a new church was spoken about, and Joseph turned his attention to producing a book.

In 1828, when more and more people were becoming interested in Joseph's charismatic experiences and the book he had begun to translate, believers joined together in what could hardly be considered a religious organization, although by then it was understood that the Lord was about to "establish my church among them." (D&C 10:53.) However, the extent to which a formal organization was contemplated was not entirely clear to these early followers. "Behold this is my doctrine—whosoever repenteth and cometh unto me, the same is my church." (D&C 10:67.) Therefore, in 1828 Mormonism could be characterized more as a "gathering" than an organization.[1]

By mid-1829 the practice of baptism had begun. Dozens of new converts were baptized into a community of believers known as "the Church of Christ." The church had no formal organization. After the Book of Mormon was published, a Church with officers was formally established on April 6, 1830, according to divine instruction. In the remaining months "branches" were organized in Manchester, Colesville, and Fayette, New York.[2] It was just before the formal organization of the Church and during the latter part of 1829 that Oliver Cowdery was assigned the responsibility of drafting, under the spirit of revelation, what became known as section 20. The document was intended to be a summary of some basic doctrines and a set of operating instructions for the new Church.

---

1. See Quinn, *The Mormon Hierarchy: Origins of Power*, 6.
2. See Quinn, *The Mormon Hierarchy: Origins of Power*, 7.

What became known as "the Articles and Covenants of the Church of Christ" resembled both in form and language the confessions of faith, or creeds, of other Christian denominations. The document mentioned the fall of Adam, the nature of man, the atonement of Christ, resurrection, redemption, justification, and sanctification.[1] However, the doctrines set forth separated Mormonism from other religions. Infant baptism was rejected and Calvinist belief in predestination was rejected in favor of a theology that embraced "human freedom and responsibility."[2]

By November 1, 1831, when Section 1 was received to serve as the "preface" for the publication of the Book of Commandments (first Doctrine and Covenants), it was apparent that mission of the Church had already expanded to include preparations for the Second Coming. Church leaders were instructed to send out authorized disciples to be a "voice of warning" to a wicked world (Section 1: 4, 6, 14-16) in preparation for the day when peace would be taken from the earth (Section 1:13, 37-39). In the meantime, first generation Mormons were building the "foundation of this church" so that it could spread across the "whole earth" (Section 1:30). As time passed, the Church would continue to unfold in many unanticipated directions. By the time Joseph was martyred, the work of the Church would include new doctrines about multiple heavens, men and women being co-eternal with God, strange marriage practices, and temple covenants and rituals intended to save the living as well as the dead. (See Section 76; 93: 107; 124; 128; 138)

The physical location of the organization of the Church was, until recently, a matter of some dispute. Joseph Smith in his 1838 history said the Church was organized at the Whitmer house in Fayette. Later, in 1842, in a letter to John Wentworth, a Chicago newspaperman, Joseph said it was in Manchester. Some historians have suggested that the Fayette meeting came shortly after the organizational meeting in Manchester. However, the generally accepted view is that the Church was formally organized in Fayette.[3] This position was substantiated by the publication of the Joseph Smith Papers.[4]

Joseph's account of the meeting states that it was opened with "solemn prayer." Joseph then asked whether those present would accept him and Oliver as teachers and whether or not they wanted to organize. Unanimous approval was given, and Joseph ordained Oliver an elder and Oliver ordained Joseph an elder. A second revelation that followed section 20 further specified that Joseph should be referred to as the "first elder" and

---

1. Bushman, *Joseph Smith: Rough Stone Rolling*, 112.
2. Bushman, *Joseph Smith: Rough Stone Rolling*, 112.
3. See Bushman, *Joseph Smith: Rough Stone Rolling*, 109.
4. See www.ldschurchnews.com (May 22, 2009).

Oliver as the "second elder" in the Church organization. The group participated in the sacrament of the Lord's Supper. Some prophesied. Joseph gave instructions on how to build up the Church. Others were ordained to the priesthood. Following the organizational meeting, Joseph Smith Sr. was baptized in a small stream on Hyrum's farm. Martin Harris, Orrin Porter Rockwell, and Lucy Smith were also baptized.[1]

Section 20 was presented to the first conference of the Church on June 9, 1830. Read and adopted by the unanimous voice of the Saints, it was the first revelation of this dispensation to be canonized by the members of the Church.

Church organized with apostles, elders, priests, and teachers

****Initially the Church organization followed Book of Mormon lines: elders, priests, and teachers. The elders, an office not associated with the Aaronic or Melchizedek Priesthoods at this time, were to meet in quarterly conferences to conduct Church business. There was no provision for a professional ministry. The practice of ordaining every worthy male a minister was established at an early time. The custom of referring to Joseph and Oliver as the first and second elders was reinforced when in a revelation received by Joseph each was designated an "apostle." Since the organization of a Quorum of Twelve Apostles came later, in this context the term *apostle* probably meant that they were messengers and witnesses of Jesus. (See commentary on D&C 18.) By 1835 the Church organization would continue to be expanded into governing quorums, among them the First Presidency, Quorum of the Twelve, and Quorum of the Seventy. (See D&C 107.)

In June 1829 in Section 18 Oliver Cowdery had been commanded to "rely upon the things that are written ... for in them are all things ... for the foundation of my church." (Section 18:3-4) In response Cowdery examined Book of Mormon passages that Joseph had recently translated as source material for the "Articles of the Church of Christ" which later became Section 20 and was used as the first handbook of instructions for the church. The Articles set out the ritual of baptism, the sacrament prayers on the bread and the water and several offices such as priest and teacher.[2] The sacrament prayers and baptismal ritual were copied verbatim.

---

1. See Bushman, *Joseph Smith: Rough Stone Rolling*, 110.
2. Hubbard and Dirkmaat, *From Darkness unto Light: Joseph Smith's Translation and Publication of the Book of Mormon*, 147.

Joseph, a prophet and seer

Bushman points out that the most important title Joseph had was "seer, a translator, a prophet." The reference to Joseph as a "seer" and "translator" was an indication of his unique gift of being able to make known the meaning of ancient texts. (See D&C 21:1; 124:125; 127:12; 135:3.) No other Mormon leader has ever claimed this gift. It was an office and gift referred to in the Book of Mormon. Joseph's experience as a "seer" followed the pattern in Mosiah where Ammon was given twenty-four Jaredite plates, which were taken to the "king of the people who are in the land of Zarahemla" to be translated. The text makes it clear that "a seer is greater than a prophet" because "a seer can know of things which are past, and also of things which are to come, and by them shall all things be revealed." (See Mosiah 8:13–18; see also commentary on D&C 21.)

The title "prophet" encompassed Joseph's extraordinary ability to teach, foretell the future, see visions, and enjoy other gifts of the Spirit. At first, Joseph's influence was based primarily on these extraordinary spiritual gifts and powers. The people listened to his prophetic voice as he revealed God's will and wishes. "He governed through his power to speak for God."[1]

After the Church was organized, his influence grew because he was the leader of a dynamic organization that responded to his direction. By the time Joseph and the Mormons settled Nauvoo, Illinois, he was the president of a governing quorum of three, the highest authority in the Church. He was also mayor and commander of the Nauvoo Legion.

Retroactive changes in the Doctrine and Covenants

It was intended that the first edition of the Doctrine and Covenants (referred to as the Book of Commandments) be printed in 1833. The project was in process when in July 1833 a mob destroyed the press and scattered the manuscript. As a result, very few of these books are available today. Two years later (1835), Joseph Smith instructed the brethren to form a committee to publish an updated book of his revelations.

The second edition was significantly different from the book in process in 1833 in a number of respects. First, between 1833 and 1835 Joseph had received more revelations, some of which would be included in the 1835 edition. Second, Joseph's understanding had increased. As a result, he edited and added material to some of his earlier revelations. For example, by 1835 Joseph had more information about offices in the Melchizedek Priesthood. Consequently, he went back and referred to Melchizedek Priest-

---

1. See Bushman, *Joseph Smith: Rough Stone Rolling*, 111.

hood offices in section 20, which when first published only mentioned Aaronic Priesthood offices. Of particular interest was the inclusion of an additional Aaronic Priesthood office, that of deacon. (See D&C 20:57.) Information on the law of common consent was also incorporated. (See D&C 20:65.)

Although today the office of elder is thought of in connection with the Melchizedek Priesthood, this was not the case when the Church was organized in 1830. It was sometime later that the office of elder was designated part of the higher or Melchizedek Priesthood.[1]

Joseph Smith's view on creeds of Christendom

A creed is a statement that defines core beliefs of members of a religious organization. Derived from the Latin *credo*, meaning "I believe," it is an official confession of faith. Creeds are generally short, formal, authoritative statements setting forth main points of belief.[2] Confessions of faith during the first 150 years of the history of the Christian church were not fixed or formalized, although the wording for the ordinance of baptism and the Lord's Supper were most probably written down and repeated word for word from a very early date. The first evidence "for the employment" of "formulas" that "became fixed" is the "Apostles' Creed"—a set of questions asked of a candidate before baptism, evident in Rome at the beginning of the third century.[3]

Even though creeds were common during the time of Joseph Smith, his religious experience pointed him in an entirely different direction. His ministry was unique because his revelatory powers allowed him to commune with God directly and unequivocally. He accepted the notion that inquiry and thought often preceded communications from heaven

---

1. See Quinn, *The Mormon Hierarchy: Origins of Power*, 27–29.
2. See Ferguson, *Encyclopedia of Early Christianity*, 300–30.
3. Ferguson, *Encyclopedia of Early Christianity*, 301. It was also about this time that the early Christian church formulated its view of the Godhead when a council under the head of the Emperor Constantine adopted the Nicene Creed, which has become the most influential statement in Christendom on what God is. (See Ferguson, *Encyclopedia of Early Christianity*, 301.) Such creedal formulaic pronouncements grew out of disputes between various factions during the early development of Christianity. The Nicene Creed is a perfect example. Competing doctrines had arisen about Jesus' relationship to the Father and to what extent he was separate from the Father. The Nicene Creed represented a compromise position on these and other disputed issues of the day. The statement was seen as authoritative, partially because it had the backing of the Emperor Constantine, who was anxious to find a solution to the divisions over doctrine that had split Christianity into competing parts. Creeds therefore grew out of contentious debates on doctrines and deeply felt differences of opinion. Once the issues were settled in a written creed, the dispute was settled and the answer written in stone. The subject was closed and the solution was final. Those who agreed with the creed were considered orthodox and those that did not were excommunicated.

(D&C 9), but in the final analysis his experience led him to place his trust in direct revelation, not in councils, edicts, and creeds.

Revelation also led Joseph Smith to the conclusion that a full understanding of the gospel developed over time as more and more information from heaven was revealed. Joseph was fond of saying, "It is not all to be comprehended in this world."[1] Revelation came "line upon line," one concept at a time. Revelation was not a one-time event but a process that occurred over a lifetime. Therefore, the spirit of Mormonism was not one expressed in the cramped finality of creeds but rather was one of anxious exploration for further light and knowledge.

Section 20 was never meant to be a creed (meaning the final word). It was a reflection of the level of understanding members of the Church had in 1830. By 1835 the organizational structure of the Church had moved far beyond a list of Aaronic Priesthood offices and now included a description of five governing quorums with complementary yet different functions. (See D&C 107.) Earlier revelations had been supplemented by more instruction from heaven. It was for this reason that Joseph would feel free to go back and make additions and deletions to section 20 and some of his other earlier revelations. It was a way of providing further context and understanding of what the Lord intended.

The significance of April 6, 1830

Most members of the Church believe Jesus was born on the same date that the Church was officially organized. Support for this position is found in the observation that the Church was formed "one thousand eight hundred and thirty years since the coming of our Lord." (D&C 20:1.) Taken literally, such a statement fixes the birthday of the Savior on April 6. Some non-Mormon New Testament scholars would agree that Jesus was born in the spring of the year; some even pinpoint April. Those taking this position argue that the flocks pasturing at night, described at the time of Jesus' birth, suggests that the birth occurred in a warmer season, not in winter, when it was customary for animals to graze more during the day.[2]

Restoration of the Melchizedek Priesthood

As discussed earlier, there is some question among Mormon historians as to whether or not the Melchizedek Priesthood was restored prior to the

---

1. See Ehat and Cook, *Words of Joseph Smith,* 341, 350, 358.
2. It was not until much later that Roman Christians adopted December 25 as a time to celebrate the birth of Jesus. (See Keener, *The IVP Bible Background Commentary,* 194.)

organization of the Church. Robinson and Garrett and others point to the language in section 20 that asserts that Joseph Smith "was called of God, and ordained an apostle of Jesus Christ, to be the first elder of this church." (Verse 2.)[1] In any case, we do know that the Melchizedek Priesthood was restored by at least September 1830, based on the reference in Doctrine and Covenants 27:12 (a revelation dated August 1830) to the restoration of the Melchizedek Priesthood in the past tense. As stated earlier, the fact that Joseph is referred to in verse 2 as an elder is not necessarily an indication that he held the Melchizedek Priesthood because this office was at first associated with the Aaronic Priesthood.

Reference to the First Vision

The language, "After it was truly manifested unto this first elder that he had received a remission of his sins, he was entangled again in the vanities of the world," is probably a reference to the First Vision, in which Joseph Smith was specifically promised a remission of his sins. (See D&C 20:5 and commentary on the First Vision; see also JS–H 1:28–30.)

Fulness of the gospel

The term "fulness of the gospel" at this stage in the development of the Church is a reference to faith, repentance, baptism, and the gift of the Holy Ghost. (See D&C 27:5.) Obviously, much more would yet be revealed in the Dispensation of the Fulness of Times to the Prophet Joseph Smith. (See D&C 76, 93, 128, 131, 132, 138, etc.)

List of beliefs

Doctrine and Covenants 20:17–36 spells out a list of beliefs espoused by the Church. They are as follows:
 1. There is a God.
 2. God created men and women.
 3. God gave men and women a commandment that they should love others.
 4. Men and women are commanded to worship the only true God, not some other variation.
 5. Men and women become sensual and devilish and fallen by transgressing the laws of God. By implication, this means that prior to the Fall, men and women do not necessarily have evil dispositions but are basically good.

---

1. See Robinson and Garrett, *A Commentary on the Doctrine and Covenants*, 1:129.

6. Jesus' mission gives all men and women the opportunity to be saved provided they believe the prophets, repent of their sins, worship the Father in Jesus' name, and endure to the end.

7. Men and women are justified (or given the opportunity to be saved) through the Lord Jesus Christ.

8. Men and women are sanctified by living the gospel but may fall from grace.

The list is most notable for its rejection of predestination, punishment of mankind for Adam's sin, the idea that men and women are by nature sensual and devilish, and its emphasis on individual agency. The list reflects the doctrines that were important to the new Church as constituted at its inception in April 1830.

Jesus suffered temptation

Jesus "suffered temptations but gave no heed to them." (Verse 22; see also Hebrews 2:17–18; 4:15; Alma 7:11–12.)

Certificates and licenses

Section 20 refers to the issuing of "certificates" and "licenses" (verses 63–64). "Although the terms . . . were often used interchangeably," a certificate was used as commonly as a membership record is today.[1] A license, on the other hand, was issued to an office holder or missionary. In addition, sometimes certificates or licenses were required from a governmental entity before a minister could engage in missionary work. For example, it was necessary for Brigham Young to obtain a government-issued license before he could preach in Preston, England.[2]

The need to regulate who was and was not a member of the Church and who could or could not lead a branch of the Church was critical in situations where some Saints assumed privileges of leadership without permission, or even the knowledge, of Joseph and Oliver, the First and Second Elders of the Church. In the early days of the Restoration, and as missionaries preached in Ohio, branches of the Church and local leadership sprung up without the approval of the leaders of the Church. As George Ellsworth pointed out, licenses and certificates helped "transition from a freelance to an organized system."[3] Regulating the internal affairs

---

1. Cannon, "Licensing in the Early Church," *BYU Studies*, 22:1:99.
2. Ibid.
3. Ibid., 104.

of the Church made it possible for members to move from one branch to another and to identify themselves as bona fide members.[1]

Church handbook

Section 20 is a book of instructions for the new church and describes how the Church should operate and administer its ordinances. Baptism, the sacrament of the Lord's Supper, conference schedules, church licensure, the minimum age for baptism, and the blessing of children are all described.

SECTION 21: WHITMER HOME, FAYETTE, NEW YORK, APRIL 6, 1830

Heading

Leaders in the new Church appointed.

The big question

Question: What is the structure of the Church?
Answer: Joseph Smith is to head the Church as the "First Elder" and Oliver Cowdery is to be the "Second Elder" in the Church.

Introduction

This revelation was given to Joseph Smith the Prophet, at Fayette, New York, April 6, 1830, at the Whitmer home in Fayette, New York, at the conclusion of the official organization of the Church. About forty to fifty persons were present. By unanimous vote Joseph Smith and Oliver Cowdery were designated the presiding officers of the Church, to be referred to respectively as the "First" and "Second" elders. By the laying on of hands, Joseph ordained Oliver an "elder" and Oliver similarly ordained Joseph. After administration of the sacrament, Joseph and Oliver, by the laying on of hands, bestowed the Holy Ghost upon and confirmed some of those present who had been baptized. Robert Woodford describes section 21 as a revelation in which "the proceedings of the day were confirmed and further directions given."[2]

---

1. Ibid., 105.
2. See headnote to Section 21 and Woodford, *The Historical Development of the Doctrine and Covenants*, 352–53.

Historical background

Section 21 was received at the close of the official organizational meeting of the Church. On this occasion some in attendance were appointed to pray. Joseph and Oliver were sustained as teachers and leaders of the new Church. The sacrament of the Lord's Supper was administered and the gift of the Holy Ghost given to some who had previously been baptized.

Various accounts of the organization of the Church

Joseph Smith recounted:

> Whilst the Book of Mormon was in the hands of the printer, we still continued to bear testimony and give information, as far as we had opportunity; and also made known to our brethren that we had received a commandment to organize the Church; and accordingly we met together for that purpose, at the house of Mr. Peter Whitmer, Sen., (being six in number,)[1] on Tuesday, the sixth day of April, A.D., one thousand eight hundred and thirty. Having opened the meeting by solemn prayer to our Heavenly Father, we proceeded, according to previous commandment, to call on our brethren to know whether they accepted us as their teachers in the things of the Kingdom of God, and whether they were satisfied that we should proceed and be organized as a Church according to said commandment which we had received. To these several propositions they consented by a unanimous vote. I then laid my hands upon Oliver Cowdery, and ordained him an Elder . . . after which, he ordained me also to the office of an Elder. . . . We then took bread, blessed it, and brake it with them; also wine, blessed it, and drank it with them. We then laid our hands on each individual member of the Church present, that they might receive the gift of the Holy Ghost, and be confirmed members of the Church of Christ. The Holy Ghost was poured out upon us to a very great degree—some prophesied, whilst we all praised the Lord, and rejoiced

---

1. There were more than six present, but the laws of New York required six official organizers who are referred to by this reference. Robinson and Garrett explain that "it should be noted that there were more than six individuals present at this meeting. On 6 April 1830, there were believers in New York state—some of them already baptized but not confirmed—in Manchester/Palmyra, mainly Smiths; Fayette, mainly Whitmers; and Colesville, mainly Knights. Six of these signed the certificate of incorporation as responsible parties on 6 April, to satisfy New York state law. More than twenty individuals were actually present at the organization meeting, however, with some of these others also receiving confirmation into the Church. Thus, the number six does not represent the actual number of members confirmed on 6 April, but rather the number of members who signed the document as legal representatives of the Church to the state of New York." (See Robinson and Garrett, A Commentary on the Doctrine and Covenants, 1:148–49.) Other Mormon historians put the number of those present between forty to fifty, not twenty, as Robinson and Garrett suppose. (See, for example, Bushman, The Beginnings of Mormonism.)

exceedingly. Whilst yet together, I received the following commandment [D&C 21].[1]

Joseph Knight Sr. recorded:

Now in the Spring of 1830, I went with my team and took Joseph out to Manchester to his father. When we were on our way he told me that there must be a Church formed, but did not tell when.... On the sixth day of April 1830, he began the Church with six members and received the following revelation [D&C 21]. They all kneeled down and prayed, and Joseph gave them instructions how to build up the Church and exhorted them to be faithful in all things, for this is the work of God.[2]

Give heed to the words of Joseph Smith

In the beginning the Church was more of a collection of believers than an organized group. With a lack of structure the emphasis was on universal revelation, not charismatic leadership, although Joseph was certainly highly renowned for his spiritual powers and visionary gifts. As the Church was organized, emphasis was placed on Joseph Smith's role as the head of a society. "Wherefore, meaning the church, thou shalt give heed unto all his words and commandments ... as he receiveth them, walking in all holiness before me; for his word ye shall receive, as if from mine own mouth, in all patience and faith."[3] (Verses 4–5.) This put the spotlight on one man, Joseph. He would continue up until the organization of the First Presidency to govern the Church, assisted by Oliver Cowdery, the Second Elder. (See D&C 107:27–31.) By 1835 there was a shift in leadership emphasis from one individual to governing quorums. Instead of just one person being preeminent, all members of the First Presidency were "accounted as equal with thee [Joseph] in holding the keys of this last kingdom." (D&C 90:6; see also D&C 107:9–10, 21–22, 33, 65, 82, 91; 112:20, 30; 115:15; 124:84, 126.)

Joseph Smith a "translator"

Of all of Joseph Smith's responsibilities, his calling as "translator" was his most unique and defining characteristic as a prophet. (See verse 1.)

---

1. See Smith, History of the Church, 1:74–78.
2. See Robinson and Garrett, A Commentary on the Doctrine and Covenants, 1:148.
3. The unsurpassed place of Joseph in the new Church is emphasized again at the end of Section 21. The text makes it clear that Joseph is over Oliver, the "first unto you [Oliver], ... the first preacher of this church." (See verses 11–12.)

A translator, sometimes referred to as a seer, had the gift to reveal[1] the meaning of ancient texts. Joseph is the only prophet in our dispensation to exercise this gift, which produced the Book of Mormon, the Book of Moses, the Inspired Version of the King James Bible [now known as the Joseph Smith Translation or JST] and the Book of Abraham. (For a more complete discussion, see commentary on D&C 8 and 9.)

Oliver, mine apostle

Apostle in this context does not refer to membership in the Quorum of the Twelve, which is an ordained office within the Church. The Quorum of the Twelve was not organized until 1835. Rather, here it is a reference to Oliver as a *special witness* to some of the key events of the Restoration—the appearance of John the Baptist and the restoration of the Aaronic Priesthood, and the appearance of Peter, James, and John and the restoration of the higher priesthood.[2]

SECTION 28: WHITMER LOG HOME, FAYETTE, NEW YORK, SEPTEMBER 1830

Heading

Hiram Page received revelations through his seer stone, which revelations he falsely claimed should govern the Church.

Introduction

This revelation was given through Joseph Smith the Prophet to Oliver Cowdery at the Whitmer home in Fayette, New York, September 1830. Hiram Page, a member of the Church and one of the Eight Witnesses of the Book of Mormon, had a seer stone through which he professed to be receiving revelations for the entire Church. Several members, including Oliver Cowdery, had been deceived by these claims. Just prior to an appointed conference, Joseph inquired of the Lord concerning the matter and received section 28.

---

1. When Joseph Smith said he "translated" a document he did not mean that he studied out the ancient language and rendered it into English. Rather, he meant that God revealed to him the meaning of an ancient document. Sometimes Joseph had the actual text (for example, the gold plates) in his possession. On other occasions he did not (for example, the book of Moses).

2. Smith, *History of the Church*, 2:379–81.

The big question

Question: What is the structure of the Church?
Answer: The Lord clarifies that Joseph is the only person who may receive revelations for the *entire* Church.

Historical background

Between June 1829 and June 1830, the Smiths had been invited by the Whitmers to live with them in Fayette, New York, so that Joseph could escape persecution in Harmony, Pennsylvania, and find a more tranquil place to finish translating the Book of Mormon. By July 1830 Joseph had finished the translation, arranged for its publication, and organized the Church, and Joseph and Emma had returned to their home in Harmony. The Smiths undoubtedly had hoped that the ill feelings about Joseph Smith and the Mormons had subsided in their absence, but this was not the case. During July and August 1830 anti-Mormon sentiment grew in intensity, and once again Peter Whitmer Sr. intervened and invited the prophet and his wife to come to live with them again in Fayette.

When Joseph Smith arrived back again in Fayette he found that his authority as the First Elder in the Church was being challenged by Peter Whitmer Sr.'s son-in-law, Hiram Page, one of the Eight Witnesses of the Book of Mormon. Page, like Joseph, claimed to use a seer stone to receive revelation binding on all members of the Church.[1] At first, Joseph tried  to sidestep the issue. However, he changed his mind when he found out that his "second-in-command" (Second Elder) Oliver Cowdery and other prominent Mormons were taking Page's revelations seriously.

Newel Knight of Colesville, New York, one of the Prophet's long-time friends, had arranged his affairs to come to Fayette to see the Prophet. When he arrived, he found "Brother Joseph in great distress of mind on account of Hyrum Page who had managed to get up some dissention of feeling among the brethren by giving revelations concerning the govern-

---

1. Page's stone is now in the hands of the Community of Christ (formerly the Reorganized Church of Jesus Christ of Latter Day Saints), in their Department of History. It is described as a "flat stone about seven inches long, four wide, and one-quarter inch in thickness. It is dark gray in color with waves of brown and purple gracefully interwoven across the surface." The stone is further described as having a hole drilled through one end of it as if a string had been threaded through it." (See Woodford, *The Historical Development of the Doctrine and Covenants*, 406.) Whether the string was to hold the instrument around someone's neck or not is not entirely known. It was not uncommon for seer stones like Page's to have a hole in them, sometimes used as a peep hole through which the user would look and see a vision.

ment of the Church . . . which he claimed to have received through the medium of a stone he possessed."[1]

Joseph Smith, in an effort to establish his authority, inquired of the Lord as to what he should do. Section 28 was received shortly thereafter and just prior to a scheduled general conference of the Church. Page's stone and his purported revelations became an order of business at the conference. Joseph Knight reported that "after considerable investigation and discussion, Brother Page and all the members of the Church present renounced the stone, and the revelations connected with it."[2]

The situation was serious and had the potential to splinter the Church into independent authorities thinking they had the right to correct Joseph. This was not the first time that this issue had surfaced. Earlier, Oliver Cowdery had received the title of Second Elder (D&C 20) and as such he felt comfortable correcting Joseph's errors. While Joseph was working on a compilation of the revelations, Oliver wrote to him about what he considered a mistake in one of the revelations. The objectionable passage concerned qualifications for baptism. It required that members "truly manifest by their works that they have received of the Spirit of Christ unto a remission of their sins." Oliver may have felt that the condition of requiring people to show by their works their worthiness to be baptized verged dangerously close to the traditional Puritan practice of insisting on evidence of grace, which gave ministers great power over their congregations. Oliver wanted the language modified or taken out.[3] Joseph wrote back, asking Oliver by what authority he challenged the accuracy of the revelations. Realizing that such rival claims could lead to anarchy, Joseph even made a trip to Fayette, New York, to straighten the matter out face to face. When he arrived, he found that Oliver had convinced the entire Whitmer family of his point and Joseph was hard pressed to convince his followers that the language should be left in.[4] Later, upon Joseph's arrival in Fayette again in September, he found Oliver and the Whitmers studying Page's revelations. He interpreted this state of affairs as a challenge to his own authority as the leader of this new Church.[5]

---

1. See Woodford, *The Historical Development of the Doctrine and Covenants*, 404–5.
2. See Woodford, *The Historical Development of the Doctrine and Covenants*, 405.
3. See Bushman, *Joseph Smith: Rough Stone Rolling*, 120.
4. See Bushman, *Joseph Smith: Rough Stone Rolling*, 120.
5. Apparently, Page had a "roll of papers" full of revelations that had been revealed to him through the medium of his seer stone. Bushman points out that Joseph had put aside his seer stone after completing the Book of Mormon. David Whitmer, however, thought this a "big mistake" and believed that only the revelations received through seer stones were trustworthy. (See Bushman, *Joseph Smith: Rough Stone Rolling*, 120.) The fact that Page and others asserted themselves was not evidence of ill will toward the prophet. Prior to and after the formal organization of the Church, the driving principle of universal revelation meant

There is no doubt that Joseph was agitated over the situation. He was concerned that he would not be able to convince people to follow his lead, especially in light of his confrontation with Oliver and the Whitmers over certain language in one of his revelations. Newel Knight recorded that the evening before the conference Joseph spent "the greater part of the night" in "prayer and supplication." The next day Joseph raised the issue of leadership with those attending the conference and presented section 28 to them. With Oliver's support, Page's revelations were rejected by the voice of the conference and Joseph was recognized as the appropriate person "appointed . . . to receive and write revelations and commandments for this Church." As Bushman stated, "Charisma [spiritual gifts] was to be focused, not left free to run wild."[1] The conference spelled out Joseph's right to have the last word.

Joseph to receive commandments

Section 28 leaves no doubt that Joseph is "to receive commandments and revelations in this church" and "no one" else. (Verse 2.) However, this did not mean that others were to stop having personal revelations. Oliver is counseled: "If thou art led at any time by the Comforter to speak or teach . . . by the way of commandment unto the church, thou mayest do it" (see verse 4), but "thou shalt not write by way of commandment, but by wisdom; and thou shalt not command him who is at thy head, and at the head of the church." (Verses 5–6.) The distinction between speaking by way of commandment and writing by way of commandment is an interesting one. Section 28 made it clear that Oliver's revelations should not be put in writing. Then, when the time came to canonize certain revelations, only Joseph's, as the first elder, would be eligible. (See also commentary on section 21 about the changing nature of Joseph's role as a Church leader.)

---

that Joseph was not the only person privileged to receive the "mind and will of God." Sorting out which revelations would take precedence raised an important issue. Later in 1833 Joseph expressed the principle in this way, "I will inform you that it is contrary to the economy of God for any member of the Church, or any one, to receive instructions for those in authority, higher than themselves; therefore you will see the impropriety of giving heed to them; but if any person have a vision or visitation from a heavenly messenger, it must be for his own benefit and instruction; for the fundamental principles, government, and doctrine of the Church are vested in the keys of the kingdom." (See Smith, *Teachings of the Prophet Joseph Smith*, 21.)

1. See Bushman, *Joseph Smith: Rough Stone Rolling*, 121.

The land of Zion near the "borders by the Lamanites"

Identifying and establishing the land of Zion would soon become a major focus of the Church. In section 28 the Lord revealed the general vicinity of Zion: "It shall be on the borders by the Lamanites." (Verse 9.) At the time, this description would have located Zion somewhere on the western border of Missouri, which was considered the outermost edge of civilization. Later, in Doctrine and Covenants 84, Zion would be designated by the Lord with greater specificity. (See D&C 84:2–4; 52:3–8, 22–33; 56:5–7. For a discussion identifying the Lamanites, see commentary on D&C 30–31 and 32.)

Section 29: Whitmer Log Home, Fayette, New York, September 1830

Heading

A revelation on the signs preceding the Second Coming, and a discussion of various doctrinal matters: the resurrection and final judgment, the spiritual nature of all things, the premortal life of God's children, the fall and atonement, and little children's innocence and redemption through the Atonement.

The big question

Question: Why a church?
Answer: To prepare a people for the Second Coming of Jesus Christ.

Introduction

This revelation was given through Joseph the Prophet in the presence of six elders in the Whitmer log home at Fayette, New York, September 1830.[1] It was given some days prior to the September 26, 1830, conference. Instructions are given on various doctrines ranging from the signs and plagues preceding the Millennium to the innocence of little children before the Lord.

---

1. Smith, *History of the Church*, 1:111–15.

Historical background

By September 1830 Joseph and his family had moved from Harmony, Pennsylvania, back to Fayette, New York. (See commentary on D&C 28.) Section 29 came in anticipation of a scheduled general conference of the Church on September 26, 1830. At the conference Joseph was appointed as the person authorized to receive revelations for the Church.[1] The first conference of the Church, held just three months earlier, "had been the occasion of a Pentecostal outpouring of the Holy Spirit," and so the Saints looked forward to this conference with great anticipation.[2]

The establishment of a Church in preparation for the Second Coming

Section 29 raised the Saints' expectation that the Second Coming was near. "For the hour is nigh and the day soon at hand when the earth is ripe; and all the proud and they that do wickedly shall be as stubble; and I will burn them up, saith the Lord of Hosts, that wickedness shall not be upon the earth." (Verse 9.) The Saints were informed that the Church must be established so that the elect could be gathered together in order to escape the calamities that surely would come prior to Christ's second coming. "Wherefore the decree hath gone forth from the Father that they shall be gathered in unto one place upon the face of this land, to prepare their hearts and be prepared in all things against the day when tribulation and desolation are sent forth upon the wicked." (Verse 8.) Missionaries were called (verse 4) to gather "mine elect" and increase Church membership before the day of the Lord. (See verses 7, 11.)

Prior to the "great and dreadful day" (D&C 2:1) of the Second Coming, "the sun shall be darkened and the moon shall be turned into blood." (Verse 14.) Men and women will weep, and there shall be "a great hailstorm sent forth to destroy the crops of the earth." (Verse 16.) The Lord will "take vengeance upon the wicked," and "flies" will "eat their flesh, and shall cause maggots to come in upon them." (Verse 17–18.) The "abominable church" will be "cast down," and then the Lord will rule for a thousand years. (Verses 21, 11.)

---

1. See Preece, *Learning to Love the Doctrine and Covenants*, 55; and commentary to section 28.
2. See Smith and Sjodahl, *Doctrine and Covenants Commentary*, 145.

Doctrinal matters

Section 29 also taught some of the distinguishing doctrines of the new Church to those who had been called as missionaries. This section was revealed just after Joseph had received Moses 3–5.[1] Much of section 29 restates in shorthand fashion the doctrines of the earlier chapters in the book of Moses. For example, the statement that God's work has no end is explained in far more detail in the book of Moses. "Worlds without number have I created.... And as one earth shall pass away, and the heavens thereof even so shall another come; and there is no end to my works, neither to my words." (Moses 1:33, 38.) The concept in Doctrine and Covenants 29:31–32 of a spiritual creation preceding the temporal is also found in Moses 3:5. Information about the premortal life mentioned in Doctrine and Covenants 29:36–39 is described in more detail in Moses 4:1–4.

In section 29, predestination is rejected and the agency of man is taught. (See verses 36–39.) Also rejected is the idea that little children are tainted by Adam's sin as well as its logical corollary, the need for infant baptism. "Little children are redeemed from the foundation of the world through mine Only Begotten; wherefore, they cannot sin for power is not given unto Satan to tempt little children, until they begin to become accountable before me." (Verses 46–47.)

SECTIONS 30–31: WHITMER LOG HOME, FAYETTE, NEW YORK, SEPTEMBER 1830

Heading

David Whitmer, Peter Whitmer Jr., and John Whitmer called to preach to the Lamanites.

The big questions

Question: Who is a worthy vessel?
Answer: David Whitmer, although he is chastened by the Lord for his failure to serve diligently. (See D&C 30:1–2.)
Question: Why a church?
Answer: To preach the gospel.

---

1. Moses 3–5 was received while Joseph Smith was in Harmony, Pennsylvania, between June and August 1830.

Introduction

Section 30 is a revelation given through Joseph Smith the Prophet to David Whitmer, Peter Whitmer Jr., and John Whitmer in the Whitmer log home at Fayette, New York, September 1830. The revelation followed a three-day conference at Fayette.[1] Originally this material was published as three revelations, but it was combined into one section in the 1835 edition of the Doctrine and Covenants.

Section 31 is a revelation given through the Prophet Joseph Smith to Thomas B. Marsh after the conference in September 1830.[2] Thomas Marsh had been baptized earlier in the month and had been ordained an elder in the Church before this revelation was given.

Historical background

Section 30 contains words of correction and encouragement to Peter Whitmer's sons, David, Peter Jr., and John. Section 31 was intended to serve the same purpose for Thomas B. Marsh, who later became the president of the Quorum of the Twelve Apostles.[3]

Marsh responded favorably to the message that the church of the New Testament had been restored. He became acquainted with the Church when he moved from his home in Massachusetts to New York state, where he first heard about the Book of Mormon. In the fall of 1829 he went to Palmyra, visited the Grandin Press where the Book of Mormon was being published, and met Martin Harris. Marsh acquired early proof sheets of the book, consisting of sixteen pages. It was on this basis that he was converted and moved his entire family to the Palmyra area, where they stayed for a while with the Smiths. Marsh was baptized by David Whitmer in Cayuga Lake on September 3, 1830, and shortly thereafter ordained an elder by Oliver Cowdery.[4]

In section 30 David Whitmer is criticized for paying too much attention to "the things of the earth" and not enough to "your Maker, and the ministry." (Verse 1.) Furthermore, he had failed to give "heed unto my Spirit." (Verse 1.) He is commanded to "ponder upon the things which you have received." (Verse 3.) Like others before him who had allowed the temptations of the world to overtake them for a time, David is reassured that if he will repent he is still a worthy vessel and that the Lord has a

---

1. Smith, *History of the Church*, 1:115–16.
2. Smith, *History of the Church*, 1:115–17.
3. Marsh later apostatized from the Church in 1838. Eighteen years later he was rebaptized at Winter Quarters in Florence, Nebraska, and traveled to Utah.
4. See Robinson and Garrett, *A Commentary on the Doctrine and Covenants*, 1:214.

work for him to accomplish. "And you shall attend to the ministry in the church, and before the world, and in the regions round about." (Verse 4.)

A mission to the Lamanites

In the same section, Peter Whitmer Jr. is instructed to accompany Oliver Cowdery on a mission to the Lamanites and John Whitmer is called to preach the gospel. The reference to the Lamanites is no small matter. According to the Book of Mormon, conversion of the Lamanites was a sign of the times and a necessary prerequisite to the Second Coming. Bushman explained: "The general import of the Israel story was that the world had come to a turning point when the favor of God was shifting from one people to another. The Gentiles were falling, and forgotten Israel was being restored. The Gentiles must serve these lost ones, the outcasts, and then join them or lose their place in history."[1]

Although the Book of Mormon never mentions the word *Indian*, early Saints believed that the American Indians were these outcast remnants of the house of Israel.[2] Oliver Cowdery's and Peter Whitmer's call was looked upon by them as providential. They, along with others, would gather the American Indians into the fold so that they could be instrumental in establishing the modern-day Zion and eventually join the Saints in Jackson County, Missouri, in building the New Jerusalem. It was because of the Lamanites' favored position in world history that Joseph had called missionaries to preach to the American Indians. (See D&C 31–32.) Others had also been called for this purpose, among them Ziba Peterson and Parley

---

1. See Bushman, *Joseph Smith: Rough Stone Rolling*, 104.
2. How many of the Indians were or were not related to the Lamanites on the borders of the Western Reserve is not known. Most LDS scholars agree that the Lehites did not populate all of the Americas but lived and developed in a rather small geographical area somewhere in Central and or South America. There is an expanding appreciation that Lehi and his descendants were not alone in the Americas but rather a small incursion into larger, existing populations. This was a subject that occupied the attention of the Prophet Joseph, who assumed that some American Indians were descendants of Book of Mormon populations. Even Joseph Smith's best thinking on this subject seemed to expand and or change during his lifetime. Frederick G. Williams attributed a statement to the Prophet in which he said that it was his opinion that "Lehi and his company . . . landed on the continent of South America, in Chile, thirty degrees, south latitude." Williams later claimed that this statement was made to him by an angel rather than by Joseph. In any case, it seems as though the question of who the actual descendants of the Lamanites were was talked about and debated within the Church. In 1842, an editorial in the Church newspaper, the *Times and Seasons* (September 15, pages 921–22) said that "Lehi . . . landed a little south of the Isthmus of Darien [Panama]," a suggestion with which some mainstream Book of Mormon scholars such as John L. Sorenson might agree. This theory, of course, places the landing of Lehi and his party some 300 miles north of the point in Chile mentioned by Williams. (See Sorenson, *An Ancient American Setting for the Book of Mormon*, 1–2.) For a more complete discussion on this point see commentary on section 32.

P. Pratt. (See D&C 28:8; 30:5; 32:1–3.) These missionaries were instructed to travel to the "borders by the Lamanites," which was understood to be "between Missouri and the Indian territory to the west."[1] Converting the Indians and building New Jerusalem were all wrapped into one grand narrative. (See 2 Nephi 3:5–6, 23; 25:21; 26:14–16; Enos 1:13–18; W of M 1:6–8; D&C 3:16–20.)

The mission to the Lamanites was decidedly unsuccessful.[2] Government Indian agents were in control of the area where the Indians resided, and the missionaries sent to teach them had not obtained the required permit to enter Indian lands to teach the gospel. Government authorities immediately informed the missionaries that they were in violation of the law and ordered them to desist until they could secure permission from General William Clark, superintendent of Indian Affairs in St. Louis.[3] However, the mission to the Lamanites did create an awareness of how important the "remnants of Jacob" would be prior to the Second Coming. Just as important, many others heard the gospel as the band of missionaries preached along the way to the "borders of the Lamanites." Within weeks at least 127 persons had been converted. Prominent among these was Sidney Rigdon, who would later become a member of the First Presidency of the Church. Other converts included Isaac Morley, Levi Hancock, Lyman Wight, and John Murdock, all well-known residents of Kirtland, Ohio, who later would also play important roles in the Church. (See also commentary on D&C 32.)

Section 31 and Thomas B. Marsh's call to be a missionary

Section 31 tells Marsh to "lift up your heart and rejoice, for the hour of your mission is come; and your tongue shall be loosed, and you shall declare glad tidings of great joy unto this generation." (Verse 3.) The Lord then promises him success in his labors as a new missionary for the Church. (See verse 7.) He is told to declare the new truths that had been revealed to the Prophet Joseph. (See verse 4.)

---

1. See *Church History in the Fulness of Times*, 79; see also D&C 28:9.
2. See *Church History in the Fulness of Times*, 87.
3. See *Church History in the Fulness of Times*, 86.

Section 32: Whitmer Log Home, Fayette, New York, October 1830

Heading

Parley P. Pratt and Ziba Peterson called to preach to the Lamanites.

Introduction

This revelation was given through the Prophet Joseph to Parley P. Pratt, Oliver Cowdery, Peter Whitmer Jr., and Ziba Peterson at the Whitmer log home, Fayette, New York, in October 1830.[1] Great interest and desires were felt by the elders respecting the Lamanites, of whose predicted blessings—such as helping to build the New Jerusalem—the Church had learned from the Book of Mormon. (See 3 Nephi 20.) Supplication was made for the Lord to indicate his will concerning whether elders should be sent at that time to the Indian tribes in the West. This revelation followed.

Historical background

Ever since the publication of the Book of Mormon, members of the Church were interested in identifying people in the Americas who may be the remnant offspring of the Lamanites, the last generation of people talked about in the Book of Mormon.[2] In fact, one of the primary reasons for the coming forth of this ancient record was to bring the Lamanites to a knowledge of their forefathers and into the restored kingdom of God in preparation for the Second Coming of Christ and his thousand-year millennial reign. (See D&C 19:26–27.) From this perspective, it is not surprising that "within six months of the Church's organization, missionaries were sent to people thought to have Lamanite ancestry."[3] (D&C 28:8; 32:2.) Section 32 extends a mission call to two prominent members of the Church, Parley P. Pratt[4] and Ziba Peterson, to preach to the Lamanites.

---

1. See Smith, *History of the Church*, 1:118–20.
2. The term *Lamanites* appears in D&C 3:20; 10:48; 19:27; 28:8–9; 30:6; 49:24; 54:8.
3. *Encyclopedia of Mormonism*, 805.
4. Parley P. Pratt, a burly young man who was six feet tall with deep eyes and a strong-set jaw, would become one of Mormonism's most ardent advocates. Prior to his conversion he was a devoted Baptist who joined with Sidney Rigdon and the Campbellites. He married Thankful Halsey, a widow ten years his senior, and they moved to the Cleveland, Ohio, area. On a visit to New York to visit relatives he heard about the Book of Mormon and decided that he should go to Palmyra to investigate the matter further. Thereafter, he became a convert to Mormonism. His enthusiasm for his newfound religion prompted him to "preach the gospel" to his relatives, but the only convert he made among them was his younger, nineteen-year-old brother, Orson Pratt, a person of slight build, a sensitive face, and large, gentle eyes. Parley

Prior to that time two other well-known figures, Oliver Cowdery and Peter Whitmer Jr., had received similar calls. (See D&C 28:8–10; 30:5–6.)

Although missionary efforts to the Lamanites proved unsuccessful,[1] these labors turned out to be exceptionally important in the development of the Church. On the way to Missouri, the band of missionaries stopped in Mentor, Ohio, near Kirtland, and visited Parley P. Pratt's friend and mentor, a Campbellite minister by the name of Sidney Rigdon. Within a short time Sidney Rigdon, Edward Partridge,[2] Frederick G. Williams, and over 120 of Rigdon's congregation were converted to Mormonism, doubling the population of the Church.[3] Rigdon and Williams went on to become members of the First Presidency, and Partridge became the first Presiding Bishop of the Church.

The result of these conversions was that the Church included more members in and around the Kirtland, Ohio, area than in any of the other places where Mormonism's first converts had been made—New York and the northern Pennsylvania area. Therefore, it made sense when, just a few months later, in December 1830, Joseph received a revelation commanding all the Saints in the East to gather with the Saints in the Kirtland region. (See D&C 37.) In Kirtland, under one "roof," the Prophet could exert direct and daily influence over his followers and thereby fortify the fledgling Church.

---

and his brother Orson went to Fayette for the September 1830 conference, at which the Prophet Joseph called Parley Pratt as a missionary to the Lamanites.

1. Although the group labored with the Indians, they did not show much interest, and U.S. Indian agents told the Mormons that it was against the law to preach to them, so the Mormon missionaries headed back to Fayette.

2. Sidney Rigdon told Edward Partridge, a friend and fellow Campbellite, about his recent conversion to Mormonism. Partridge was a hatter about Sidney's age. Partridge was skeptical but agreed to go with Sidney Rigdon to meet the Prophet Joseph. Both joined the Church.

3. When Parley P. Pratt arrived in Ohio, he sought out Sidney Rigdon to tell him of his newfound religion. Rigdon was a tall man of thirty-seven years. He was well educated and a self-assured religious leader of the Campbellites. He preached in Mentor, not far from Kirtland. He was a thorough student of the Bible and proficient in history and English grammar. He had studied theology under a Baptist minister, got a license and was a preacher of remarkable eloquence. Parley P. Pratt gave Rigdon a Book of Mormon. At first he was put off by it, but was persuaded that a person of Joseph's background and education could not have written it. He was converted, left his congregation, gave up a house that his congregation had built for him, and became one of Mormonism's three most important leaders along with Joseph and Oliver Cowdery.

Who are the Lamanites?

Joseph Smith assumed that at least some of the Lamanites could be found among the Indian tribes located on the Western Reserve, an area near Independence, Missouri.[1] Joseph Smith's expectation that these Indians were in fact related in some way to Book of Mormon peoples changed.[2] As time passed the Prophet considered the possibility that the remnant of the Lamanites might also be located in South America as well. In 1841 the Prophet suggested that newly discovered temples in Mesoamerica were the work of Book of Mormon peoples.[3] Frederick G. Williams reported that Joseph said that "Lehi and his company . . . landed on the continent of South America, in Chile, thirty degrees, south latitude." Some time later, however, in the *Times and Seasons*, an early Church publication for which the Prophet assumed editorial responsibility, an article appeared asserting that "Lehi . . . landed a little south of the Isthmus of Darien (Panama)." This location is three thousand miles north of the point in Chile. Varying statements on this topic indicate that Joseph's ideas about the location of Book of Mormon peoples and their descendants was not settled.[4]

The assumption that some of the Indians who lived on the Western Reserve were Lamanites becomes more plausible, however, if one carefully defines the term and how it is used in the Doctrine and Covenants. It is important to take into consideration that the term *Lamanite* was used in a number of different ways in the Book of Mormon. Initially this designation was used narrowly to refer to the direct descendants of Laman and Lemuel. Nevertheless, within two or three generations the term was used less genealogically and designated a religious/political faction that opposed the Nephites and the church of Christ. After Jesus' appearance to the Book of Mormon people, Lamanites were a mixture of the descendants of Lehi, Ishmael, Zoram, Mulek, and perhaps some Jaredites. Furthermore, as Jeffery Meldrum and Trent D. Stephens suggest, "From the point of view of the Nephite record keepers and defenders of the Christian faith these dissenters [Lamanites] would likely encompass any [other] indigenous populations[5] that were not counted among members of church of Christ or that did not demonstrate allegiance to the Nephite system of government.

---

1. See Smith, *Teachings of the Prophet Joseph Smith*, 17, 92–93.

2. It is accepted by most anthropologists that the ancestors of American Indians are not of Near Eastern descent but are of Asian background, coming to America by way of the Behring Straits. This does not preclude other ancestral origins.

3. See Jessee, *Personal Writings of Joseph Smith*, 501–2.

4. See Sorenson, *An Ancient American Setting for the Book of Mormon*, 1–5.

5. It is generally accepted by Book of Mormon scholars that a careful reading indicates Nephi and his family eventually came into contact with indigenous peoples in the New World. (See Sorenson, *The Book of Mormon in an Ancient American Setting*; and Meldrum and Stephens, *Who Are the Children of Lehi?*)

This 'them-versus-us' concept is somewhat like the monikers of 'Jew and Gentile.'"[1] That this much more inclusive definition of the term *Lamanite* is the preferred usage in the Doctrine and Covenants is supported by section 10, which explains that the Book of Mormon is to come forth to convert the "Lamanites, and also all that had become Lamanites because of their dissensions." (Verse 48.) This broad understanding of the term could have easily applied to some of the Indians on the Western Reserve, regardless of their genealogical connections.

Section 33: Whitmer Log Home, Fayette, New York, October 1830

Heading

Ezra Thayre and Northrop Sweet called as missionaries.

The big question

Question: What is the structure of the Church?
Answer: Members are called to be missionaries and to build up the Church in preparation for the Second Coming.

Introduction

This revelation was given through Joseph to Ezra Thayre and Northrop Sweet in Fayette, New York, in October 1830.[2] The Lord is ready to instruct those who seek in faith. Laborers are called to declare the gospel in the eleventh hour. The Church is established and the elect are to be gathered. Prepare for the Second Coming.

---

1. See Meldrum and Stephens, *Who Are the Children of Lehi?* 18.
2. Smith, *History of the Church*, 1:126–27.

Historical background

Ezra Thayre and Northrop Sweet were members of the Church living in Palmyra, New York. Desirous to know what the Lord expected of them, they consulted the Prophet, who was living in Fayette, New York. Joseph inquired of the Lord and received section 33.[1] The revelation instructs Thayre and Sweet to build up and establish the Church, preach the gospel, and gather the elect in preparation for the Second Coming.[2]

Ezra Thayre was born in October 1791 in Randolph, Vermont. Hyrum Smith introduced the gospel to him and provided him with a Book of Mormon. Thayre recorded:

> When Hyrum began to speak, every word touched me to the inmost soul. I thought every word was pointed to me.... The tears rolled down my cheeks.... When Hyrum got through, he picked up a book and said, "Here is the book of Mormon." I said, "Let me see it." I then opened the book, and I received a shock with such exquisite joy that no pen can write and no tongue can express. I shut the book and said, "What is the price of it?" "Fourteen shillings," was the reply. I said, "I'll take the book." I opened it again, and I felt a double portion of the Spirit, that I did not know whether I was in the world or not. I felt as though I was truly in heaven.[3]

Thayre was baptized by Parley P. Pratt in 1830. He experienced opposition from friends and family and was reassured of the truth of Mormonism by the appearance of an angel.[4]

Northrop Sweet was a farmer living in the Palmyra area. Parley P. Pratt baptized him in October 1830; he was ordained an elder in June 1831 and moved to Kirtland. There he claimed to have received a revelation to start a new church along with Wycom Clark and four others, which

---

1. See Smith, *History of the Church*, 1:126.
2. Thayre acted upon the revelation and en route from New York to Ohio he preached at several homes and baptized a number of people into the Church. See Black, *Who's Who in the Doctrine and Covenants*, 319.
3. See Black, Who's Who in the Doctrine and Covenants, 319.
4. See Black, *Who's Who in the Doctrine and Covenants*, 319. Thayre remained faithful to the main body of the Church until after the Martyrdom, when he refused to follow Brigham Young and the Twelve to the Great Basin. He later affiliated with the Reorganized Church of Jesus Christ of Latter Day Saints. Prior to his apostasy he was deeply involved in the Church. He was ordained a high priest and thereafter called to go on a proselytizing mission with Thomas B. Marsh (see D&C 52:22), but he failed to serve for financial reasons. The Lord rebuked Thayre for sins of pride and selfishness. (See D&C 56:5, 8–10.) Thayre repented and another call to serve with Marsh was extended. (See D&C 75:31.) Thayre volunteered to march with Zion's Camp. When the horses became ill, he concocted a home remedy called his "18x24," and the animals recovered after taking it. When the camp arrived at Fishing River on June 22 1834, Thayre, along with several others, fell ill with cholera. He went to the river and dipped himself in it and finding that it helped continued until well again. (See Black, *Who's Who in the Doctrine and Covenants*, 320.)

they called The Pure Church of Christ. The name of the Church implies that they felt that Joseph was teaching doctrines that went beyond those "pure" doctrines found in the New Testament.[1] The denomination died out and Sweet left Kirtland in about 1834.[2]

Open your ears and mouths

Both Thayre and Sweet are admonished to "open [their] ears and hearken to the voice of the Lord [their] God" and then to "open [their] mouths" as missionaries. (Verses 1, 8–9.) They were promised that if they were faithful they would become like "Nephi of old, who journeyed from Jerusalem in the wilderness." (Verse 8.) Missionary opportunities were described as a "field . . . white already to harvest." (Verse 3.) However, there would be obstacles. The "vineyard has become corrupted . . . and there is none which doeth good save it be a few; and they err in many instances because of priestcrafts, all having corrupt minds." (Verse 4.)

SECTION 34: WHITMER LOG HOME, FAYETTE, NEW YORK, NOVEMBER 4, 1830

Heading

Orson Pratt baptized and called as a missionary to preach the gospel in preparation for the Second Coming of Christ.

Introduction

This revelation was given through Joseph Smith the Prophet to Orson Pratt in the Whitmer log home at Fayette, New York, on November 4, 1830.[3] Brother Pratt was nineteen years old at the time. He had been

---

1. Over time, as the Church developed and Joseph was given further revelations, Sweet was not alone in his concerns that what had started out to be a simple gospel had become more complicated and moved beyond the confines of the New Testament. Perhaps he was fortified in his belief by the simple and straightforward description of the gospel in this revelation to him. "Yea, open your mouths and they shall be filled, saying: Repent, repent, and prepare ye the way of the Lord, and make his paths straight; for the kingdom of heaven is at hand; Yea, repent and be baptized every one of you, for a remission of your sins; yea be baptized even by water, and then cometh the baptism of fire and of the Holy Ghost. Behold, verily, verily, I say unto you, *this is my gospel;* . . . and upon this rock I will build my church." (D&C 33:10–13; emphasis added.)

2. See McCune, *Personalities in the Doctrine and Covenants,* 135–38; Black, *Who's Who in the Doctrine and Covenants,* 310–11.

3. Smith, *History of the Church,* 1:127–28.

converted and baptized when he first heard about the restored gospel from his older brother, Parley P. Pratt, six weeks before.

The big question

Question: Why a church?
Answer: To preach the gospel in preparation for the Second Coming.

Historical background

In autumn 1829 Orson Pratt became very concerned about God and religion and began to pray fervently. He recorded that at night he would often retire to a solitary place and pray for hours, his greatest desire at the time being that the Lord manifest his will concerning him. In September 1830 his older brother Parley P. Pratt and another elder came into the area preaching the gospel. Orson was impressed and was "convinced of the divine authenticity of the doctrine they taught"[1] and was baptized on September 19, 1830. In October he traveled westward over two hundred miles to meet the Prophet Joseph Smith in Fayette, New York, and became intimately acquainted with him. On November 4, 1830, Orson asked the Prophet to inquire of the Lord on his behalf, and section 34 was given.

Section 34 commends Orson for his belief and calls him to preach the gospel. (See verses 4–5.) His ministry is to help prepare the way for the Second Coming of Christ. (See verse 6.) He is to teach and prophesy by the power of the Holy Ghost. (See verse 10.)

Sections 35–36: Fayette, New York, December 1830[2]

Heading

Sidney Rigdon called to assist Joseph Smith as his scribe as Joseph continued his revision of the King James Bible. Rigdon and Edward Partridge called to do missionary work.

---

1. See McConkie and Ostler, *Revelations of the Restoration*, 259.
2. We now know that Sections 35 and 36 were received December 9, 1830. See Woodford, "Discoveries from the Joseph Smith Papers Project," 29.

The big question

Question: Why a church?
Answer: To preach the gospel, baptize, and confer the gift of the Holy Ghost.

Introduction

Section 35 was given to Joseph Smith on behalf of Sidney Rigdon at or near Fayette, New York, in December 1830. As a preface to his record of this revelation the Prophet wrote: "In December Sidney Rigdon came [from Ohio] to inquire of the Lord, and with him came Edward Partridge.... Shortly after the arrival of these two brethren, thus spake the Lord."[1] Rigdon was instructed to baptize and confer the Holy Ghost.

Section 36 was given through Joseph Smith the Prophet to Edward Partridge, near Fayette, New York, in the same month, December 1830.[2] Edward Partridge is called "a pattern of piety, and one of the Lord's great men." Partridge is told that every man who receives the gospel and the priesthood should be called to go forth and preach the gospel.

Historical background

Sidney Rigdon became converted and was baptized when he encountered his old friend Parley P. Pratt, who was headed west to preach the gospel to the Lamanites. Rigdon expressed his enthusiasm for his newfound religion to Edward Partridge[3] and invited him travel to Fayette, New York, with him to meet Joseph Smith.[4] Upon their arrival they sought

---

1. Smith, *History of the Church*, 1:128–31.
2. Smith, *History of the Church*, 1:131.
3. Edward Partridge was from nearby Painesville, Ohio.
4. Regarding Partridge's visit to New York, Lucy Mack Smith recorded: "In December of the same year [1830], Joseph appointed a meeting at our house. While he was preaching, Sidney Rigdon and Edward Partridge came in and seated themselves in the congregation. When Joseph had finished his discourse, he gave all who had any remarks to make, the privilege of speaking. Upon this, Mr. Partridge arose, and stated that he had been to Manchester, with the view of obtaining further information respecting the doctrine which we preached; but, not finding us, he had made some inquiry of our neighbors concerning our characters, which they stated had been unimpeachable, until Joseph deceived us relative to the Book of Mormon. He also said that he had walked over our farm, and observed the good order and industry which it exhibited; and, having seen what we had sacrificed for the sake of our faith, and having heard that our veracity was not questioned upon any other point than that of our religion, he believed our testimony, and was ready to be baptized, 'if,' said he, 'Brother Joseph will baptize me.' 'You are now,' replied Joseph, 'much fatigued, brother Partridge, and you had better rest to-day, and be baptized tomorrow.' 'Just as Brother Joseph thinks best,' replied Mr. Partridge, 'I am ready at any time.' He was accordingly baptized the next day." (See Robinson and Garrett, *A Commentary on the Doctrine and Covenants*, 1:245–46.)

guidance from the Prophet, who received sections 35 and 36. Partridge was baptized on December 11, 1830.

At this time the Prophet was engaged almost daily in revising the King James Bible through the spirit of revelation. The process, which Joseph referred to as a "translation," began as early as June 1830, and both Oliver Cowdery and John Whitmer had served as scribes. Both of these men had recently been called to preach to the Lamanites. (See D&C 28:8; 30:9–11.) Therefore, the Lord called Sidney Rigdon to serve as Joseph's scribe. (D&C 35:20.)

Inspired Version of the Bible or Joseph Smith Translation (JST)

The Lord had commanded Joseph Smith to study the Bible and make inspired changes. The end product of this project is known as the Inspired Version or Joseph Smith Translation of the Bible.[1] Although members of the Church refer to this work as a "translation," to do so is somewhat misleading. Joseph was not translating in the sense that he rendered an English version of the Bible from some Greek or Hebrew manuscripts. Rather, he studied the text and made inspired interpolations.[2]

The very idea that Joseph could read the Bible and make additions and deletions demonstrates that he did not believe that the Old and New testaments were inerrant. It was always his understanding that the Bible was the word of God only insofar as it was "translated correctly." (A of F 8.) He explained: "I believe the Bible as it read when it came from the pen of the original writers. Ignorant translators, careless transcribers, or designing and corrupt priests have committed many errors."[3] Joseph thought "it was apparent that many points touching the salvation of men, had been taken from the Bible, or lost before it was compiled."[4]

Rigdon given authority to confer gift of the Holy Ghost

Before Sidney Rigdon's conversion to the Church, he had been a preacher in the Reformed Baptist movement in the Kirtland area. When he formed a communal order called "the Family" in August 1830, it caused a break with

---

1. Joseph's study of the Bible raised many theological questions, which prompted him to inquire of the Lord. Some of the most important revelations in the Doctrine and Covenants came in answer to questions raised as Joseph carefully studied the Bible text. See Section 76 for example.

2. The Inspired Version of the Bible differs from the King James Version in at least 3,410 verses and consists of additions, deletions, and rearrangements. Sometimes changes are minor and at other times entire chapters are added or reconstructed.

3. Smith, *Teachings of the Prophet Joseph Smith*, 327.

4. Smith, *Teachings of the Prophet Joseph Smith*, 9–11.

the Reformed Baptist movement sponsored by well-known primitivist[1] preacher Alexander Campbell. The Lord comments on Rigdon's previous experience as a minister of the gospel: "Thou didst baptize by water unto repentance, but they received not the Holy Ghost; but now I give unto thee a commandment, that thou shalt baptize by water, and they shall receive the Holy Ghost by the laying on of the hands, even as the apostles of old." (D&C 35:5–6.) Even though Rigdon had preached as a Protestant minister and prepared many people to come into the restored gospel (D&C 35:3–4), it was now necessary for him to be given proper authority to bestow the Holy Ghost with God's full approval.

Section 37: Fayette, New York, December 1830

Heading

Members of the Church are called to gather in Ohio.

Introduction

This revelation was given to Joseph Smith the Prophet and Sidney Rigdon near Fayette, New York, December 1830.[2] Members of the Church are instructed to gather in Ohio.

The big question

Question: What is the structure of the Church?
Answer: A united group of believers who congregate together in "gathering places."

Historical background

Section 37 commands members of the Church to gather together in one place—the Kirtland, Ohio, area. The headquarters of the Church would be established there for several years, and it would become a place of refuge and mutual protection. The move would also centralize Joseph's authority. Before this, members were isolated from one another and lived in various communities in the state of New York, primarily in the Palmyra/Manchester area, Colesville, and Fayette, New York. Without

---

1. A "primitivist" at the time of Joseph Smith was a person who believed in the importance of living by the tenets of Christianity as the religion was originally formulated by Jesus and first-generation Christians.
2. Smith, *History of the Church*, 1:139.

modern communication devices, the distance between these locations made it difficult, if not impossible, for Joseph to directly influence the affairs of the disparate branches. As a result, local leaders had wide discretion and sometimes instituted policies that Joseph felt were inconsistent with his revelations. In some cases, local leaders claimed inspiration from God that contradicted what Joseph intended. The move to Kirtland would allow him to live and work in close proximity with his followers. He could come to know the few hundred faithful on a personal basis. Living together in one place would unify God's people and help put a stop to any divisions in policy or doctrine.

The gathering to the Kirtland area also made sense from a practical point of view. At this time there were only about seventy members of the Church in New York and, due to the success of the missionaries to the Lamanites, three times as many living in and around Kirtland. Directing the eastern members to go west meant that the fewest number of members would be inconvenienced by such a move.

The Kirtland area, however, would be only a temporary gathering place. When the Saints began to arrive in May 1831, Joseph received a revelation informing him that Ohio would be a gathering place only "for a little season." (D&C 51:16.) Just two months later, in July 1831, it was revealed that Jackson County, Missouri, had been "appointed and consecrated for the gathering of the saints." (D&C 57:1–3.) Jackson County was to be the place of the literal gathering of Israel, the New Jerusalem, Zion, a place where Jesus would come at his Second Coming. (See 3 Nephi 20:22; Ether 13:3.) Consequently, Joseph gave permission for some living in the Kirtland area to relocate in Jackson County. For the next seven years there would be two gathering places.

Bible translation stopped for a time

In early December 1830, Sidney Rigdon was commanded to act as scribe to record Joseph's inspired changes to the Old and New Testaments, known as the Inspired Version of the Bible or the Joseph Smith Translation. From that point on, opposition to the Church increased in Colesville and Fayette, New York. (See D&C 37:1; 38:13, 28–29.) Such pressing concerns made it necessary to cease translation on the Bible for a period of time while the Prophet devoted all of his time to strengthening the Church.[1]

---

1. It is also interesting to note that at this time in Church history there was "much conjecture and conversation . . . concerning the books mentioned, and referred to, in various places in the Old and New Testaments, which were now nowhere to be found." (See Smith, *History of the Church*, 1:132–39.) For example, the book of Jude refers to the words of Enoch, the seventh from Adam, but Enoch's words are not found in the Bible. The Saints referred to

Section 38: Whitney Log Home, Fayette, New York, January 2, 1831

Heading

Conference of the Church.

The big question

Question: Why a church?
Answer: To prepare for the Second Coming and to organize a Zion-like people with no poor among them.

Introduction

This revelation was given through Joseph Smith the Prophet, in the Whitney home, at Fayette, New York, January 2, 1831.[1] The occasion was a conference of the Church. Section 38 affirms that Jesus Christ created all things and counsels members of the Church to esteem each other as brothers and sisters. Wars are predicted. The gospel will be preached among all nations. The Church is commanded to care for the poor and needy.

Historical background

During December 1830 Joseph Smith and Sidney Rigdon were recording inspired revisions to the book of Genesis. At this time Joseph received a revelation restoring information about Enoch's Zion society contained in an ancient lost book, the book of Moses (now Moses 6–7 in the Pearl of Great Price). During the same month, Joseph received section 37, which commanded the Saints in the East to leave their homes and gather to the Kirtland, Ohio, area to establish their own Zion-like community.

In early January 1831 a conference of the Church was held in Fayette, New York. The Saints were anxious to learn more concerning the "gathering" to Ohio. In response, and in the presence of the congregation, Joseph dictated section 38 under the spirit of revelation.[2] No minutes of the meeting were kept. However, Joseph said of this occasion, "The year 1831

---

such books as the "lost books." Much to the delight of Joseph Smith's followers, as part of the revisions and additions to the Old and New Testaments in December 1830, Sidney Rigdon had written down the Prophet's dictation of the words of Enoch which is now chapter 7 of Moses in the Pearl of Great Price.

1. Smith, *History of the Church*, 1:140–43.
2. See Woodford, *The Historical Development of the Doctrine and Covenants*, 491.

opened with a prospect great and glorious for the welfare of the kingdom; for . . . a conference was held . . . at which the ordinary business of the Church was transacted; and in addition, the following revelation [D&C 38] was received."[1] At this conference members were once again instructed to gather in Ohio.[2]

Most of those who attended the conference were spiritually fed. John Whitmer said of this gathering that "the solemnities of eternity rested on the congregation."[3] However, some members of the Church were not convinced and claimed that Joseph had "invented" this revelation "to deceive the people" in order to financially benefit himself.[4] Most of the members did not feel this way. They believed that "the Lord had manifested his will to the people" and began making preparations to move to Ohio.[5]

The exodus to Ohio involved sacrifice of property and physical hardship. After the conference closed, Newel Knight made a diary entry that was typical: "Having returned home (Colesville) from the conference (held at Fayette . . .) in obedience to the commandment which had been given, I, together with the Colesville Branch, began to make preparations to go to Ohio. . . . As might be expected, we were obliged to make great sacrifices of our property."[6]

To complicate matters, the winter of 1830–31 was one of the most severe recorded in the eastern states.[7] Four feet of snow remained on the ground through February. The Saints recorded that freezing rains in January enabled wolves to run on the crust of the snow, while heavier game were entrapped and unable to escape predators. Newspaper publications were suspended when the mail could no longer be delivered.[8]

Like some of Joseph's earlier revelations (D&C 29 and 33), the gathering described in section 38 was in anticipation of the Second Coming of Christ: "The day soon cometh that ye shall see me." (Verse 8.) Because of these revelations, the Saints expected to see, within a reasonably short period of time, the pestilences described in the Bible and Book of Mormon, as well as those explicitly described in section 29—flies, maggots, signs in heavens, hailstorms, and devouring fire. (See D&C 29:14–21.) In light of such looming catastrophes, the Saints were motivated to gather together in one place for refuge against the predicted upheavals. "But if ye are

---

1. See Woodford, *The Historical Development of the Doctrine and Covenants*, 490.
2. See Robinson and Garrett, *A Commentary on the Doctrine and Covenants*, 1:255.
3. See Woodford, *The Historical Development of the Doctrine and Covenants*, 491.
4. See Woodford, *The Historical Development of the Doctrine and Covenants*, 491.
5. See Woodford, *The Historical Development of the Doctrine and Covenants*, 491.
6. See Woodford, *The Historical Development of the Doctrine and Covenants*, 492.
7. See Preece, *Learning to Love the Doctrine and Covenants*, 69.
8. See Newell and Avery, *Mormon Enigma: Emma Hale Smith*, 37; and Preece, *Learning to Love the Doctrine and Covenants*, 69.

prepared ye shall not fear.... That ye might escape ... —wherefore, for this cause ... ye should go to the Ohio."[1] (D&C 38:30–31.)

No poor in Zion

The move to Ohio also gave the Saints an opportunity to further implement the ideal Christian society and government of God on earth.[2] At this place the Saints would hear the voice of the Lord and "have no laws but my laws when I come, for I am your lawgiver, and what can stay my hand?" (Verse 22.) The poor would be cared for in a manner similar to the ideal community that had recently been described by the Prophet Joseph in the book of Enoch in the Pearl of Great Price. "And the Lord called his people ZION, because ... there was no poor among them." (Moses 7:18.) Likewise, in the Zion at Ohio every member was to "esteem his brother as himself"; therefore, the Church must "look to the poor and the needy, and administer to their relief that they shall not suffer." (Verses 16, 22, 24–25, 35.) A month later the law of consecration would be revealed, giving specific instructions on how the Saints should organize their economic affairs to care for everyone. (See D&C 42:30–42.)

SECTIONS 39–40: FAYETTE, NEW YORK, JANUARY 5, 1831[3]

Heading

James Covel invited to join the Church but disaffiliates himself shortly thereafter.

---

1. The motivation to move to avoid the plagues of the Second Coming is also found in D&C 38:33. "And from thence, whosoever I will shall go forth among all nations, and it shall be told them what they shall do; for I have a great work laid up in store, for Israel shall be saved, and I will lead them whithersoever I will, and no power shall stay my hand." Another possible motivation was the promise that those who came to Ohio would have riches if they would avoid pride: "And if ye seek the riches which it is the will of the Father to give unto you, ye shall be the richest of all people, for ye shall have the riches of eternity; and it must needs be that the riches of the earth are mine to give; but beware of pride, lest ye become as the Nephites of old." (Verse 39.) And again: "And I hold forth and deign to give unto you greater riches, even a land of promise, a land flowing with milk and honey, upon which there shall be no curse when the Lord cometh." (Verse 18.)

2. Another function of the gathering to Ohio was to separate the Saints from "among the wicked" so that they could better "save" themselves by not being drawn into the sinful temptations of the world. "Be ye clean that bear the vessels of the Lord." (See verse 42.)

3. The first revelation to James Covill (Section 39) was received January 5, 1830, and we now know that Section 40 was received the following day on January 6. We also have evidence that James Covill was a Methodist preacher, not a Baptist, as had been previously assumed. See Woodford, "Discoveries from the Joseph Smith Papers Project," 29.

Introduction

These revelations were given through Joseph Smith to James Covel, at Fayette, New York, January 5, 1831.[1] Covel is commanded to be baptized and work in the Church. Covel declines the invitation.

Historical background

Not long after the Church conference held on January 2, 1831, Joseph met and conversed with Methodist minister James Covel about joining the Church. Joseph recorded that Covel agreed that he would "obey any command that the Lord would give to him through me."[2] Joseph inquired of the Lord and received section 39, commanding Covel to "Arise and be baptized." (Verse 10.) We have no information on whether or not Covel was baptized but we do know that he quickly abandoned any interest in the Church. Concerned and in a quandary as to why Covel changed his mind about Mormonism, Joseph and Sidney Rigdon inquired of the Lord; they were told that Covel feared that association with Saints would bring persecution upon him.[3]

James Covel, like many Methodists, may have been especially attracted to the Mormons. The more evangelical branch of the Methodist Church, with its emphasis on the gifts of the Spirit and its acceptance of "dreams and visions as legitimate manifestations from God to an individual" had much in common with the Mormons.[4] Brigham Young (and his brothers), Solomon Chamberlain, and John Taylor "left mainstream Methodism and united with smaller schismatic Wesleyan groups in the search for truth in the years leading up to their introduction to Mormonism."[5] In fact, the first three presidents of the restored Church and eight members of its first Quorum of the Twelve had been Methodists.[6] As a youth, Joseph was somewhat partial to the Methodists and later told Methodist preacher Peter Cartwright that "we Latter-day Saints are Methodists, as far as they have gone, only we have advanced further."[7]

On the other hand, the Lord's command to Covel that he "arise and be baptized" and thereafter serve a mission may have pushed him out of the

---

1. Smith, *History of the Church*, 1:143–45.
2. See Woodford, *The Historical Development of the Doctrine and Covenants*, 504.
3. See D&C 40:2; and Woodford, *The Historical Development of the Doctrine and Covenants*, 504.
4. Jones, "Mormonism in the Methodist Marketplace," *BYU Studies* 51:1:84.
5. Ibid., 85.
6. Ibid., 83.
7. Ibid.

Church. Methodist and Mormon views "diverged sharply" on baptism.[1] Methodists were comfortable with infant baptism, baptism by sprinkling, and pouring or immersion. On this point the Methodists were unbending, and they clashed with and had a history of antagonism with the Baptists.

On the issue of missionary work, Mormons and Methodists relied on untrained ministers to travel the countryside, solicit appointments, and preach. Bushman even suggested that the Methodists might have been the model for the Mormons on what was expected in missionary work. In any case, it was arduous service. Covel had been a traveling minister/missionary of some sort for the Methodists for forty years, and the thought of doing it for the Mormons must have been daunting at age sixty-one.[2]

Covel's rejection of the gospel meant that the promises of the Lord made to him would not be fulfilled. He had been promised a "greater work," involving preaching "the fulness of my gospel" (39:11.) In addition, he was assured "that power shall rest upon thee; thou shalt have great faith, and I will be with thee and go before thy face" (39:12). These promises were never realized, but the Lord assured Joseph and Sidney Rigdon that "it remaineth with me to do with him as seemeth me good" (D&C 40:3). Covel rejoined the Methodists with even more "devotion and energy than ever before."[3]

---

1. Ibid., 86.
2. Ibid., 91.
3. Ibid., 95.

Part 6

The Kirtland, Ohio, Period

Chapter 22

Building a Church Organization: Kirtland, Ohio, 1831–1837

With little room for interpretation, the word of the Lord to Joseph in December 1830 was explicit and came by way of commandment. Move to Ohio. (See D&C 37.) Although some would resist, saying that Joseph was trying to deceive the people to enrich himself, and although people were reluctant to leave their farms and sell their property for a loss as part of a mass exodus, most of the New York Saints reconciled themselves to the command and made preparations to leave.[1] In part, they were motivated by a belief in the impending Second Coming and a need to gather as a group in a specific place for refuge and protection from the predicted judgments of God that would surely be poured out upon the earth.[2] Although their millennial expectations were not met, in retrospect, moving to a central location in Kirtland, Ohio, was an essential step in the development of the new Church.

Prior to the move, the Saints were spread out in a number of cities distant from one another at a time when travel was by stage coach. Pockets of Saints lived in the New York area and in northern Pennsylvania. Joseph found it difficult to exert his influence effectively in a situation where

---

1. See *Church History in the Fulness of Times*, 89.
2. Joseph had already started talking about the New Jerusalem, which was to be a refuge against the coming calamities. As Bushman pointed out, "The conversion of Indians, the building of the New Jerusalem, and the gathering of the elect came together in a single plan to prepare the world for the Savior's Second Coming." (Bushman, *Joseph Smith: Rough Stone Rolling*, 123.) The intensity of feeling on this subject was increased at the January 2, 1831, conference of the Church held in the Peter Whitmer Jr. home in Fayette. There, Joseph received what became section 38, which talked about a place where the Saints could gather and "escape the power of the enemy, and be gathered unto me a righteous people." The revelation further prophesied that the time was soon coming when wars would erupt prior to the Second Coming, interrupting the activities of everyday life. Under these circumstances, why not flee the coming destruction and gather on holy ground, a place of safety, a place that was described as "a land of promise, a land flowing with milk and honey"? (D&C 38:18.)

the Saints were spread out. Without his direct leadership, some members began to challenge his authority. Even those close to him, including Oliver Cowdery and others less acquainted with the Prophet, such as Hyrum Page, questioned Joseph's right to give direction in certain areas. For example, Oliver felt he could correct Joseph's revelations, and Hiram Page took it upon himself to obtain "revelations" for the entire Church. Since Mormons believed it was not necessary to contact God through an intercessory, the Whitmers and other leading families of the Church were willing to accept Page's revelations at face value. It was under these circumstances that the move to Ohio made it possible for Joseph Smith to gain greater control over the members of the new Church.

Furthermore, it also made practical sense to gather in the Ohio region to escape the criticism and outright persecution that had arisen in Palmyra, Colesville, and Harmony. Early on, Joseph and a number of his followers had experienced severe persecution. Conflict and an effort by Joseph's enemies to steal the plates when he was living in Palmyra  had forced Joseph and Emma to move to Harmony, Pennsylvania. It was not long before ill feelings in Harmony necessitated a move to Fayette, New York, so that Joseph could finish translating the Book of Mormon. A larger concentration of Saints in one place, Ohio, held out the promise of tranquility and greater social acceptance.

In addition, Joseph's call for missionaries to be sent west to convert the Lamanites proved successful, not because the Indians were converted, but because others were converted along the way.[1] On their journey westward, Parley P. Pratt made contact with an old friend, a minister by the name of Sidney Rigdon, who read the Book of Mormon and joined the Church along with many of his associates. Pratt reported, "The people thronged us night and day, insomuch that we had no time for rest and retirement. Meetings were convened in different neighborhoods, and multitudes came together soliciting our attendance; while thousands flocked about us daily; some to be taught, some for curiosity, some to obey the gospel, and some to dispute or resist it."[2] Soon there were about three times more members in the Ohio area than there were in New York and Pennsylvania put together. Inviting the Saints in the East to come west made sense.

Finally, Joseph was looking for the place where God had told him to

---

1. Oliver Cowdery (D&C 28:8), Peter Whitmer Jr., Ziba Peterson, and Parley P. Pratt (D&C 30:5; 32:1–3) had been called to preach to the Lamanites. When they arrived on the Indian reservations on the western border of Missouri, they were informed that it was unlawful for them to preach to the Indians.

2. *Church History in the Fulness of Times*, 81.

establish a Zion-like city. In the fall of 1830, he had received the Book of Enoch—110 verses in the Book of Moses—which described the ancient prophet Enoch's utopian society. It was Joseph's conviction that a similar social order had to be established before the Second Coming of Christ. A move to Ohio would facilitate this vision.

Although Joseph's vision of what a God-like society should be was partially implemented in Kirtland, Ohio, and the surrounding areas, ultimately the enterprise would fail. Poverty, economic rivalry, the Panic of 1837, the collapse of the Church's banking institution (the Kirtland Safety Society), and the resulting apostasy and persecution would make it impossible for the Saints to carry on in their new found Zion.

Chapter 23

The Big Questions: Kirtland, Ohio

How Do We Live Together and Build Zion Now That We Have Gathered?

Once the Saints had started to gather, Joseph received a set of laws in section 42 that regulated the social and economic relationships in the community. Spiritual and economic equality were espoused in the law of consecration. (See D&C 78.) The Ten Commandments were reiterated, and specific rules about respecting the property of others and how members should resolve disputes among themselves were set forth. (See D&C 42.) The Lord also gave specific instructions on how the Saints were to treat outsiders who persecuted them and engaged in violence against them. (See D&C 98.) To perfect the Saints spiritually, the Kirtland Temple was built and a spiritual endowment of power was promised. (See D&C 109; 110.) Old doctrines were refined and new doctrines introduced. Joseph continued to expand and refine the organizational structure of the Church. Offices in the Melchizedek Priesthood were added, and by March 1835 the primary governing quorums and their relationships to each other were set forth. (See D&C 107.) The location of Zion, the New Jerusalem that should be built in preparation for the Second Coming, was revealed and instructions were given on how Zion should be established.

After Joseph arrived in Kirtland, Ohio, his revelations began to address the community of believers rather than individuals directly. For the first time, his revelations began, "Hearken and hear, O ye my people, saith the Lord and your God" (section 41:1). The first Kirtland revelations also singled out specific groups within the larger community of believers. A February 1831 revelation on the law of consecration begins, "Hearken, O ye elders of my church" (section 42:1).

What Is the Structure of the Church?

During the Kirtland, Ohio, period the organization of the Church expanded. The roles of Joseph and Oliver as the sole administrative heads of the Church lessened and were replaced by governing boards (priesthood quorums)—the First Presidency, the Quorum of the Twelve, the Seventy, and local stake presidencies and high councils. The idea that quorum decisions ought to be made by unanimous consent was instituted. Decision-making authority expanded to include more Church members in the day-to-day operations of the Church. A lay ministry was firmly established. Many men were called to go on missions to proselyte potential converts. As many as were willing became active participants in the newly established kingdom of God.

The Kirtland Ashery, in Kirtland, Ohio. The Ashery was given to the Church by Newel K. Whitney as part of the law of consecration. Ashes from stoves and wood burnings on farms were sold to the ashery and baked into potash or pearl ash and then sold to textile manufactures in the East, which used the product to make glass and soap. Profits were used to help finance the construction of the Kirtland Temple.

The John Johnson Inn, in Kirtland, Ohio. The original inn was constructed by Peter French in 1813. The Mormons purchased it in 1833. It was used as a temporary printing office after the Church press in Independence, Missouri, was destroyed by a mob in 1833. A Church newspaper, The Evening and Morning Star, *was printed here from December 1833 to September 1834. The Egyptian mummies that Joseph purchased from Michael Chandler were on display here.*

The Kirtland Schoolhouse, located in Kirtland, Ohio, was used for educational purposes as well as for meetings for first-generation Mormons.

Chapter 24

Whitney Home, Kirtland, Ohio, February 1831–December 1831

Section 41: Whitney Home, Kirtland, Ohio, February 4, 1831

Heading

Members of the Church living in communal orders and sharing wealth equally experience ill will between the participants. The Lord condones the practice of communal orders and promises to reveal more about the principles of consecration. The first bishop of the Church appointed.

The big questions

Question: How do we live together and build a community now that we have gathered?
Answer: Live together in communal orders in which wealth is shared equally.
Question: What is the structure of the Church?
Answer: Bishops should be appointed to help administer the temporal affairs of the Church.

Introduction

Revelation given through Joseph Smith the Prophet to the Church in the Whitney home, Kirtland, Ohio, February 4, 1831.[1] The Kirtland Branch of the Church at this time was growing. Prefacing this revelation the Prophet wrote: "The members were striving to do the will of God, so far as they knew it, though some strange notions and false spirits had crept in among them . . . [and] the Lord gave unto the Church the following." The elders

---

1. Smith, *History of the Church*, 1:146–47.

are told to govern the Church by the spirit of revelation and promised that in the future the Lord will reveal more about the basic principles of economic equality and communal orders. Edward Partridge was named the first bishop.

Background

Prior to Joseph and Emma's arrival in Kirtland, some of the Saints had been experimenting with and living in communal orders. Prior to the time that Sidney Rigdon was a member of the Church, he and some members of his congregation had established communal orders in which all property was shared equally between the participants. These orders were referred to as "the family" or "family commonwealth." Isaac Morley, a follower of Rigdon, lived in such a commonwealth along with other supporters on his farm,[1] located a few miles north of Kirtland. After Rigdon, Morley, and their followers all joined the Church, they continued to live in their communal economic orders.

Unfortunately, Rigdon's experiment had not gone particularly well. Some of the members of the society had taken the property of others without first asking permission on the assumption that all had equal rights to whatever property was part of the order. Bad feelings, a spirit of noncooperation, and confusion about how members of the society should treat property arose. Section 41 acknowledges this difficulty and informs those in the order that a revelation on the matter would be forthcoming (which it did in section 42). In anticipation, the members were told to "assemble yourselves together to agree upon my word; and by the prayer of your faith ye shall receive my law." (D&C 41:2.)

Section 42 followed just four days later and established a rule that members of the order should ask permission before they borrowed or took property that was under the control of another person. It was at this point that the "family" or "family commonwealth" was modified and eventually supplanted by a new and improved "law of consecration."

Levi Hancock, when visiting Kirtland in 1831, described some of the specific problems faced by Rigdon's communal experiments.

> While I was in the room at "Father Morley's" as we all called him . . . Heman Bassett came to me and took my watch out of my pocket and walked off as though it was his. I thought he would bring it back soon but was disappointed as he sold it. I asked him what he meant by selling my watch. "O," said he, "I

---

1. Isaac Morley had owned this farm since 1812.

Whitney Home: Kirtland, Ohio, February 1831–December 1831

The Newel K. Whitney Home located in Kirtland, Ohio. Joseph Smith and his wife Emma and their five children arrived in Kirtland in February 1831 and lived in this home for a few weeks.

thought it was all in the family." I told him I did not like such family doings and I would not bear it.[1]

Such disagreements on who controlled what property undoubtedly made members of these orders anxious to know how the Lord felt about such matters. The answer that came was specific and clarified that even in communal living situations where property was held in common, it was necessary that each member of the order be given stewardship and control over his or her portion, especially personal items. "Thou shalt not take thy brother's garment; thou shalt pay for that which thou shalt receive of thy brother." (D&C 42:54.)

Joseph and Emma move to Kirtland

Joseph was eager to live with the Saints who were gathering to Kirtland. The prospects for Emma were less inviting. She had moved on account of Joseph seven times in the first four years of marriage. Further, Emma was just recovering from a month-long illness and was six months pregnant. Facing the three-hundred mile trip during one of the worst winters on record must have been daunting at best. Joseph Knight provided a sleigh, and at the end of January, Joseph, Emma, Sidney Rigdon, and Edward Partridge set out for Kirtland.[2]

In early February, when they arrived, Joseph "sprang from the sleigh" and went into the local store of Newel K. Whitney. Joseph exclaimed. "Newel K. Whitney! Thou art the man," and extended the hand of fellowship. Whitney replied, "You have the advantage of me. . . . I could not call you by name as you have me." Joseph introduced himself as "the Prophet" and said, "you prayed me here, now what do you want of me?" Joseph then explained that while in New York he had seen Newel in a vision praying for him to come to Kirtland.[3] Realizing this to be the case, the Whitney's welcomed the Smiths and invited them to live temporarily in their home.

When Joseph extended his hand and said to Whitney, "Thou art the

---

1. The Historical Development of the Doctrine and Covenants, 84.
2. See *Church History in the Fulness of Times*, 90.
3. Elizabeth Ann Smith Whitney, who came to be known as "Mother Whitney," recounted her first contact with Mormonism. She and her husband, Newel, were Campbellites and members of Sidney Rigdon's congregation. On hearing the gospel preached, she and her husband were converted. Mother Whitney told the story that one night prior to the arrival of Mormon missionaries (Oliver Cowdery and others) she and Newel had been praying to learn how they might obtain the gift of the Holy Ghost. They "saw a vision as a cloud of glory" resting upon their house, and heard a voice from heaven saying, "Prepare to receive the word of the Lord, for it is coming." Shortly afterwards, Oliver Cowdery and associates came, taught them the gospel, and gave them a Book of Mormon. (See Preece, *Learning to Love the Doctrine and Covenants*, 72; Smith, *History of the Church*, 2:486.)

man," he was probably drawing on the Book of Mormon story of Alma encountering Amulek, who greeted him by saying, "Thou art the man whom an angel said in vision: Thou shalt receive. Therefore, go with me into my house and I will impart unto thee of my food. . . . And it came to pass that the man received him into his house; . . . and he brought forth bread and meat and set before Alma"[1] (Alma 8:20–21). Like Alma in the Book of Mormon story, Joseph and Emma stayed at the Whitney home for some weeks, and Joseph reminisced that his family "received every kindness and attention which could be expected and especially from Sister Whitney."[2]

Partridge called as the first bishop of the Church

The office of bishop would evolve over time, but from the beginning involved a central role in the day-to-day operation of the Church. When the Church was small, "bishops were concerned primarily with the temporal needs of the Church, and spiritual needs were left to the Prophet."[3] Edward Partridge was called as the first bishop and was placed in charge of a storehouse to help the poor. (See D&C 42:10, 30–39.) As the Church grew, more bishops were needed, and in December 1831 Newel K. Whitney was also appointed. (See D&C 72:8.) Partridge served in the Missouri area and Whitney in Ohio and the eastern states. (See D&C 20:66.) During the Kirtland era their main function was to administer the affairs of the communal living orders.

The first responsibilities of bishops involved temporal matters such as paying bills, buying and selling land and goods, supervising construction projects, printing Church materials and most importantly assisting the poor.[4] Later, in Nauvoo (1839–1846), the office of bishop would become associated with political subdivisions called "wards" instead of regions (such as Ohio and Missouri). By this time communal living orders had all but ceased and in their place the law of tithing was practiced. Tithing was collected by the bishops. Bishops continued to focus much of their time and efforts on providing for the poor. Bishops rarely presided over or conducted Church services. Such meetings were held outdoors on a citywide basis or in individual homes. Bishops collectively organized and directed the work of deacons, teachers, and priests quorums in the city.[5]

When the Saints settled in the Great Basin in 1847 the norm became for

---

1. Staker, *Hearken, O Ye People*, Kindle locations 7362–67.
2. *History of the Church*, 1:146.
3. See *Encyclopedia of Mormonism*, 1:119.
4. See *Encyclopedia of Mormonism*, 1:119.
5. See *Encyclopedia of Mormonism*, 1:119.

bishops to be assigned to each settlement. Salt Lake City, the largest settlement, was divided into nineteen wards in 1849, with a bishop appointed in each ward. At first each settlement or ward had a president and bishop. The president would organize and preside at meetings. The bishops still concentrated their time and attention on temporal matters, but eventually the bishops would also take on more spiritual responsibilities and became the primary head of a congregation.

Bishop Partridge was born on August 27, 1793, in Pittsfield, Massachusetts. He was a hatter by trade and eventually moved to Painesville, Ohio, where he opened a store. In 1828 he and his wife, Lydia, joined the Campbellite congregation and were later converted by Oliver Cowdery. He was baptized by the Prophet in December 1830 and two months later was called as the first bishop of the Church.[1]

Section 42: Whitney Home, Kirtland, Ohio, February 9, 1831[2]

Whitney Home, Kirtland, Ohio, February 9, 1831[3]

Heading

Principles of communal living expounded and the law of consecration introduced. Important ethical teachings mentioned in the Ten Commandments and elsewhere are reiterated to God's people in a modern day. The Saints instructed to care for each other temporally and to heal and nurture the sick.

Anchor section

Memorize: Law of Consecration/Commandments

---

1. See Garr, Cannon, and Cowan, *Encyclopedia of LDS History*, 897–98.
2. Section 42 is a composite of two revelations, one received February 9, 1831, and the other on February 23. What is not generally known is that a portion of this section has never been published and another portion, which was printed in the Book of Commandments, was deleted from the Doctrine and Covenants. (See Woodford, "Discoveries from the Joseph Smith Papers Project," 30.)
3. Section 42 is a composite of two revelations, one received February 9, 1831, and the other on February 23. What is not generally known is that a portion of this section has never been published and another portion, which was printed in the Book of Commandments, was deleted from the Doctrine and Covenants. (See Woodford, "Discoveries from the Joseph Smith Papers Project," 30.)

The big question

Question: How do we live together and build a community now that we have gathered?

Answer: Establish communal living orders where wealth is shared equally, live by the ethical standards in the Ten Commandments and elsewhere, and care for each other.

Introduction

Revelation given through Joseph Smith the Prophet in the Whitney home, Kirtland, Ohio.[1] The revelation was received in the presence of twelve elders and in fulfillment of the Lord's promise previously made that the "law" and further instructions on communal living orders would be given in Ohio. (See D&C 38:32; 41:3.) The Ten Commandments are given anew in this dispensation. The law of consecration is introduced for the first time. Procedures on healing the sick are set forth.

Background

Most of section 42 was received by the Prophet on February 9, 1831, in the presence of twelve elders.[2] John Whitmer recorded the event and said that "the Elders were called together, and united in mighty [prayer] and were agreed, as touching the reception of the Law; therefore, thus saith the Lord your God."[3] Receiving revelations in the presence of others after counseling together with his brethren was a practice Joseph often engaged in. When the time came, Joseph would dictate the revelation slowly, word by word, and a clerk would take it down.

John Whitmer said that section 42 was not well accepted by some of the members of the Church, who balked at the suggestion that their property should be shared in common with other members of the Church. This may be one reason Joseph did not require all of his followers to enter into communal living orders. Those Saints who could accept it were instructed to gather together on farms just outside the city of Kirtland

---

1. Smith, *History of the Church*, 1:148–54. Section 42 is actually a series of revelations. Verses 1–73 were received at the February 9 meeting in the presence of the elders. Verses 74–93 were received two weeks later on February 23. (See Robinson and Garrett, *Doctrine and Covenants Commentary*, 2:10; Woodford, *The Historical Development of the Doctrine and Covenants*, 527–34.)
2. Smith, *History of the Church*, 1:148–54.
3. Robinson and Garrett, *Doctrine and Covenants Commentary*, 2:9.

to implement the practice.[1] Joseph certainly was not the first religious leader in the nineteenth century to endorse communal living, and his vision differed considerably from some of the others who imagined a utopian society. Richard S. Van Wagoner points out that Joseph's law of consecration differed from some of the systems proposed by others because it "combined elements of both individualism and collectivism."[2] Although all real and personal property was deeded in fee simple absolute to the Church, members were leased back what they needed as "stewards" rather than owners or profiteers. Bishops were appointed to control allocation of land and personal property. Stewards would use the property, and any excess revenues generated or properties acquired were given back to the bishop at designated intervals.[3]

Under this system, private accumulation of capital was impossible. Excess capital was concentrated under the control of the Church structure. Church leaders would decide how excess capital should be used for the benefit of the whole. This system was meant to ensure that no segment of the society would be disenfranchised or lack for the necessities of life. "For I will consecrate of the riches of those who embrace my gospel among the Gentiles unto the poor of my people who are of the house of Israel." (See verse 39.)

The legal instrument that governed the law of consecration was called a "Deed of Stewardship or Lease and Loan Agreement." This legal instrument listed all of the property deeded over to the Church by the individual, which literally included the clothes off his or her back—all real and personal property was gifted to the Church. In return, the Church leased or loaned back what individual members and their families needed. The sweeping nature of the arrangement made it necessary for the Church to lease back everything from clothing to kitchen utensils. In such a "Deed of Stewardship," Joseph Knight Jr. gave all he had to the Church, and the Church leased back a parcel of land and in addition various items needed to sustain life such as

sundry articles of crockery, tin ware, knives, forks and spoons, valued nine dollars forty three cents. Sundry articles of iron ware and household furniture valued twelve dollars ninety two cents,—one bed and bedding valued nineteen dollars,—sundry articles of clothing valued twenty two

---

1. See Robinson and Garrett, *Doctrine and Covenants Commentary*, 2:9–10. (See commentary on D&C 41 for a discussion of members of the Church who lived in communal living orders prior to the receipt of this revelation.)

2. Van Wagoner, *Sidney Rigdon: A Portrait of Religious Excess*, 85.

3. For example, stewards would be assigned farmland for cultivation. A steward, in consultation with the bishop, would keep what he and his family needed and all excess goods would be given to the Church, placed in the bishop's storehouse for distribution to others, especially the poor.

Whitney Home: Kirtland, Ohio, February 1831–December 1831

dollars thirteen cents,—Grain valued seven dollars,—sundry articles of joiner tools valued twenty dollars forty four cents,—one cow valued twelve dollars.[1]

It is important to note that the property once leased to Knight was under his control and could not be summarily confiscated by other members of the community for other purposes. Nevertheless, under this system of property distribution, Knight could not keep or "accumulate more than needful for the support and comfort of myself and family." Any excess would be appropriated by the Church for other uses.[2]

Specific instructions on how to avoid bad feelings between members of communal orders

The sharing of property made some members critical of how much or how little each member possessed in comparison with others. The opportunity for giving and taking offense was real. Specific instructions on the subject were given. "And if thy brother or sister offend thee, thou shalt take him or her between him or her and thee alone. . . ." (Verse 88.) If this did not resolve the issues, then a system of appeals was instituted whereby the members could take the matter up the chain of command. (See verses 88–92.)

When the instructions on what to do if offended were first published in the *Morning and Evening Star* in 1832, the language did not refer to the female gender. Verse 88 reads, "And if thy brother offend thee, thou shalt take him between him and thee alone; and if he confess thou shalt be reconciled."

When the Doctrine and Covenants was revised in 1835, the verse was changed to make specific reference to the sisters as well as the brethren. The verse now reads, "And if thy brother *or sister* offend thee, thou shalt take him *or her* between him *or her* and thee alone; and if he *or she* confess thou shalt be reconciled." (Emphasis added.)

Note that the addition of the specific reference to the female gender is carried through verse 92, the verse that concludes the discussion on the subject of offenses. Apparently, absolute clarity that both genders were subject to this system of reconciliation was necessary.

Also note that it is the responsibility of the one offended to take the matter up with the person who gave the offense. Why? Because in many instances the person giving offense may not know that he or she has offended his brother or sister. Once on notice, the offender can correct the

---

1. See Arrington, Fox, and May, *Building the City of God*, 368.
2. See Arrington, Fox, and May, *Building the City of God*, 368.

situation, explain, or make a heartfelt apology. This done, the offended person is obligated to forgive the offender. "I, the Lord, will forgive whom I will forgive, *but of you it is required to forgive all men.*" (D&C 64:10; emphasis added.)

In most instances the scriptures speak in general terms—love your neighbor, forgive others, and be kind. In such instances individuals are left to decide on the appropriate course of action in any given situation. However, this is not the case when a person has been offended. Greater specificity is warranted in such a situation because it is naturally difficult for an offended party to initiate a conversation with an offender. What generally happens is that the offended party speaks to anyone *but* the offender. Backbiting becomes the chosen remedy.[1] (See D&C 20:54.) Extra encouragement to the offendee to clear the air directly with the offender is generally necessary. The objective of these instructions on what to do when offended is to avoid the festering resentments that undermine personal relationships and the spirituality of the Church as a whole.

The success of communal living orders in Kirtland

Ultimately, the Kirtland communal orders failed. The Saints were simply unable to implement the program without selfishness and division entering in. This said, Joseph knew that Zion could not be built up upon any other principle. Therefore, some of the Saints in Kirtland were asked to leave the area and practice the law of consecration in Jackson County, Missouri, the place designated in the revelations as the New Jerusalem. Here the Saints would establish communal orders in preparation for and anticipation of the Second Coming. Unfortunately, the system failed in Missouri as well, and the Saints were forced out of the territory to Nauvoo and then to the Great Basin.

After the Saints reached the Great Basin in 1847, Brigham Young initiated various communal experiments in different places and at different times; some of these even lingered into the early part of the twentieth century.[2] Today, Mormon economic idealism is seen in the persistence of

---

1. Backbiting by its very nature is destructive because it does not give the person responsible for the offense the opportunity to explain or, if necessary, ask for forgiveness.

2. In Utah communities in the 1850s and 1860s, "Brigham Young described the ideal united order on numerous occasions and in explicit terms. The model for his vision was the 'well regulated family,' an institution characterized by sharing of resources according to need, contributions of labor according to ability, and a concern for the welfare of others in the group that transcended selfishness and promoted harmony and unity. The physical environment of an ideal order would be similar to that of a family as well, with a common kitchen serving both as a symbol of equality in consumption and labor and as a hearth, the center of the family social and spiritual life. Private apartment houses or rooms would

the law of tithing, fast offerings, and the magnitude of Church-sponsored projects to assist the helpless, the educationally and socially disadvantaged, and the poor. But members are reminded of the higher law each time they participate in an endowment session, which commits the faithful to live the law of consecration at some point in the future if asked to do so.[1]

---

accommodate the members for sleeping and more personal aspects of their lives, but the social experiences of Order members were to take place in the community environment rather than within the nuclear family." (Arrington, Fox, and May, *Building the City of God*, 203.)

1. The transition from an equal distribution of goods to capitalism was not always easy for Latter-day Saints. Typical of statements just prior to and after the turn of the nineteenth century are those of Orson Pratt, a member of the original Quorum of the Twelve, and Charles Nibley, a member of the First Presidency in the early 1900s. Orson Pratt said, "Division of property, like a division in doctrine, is a plan of the devil, followed by Gentiles." (Pratt, *New Jerusalem* and *Equality and Oneness of the Saints*, 59.) Charles Nibley, reacting against the social injustice that characterized the United States during this period, said, "We have hundreds of thousands of tramps abroad in the land which are not so much of a credit to us. . . . I know that there are more luxuries in the world than there used to be, but are the poor any better off than formerly? Let the armies of tramps answer. Let the miserable tenants of garrets and cellars in our great cities answer. . . . If this is our country and we govern it, why cannot we govern it in such a way that we shall at least be sure of bread enough to eat? . . . justice is demanded; something like an equal distribution of this world's goods is demanded; and no amount of sophistry—of 'sovereign ruler' talk will put the great question off much longer. . . . Liberty, I am told, is a divine thing. Liberty, when it becomes the 'liberty to die by starvation' is not so divine. . . . With our horses, after we have got a summer's work out of them, we feed them and care for them during the winter months while there is no work. A horse is too valuable to let die of starvation. But a *man*, made in the image of God, after he has worked for me during seasons of prosperity, now when dull times come I discharge him—turn him off caring little, it would seem, whether he lives or dies. . . . If it is noble to simply pile up your thousands, your millions and gain thereby the hatred of your poor fellow mortals until they are anxious to make an end of you, then I for one do not wish to belong to that class of nobility. No true Latter-day Saint can belong to such a class. And yet we are prone to worship money and the power of money. We too often look after the successful man more than the worthy man, and if he has only 'made money' we are somewhat anxious to elevate him to the first seats in the synagogue. . . . The question must get to be, not 'how much money have you made?' but 'how much work have you done?' . . . O, my friends we must have some other method of computing wages than supply and demand. . . . Upon the Latter-day Saints devolves the labor of changing the political economy of the world. What have we done thus far towards making that change? Comparatively nothing. . . . a prosperity which makes here a millionaire and there a million tramps is surely enough the 'prosperity of fools,' and it '*shall* destroy them.' . . . How to bring about this change is the grand question. There is one way and only one that will be found in a system where laborers and master have a common interest; where the profits on all the work that is done shall inure not to one man or a corporation of ten or fifty, but to the society as a whole; where individual interest shall sink and one common brotherhood, each man having an equal interest in the work—will yet be found to be the true system of work and wages. . . . And the man who is so narrow in his soul that in the broadest stretch of his imagination, he can only reach to 'me and my wife, my son John and his wife,' is not fitted for such a new brotherhood." (Nibley, "Logan Temple Lectures," *The Contributor* 7:423–29.)

Attitudes about property since the law of consecration was discontinued

After the discontinuance of the law of consecration, the First Presidency still spoke out from time to time on issues involving the appropriate use of personal and public resources. Such concerns focused on the corrupting influence of too much wealth in the hands of a few and the unwillingness of those who have much to share with those who have little. As a general principle, the First Presidency has recognized that people are better off generally in societies where wealth is most equally distributed. For example, they have said, "The experience of mankind has shown that the people of communities and nations among whom wealth is the most equally distributed enjoy the largest degree of liberty, are the least exposed to tyranny and opposition, and suffer the least from luxurious habits which beget vice."[1] The idea is that resources should be used to the degree possible for the benefit all members of society.

Concerns about the concentration of wealth by a few has also been identified as a cause for alarm and has been described as "one of the great evils with which our nation is menaced."[2] The ideal of liberty is "endangered by the monstrous power which this accumulation of wealth gives to a few individuals and a few powerful corporations."[3] The reason given is that wealth "threatens to give shape to . . . legislation, both state and national."[4] The First Presidency warns that "if this evil should not be checked, and measures not taken to prevent the continued enormous growth of riches among the class already rich, and the painful increase of destitution and want among the poor, the nation is liable to be overtaken by disaster; for, according to history, such a tendency among nations once powerful was the sure precursor of ruin."[5] This statement, made in 1851, proved prophetic. Just eighty years later, the nation suffered through significant economic disparity during the depression.

On a personal level, Latter-day Saints are advised that the wealth placed in individual's hands is "good" but potentially seductive and spiritually corrosive. "I am afraid that many . . . have begun to worship [wealth] as false gods, and they have power over us. Do we have more of these good things than our faith can stand?"[6] The Saints are counseled to use their resources to build up the kingdom of God and to remember that "all are not equally prosperous" and that those with enough and to spare have a

---

1. Bergera, *Statements of the LDS First Presidency*, 483.
2. Bergera, *Statements of the LDS First Presidency*, 483.
3. Bergera, *Statements of the LDS First Presidency*, 484.
4. Bergera, *Statements of the LDS First Presidency*, 484.
5. Bergera, *Statements of the LDS First Presidency*, 484.
6. Bergera, *Statements of the LDS First Presidency*, 482.

duty "to care for the sick and sorrowing, and prevent as far as possible human suffering."[1]

Commandments reiterated to modern Israel

The importance of the fundamental ethical teachings of Judaism and Christianity, as recorded in the Ten Commandments and elsewhere, are given special emphasis in section 42 and are reiterated to modern Israel. "Thou shalt not kill," "steal," "lie," "commit adultery," and "speak evil of thy neighbor." (Verses 18–27.) In sum, "If thou lovest me thou shalt serve me and keep all my commandments." (Verse 29.)

Thou shalt not kill The command "Thou shalt not kill" is stated in connection with the observation that "he that kills shall not have forgiveness in this world, nor in the world to come." (Verse 18.) Taken at face value, the idea that a person who kills may not be forgiven seems overly broad and is inconsistent with other canonized statements on the subject. For example, Ammon said, "And behold, I also thank my God, that ... we have been convinced of our sins, and of the many murders which we have committed. And I also thank my God ... that he hath granted unto us that we might repent of these things, and also that he hath forgiven us of those our many sins and murders which we have committed, and taken away the guilt from our hearts, through the merits of his Son." (Alma 24:9–10.) Therefore, it is fair to conclude that the blanket statement "he that kills shall not have forgiveness" also allows for certain exceptions based on the particular situation. Clearly, intent, forethought, killing in self-defense, and mental illness are all factors that will be taken into consideration.

The seriousness of this sin is expressed in the approval of capital punishment, "He that killeth shall die." (Verse 19.) Presumably, however, this extreme penalty would be exercised only in cases where intent and forethought are present. The added considerations of intent are specifically mentioned elsewhere in the canon. "Wo unto the murderer who *deliberately* killeth, for he shall die." (2 Nephi 9:35; emphasis added.)[2]

---

1. Bergera, *Statements of the LDS First Presidency*, 483.
2. The idea that being forgiven for murder fits into a more stringent category was commented on by the Prophet Joseph. "The doctrine of eternal judgment was perfectly understood by the apostle, is evident from several passages of scripture. Peter preached repentance and baptism for the remission of sins to the Jews, who had been led to acts of violence and blood, by their leaders, but to the Rulers he said, 'I would that through ignorance ye did it, as did also those ye ruled.—Repent, therefore, and be converted that your sins may be blotted out, when the times of refreshing (redemption), shall come from the presence of the Lord, for he shall send Jesus Christ, who before was preached unto you etc.' The time of redemption here had reference to the time, when Christ should come; then and not till then would their sins be blotted out. Why? Because they were murderers, and no murderer hath eternal life.

A complicating factor that must be mentioned in reference to appropriate punishment for premeditated murder is the concept of blood atonement. Blood atonement expresses the idea that there are certain sins that are so grievous that the sinner is placed beyond the power of the atonement. In such circumstances partial recompense can be made if the sinner is subjected to capital punishment and sheds his own blood. Bruce R. McConkie and others taught that murder is one of these sins. He explains:

This principle can only operate in a day, as that of Moses, when there is no separation of Church and state and when the Church has power to take life. Of conditions in our day, and as to how this law applies to us, President Joseph Fielding Smith says: "We cannot destroy men in the flesh, because we do not control the lives of men and do not have power to pass sentences upon them which involve capital punishment. In the days when there was a theocracy on the earth, then this decree was enforced. What the Lord will do in lieu of this, because we cannot destroy in the flesh, I am unable to say, but it will have to be made up in some other way." (*Doctrines of Salvation*, 2:97.)[1]

Sexual sin, adultery and fornication Adultery or fornication is discussed in section 42 in no fewer than eight verses. (See verses 22–26, 74–75, 80.) Provision is made for repentance. But repeated and continued instances of adultery merit excommunication. (See verses 23–26, 74–75, 80.) Such sins are serious and are entirely inconsistent with the ideal of reserving sexual relationships for marriage partners only. "Thou shalt love thy wife with all thy heart, and shalt cleave unto her and none else." (Verse 22.)[2]

The seriousness of adultery in Mormon theology stems from the belief that family relationships are the well-springs of happiness around which social life revolves in this life and the next. Since infidelity is often the most destructive event to occur in marriage, and frequently leads to divorce, adultery is considered most serious. In 1886, the First Presidency said:

Even David, must wait for those times of refreshing, before he can come forth and his sins be blotted out; for Peter speaking of him says, 'David hath not yet ascended into Heaven, for his sepulchre is with us to this day:' his remains were then in the tomb. Now we read that many bodies of the saints arose, at Christ's resurrection, probably all the saints, but it seems that David did not. Why? because he had been a murderer.... for such characters cannot be forgiven, until they have paid the last farthing." (Ehat and Cook, *Words of Joseph Smith*, 72–73.)

1. See McConkie, *Doctrinal New Testament Commentary*, 3:344–45.
2. See also verse 23: "And he that looketh upon a woman to lust after her shall deny the faith, and shall not have the Spirit; and if he repents not he shall be cast out." As Robinson and Garrett point out, this involves more than the occasional stray thought but rather acts intended to bring about an illicit relationship. (See Robinson and Garrett, *Doctrine and Covenants Commentary*, 2:20.)

To a people who believe, as we do, that true marriage was divinely instituted for the multiplication of mankind, and is not a union for time alone, but reaches into the eternities, the disruption of families by divorce is an evil of not ordinary character, not only bearing a harvest of sorrow and suffering in this life, but also having a far-reaching influence into the world beyond the grave, and possibly involving others in ruin who had no voice in the separation or power to avert its occurrence.[1]

Consequently, the Church has always looked with disapproval upon anything, especially sexual transgression, that weakens the bonds of family life.

On the other hand, the Church has always been cautious not to define what is sexually appropriate or not appropriate between partners in marriage and recognizes that procreation is not only for producing offspring but also a way of expressing "love for one another—to bind husband and wife together in loyalty, fidelity, consideration, and common purpose."[2]

Since bishops and stake presidents are authorized to ask Latter-day Saint couples if they have been sexually loyal to their spouse prior to giving permission for members to enter the temple, the First Presidency cautioned that such questions should be narrowly focused: "In conducting worthiness interviews . . . you should never inquire into personal, intimate matters involving marital relations between a man and his wife. You should never deviate from or go beyond the specific questions contained in the temple recommend book."[3]

The statement goes on to explain that if in the course of an interview a spouse should ask about the "propriety" of "specific conduct, you should not pursue the matter but should merely suggest that if the member has enough anxiety about the propriety of the conduct to ask about it, the best course would be to discontinue it."[4]

Joseph Smith Translation

The words "Thou shalt ask, and my scriptures shall be given as I have appointed" most probably refer to the Joseph Smith Translation of the Bible. (See verse 56.) In addition, the Lord advises that the Joseph Smith Translation was not complete enough to "teach" at this point in time. (See verse 57.) "And it is expedient that thou shouldst hold thy peace concerning them, and not teach them until ye have received them in full." (Verse 57.)

---

1. Bergera, Statements of the LDS First Presidency, 118.
2. Bergera, *Statements of the LDS First Presidency*, 418.
3. Bergera, *Statements of the LDS First Presidency*, 420.
4. Bergera, *Statements of the LDS First Presidency*, 420.

The issue of not teaching from the Joseph Smith Translation "until ye have received them in full" is somewhat confusing. On July 2, 1833, Joseph Smith, Sidney Rigdon, and Frederick G. Williams wrote a letter to the brethren in Zion, or Jackson County, Missouri. "We this day finished the translating of the Scriptures, for which we returned gratitude to our Heavenly Father."[1] But as Robinson and Garrett point out, "It is likely the word 'finished' meant they had made the changes appropriate at that time."[2] This interpretation is supported by the fact that Joseph did not consider the 1833 translation complete and continued to make further changes until his death in 1844. As Robert J. Matthews points out, "Joseph had spoken with Brigham Young 'about going through the translation of the scriptures again and perfecting it upon points of doctrine which the Lord had restrained him from giving in plainness and fulness at the time of which we write,' which was February 2, 1833."[3]

On healing the sick

Those that are ill are not always promised health. "And whosoever among you are sick, and have not faith to be healed, but believe, shall be nourished with all tenderness, with herbs and mild food." (Verse 43.) The reference to "herbs" reflects the common practice in Joseph's day to use various herbal remedies to help heal the sick. The use of herbs with healing properties is ancient and was used prior to the advancement of modern science. For example, herbs were used to promote the flow of urine, raise pH, invigorate and strengthen, increase perspiration, promote digestion, and sooth the nerves. General tonic herbs included barberry, nux rosemary, tansy, snake root, Beth root, box leaves, celery, bugle, chamomile, Culver's root, angostura, and English alder. Buchu, night-blooming cereus, celery, coffee, garlic, and Paraguay tea were used as diuretics.

Joseph Smith had the gift of healing others, and to be healed himself. On June 12, 1837, the Prophet Joseph was taken ill and was not able to leave his room. His afflictions continued to increase and were very severe, so much so that he was unable to raise his head from his pillow. Some of the brethren of the Church called to "bid me farewell" he said. Joseph "continued to grow worse and worse until my sufferings were excruciating." The Prophet called on some of the brethren to administer to him. He continued in bed and was nursed back to health with herbs and mild food. In just a few days his illnesses eased and he was able to resume

---

1. Robinson and Garrett, *Doctrine and Covenants Commentary*, 2:28.
2. Robinson and Garrett, *Doctrine and Covenants Commentary*, 2:28.
3. See Robinson and Garrett, *Doctrine and Covenants Commentary*, 2:29.

his labors. He commented: "This is one of the many instances in which I have suddenly been brought from a state of health, to the borders of the grave, and as suddenly restored, for which my heart swells with gratitude to my heavenly Father, and I feel renewedly to dedicate myself and all my powers to His service."

Joseph went on to comment that some of his enemies took the opportunity when he was ill to suggest that his afflictions were brought upon him because of transgression, a notion Joseph rejected.[1]

On other occasions, when it was not the will of the Lord, Joseph was not readily healed. Just before the march of Zion's Camp was disbanded, many of the brethren became ill. The situation was described as follows:

> This night the cholera burst forth among us, and about midnight it was manifested in its most virulent form. Our ears were saluted with cries and moanings and lamentations on every hand; even those on guard fell to the earth with their guns in their hand, so sudden and powerful was the attack of this terrible disease.... I attempted to lay on hands for their recovery, but I quickly learned by painful experience, that when the great Jehovah decrees destruction upon any people, and makes known His determination, man must not attempt to stay His hand. The moment I attempted to rebuke the disease I was attacked, and had I not desisted in my attempt to save the life of a brother, I would have sacrificed my own. The disease seized upon me like the talons of a hawk, and I said to the brethren: "If my work were done, you would have to put me in the ground without a coffin."[2]

The ordeal continued:

> As it was impossible to obtain coffins, the brethren rolled the corpses in blankets, carried them on a horse-sled about half a mile, buried them on the bank of a small stream, which empties into Rush creek, all of which was accomplished by dark. When they had returned from the burial the brethren unitedly covenanted and prayed, hoping the disease would be stayed; but in vain, for while thus covenanting, Eber Wilcox died; and while some were digging the grave, others stood sentry with their fire arms, watching their enemies....
>
> The cholera continued its ravages for about four days... I told them if they would humble themselves before the Lord and covenant to keep His commandments and obey my counsel, the plague should be stayed from that hour, and there should not be another case of the cholera among them. The brethren covenanted to that effect with uplifted hands, and the plague was stayed.[3]

The recognition that the sick would not always be healed (v. 43) was an

---

1. See Smith, *History of the Church*, 2:492–93.
2. Smith, History of the Church, 2:114.
3. Smith, History of the Church, 2:115–16; 119, 120.

issue that needed to be addressed so that the Saints were prepared to accept the times when God chose not to honor such requests. One such instance involved Joseph's ordination of John Murdock and the healing blessing he bestowed just afterward. At age seventeen, this former Campbellite "fell on a scythe and became a cripple by a severe wound in my wrist, having cut two of the main leaders I came near bleeding to death." Joseph took hold of the damaged hand, which was "twisted and useless," pulled it out straight, and commanded that it be healed—to no avail.[1]

The recognition that the sick would not always be healed (v. 43) was an issue that needed to be addressed so that the Saints were prepared to accept the times when God chose not to honor such requests. One such instance involved Joseph's ordination of John Murdock and the healing blessing he bestowed just afterward. At age seventeen, this former Campbellite "fell on a scythe and became a cripple by a severe wound in my wrist, having cut two of the main leaders I came near bleeding to death." Joseph took hold of the damaged hand, which was "twisted and useless," pulled it out straight, and commanded that it be healed—to no avail. Instead, it became impossible for him speak.[2]

Murdock's experience was in stark contrast to the Montrose healing along the banks of the Mississippi River in 1839 when Joseph healed the sick by the dozens, some nigh unto death. Two of the more remarkable were the healing of Elijah Fordham and Joseph B. Noble. Many of the saints had bilious fever and many had died. Noble noted in his diary that two of his children had died and his wife had asked him in tears if "I was dying." A next-door neighbor was also very sick and his loved ones were preparing burial clothes for him. Joseph went to Fordham's home and commanded in the name of Jesus that he "arise and walk. He immediately jumped from his dying bed, kicked off the drafts from his feet, and came into my house." Joseph led the way.

> As soon as I saw him the tears of joy burst from my eyes. In a moment he was by my bedside, and took me by the hand. Without waiting for the other brethren to get to my bed, he commanded me, in the name of Jesus Christ, to arise and walk. I arose, and while putting on my clothes I fainted. When I regained consciousness I was on the bed, and Joseph was standing close to me. As soon as my eyes met his he said, "Wherefore didst thou doubt?" and again commanded to arise.
>
> While he was speaking I felt the healing virtue flowing through every part of my system. I immediately arose and walked, rejoicing and praising the Lord with all of my heart, for His blessing resting upon me by which I was made whole.[3]

---

1. Mark Lyman Staker, *Hearken, O Ye People: The Historical Setting of Joseph's Ohio Revelations*, Kindle Locations 5442–49.
2. Staker, *Hearken, O Ye People*, 5442–49.
3. Joseph Bates Noble, *Juvenile Instructor*, 15:112.

On teaching the gospel

Those who teach the gospel are to be authorized to do so in a way that is "known to the Church"; they are to be ordained or set apart for that purpose. (See verse 11 and D&C 20:65.) Teachers are to teach from the scriptures—the Bible, Book of Mormon, Doctrine and Covenants ("Church articles"—verse 13).[1] The Pearl of Great Price was not extant at this time, but the idea is to teach from the canon. Teachers are to seek the Spirit in their presentations. "And the Spirit shall be given unto you by the prayer of faith; and if ye receive not the Spirit ye shall not teach." (Verse 14; see also D&C 11:21; 2 Nephi 33:1.)

SECTION 43: WHITNEY HOME, KIRTLAND, OHIO, FEBRUARY 1831

Heading

Only Joseph Smith receives revelations that bind the entire Church. Missionaries are sent out to warn of the impending Millennium.

The big question

Question: What is the structure of the Church?
Answer: Joseph Smith (First Elder) is the recognized leader and revelator for the Church.[2]

Introduction

Revelation given through Joseph Smith the Prophet at the Whitney home in Kirtland, Ohio, in February 1831.[3] At this time some members of the Church were disturbed by people making false claims as revelators. The Prophet inquired of the Lord and received this communication addressed to the elders of the Church. The first part deals with who is authorized to receive revelations for the Church as a whole and the second part contains a warning that the elders are to give to the nations of the earth.

---

1. The Doctrine and Covenants at this time was known as *Articles and Covenants of the Church*.
2. Joseph Smith was the First Elder and Oliver Cowdery the Second Elder—the governing head of the Church. (See D&C 20:2–3, 5; 21:11.) The First Presidency would not be organized until March 1832, two years after the founding of the Church.
3. Smith, *History of the Church*, 1:154–56.

Background

By February 1831 Joseph Smith had arrived in Kirtland, Ohio, and the gathering was underway. It would not be long before the Saints from the New York area would begin to arrive (May-June 1831). The gathering and the rapid growth of the Church presented challenges and problems. Spiritual manifestations were common in Joseph's day, and "strange notions and false spirits" beset some of the local branches of the Church.[1] Some of the new members had "wild enthusiastic notions" about the effects of the Holy Spirit. John Corrill reported that a few young people claimed they saw visions: "They conducted themselves in a strange manner, sometimes imitating Indians in their maneuvers, sometimes running out into the fields, getting on stumps of trees and there preaching as though surrounded by a congregation,—all the while so completely absorbed in visions as to be apparently insensible to all that was passing around them."[2]

In this spiritually charged environment, a recent convert and self-proclaimed prophetess, Sister Hubble, claimed authority to reveal commandments and be a teacher in the Church. John Whitmer said that she "appeared to be very sanctimonious and deceived some who were not able to detect her in her hypocrisy."[3] A few others, however, were more impressed with her claims. The Prophet commented that she spoke about "curious matters" and had a divisive influence. Joseph inquired of the Lord and received section 43. "There is none other appointed unto you to receive commandments and revelations until [Joseph Smith] be taken, if he abide in me." (Verse 3.) According to John Whitmer, the revelation had a calming effect and "unity and harmony prevailed."[4]

The issue of who in the Church should be its authorized spokesman was not new. A few months earlier, a similar situation had arisen concerning Hiram Page, who used a seer stone through which he claimed to receive revelations for the Church. Page was also informed that Joseph was the only person who could speak for the entire Church. (See D&C 28:2.) Since the Page episode occurred in Fayette, New York, it is fair to assume that the new converts joining the Church in Ohio were not generally familiar with this precedent.

One of the appeals of early Mormonism was its appreciation that all are entitled to personal revelation. No priest intercessory was necessary for an individual to contact God. This principle would be reiterated just nine months later in November 1831. "Every man might speak in the name

---

1. *Church History in the Fulness of Times*, 92.
2. *Church History in the Fulness of Times*, 92.
3. *Church History in the Fulness of Times*, 92.
4. See Robinson and Garrett, *Doctrine and Covenants Commentary*, 2:35.

of God ... that faith ... might increase in the earth." (D&C 1:20–21.) In such a liberal spiritual environment, deciding which revelations governed the Church was an important consideration. If order were to prevail, it was necessary for all to understand that Joseph had the final say. "No one shall be appointed to receive commandments and revelations in this church excepting my servant Joseph Smith, Jun., for he receiveth them even as Moses." (D&C 28:2; see also D&C 21:4–5.) Joseph was the person "through ... whom I have appointed unto you to receive commandments and revelations from my hand." (D&C 43:2.) As time progressed, authoritative revelation for the Church as a body would become institutionalized and less dependent upon one individual. Revelations for the entire Church would come through the governing quorums of the Church, provided there was unanimous agreement within the presiding quorums. (See D&C 107:27–31.) As time progressed, members understood more clearly that their individual revelations were to guide their personal lives and individual callings in the Church; but they were not to be considered binding upon the Church generally, especially when a personal revelation was in direct conflict with the revelations and policies of the hierarchy.

Joseph Smith at the head of the Church

Section 43 makes it clear that Joseph Smith is the preeminent leader of the Church. "Through him [Joseph] I have appointed ... to receive commandments and revelations from my hand." (Verse 2.) This revelation also clarifies that in the event Joseph is unable to lead, then he will "appoint another in his stead." (See verse 4.) This procedure is in place so that the members will not "be deceived." (See verse 6.) Order will prevail in the Church because those who are called to teach will "come in at the gate and be ordained." (See verse 7.) In other words, baptized members (with baptism being "the gate") will be officially authorized "through him whom I have appointed" to act, meaning Joseph Smith. Therefore, "uphold [Joseph] before me by the prayer of faith." (See verse 12.)

Saints to meet together to instruct and edify each other

Members of the Church are to meet together to "instruct and edify each other." (See verse 8.) In this way each member will be more knowledgeable about the laws of the Church and "sanctified by that which ye have received." (See verse 9.) And in this way "glory" will be "added to the kingdom." (See verse 10.)

Saints to uphold Joseph spiritually and temporally

The Saints are commanded to uphold Joseph spiritually. "Uphold him before me by the prayer of faith." (Verse 12.) In addition, they are to provide temporal support for Joseph as well—"food and raiment, and whatsoever thing he needeth to accomplish the work wherewith I have commanded him." (Verse 13.) By so doing Joseph will be given the time to search out and reveal the "mysteries of the kingdom"—those things that are important to the establishment of the kingdom of God on earth but not yet made manifest.

Missionaries instructed to teach and sanctify themselves

The missionaries are sent forth "to teach" and not "to be taught." (See verse 15.) Therefore, it was incumbent upon missionaries to study the gospel and learn the principles involved. They were also to be taught by the spirit of revelation. "Sanctify yourselves and ye shall be endowed with power." (Verse 16.)

The message

Millennial expectations were high. The elders (missionaries) were to proclaim the message. "Ye are not sent forth to be taught, but to teach the children of men." (Verse 15.) The warning voice was to be raised about the impending Millennium. "Prepare yourselves for the great day of the Lord." (Verse 20.) "For in mine own due time will I come upon the earth in judgment.... For the great Millennium ... shall come." (Verses 29–30.) "And the wicked shall go away into unquenchable fire." (Verse 33.)

During the Millennium men and women will be judged. Satan will be "bound, and when he is loosed again he shall only reign for a little season, and then cometh the end of the earth." (Verse 31.) The earth will pass away and those who are righteous will not taste of death but be "changed in the twinkling of an eye." (Verse 32.) The wicked will be segregated out from among the righteous and be consigned to an awful place–a place of "unquenchable fire, and their end no man knoweth on earth, nor ever shall know, until they come before me in judgment." (Verse 33.)

This message about God's future designs, Joseph taught, would involve all the nations of the earth; it was a continuing theme throughout the Prophet's life. Just two years prior to his death he said, "It has been the design of Jehovah, from the commencement of the world, and is His purpose now to regulate the affairs of the world in His own time, to stand as a head of the universe, and take the reins of government in His own hand. When that is done, judgment will be administered in righteousness; anarchy and confusion will be destroyed, and 'nations will learn war no more.'"[1]

Section 44: Whitney Home, Kirtland, Ohio, February 1831

Heading

Saints told to prepare to implement the law of consecration and to send out missionaries to grow the Church.

The big question

Question: How do we live together and build a community now that we have gathered?

Answer: Implement the law of consecration and send out missionaries to grow the Church.

Introduction

Revelation to Joseph Smith the Prophet, received at the Whitney home in Kirtland, Ohio.[2] In accordance with the revelation set forth, the Church appointed a conference to be held in the month of June following. The Lord encourages the Saints to live the law of consecration. Missionary work is urged and many converts are promised. (See verses 3–4.)

Background

In Doctrine and Covenants 20:61 the Lord revealed that Church conferences were to be held on a quarterly basis. However, up to this time conferences had not been held for the general membership or groups of members within the Church on a regular basis.[3] It had been the practice of the Church to schedule a new conference at the conclusion of the one preceding. But the command to gather in Ohio had disrupted the practice. Section 44 prompted Joseph to set a date for a conference in June 1831.[4]

Just days earlier, section 42, which was on the law of consecration, had been received. Implementing the plan would prove difficult because there

---

1. Smith, *Teachings of the Prophet Joseph Smith*, 250–51.
2. Smith, *History of the Church*, 1:157.
3. Prior to this time Church conferences had been held on June 9, 1830; September 26, 1830; and January 2, 1831.
4. The elders met in Kirtland on June 3–6, 1831.

were not enough Ohio Saints to consecrate sufficient land to support all of the new converts in addition to the members of the Church coming from the East to settle in the Kirtland area. (See D&C 37:3.) Therefore, the success of the Church was in part dependent upon its continued growth. Section 44 commanded missionaries to "go forth into the regions round about and preach" the gospel. (See verse 3.) Many converts were promised. (See verse 4.) Until there were enough members to implement the law of consecration, the Saints must not lose track of the poor and needy. (See verses 4–6 and D&C 42:30.)

Section 70: Whitney Home, Kirtland, Ohio, November 12, 1831

Heading

The Literary Firm organized to publish the Inspired Version of the Bible, a hymnal, newspaper, and any other materials deemed important for the benefit of the Church.

The big question

Question: How do we live together and build a community now that we have gathered?
Answer: Make Church publications available to the members.

Introduction

Four special conferences were held from November 1 to 12, 1831. In the last of these assemblies, the great importance of the Book of Commandments, later the Doctrine and Covenants, was considered. The elders voted to publish the Book of Commandments. Joseph taught that this book would be the "foundation of the Church in these last days, and a benefit to the world showing that the keys of the mysteries of the kingdom of our Savior are again entrusted to man."[1] (D&C 67 and commentary.)

Background

In November 1831 Joseph held a special conference of the Church to conduct business. A "stewardship" was organized to publish some of Joseph's revelations, as well as other Church materials. A committee consisting of

---

1. Smith, *Teachings of the Prophet Joseph Smith*, 7.

Joseph Smith, Oliver Cowdery, Martin Harris, John Whitmer, and Sidney Rigdon founded the Literary Firm. It was intended that members of the committee be compensated for their labor from any profits. Any excess amounts were to be used for the "Church at large."[1] (See verses 7–8.)

The Literary Firm was one of a number of businesses[2] organized by the Church for a specific purpose in conjunction with the establishment of the law of consecration. Therefore, it was stressed that such business associations were a part of and not "exempt" from laws of stewardship and consecration. (See verse 10.) The aim was clear: "In your temporal things you shall be equal, and this not grudgingly." (See verse 14.) In this regard, members were warned that if they were not willing to participate in these economic orders willingly, "the abundance of the manifestations of the Spirit shall be withheld." (See verse 14.)

Church publications to be sold

The law of consecration did not mean that legal tender was not necessary to purchase items within the community. Therefore, it was intended that Church publications be put up for sale. "Wherefore, a commandment I give unto them, that they shall not give these things unto the church, neither unto the world." (Verse 6.)

Section 72: Whitney Home, Kirtland, Ohio, December 4, 1831

Heading

Bishops called to administer the law of consecration.

The big question

Question: What is the structure of the Church?

---

1. See Cook, *Revelations of the Prophet Joseph Smith*, 112–13. In connection with these events, Joseph Smith noted that "Brother Oliver had labored with me from the beginning in writing, etc. Brother Martin has labored with me from the beginning and Brother John Whitmer and Sidney Rigdon also for a considerable time, and as these sacred writings are now going to the Church for its benefit, that we may have claim on the Church for recompense—if this conference think these things worth prizing to be had on record to show hereafter—I feel it will be according to the mind of the Spirit, for by it these things were put into my heart which I know to be the Spirit of truth." (Smith, *History of the Church*, 1:236.)

2. Specialized businesses involving groups of people cooperating in a single enterprise were sometimes referred to as "united orders" to distinguish them from the more general situation where individuals consecrated properties to the Church.

Answer: Bishops called to administer the law of consecration in Kirtland, Ohio, as well as in Zion—Independence, Missouri.

Introduction

Revelation given through Joseph Smith the Prophet in the Whitney home at Kirtland, Ohio.[1] Several elders and members had assembled to learn their duty and to be further edified in the teachings of the Church. This section is a compilation of two revelations received on the same day. Verses 1–8 make known the calling of Newel K. Whitney as a bishop. Verses 9–26 give instruction on a bishop's duties. Elders in the Church must give an account of their stewardship or calling. The bishop is to establish a storehouse, care for the poor, and certify members' worthiness.

Background

By the time section 72 had been received (December 1831), Joseph understood that Jackson County, Missouri, was to be the New Jerusalem—Zion. (See D&C 57:1–3.) At the Prophet's urging, the Colesville Saints were sent to settle there; they arrived in July 1831. On June 19, 1831, Joseph Smith, Sidney Rigdon, Edward Partridge, Martin Harris, Joseph Coe, William W. Phelps, and Sidney Gilbert and his wife, Elizabeth, started for the newly designated Zion themselves, making nearly a nine-hundred mile journey from Kirtland. The group arrived in Zion on August 2, 1831. Sidney Rigdon dedicated the land for a place of gathering and Joseph dedicated the temple site. During the latter part of August, Joseph returned home to Kirtland.

During his stay in Independence, the Prophet appointed one of his traveling companions, Edward Partridge, to serve as the bishop in Zion for the purpose of administering the law of consecration. Partridge had previously been called as the first bishop in the Church on February 4, 1831, and assigned to serve in Kirtland. (See D&C 41:9.) Partridge's change in assignment necessitated calling a bishop in Kirtland, and therefore Newel K. Whitney was selected.[2] (See verse 2.) At this point in the early development of the Church organization, it was not clear whether or not Bishop Whitney was subservient to or equal to Bishop Partridge in Independence, Missouri. Section 72 addresses this ambiguity in verses 5–6

---

1. Smith, *History of the Church*, 1:239–41.
2. It should be noted that Bishop Whitney was called as a result of a conference of high priests who had been asked by the Prophet Joseph to assemble themselves together for the purpose of conducting the business of the Church. This practice of conducting Church business in mini-conferences, as noted elsewhere, was characteristic of Joseph's leadership style and was later formalized in the governing quorums. (See D&C 107:27–31.)

and makes clear that Bishop Whitney was to report to Bishop Partridge, a step in the direction of the idea of a presiding bishop as we know it today.

It should be remembered that during this period in Church history, wards had not been organized and therefore bishops had general jurisdiction in the areas where they were appointed. There duties were to care for the poor and to administer the law of consecration. It would not be until Nauvoo that wards were organized and the function of bishops tied to a specific area designated as a "ward." The bishop's duties are to "receive the funds . . . take an account of the elders . . . administer to their wants . . . [and care for] the poor and needy."[1] (Verses 10–12.)

The distance between Kirtland and Independence and the rapid growth of the Church made it impossible for the bishop in Zion to know which members from Kirtland were in good Church standing or for the bishop in Kirtland to know which members from Zion were in good Church standing. Therefore, section 72 provides that when members traveled to Zion, they carry a "certificate" from Bishop Whitney to Bishop Partridge, or vice versa, which introduced them and confirmed that the bearer was entitled to membership privileges. (See verses 17–19, 25.)

---

1. A bishop is also called to be a judge. (See D&C 58:17; 64:40.)

Chapter 25

Morley Farm: Kirtland, Ohio, March 1831–September 1831

Section 45: Morley Farm, Kirtland, Ohio, March 7, 1831

Heading

Signs of the Second Coming set forth and the desolation of the earth described. The Saints are commanded to gather and build the New Jerusalem in Jackson County, Missouri. As part of the events of his Second Coming, Jesus will visit the New Jerusalem.

Anchor section

Memorize: Second Coming

The big question

Question: How do we live together and build a community now that we have gathered?
Answer: Prepare for the Second Coming. Build the New Jerusalem in Jackson County, Missouri.

Introduction

Revelation given through Joseph Smith on the Morley farm near Kirtland, Ohio, on March 7, 1831.[1] Prefacing his record of this revelation, the Prophet states that "at this age of the Church many false reports, lies, and foolish stories were published in the newspapers and circulated in every

---

1. Smith, *History of the Church*, 1:158–63.

direction, to prevent people from investigating the work, or embracing the faith. But to the joy of the saints . . . I received the following."

The move from Kirtland to the Morley farm

Section 45 was given about a month after the Prophet Joseph and Emma arrived in Kirtland on February 1, 1831. The prophet's wife, Emma, was pregnant, and the Smiths had no place to stay. Sidney Gilbert, one of the proprietors of the Gilbert and Whitney store, invited Joseph and Emma to stay with his family. They gratefully accepted the invitation, but when Emma arrived she realized the Gilberts had also invited the Rollins family to stay with them. Emma felt uncomfortable and the Smiths returned to the Elizabeth and Newel K. Whitney home, where they were warmly welcomed. It turned out, however, that the living situation was not particularly easy. Elizabeth's elderly aunt, Sarah, a religious skeptic and anti-cleric, received Joseph coldly. After a short time Joseph obtained a revelation that commanded that a home be provided the Smiths so that Joseph could care for the needs of his family and find enough quiet time to continue translating the Bible. (See D&C 41:7.) Accordingly, the Smiths moved into a small cabin located on the Morley farm, just a few miles outside Kirtland.[1]

During the Smiths' stay at the Morley farm, Emma's pregnancy was complicated by ill health. On April 30, 1831, she gave birth to twins, a boy and a girl. Within three hours both died. Emma was despondent. Her first pregnancy had resulted in the loss of her firstborn, who lay buried in a cemetery near the Smith home in Harmony, Pennsylvania. Now the loss of her twins overwhelmed her with sadness. Coincidentally, another brother in the Church, John Murdock, had recently lost his wife who died just after giving birth to twins. Murdock was not in a position to adequately care for the newborns and offered them to the Smiths. Emma gladly took the babies; she named the girl Julia and named the boy after her husband, Joseph. She raised the children as her own.

Meanwhile, Joseph settled in and resumed his translation of the Bible. Not much progress was made. Between April 4 and April 7 he and his scribe, Rigdon, had completed only the first eight chapters of Matthew, and by September 26 they had advanced only to Matthew 26.[2]

---

1. See Bushman, *Joseph Smith: Rough Stone Rolling*, 146.
2. Woodford takes the position that section 45 was not received in connection with the work Joseph Smith was doing on the JST but to counter "false reports and foolish stories." (See introduction to D&C 45.) He believes that at this time Joseph Smith was not working on the New Testament translation but rather the Old. "However, in verses 60 and 61 of section 45 the following is revealed: 'And now, behold I say unto you, it shall not be given unto you to know any further concerning this chapter, until the New Testament be translated, and in it

The Morley farm, just outside Kirtland, Ohio. Joseph Smith lived here from March 1831 to September 1831. First-generation Mormons were invited to live on the farm and establish the law of consecration. The fourth conference of the Church was convened here in a small schoolhouse, where men were ordained to the high priesthood for the first time.

Joseph's efforts to revise and add his revelatory insights to the text of the New Testament produced wonderful results. First, Joseph became intimately acquainted with the text and content of the Bible, something he had not done in his youth. In describing her son, Joseph's mother, Lucy, had said Joseph was not particularly interested in reading. Second, Joseph's study of the Bible raised questions in his mind about the meaning and accuracy of the text. He noticed inconsistencies and questioned whether certain passages correctly reflected the will of God. Prayer and revelation followed.

Section 45 and the signs of the times

Section 45 and others like it were of great interest to the new Church. In it the Lord commanded the Saints continue to gather "out from the eastern lands" and settle in Kirtland. Once there, some were commanded

---

all these things shall be made known; wherefore I give unto you that ye may now translate it, that ye may be prepared for the things to come.' The next day, March 8, Joseph Smith and Sidney Rigdon began work on the New Testament, and in a matter of days they reached Matthew 24." (Woodford, "Discoveries from the Joseph Smith Papers Project," 33–34.)

to move farther west to a spot referred to as Zion, the New Jerusalem. (See verse 64.) There, the Saints would build a holy city that would become "a land of peace, a city of refuge, a place of safety for the saints." (Verse 66.) Then, the Savior would return and the Millennium would be ushered in. No doubt such promises motivated the Saints to give up their homes in the East and go to Kirtland. After all, if the cataclysmic events preceding Jesus' Second Coming were about to destroy the earth, their homes were at risk. The only place where true safety could be found was in Zion.

The expectation of the cataclysmic events and bloodshed preceding the Second Coming heightened the Saints' interest in local, national, and world events. Joseph's concerns "about 'troubles among the nations' on a global scale and the 'ravages of the cholera' in the world's major cities with plague as far away as India were as much a part of his conversation as were current political crises in the United States."[1] Five months after this revelation was received, unrest caught the attention of the entire nation when a slave rebellion occurred in Southampton County, Virginia, involving a slave named Nat Turner. Fifty-five whites were shot, stabbed, or clubbed to death. Turner fled and was arrested in October for leading the bloodiest slave revolt in U.S. history. He was hanged for his part in the uprising. These and other events stoked the fires of millennialism.

Joseph Smith was not alone when it came to forecasting the Second Coming. In August of 1831 William Miller, an American Baptist minister preached his first sermon on the Second Coming of Christ in Dresden, New York that marked the commencement of the Advent Movement in the United States. Later Miller would unsuccessfully predict the exact date in 1843 when Christ would come a date specifically rejected by the prophet Joseph.

By the end of the decade, despite calamitous events around the globe, the Saints would face the stark realization that their millennial expectations would not to be realized as they had anticipated. They would settle and be brutally driven out of Zion, the New Jerusalem (Jackson County). Members of the Church would come to realize that the expectations about the end of time, fanned by the flames of Joseph's revelations, would not come to pass in their lifetime. A more conservative approach was closer to what the Lord actually had in mind. In their enthusiasm, the Saints had not paid enough attention to the parts of Joseph's revelations that warned that "the hour and the day no man knoweth, neither the angels in heaven, nor shall they know until he comes." (D&C 49:7.) For reasons to be explored in connection with some of Joseph's later revelations, the Lord's Second Coming was not just around the corner.

---

1. Staker, *Hearken, O Ye People*, Kindle locations 6069–71.

Signs that will precede the Second Coming

Prior to the Second Coming the Saints will be gathered. In that day, there shall be heard of wars and rumors of wars. The whole earth will be in commotion. Men's hearts will fail them. People will say that Christ has delayed his coming until the end of the earth. (See verse 26.) The love of men will "wax cold" and "iniquity shall abound." (See verse 27.) There will be an overflowing scourge, and a desolating sickness will cover the land. However, members of the Church will stand in holy places while the wicked lift up their voices, curse God and die. (See verse 32.) Earthquakes will occur in diverse places and "many desolations" will cover the earth. Yet people will not believe in God, and they will take up the sword and kill one another. (See verse 33.) Finally, there will be signs and wonders in the heaven. (See verse 40.) Blood, fire, vapor, and smoke will prevail. (See verse 41.) The sun will be darkened and the moon turned into blood and the stars fall from heaven. (See verse 42.) Then the Lord himself will come and set forth his foot upon the Mount Olivet and it shall "cleave in twain . . . and reel to and fro, and the heavens also shall shake." (Verse 48.)

Reference to the Civil War

The Saints are informed that that in "not many years hence ye shall hear of wars in your own lands," undoubtedly a reference to the American Civil War. (Verse 63.) Warnings of this forthcoming event would come more explicitly in December 1832, when Joseph received the Civil War prophecy. (See D&C 87.)

The "heathen nations" will have part in the first resurrection

Two resurrections await mankind—the first or resurrection of the just, and the second or resurrection of the unjust. (See D&C 76; John 5:28–29; Revelation 20.) The first resurrection is divided into the morning and afternoon. Those being resurrected with celestial bodies will come forth in the morning. They are Christ's, the first fruits, and will reign as kings and priests, queens and priestesses during the millennial era. This group is also made up of those who "died in their sins, without a knowledge of the truth, or in transgression, having rejected the prophets," who "were taught faith in God, repentance from sin, vicarious baptism for the remission of sins, the gift of the Holy Ghost by the laying on of hands, and all other principles of the gospel that were necessary for them to know in order to qualify themselves that they might be judged according to men in the flesh, but live according to God in the spirit." (See D&C 138:32–34, 58–59;

29:13; 43:18; 76:50–70; 88:97–98; 1 Thessalonians 4:16–17; Revelation 20:3–7.) During the afternoon of the first resurrection, those who received the gospel in the spirit and "are not valiant in the testimony of Jesus" will come forth with terrestrial bodies. (See D&C 76:71–80.)

Sometime during the first resurrection, section 45 teaches, the "heathen [neither Jewish nor Christian] nations [shall] be redeemed, and they that knew no law shall have part in the first resurrection; and it shall be tolerable for them." (Verse 54.) Presumably these are those who have been taught the gospel in the spirit world and were either "valiant" or not "valiant" in the "testimony of Jesus" and therefore are raised up with either celestial or terrestrial bodies. (See D&C 76:79; 138: 32–34, 58–59.) Joseph taught that "to say that the heathens would be damned because they did not believe the Gospel would be preposterous and to say that the Jews would all be damned that do not believe in Jesus would be equally absurd; for 'how can they believe on him of whom they have not heard.'"[1] Therefore "neither Jew nor heathen can be culpable for rejecting the conflicting opinions of sectarianism, nor for rejecting any testimony but that which is sent of God."[2]

At the end of the Millennium the second resurrection begins. (See D&C 88:100–101.) These are those who have telestial bodies and were wicked and carnal in mortality. (See D&C 76:85, 81–112.) Finally, in the latter end of the resurrection of the unjust or damnation, the sons of perdition come forth who "remain filthy still." (See D&C 88:102; Alma 12:17–18.)

Events preceding and during the Millennium

Prior to Jesus' coming the wicked will slay one another, and those that "will not take his sword against his neighbor must needs flee unto Zion for safety." (Verse 68.) At Zion the righteous of the earth will be gathered in one. "And it shall be said among the wicked: Let us not go up to battle against Zion, for the inhabitants of Zion are terrible; wherefore we cannot stand." (Verse 70.)

At his coming, "the saints that have slept shall come forth to meet me in the cloud." (Verse 45.) Jesus will appear on both continents. In the east, the Jews will "look upon me and say: What are these wounds in thine hands and in thy feet? Then shall they know that I am the Lord." (Verses 51–52.)

During the Millennium, "Satan shall be bound, that he shall have no place in the hearts of the children of men." (Verse 55.) The peoples of the earth will "multiply and wax strong, and their children shall grow

---

1. Smith, *Teachings of the Prophet Joseph Smith*, 221.
2. Smith, *Teachings of the Prophet Joseph Smith*, 221.

up without sin unto salvation." (Verse 58.) "The Lord shall be in their midst and his glory shall be upon them, and he will be their king and their lawgiver." (Verse 59.)[1]

Section 46: Morley Farm, Kirtland, Ohio, March 8, 1831

Heading

Gifts of the Spirit enumerated.

The big questions

Question: How do we live together and build a community now that we have gathered?
Answer: Encourage members to seek after the best spiritual gifts to bless and edify each other.
Question: What is the structure of the Church?
Answer: Church services are open to the public. A bishop's responsibility is to discern which gifts of the Spirit are from God and which are not.

Introduction

Revelation given through Joseph Smith the Prophet to the Church at the Morley farm near Kirtland, Ohio, on March 8, 1831.[2] A pattern for conducting Church services had not yet developed, and a custom of admitting only members and earnest investigators to sacrament meetings was extant. The Lord instructs that nonmembers should not be cast out of general Church meetings. False spiritual manifestations were being experienced. Bishops were given the authority to decide which spiritual gifts were from God and which were not.

---

1. Joseph F. McConkie and Craig Ostler point out that "not all wickedness will cease at the beginning of the Millennium. Some will reject the testimony of Jesus Christ and his divine mission. The Prophet Joseph Smith taught that 'there will be wicked men on the earth during the thousand years. The heathen nations who will not come up to worship will be visited with the judgments of God, and must eventually be destroyed from the earth' (Smith, *Teachings of the Prophet Joseph Smith*, 268–69). Those who knew no law or sinned in ignorance because of traditions of their fathers will be given opportunity to receive the testimony of Jesus and be numbered among the Saints." (McConkie and Ostler, *Revelations of the Restoration*, 355.) It is also worthy of note that there is reason to believe that freedom of worship will also be enjoyed during the Millennium. (See Jeremiah 31:34.)

2. Smith, *History of the Church*, 1:163–65.

Anchor section

Memorize: Gifts of the Spirit

Background

Section 46 came in response to growing concerns on the part of Joseph Smith and others that false spiritual manifestations were creeping into the Church. Clearly, one of the primary traits of the restored gospel was the exercise of spiritual gifts—healing, prophecy, tongues, and more. But sometimes the early members' enthusiasm for and expression of "spiritual gifts" were contrary to the will of God. In recognition of this problem, Joseph Smith said that some members "were striving to do the will of God, so far as they knew it, though some strange notions and false spirits had crept in among them. With a little caution and some wisdom, I soon assisted the brethren and sisters to overcome them."[1]

Spiritual intemperance during this period in the Church's history was described in the *Painesville Telegraph* on February 15, 1831:

> [Members of the Church] would fall, as without strength, roll upon the floor, and so mad were they that even the females were seen on a cold winter day, lying under the bare canopy of heaven, with no couch or pillow but the fleecy snow. At other times they exhibited all the apish actions imaginable, making grimaces both horrid and ridiculous, creeping upon their hands and feet, etc. Sometimes, in these exercises the young men would rise and play before the people, going through all the Indian maneuvers of knocking down, scalping, jabbering after which they call speaking foreign languages by divine inspiration. At other times, they would start and run several furlongs, then get upon stumps and preach to imagined congregations, baptize ghosts, etc.[2]

Descriptions of such spiritual overindulgence were also mentioned by Parley P. Pratt, John Whitmer, and George A. Smith. Pratt reported that "some very strange spiritual operations were manifested," which he found to be "disgusting, rather than edifying."[3] He mentioned that some Saints would "swoon away" or "fall into ecstasies" and be "drawn into contortions" that were "not edifying."[4] John Whitmer told of some members wielding an imaginary "sword of Laban" while other would act like "an Indian in the act of scalping another person."[5] Others would "slide or

---

1. Van Wagoner, *Sidney Rigdon: A Portrait of Religious Excess*, 82.
2. See Van Wagoner, Sidney Rigdon: A Portrait of Religious Excess, 83.
3. Van Wagoner, *Sidney Rigdon: A Portrait of Religious Excess*, 83.
4. Van Wagoner, *Sidney Rigdon: A Portrait of Religious Excess*, 83.
5. Van Wagoner, *Sidney Rigdon: A Portrait of Religious Excess*, 83.

scoot on the floor" like a serpent." Whitmer concluded that such behaviors were not becoming of good disciples.

Joseph Smith's personal reaction to the spiritual tenor of the times was confirmed by his cousin, George A. Smith. He documented an incident involving a Latter-day Saint by the name of "Black Pete," a former slave, self-proclaimed revelator, and member of the communal order on the Morley farm. One evening "Black Pete" thought he caught sight of a black angel flying through the heavens. In a dash after the seraph he fell off a steep cliff, landed in a tree, and was fortunate enough to come out with only a few scratches.[1] All of this was too much for Joseph, who took occasion to teach the Saints the difference between "the spirit of God, and the spirit of the devil."[2] He said that people seized in a violent and unnatural manner or who uttered strange sounds were deceiving themselves if they believed they were manifesting the Spirit of the Lord.[3]

Other common spiritual gifts in early Kirtland involved shouting, jerking, dancing, singing, and barking.[4] Barking was an extension of the jerks, in which the worshipper would rock his head repeatedly and make "uncontrollable noises."[5] Sometimes a "barker" would hang on to a tree and would be ridiculed for "barking up a tree," a common phrase used to this day in a nonspiritual context.[6] As part of this religious, ecstatic experience, some claimed to see in vision letters falling from heaven, which were copied on paper and authorized the recipient to preach or baptize. Confusing the spiritual gifts with divine commissions and the right to perform saving ordinances was problematic and undermined central control over the growth of the Church.[7]

Joseph Smith's concerns about bodily contortions being associated with the devil probably dated back to the first official miracle in the Church, which involved Newel Knight, a new convert and close friend of the Prophet's. Prior to Joseph's arrival, Newel had attended a Church meeting and been asked to pray publicly. He was shy and declined. The next morning he went into the woods to pray in private. He felt guilty for not praying in public and felt a bad spirit come over him as he tried to petition heaven. Newel returned home, and his wife was alarmed by his appearance. He was "suffering very much in his mind, and his body acted upon in a very strange manner; his visage and limbs distorted and twisted in every shape

---

1. Van Wagoner, *Sidney Rigdon: A Portrait of Religious Excess*, 83.
2. Van Wagoner, *Sidney Rigdon: A Portrait of Religious Excess*, 84.
3. Van Wagoner, *Sidney Rigdon: A Portrait of Religious Excess*, 84.
4. Staker, *Hearken, O Ye People*, Kindle location 1325.
5. Ibid.
6. Ibid.
7. Ibid., 2514.

and appearance possible to imagine; and finally he was caught up off the floor of the apartment [room], and tossed about most fearfully."[1]

This startling event caused a commotion, and relatives and friends gathered to see what was going on. The Prophet was informed of the situation and arrived at the Knights' to see for himself. Joseph caught hold of Newel's hand, said Newel was possessed of an evil spirit, and commanded the Devil to depart in the name of Jesus Christ. Newel said that he saw an evil spirit depart and vanish. Joseph affirmed that the devil had been cast out by the "power of godliness."[2]

After the evil spirit was cast out, Newel said he felt weak and went to bed. Later on the same day, the Spirit of the Lord came over him and he reported seeing the visions of eternity and was "for some time enwrapt in contemplation, insomuch that I knew not what was going on in the room." During this vision his body was once again elevated until he felt the ceiling beams pressing against his body.[3]

Joseph's desire to restrain inappropriate spiritual expression, however, was not meant to squelch the Spirit. Unlike the Campbellites, Mormons believed that the gifts of the Spirit should be an important part of the restoration of what Jesus taught. Mormon preachers emphasized receiving a witness from God for oneself. After all, the Book of Mormon promised the reader that upon prayerful inquiry, God would "manifest the truth" of the book "by the power of the Holy Ghost" (Moroni 10:4). Specifically, the book warned that in the last days people would cease to believe in miracles because "they dwindle in unbelief, and depart from the right way" (Mormon 9:20).

Dr. Samuel Underhill, an Owenite, said Mormon missionaries relied on an internal feeling of certainty that they defined as the Spirit of God. He listened to the missionaries and "felt something" but dismissed it as human emotion, not a divine communication from heaven. In speaking about why the Mormons were gaining converts, he said: "You wonder at the success of the New System of the Mormonites! I wonder not at all. . . . It is not the golden bible . . . not the eloquence of their preachers . . . not the result of studied . . . understanding. . . . You ask then what then can it be? I'll tell you . . . what it is. . . . Let me ask you did you never feel in a religious meeting an unexpected mighty solemn feeling, a kind of vivid flame glowing in every part of your frame. Did it never make you tremble, did you never see others tremble like an aspen leaf . . . have you not witnessed the thrilling shriek, the convulsive sobs, the broken

---

1. *Church History in the Fulness of Times*, 69.
2. See *Church History in the Fulness of Times*, 69.
3. See *Church History in the Fulness of Times*, 70.

words?"[1] Underhill's description was a common occurrence and is not unlike what modern-day converts feel, except for perhaps the "thrilling shriek" and "convulsive sobs."

It was in the context of discerning between appropriate and inappropriate spiritual happenings that the Prophet inquired of the Lord, and section 46 was received. The revelation encouraged members to seek after the best gifts and gave bishops the responsibility to see that such things were not abused. "And unto the bishop of the church . . . [is] . . . given . . . to discern all those gifts lest there shall be any among you professing and yet be not of God." (Verse 27.)

The function of spiritual gifts

The purpose the spiritual gifts are to bless, benefit, and comfort, and they should be used in the service of others. Gifts sought solely as a demonstration of God's power is forbidden. "For verily I say unto you, they [gifts] are given for the benefit of those who love me and keep all my commandments, and him that seeketh so to do; that all may be benefited that seek or that ask of me, that ask and not for a sign that they may consume it upon their lusts." (Verse 9.)

Obtaining the gifts of the Spirit

Spiritual gifts cannot be obtained on command and are most often experienced as a byproduct by those who genuinely serve others. Therefore, it is not unusual for people to report that the gifts of the Spirit are most prevalent during times of intense service—full-time missionary labor or while involved in more demanding Church-related activities.

This said, it should also be recognized that the gifts may be employed in our temporal pursuits as well. There simply is no clear line of demarcation between the spiritual and the temporal. As Brigham Young once explained, a religion that cannot save a person temporally cannot save him or her spiritually. Salvation consists of both. "Wherefore, I say unto you that all things unto me are spiritual, and not at any time have I given unto you a law which was temporal." (D&C 29:33–35.) For these reasons it is always appropriate for Latter-day Saints to exercise faith and to expect spiritual help in both the temporal and spiritual affairs of life.

David O. McKay, the ninth president of the Church, gave some good counsel on what we may or may not expect in reference to spiritual intercession. He explained what happened when he first sought a testimony

---

1. Staker, *Hearken, O Ye People*, Kindle location 2541.

of the gospel, which suggests a pattern on how and when spiritual experiences come. As a young man herding cattle he climbed a steep hill and stopped to let his horse rest. An intense desire came over him to receive a manifestation of the truthfulness of the gospel. He dismounted, threw his reins over his horse's head, and knelt and prayed "fervently and sincerely and with as much faith as a young boy could muster." At the conclusion of the prayer he got up onto his horse again. "No spiritual manifestation has come to me," he confessed. "If I am true to myself, I must say I am just the same old boy that I was before I prayed."

It was not until he was serving as a full-time missionary that he received a witness of the Spirit confirming the truthfulness of the gospel. At the time he had been given increased responsibility as the president of the Scottish Conference. Of this experience he said, "I remember as if it were but yesterday, the intensity of the inspiration of that occasion. Everybody felt the rich outpouring of the Spirit of the Lord. Never before had I experienced such an emotion." He explained that his testimony came as "a natural consequence to the performance of duty." He devoted himself to the work of the Lord and conviction followed. President McKay continued in service to the Church throughout his life and continued to experience the gifts of the Spirit. On May 10, 1921, he was blessed with a sublime vision of the Savior.[1]

Finally, the gifts of the Spirit are not reserved only for those who are spiritually strong but also for those who sincerely endeavor to do the will of the Lord. There is comfort in the assurance that the gifts are not only for those who "love me [God] and keep *all* my commandments" but also for those who *"seeketh so to do."* (See D&C 46:9; emphasis added.) The Lord is generous.

The gift of knowing the "differences of administration"

The function and use of most of the gifts set forth in section 46 are self-evident. However, the gift of the "differences of administration" is not as easily understood. This gift involves knowing in any set of circumstances what course of conduct would most effectively bless and strengthen others. "Differences of administration" is most often thought of in connection with Church administration but also applies in other situations as well. "And there are different ways that these gifts are administered; but it is the same God who worketh all in all." (Moroni 10:8.) Consequently, there are as many spiritual gifts as there are different situations, and no complete list is

---

1. Clair Middlemiss, *Cherished Experiences*, (Salt Lake City: Deseret Book, 1955).

possible. As H. George Bickerstaff noted, "Clearly the Spirit can grant any gift that would fill a particular need: hence no exhaustive list is possible."[1]

All meetings should be conducted according to the Spirit

In highly structured situations it is more difficult for the Spirit to direct. Flexibility allows for this opportunity. It is for this reason that "it always has been given to the elders of my church from the beginning, and ever shall be, to conduct all meetings as they are directed and guided by the Holy Spirit." (D&C 46:2.) This policy was first introduced at the organization of the Church (D&C 20:44–45) and is also repeated in the Book of Mormon. "And their meetings were conducted by the church after the manner of the workings of the Spirit, and by the power of the Holy Ghost; for as the power of the Holy Ghost led them whether to preach, or to exhort, or to pray, or to supplicate, or to sing, even so it was done." (Moroni 6:9.)

The equality of the gifts and Paul's comparison of the gifts of the Spirit to the human body

As mentioned previously, the purpose of the gifts is to bless, comfort, and encourage. To this end, each person is given a gift to uplift others. The Apostle Paul makes this point by comparing the gifts of the Spirit to various parts of a human body—the eyes, ears, nose, and so forth. He explains that each body part works in unison together so that the body might function properly.

This metaphor suggests that each member is uniquely fit to perform various functions and that no function, regardless of how lowly, can be left out. "But all these worketh that one and the selfsame Spirit, dividing to every man severally as he will. For as the body is one, and hath many members, and all the members of that one body, being many, are one body: so also is Christ." (1 Corinthians 12:11–12.) Furthermore, "And the eye cannot say unto the hand, I have no need of thee: nor again the head to the feet, I have no need of you. Nay, much more those members of the body, which seem to be more feeble, are necessary: And those members of the body, which we think to be less honourable, upon these we bestow more abundant honour; and our uncomely parts have more abundant comeliness." (1 Corinthians 12:21–23.)

The New Living Translation makes the point even more clearly. "In fact, some of the parts that seem weakest and least important are really the most necessary. And the parts we regard as less honorable are those

---

1. *Encyclopedia of Mormonism*, 5:544.

we clothe with the greatest care.... So God has put the body together in such a way that extra honor and care are given to those parts that have less dignity. This makes for harmony among the members, so that all the members care for each other equally." (1 Corinthians 12:22–25.)

Open attendance at public meetings

At this time in the Kirtland area some congregations were excluding members of the public from attending general Church meetings. Perhaps such limits grew out of concerns that nonmembers had attempted to disrupt Mormon services and therefore only members and earnest investigators should be admitted. This approach was contrary to advice given in the Book of Mormon when Jesus visited the Nephites and the Lamanites after his resurrection. Jesus commanded that "none . . . should go away" and further that members should not "cast" anyone "out from among you, but ye shall minister unto him." (3 Nephi 18:25, 30.) These same sentiments are repeated in this section. "Nevertheless ye are commanded never to cast any one out from your public meetings, which are held before the world." (D&C 46:3–6.)

SECTION 47: MORLEY FARM, KIRTLAND, OHIO, MARCH 8, 1831

Heading

John Whitmer appointed Church historian.

Introduction

Revelation given through the Prophet Joseph at the Morley farm located near Kirtland, Ohio.[1] Prior to this time Oliver Cowdery had acted as Church historian and recorder. John Whitmer had not sought an appointment as historian, but, being asked to serve in this capacity, he had said that he would obey the will of the Lord in the matter. He had already served as a secretary to the Prophet in recording many of the revelations received in Fayette, New York.

---

1. Smith, *History of the Church*, 1:166.

The big questions

Question: What is the structure of the Church?
Answer: A Church historian should be appointed to chronicle the history of the Church.

Background

Prior to this time Oliver Cowdery had been acting as Church historian.[1] John Whitmer at the time was serving as a records clerk. Joseph advised Whitmer that he should, in addition, chronicle the history of the Church. Whitmer was reluctant at first, but said he would serve if it was the will of the Lord.[2] Joseph inquired and section 47 was received. "Behold, it is expedient in me that my servant John should write and keep a regular history." (Verse 1.)

Recording the history of the Church had been a priority from the beginning. (See D&C 123:1–7.) On the day the Church was organized, April 6, 1830, Joseph had been commanded to keep a journal on the rise of the Church. Whitmer's calling continued the practice.

Whitmer started his official duties on June 12, 1831, and served in this capacity until his excommunication on March 10, 1838. During his seven-year tenure he recorded only a hundred pages of text, of which a number of pages were torn out and lost. In November 1831, in a revelation to Joseph, the Lord encouraged Whitmer in his duties. "Wherefore, I, the Lord, will that my servant, John Whitmer, should . . . continue in writing and making a history of all the important things which he shall observe and know concerning my church." (D&C 69:2–3.) The Whitmer manuscript eventually found its way into the hands of the Community of Christ Church. His history was published in 1908.[3]

John Whitmer's commission to keep a history was reiterated in a second revelation given in November of 1831 wherein he was commanded to "continue in writing and making a history." (Section 69:3)

---

1. Cowdery kept the official history of the Church up to mid-1831. His record was lost and has never been located. During his second term in office, he wrote a series of eight historical letters that were later published in the *Messenger and Advocate* in 1834. (See *Encyclopedia of Mormonism*, 2:588.) (See verse 3.)

2. John Whitmer recorded the following on his feelings about being called as the Church Historian. "I was appointed by the voice of the Elders to keep the Church Record. Joseph Smith Jr. said unto me you must also keep the Church history. I would rather not do it but observed that the will of the Lord be done, and if he desires it, I desire that he would manifest it through Joseph the Seer. And thus came the word of the Lord." (Robinson and Garrett, *Doctrine and Covenants Commentary*, 2:84.)

3. See *Encyclopedia of Mormonism*, 2:589.

Morley Farm: Kirtland, Ohio, March 1831–September 1831

Section 48: Morley Farm, Kirtland, Ohio, March 1831[1]

Heading

Share what you have with the Saints migrating to Kirtland, Ohio, from the East. Prepare financially to purchase land at the location of the New Jerusalem.

The big question

Question: How do we live together and build a community now that we have gathered?

Answer: Share what you have with the Saints migrating to Kirtland from the East.

Introduction

Revelation given through Joseph Smith the Prophet at the Morley farm located near Kirtland, Ohio, in March 1831. The Prophet Joseph had inquired of the Lord as to the mode of procedure in procuring lands for the settlement of the Saints. This was an important matter in view of the migration of members of the Church from the eastern states in accordance with the command that they should assemble in Ohio. (See D&C 37:1–3; 45:64.)

Background

In March 1831, the question of where the Saints arriving in Kirtland from the East could settle was a pressing concern. Joseph and his family had been in Kirtland for only a couple of months and others were following. Obedient to the command to gather in Ohio, the Colesville, New York, Saints and others were arriving daily and in need of food and shelter. (See D&C 37:3; 38:32, 37; 39:15; 45:64.) The newcomers for the most part were poor. Uprooted from their homes in the East and other parts of the country, many had sold their land and possessions at a loss and arrived in Kirtland with no visible means of support. Although the law of consecration had been revealed just weeks before (see D&C 42) it was not implemented in Kirtland because there were insufficient properties in the area to provide for the local Saints, let alone the many that were headed to Zion. Faced with

---

1. "We can now accurately date this section on March 10, 1831." (Woodford, "Discoveries from the Joseph Smith Papers Project," 30.)

these issues and concerns, the Saints were commanded to share their lands with the incoming Saints, continue to purchase lands, and build a city.[1]

It was already known by this time that the Lord intended to establish the New Jerusalem (Zion), but the exact place was not known. In this regard the Saints were advised to "save all the money that ye can" so that when the location of Zion was specifically revealed the land could be purchased. (See verses 4–5.)

Section 49: Morley Farm, Kirtland, Ohio, March 1831[2]

Heading

Missionaries sent to the Shaker community and are rejected.

The big question

Question: What is the structure of the Church?
Answer: Send missionaries out to grow the Church.

Introduction

Revelation given to Joseph Smith the Prophet for Sidney Rigdon, Parley P. Pratt, and Leman Copley at the Morley farm located near Kirtland, Ohio, in March 1831.[3] Leman Copley had embraced the gospel, but still held to some of the teachings of the Shakers (United Society of Believers in Christ's Second Appearing), to which he had formerly belonged. Some of the beliefs of the Shakers were that Christ's Second Coming had already occurred and that he had appeared in the form of a woman, Ann Lee. Baptism by water was not considered essential, nor were members allowed to eat pork, and many did not eat any meat. Celibacy was considered to be a higher good than marriage. The Prophet wrote, "In order to have a more perfect understanding on the subject, I inquired of the Lord, and received the following." This revelation refutes some of the basic concepts of the Shaker group. Rigdon, Pratt, and Copley took a copy of this revelation to the Shaker community near Cleveland, Ohio, and read it to them in its entirety, but it was rejected.

---

1. See Robinson and Garrett, *Doctrine and Covenants Commentary*, 2:86–87.
2. "Although the current Doctrine and Covenants dates this revelation in March 1831, we can show it was actually received May 7, 1831." (Woodford, "Discoveries from the Joseph Smith Papers Project," 30.)
3. Smith, *History of the Church*, 1:167–69. Some date this revelation in May 1831.

Morley Farm: Kirtland, Ohio, March 1831–September 1831

Background

Leman Copley, once a Shaker and a recent convert to the Church, approached Joseph to discuss with him his reticence to preach the gospel. He suggested that missionaries be sent to the members of his former church, but he was not anxious to participate. Subsequently, Copley was convinced to accompany two missionary powerhouses, Sidney Rigdon and Parley P. Pratt, on a mission to the Shakers.

The Shakers were an offshoot of the Quaker group that was started by George Fox in England in the seventeenth century. The Shakers, like their cousins, the Quakers, wore distinguishing dress. The men wore a white turtleneck-like collar with a white bowtie, tall top hat, and a long black suit coat that completely covered their buttocks. The women wore brown dresses that reached to the ankles and a white inner bonnet covered by either a brown or black outer bonnet with a deep rim. When Shakers worshiped they would physically shake and tremble. They also practiced an ecstatic dancing and frenzy that led to twirling, shouting, and tongues. Although a conservative group for their times, they believed in the equality of women.

Ann Lee assumed leadership of the Shakers. Lee was the daughter of a blacksmith/handyman, had no schooling, worked as a cook, and was a hatter. All four of her children died in childbirth, and her husband deserted her. Her followers believed that she was the Messiah and that the Millennium had already started.[1] The group lived in a communal living order and considered sexual relations to be at the root of most evil. Although they did not forbid marriage, they taught that celibacy was superior. They despised violence and were pacifists, viewed wealth and luxury as sin, denied the doctrines of the trinity (believed in one God only), believed that spiritual feelings were a more sure source of truth than the scriptures, and rejected the atonement and the resurrection of the flesh. Sickness and disease were considered the product of sin. Shakers avoided meats, especially pork, because it was taught against in Leviticus.

Persecuted in England, Mother Ann, as she was called, claimed to have received a revelation to come to America in 1774 to establish the Church of the United Society of Believers in Christ's Second Appearing—the Shakers' official name. In 1831 they had well over five thousand members and outnumbered the fledgling Mormons.[2]

---

1. They taught that since Christ had come the first time in the form of a man, his second appearance would be in the form of a woman. In support they reasoned that God was both male and female based upon Genesis 1:27: "In his own image . . . created he them" both male and female.
2. See Preece, *Learning to Love the Doctrine and Covenants*, 91.

Some time in May 1831, Copley, Rigdon, and Pratt were dispatched to go preach the gospel to the Shaker settlement, just a few miles outside of Kirtland. The Lord promised, "Behold, I will go before you and be your rearward; and I will be in your midst, and you shall not be confounded." (Verse 27.) Upon their arrival, the Mormon missionaries met with the Shakers in one of their meetings and read section 49 to them verbatim. However, the Shakers vigorously rejected the revelation.

According to Shaker leader Ashbel Kitchell, Rigdon and Copley arrived on Saturday and agreed not to interrupt the meeting on Sunday. Pratt, however, arrived on Sunday morning and asked permission to read section 49 to the members of the congregation at the end of the meeting. Apparently, Rigdon read the section and the Shakers protested. Pratt stood and shook his coattail and the dust from his feet as a testimony against the Shaker congregation. Kitchell was offended and rebuked Pratt, who left abruptly. Rigdon and Copley stayed for supper in continuation of their missionary efforts, but the Shakers were unmoved by any efforts.

When Copley returned to Kirtland he was asked by Joseph to use his land located in Thompson, Ohio, for the establishment of a communal order patterned after the instructions that had been given in connection with the law of consecration.[1] Consequently, the Colesville, New York, Saints were invited to settle there. At first Copley complied, but he later changed his mind and evicted the hundred or so people that had made their abode there. It was not long afterwards that members of the Colesville group were sent to settle and build up the new Zion in Jackson County, Missouri.

Copley was disfellowshipped but regained full fellowship by October 1832. In 1834 he was accused of bearing false witness against Joseph in a civil trial and was excommunicated. He apologized and was accepted back into the faith. Copley never went with the body of the Saints to Missouri and died in Ohio in 1860. According to Richard Van Wagoner, at some point he rejoined the Shaker faith.[2] He was buried in Thompson, Ohio.

Shaker doctrines addressed

The following Shaker doctrines were accepted or rejected:

1. *The Millennium was in progress and Jesus had come in the form of Ann Lee*. Section 49 spells out that Jesus had not come and the Millennium was not in progress. As to the time of the Second Coming, "The hour and the day no man knoweth, neither the angels in heaven, nor shall they know until he comes." (Verse 7.) All of these events were yet to come. On the

---

1. Copley's farm comprised about 759 acres and was located just outside Kirtland.
2. Van Wagoner, *Sidney Rigdon: A Portrait of Religious Excess*, 94.

issue of Jesus coming in the form of a woman, Ann Lee, section 49 made clear "the Son of Man cometh not in the form of a woman." (Verse 22.)

2. *Celibacy is preferable to marriage.* Section 49 spells out that celibacy is not of God and that marriage is ordained of God. "Whoso forbiddeth to marry is not ordained of God, for marriage is ordained of God unto man." (Verse 15.)

3. *People should abstain from meats.* Section 49 spells out that "whoso forbiddeth to abstain from meats, that man should not eat the same, is not ordained of God." (Verse 18.)

4. *Communal orders were divinely approved social communities.* On this point section 49 seems to agree. "But it is not given that one man should possess that which is above another, wherefore the world lieth in sin." (Verse 20.)

The role of the remnant of Jacob and the Second Coming

Regarding the Second Coming, section 49 provides information on the remnant of Jacob or the Lamanites. Prior to Jesus' return, this group will "flourish in the wilderness, and the Lamanites shall blossom as the rose." (Verse 24.) Faithful latter-day Gentiles are to take the gospel to this group. (See 2 Nephi 20:20–22; 21:11–12; 3 Nephi 16:4; 5:24–26.) The Lamanites will become strong in the faith, and faithful Gentiles will be numbered among them to assist them in building up the New Jerusalem. (See 3 Nephi 21:6, 22–23.) Unrighteous Gentiles who do not accept the gospel are warned that Jacob will come among them like a "lion among the flocks of the sheep." (See 3 Nephi 20:15–16; 21:12.)

SECTION 50: MORLEY FARM, KIRTLAND, OHIO, MAY 1831[1]

Heading

False spiritual manifestations abroad in the Church at Kirtland.

Anchor section

Memorize: False revelation

---

1. "The precise date of this revelation is May 9, 1831." (Woodford, "Discoveries from the Joseph Smith Papers Project," 30.)

The big question

Question: How do we live together and build a community now that we have gathered?

Answer: By carefully discerning which spiritual gifts are from God and which are not.

Introduction

Revelation given through the Prophet Joseph at the Morley farm located near Kirtland, Ohio, on May 9, 1831.[1] The Prophet stated that some of the elders did not understand the manifestations of different spirits abroad in the earth and that this revelation was given in response to his inquiry of the Lord on this matter. Many spiritual manifestations, false and true, were known among the Saints (visions and revelations). The Lord explains how to discern true spiritual experience from the counterfeit. That which edifies is of God; that which does not is not of God.

Background

Between the time when missionaries went to preach to the Lamanites in November 1830 and the Prophet arrived in Kirtland in February 1831, the Kirtland Saints were left to themselves and were without strong central leadership. As a result, the Church drifted, false religious ideas took hold, and counterfeit spiritual experiences were mistaken for manifestations from God. When Parley P. Pratt returned from his mission to the Shakers (D&C 49) he described "strange spiritual operations" occurring in Kirtland that were "disgusting, rather than edifying." Members of the Church would "swoon away, and make unseemly gestures, and be drawn or disfigured in their countenances. Others would fall into ecstasies and be drawn into contortions, cramps, fits, etc." Some had visions and revelations that were not uplifting, and it seemed to Pratt that there was a "false and lying spirit" abroad in the Church.[2] (See commentary on section 46.)

Levi Hancock,[3] a convert who was baptized by Parley P. Pratt and later

---

1. Smith, *History of the Church*, 1:170–73. Although the exact date of the revelation is not mentioned in the Doctrine and Covenants, *The Evening and Morning Star*, in which section 50 first appeared, gave the date of this revelation as May 9, 1831.

2. See *Autobiography of Parley P. Pratt*, 48.

3. Levi Hancock was introduced to Mormonism by his brother Alvah, who asked him if he had heard the news about a "book . . . they call [a] history and a record of the people that once inhabited this land." As Alvah spoke, Levi Hancock "gathered faith and there seemed to fall on me something pleasant and delightful. It seemed like a wash of something warm took me in the face and ran over my body which gave me a feeling I cannot describe. The

one of the seven presidents of Seventy, was another eyewitness who questioned the propriety of some of the spiritual gifts operating among the Latter-day Saints. He reported that while he was engaged in preaching the gospel three young missionaries, Herman Basset, age sixteen (D&C 52:37), Edson Fuller, age twenty-one (D&C 52:28), and Burr Riggs, age twenty (D&C 75:17), claimed revelations, the visitation of angels, and engaged in strange behaviors such as falling down and frothing at the mouth.

> One of them who acted the worst was Burr Riggs. I have seen him jump up from the floor, strike his head against the joist in the Baldwins new house and swing some minutes, then fall like he was dead. After an hour or two he would come to [and] ... would prophesy and tell what he had seen. At other times he appeared to be so honest and sincere I was led to believe all he said, but concluded that all could not be blessed and perhaps I was not as pure as those young men ...
>
> Edson Fuller would fall and turn black in the face. Heman Bassett would behave like a baboon. He said he had a revelation he had received in Kirtland from the hand of an angel [and] ... would read it and show pictures of a course of angels declared to be Gods, then would testify of the truth of the work and I believed it all, like a fool.
>
> I dare not come out against any thing that an Elder should say for fear I should speak against the Holy Ghost.[1]

Such so-called spiritual happenings, while perhaps amusing, raised credibility issues, caused some to doubt, and were disruptive to the harmony of the Church. As late as 1842 Joseph recalled and commented on spiritual abuses in Kirtland. Joseph acknowledged that "The Church of Jesus Christ of Latter-day Saints has also had its false spirits."[2]

Pratt and others went to the Prophet because they desired some guidance on how to discern the source of spiritual experiences. Pratt reported:

> Feeling our weakness and inexperience, and lest we should err in judgment

---

first word[s] I said ... [were], 'It is the truth, I can feel it.'" He was baptized on November 16 1830, by Parley P. Pratt and "preached from place to place." He was a member of Zion's Camp and was remembered for making a flag for the camp that had a white background, an eagle, and the word "Peace" inscribed upon it. He became one of the Seven Presidents of Seventy in February 1835. (See D&C 124:138–39.) He served in the Nauvoo Legion and the Mormon Battalion and later came west and settled in Payson and Manti. He served three terms in the territorial legislature and in 1872 was ordained a patriarch. In 1882 he died at age seventy-nine. (See Black, *Who's Who in the Doctrine and Covenants*, 114–16.)

1. Autobiography of Levi Ward Hancock, 41, as quoted in McConkie and Ostler, Revelations of the Restoration, 382–83.

2. Smith, *Teachings of the Prophet Joseph Smith*, 213. "Soon after the Gospel was established in Kirtland, and during the absence of the authorities of the Church, many false spirits were introduced, many strange visions were seen, and wild, enthusiastic notions were entertained." (Smith, *Teachings of the Prophet Joseph Smith*, 214.)

concerning these spiritual phenomena, myself, John Murdock, and several other Elders, went to Joseph Smith and asked him to inquire of the Lord concerning these spirits or manifestations. After we had joined in prayer in his translating room [where Joseph worked on the Inspired Version of the Bible], he dictated in our presence the following revelation: each sentence was uttered slowly and very distinctly, and with a pause between each sufficiently long for it to be recorded by an ordinary writer in long hand.[1]

The revelation Parley P. Pratt refers to is section 50. The revelation frankly admits that some of the spiritual manifestations in the Church were "false spirits, which have gone forth in the earth, deceiving the world." (Verse 2.) And that "Satan hath sought to deceive you, that he might overthrow you." (Verse 3.) All these things are "abominations in the church that profess[es] my name." (Verse 4.)

Discerning spirits

Joseph Smith, a visionary himself, never doubted the reality of the appearance of angels, visions, healings, tongues, prophecy, and other manifestations of the gifts of the Spirit. However, he also realized that all such gifts were not always of God and could be spiritually damaging. He said, "Men are ignorant of the nature of spirits; their power, laws, government, intelligence, etc., and imagine that when there is anything like power, revelation, or vision manifested, that it must be of God." He commented that many sincere believers have been misled by false spirits. "Long pilgrimages have been undertaken, penances endured, and pain, misery and ruin have followed in their train; nations have been convulsed, kingdoms overthrown, provinces laid waste, and blood, carnage and desolation are habiliments in which it [false revelation] has been clothed."[2] He said nothing was more damaging than mistaking the power of darkness for the power of light.[3]

Section 50 instructs members of the Church on how to recognize whether or not spiritual manifestations are from God or some other source. When the Spirit of the Lord is present, all are *edified*. If this is not the case, then it is more likely that the spirit is false. (See verses 22–23.) If a person

---

1. See Autobiography of Parley P. Pratt, 61–62.
2. Smith, *Teachings of the Prophet Joseph Smith*, 205.
3. Joseph said, "A man must have the discerning of spirits before he can drag into daylight the hellish influence and unfold it unto the world in all its soul-destroying, diabolical, and horrid colors; for nothing is a greater injury to the children of men than to be under the influence of a false spirit when they think they have the Spirit of God. Thousands have felt the influence of its terrible power and baneful effects." (Smith, *Teachings of the Prophet Joseph Smith*, 205.)

is troubled by a spiritual manifestation, he or she should ask God to experience the same spirit. If it is not of God, the individual will not receive that spirit. (See verses 29–31.) In such a situation, the individual should reject the spiritual display and proclaim against it. (See verse 32.)

To *edify*, according to Webster's 1828 edition, is to build up, instruct, improve the mind in knowledge (particularly in moral and religious knowledge), and to promote faith and holiness. The term *edify* is also connected to *"light."* (See verse 24.) To illuminate clears up confusion, anxiety, and uncertainty. It brings assurance and clarity to any given situation. The message harks back to a similar warning about spiritual gifts enunciated by Paul, "Even so ye, forasmuch as ye are zealous of spiritual *gifts*, seek that ye may excel to the *edifying* of the church." (1 Corinthians 14:12.) In other words, the spiritual gifts are for our growth and development, and if a gift tears down, belittles, and leads to confusion and uncertainty, it is not of God.

Judging whether or not something is or is not edifying is not left up to the individual alone. The approach suggested in section 50 involves the idea of *mutual edification*. That is, if the spirit is of God, all should feel edified—there should be a unity of feeling. "Wherefore, he that preacheth and he that receiveth, understand one another, and *both are edified and rejoice together.*" (Verse 22; emphasis added.) This check and balance offers extra assurance that a gift is appropriate. Joseph always emphasized that "there was nothing indecorous in the proceeding of the Lord's prophets in any age; neither had the apostles nor prophets in the apostles' day anything of this kind."[1]

During Joseph's lifetime he would return again and again to this subject of carefully discerning between manifestations that were of God and those that were not. He spoke about "keys" or methods for discerning the source of revelations and spiritual gifts. One was whether or not "any intelligence" had been communicated. "Are the curtains of heaven withdrawn, or the purposes of God developed?" Another involved the stabilizing influence of priesthood authority. "No man nor set of men without the regular constituted authorities, the Priesthood and discerning of spirits, can tell true, from false spirits. This power was possessed in the Apostles' day."[2] A further key involved the extent to which a person was familiar with the true gifts so that he or she could distinguish them from the false—being aware of Satan's "angelic form, the sanctified look and gesture, and the zeal that is frequently manifested by him for the glory of God, together with the prophetic spirit, the gracious influence, the godly appearance,

---

1. Smith, *Teachings of the Prophet Joseph Smith*, 209.
2. Smith, *History of the Church*, 572, 574, 579–80.

and the holy garb, which are so characteristic of [God's] proceedings and his mysterious windings."[1] Finally, did the so-called spiritual expression square with what is contained in the scripture? In judging the veracity of a revelation of a woman by the name of Jemimah, Joseph evaluated a notion she had about the resurrection by commenting that "the idea of her soul being in heaven while her body was [living] on earth, is . . . preposterous."[2] He then turned to the scripture for support and pointed out that what Jemimah claimed was inconsistent with what happened when the Savior's spirit departed his body prior to the resurrection.[3]

SECTION 52: MORLEY FARM, KIRTLAND, OHIO, JUNE 7, 1831[4]

Heading

The ordination of men to the "high priesthood." The general location of Zion revealed.

The big question

Question: What is the structure of the Church?
Answer: Men are ordained to the "high priesthood."

Introduction

Revelation given through Joseph Smith the Prophet, to the elders of the Church, on the Morley farm near Kirtland, Ohio, on June 6, 1831.[5] A conference had been held in the schoolhouse on the Morley farm beginning on the third. At this conference men were "ordained to the "high priesthood" and certain manifestations of false and deceiving spirits were discerned and rebuked.

---

1. Smith, *Teachings of the Prophet Joseph Smith*, 205.
2. Smith, *Teachings of the Prophet Joseph Smith*, 210.
3. See Smith, *Teachings of the Prophet Joseph Smith*, 210.
4. "We now accept June 6, 1831, as the date of this revelation, not June 7 as in the current Doctrine and Covenants." (Woodford, "Discoveries from the Joseph Smith Papers Project," 30.)
5. Smith, *History of the Church*, 1:175–79. The receipt date (June 7th) of section 52 given in the heading of the Doctrine and Covenants is incorrect. As indicated in the *History of the Church*, this revelation was received the day after the conference was held, beginning on Friday, June 3, and ending on Sunday, June 5. Therefore, the revelation had to have been received on Monday June 6, a date also supported by other contemporaneous accounts. (See Smith, *History of the Church*, 1:175–77.)

Morley Farm: Kirtland, Ohio, March 1831–September 1831

Background

In early June, forty-four elders, four priests, and fifteen teachers met in a log schoolhouse on Isaac Morley's farm seeking a spiritual endowment. The school was small and designed to hold no more than 25 children and a teacher. "More than sixty and perhaps as many as eighty adults worked their way into the fourteen-foot-square log structure. Men sat on rough-hewn benches, windowsills, or the ground outside near the open windows and doors."[1]

It was on this occasion that Joseph prophesied that Lyman Wight would see the Savior, and so he did. Wight became stiff and white in appearance and said that he had, in fact, viewed the Savior. Joseph confirmed Wight's experience by reporting, "I now see God, and Jesus Christ at his right hand."[2] Shortly thereafter, what had begun as a spiritual gathering was interrupted by confrontations with Satan. While Joseph was ordaining Harvey Whitlock to the high priesthood, Whitlock was seized by an evil spirit. "He turned as black as Lyman was white. His fingers were set like claws. He went around the room and showed his hands to people and could not speak. His eyes were in the shape of oval O's."[3] At Hyrum's urging, Joseph bowed his head, laid his hands upon Whitlock's head, and commanded Satan to depart. Whitlock returned to normal countenance and behavior.[4] As soon as this was accomplished, another member of the congregation, Leman Copley, a stout man weighing over three hundred pounds, was seized upon by an unseen power, somersaulted in the air, and fell on his back over a bench. It was reported that confrontations with evil spirits continued throughout the day and into the night.[5] Some of the members were so traumatized by this experience that they left the Church.

In June 1831, few members held an official office in the Church. Joseph Smith was the First Elder and Oliver Cowdery the Second Elder, but shortly thereafter, other members were set apart only intermittently as officers of the Church. Mark Lyman Staker points out, "Minutes of other Church meetings in Ohio "typically identified office-holders with the generic term 'elder,' meaning a general officer of a church (its most common use

---

1. Staker, *Hearken, O Ye People*, Kindle locations 5378–81.
2. Bushman, *Joseph Smith: Rough Stone Rolling*, 156.
3. Bushman, *Joseph Smith: Rough Stone Rolling*, 156.
4. Bushman, *Joseph Smith: Rough Stone Rolling*, 157.
5. See Bushman, *Joseph Smith: Rough Stone Rolling*, 157. Parley P. Pratt recorded in his autobiography, "There also were some strange manifestations of false spirits which were immediately rebuked." (Preece, *Learning to Love the Doctrine and Covenants*, 98.) In *John Whitmer's History of the Church*, he reports that Satan caused Harvey Whitlock and John Murdock to lose their ability to speak for a time. Joseph commanded the devil to depart, much to the joy of the persons attending the conference. (See Preece, *Learning to Love the Doctrine and Covenants*, 98.)

at the time). The list of those present at this conference, however, and the offices they held suggest a particular interest in distinctions between offices and the tendency in Ohio to ordain elders instead of priests or teachers. According to the minutes, forty-four elders attended along with fifteen teachers and four priests. More than half the elders were Ohio converts, while only two teachers (Daniel Stanton and Stephen Burnett) and only one priest (Caleb Baldwin) were ordained in Ohio. During the June conference, Stanton was ordained an elder, making the difference in numbers even more pronounced."[1]

During the meeting, Joseph ordained five men to the high priesthood. Lyman Wight ordained eighteen others, Joseph Smith included.[2] Bushman points out that:

> The ordinations to the high priesthood marked a milestone in Mormon ecclesiology. Until that time, the word "priesthood,"[3] although it appeared in the Book of Mormon, had not been used in Mormon sermonizing or modern revelations. Later accounts applied the term retroactively, but the June 1831 conference marked its first appearance in contemporary records ... before 1831 men were called to church offices—elders, priests, and teachers—given authority, and licensed without reference to a bestowal of priesthood.[4]

Bushman suggests that this may have been because the idea of priesthood was associated with Roman Catholicism and looked upon with suspicion by Protestants. Many Mormon converts were uncomfortable with the idea of priests administering sacraments for the reason that "priesthood" was associated with priestcraft—"priests" who used their influence to control secular and/or political affairs to their own benefit.[5]

From this point forward, Joseph began to suggest that the idea of priesthood encompassed more than simply authorization to act in a particular office. Priesthood also involved the bestowal of spiritual power. Bushman correctly observed that just a year later, Joseph would receive a revelation

---

1. Mark Lyman Staker, *Hearken, O Ye People: The Historical Setting of Joseph Smith's Ohio Revelations*, Kindle locations 5386–92.

2. See Bushman, *Joseph Smith: Rough Stone Rolling*, 157.

3. Section 2 records the words of Moroni spoken to Joseph Smith during the night of September 21 and 22, 1823, in which the word "priesthood" is used. Section 2 was first included in the Doctrine and Covenants in 1876. (See Woodford, The Historical Development of the Doctrine and Covenants, 126.) The word "priesthood" is also used in section 13, in which John the Baptist in May 1829 restored the Aaronic Priesthood. However, this section was not included in the Doctrine and Covenants until 1876, when it was "lifted out of the history of the Prophet." (Woodford, The Historical Development of the Doctrine and Covenants, 235.) The reference to the word "priesthood" in D&C 20:67 was added in 1835, as was the reference to "priesthood" in D&C 27:8.

4. See Bushman, Joseph Smith: Rough Stone Rolling, 157–58.

5. See Bushman, *Joseph Smith: Rough Stone Rolling*, 159.

that made known that it was in the ordinances of the priesthood that "the power of godliness is manifest. And without the ordinances thereof and authority of the priesthood, the power of godliness is not manifest unto men in the flesh." (D&C 84:20–21.) Eventually, this tie between priesthood, power, and ordinances would be institutionalized in Mormon temples. In a temple setting, both the Aaronic and Melchizedek priesthoods would involve rituals through which members of the Church would enter into covenants, the end purpose of which was to sanctify and empower them to become gods and goddesses. The priesthood, when thought of in a temple context, is referred to as the "fulness of the priesthood" to distinguish it from the use of the word "priesthood" when it refers to holding an office in the Church. (See D&C 124.)

It should be acknowledged that some Mormon historians take the position that at the June conference the word "priesthood" was used and priesthood was "bestowed as if it was an addition to previous authority," implying that it had not been extant a year or two earlier, prior to the formal organization of the Church.[1] In support of this proposition, Richard Bushman, D. Michael Quinn, and others point out that Joseph is recorded to have said that it was on the Morley farm at this June conference that "the Melchizedek Priesthood was conferred for the first time."[2] Others who were also present, such as Parley P. Pratt, recalled the events in the same way. Of this episode Pratt wrote that "several were then selected by revelation, through President Smith, and ordained to the High Priesthood after the order of the Son of God; which is after the order of Melchizedek. This was the first occasion in which this priesthood had been revealed and conferred upon the Elders in this dispensation."[3]

The usual explanation of these events, however, is that Joseph meant to say "high priest" not "high priesthood."[4] This confusion may indicate that the division between the Aaronic and Melchizedek priesthoods was not entirely clear at this point in time. As has been previously discussed, when the Church was first organized, the office of "elder" was associated

---

1. See Bushman, *Joseph Smith: Rough Stone Rolling*, 158.
2. See Bushman, *Joseph Smith: Rough Stone Rolling*, 158. Joseph Smith wrote that during this conference, "the Lord displayed His power to the most perfect satisfaction of the Saints. The man of sin was revealed, and *the authority of the Melchizedek Priesthood was manifested and conferred for the first time upon several of the Elders.* It was clearly evident that the Lord gave us power in proportion to the work to be done, and strength according to the race set before us, and grace and help as our needs required. . . . Faith was strengthened; and humility, so necessary for the blessing of God to follow prayer, characterized the Saints. The next day, as a kind continuation of this great work of the last days, I received the following"—section 52. (Smith, *History of the Church*, 1:175–77; emphasis added.)
3. Bushman, *Joseph Smith: Rough Stone Rolling*, 158.
4. See Bushman, *Joseph Smith: Rough Stone Rolling*, 158.

with the Aaronic Priesthood, not the Melchizedek. (See D&C 20:38, and commentary.)

In any event, the idea of priesthood would become "one of the defining principles of Mormonism."[1] And despite the fact that Protestants had an aversion to it, Joseph "continued to expand priesthood down to his final days in Nauvoo. The June 1831 conference ordinations hinted at the direction his theology would take."[2] As Bushman observed: "One of [Joseph's] gifts was to sense the power in biblical passages that others had long overlooked. His inspiration told him to restore priesthood to the central position it had occupied in ancient Hebrew religion, and the idea appealed to the searching nineteenth-century Christians who came to Mormonism. In priesthood, they found a key to the godly powers they longed for."[3]

By the time Joseph exited the scene, the idea of priesthood as both *power* and *authority* would be an essential component around which the Church would coalesce and through which direction would be given to the Church.

Fourth conference of the Church and the general location of Zion revealed

This June conference had been announced in February 1831. (See D&C 44.) Prior major conferences had been held in Fayette, New York, on June 9, 1830, September 26, 1830, and January 2, 1831. Prior such gatherings were often held over a period of a few days and should not be seen as analogous to the general conference sessions of the Church today. For example, the conference on the Morley farm was attended by sixty-three brethren (elders, priests, teachers) and was not so much for the general instruction of the Church but rather to confer about and conduct Church business.

At the conference, Joseph prophesied that John the Revelator was then among the Ten Tribes to help prepare them for their return. Lyman Wight falsely prophesied that some in the congregation would live until the Savior came in glory, an extravagant prediction that went contrary to the scriptural injunction that no one, not even the angels in heaven, know the day nor the hour. He also prophesied correctly that some of the Saints would suffer martyrdom.[4]

---

1. See Bushman, *Joseph Smith: Rough Stone Rolling*, 159.
2. Bushman, *Joseph Smith: Rough Stone Rolling*, 159.
3. Bushman, *Joseph Smith: Rough Stone Rolling*, 159.
4. See Preece, *Learning to Love the Doctrine and Covenants*, 98.

Twenty-eight missionaries called to preach on their way to the land of Zion

Section 52 extends calls to twenty-eight missionaries to leave their homes and travel the one thousand miles from Kirtland to the Independence, Missouri, area. They were instructed to preach the gospel two-by-two along the way and to take different routes to broaden their contact with potential converts. (See verse 33.)

Missourians referred to as "enemies"

The Saints would live in the land of Zion in Missouri from June 1831 to 1834, when they would be driven north. By 1838, they would have to leave the state altogether after the "extermination order" was issued by Governor Lilburn W. Boggs on October 27, 1838. A foreshadowing of what was to come is mentioned: "If ye are faithful ye shall assemble yourselves together to rejoice upon the land of Missouri . . . which is now the land of your enemies." (Verse 42.)

Counsel on the difference between true and false spirits

Considering the fact that evil spirits had afflicted the conference, it is not surprising that discerning the good from the evil is specifically addressed in this revelation and mirrors the counsel given on the subject in section 50. "And, again, I will give unto you a pattern in all things, that ye may not be deceived: for Satan is abroad in the land, and he goeth forth deceiving the nations." (Verse 15.) Once again the Saints are instructed that those who are "contrite," whose language is "meek," and who "edifieth" are of God. The ultimate test is in the outcome: "He that trembleth under my power shall be made strong, and shall bring forth fruits of praise and wisdom, according to the revelations and truths which I have given you." (Verse 17.) Those who advance the kingdom and act in accordance with the revelations are of God. "Wherefore, by this pattern ye shall know the spirits in all cases under the whole heavens." (Verse 19.)

Section 53: Morley Farm, Kirtland, Ohio, June 1831[1]

Heading

Sidney Gilbert ordained an elder and called to travel to Independence, Missouri, and serve as a bishop's agent.

The big question

Question: What is the structure of the Church?
Answer: Agents appointed to assist the bishop.

Introduction

Revelation given through the Prophet Joseph to Sidney Gilbert, on the Morley farm outside of Kirtland in June 1831.[2] At Sidney Gilbert's request, the Prophet inquired of the Lord as to Brother Gilbert's work and appointment in the Church. He was told that he should be ordained an elder[3] and serve as a bishop's agent.

Background

Sidney Gilbert was converted when Joseph sent Parley P. Pratt and others out to preach to the Lamanites. (See D&C 28:8; 30:5; 32:1–3.) He was in his early forties, lived in Kirtland, and was a partner with Newel K. Whitney in the ownership and operation of the N. K. Whitney & Co. general store. Gilbert attended the conference in June and had not been given an assignment. He approached Joseph and asked that he inquire of the Lord on his behalf. It was revealed that he should be ordained an elder. He was ordained on June 6, 1831, just after section 53 was received. A few days later, on June 19, Gilbert went to Missouri with Joseph and others. He settled in the Independence, Missouri, area, and opened another store called Gilbert and Whitney (D&C 57:6–8), which also served as a bishops' storehouse.[4] During the persecutions in Missouri in July 1833 mobs ransacked his store, broke windows, and dumped the goods from his store into the street. While he was a good businessman, he did not

---

1. "We now date this section June 8, 1831." (Woodford, "Discoveries from the Joseph Smith Papers Project," 30.)
2. Smith, *History of the Church*, 1:179–80.
3. An "elder" at this point in time was an office in the Aaronic Priesthood. (See commentary on D&C 20.)
4. Gilbert worked under the direction of Bishop Partridge, who had just been appointed bishop. (See D&C 52:24.)

like preaching. It was reported that he said he would rather die than preach as he had been instructed to do. (See verse 3.) Ironically, Gilbert died a short time later, when he contracted cholera and was laid to rest on June 29, 1834.[1]

Calling and election in the Church

In context, the reference to Gilbert's "calling and election in the church" is not a reference about the certainty of his salvation.[2] In this context Gilbert was "called and elected" to establish a storehouse in Zion and to assist Bishop Partridge. (See verse 1.)

SECTION 54: MORLEY FARM, KIRTLAND, OHIO, JUNE 1831[3]

Heading

The Colesville Saints are commanded to leave Kirtland, Ohio, and travel to Missouri (Zion) to establish the law of consecration.

The big questions

Question: How do we live together and build a community now that we have gathered?

Answer: Establish the law of consecration and share temporal blessings equally.

Introduction

Revelation given through Joseph Smith the Prophet to Newel Knight on the Morley farm, in Kirtland in June 1831.[4] Members of the Church in the branch at Thompson, Ohio, were divided on questions having to do with the consecration of properties. Selfishness and greed were manifest, and Leman Copley had broken his covenant to consecrate his large farm as a place of inheritance for the Saints. As a consequence, Newel Knight (president of the branch at Thompson) and other elders had come to the

---

1. See Smith, *History of the Church*, 2:118; see also Robinson and Garrett, *Doctrine and Covenants Commentary*, 2:124–25.
2. For a discussion on making one's "calling and election sure," see commentary on section 131.
3. "This section can be dated June 10, 1831." (Woodford, "Discoveries from the Joseph Smith Papers Project," 30.)
4. Smith, *History of the Church*, 1:180–81.

Prophet asking how to proceed. The Prophet inquired of the Lord, and the members were told to keep their covenant of consecration and be patient in tribulation.

Background

When the Colesville, New York, Saints (about sixty in number) arrived in Kirtland in mid-May 1831, they settled in Thompson, a farming community just outside Kirtland, on Leman Copley's 759-acre property.[1] Bishop Edward Partridge tried to inaugurate the law of consecration, and Copley refused. Copley had previously agreed to share his land in Thompson with the Saints arriving from the East. The agreement called for Copley to consecrate half of his farm and sell the other half to the Church on fair terms. However, when Copley had returned from his Shaker mission (see D&C 49), he was disillusioned and, having once been a member of the Shaker faith, wondered if his former church was right.[2] "To make matters worse, when Leman returned to Thompson many of the members there, people who were living on his land through his generosity, blamed him for deceiving them with the hope of converting the Shakers."[3] Therefore, when Bishop Partridge began to divide up Copley's land according to the principles of the law of consecration as previously agreed, Copley, who had not yet legally conveyed his property to the Church, retracted his offer. Bitter exchanges followed as Copley ordered the Colesville Saints off his land and charged them rent even though improvements had been made to his property—crops planted and fences built. Newel Knight, the leader of the Colesville Saints, and other elders asked Joseph to inquire of the Lord and section 54 was given.

Section 54 commands the Colesville Saints to leave Kirtland and "take [their] journey into the regions westward, unto the land of Missouri, unto the borders of the Lamanites," where it was intended that they would settle and live the law of consecration. (See verse 8.) On July 3, 1831, the Colesville Saints pulled up stakes and started for Missouri.[4]

The Colesville Saints' journey to Missouri was arduous. Many left carrying their belongings on their backs and provisions in twenty-four wagons

---

1. The Saints in Seneca County were assigned to live on the Morley farm.
2. See Robinson and Garrett, *Doctrine and Covenants Commentary*, 2:127; *Church History in the Fulness of Times*, 99.
3. See Robinson and Garrett, *Doctrine and Covenants Commentary*, 2:127.
4. On June 19, 1831, Joseph Smith, Sidney Rigdon, Edward Partridge, Martin Harris, Joseph Coe, William W. Phelps, and Sidney Gilbert and his wife, Elizabeth, started for Missouri, some 900 miles away. (See *Church History in the Fulness of Times*, 104.)

that went via the Ohio and Mississippi rivers to St. Louis and then to Independence, Missouri. They arrived in the middle of July.[1]

Colesville Branch told to repent and travel to the land of Zion (Missouri)

The Colesville Branch had been unkind to Leman Copley in reaction to the failure of the Shaker mission and Leman's unwillingness to deed his property to the Church. "And if your brethren desire to escape their enemies, let them repent of all their sins, and become truly humble before me and contrite." (Verse 3.) The Lord rebuked the Colesville Saints and Leman Copley for "breaking the covenant" and particularly chastised Copley, for "it had been better for him that he had been drowned in the depth of the sea." (Verse 5.)

The Lord then encouraged the Colesville Saints to keep "the covenant" and promised them if they would do so "they shall obtain mercy." (See verse 6.) "Wherefore, go to now and flee the land . . . and take your journey." (Verse 7.) "And thus you shall take your journey into the regions westward, unto the land of Missouri, unto the borders of the Lamanites." (Verse 8.)

SECTION 55: MORLEY FARM, KIRTLAND, OHIO, JUNE 1831[2]

Heading

William W. Phelps called to be the printer for the Church.

The big question

Question: What is the structure of the Church?
Answer: The Church should establish a publishing house to print Church materials.

Introduction

Revelation given through the Prophet Joseph to William W. Phelps at the Morley farm just outside of Kirtland in June 1831.[3] William W. Phelps, a printer, and his family had just arrived in Kirtland. The Prophet sought

---

1. See *Church History in the Fulness of Times*, 104.
2. "The accepted date is now June 14, 1831." (Woodford, "Discoveries from the Joseph Smith Papers Project," 30.)
3. Smith, *History of the Church*, 1:184–86.

the Lord for information concerning him. Phelps was instructed to be baptized, be ordained an elder, publish books, and settle in Missouri.

Background

William Phelps probably attended at least some of the conference sessions in June 1831, even though he had just recently arrived with his family from Canandaigua, New York, and was not yet a member of the Church. Prior to this time he had purchased a copy of the Book of Mormon from Parley P. Pratt, read it, and believed it. He was so enthusiastic that he sat up all night comparing passages in the Book of Mormon with passages in the Bible.[1] At the close of the conference or shortly thereafter, Phelps presented himself to the Prophet "to do the will of the Lord."[2] In response, section 55 was received. Phelps was commanded to be baptized, be ordained an elder, become Church printer, and move to Independence, Missouri, there to assist Oliver Cowdery. Cowdery had been residing in Independence for about six months. He was the Second Elder in the Church, second only to Joseph Smith in terms of general leadership and authority. The record indicates that Phelps was ordained on June 6, 1831, along with several others.[3] He accompanied the Prophet on his journey from Kirtland to Missouri in June 1831.

Phelps was well prepared for his new Church assignment to be the printer. He was an experienced writer, editor, and publisher and had been the editor of *The Ontario Phoenix*, an anti-Masonic paper in Canandaigua, New York. He became known as the "printer unto the church" and would later become the publisher of the Church's first newspaper, *The Evening and Morning Star*. He wrote a number of Mormon hymns, among them, "Praise to the Man," "Gently Raise the Sacred Strain, and "The Spirit of God."

SECTION 56: MORLEY FARM, KIRTLAND, OHIO, JUNE 1831[4]

Heading

Ezra Thayre criticized for his pride and selfishness as it pertained to his participation in a communal order. He puts off a mission call.

---

1. See Black, *Who's Who in the Doctrine and Covenants*, 223.
2. See Robinson and Garrett, *Doctrine and Covenants Commentary*, 2:131; Cook, *Revelations of the Prophet Joseph Smith*, 86–88.
3. See Robinson and Garrett, *Doctrine and Covenants Commentary*, 2:131–32.
4. "We can now date this revelation June 15, 1831." (Woodford, "Discoveries from the Joseph Smith Papers Project," 30.)

The big question

Question: How do we live together and build a community now that we have gathered?

Answer: Live the law of consecration. Encourage the rich to give their property to the poor. Encourage the poor to be satisfied with what they have and to labor diligently.

Introduction

Revelation through Joseph Smith the Prophet given on the Morley farm, just outside of Kirtland in June 1831.[1] Ezra Thayre had been appointed to travel to Missouri with Thomas B. Marsh (D&C 52:22). However, he was unwilling to do so because of his involvement in a community living the law of consecration. The prophet inquired and this revelation followed.

Background

In June 1831, Ezra Thayre and Thomas B. Marsh were called as companions to preach the gospel in Missouri.[2] (See D&C 52:22.) Thayre refused to go at the time appointed, and it was necessary to assign Marsh another companion, Selah J. Griffin. Thayre's inability to start his mission grew out of a dispute involving his interest in part of a piece of property originally owned by Frederick G. Williams, which was shared by at least three parties. Thayre wanted to make sure that he had perfected his interest in his portion of the real estate before he left on his mission, which delayed his departure.[3] Section 56 rebukes Thayre for his "pride" and "selfishness." (See verse 8.) Four months later, on October 10, 1831, a conference of elders in Kirtland criticized Thayre for his unwillingness to immediately go on his mission but no other action was taken.[4] In January 1832 he

---

1. See Smith, *History of the Church*, 1:186–88.

2. As many as fourteen pairs of missionaries had been called to journey to the western boundaries of the United States (Jackson County, Missouri area). Ezra Thayre was one of the Colesville, New York, Saints. He was baptized by Parley P. Pratt in 1830. After he joined the Church he was severely criticized by his family and friends but was convinced to remain faithful by the appearance of an angel. (See Black, *Who's Who in the Doctrine and Covenants*, 319.)

3. Thayre had a fair amount of cash, probably from the sale of his property when he left New York. He agreed to consecrate his holdings to the Lord and received in return a promised interest in the Williams farm.

4. Robinson and Garrett, *Doctrine and Covenants Commentary*, 2:134.

responded favorably to another call to serve a mission with Thomas B. Marsh.[1] (See D&C 75:31.)

Prior to this time, in a revelation not included in the Doctrine and Covenants, Joseph Smith Sr. was commanded to manage the Frederick G. Williams farm. Members of the Smith, Williams, and Thayre families were appointed to live together in the same house until the Church could build a separate house for Ezra Thayre on the same property.[2] Also, a share of the property was to be deeded in stewardship to Frederick G. Williams, who still legally owned it all but had left it to the Church when he departed for his mission to Missouri.[3] Thayre's hesitation to immediately leave on his mission is illustrative of some of the problems the Saints were having trying to live the law of consecration.

Counsel to the rich and poor regarding the law of consecration

Section 56 acknowledges the problems the Saints were having living the law of consecration. "Behold, thus saith the Lord unto my people—you have many things to do and to repent of." (Verse 14.) The rich are told that if they are unable to consecrate their properties to the poor, "your riches will canker your souls; and this shall be your lamentation in the day of visitation, and of judgment, and of indignation: The harvest is past, the summer is ended, and my soul is not saved!" (Verse 16.) The poor are admonished to be satisfied with what they have and commanded not to covet "other men's goods." (See verse 17.) Furthermore, the poor are admonished to "labor with your own hands." (See verse 17.)

God revokes commands

The Lord adjusts his commands to "compensate for and adjust to the consequences of the choices made by the rebellious who have failed to fulfill their responsibilities. Accordingly, the innocent and repentant are given new assignments within the Lord's vineyard."[4] In this instance, missionary assignments are revised. "Wherefore I, the Lord, command

---

1. One year later Thayre was appointed to negotiate and purchase land in Kirtland, on which the Kirtland Temple was built. (See Black, *Who's Who in the Doctrine and Covenants*, 320.) He continued faithful, although he was briefly disfellowshipped; he moved to Missouri with the Saints and later to Nauvoo, where he was a member of the Council of Fifty. However, he was not willing to support Brigham Young after Joseph was murdered and stayed in the East, joining what was then known as the Reorganized Church. (Robinson and Garrett, *Doctrine and Covenants Commentary*, 2:135–36.)
2. See Cook, *Revelations of the Prophet Joseph Smith*, 88–89.
3. See Robinson and Garrett, *Doctrine and Covenants Commentary*, 2:134.
4. McConkie and Ostler, *Revelations of the Restoration*, 407.

and revoke, as it seemeth me good." (Verse 4.) Joseph F. McConkie points out that this same principle was at work when the children of Israel were commanded to posses the land of Canaan. They feared the might of the walled cities, and "all the children of Israel murmured against Moses and against Aaron: . . . and they said one to another, Let us make a captain, and let us return into Egypt." (Numbers 14:2, 4.) As a result the Lord revoked this command, and they did not enter the promised land. Instead they wandered in the wilderness for forty years.

The former commandment

"The former commandment" mentioned in verse 8 was a revelation concerning Kirtland farms recorded in the *Kirtland Revelation Book* and not included in the Doctrine and Covenants.

SECTION 63: MORLEY FARM, KIRTLAND, OHIO, AUGUST 1831[1]

Heading

Some of the Saints commanded to go to Zion in Jackson County, Missouri. Members of the Church are warned against seeking after signs.

The big question

Question: How do we live together and build a community now that we have gathered?
Answer: Continue to assemble and build up Zion in Jackson County, Missouri. Do not seek after miraculous signs.

Introduction

Revelation given through the Prophet Joseph on the Morley farm just outside of Kirtland, Ohio, in August 1831.[2] The Prophet, Sidney Rigdon, and Oliver Cowdery had returned to Kirtland on August 27, 1831, from their visit to Missouri. Prefacing his record of this revelation, the Prophet wrote: "In these infant days of the Church, there was a great anxiety to obtain the word of the Lord upon every subject that in any way concerned our salvation; and as the land of Zion was now the most important

---

1. "There is evidence that this revelation was given August 30, 1831." (Woodford, "Discoveries from the Joseph Smith Papers Project," 30.)
2. See Smith, *History of the Church,* 1:206–11.

temporal object in view, I inquired of the Lord for further information upon the gathering of the Saints and the purchase of the land, and other matters." The Saints are instructed to continue to assemble in Jackson County, Missouri (verses 23, 36), and to send "all the moneys which can be spared" to build up Zion. (See verse 40.)

Background

On August 27, 1831, Joseph Smith had just arrived back in Kirtland from Jackson County, Missouri, having seen for the first time the place where the New Jerusalem would be built in preparation for the Second Coming. A few weeks prior, Sidney Rigdon had been given the go ahead to "write a description of the land of Zion, and a statement of the will of God, as it [was] made known by the Spirit unto him," which was to be used to encourage the Saints to give money[1] to the project.[2] (See D&C 58:50–52.) Section 63 completes the fundraising proposal by calling Newel K. Whitney and Oliver Cowdery to head up the effort.[3]

Apostasy in Kirtland

While Joseph Smith was in Jackson County, Missouri, and absent from Kirtland some of the Saints began to fall away from the Church. One of the leading apostates during this period was a man by the name of Ezra Booth, a former Methodist minister who had been converted when he witnessed Joseph instantly heal the partially paralyzed arm of Elsa Johnson. Booth had been sent in company with other missionaries to preach the gospel while on his way to Missouri. (See D&C 52:3, 23.) The physical stress of having to walk and preach took its toll, and Ezra began to find fault with the leaders of the Church. He was also disappointed that he was not experiencing the gifts of the Spirit to the extent that he desired. The Prophet Joseph commented that Booth did not appreciate

---

1. Zion was not to be taken by force but purchased. "Wherefore, the land of Zion shall be obtained by purchase. . . . And if by purchase, behold you are blessed; and if by blood, as you are forbidden . . . your enemies are upon you, and ye shall be scourged from city to city, and from synagogue to synagogue, and but few shall stand to receive an inheritance." (D&C 63:29–31.)

2. Rigdon failed on his first attempt to write his description of the land of Zion. He had included in his statement a rather long "apocalyptical essay calling sinners to repentance." (Van Wagoner, *Sidney Rigdon, A Portrait of Religious Excess*, 103.) Having gone beyond the mark, he was reprimanded and had to start over again. (See D&C 63:55–57.) "I, the Lord, am not pleased with my servant Sidney Rigdon; he exalted himself in his heart, and received not counsel, but grieved the Spirit." (Verse 55 and 56; see also Van Wagoner, 103.)

3. See Woodford, *The Historical Development of the Doctrine and Covenants*, 791–92.

that "faith, humility, patience, and tribulation go before blessing."[1] By September Booth had apostatized and published nine letters in the *Ohio Star* in Ravenna, from October 13 to December 8, 1831, setting forth his objections to Mormonism.[2]

Others in the Church who were disposed to fall away were also warned in section 63. Too many of the Saints, like Ezra Booth, were mocking the sacred. "Remember, that which cometh from above is sacred, and must be spoken with care, and by constraint of the Spirit." (Verse 64.) "For behold, verily I say, that many there be who are under this condemnation, who use the name of the Lord, and use it in vain, having not authority. Wherefore, let the church repent of their sins, and I, the Lord, will own them; otherwise they shall be cut off." (Verses 62–63.)

Section 63 addresses some of Ezra Booth's misgivings, as well as concerns of others who were similarly uncertain about Mormonism. The "unbelieving" are told to "hold their lips, for the day of wrath shall come upon them as a whirlwind, and all flesh shall know that I am God." (Verse 6.) Sign seeking is specifically addressed, advice of particular significance to Ezra Booth, who had been converted because he witnessed a miraculous healing and was disappointed that he had not experienced more of the same since he had joined the Church. "And he that seeketh signs shall see signs, but not unto salvation." (Verses 7–9.) Furthermore, "I the Lord, am not pleased with those among you who have sought after signs and wonders for faith, and not for the good of men unto my glory." (Verse 12.) Others in Kirtland were warned about adultery and other sins. (See verses 13–16, 22.)

Seeking after signs

Seeking after a sign is a way of testing the Lord. Those seeking after a sign demand that the Lord perform a miracle before they will believe. Jesus specifically rejected this approach when he was tempted in the wilderness for forty days. In response to Satan, "Jesus said unto him, It is written again, Thou shalt not tempt the Lord thy God." (Matthew 4:7.) On this point, section 63 instructs that unyielding faith "cometh not by signs, but signs follow those that believe." (Verse 9.) Signs therefore are not for confirming God's reality but are a result of faith directed in service to

---

1. See *Church History in the Fulness of Times*, 114.
2. See *Church History in the Fulness of Times*, 113–14. Booth's letters were later incorporated into the first anti-Mormon book, Eber D. Howe's *Mormonism Unvailed*, published in 1834. (See *Church History in the Fulness of Times*, 114.) Ultimately it was necessary for Joseph Smith and Sidney Rigdon and other missionaries to blunt Booth's efforts. Booth's negative influence contributed to the violence that erupted in Hiram on March 24, 1832, when Joseph and Rigdon were dragged from their abodes on the Johnson farm and tarred and feathered.

humankind. "I, the Lord, am not pleased with those among you who have sought after signs and wonders for faith, and not for the good of men unto my glory." (Verse 12.)

The Mount of Transfiguration

The appearance Moses and Elijah and others on the Mount of Transfiguration is a moment of considerable import in Mormon theology. It was on this occasion that Peter, James, and John beheld Jesus' glory. (See John 1:14; 2 Peter 1:16.) Joseph Smith taught, in addition, that Peter, James, and John themselves were "transfigured before him," given the keys of the kingdom, and received their endowments.[1] Section 63 adds more information about this transcendent event and informs us that on this occasion Peter, James, and John also saw "When the earth shall be transfigured, even according to the pattern which was shown unto mine apostles upon the mount; of which account the fulness ye have not yet received." (Verse 21.)

Titus Billings told to dispose of land

Titus Billings was a native of Kirtland who lived on the Morley farm. When Isaac Morley was sent to Missouri, Billings was left in charge of the Morley farm, where the Saints were living in a communal order. Titus was instructed to sell the land so that the proceeds could be used to purchase land in Independence (see verse 40) and so that the members who were then living on the Morley farm would have funds to prepare for their move to Zion.[2] (See also verses 39–40.)

At this time Joseph and Emma, as well as the Rigdon family, were living in small houses on the Morley farm. Section 63 instructs them to find new residences "through prayer by the Spirit." (See verse 65.) On Joseph's return from his visit to Zion, he moved in with the John Johnson family in Hiram, Ohio, which was about thirty miles southeast of Kirtland. Rigdon followed and lived in a small cabin at the same location.

---

1. See Smith, *Teachings of the Prophet Joseph Smith*, 158; Smith, *Doctrines of Salvation*, 2:165.
2. Robinson and Garrett, *Doctrine and Covenants Commentary*, 2:201.

In the Millennium, men and women will live to the "age of a man" and be changed in the twinkling of an eye

With the Saints' attention firmly fixed on building up the New Jerusalem and the approaching Millennium,[1] the Lord revealed that during the Millennium men and woman will live to a ripe old age and not suffer death but rather will be changed in the "twinkling of an eye." (See verses 50–51.) Isaiah, when speaking about the Millennium, said that a child will live to be a hundred years old. (See Isaiah 65:20; Psalm 90:10.)

Section 64: Morley Farm, Kirtland, Ohio, September 11, 1831

Heading

Joseph prepares to move from the Morley farm to live on the Johnson farm, also just outside of Kirtland.

Anchor section

Memorize: Forgive others

The big question

Question: How do we live together and build a community now that we have gathered?
Answer: Forgive each other unconditionally.

Introduction

Revelation given through Joseph Smith the Prophet to the elders of the Church, at the Morley farm located near Kirtland, Ohio, on September 11, 1831.[2] The Prophet was preparing to move to Hiram, Ohio, to renew his work on the translation of the Bible, which had been laid aside while he had been in Missouri. A company of brethren who had been commanded to journey to Zion (Missouri) was earnestly engaged in making preparations to leave in October.

---

1. "These things [Zion and the Millennium] are the things that ye must look for; and, speaking after the manner of the Lord, they are now nigh at hand, and in a time to come, even in the day of the coming of the Son of Man." (Verse 52.)
2. Smith, *History of the Church*, 1:211–14.

Background

Section 64 was given the day before Joseph Smith moved from the Morley farm to live with the John Johnson family in their home in Hiram, Ohio, about thirty miles southeast of Kirtland.[1] The move was occasioned because the Lord had commanded that the Morley farm be sold. The Morley farm had been organized as a communal living order, and in conjunction with the sale of the property a number of its members had been asked by Church authorities to resettle in the new Zion located in Jackson County, Missouri, and to reinstitute the communal order there. Sidney Rigdon followed Joseph to the Johnson farm and took up residence in an old log cabin there.[2] The Smiths and the Rigdons would live in their new homes from September 12, 1831, through March 1832, six and a half months.

September was a busy time in Kirtland. Joseph had recently visited Zion in Missouri. Upon his return he spent a significant amount of time raising funds to purchase more land in Missouri. Members of the Church were being called to migrate there, among them Edward Partridge, Sidney Gilbert, and W. W. Phelps. Undoubtedly, the Prophet's move from the hustle and bustle of Kirtland to Hiram would afford him some time to think and continue working on his inspired revision of the Bible.

The Inspired Version of the Bible

By December 1830 Joseph Smith was commanded to start his work on the Joseph Smith Translation (JST) or Inspired Version (IV) of the Bible.[3] From that time forward he had made an effort to continue working on the project, but he had been interrupted by his move from New York to Ohio in early 1831 and by his visit to Missouri in the summer of that same year. His move from Kirtland to Hiram would provide a quiet place away from the press of Church business. The Johnson farm proved to be a good place for the Prophet to reside because it was far enough away from Kirtland (thirty miles southwest) to allow Joseph uninterrupted time to

---

1. John Johnson owned a 304-acre farm in Hiram, Ohio.
2. Sidney Rigdon was married to Phoebe. They had six children.
3. The word "translation" in this context needs clarification. Joseph Smith was not translating the Bible from the original Greek or Hebrew into English. Rather, he made changes in the text and sometimes added passages by the spirit of revelation. Joseph Fielding Smith described what Joseph was doing when he said, "By translation is meant a revision of the Bible by inspiration or revelation." (Woodford, *The Historical Development of the Doctrine and Covenants*, 811.)

think and meditate and close enough to Kirtland that Joseph could go there when occasion required.[1]

Forgive each other unconditionally

The need for a revelation on unconditional forgiveness was particularly relevant at this time in Church history. First, Joseph and his brethren had been in an altercation on their way back from Missouri, which indisputably caused bad feelings. Second, living the law of consecration resulted in some members accusing others of selfishness. Third, some Mormons had apostatized and were deliberately attacking the Church, which caused some members to want to retaliate against them for not being loyal to the faith.

As mentioned in the previous paragraph, the situation that may have precipitated this revelation involved a contentious situation that had arisen between Joseph and a group of elders while traveling back from Missouri in canoes to the Kirtland area. (See D&C 60:5.) On August 11, 1831, on the third day of their journey, there are two accounts of what happened. In one the canoe in which Joseph and Sidney were riding hit a "sawyer," or partially submerged tree, and was nearly overturned.[2] In the other account, the canoe in which the Prophet and Sidney Rigdon were riding hit a tree bobbing in the river and capsized, almost drowning Joseph and Sidney.[3] In any case, Joseph and Rigdon found themselves in harm's way, as did some of their other fellow travelers. As a result, the bedraggled party stopped at McIlwaine's Bend (Miami Bend) about forty miles above Chariton, Missouri, to get their bearings and to rest on the banks of the river.

Unfortunately, the stress and strain of this incident caused Joseph and his brethren to come into conflict. Ezra Booth described the situation in a letter to Edward Partridge written on September 20, 1831: Booth said:

> The morning after they left Independence, the conduct of some of the elders displeased Oliver who uttered a malediction something like, "As the Lord God liveth, if you do not behave better, some accident will befall you." In the afternoon of the third day while negotiating some treacherous waters, Joseph took command and issued some orders which were resented by the brethren in one of the canoes who refused to obey, and in so doing became tangled in some brush and almost capsized. This frightened Joseph who ordered them

---

1. The Johnson farm was also a place where Joseph felt welcome. John Johnson was a friend and his wife, Elsa, had been miraculously healed by the Prophet some time before. The Johnsons no doubt were enthusiastic about the prospect of the Prophet living with them. When Joseph arrived, he and Emma were given a bedroom on the main floor and an entire room upstairs as an office where Joseph and Rigdon transacted the business of the Church and translated the Bible.
2. See Robinson and Garrett, *Doctrine and Covenants Commentary*, 2:174.
3. See Cook, *Revelations of the Prophet Joseph Smith*, 96.

all ashore, while some of the brethren felt they should continue. Once on shore, at McIlwaine's bend, tempers flared and words were exchanged. Joseph and Oliver were accused of being "highly imperious and quite dictatorial." Joseph was also called a coward. After much emotional discussion, apologies were made, and a reconciliation of sorts reached.[1]

Communal living orders also took their toll on some personal relationships. Constant association, close living quarters, and sharing resources proved difficult. John Whitmer wrote that arguments arose over who could or could not exercise control over property. In May 1831 conflicts arose when Bishop Partridge attempted to implement the law of consecration among the Colesville Saints on the Thompson farm located near Kirtland. One of the issues revolved around Leman Copley's promise to pledge his property to the order and then changing his mind, which left many of the Saints without a home. (See D&C 51:3.)[2]

Finally, negative stories were circulating in the press about the Mormons, and many people were leaving the Church. Norman Brown left the Church because his horse died on the trip to Zion. Joseph Wakefield exited the faith because he saw Joseph playing with children and felt it inconsistent with Joseph's serious calling as a prophet. Simonds Ryder denied that Joseph had the spirit of revelation because he misspelled his name on his commission to preach. Ezra Booth, a former Methodist minister, left the Church and wrote a series of letters that reflected negatively on Church members. Undeniably, people in and out of the Church harbored bad feelings for one another.[3]

It was at this time that Joseph was forgiven of his sins, and members of the Church who had been critical of Joseph were told to repent and forgive others for wrongs real or imagined. (See verses 5–7, 15–21.) "Wherefore, I say unto you, that ye ought to forgive one another; for he that forgiveth not his brother his trespasses standeth condemned before the Lord; for there remaineth in him the greater sin. I the Lord will forgive whom I will forgive but of you it is required to forgive all men." (See verses 9–10.) Looking forward, this counsel would only become more essential as time moved on. Persecution, poverty, bloodshed, exhaustion, deceit, selfishness, envy, and loss would all test the resolve of the members of the Church to follow the example of Jesus in all things.[4]

---

1. See Preece, Learning to Love the Doctrine and Covenants, 117.
2. See Anderson, *Joseph Smith's Kirtland*, 129–31.
3. *Church History in the Fulness of Times*, 113.
4. A classic story about forgiveness involving the Prophet Joseph and Orson Hyde follows. Upon Orson's return from England to Kirtland in 1838, Ohio he found the Church in turmoil. Dissenters were calling Joseph Smith a fallen prophet. The Kirtland Bank had failed, and people were looking to place blame. The Saints were taking up roots in Kirtland and were

on their way to Far West, Missouri, the new headquarters for the Church. Orson embarked for Missouri and became ill, suffering from a fever that became worse and worse. Upon his arrival, he found that Church leadership had changed. Unrepentant leaders had been released and replaced. Four new members had been appointed to fill vacancies in the Twelve. Violence against the Saints continued to increase. And Orson's illness prevented him from attending his meeting in Far West with the Prophet and his brethren of the Twelve. The Prophet visited Orson whenever he could, but the press of business left little time for this.

"Subtle changes in Orson's feelings about the Prophet crept into his thoughts." Thomas B. Marsh, president of the Twelve, took an interest in Orson. Marsh was miffed at the Prophet. On July 25, just before Orson arrived in Far West, Thomas' wife had been brought before a Church court for withholding cream strippings from a friend, with whom she had agreed to share equally to make cheese. Joseph agreed with the court's findings, and Marsh was deeply offended. Finding himself in an impossible position, he stood by his wife. In addition, he criticized the Prophet and conveyed his feelings to Orson. Orson's fevers continued and caused an "increase in his confusion." Marsh continued to visit and complain to Orson.

On October 15, word reached Far West that homes in nearby Di-Ahman (a Church settlement) had been burned, plundered, and razed to the ground. Marsh was afraid that violence would come to Far West as well. He convinced Orson and their respective families to leave Far West and seek safety in nearby Richmond, a non-Mormon settlement. Orson seemed agitated and was probably misled by Marsh's intentions, because he had been led to believe that they were going to settle only three miles out of town, safe from any mobs that might come to the center of town at Far West. In Richmond, apostates befriended Marsh and Hyde. The apostates tried to get them to deny that Joseph Smith had seen angels. They did not. But the apostates did convince them to admit that Joseph was a fallen prophet, opinions based on their perceived criticisms of the Prophet. After all, the Kirtland Bank had failed. The Saints had been pushed out of their city of Zion in Jackson County, Missouri, and Christ had not come.

Thomas B. Marsh and Orson Hyde were visible figures in Mormonism. Marsh was the President of the Quorum of the Twelve and Hyde a member of the Twelve. Marsh decided to sound a warning voice and disclose to the public the "insidious designs" of Joseph Smith. Consequently, he wrote and signed an affidavit to this effect and convinced Orson to sign as well. Orson's illness had continued, and by this time Orson's "clothes hung limply from his emanciated frame as he watched, physically and mentally exhausted, spiritually numb." Orson hesitated to sign but did so. Later he wrote to his sister, "I have left the Mormons . . . [and] Joseph Smith Jr. for conscience sake, and that alone, for I have come to the conclusion that he is a very wicked man."

The situation between the Saints and the Missourians continued to deteriorate, and violence broke out. News reached Marsh and Hyde that David W. Patten, a member of the Twelve, had been killed in a skirmish with non-Mormons. Tensions were on the rise. A few days later, a "startling event" occurred. Marsh and Hyde were sitting in a log cabin in silent meditation. Orson recounts that Thomas "sat upright as though reacting to a slap on the shoulder. Orson saw no other person, but he felt the hallowed presence of a being of spirit. Then he heard a man's voice implore, with deep anxiety and solicitude, "Thomas! Thomas! Why have you so soon forgotten?" The color drained from Marsh's face. When he spoke he did so solemnly and he told Orson that David Patten, their fellow brother and apostle who had recently been killed had visited them. Marsh went on to explain that at an earlier time he and Patten "had made a covenant to remain true and faithful until the end."

Although troubled, Marsh was not moved enough to change his opinion. He and Hyde eventually learned that their affidavit had reached Governor Lilburn W. Boggs, Governor of the State of Missouri. This affidavit, signed by such high-profile Mormons, helped convince Boggs that the Mormons should be forced out of the state. He signed what is known as the "Extermination Order," authorizing the Mormons to be killed on sight or driven from the state. Within days Far West was attacked by non-Mormons. Mormons were slaughtered at

Forgiveness needed at all levels, high and low

Section 64 makes clear that forgiveness is a principle that applies at every level of Church leadership. The Lord makes reference to a situation that existed among Jesus' Twelve where forgiveness was counseled. After Jesus and his disciples arrived in Capernaum, they settled into the house where they would be staying and Jesus asked them what they had been discussing out on the road. The disciples didn't answer because "they had been arguing about which one of them was the greatest." (NLT Mark 9:33–37.) Jesus sat down and called the Twelve over and rebuked them, saying that "Anyone who wants to be the first must take last place and be the servant of everyone else." (NLT Mark 9:35.)

Haun's Mill. Joseph, Hyrum Smith, and Sidney Rigdon were jailed. A number of Saints were killed, raped, and beaten; and eventually all were forced out of Far West, across the Missouri River, and on to Commerce, Illinois, later renamed Nauvoo.

Orson tried to make a new life for himself. During the winter of 1838–39 his health slowly improved. He found employment as a school teacher. But, he "felt empty, and his changes in mood plagued him. In moments of anger, he wanted to scourge the Mormons. In moments of sadness, he remembered the joys he had shared with them. Sometimes his perplexed mind reeled in such turmoil that he could neither work nor sleep. Frequently he found himself weeping without seeming cause, and he asked himself: 'Why in God's name is it so? What have I done that I am left in this situation, or . . . Suffered to fall into this dilemma.'" Orson became introspective. When he had been called to be an apostle he had been warned that he should "beware . . . Be always prayerful; be always watchful . . . [T]he enemy will rage."

He concluded that he had not followed this advice and sinned. "The impact of this cold reality made his sickness of body as nothing compared with his sickness of soul." Orson prayed to the Lord as never before. An answer came by way of a vision. In it he received specific instruction that "if I did not make immediate restitution to the Quorum of the Twelve, I would be cut off [from the Church and everlasting blessings] with all my posterity." He also saw that after death he would be cast down to hell as "a consequence of his denial, in essence, of his past immense spiritual enlightenment."

Orson decided that he must immediately seek forgiveness of the Twelve and Joseph Smith. "He bundled his frail body for protection from the weather, carried a knapsack of necessities, and trudged the seventy-five westward miles to Richmond. He managed the courage to visit the Richmond jail, where he conversed with" another member of the Twelve, Parley P. Pratt, "through the crevices in the thick walls." Even though incarcerated partially as a result of Orson's affidavit against the Mormons, Parley was kind and forgiving of Orson's behavior. Orson walked on toward Far West, where he sought the forgiveness of Brigham Young and Heber C. Kimball, senior apostles. It was given. When Heber first saw Orson, his "eyes widened in surprise. Then his smile beckoned through his tears, and the two men embraced." Here he "viewed burned skeletons of houses, strewn haystacks, and furniture broken to rubble."

Orson realized that it was now necessary for him to meet Joseph. He was apprehensive, to say the least. How would Joseph receive him? Orson made his way to Nauvoo, then called Commerce. He arrived at the Smith home on the banks of the Mississippi River. "Orson opened the Smith gate. He had barely stepped into the yard when a door opened. Brother Joseph came running to meet him, his arms out in welcome. 'O Brother Hyde, how glad I am to see you!' the Prophet exclaimed, as he wrapped his arms around Orson's neck. Both men 'wept like children.'" Joseph said that he came out of the door so quickly when Orson had just opened the gate "because the Lord had told him of Orson's approach, and he had been watching out the window." (See Stevens, *Orson Hyde: The Olive Branch of Israel*, 98–109.)

Apostolic wrangling was a challenge for Joseph Smith and is addressed in section 112. The Twelve are admonished to "be thou humble" and to pray for each other. (See D&C 112:10–12.) The Twelve were admonished "sharply . . . for all their sins" and told to be more faithful, especially in light of the fact that some had tried to "exalt" themselves. (See D&C 112:12, 15.)

Chapter 26

Whitney Store: Kirtland, Ohio, September 1832–December 1833

Section 84: Whitney Store, Kirtland, Ohio, September 22, 23, 1832

Heading

Elders had begun to return from their missions in the eastern states and to make reports of their labors.

The big question

Question: What is the structure of the Church?
Answer: Members should preach the gospel and fund missionary efforts.

Anchor section

Memorize: Oath and Covenant of the Priesthood

Introduction

Revelation given through Joseph Smith the Prophet in Kirtland, Ohio, September 22 and 23, 1832, in the "revelation room" located on the second floor of the Whitney store, in Kirtland, Ohio.[1] The breaking point between the part of the revelation received on the 22nd and the 23rd is between verse 102 and 103.[2] During the month of September, elders had begun

---

1. Smith, *History of the Church*, 1:286–95.
2. Section 84 has always been dated September 22 and 23, 1832. But we now know the breaking point is between verses 102 and 103. (See Woodford, "Discoveries from the Joseph Smith Papers Project," 32.)

to return from their missions in the eastern states and to make reports of their labors. It was while they were together in this season of joy that the following communication was received.

Background

During the summer of 1832 Joseph had spent two weeks in the Jackson County, Missouri, area "sitting in council" with the Saints, where he established a united order (D&C 78) and provided for the establishment of a bishop's storehouse in Independence, Missouri, and Kirtland, Ohio.[1]

On his way home to Kirtland, however, his journey was prolonged. His traveling companion, Bishop Newel K. Whitney, injured himself in a runaway stage coach accident. While the unrestrained coach was moving at full speed, Whitney jumped off and caught his foot in a wheel, breaking his foot and leg in several places. Joseph followed but was unharmed. Sidney Rigdon, who was also with them, managed to escape physical harm. Joseph sent Sidney Rigdon on his way to Kirtland and remained behind with Whitney during a month-long convalescence in Greenville, Indiana. While there, Joseph became deathly ill with food poisoning, got up from the table, rushed to the door, and vomited blood so violently that he dislocated his jaw. He pushed his jaw back into place and went back to the bedside of Whitney, who laid hands on Joseph and instantly healed him from his affliction. Over the next few days Joseph lost a considerable amount of hair from his head.[2] Both decided it was time to leave Greenville and start for home. The pair arrived in the Kirtland area in September 1832.

Prior to this time Joseph and his family had been living on the Johnson farm in Hiram, outside of Kirtland. Upon his return he took the opportunity to move his family to their new quarters located on the second floor above the Whitney store in Kirtland. It was time for Joseph to move back to the city where most of the Saints resided so that he could be more involved in the day-to-day activities of the Church.

During this period of Church history, the elders were involved in intense missionary efforts. As many as were able spread the news of the restoration of the gospel as far and wide as possible. Those with limited means preached in communities close to their homes and when out of money returned back again to replenish their resources. Others were sent to far distant locations and told to preach along the way. Missionaries were sent to every state in the Union (even to the Fox Islands, just off the coast of Maine), and to upper Canada and Great Britain. Between 1831 and 1837

---

1. See Robinson and Garrett, *Doctrine and Covenants Commentary*, 3:22.
2. See Bushman, *Joseph Smith: Rough Stone Rolling*, 185.

some twenty thousand converts were baptized.[1] Just prior to the receipt of section 84, elders began to return from missions in the eastern states and present histories of their several experiences and successes. Kirtland was literally "saturated" with missionaries.[2] Joseph described it as a season of joy. It was a time when the Saints were focused on missionary work and whether or not converts ought to come and settle with the main body of the Saints in the Kirtland area.

Instructions on missionary work

The brethren are commanded to "go . . . into all the world" to do missionary work. (See verse 62.) Those who believe will be "baptized by water for the remission of sins" and "shall receive the Holy Ghost." (Verse 64.) Signs will follow those that believe. (See verses 65–73). Missionaries are instructed to preach without "purse or scrip," or without money or a satchel (suitcase).[3] (See verse 78.) Missionaries are promised physical and spiritual blessings if they are faithful. They "shall not go hungry, neither athirst." (Verse 80.) The Spirit will help them know what to say "in the very hour that portion that shall be meted unto every man." (Verse 85.) The Lord will prepare the way "for I will go before your face. I will be on your right hand and on your left, and my Spirit shall be in your hearts, and mine angels round about you, to bear you up." (Verse 88.) The families of missionaries should help support their relatives in the mission field. (See verse 103.) Those without family financial support should petition the "bishop in Zion" for assistance. (See verse 104.) Missionaries should go two by two and "if any man among you be strong in the Spirit, let him take with him him that is weak, that he may be edified in all meekness, that he may become strong also." (Verse 106.) Although this section anticipates that "high priests," those who have the higher priesthood, and the "elders" will proselyte (verses 63, 111), they may take with them those who hold the "lesser priesthood" or "lesser priests." (See verses 107, 111.) Deacons and teachers should stay behind and are "appointed to watch over the church, to be standing ministers unto the church." (Verse 111.) It should be remembered that during this period in Church history members of the lesser priesthood are adults. Even the bishop (Newel K. Whitney) is commanded to proclaim the gospel to New York, Albany, and Boston (verse 114) after

---

1. See Allen and Leonard, *Story of the Latter-day Saints*, 73.
2. See Allen and Leonard, *Story of the Latter-day Saints*, 73.
3. To avoid the impression that missionaries are vagabonds and beggars wandering the earth in search of food, money, and a place to sleep, this policy has been changed and missionaries are provided the necessities of life during their missionary service.

he has cared for the Church by "searching after the poor to administer to their wants by humbling the rich and the proud." (Verse 112.)

Build the New Jerusalem

About a year earlier, in August 1831, Joseph Smith, Sidney Rigdon, and his brethren dedicated Jackson County, Missouri, and its environs for the gathering of the Saints and the establishment of a temple at the heart of what would become the New Jerusalem. The "city New Jerusalem shall be built by the gathering of the Saints, beginning at this place, even the place of the temple, which temple shall be reared in this generation." (Verse 3.) The temple lot had been more particularly described almost one year before. "Behold, the place which is now called Independence is the center place; a spot for the temple is lying westward, upon a lot which is not far from the courthouse." (D&C 57:3.) Ultimately, enemies of the Church would prevent the Saints from building a temple and the New Jerusalem. The commandment to establish the New Jerusalem would be revoked, at least for a season. (See D&C 124:49–51.)[1]

The Saints' enthusiasm for building the city of the New Jerusalem was no doubt increased by statements in the Book of Mormon and the Bible on the subject. The scriptures promised the Latter-day Saints that in preparation for Jesus' return they were chosen to help prepare the foundation of this remarkable city. (See Ether 13:3–11; Moses 7:62–65; see also Isaiah 2:3; Zechariah 12–14.) The New Jerusalem in the Americas was to be the counterpart of the Old Jerusalem in Israel where the Lord promised that the Jews would gather prior to the Second Coming.[2] (See Zechariah 12–14.) Once established, the Saints understood that the Old and New Jerusalem would function as the two great capitals of the world during the Millennium.[3] (See Isaiah 2:3.)

---

1. The temple site is now owned by the Church of Christ, Temple Lot, a group also known as the Hedrickites, named after one of its founders Granville Hedrick.
2. See Smith, *Teachings of the Prophet Joseph Smith*, 17.
3. See McConkie, *Mormon Doctrine*, 481.

Temples to be built at the center of the New Jerusalem

By June 1833, Joseph would inform the Saints that more than one temple would be built at the site of the New Jerusalem. Separate temples or buildings would be constructed as administrative centers for the different quorums of the priesthood—the First Presidency, apostles, bishops, elders, teachers, and deacons.[1] In all, Joseph foresaw twenty-four temples.[2] Since the endowment ritual had not been made known, the buildings Joseph describes are not temples in the modern sense. (See D&C 124:25–48.) However, it is good logic to suppose that when the New Jerusalem is built, temples in which saving ordinances for the living and the dead are performed will also play a prominent role at the center spot of Zion.

Temple to be built in "this generation"

Section 84 appears to set a timetable for the accomplishment of the building of a temple at the place of the New Jerusalem—no more than a generation. "Verily this is the word of the Lord, that the city New Jerusalem shall be built by the gathering of the Saints, beginning at this place, even the place of the temple, which temple will be reared in this generation. For verily, this generation shall not all pass away until an house shall be built unto the Lord, and a cloud shall rest upon it, which cloud shall be even the glory of the Lord, which shall fill the house." (Verses 3–4.) Although temples would be built within the next few years in Kirtland and Nauvoo, and although each temple would be blessed with mighty spiritual manifestations, a temple has never been erected at the location where the New Jerusalem will be built.

It is fair to assume that Joseph and his people believed that they were about to erect a temple and start building the New Jerusalem within their lifetime. After all, section 84 promised that such things would come to pass "in this generation"—often times defined as the average time in which children are ready to replace their parents, or about twenty-five to thirty years. (See verse 4.) Moreover, the exact location of the temple and the city had recently been revealed and some of the Saints were being called to leave their homes and settle there. Furthermore, Joseph expressed his opinion in 1835 that the coming of the Lord was nigh—"even fifty six years should wind up the scene."[3]

---

1. The Prophet Joseph Smith also taught that members of the Aaronic Priesthood would offer one last blood sacrifice in a temple built in Independence, Missouri, in preparation for the Second Coming of Christ. (See Smith, *Teachings of the Prophet Joseph Smith*, 171–73.)
2. See Smith, *History of the Church*, 1:357–62.
3. "President Smith then stated that the meeting had been called, because God had

Even after it became reasonably clear that the temple would not be erected in the time frame the Saints had expected, Orson Pratt and others still held out hope even after the Saints had arrived in Salt Lake City. "Here then we see a prediction, and we believe it. Yes! The Latter-day Saints have as firm faith and rely upon this promise as much as they rely upon the promise of forgiveness of sins. . . . We just as much expect that a city will be built, called Zion, in the place and on the land which has been appointed by the Lord our God, and that a temple will be reared on the spot that has been selected . . . in the generation when this revelation was given." Then Elder Pratt rebuked the doubters, saying, "But says the objector, 'thirty-nine years have passed away.' What of that? The generation has not passed away; all the people that were living thirty-nine years ago have not passed away; but before they do pass away this will be fulfilled."[1]

Clearly, the temple was not built as predicted at the site of the New Jerusalem if a *generation* is taken to mean a time period of about twenty-five to thirty years. Therefore, is there an alternative interpretation of these verses that is satisfying? A number of explanations have been suggested.[2] Short of simply saying that the prediction was wrong, the most straightforward is to propose that the use of the word "generation" in this context was used loosely to mean a period of time or "dispensation" or that the descendants from the first generation of Mormons would build this temple at some point in the future. This approach is not inconsistent with the way in which the word *generation* was used at the time of Joseph Smith. The 1828 edition of the *American Dictionary of the English Language* allows for all of such usages of the word generation.[3] (See also commentary on D&C 111.)

---

commanded it; and it was made known to him by vision and by the Holy Spirit . . . and it was the will of God that [they] should be ordained to the ministry, and go forth to prune the vineyard for the last time, or the coming of the Lord, which was nigh—even fifty-six years should wind up the scene." (*History of the Church*, 2:182.)

1. *Journal of Discourses*, 14:275. This sermon was delivered in 1871, two years after the Hedrickites gained possession of the "temple lot."

2. In reference to verse 4, Robinson and Garrett opine, "This passage can be understood to constitute a *commandment* rather than a *prophecy*, as indicated in Doctrine and Covenants 124:51. Even though the Lord said, 'Thou shalt not commit adultery,' it does not make God incorrect every time someone commits this sin, because that statement also is a commandment rather than a prophecy. . . . In the case of the temple in Zion, the failure to obey the commandment to build a temple in Zion appears to be due in part to the opposition of enemies as well as to collective unfaithfulness of the Saints (see D&C 101:2, 6–8; 124:49–51.)" In reference to verse 5, Robinson and Garrett state that "if any part of verses 3–5 were to be understood prophetically, it would be [verse 5], which does not specify the location of the temple being described here. One way or another, at Independence or somewhere else, a temple for receiving God's choicest blessings was going to be built by that generation of Saints. The temples in Nauvoo, St. George, Manti, Logan, and Salt Lake—and perhaps others, depending on the definition of *generation*—would all fulfill the specifics of verse 5." (Robinson and Garrett, *Doctrine and Covenants Commentary*, 3:26–27.)

3. "Generation, n. (1) The act of begetting; procreation, as of animals. (2) Production;

The priesthood defined as the "power of God unto salvation," not only an office of authority

Section 84 continues to expand the Saints' understanding of priesthood as it was first spoken of during a conference in June 1831 on the Morley farm. At this conference, Joseph ordained five men to the *high priesthood* and Lyman Wight ordained eighteen others, Joseph included.[1] Bushman points out that these ordinations were a milestone in Mormon ecclesiology because until this time the word "priesthood," although it appeared in the Book of Mormon, had not been used extensively in any of the modern revelations. The June conference marked one of its first appearances in contemporary records. Later accounts applied the term retroactively. Before June 1831, men were called to Church offices—elders, priests, and teachers. They were given "authority" and "licensed" but without reference to a bestowal of priesthood.[2] Hence, it was at this conference that Joseph began to suggest that priesthood, apart from offices in the Church, incorporated a godly power that could help men come into the presence of God.

Section 84, which came just over a year after the idea of *higher priesthood* was introduced at the June conference on the Morley farm, continued to expand Joseph's understanding of what the concept of priesthood ultimately entailed. Section 84 unquestionably talks about *priesthood* as office or authority in the Church. Priesthood also includes rituals wherein "the power of godliness is manifest. And without the ordinances thereof, and the authority of the priesthood, the power of godliness is not manifest unto men in the flesh." (Verses 19–22.) Offices became secondary and were for the first time referred to as "appendages" to the priesthood. (See verses 29–30.) By December 1845 the idea of priesthood rituals and ordinances would become institutionalized in Mormon temples, where the highest orders of the Mormon priesthood are practiced. In the temple setting priesthood is not talked about in connection with Church office but rather defined in terms of covenants and promises intended to make people more holy, more sanctified, more like God. This expanded understanding of priesthood is referred to as the "fulness of priesthood" to distinguish it from the idea that priesthood only entails the notion of Church office and authority. (See D&C 124.)

---

formation; as the *generation* of sounds or of curves or equations. (3) A single succession in natural descent, as the children of the same parents; hence, an age. Thus we may say, the third, the fourth, or the tenth *generation*. Gen. xv.16. (4) The people of the same period, or living at the same time. O faithless and perverse generation. Luke ix. (5) Genealogy; a series of children or descendants from the same stock." (Noah Webster, *American Dictionary of the English Language*, 1828 edition.)

1. See Bushman, *Joseph Smith: Rough Stone Rolling*, 157.
2. See Bushman, *Joseph Smith: Rough Stone Rolling*, 157–58.

Information about the Aaronic and Melchizedek priesthoods

In addition to expanding the definition of *priesthood*, section 84 placed it in historical context, informing Joseph about its function in other dispensations of time. Joseph learned that Abraham received the priesthood from Melchizedek.[1] Melchizedek was the king of Shiloam or Salem (ancient Jerusalem) who called his people to repentance and built a righteous society. (See D&C 84:14; Alma 13:14–19; JST Genesis 14:25–40.)[2] He learned that the priesthood "continueth in the church of God in all generations, and is without beginning of days or end of years." (Verse 17.) The difference between a greater and lesser priesthood is explained. The "lesser priesthood" was "confirmed ... upon Aaron and his seed, throughout all their generations, which priesthood also continueth and abideth forever with the priesthood which is after the holiest order of God" or *greater priesthood*. (See verses 18, 26.) The "greater priesthood" brings people into the presence of God. (See verses 19, 22.) The "lesser priesthood" brings people into the presence of "ministering angels." (See verse 26.) Moses held the *greater priesthood*, but his people "hardened their hearts" and "therefore, [God] took ... the Holy Priesthood [higher or greater priesthood]" away from them and replaced it with the "lesser priesthood." (See verses 24–26.) The faithful in Joseph's day could obtain the lesser and the greater priesthoods and become "the seed of Abraham" and become the "elect of God."[3] (See verses 33–34.) To those so privileged, they would receive "all that my Father hath." (See verse 38.) Receiving priesthood required an "oath and a covenant" discussed below. (See verses 39–44.)

The Campbellites and the development of the idea of priesthood

The Campbellites, a nickname for the Disciples of Christ, were founded in the early 19th century by Thomas and Alexander Campbell. Sidney Rigdon, a leading member of the Disciples of Christ and an early convert to

---

1. By August 1843 Joseph was teaching that Abraham had received the highest ordinances of the temple from Melchizedek. For a more detailed discussion, see commentary on the fulness of the priesthood in section 124. (See also Ehat and Cook, *The Words of Joseph Smith*, 244–47; notes on 303–8; and JST Genesis 14:25–40.)

2. Robinson and Garrett, *Doctrine and Covenants Commentary*, 3:28.

3. In the context of D&C 84:33–35, "Sons of Moses and of Aaron" is a reference to the Melchizedek (higher) and Aaronic (lesser) priesthoods. The expression "seed of Abraham" is a blessing received by those who "obtain these two priesthoods—blessings associated with the Abrahamic covenant. By 1843 Joseph would speak about "three grand orders"—the Levitical (Aaronic), Melchizedek, and Patriarchal ("the power of endless life" or eternal procreation.) Patriarchal privilege was obtained by entering into this order of the priesthood [meaning the "new and everlasting covenant of marriage.]" (See D&C 131:2; 132.) When Joseph explained this idea he said, "Go to and finish the temple ... and you will then receive more knowledge concerning this priesthood." (See Smith, *Teachings of the Prophet Joseph Smith*, 322–23.)

Mormonism, brought hundreds of his fellow Campbellites into the Church with him. Sidney quickly became a close associate in the leadership of the Church with Joseph Smith. Because Mormon doctrines and practices were not well defined or entrenched at first, Campbellite ideas, doctrines, and practices heavily influenced the thinking of Joseph and his followers. The explanation of the priesthood as found in section 84 is conceivably the Lord's response through Joseph to some of these Campbellite beliefs. Mark Lyman Staker pointed out that, given the environment in which section 84 was revealed, it is certainly not unreasonable that Joseph sought inspiration about the place of priesthood in the restored Church to satisfy the "hunger of new converts to Mormonism to understand how their revealed religion was similar or differed from their earlier beliefs as espoused by Campbell."[1]

In February 1831, Alexander Campbell made a well-known attack on the Book of Mormon. He claimed it could not possibly be the word of God because it conveniently resolved some of the religious controversies of his day, was full of "Josephisms," and misconstrued the concept of priesthood as it was taught in the Bible.[2] On the issue of priesthood, Campbell supposed that the Bible supported the idea that his own authority was based on a concept called the "priesthood of all believers," a Protestant doctrine used to circumvent the authority of the Catholic Church. It proposed that every individual had direct access to God without ecclesiastical mediation and that each individual shares the responsibility of ministering to the community of believers[3]—nothing more, nothing less.

Campbell acknowledged that a more structured and tiered view of priesthood was found in the Bible. He freely admitted that the Old and New Testaments speak about "patriarchal," "Aaronical," Melchizedek, and Messianic priesthoods. But he believed that these ancient priesthoods became irrelevant when Jesus was born and established his gospel.[4] This meant that "the covenant made with Abraham was fulfilled and no longer significant." Judaism had been abolished, and there was "no need to maintain priesthood ties with previous dispensations and no need to pass authority from one generation to the next to keep the ancient order of things" alive.[5]

Campbell's view on priesthood put him at add odds with the Book of Mormon, which he criticized for depicting a priesthood that could be

---

1. Ibid., Kindle locations 5222–23. *[what does ibid. refer to here, Staker? If so, Staker should be note no 1, and then note no. 2 could be ibid.]*
2. Staker, *Hearken, O Ye People*, Kindle locations 5109–10.
3. Ibid., 5132.
4. Ibid., 5158–61.
5. Ibid., 5163–64, 5186–87.

passed on from one generation to the next and did not end with the earthly advent of Jesus.[1] Joseph would later use some of the same terminology that Alexander Campbell used to describe priesthood offices found in the Bible, but he defined these terms much differently. Not unexpectedly, Joseph's conception of priesthood was more in line with the Book of Mormon, which espoused a priesthood as it is depicted by the prophet Alma: a "high priesthood being after the order of his Son, which order was from the foundation of the world; or in other words, being without beginning of days or end of years, being prepared from eternity to all eternity"[2] (Alma 13:7). It was a priesthood that did not discount Jacob or Israel, as the Campbellites did, but "placed Israel at the center of all God did, confirming that the ancient covenant would be renewed and continued."[3] By the 1840s, filling out the role of priesthood became a central part of Joseph Smith's mission (see sections 107 and 124). Contrary to Campbell's understanding, the priesthood was not obsolete but rather the unifying principle that tied together all past and future dispensations of time.

The oath and covenant of the priesthood

The oath and covenant of the priesthood mentioned specifically in verses 33–39 is a mutual promise between God and man. Men promise that they will (1) obtain the Aaronic, Melchizedek, and patriarchal priesthoods, (2) magnify their callings in these priesthoods, (3) study the scriptures, and (4) "live by every word that proceedeth forth from the mouth of God." (See verses 33, 43–44). In return, God swears an oath and promises men exaltation, or in other words, the "Father's kingdom" or "all that my Father hath." (See verse 38.)

The oath and covenant of the priesthood is patterned after the covenant-making process described in Genesis

The oath and covenant of the priesthood follows an ancient pattern described in Genesis. Understanding the parallel between the ancient and modern covenants deepens our understanding of section 84 and informs us about how God puts his children under an obligation to live his commandments.

Contemporary ideas about covenants or contracts differ from those set out in the ancient world. A modern understanding involves a situation

---

1. Ibid., 5197–99.
2. As early as 1831 in his revelation on Moses, Joseph described a priesthood that "was in the beginning [and] shall be in the end of the world also" (Moses 6:7).
3. Staker, *Hearken, O Ye People*, Kindle locations 5277–79.

where two or more parties bargain and enter into a mutual agreement to perform certain promises. By way of contrast, in Old Testament times a covenant was not bargained for but rather imposed by a superior power. The terms and conditions were solely the creation of only one party to the agreement. Therefore, men and women were invited to join the covenant but by so doing were not able to alter its terms and conditions. In other words, "God takes the sole initiative in covenant making and fulfillment." The covenant therefore emphasizes the "authority and grace of God in making and keeping the covenant." Thus, while man's willingness to obey the terms and conditions of the covenant are necessary for its fulfillment, "yet man's action is not causative. God's grace always goes before and produces man's response."[1]

The concept of an oath is also distinct from the Old Testament perspective. When we think of oath taking, we picture a person taking the stand and swearing to tell the truth. In the Old Testament times, the idea of oath taking was used more broadly to mean that a person would swear to bring about the promised reward or exact certain punishments depending upon how well the participants lived by the terms and conditions of the covenant. After the covenant was entered into, a person, or in our case God, would swear that he would deliver or bring about the reward or punishment for living or not living by the promises made.[2]

An examination of Old Testament-like covenants and the oath and covenant of the priesthood as revealed in section 84 demonstrates that both are ancient in character. For that reason, it is instructive to examine the specific elements involved in ancient covenant making and compare each to the oath and covenant as it is expressed in section 84.

Ancient covenants included the following stipulations:
1. A preamble;
2. A historical prologue;
3. Demands or stipulations;
4. Divine witness; and
5. Blessings and curses.

Once the covenant was written down, it was made public by reading it aloud and by depositing the text in a public place.

Chaim Potok in his popular book *Wanderings* discusses what is involved. The *preamble* identified the covenant giver. For example, "These are the words of the sun-god...."[3]

The *historical prologue* recounted the covenant giver's past deeds for

---

1. Unger and White, *Expository Dictionary of the Old Testament*, 83.
2. See Unger and White, *Expository Dictionary of the Old Testament*, 83. See also Deuteronomy 4:31.
3. See Potok, *Wanderings*.

the benefit of the vassal. It was designed to have "the past serve as the foundation for the present obligation."[1] It served the purpose of causing a sense of gratitude in the vassal and put him under an obligation to "comply with the wishes of his benefactor."[2] For example, "Aziras was the grandfather of you, Duppi-Tessub. He rebelled against my father, but submitted again to my father."[3]

The *demands or stipulations* set forth explicitly the terms and conditions of the covenant.

Depositing the text and the public reading was accomplished when the covenant or treaty was placed in the sanctuary or shrine so that its contents could be published to the general population. Potok said that at regular intervals it was read in the presence of the king. It is not unlike Josiah in the book of Kings renewing the covenant when he read to the people the words of the Book of the Covenant that had been found in the temple of the Lord.[4] It is also reminiscent of King Benjamin addressing his people in the Book of Mormon.

Divine witness involved deities attesting to the terms of the treaty or covenant. The idea was that if God was cognizant of the agreement, then "there was no god left that the vassal could appeal to for protection if he wanted to violate his solemn oath."[5] The function of a witness was to observe the behavior of the covenant takers and mete out appropriate rewards and/or punishments.

Blessings or curses were promised those that either lived or broke the terms of the covenant. The consequent results of either living or not living by the terms of the covenant were described in detail.[6] Potok described blessings and curses in his book:

> BLESSINGS AND CURSES: The treaty is sacred law. The gods will curse and wreak vengeance upon the vassal who breaks it, and bring blessings upon the vassal who upholds it. The vassal would take an oath to uphold the covenant. This oath was part of a ceremony in which the parties ate together, drank together, smeared oil on themselves, or sacrificed a young donkey. The vassal might drink water in order to have the curse enter his body. Most often an animal was cut up, and the one who took the oath was identified by a

---

1. See *Anchor Bible Dictionary* 1:1180.
2. See *Anchor Bible Dictionary*, 1:1181.
3. See Potok, *Wanderings*.
4. The king stood by the pillar and renewed the covenant in the presence of the Lord—to follow the Lord and keep his commands, regulations, and decrees with all his heart and all his soul, thus confirming the words of the covenant written in this book. Then all the people pledged themselves to the covenant. (See New International Version 2 Kings 23:1–4.)
5. *Anchor Bible Dictionary*, 1:1181.
6. See *Anchor Bible Dictionary*, 1:1181.

gesture of some kind—perhaps a finger across the throat—with the bloody pieces. May he be cut up as this animal is cut up if he breaks his oath.[1]

The Oath and Covenant of the Priesthood in section 84 follows the ancient pattern of covenant making.

The *preamble* is contained in verses 1–2 and identifies the giver of the covenant: "A revelation of Jesus Christ unto his servant Joseph Smith, Jun., and six elders . . . as he has spoken by the mouth of his prophets."

The *historical prologue* begins in verse 6 and continues through verse 32. It follows verses 3–5, which briefly identify Jackson County, Missouri, as the location of the New Jerusalem. The historical prologue recounts the history of the priesthood beginning with Moses through Abraham and Melchizedek. It describes the powers associated with the Aaronic and Melchizedek priesthoods anciently and recounts the mission of John the Baptist. The history concludes with a statement about the sons of Aaron or holders of the Aaronic Priesthood offering a blood sacrifice at the temple before the coming of the Lord.

The *demands and stipulations* of the covenant are set out with specificity in verses 33 and 43–44, wherein the Lord requires those who are to receive of his fulness to (1) obtain the Aaronic, Melchizedek, and patriarchal priesthoods, (2) magnify their callings in the priesthoods, (3) give heed to or study the scriptures or words of eternal life, and (4) live all the commandments.

The part of ancient covenant making that involves *depositing the text and publication* is accomplished by placing the oath and covenant in the canon of scripture, and in this way making it public.

Divine witness is addressed in verses 39–40, where the Lord himself witnesses and swears an oath that he will honor the terms of the covenant. If God's people live by the conditions of the covenant, then he will bring about the promised blessings of exaltation.

The *blessings and curses* are set out in verses 34–38 and 41–42. Those who live the covenant will enjoy the blessings Moses, Aaron, and Abraham and be the "elect of God." Such will receive the Lord and the Lord's servants, and everything "that my Father hath shall be given him." Covenant keepers will be joint heirs with God and Jesus Christ. (See Romans 8:14–17; 2 Corinthians 3:18; Galatians 4:7; Ephesians 3:19; 4:11–13.) Those who disobey the covenant and "altogether turneth therefrom, shall not have forgiveness of sins in this world nor in the world to come." (Verse 41.)

Verse 41 deserves some additional analysis because it can be read to mean that people who enter into the oath and covenant of the priesthood

---

1. See Potok, *Wanderings*.

and forsake it are sons of perdition because those who "altogether turneth therefrom, shall not have forgiveness of sins in this world nor in the world to come." In this context note that the Prophet Joseph Smith taught that "all sins shall be forgiven, except the sin against the Holy Ghost; for Jesus will save all except the sons of perdition."[1] Sinning against the Holy Ghost is a term of art, and Joseph carefully delineates its meaning. He explains that to sin against the Holy Ghost a person "has got to say that the sun does not shine while he sees it; he has got to deny Jesus Christ when the heavens have been opened unto him, and to deny the plan of salvation with his eyes open to the truth of it."[2]

In other words, those beyond the saving grace of God are those who have had superlative spiritual experience and had their callings and elections made sure and then turn away from God and the restored gospel.

The Spirit giveth light to every person

The Lord teaches that all, those in and out of the Church, are susceptible to his Spirit. In this context the "Spirit" referred to is probably the Spirit of Christ as well as the Holy Ghost. Although after baptism members of the Church are given a special endowment of the Holy Ghost by the laying on of hands, James Talmage explains in *The Articles of Faith* that the Holy Ghost may also minister to the unbaptized.

> In another sense the Holy Ghost has frequently operated for good through persons that were unbaptized; indeed, some measure of His power is given to all mankind; for, as seen already, the Holy Spirit is the medium of intelligence, of wise direction, of development, of life. Manifestation of the power of God, as made plain through the operations of the Spirit, are seen in the triumphs of ennobling art, the discoveries of science, and the events of history; with all of which the carnal mind may believe that God takes no direct concern. Not a truth has ever been made the property of humankind except through the power of that great Spirit who exists to do the bidding of the Father and the Son. And yet the actual companionship of the Holy Ghost, the divinely-bestowed right to His ministrations, the sanctifying baptism with fire, are given as a permanent and personal possession only to the faithful, repentant, baptized candidate for salvation; and with all such this gift shall abide unless it be forfeited through transgression.[3]

---

1. Smith, *Teachings of the Prophet Joseph Smith*, 358.
2. See Smith, *Teachings of the Prophet Joseph Smith*, 358.
3. See Talmage, *Articles of Faith*, 149.

Pay attention to the Book of Mormon

Grant Underwood engaged in a project designed to calculate Book of Mormon usage versus Bible usage by first-generation Mormons. His research concluded that Church writers quoted the Book of Mormon once for every nineteen times the Bible was referenced. This ratio is not particularly surprising in light of the ubiquitous influence of the King James Bible in Joseph Smith's day. It is in this context that Saints are told to "remember the new covenant, even the Book of Mormon." (See verse 57.) The Lord chides the Saints for having "treated lightly the things you have received." (See verse 54; see also D&C 42:12.) It is also interesting to observe that even after this revelation was given the ratio between Book of Mormon usage and Bible usage did not change through at least 1846.[1]

Washing feet

In some instances, when moved upon by the Spirit but not otherwise, the elders are to cleanse their feet as a witness against those who reject their testimony. (See D&C 24:15; 75:20; Matthew 10:14–15; Mark 6:11; Luke 9:5; 10:10–12; Acts 13:51.)

Election of grace

The term *election of grace* as it is used in Doctrine and Covenants 84:99 hints that some were called (elected) in a premortal existence to perform certain missions in this life. (See Romans 9; Abraham 3:22–24.) This idea is not to be confused with *predestination*, the concept that God arbitrarily selects certain individuals to be saved and others to be damned regardless of any effort or desire on their own part. Those elected by "grace" or love of God may or may not accomplish their predesignated missions, depending on their personal choices.

The "election of grace" should not be confused with the doctrine of having one's *calling and election made sure*. *Calling and election* means that after a person has been "thoroughly proved" and the Lord is satisfied that he will "serve Him at all hazards," he or she is assured of the blessing of *eternal life* or association in the highest degree of the three degrees of the celestial kingdom.[2] (See D&C 131 and commentary for D&C 131:5–6.)

---

1. See Underwood, "Book of Mormon Usage," 53–59.
2. See Smith, *Teachings of the Prophet Joseph Smith*, 150.

The desolation of abomination

The term *desolation of abomination,* found in Doctrine and Covenants 84:117, is a reference to imagery used in Daniel 11:31 and repeated in Matthew 24:15. Bruce R. McConkie said this phrase described the "corruption and befoulment" that would bring about the downfall and "ruination" of the earth.[1] He believed that the "conditions of desolation" were to "occur twice in fulfillment of Daniel's words."

> The first was to be when the Roman legions under Titus, in 70 A.D., laid siege to Jerusalem, destroying and scattering the people, leaving not one stone upon another in the desecrated temple, and spreading such terror and devastation as has seldom if ever been equalled on earth. Of those days Moses had foretold that the straitness of the siege would cause parents to eat their own children and great loathing and evil to abound. (Deut. 28.) . . .
>
> Then, speaking of the last days, of the days following the restoration of the gospel and its declaration "for a witness unto all nations," our Lord said: "And again shall the abomination of desolation, spoken of by Daniel the prophet, be fulfilled." (Jos. Smith 1:31–32.) That is: Jerusalem again will be under siege . . ."houses rifled, and the women ravished; and half of the city shall go forth into captivity" . . . (Zech. 14.) It will be during this siege that Christ will come, the wicked will be destroyed, and the millennial era commenced.[2]

SECTION 85: WHITNEY STORE, KIRTLAND, OHIO, NOVEMBER 27, 1832

Heading

The Saints should divide their inheritance in Zion, Jackson County, Missouri. "One mighty and strong" predicted.

Introduction

Revelation given through Joseph Smith in the "revelation room" at the Whitney store in Kirtland, Ohio.[3] This section is an extract from a letter the Prophet Joseph wrote to W. W. Phelps, who was living in Independence, Missouri. It was given to answer questions about those Saints who had moved to Zion but who had not received their inheritances according to the established order in the Church. Inheritances in Zion were to be

---

1. See McConkie, *Mormon Doctrine,* "Abomination of Desolation," first edition.
2. See McConkie, Mormon Doctrine, "Abomination of Desolation," first edition.
3. Smith, *History of the Church,* 1:298–99.

received through consecration. At some time in the future, "one mighty and strong" may give the Saints their inheritances in Zion.

The big question

Question: How do we live together and build a community now that we have gathered?

Answer: By dividing inheritances and entering into the law of consecration.

Background

On November 6, 1832, Joseph returned from a short mission in New York, Albany, and Boston. Sometime during the next three weeks, Joseph received letters from Church leaders in Missouri (Zion) reporting on the situation there.[1] This revelation is an extract from a letter from Joseph to W. W. Phelps, the Church printer and one of the leading brethren living in Zion, who had been asked to help Bishop Edward Partridge distribute inheritances according to the law of consecration. The letter was necessitated by the fact that some had complained to Joseph about whether or not Bishop Partridge was being fair in the way he distributed property among Church members. Phelps received Joseph's letter in December 1832 and published portions of it in the January 1833 issue of the *Evening and Morning Star.* In 1876 Orson Pratt was directed by Brigham Young to include portions of this letter as section 85 in the Doctrine and Covenants.[2]

Parts of section 85 were originally directed to John Whitmer, the Church historian or "the Lord's" clerk. (See verse 1.) Whitmer was living in Zion, Jackson County, Missouri, and as historian had been given the responsibility to keep a "regular history." (See D&C 47:1.) Section 85 reiterates his responsibility to "keep a history, and a general church record." (See verse 1.) However, his record-keeping duties are expanded to include financial and membership records.[3] (See verses 3–12.) "It is the duty of the Lord's clerk . . . to keep [records about] all those who consecrate properties." (Verse 1.)[4]

---

1. See Smith, *History of the Church*, 1:297.
2. See Robinson and Garrett, *Doctrine and Covenants Commentary*, 3:70.
3. Membership records in these verses are referred to as "genealogy" records. As of this date, the concept of vicarious ordinance work for the dead had not yet been introduced.
4. Oliver Cowdery communicated with John Whitmer on a number of occasions about his responsibilities as historian. In a letter dated January 1834, Cowdery explains in more detail what the Prophet envisioned concerning record keeping. There were at least three levels at which a "book of remembrance" or history was to be kept. "You have requested instruction on the subject of Church Records: I have just conversed with bro. Joseph concerning the

It was considered a privilege to be called to go to Jackson County, Missouri, and build up Zion. (See D&C 72:24.) Those who went were to be debt-free and have the means to purchase land in Missouri upon their arrival. Robinson and Garrett point out that ideally they were to bring with them enough food and clothing to last for a year. In addition, they were to bring with them recommends from Church authorities in Kirtland attesting to their worthiness and good standing. (See D&C 72:3–6, 16–18, 24–26.) However, this was not always the case. Many came with great enthusiasm but were unprepared financially. The number of poor members arriving were a "financial drain" and "threatened the very establishment of Zion."[1] When those with very little or no means arrived, such members could not be tithed (see verse 3), calling into question whether or not they should be accepted into consecrated orders. Note here that "tithed" does not refer to the common practice in the Church today of giving a tenth of one's income to the Church. Rather the expression is used more generally to mean to donate or to give one's property to the Church.

In the larger context, this letter also motivated members of the Church living in Zion to willingly give their property to the bishop and receive back their portion (inheritance). For those unwilling to do so, even though they may hold high office in the Church, they will be "cut asunder" and be numbered with the unbelievers, "where [there will be] wailing and gnashing of teeth." (Verse 9.) The Lord compared those members cut off to the Jews who returned to Jerusalem from captivity in Babylon and were prohibited from priesthood-related service in the temple because they could not prove from the genealogical records that they were of Levi—"they had lost their genealogical records, so they were not allowed to serve as priests." (See NLT Ezra 2:62; Nehemiah 7:64.)

"One mighty and strong"

The phrase "one mighty and strong" is not defined precisely in section 85 and therefore has given rise to a number of competing interpretations.

---

same; and he has given me instruction upon his letter [D&C 85] published in the 8th No. of the Star.... I will say... that it is necessary to keep the names of the Saints, & when a child is brought forward to be blessed by the Elders, it is then necessary to take their name upon the Church Record. Put down the name of the man, his place of birth... family.... If he apostatizes write opposite his name that he has. If he begets children after that and they do not come into the Church their names are not known with their brethren in the book of remembrance. The names of the Saints are to be kept in a book that contains the law of God, this is what is meant in bro. Joseph's letter.... Each family will have its record with the law of the Lord in it; each branch of the Church the same in every city; and each city one general record kept by a general clerk." (Cook, *Revelations of the Prophet Joseph Smith*, 178.)

1. See Robinson and Garrett, *Doctrine and Covenants Commentary*, 3:72.

On its face, the phrase refers to an individual whom the Lord "will send" to "set in order the house of God, and to arrange by lot the inheritances of the saints." (Verse 7.) The phrase was largely forgotten until it was used by Mormon fundamentalists to try to justify their claims that at some future point in time, prior to the Second Coming, one of their own persuasion would be raised up to set in order The Church of Jesus Christ of Latter-day Saints.[1] According to this view, sweeping changes will transform the Church in Salt Lake City and in the world. The "one mighty and strong" will arrive in Jackson County, Missouri, arrange the lots of inheritance, direct the construction of the temples, exert his authority over the established quorums of the Church, and welcome Jesus to earth at the Second Coming.[2]

In response to the controversial claims of such fundamentalist opponents, the First Presidency in 1905, consisting of Joseph F. Smith, John R. Winder, and Anthon H. Lund, issued a statement on the subject. The Presidency suggested two interpretations. In the first instance the "one mighty and strong" was a warning to Bishop Edward Partridge that if he did not repent another would stand in his place. In the second instance, if there are those who still insist that section 85 indicates that the "one mighty and strong" is an event relating to the future, "let the Latter-day Saints know that he will be a future bishop of the Church who will be with the Saints in Zion . . . when the Lord shall establish them in that land."[3]

The only information we have from the Prophet Joseph on this subject suggests that the warning that a person who sins or "puts forth his hand to steady the ark of God, does not mean that any one had at the time, but it was given for a caution to those in high standing to beware, lest they should fall by the shaft of death."[4] In context, the person who stood in need of a warning to repent to avoid replacement was Bishop Edward Partridge, whose method of administering the law of consecration was being challenged and criticized. However, Partridge apparently did repent for any unnamed faults and less than two years later, on November 7, 1835, the Lord stated in an uncanonized revelation that he was "well pleased with . . . my servant Edward Partridge, because of the integrity of [your heart] in laboring in my vineyard, for the salvation of the souls of men."

---

1. No single verse is referred to any more often by apostate fundamentalists. (See Merrill and Harper, "It Maketh My Bones to Quake," 87.)
2. See www.mormonfundamentalism.com/NEWFILES/OneMightyAndStrong.htm.
3. Clark, *Messages*, 4:112, 115–17.
4. Cook, *Revelations of the Prophet Joseph Smith*, 179.

The revelation adds that Partridge's "sins [were] forgiven."[1] His repentance then meant that the need for "one mighty and strong" was now moot.

Orson Pratt and W. W. Phelps were of the opinion that the "one mighty and strong" would yet come to Missouri. Pratt said, "The time will come for the Saints to receive their stewardships, when they shall return to the lands from whence they have been driven; but the inheritances will not be given, until the Lord shall first appoint to the righteous dead their inheritances, and afterwards the righteous living will receive theirs" under the direction of "one mighty and strong."[2] Phelps agreed. "[N]ow this revelation was sent to me in Zion, and has reference to the time when Adam . . . comes at the beginning of our Eternal Lot[s] of inheritance,—according as our names are found in the [Book of the] Law of the Lord, while the fools that received the priesthood, like the fool that took his 'one Talent' and hid it;—or reached out to steady the ark, will find themselves where the rich man did—in hell, with plenty of fire–but no water."[3]

Robinson and Garrett add another possible interpretation. If the language referring to the "one mighty and strong" has any future fulfillment it should be seen as a title for the Savior, "the mighty One of Israel" who is Jehovah or Christ. (See Genesis 49:24; Psalm 24:8; Isaiah 1:24; D&C 36:1; see also Isaiah 9:6; 10:21; 28:2–17.) Consequently, this verse may refer to a time when the Savior himself, either directly or through his authorized agents, will establish the law of consecration during the Millennium or sometime prior thereto in preparation for this great event.[4]

---

1. See Smith, *History of the Church*, 2:302–3.
2. See *Journal of Discourses*, 21:150–51.
3. Letter from W. W. Phelps to President Brigham Young, Great Salt Lake City, May 6, 1867. LDS Church Archives and www.mormonfundamentalism.com/NEWFILES/ OneMightyAndStrong.htm.
4. Robinson and Garrett, *Doctrine and Covenants Commentary*, 3:73–74. If in fact this event does allude to a future "one mighty and strong," he will "arrange by lot the inheritances of the saints." (Verse 7.) Robinson and Garrett point out that "by lot" means by chance, "as in drawing straws or drawing names from a hat." (Robinson and Garrett, *Doctrine and Covenants Commentary*, 3:75.) This process for selecting the piece of ground assigned to participants in the order eliminates any favoritism on the part of the bishop in dividing up the resources of the community. The idea behind casting lots was that God would intervene and assure a right outcome. For example, in Acts when the Twelve were choosing another apostle they "all prayed for the right man to be chosen" and then "cast lots." (NLT Acts 1:25–26.)

Section 86: Whitney Store, Kirtland, Ohio, December 6, 1832

Heading

Joseph Smith continues to make inspired changes and additions to the New Testament. He reinterprets the parable of the wheat and the tares in the context of the restoration.

Introduction

Revelation given through Joseph Smith the Prophet in the Whitney store in Kirtland, Ohio, on December 6, 1832.[1] This revelation was received while the Prophet was reviewing and editing the manuscript of his inspired interpretation of various passages in the Bible. The Lord explains the meaning of the parable of the wheat and the tares. Priesthood blessings will be offered to those who are in the direct line of Abraham as well as to others who will be adopted in.

Background

In December 1832 Joseph continued to make inspired changes in the New Testament with his counselor in the First Presidency, Frederick G. Williams, acting as scribe. The process yielded an increased understanding of the parable of the wheat and the tares in Matthew 13:24–30 and 36–43 and related it to the reestablishment of Jesus' church on the earth through the Prophet Joseph Smith.

The well-known parable is sometimes referred to as the story of the wheat and the tares (weeds). Its traditional interpretation comes from the text in the New Testament itself. Jesus likened the Church on earth to a farmer who planted good seed in his field. But that night as everyone slept, an enemy came and planted weeds among the wheat. When the crop began to grow and produce grain, the weeds also took root. The farmer's servant asked the farmer if he should pull out the weeds. The farmer forbade it because excising the weeds would harm the wheat as well. Rather, the farmer told the servant to let the wheat and the weeds grow together until the day of the harvest.

Jesus explains that he is the farmer who planted the good seed. The field is the world and the good seed the righteous members of his kingdom or church. The weeds are sinners who belong to the evil one. The enemy

---

1. See Smith, *History of the Church*, 1:300.

who planted the weeds is the devil. The harvest is the end of the world, and the harvesters are the angels. The point of the parable is that the good and the bad will coexist in the Church until separated by out by fire at the Second Coming.

Section 86 places this parable in the context of the apostasy and restoration of the gospel. Section 86 explains that apostles and, by extension, other followers of Jesus also sow good seeds or bring the righteous into the Church or kingdom. (See verse 2.) The revelation explains that the "weeds," or those over whom Satan has power, would overtake the Church and drive it "into the wilderness." The "wilderness" is a place apart from the evils of the world. It is a metaphor that explains that the Church was removed off the face of the earth and held in abeyance until it could be restored in the last days. (See D&C 86:3; Revelation 12:6, 14; JST Revelation 12:5–7.)

The closing verses in section 86 acknowledge that the house of Israel has been scattered and lost for many centuries. However, the literal descendants of Abraham, those who by lineage have claim on the priesthood, are not lost to God. They will help restore the true gospel in the latter days; and provision will be made for those who are not direct descendants to be adopted into the house of Israel so that they also will have all the blessings of the gospel. (See Galatians 3:24–29; Abraham 2:9–11.)

Section 87: Whitney Store, Kirtland, Ohio, December 25, 1832

Heading

Prophecy on the American Civil War and other wars that will follow.

Introduction

Revelation and prophecy on war, given through Joseph Smith the Prophet at the Whitney store in Kirtland, Ohio, on December 25, 1832.[1] This section was received at a time when the brethren were reflecting and reasoning upon African slavery in America and the slavery of men throughout the world. A civil war is foretold between the Northern and Southern states, followed by a continuing cascade of calamities and war to befall the inhabitants of the earth.

---

1. See Smith, *History of the Church*, 1:301–2.

Section 87 was first published as part of Pearl of Great Price

In the *Millennial Star*,[1] a Mormon publication printed and distributed in England, an advertisement announced that a new book was about to published called the Pearl of Great Price. The advertisement included a reference to the prophecy on war contained in section 87, stating that it had "never appeared in print." Shortly thereafter, the Pearl of Great Price, with this prophecy in it, was published by Franklin D. Richards, in Liverpool, England. The prophecy first appeared in the 1876 edition of the Doctrine and Covenants. The earliest extant copy of the revelation is in the handwriting of Sidney Gilbert and was made sometime before June 12, 1833.

Background

Section 87 was received during a time in American history when people in and out of the Church were concerned about the future of slavery in the Southern states. The North vehemently opposed the practice, while the South defended it. Resentful of the influence of the Northern states in the national legislature, South Carolina threatened to secede from the union when Congress passed a tariff adversely impacting the economy of their state. Fear of civil war spread across the nation. Like others, Joseph Smith concluded that the "United States . . . was threatened with immediate dissolution."[2] It was under these circumstances that he prophesied the coming of the American Civil War, a prophecy that he repeated eleven years later at Ramus, Illinois, on April 2, 1843.

"I prophesy, in the name of the Lord God, that the commencement of the difficulties which will cause much bloodshed previous to the coming of the Son of Man will be in South Carolina. It may probably arise through the slave question. This a voice declared to me, while I was praying earnestly on the subject, December 25, 1832." (D&C 130:12–13.)

Specifics of the prophecy address the following:

1. A civil war will shortly come about. (See verse 1.)
2. The war/rebellion will begin in South Carolina. (See verse 1.)
3. The war will end in the death and misery of many souls. (See verse 1.)
4. The time will come when war shall be poured out upon all nations. (See verses 2–3.)
5. The Southern states will divide against the Northern states. (See verse 3.)

---

1. *Millennial Star* 13 (1851): 216–17.
2. See Smith, *History of the Church*, 1:301.

6. The Southern states will call upon Great Britain for assistance. (See verse 3.)

7. Slaves will rise up against their masters. (See verse 4.)

8. The remnants "left on the land will marshal themselves, and shall become exceedingly angry, and shall vex the Gentiles with a sore vexation." (See verse 5.)

9. Famine, plague, thunder, and vivid lightning will be experienced by the inhabitants of the earth. (See verse 6.)

10. In the process, the blood of the Saints will be spilt by their enemies. (See verse 7.)

It is of note that even though in 1832 it appeared that a potential schism between North and South would arise over trade issues, Joseph never connected his predicted rebellion of South Carolina with tariff issues. Rather, he identified slavery as the root cause of the coming difficulties. Years later, in 1860, Brigham Young said section 87 came when "the brethren were reflecting and reasoning with regard to African slavery on this continent, and the slavery of the children of men throughout the world."[1]

Joseph's prophecy on the Civil War was accepted as the word of God by the Saints. Mormon missionaries carried manuscript copies of it with them as they taught the gospel and frequently read it to various congregations throughout the United States. During the ensuing years Joseph warned friends and relatives to flee South Carolina in anticipation of a war.

Joseph continued to consider the subject of war and prophesied some time later that some of the battles associated with an American civil war would devastate Jackson County, Missouri, as a punishment for the part some of them played in persecuting the Saints. He said that the Missourians' "fields and farms and houses will be destroyed and only the chimneys will be left to mark the desolation." During the Civil War, Missouri was a key state in the Union cause. The three major waterways of the country, the Missouri, Mississippi, and Ohio rivers, either passed through or touched the state. Consequently, during the Civil War Confederate and Union armies battled to control the waterways in this strategic area of the country, which resulted in devastating destruction.

Joseph's prophecy given in 1832 was realized twenty-eight years later. The Southern states attempted a divide with the Northern States, and the predicted conflict began with a rebellion in South Carolina. On April 12, 1861, at 4:40 in the morning, the Southern forces opened fire on Fort Sumter, which was operated by the federal government. At least 4,000 rounds of cannonballs were fired at this lonely fortress located at the mouth of Charleston harbor, South Carolina. Thirty-six hours later this

---

1. *Journal of Discourses*, 8:58.

outpost was forced to surrender. Three days following the attack, President Abraham Lincoln called for 75,000 men to enlist in the army.

Joseph also accurately predicted that the Civil War would terminate in the death and misery of many souls. The number of men called into service during the war was about 2.6 million. Of these, about 1.4 million saw actual service, 620,000 were killed on the battlefield or died from complications associated with the blood and carnage.

Also foreseen was the degree to which slaves would participate in the conflagration. Approximately 180,000 blacks, about 10 percent of the Northern manpower, joined the Federalist cause. By the end of the war there were 140 black regiments. The Secretary of War, General David Hunter, paid tribute to the "colored regiments" and observed that "they are imbued with a burning faith that now is the time appointed by God, in His All-wise Providence, for the deliverance of their race."[1]

Joseph Smith also said in connection with the American Civil War that the Southern States would call upon other nations for assistance, including Great Britain. As early as May 1861, the Southern Confederacy sent a number of commissioners abroad to seek recognition and aid from foreign powers. P. A. Rost of Louisiana was sent to France, A. Dudley Mann of Virginia was sent to Holland and Belgium, and T. Butler King of Georgia was sent as a roving commissioner with the job of keeping in touch with a number of other nations. In 1861 William Yancey of Alabama was sent to England. Later that same year, James M. Mason and John Slidell were sent as ambassadors to England and France respectively to appeal for assistance. Though Mason and Slidell did not succeed in securing direct assistance from Great Britain, it is well known that the British were in sympathy with the Confederate cause and allowed two war vessels, the *Alabama* and the *Florida*, to be built there. These two vessels did immense damage to the Northern states shipping interests. The *Alabama* alone captured sixty-five merchant vessels and destroyed millions of dollars worth of property.[2]

The prophecy on the Civil War was not purely a prediction about a future civil war between North and South. The prophecy informs us that eventually war will be poured out upon all nations. Fifty-three years after the American Civil War, the nations of the earth would be involved in World War I, followed by World War II, the Korean War, the Vietnam War, and the war in Iraq and Afghanistan, to name but a few. Many other nations in the less-developed world have also seen much bloodshed. No one can contest the fact that the twentieth century has been the bloodiest

---

1. See *BYU Studies*, 6:3:191.
2. See Cooper's *American Politics*, 1:197, cited in B. H. Roberts, *New Witnesses for God*, 1:329.

period in world history. In reference to the wars that would follow, Joseph predicted that Great Britain, the most powerful nation of his time, would call upon other nations of the earth to help protect and defend their interests. Surely this part of the prophecy was literally fulfilled in the two great world wars of the twentieth century.

An ambiguous part of Joseph's prophecy concerns "remnants who are left on the land" who rise up and "vex the Gentiles." (See verse 5.) This language may refer to the American Indians and their bloody retreat as settlers pushed them farther and farther west. The relocation of Indians was started in earnest in 1830, when the Congress passed the Indian Removal Act. The prophecy may also refer to a time spoken about in the Book of Mormon that foresees the "remnants of Jacob" or Lamanites waging war from within against the Gentiles before the Second Coming.[1] (See 3 Nephi 20:10–20; 5:23–24; Mormon 5:24.)

SECTION 88: WHITNEY STORE, KIRTLAND, OHIO, DECEMBER 27 AND 28, 1832, JANUARY 3, 1833

Heading

Concerns about the Second Coming addressed. The school of the prophets established.

The big question

Question: What is the structure of the Church?
Answer: Schools must be built to educate the Saints in temporal and spiritual matters.

Introduction

Revelation given through Joseph Smith the Prophet in the "revelation room" of the Whitney store located in Kirtland, Ohio.[2] It was designated by the Prophet as the "olive leaf ... plucked from the Tree of Paradise, the Lord's message of peace to us." It was sent to comfort the Saints, and speaks of the Holy Spirit of Promise, the Light of Christ, sanctifying oneself by obeying law, the importance of both spiritual and temporal education, and the framework for the school of the prophets.

---

1. This may refer to America's neighbors south of the border and to Hispanics within the United States.
2. See Smith, *History of the Church,* 1:302–12.

The Whitney Store, located in Kirtland, Ohio. The proprietor of the store, Newel K. Whitney, prepared an apartment here for Joseph and Emma's family in 1832. They lived here until the following year. The upper room with the desk in it became the headquarters of the Church. During the winter of 1832–33, the School of the Prophets met on the second floor in the room with benches in it.

Anchor section

Memorize: Calling and election; Light of Christ; resurrection; learn doctrine; eternal law; school of the prophets

Section 88 received over a few days' time

This revelation was received by Joseph Smith in the "revelation room" on the second floor of the Whitney store. The revelation was not all received at the same time but spread over a few days, December 27 and 28, 1832, and January 3, 1833. Note that verses 138–41, describing the washing of feet as an initiation ritual to become part of the school of the prophets, was added after January 3, 1833, before the publication of the 1835 edition. The washing-of-feet language was part of the original revelation but for an unknown reason was not originally included in any prior publications of this revelation.[1]

Background

In December 1832 Joseph Smith continued to work on his revisions to the Bible. It was a time when Joseph received revelations about the last days. For example on December 6, 1832, he recorded section 86 concerning the judgments to come when the unrighteous would be punished. On Christmas day he penned section 87, prophesying future wars. Jedediah M. Grant recorded that at about this time "the Prophet stood in his own house when he told several of us of the night the visions of heaven were opened to him, in which he saw the American continent drenched in blood, and he saw nation rising up against nation. . . . The Prophet gazed upon the scene his vision presented, until his heart sickened, and he besought the Lord to close it up again."[2]

The focus on the last days and the destruction to come concerned Joseph and the members of the Church. A council of ten leading high priests met to plead with the Lord for more understanding. Section 88 came by way of reassurance to help calm some of the anxiety the members felt. The Saints would be comforted. God was in charge. The faithful would receive blessings. It was in this spirit that Joseph referred to this revelation as the "olive leaf," a universal symbol of peace.

Section 88 was given at a time when a group of high priests held a confer-

---

1. See Robinson and Garrett, *Doctrine and Covenants Commentary,* 3:96.
2. *Journal of Discourses,* 2:147.

ence in what was called the "revelation room," a small room on the second floor of the Whitney store. F. G. Williams, clerk of the conference, wrote:

> Brother Joseph arose and said, to receive revelation and the blessing of heaven it was necessary to have our minds on God and exercise faith and become of one heart and of one mind. Therefore, he recommended all present to pray separately and vocally to the Lord for to receive his will unto us concerning the up building of Zion and for the benefit of the saints and for the duty and employment of the Elders. Accordingly we all bowed down before the Lord, after which each one arose and spoke in his turn his feelings, and determined to keep the commandments of God. And thus proceeded to receive a revelation . . . the revelation not being finished the conference adjourned till tomorrow morning at 9 o'clock A.M. . . . and commenced by prayer thus proceeded to receive the residue of the above revelation.[1]

These circumstances are alluded to in the first two verses of section 88. Reference is made to the high priests assembled. "Verily, thus saith the Lord unto you who have assembled yourselves." (Verse 1.) And the Lord acknowledges that the prayers Joseph asked those assembled to utter were heard by the Lord. "[T]he alms of your prayers have come up into the ears of the Lord." (Verse 2.)

The other Comforter, the Holy Spirit of Promise, and making your calling and election sure

The phrase *Holy Spirit of Promise* is one of many titles for Holy Ghost and is defined differently depending upon the context. There are two distinct meanings. In this section the term is a reference to the promise of eternal life, or making one's calling and election sure. In section 132 this term expresses the idea that God will not recognize gospel ordinances unless such rituals are ratified by the Holy Ghost. Authority alone is not enough. Divine acceptance depends on personal worthiness and the seal of the Holy Ghost confirms that a recipient of blessings is sincere and genuine. (See D&C 132:7.)[2]

---

1. See Cook, Revelations of the Prophet Joseph Smith; Woodford, The Historical Development of the Doctrine and Covenants, 1127.

2. The concept that God approves only of acts ratified by the Holy Ghost applies broadly to "all covenants, contracts, bonds, obligations, oaths, vows, performances, connections, associations." (D&C 132:7.) Note that the ratification of earthly performances and covenants are conditional and depend on continued worthiness. "We know also, that sanctification through the grace of our Lord and Savior Jesus Christ is just and true, to all those who love and serve God with all their mights, minds, and strength. But there is a possibility that man may fall from grace and depart from the living God." (D&C 20:31–32; see also commentary on D&C 131:5.)

As used in section 88, the term *Holy Spirit of Promise* is linked to the two comforters Jesus promised his disciples in the Gospel of John. The *First Comforter* is the Holy Ghost. (See John 14:16.) The *Second Comforter* is Jesus himself, who guarantees that after his death he will personally make appearance to the righteous. (See John 14:18–23.)[1] Those so privileged receive "the promise which I give unto you of eternal life" (verse 4), or salvation in the highest degree of the celestial kingdom, a promise referred to as having one's *calling and election made sure*. Those who receive this promise of exaltation are said to be members of the *Church of the Firstborn*, or "the inner circle of faithful saints who are heirs of exaltation and the fulness of the Father's kingdom."[2] Paul taught the same doctrine in Ephesians. He says that the faithful Saints "were sealed with that holy Spirit of promise," which was the surety of their "inheritance until the redemption of the purchased possession." (See Ephesians 1:12–14.)[3]

The Light of Christ

The Light of Christ[4] is defined and thought of by Mormons as a divine energy or power that fills the immensity of space, "is in all things, . . . is the law by which all things are governed," and gives life and light to all things. (Verses 12, 13.)[5] B. H. Roberts refers to the Light of Christ as a creative power, a governing power, a life-giving power, an "intelligence-inspiring power."[6] (See verse 13.) It is said that this power influences the conscience by which an individual instinctively knows good from evil. It is a power that guides people to truth and ultimately into the restored gospel of Jesus Christ.[7]

---

1. McConkie and Ostler, *Revelations of the Restoration*, 627. Joseph Smith taught, "Now what is this other Comforter? It is no more nor less than the Lord Jesus Christ Himself; and this is the sum and substance of the whole matter; that when any man obtains this last Comforter, he will have the personage of Jesus Christ to attend him, or appear unto him from time to time, and even He will manifest the Father unto him, and they will take up their abode with him, and the visions of the heavens will be opened unto him, and the Lord will teach him face to face, and he may have a perfect knowledge of the mysteries of the Kingdom of God." (Smith, *History of the Church*, 3:381.) A person who has experienced this Second Comforter is said to have had his calling and election made sure and is "sealed up" to eternal life. (See Smith, *History of the Church*, 3:380.)

2. McConkie, *Mormon Doctrine*, 139.

3. See *Encyclopedia of Mormonism*, 2:651.

4. The *Light of Christ* is sometimes referred to as the *Spirit of Christ*.

5. "The Light of Christ is the divine energy, power, or influence that proceeds from God through Christ and gives life and light to all things. The Light of Christ influences people for good and prepares them to receive the Holy Ghost. One manifestation of the Light of Christ is what we call a conscience." (LDS.org)

6. See *Encyclopedia of Mormonism*, 835.

7. "The Light of Christ became a doctrine of the *Latter Day Saint* movement, including *The Church of Jesus Christ of Latter-day Saints*, that most people would call *conscience*. This

The *Light of Christ* is not to be confused with the *Holy Ghost, gift of the Holy Ghost,* or the spirit personage of Jesus Christ.[1] In Mormon theology each member of the Godhead is a distinct and separate personage. In the case of the *Father* and the *Son,* both have a resurrected body of flesh and bones. The *Holy Ghost* is a personage of spirit (refined mater). The Spirit of the *Holy Ghost* operates in a way similar to the *Light of Christ,* sometimes referred to as the *Spirit of Christ.* The *gift of the Holy Ghost* is the promise given to newly baptized members of the Church that if they live righteously they will have an increased association or companionship with the influence of the Holy Ghost, referred to as a "gift."

The expressions *Spirit of the Lord, Spirit of God,* and the *Spirit of Christ* are often times used interchangeably in scripture and conversation and most often do not change the sense of what is being communicated. By paying attention to the context, it is sometimes possible to discern which member of the Godhead is being referred to.

Primacy of eternal law

Section 88 emphasizes the importance of eternal laws that govern the physical, social, moral, and spiritual aspects of the universe. Taken at face value, this idea comports with a modern understanding of how things operate in a cause and effect way. However, in a Mormon context this idea is more far reaching than might be immediately supposed. Section 88 teaches that "all beings," including God, are subject to eternal law.[2] "All beings who abide not in those conditions [eternal laws] are not justified."

---

doctrine teaches that the light of Christ 'lighteth every man that cometh into the world.' (Holy Bible, King James Version, John 1:9) "Wherefore, every thing which inviteth and enticeth to do good, and to love God, and to serve him, is inspired of God." (*Book of Mormon,* Moroni 7:13.) 'The Spirit of Christ is given to every man, that he may know good from evil.' (Moroni 7:16)" (Wikipedia, http://en.wikipedia.org/wiki/Light_of_Christ.)

1. President Joseph F. Smith (1838–1918) taught: "We often say the Spirit of God when we mean the Holy Ghost; we likewise say the Holy Ghost when we mean the Spirit of God. The Holy Ghost is a personage in the Godhead, and is not that which lighteth every man that cometh into the world. It is the Spirit of God which proceeds through Christ to the world, that enlightens every man that comes into the world, and that strives with the children of men, and will continue to strive with them, until it brings them to a knowledge of the truth and the possession of the greater light and testimony of the Holy Ghost." (Smith, Gospel Doctrine [1939], 67–68.)

2. See also Alma 42:22: "But there is a law given, and a punishment affixed and a repentance granted; which repentance, mercy claimeth; otherwise, justice claimeth the creature and executeth the law, and the law inflicteth the punishment; if not so, the works of justice would be destroyed, and God would cease to be God." The idea of "mercy" in this verse is a reference to the idea that Jesus brought about "mercy" by atoning for the sins of the world "to appease the demands of justice, that God might be a perfect, just God, and a merciful God also." (Verse 15.)

(Verse 39.) Making God subservient to eternal law is a major departure from traditional Christianity, which insists that God is the author of laws and hence above them.

The Mormon view on the subject of law is reflected in a lesson manual for the priesthood authored by John A. Widtsoe in 1915 called *A Rational Theology*.[1] In chapter 5, entitled "The Great Law," he outlines a Mormon understanding of the relationship of law to man and God and its importance to human development. Widtsoe explains that the universe is ordered. He describes it as "a universe controlled by intelligence under the law of cause and effect." This means that the same act, under the same conditions, will produce the same results. God and man are subject to these laws, and God is God because he knows about all of the laws of the universe, is obedient to them, and is therefore powerful—able to exercise control over the environment. Men become like God by learning and conforming to eternal law just as God has done before them. Widtsoe explains that "man, as he gathers experience, becomes more powerful in using the forces of nature in the accomplishment of his purposes. With this thought in mind the great law becomes one of increasing power, or progressive mastery over the universe."[2] Conversely, "The extent of man's growth or progression will depend upon the degree his will is exercised intelligently, upon the things about him. It is therefore conceivable that by the misuse of will, man may lose some of his acquired powers, the negative of the law of progression."[3]

B. H. Roberts concurred. He said that one of the "impressive things about the universe is . . . the fact of order within it."[4] The order to which he refers is cause and effect. This regularity is the foundation of existence and the foundation of science, morals, and theology. As David L. Paulsen said, it is the reign of law that "enables one to predict the future, interpret the past, and to understand the present."[5] This thought about the rule

---

1. Widtsoe was a member of the Twelve and a highly regarded Mormon theologian, along with B. H. Roberts and James E. Talmage.

2. See Widtsoe, *Rational Theology* (1937), 20.

3. See Widtsoe, *Rational Theology* (1937), 21; Joseph Smith explained how God advanced by adhering to eternal laws based on his comprehension and mastery of law and provided a way for his spirit sons and daughters to do likewise. "The first principles of man are self-existent with God. God himself, finding he was in the midst of spirits and glory, because he was more intelligent, saw proper to institute laws whereby the rest could have a privilege to advance like himself. The relationship we have with God places us in a situation to advance in knowledge. He has power to institute laws to instruct the weaker intelligences, that they may be exalted with himself, so that they might have one glory upon another, and all that knowledge, power, glory, and intelligence, which is requisite in order to save them in the world of spirits." (See Smith, *Teachings of the Prophet Joseph Smith*, 354.)

4. Roberts, *The Truth, the Way, and the Life*, xcix.

5. Roberts, *The Truth, the Way, and the Life*, xcix.

of law is more fully explained in section 88 than anywhere else in the canon of scripture. It is a core principle of existence, the source and origin of God's power, and the means by which God's children advance and become more like him.

Section 88 speaks about law in the following circumstances:

1. There is a relationship between living a celestial law and being able to clothe a spirit with a celestial body in the resurrection (verses 20–24, 28);

2. If a person refuses to live by the law, it is like refusing to accept a gift. "For what doth it profiteth a man if a gift is bestowed upon him, and he receive not the gift?" (verses 32–33);

3. God's children are sanctified when they live by the moral laws (verses 34–35);

4. Eternal laws govern the entire universe (verses 36–38, 42); and

5. "All beings," including God, are subject to the law (verse 39).

The "digging in the field" parable

The "digging in the field parable" is an admonition that now is the time for those who have the gospel to repent and draw near to the Lord. The idea is that it does not matter what others may do, for the Lord will give all people at some time, either here or in the next life, an opportunity to find the truth, "every kingdom in its hour, and in its time, and in its season." (See verses 51–61.) But the point is that the Saints' opportunity is in the present and should not be lost. Therefore, the revelation counsels the Saints to "call upon me while I am near." (See verse 62.)

Coming to God involves inquiry, focus on the things of God, repentance, and serious effort. (See verses 63–69.) Those who commit will receive blessings. The time will come when the righteous will "see him [Jesus]; for he will unveil his face unto you, and it shall be in his own time, and in his own way, and according to his own will." (See verse 68.)

The Second Coming

Thoughts about the Second Coming during this period in Church history were front and center. "For not many days hence" the earth will "tremble" and "stars" fall from heaven. (See verse 87.) "Earthquakes ... shall cause groanings" and there will be "thunderings ... lightnings ... tempests" and "the waves of the sea heaving themselves beyond their bounds." (See verse 89.) The mother of abominations will fall, and Jesus will come. (See verses 94–95, 105.) The graves will be opened, Satan will be bound, and God will complete his purposes upon the earth. (Verses 97, 110.)

The school of the prophets

Section 88 established the school of the prophets to instruct members on spiritual and temporal matters, and to help prepare missionaries to preach the gospel in a diverse world. The school was sometimes referred to as the school of the elders.

The first school met on January 23, 1833, in the Whitney store in Kirtland. Students came fasting at sunrise and normally continued until about 4:00 P.M. Zebedee Coltrin remembers that "before going to school we washed ourselves and put on clean linen."[1] Blessings were pronounced. The prophet invited each person present to receive the ordinance of washing of feet as a ritual by which they became a member of the school. The day was concluded by partaking of the Lord's Supper, after which they sang a hymn and were dismissed.[2]

Of the washing of feet, Joseph and Samuel H. Smith reported that those present were told that they should "call a solemn assembly and every man call upon the name of the Lord and continue in prayer that they should sanctify themselves and wash their hands and feet for a testimony that their garments were clean from the blood of all men."[3]

The school was opened and sometimes dismissed with uplifted hands in token of the everlasting covenant to bear one another's burdens. This procedure is set out in Doctrine and Covenants 88:132–33. Powerful manifestations of the Holy Spirit were experienced, along with the gift of tongues and the interpretation thereof.[4]

The school met through the winter and early spring of 1833. Orson Hyde was the instructor. Enrollment never exceeded about twenty-five. All were initiated through the washing of feet and then reaffirmed their

---

1. See Cook, *Revelations of the Prophet Joseph Smith*, 187.

2. The sacrament was administered after the ancient order. Warm bread was used so that it broke easily into fist-size pieces and each person participating had a glass of wine. (See Cook, *Revelations of the Prophet Joseph Smith*, 187.)

3. Woodford, *The Historical Development of the Doctrine and Covenants*, 1128. Some Mormon historians have pointed out that Joseph may have used the washing of feet ordinance as a ritual for making school members' calling and election sure. This inference is based on language from the minutes of the January 23, 1833, meeting of the school. "Tongues proceeded to washing hands faces feet in the name of the Lord . . . each one washing his own after which the president girded himself with a towel and again washed the feet of all the Elders wiping them with the towel. . . . The President said after he had washed the feet of the Elders, as I have done so do ye wash ye therefore one another's feet pronouncing at the same time through the power of the Holy Ghost that the Elders were all clean from the blood of this generation but that those among them who should sin willfully after they were thus cleansed and sealed up unto eternal life should be given over unto the buffetings of Satan until the day of redemption. Having continued all day in fasting and prayer before the Lord at the close . . . partook of the Lord's supper." (Cook, *Revelations of the Prophet Joseph Smith*, 186.)

4. See Woodford, *The Historical Development of the Doctrine and Covenants*, 1129.

mutual love and goodwill by exchanging the formal salutation referred to at the commencement of each class.

The school ended in April 1833, when the brethren were sent on missions. Two later schools known as the school of the elders or school of the prophets convened in Jackson County, Missouri, during the summer of 1833 and in Kirtland from late fall to early spring in 1834–35 and 1835–36. The enrollment was enlarged and expanded. Secular as well as religious curriculum was offered. These later schools did not observe the earlier initiation rite and formalized salutations. Parley P. Pratt led the Missouri school and Joseph Smith, Sidney Rigdon, Frederick G. Williams, and William E. McLellin taught in Kirtland. During the 1834–35 school year, students in Kirtland heard the lectures later published in the Doctrine and Covenants as the Lectures on Faith.

The school of the prophets did not meet again until the Church moved west. Brigham Young reorganized the school in connection with the University of Deseret. The classes later separated from the university, and branch classes were held in major Mormon communities. The schools were dissolved in the summer of 1872 and reorganized on a smaller level in the fall for General Authorities and other invited priesthood leaders; by 1884, under the administration of John Taylor, they were completely disbanded.

Spiritual power and the school of the prophets

The teaching principles set out in connection with the establishment of the school of the prophets are notable. The teacher's responsibility was to seek the Lord in prayer and invite the spirit of revelation into the teaching process. The relationship between the students and between the teacher and students rested on Christian fellowship and a determination to support, love, and strengthen one another. Furthermore, the relationship between the teacher and student was somewhat egalitarian. Although the teacher instructed, students were given an opportunity to speak and edify each other. There was a mutual responsibility for both student and teacher to edify and instruct.

Joseph Smith often emphasized principles by constructing inspired rituals around fundamental religious beliefs making abstractions more concrete and meaningful. Such is the case here. The instructor's responsibility was to teach with the Spirit of God, and a method was provided to bring this about. (See verse 129.) The teacher was instructed to kneel in prayer prior to entering the classroom. (See verse 131.) The bond of fellowship was given emphasis and ritualized by instructing the teacher to greet the students by standing with uplifted hands and stating the following:

Art thou a brother or brethren? I salute you in the name of the Lord Jesus Christ, in token or remembrance of the everlasting covenant, in which covenant I receive you to fellowship, in a determination that is fixed, immovable, and unchangeable, to be your friend and brother through the grace of God in the bonds of love, to walk in all the commandments of God blameless, in thanksgiving, forever and ever. Amen. (Verse 133.)

The dual role of teacher and student to cooperate, respect each other's views, and edify each other was not ritualized, but specific instruction on that role was given—all should have an opportunity to speak. (See verse 122.) By inviting teacher-student interaction, students were given an opportunity to contribute insights that further enriched the subject matter and instruction.

This approach to teaching brought about awe-inspiring results. During the process many present commented on the spirit felt. Some prophesied, and yet others saw the heavens opened. At the Kirtland school of the prophets on January 23, 1833, Joseph Smith and a small number of men convened to organize the school. They opened with prayer, and some spoke in tongues.[1] The most remarkable events of the meeting were recorded by Zebedee Coltrin:

> About the time the school was first organized some wished to see an angel, and a number joined in a circle, and prayed when the vision came, two of the brethren shrank and called for the vision to close or they would perish. . . . Joseph having given instructions, and while engaged in silent prayer, kneeling, with our hands uplifted each one praying in silence, no one whispered above his breath, a personage walked through the room from east to west, and Joseph asked if we saw him. I saw him and suppose others did, and Joseph answered that is Jesus, the Son of God, our elder brother. Afterward Joseph told us to resume our former position in prayer, which we did. Another person came through; He was surrounded as with a flame of fire.[2]

In connection with this appearance of the Father and the Son, Coltrin said that he "experienced a sensation that it might destroy the tabernacle as it was of consuming fire of great brightness. . . . This appearance was so grand and overwhelming that it seemed I should melt down . . . and the sensation was so powerful that it thrilled through my whole system and I felt it in the marrow of my bones."[3] The prophet explained that those who had seen the Father and the Son were now prepared to be "Apostles of Jesus Christ."[4]

---

1. See Cook, *Revelations of the Prophet Joseph Smith*, 186.
2. Cook, Revelations of the Prophet Joseph Smith, 187.
3. Cook, *Revelations of the Prophet Joseph Smith*, 187–88.
4. Cook, *Revelations of the Prophet Joseph Smith*, 188.

The curriculum of the school of the prophets

It was intended that the curriculum of the school be broad and involve religious as well as secular instruction. Addressing the religious side, the revelation said that all should be taught "in theory, in principle, in doctrine, in the law of the gospel, in all things that pertain unto the kingdom of God." (Verse 78.) Addressing the secular, the revelation said that students should learn "of things both in heaven and in the earth, and under the earth; things which have been, things which are, things which must shortly come to pass; things which are at home, things which are abroad; the wars and the perplexities of the nations, and the judgments which are on the land; and a knowledge also of countries and of kingdoms." (Verse 79.) The command to learn about everything from geology, mining, and history through political science, foreign affairs, and science was taken seriously, and a broad range of classes were offered. In 1836–37 the school of the prophets provided class-work for the nearly 150 students. Along with classes on theology, Greek, Latin, English, arithmetic, geography, classical languages, and history were taught.[1]

The immediate aim of the school was to educate missionaries so that they would "be prepared in all things" to "magnify" their "calling." (See verse 80.) In this way the work of the Lord would be advanced. Missionaries would be equipped to engage the peoples of the world and most effectively "warn the people" of the restoration of the gospel, its implications, and the impending return of the Lord Jesus Christ. (See verse 81.) The command to teach a wide-ranging curriculum and to "teach one another words of wisdom . . . out of the best books" was a tradition that most certainly led to the establishment of a university in Nauvoo and later universities sponsored by the Church all over the western part of the United States. (See verse 118.)

Schools in Kirtland and Nauvoo

The school of the prophets[2] spawned other educational institutions in Kirtland and in Nauvoo. The Kirtland School, later called the Kirtland High School opened in 1834 and was unique for its times. As Givens points out, "the first modern high school had opened a bare thirteen years earlier

---

1. See Cook, *Revelations of the Prophet Joseph Smith*, 190.
2. "The school of the prophets' first session lasted only a few months, and it then reopened in November 1834 with two divisions. The school of the elders focused on theological training for missionary work—with a focus on seven Lectures on Faith, which were given canonical status by their inclusion in the Doctrine and Covenants the next year." (Givens, *People of Paradox*, 74.) The other division became the Kirtland High School.

in Boston."[1] More children than could be accommodated enrolled in the high school, and in February 1835 about 100 children began instruction there under William McLellin. A broad curriculum typical for the time was taught—penmanship, arithmetic, English grammar, geography, history, Latin, and the classics. In the winter of 1836–37 the high school met in the attic story of the Kirtland Temple and by this time had grown to 140 students.[2]

By the time the Saints moved to Nauvoo, education was stressed to an even greater extent. Joseph founded the University of Nauvoo at a time in the United States when most colleges were poverty-stricken and precarious. Although the Nauvoo University had no campus, it was a serious undertaking. Many public buildings were conscripted into service, such as the Masonic Hall, the Concert Hall, the Seventies Hall, the red brick store, and the unfinished temple, as well as private homes. The curriculum was ambitious and included chemistry, geology, mathematics, literature, philosophy, history, religion, music, and foreign languages (German, French, Latin, Greek, and Hebrew).[3] All of this reflected a rather liberal bent toward education by the Mormons in a country where numbers of Baptists and Methodists downplayed education, sometimes expressing outright hostility, and talked about the "evils" of human learning.[4] Even more impressive was the fact that women were not segregated or excluded. Sarah Kimball, for example, attended the school of the prophets alongside the brethren while still a teenager. Women were admitted to the Kirtland High School, and Eliza R. Snow ran her own "select school" for young women. Half the students enrolled in Nauvoo's schools were female.[5]

Education for Joseph is a religious precept

The importance of education would become more essential as Joseph's theological concepts developed. By the time the Saints gathered in Nauvoo, continuing education would become a religious tenet. Joseph would teach that this "earthly sojourn" is "basically an educative process. Knowledge is necessary to mastery, and the way to deification is through mastery, for not only does education aid man in fulfilling the present tasks, it advances him in his eternal progress."[6] The education required as part

---

1. Givens, *People of Paradox*, 79.
2. See Givens, *People of Paradox*, 79.
3. See Givens, *People of Paradox*, 83–84.
4. See Givens, *People of Paradox*, 67–68.
5. See Givens, *People of Paradox*, 78.
6. Thomas O'Dea, *The Mormons* (Chicago: University of Chicago Press, 1957), 147–48, as quoted in Givens, *People of Paradox*, 70.

of this unfolding development of men and women embraced more than just "religious" or "spiritual" knowledge. It required a life of "patient, steadfast, laborious acquisition of all knowledge. And this particular brand of perfectionism, which incorporates the sacred and the worldly and which reconciles certainty with ceaseless searching, is the pattern that Joseph initiated and emulated almost from the foundation of Mormonism."[1]

Section 89: Whitney Store, Kirtland, Ohio, February 27, 1833

Heading

Health code revealed for the physical well-being of members of the Church.

Introduction

Revelation to Joseph Smith.[2] As a consequence of the early brethren using tobacco in their meetings, the Prophet was led to ponder upon the matter. Consequently, he inquired of the Lord concerning the situation. This revelation, known as the Word of Wisdom, was the result.

Anchor section

Memorize: Word of Wisdom

Background

Intemperance was a pressing social issue in Kirtland and elsewhere in the United States during the early 1830s when section 89 was received. By 1833 there were five thousand local temperance societies boasting over a million members. Healthy diets were touted, which recommended eating fruits and vegetables as well as small amounts of meat. Some local churches such as the Campbellites discouraged drinking alcoholic beverages and joined the Kirtland Temperance Society. The temperance movement was so successful that it closed the local distillery in Kirtland as well as the distillery in Mentor a few miles away. Even though some Latter-day Saints

---

1. Givens, *People of Paradox*, 72.
2. See Smith, *History of the Church*, 1:327–29.

belonged to the Kirtland Temperance Society, some of its leaders complained of lack of Mormon support and the society disbanded in 1835.[1]

Samuel Underhill, a prominent member of the Owenite community with connections to the Morley farm near Kirtland, preached on diet and health. He became a force in the temperance movement because he expanded beyond alcohol the list of deleterious substances. He wanted to limit the consumption of meat and pork in particular.[2] He also advised against coffee, tea, and tobacco (smoked or chewed).[3] In 1829 he wrote a tract against the use of these substances and even went so far as to criticize not only "strong drink" but also wine used by the Mormons for the sacrament in branches and wards until it was discontinued just after the beginning of the 20th century. He said water was good enough to drink and that water, along with exercise and a simple diet, would lead to happiness.[4]

For members of the Church such health concerns came into focus because many of those who attended the school of the prophets in the Whitney store chewed tobacco and spit it out onto the floor. Joseph's wife, Emma, was often left to clean up the wet used chewing tobacco and complained to her husband. Brigham Young gives an account of the circumstances:

> The first school of the prophets was held in a small room . . . in a house. . . . The brethren came . . . for hundreds of miles to attend school in a little room probably no larger than eleven by fourteen. When they assembled together in this room after breakfast, the first they did was to light their pipes, and, while smoking, talk about the great things of the kingdom, and spit all over the room, and as soon as the pipe was out of their mouths a large chew of tobacco would then be taken. Often when the Prophet entered the room to give the school instructions he would find himself in a cloud of tobacco smoke. This, and the complaints of his wife at having to clean so filthy a floor, made the prophet think upon the matter, and he inquired of the Lord relating to the conduct of the Elders in using tobacco, and the revelation known as the Word of Wisdom was the result.[5]

The Zebedee Coltrin account informs us that the revelation was received in a room now known as the "revelation room," which adjoined the classroom. John H. Hayes, who was present when the revelation came, reported that when the Prophet received this revelation Joseph's face "just shone with brilliance."[6]

The revelation was announced to the members of the school after they

---

1. See Allen and Leonard, *Story of the Latter-day Saints*, 95.
2. Staker, *Hearken, O Ye People*, Kindle location 3889.
3. Ibid., 3896.
4. Ibid., 110. *[are you sure this is Ibid.? note the page-number difference]*
5. Cook, Revelations of the Prophet Joseph Smith, 191–92.
6. Woodford, *The Historical Development of the Doctrine and Covenants*, 1170.

had assembled for class-work. Joseph entered carrying the revelation in his hand. "Out of the twenty-two members that were there assembled, all used tobacco more or less, except two. Joseph read the Revelation and when they heard it they all laid aside their pipes and use of tobacco."[1]

Compliance

The revelation came "not by commandment" but rather by way of advice. Consequently, the Saints at times observed its proscriptions and at other times ignored them. Strong drinks were off limits except wine, which could be used for the sacrament and was in some wards in the Church up until 1906, when the official policy changed and water was uniformly substituted. Since the Lord had warned Joseph early on that enemies of the Church may attempt to poison the Saints' sacramental wine, wine was sometimes fermented by the Saints themselves. (See verse 6 and D&C 27:3–4.) This practice also continued until just after the turn of the twentieth century.

Joseph Smith's attitude about the Word of Wisdom was somewhat typical of his other brethren and sisters. He never interpreted the revelation as requiring total abstinence, but stressed moderation and self-control.[2] One account of how Joseph handled accusations of drunkenness is informative:

"It was reported to me that some of the brethren had been drinking whiskey that day in violation of the Word of Wisdom. I called the brethren in and investigated the case, and was satisfied that no evil had been done, and gave them a couple of dollars, with directions to replenish the bottle to stimulate them in the fatigues of their sleepless journey."[3]

John Taylor's account of the Martyrdom is consistent with these sentiments. He reported that during the last days of the Prophet Joseph in Carthage Jail, the brethren partook of wine to lift their spirits.

Understanding the terminology used in the Word of Wisdom in the context of the times is revealing. "Strong drink" was the equivalent of hard alcohol and was prohibited. "Mild drink" referred to beer and was for use "for man." See verse 17. In the early part of the twentieth century, Heber J. Grant (seventh President of the Church), under the spirit of inspiration and revelation, taught that members of the Church should abstain from all alcoholic beverages.[4] "Hot drinks" were not defined but

---

1. Woodford, *The Historical Development of the Doctrine and Covenants*, 1170.
2. See Peterson, "An Historical Analysis of the Word of Wisdom," 38.
3. See Peterson, "An Historical Analysis of the Word of Wisdom," 38.
4. As recently as 1901, Apostles Brigham Young Jr. and John Henry Smith argued that the revelation did not prohibit beer. See http://en.wikipedia.org/wiki/Word_of_Wisdom. Strict abstinence from all alcoholic beverages has been a great blessing to the members of the

later came to be associated with tea and coffee and thought harmful. The revelation recommended that meat be eaten sparingly and encouraged the use of fruits and vegetables. Grain constituted the staff of life and was acknowledged as good for the use of humankind. (See verses 5, 17, 9, 10–12, 14–16.)

It was not until President Heber J. Grant's administration (1919–45) that emphasis on the Word of Wisdom became obligatory on all members of the Church. Abstinence from all alcohol, tobacco, tea, and coffee became a uniform standard of those who wished to enter the temple, with some minor exceptions.[1] By 1930, adherence to the new interpretation of the Word of Wisdom became a universal requirement for temple attendance.[2]

Over time some leaders in the Church suggested that the reason tea and coffee were prohibited was because these drinks contained concentrated amounts of caffeine. With the introduction of cola drinks in the early 1900s, cold drinks with caffeine became common, and some members of the Church abstain from cola drinks as well. No official Church position has been stated. However, leaders have counseled members to avoid deleterious substances and any harmful and or addictive products.[3]

Spiritual and temporal promises associated with the Word of Wisdom

In retrospect, stricter observance of the Word of Wisdom in the early twentieth century was prophetic, and prohibiting the drinking of all alcohol, the use of tobacco, and encouraging healthy eating habits as the world entered the twentieth century proved to be an unparalleled blessing. The health risks associated with smoking, the addictive nature of drugs, and the dangers of a diet that encourages obesity are now well known. Many Latter-day Saints have been spared cancer, alcoholism, and other modern diseases by adherence to this health law.

Section 89 warns that "conspiring men in the last days" (verse 4) will knowingly harm men and women by encouraging the use of unhealthy

---

Church who live in an age when alcoholic beverages lead in some cases to alcoholism and, at the very least, cause serious motor vehicle accidents, maiming its victims and causing death as well as other serious crimes.

1. In a letter dated February 12, 1969, to A. Harold Goodman, president of the BYU 5th Stake at the time, the First Presidency, consisting of President David O. McKay, Hugh B. Brown, and N. Eldon Tanner, wrote, "The use of a beverage from which the deleterious ingredients have been removed would not be considered as breaking the word of wisdom. This would include Sanka Coffee and a temple recommend should not be denied to those drinking Sanka Coffee."

2. See *Encyclopedia of Mormonism*, 1584.

3. See *Encyclopedia of Mormonism*, 1585.

products. Evidence of this contention hardly needs comment in light of the wide-known conspiracy of the tobacco companies to advertise and sell cigarettes, which were known to be harmful to a person's health. The promise that those who complied with the terms and conditions of the Word of Wisdom would "receive health in their navel and marrow to their bones" (verse 18) has been amply demonstrated time and time again.

Those who adhere to the Word of Wisdom are also promised spiritual as well as temporal blessings. "And all saints who remember to keep and do these sayings . . . shall find wisdom and great treasures of knowledge, even hidden treasures." (Verses 18–19.)

The Word of Wisdom is for the most part a set of health regulations, not an ethical or moral code involving basic honesty or personal regard for others. Those who are addicted to tobacco or other substances (cocaine and other illegal drugs, the misuse of prescription drugs) are not in any way morally inferior and should not be ostracized. We should look with compassion upon our brothers and sisters struggling with addictions of any kind. Persons who use deleterious substances, whether by choice or because of dependence, may in some cases be more upright than those who are able to strictly live the health provisions of the Word of Wisdom.

Textual development

A significant variation in the text is the addition in the 1876 edition of verses 1–3. Originally these verses stating that the revelation was sent by "greeting; not by commandment or constraint" were not considered part of the revelation but simply an introduction to it. The inclusion of these verses in the main body of the text was added by Orson Pratt under the direction of Brigham Young.[1] The only other text variation is the addition of a comma inserted in the 1921 edition.[2] (See discussion below.)

The significance of a comma and eating meat

Prior to the 1921 edition of the Doctrine and Covenants, the comma in verse 13 concerning the use of meat was not present. Apparently, it was added by the printer. According to T. Edgar Lyon, when Joseph Fielding Smith was shown this addition, he said: "Who put that in there?"—but he never did anything about it.[3]

Sometimes the addition or deletion of a comma makes very little or no

---

1. See Woodford, *The Historical Development of the Doctrine and Covenants*, 1171, 1175.
2. See Woodford, *The Historical Development of the Doctrine and Covenants*, 1175.
3. See Woodford, *The Historical Development of the Doctrine and Covenants*, 1175.

difference. However, in this case the use of a comma completely changes the meaning. Without the comma after the word "used" in verse 13, the revelation recommends the use of meat year round. The placement of a comma prohibits the use of meat altogether, except "in times of winter, or of cold, or famine." The text now reads: "And it is pleasing unto me that [meat] should not be used, only in times of winter, or of cold, or famine."

The placement of the comma in section 89 is inconsistent with some of the other revelations Joseph received. For example, in section 49 the Lord explicitly states that a person who "forbiddeth to abstain from meats . . . is not . . . of God." (D&C 49:18.) Furthermore, meat is "ordained for the use of man for food and for raiment, and that he might have in abundance." (D&C 49:19.) Timothy in the New Testament also warns that in the last days some, not of God, will forbid eating meat, "which God hath created to be received with thanksgiving of them which believe and know the truth." (1 Timothy 4:3.)

However, there is another side to this question. A. Jane Birch has pointed out that "the way the text was read without the comma in the decades before 1921 was identical to the way the text is read today with the addition of the comma."[1] In 1842, Hyrum Smith acting as Patriarch to the Church interpreted the Word of Wisdom to exclude the use of meat except during cold and famine. After the comma was added, leading brethren continued to interpret the verse in this way. Birch asserts that in 1921, the year the comma was actually inserted in the printed text, Apostle John A. Widtsoe and Leah D. Widtsoe commented that meats should be used sparingly in cold or famine.[2] It should be noted, however, that both Elder Widtsoe and especially his wife Leah, took a stricter view of the Word of Wisdom than most of the leaders of the Church at that time and furthermore, the idea that the comma placement was a mistake which changed the meaning was not suggested until the 1960s.[3]

Since Latter-day Saints do not believe that the scriptures are inerrant, it is important to note inconsistencies, and compare what various sacred texts have to say on a particular subject. "These commandments are of me, and were given unto my servants in their weakness, after the manner of their language, that they might come to understanding. And inasmuch as they erred it might be made known." (D&C 1:24–25.) In fact, the introduction to the Doctrine and Covenants cautions that "errors have been perpetuated in past editions." In a future edition this comma could very well be removed.

---

1. A. Jane Birch, "Question the Comma in Verse 13 of the Word of Wisdom," *Interpreter: A Journal of Mormon Scripture* 10 (2014): 133-149.
2. Ibid.
3. Ibid.

Section 90: Whitney Store, Kirtland, Ohio, March 8, 1833

Heading

First Presidency organized.

The big question

Question: What is the structure of the Church?
Answer: A First Presidency should be organized to lead the Church. Each member holds the keys of the kingdom.

Introduction

Revelation to Joseph Smith the Prophet, given in the "revelation room" at the Whitney store located in Kirtland, Ohio.[1] This revelation is a continuing step in the establishment of the First Presidency. (See also D&C 81.) As a consequence, the counselors mentioned, Sidney Rigdon and Frederick G. Williams, were ordained ten days later, on March 18, 1833.

Background

In April 1830, section 20 said that Joseph and Oliver Cowdery were apostles and elders of the Church and were respectively designated first and second elder. (See D&C 20:2–3.) This arrangement continued until January 25, 1832, by which time a number of high priests had been ordained, beginning at the Morley farm (June 1831). It was in January 1832 that Joseph was sustained and ordained President of the High Priesthood. Six weeks later, on the day section 90 was received, March 8, 1832, Jesse Gause and Sidney Rigdon were called and ordained counselors with Joseph in the Presidency of the High Priesthood, a term synonymous with the designation First Presidency. Jesse Gause was excommunicated from the Church on December 3, 1832, after serving six months in the presidency. Thereafter, Frederick G. Williams, who had been serving as Joseph's clerk in the First Presidency, was ordained to take Jesse Gause's place. Section 90 came a few months later and confirmed the callings of Sidney Rigdon and Frederick G. Williams as counselors in the presidency.[2]

Jesse Gause was a Quaker before his conversion to Mormonism. It is not known exactly when he came into the Church. Gause was eight years older than Sidney Rigdon and twenty years older than Joseph and probably was

---

1. Smith, *History of the Church*, 1:329–31.
2. Robinson and Garrett, *Doctrine and Covenants Commentary*, 3:154–55.

Joseph's first counselor based upon his age. After he became a member of the First Presidency, he was called on August 1, 1832, to serve a mission with Zebedee Coltrin; there Gause attempted to convert his wife, Minerva, to Mormonism. She refused and Matthew Houston, an elder in the Shaker community, wrote a letter to Seth Y. Wells in which he commented that Gause was "very much enraged" and "threatened to take away Minerva's child," which she presented to him but Gause ultimately refused.[1] Gause continued on his mission with Coltrin until Coltrin became ill and returned to Kirtland alone. It is believed that Gause continued east. From that point his whereabouts have been unknown to this day.[2]

The Sidney Rigdon episode

Almost a year before section 90 was received, in May 1832, Rigdon, Smith, and Newel K. Whitney ended their visit to Zion (Independence, Missouri) and headed home to Kirtland, Ohio. En route the stagecoach driver lost his grip on the reins and the horses ran headlong out of control. Joseph and Newel K. Whitney were forced to jump from the moving coach. As Whitney leaped from the horse-drawn carriage he mangled his leg in the spokes of the fast-moving wheel. Whitney was unable to travel and delayed his return. Joseph stayed behind and nursed Whitney back to health in Greenville, Indiana. Rigdon continued on to Kirtland.

Upon Rigdon's arrival in Kirtland, worry about his family precipitated one of a number of dramatic mood swings that Rigdon suffered from throughout his life. After he found his nine-year-old daughter, Nancy, seriously ill and discovered that his family had been shuffled from place to place, relying on the charitable contributions of neighbors to survive, he attended a prayer meeting on July 5, 1832, in Joseph Smith Sr.'s barn where he simply fell apart.[3] Joseph's mother recorded what happened. Sidney arrived late.

> At last he came in, seemingly much agitated. He did not go to the stand, but began to pace back and forth through the house. My husband said, "Brother Sidney, we would like to hear a discourse from you today." Brother Rigdon replied, in a tone of excitement, "The keys of the kingdom are rent from the Church, and there shall not be a prayer put up in this house this day." ... This greatly disturbed the minds of many sisters, and some brethren.[4]

---

1. See Black, *Who's Who in the Doctrine and Covenants*, 100–101.
2. See Black, *Who's Who in the Doctrine and Covenants*, 101.
3. See Van Wagoner, *Sidney Rigdon: A Portrait of Religious Excess*, 125.
4. Van Wagoner, Sidney Rigdon: A Portrait of Religious Excess, 126.

Joseph's older brother Hyrum was also present and reported that he was not persuaded by Rigdon's rant that the keys of the kingdom had somehow been lost.

On the following Saturday, when Joseph learned of the incident, he denounced Rigdon and told the Church that he had the "keys of this last dispensation, and will forever hold them, both in time and eternity."[1] Eight months later, when section 90 was received, the Lord confirmed that indeed Joseph still held the keys. "Verily I say unto you, the keys of this kingdom shall never be taken from you, while thou art in the world, neither in the world to come." (Verse 3.) Section 90 also held out hope to Rigdon, who had long since repented of his thoughtless statements. "And again, verily I say unto thy brethren, Sidney Rigdon and Frederick G. Williams, their sins are forgiven them also." (Verse 6.)

Upon reflection, some historians believe Rigdon's mental instability was the result of a bipolar disorder. Throughout his ministry Rigdon manifested a lack of steadiness, depression, and manic episodes. His mood disturbances were no doubt exacerbated when he was tarred and feathered along with Joseph on March 24, 1832. It was reported that Rigdon was dragged over a wood pile and out into the night, his head thumping on the frozen ground.[2] His condition came to the forefront on various occasions throughout his life. At times he had an inflated sense of self-esteem and was euphoric. At other times he was hostile and engaged in angry tirades. His condition would have been treated pharmaceutically today. However, such relief was not available in his time. His condition would take a severe toll on Rigdon, his family, and Church members generally, and it plagued his relationship with Joseph and close associates.

Counselors in the First Presidency are equal in holding the keys of the ministry

Just after the Church was organized, the leadership focus was on Joseph. As time passed, the decision-making functions shifted outward to priesthood quorums. (See D&C 107:27–31.) Section 90 is a step in this direction and explains that Rigdon and Gause "are accounted as equal with thee [Joseph] in holding the keys of this last kingdom." (Verse 6.)[3] Strictly

---

1. Van Wagoner, *Sidney Rigdon: A Portrait of Religious Excess*, 126.
2. See Van Wagoner, *Sidney Rigdon: A Portrait of Religious Excess*, 115.
3. The key to authorize plural marriage is only held by the President of the Church. In reference to polygamy, the Lord explains that this power is "through the medium of mine anointed, whom I have appointed on the earth to hold this power (and I have appointed unto my servant Joseph to hold this power in the last days, and there is never but one on the earth at a time on whom this power and the keys of this priesthood are conferred)." (D&C 132:7.)

speaking, the Church is not governed by individuals but by quorums. (See D&C 107.)

The expression "keys" is used in the Doctrine and Covenants in this section in a broad sense and refers to the power whereby the First Presidency governs the Church. In other words, "the keys" are the right to direct the affairs of the kingdom of God on earth.

The duty of the First Presidency

The responsibility of the First Presidency was to assist Joseph in completing his inspired translation of the Bible (verse 13), "set in order the churches, and study and learn, and become acquainted with all good books, and with languages, tongues, and people." (Verse 15.) This body was to "preside in council" (verse 16), a term defined precisely in Doctrine and Covenants 107:27–32. This quorum was admonished to avoid "highmindedness and pride" because it could be a "snare" to their souls. (See verse 17.) Finally, they were cautioned to "search diligently, pray always, and be believing." (Verse 24.)

Members of the Church should pay attention to the First Presidency

Members of the Church are counseled to "receive the oracles of God" or the First Presidency. "Let them beware how they hold them lest they are accounted as a light thing, and are brought under condemnation thereby, and stumble and fall when the storms descend, and the winds blow, and the rains descend, and beat upon their house." (Verse 5.)

Small families

The advice to "let your families be small" is not a reference to the number of children parents should or should not have. (See verse 25.) Rather, this is an allusion to the practice of inviting guests to live in homes, a practice that became quite prevalent as people migrated and gathered to Kirtland. Oftentimes newcomers did not have the means to become independent immediately, and they counted on the generosity of the members, particularly Joseph Smith Sr., who was liberal to a fault. To help relieve some of the pressure that resulted when people crowded into small homes, the Lord counsels that this practice be restricted. (See verses 25–27.)

A covenant between the members of the First Presidency

The "covenant wherewith ye [members of the First Presidency] have covenanted one with another" is a reference to the covenant made in the school of the prophets. (See verse 24; D&C 88:132–41.)

Section 91: Whitney Store, Kirtland, Ohio, March 9, 1833

Heading

Reading the Apocrypha is of particular benefit to those enlightened by the Spirit.

Introduction

Revelation given through Joseph Smith the Prophet in the Revelation Room at the Whitney store in Kirtland, Ohio, on March 9, 1833.[1] The Prophet was at this time engaged in the translation of the Old Testament. Having come to that portion of the ancient writings called the Apocrypha, he inquired of the Lord and received this instruction.

Background

Section 90 instructs Joseph to continue making inspired interpolations, revisions, and additions to the Bible, the result of which is referred to as the Inspired Version (IV) and or the Joseph Smith Translation (JST). (See verse 13.) Joseph is directed to finish the "translation of the prophets," a specific reference to the prophets in the Old Testament. The day after section 90 was received, Joseph came upon the Apocrypha, which was at the end of his King James Old Testament. Apparently, there was some question in his mind as to whether or not he should revise the fourteen books contained there.

At the time, Joseph was reading the King James Version of the Bible, which included the Apocrypha. The difference between the Catholic and Protestant canon came about because the Catholic and Eastern Orthodox traditions translated their Bible from the Septuagint, a Greek translation of the Old Testament that dated back to the second century and that included the Apocrypha, while Luther and the Protestants derived their Bible from Hebrew manuscripts that did not include the Apocrypha.

There is not unanimous agreement on which books should or should

---

1. Smith, *History of the Church*, 1:331–32.

not be listed as part of the Apocrypha. Generally speaking, 1 and 2 Esdras (sometimes called 3 and 4 Esdras) Tobit, Judith, Esther, Wisdom of Solomon, Wisdom of Jesus the Son of Sirach (also referred to as Ecclesiasticus), Baruch, the Epistle of Jeremiah, additional parts of Daniel (including the Song of the Three Holy Children), the History of Susanna, and the History of the Destruction of Bel and the Dragon, the Prayer of Manasses, and 1 and 2 Maccabees (sometimes referred to as Machabees) are included on the list. Sometimes Apocryphal books were included in the King James editions and sometimes not. For example, the 1611 King James Bible included the Apocrypha, and the 1629 edition did not. Since the nineteenth century the Apocrypha has not been included in almost all Protestant Bibles. Today the Bible used by the Catholics does include some of the books traditionally thought of as part of the Apocrypha.

Section 91 informs Joseph that it was not necessary for him to revise the Apocrypha. This decision, however, does not imply that the Apocrypha does not contain worthwhile information. "There are many things contained therein [in the Apocrypha] that are true, and it is mostly translated correctly." (Verse 1.) However, "there are many things contained therein that are not true, which are interpolations by the hands of men." (Verse 2.) Therefore, those who choose to read should seek to be "enlightened by the Spirit" and "shall obtain benefit therefrom." (Verse 5.)

Since the time of Joseph Smith, many religious books containing information about the prophets and Jesus have been discovered in addition to the Apocrypha. In fact, the Book of Mormon foresees that other books are "sealed up to come forth in their purity, according to the truth which is in the Lamb, in the own due time of the Lord, unto the house of Israel." (1 Nephi 14:26; D&C 9:2.) Since the organization of the Church, many ancient records have been found and are coming forth today. A well-known example are the Dead Sea Scrolls which were discovered in 1947 in caves located near the northern end of the Dead Sea. They contain many Old Testament books and writings. Shortly before this, thirteen ancient codices that contain about fifty texts were found in 1945 in upper Egypt; these are referred to as the Nag Hammadi collection. This immensely important discovery includes a number of early Christian texts such as the Gospel of Thomas, the Gospel of Philip, and the Gospel of Truth. Another collection of ancient records authored in and around the time of Jesus is the Pseudepigrapha. The term refers to Jewish writings of the period from about 200 B.C. to A.D. 200, which were never made a part of the Old Testament but reveal a uniquely Christian approach. Finally, of particular interest to Latter-day Saints are the so-called Forty Day Documents, which report what Jesus did and taught during his forty-day ministry on earth after the resurrection. Prayer circles, temple rituals, and predictions about the future of the kingdom of God are found therein.

By extension, the Lord's endorsement of the Apocrypha in section 91 invites members of the Church to read ancient records in the same spirit in which they would read the Apocrypha—with the aid of the Spirit of the Lord. The Pearl of Great Price is yet another example of the wisdom found in ancient manuscripts, which the Lord has seen fit to make known to members of the Church.

SECTION 92: WHITNEY STORE, KIRTLAND, OHIO, MARCH 15, 1833

Heading

United orders established as part of the law of consecration.

The big question

Question: What is the structure of the Church?
Answer: Establish united orders, economic units organized to carry out specialized economic objectives within the law of consecration.

Introduction

Revelation given to Joseph Smith the Prophet in the Revelation Room at the Whitney store in Kirtland, Ohio, on March 15, 1833.[1] The revelation is directed to Frederick G. Williams, who had recently been appointed a counselor in the First Presidency. It directs him to participate in a *united order*.

Background

Section 92 instructed Frederick G. Williams to become a member of a *united order*. The expression *united order* was used interchangeably with *united firm* and described mercantile establishments (stores) that operated as part of the law of consecration.[2] James B. Allen and Glen M. Leonard explain that by early 1832 the administration of new economic orders was becoming more complicated and required innovation. The original idea behind the law of consecration envisioned a bishop's storehouse operated by the Church to accommodate temporal needs of members of the Church, as well as helping the poor and the needy. There were also other stores

---

1. Smith, *History of the Church*, 1:333.
2. See Ehat and Cook, *The Words of Joseph Smith*, 194.

operated privately in both Ohio and Missouri which Joseph desired to integrate into the law of consecration.[1]

At first the united order or firm consisted of five members, including Bishop Whitney, Joseph Smith, and Sidney Rigdon, all in Ohio, and Oliver Cowdery and Martin Harris in Missouri.[2] The introduction of united orders consolidated Church financial concerns under Church control by making existing and potential private businesses part of the law of consecration.[3] Apparently, Frederick G. Williams, as a new member of the First Presidency, was commanded to become a "lively" or active member of this order.

During the Brigham Young period (as well as that of his immediate successors) the term *united order* was used more broadly to refer to a number of different types of cooperative enterprises established in Mormon communities in Utah, Mexico, and Canada during the last decades of the nineteenth century. The range of different economic relationships varied considerably. In some instances, all of the members of a particular economic order shared more or less equally all of their earthly goods. Under this model members ate and prayed together regularly, much like a well-regulated family. In Orderville, Utah, for example, all the participants even dressed alike. Other arrangements involved far less sharing and were set up along the lines of a joint stock company with significant cooperative characteristics. Brigham Young believed that pooling capital and labor would promote unity and self-sufficiency. These orders for the most part were short-lived.[4]

---

1. Examples of *united orders* set up by Joseph include the Printing Establishment, a Literary Establishment organized in Missouri, as well as a Literary Establishment in Ohio with a committee of six men appointed "stewards over the revelations and commandment." These six men were also responsible for all literary activities of the Church. (See Allen and Leonard, *Story of the Latter-day Saints*, 76–77.)

2. The concentration of administrative authority in Kirtland, where Bishop Whitney and Joseph Smith lived, instead of in Zion (Independence, Missouri) naturally disturbed some Church leaders in Missouri, for it seemed to downgrade Zion's emerging role as the place where Jesus would return and establish a New Jerusalem to administer the worldwide affairs of His kingdom. They criticized Joseph for failing to move Church headquarters to Missouri. (Allen and Leonard, *Story of the Latter-day Saints*, 77.)

3. Allen and Leonard, *Story of the Latter-day Saints*, 77.

4. See *Encyclopedia of Mormonism*, 1493–94.

Section 93: Whitney Store, Kirtland, Ohio, May 6, 1833

Heading

The Mormon meta-narrative, deification, eternality of matter, intelligences, spirits, premortal life, mortal life, the purpose of worship, and the resurrection.

The big question

Question: How do we live together and build a community now that we have gathered?
Answer: Parents should teach their children Mormon theology.

Introduction

Revelation given through Joseph Smith the Prophet in the "revelation room" in the Whitney store in Kirtland, Ohio, on May 6, 1833.[1] The Lord reveals information about the Mormon meta-narrative, deification, eternal intelligences, spirits, the meaning of truth, and the importance of parents teaching these concepts to their children.

Anchor section

Memorize: All may see Jesus; deification; definition of truth; intelligences; teach your children.

Background

Section 93 most likely came in response to Joseph's study of and revisions to the Bible.[2] "And verily I say unto you, that it is my will that you should hasten to translate my scriptures." (D&C 93:53.) The heading for section 93 in the 1921 edition of the Doctrine and Covenants[3] supports this idea by suggesting that the text of the revelation contains a portion of the record

---

1. Smith, *History of the Church*, 1:343–46.
2. Section 93 may also have been intended as a curriculum for the school of the prophets. On May 4, 1833, Joseph met with a group of high priests in Kirtland to plan the construction of a building to hold the school of the prophets. The group agreed to raise funds. Section 93 was received two days later, on May 6, 1833. (See Preece, *Learning to Love the Doctrine and Covenants*, 223.)
3. All subsequent reprints of the 1921 edition (1921–1980) also contain the same reference.

of John the Apostle. However, the historical record is not entirely clear on what may or may not have precipitated this revelation.[1]

Section 93 introduced doctrinal ideas that for the most part were not publicly acknowledged or discussed until the end of the Nauvoo period. The profound implications of these new ideas would eventually set Mormonism apart and more dramatically separate it from the theological mainstream of Christianity. Mormon ideas on the eternality of matter, the coeternality of intelligences with God, spirits born of heavenly parents, Gods with corporeal bodies, and the idea that all men and women may become gods and goddesses find expression in this section of the Doctrine and Covenants.[2] These new doctrines would eventually come to greater fruition just before Joseph's martyrdom in 1844. Eleven years later, and just weeks before his death in April, Joseph spoke to members and nonmembers alike about these ideas in what is perhaps his greatest and most well-known sermon, the King Follett discourse.

Men and women may see and converse with Jesus face to face

Section 93 describes God as an anthropomorphic, personal God—an exalted person—with whom men and woman may have direct discourse, face to face. Audience with God is predicated upon forsaking sin, calling upon him in prayer, and obeying his commandments. (See verse 1.) Joseph Smith became personally acquainted with God when he first saw the Father and the Son in the spring of 1820. (See JS–H 1:11–20.) In the King Follett discourse he speaks about the importance of this belief. "It is the first principle of the Gospel to know for a certainty . . . that we may converse with him [God] as one man converses with another."[3]

The invitation to speak with God is gender blind. The promise is to "every soul," without limitation. This idea that God is not a respecter of persons is also expressed emphatically in the Book of Mormon: "He

---

1. John Taylor and Orson Pratt believed the record to be that of John the Baptist. (See Cook, *Revelations of the Prophet Joseph Smith*, 194–95; Taylor, *Mediation and Atonement*, 55; and Pratt, *Journal of Discourses*, 16:58). Bruce R. McConkie felt strongly that the *John* referred to in this section was John the Baptist and not John the Beloved Apostle. "From latter-day revelation we learn that the material in the forepart of the gospel of John (the Apostle, Revelator, and Beloved Disciple) was written originally by John the Baptist. By revelation the Lord restored to Joseph Smith part of what John the Baptist had written and promised to reveal the balance when men became sufficiently faithful to warrant receiving it (D&C 93:6–18)." (*Doctrinal New Testament Commentary*, 1:70–71.)

2. The notion of deification also finds expression as early as February 1832 in D&C 76:58.

3. Smith, *Teachings of the Prophet Joseph Smith*, 345.

inviteth ... all to come unto him and partake of his goodness; and he denieth none that come unto him, black and white, bond and free, *male and female*, and he remembereth the heathen; and all are alike unto God." (2 Nephi 26:33.)

The Father and the Son are one in glory, not person

Section 93 teaches that Jesus and his Father, Elohim, are one in power and glory. "And ... I am in the Father, and the Father in me, and the Father and I are one." (Verse 3.) In what way are the Father and Son one? In glory, not in person. "The Father because *he gave me of his fulness*, and the Son because I was in the world and made flesh my tabernacle, and dwelt among the sons of men.... And John saw and bore record of the fulness of my glory." (Verses 4–6; emphasis added.) The same concept is expressed in Jesus' intercessory prayer in John 17. "I brought glory to you here on earth by doing everything you told me to do. And now, Father, *bring me into the glory we shared* before the world began." (NLT John 17:4–5.) This idea is in sharp contrast to traditional Christianity, which teaches that Jesus and his Father are one in person or substance rather than two separate individuals. (See verses 3–4; emphasis added.)

Men and women may become gods and goddesses

Section 93 teaches that men and woman may become glorified or in other words become gods and goddesses. This human transformation is brought about by individuals who follow the model of Jesus, the Great Exemplar. The pattern men and women should follow is explained. Like Jesus, individuals are born into mortality and receive a body. Thereafter, men and women should do what Jesus did—be baptized, obtain the gift of the Holy Ghost, and receive "grace for grace" or improve attribute upon attribute, until such time as they may obtain God's "fulness" or glory. (See verses 8–20.) Stated more explicitly, receiving God's "fulness" means possessing "all power, both in heaven and on earth, and the glory of the Father." (Verse 17.)[1] This step-by-step apotheosis was described in Nauvoo at the end of Joseph's life when he spoke the King Follett discourse in April 1844:

> You have got to learn how to be Gods yourselves ... the same as all Gods have done before you, namely, by going from one small degree to another,

---

1. Deification is also explicitly taught in D&C 76:55–70 (February 16, 1832) and in D&C 132:19–20 (recorded July 12, 1843, but probably received much earlier—1833).

and from a small capacity to a great one; from grace to grace, from exaltation to exaltation, until you ... sit in glory.[1]

In the same sermon Joseph also explained that becoming Godlike is like climbing up a ladder. You "begin at the bottom, and ascend step by step, until you arrive at the top."[2] He cautions that the promise of deification is not instantaneous at death. "It is not all to be comprehended in this world; it will be a great work to learn our salvation and exaltation even beyond the grave."[3]

The idea of men and women becoming gods and goddesses is generally repugnant to the Christian world. Yet Jesus taught the same principle in the Sermon on the Mount when he commanded all men and women to be perfect even as God is perfect. The King James Version translates it, "Be ye therefore perfect, even as your Father which is in heaven is perfect." (Matthew 5:48.)

It is noteworthy that some modern renditions that translate this same verse (Matthew 5:48) about the perfectibility of individuals do so in a manner that is even more consistent with Joseph's thinking; they imply that becoming like God is an evolutionary process rather than an instantaneous decision or reward for good living, as the command "Be perfect" might suggest. For example, the Emphasized New Testament: A New Translation (J. B. Rotherham) says, "Ye therefore *shall become* perfect. . . ." (Emphasis added.) Taking all of this into account, it should not be surprising that the Joseph Smith Translation (JST) points in this direction as well. "Ye are therefore commanded *to be* perfect, even as your Father which is in heaven is perfect."[4] (Emphasis added.) The Book of Mormon is even closer to what Joseph taught about becoming like God. "Therefore I would that ye *should be perfect even as I or* . . . your Father who is in heaven *is* perfect." (3 Nephi 12:48; emphasis added.)

Ernst W. Benz, a professor emeritus of Church History at the University of Marburg, answers one of the main concerns traditional Christianity harbors about the notion that men and women are potentially gods and goddesses—namely, that such a doctrine demeans Deity and self-aggrandizes man. Benz argues that such a belief has precisely the opposite effect.

---

1. Smith, Teachings of the Prophet Joseph Smith, 346–47.
2. Smith, *Teachings of the Prophet Joseph Smith*, 348.
3. Smith, *Teachings of the Prophet Joseph Smith*, 348.
4. Paul reflects what Jesus taught in Matthew 5:48, John 10:22–38, John 17, and elsewhere. When speaking about the subject, Paul talks about becoming "joint heirs" with Jesus or full participants in the same glory that Jesus had. (See Romans 8:14–17; 2 Corinthians 3:18; Galatians 4:7; Ephesians 3:11–13; Philippians 2:5–6.) Finally, as Jesus points out in John 10:34, the idea of deification may also be found in the Old Testament in Psalm 8:4–5 (NLT) and Psalm 82:6.

The concept of Imago Dei does not lead toward self-aggrandizement but toward charity as the true and actual form of God's love, for the simple reason that in one's neighbor the image of God, the Lord himself, confronts us, and that the love of God should be fulfilled in the love towards him in whom God himself is mirrored, that is, in one's neighbor. Thus, in the last analysis the concept of Imagio Dei is the key to the fundamental law of the gospel. "Thou shalt love God and thy neighbor as thyself," since thou shouldst view thy neighbor with an eye to the image which God has engraven upon him and to the promise that he has given about him. This comprehension of one's neighbor as the image of God is contained best in a phrase upon which Ernesto Buonaiuti bases one of his Eranos Lectures, the words of the Lord, not contained in the canonized Gospels but passed on to the Latin fathers of the second century, especially Tertullian. It is certainly authentic, for it represents a summary of the Lord's words just cited from the Gospel of Matthew: "Vidisti frantrem, vidisti dominum tuum"—"If thou has seen thy brother, then thou hast also seen the Lord."[1]

From this perspective, the idea of deification leads right back to the greatest commandments—love God and love neighbor.

The purpose of "worship" is self-developmental

Section 93 teaches that the worship of God is ultimately designed to help God's children become more like Him. "I give unto you these sayings [about deification] that you may understand and know how to worship, ... and in due time receive of his fulness." (Verse 19.) The idea is that worship is more than singing praises to Deity, although this may also be appropriate. Complete worship involves "putting on" the Lord Jesus Christ or disciplining oneself to become like Him. Worship therefore is self-developmental and includes service to others. Consistent with this consideration is the notion of a lay ministry and priesthood that requires ordinary people to serve as clerics.

Intelligences are coeternal with God

Joseph Smith taught that the mind of man or *intelligence* is coeternal with God Himself, who is "a self-existent being" (always existed).[2] Likewise, section 93 defines *intelligence* as the indestructible and eternal element within each man or woman—that part which is coeternal with God. "Man was also in the beginning with God. *Intelligence*, or the light of truth, was not created or made, neither indeed can be." (Verse 29; emphasis added.)

---

1. Benz, "Imago Dei: Man in the Image of God," 218.
2. See Smith, *Teachings of the Prophet Joseph Smith*, 352–53, and footnote 8.

Some Mormon educators have been reluctant to speak about this concept because there is so little information on it. John Widtsoe in *A Rational Theology* conceded that "to speculate upon the condition of man when conscious life was just dawning is most interesting, but so little is known about that far-off-day that such speculation is profitless."[1]

Nonetheless, B. H. Roberts, James Talmage, and John A. Widtsoe did assign various attributes to intelligence which, they taught, preceded spiritual birth or the organization of spiritual bodies. Each opined that intelligence was self-conscious and independent. Roberts expresses it well in his book *The Truth, The Way, The Life*:

> [Intelligences] are uncreated; self-existent entities, necessarily self-conscious.... They possess powers of comparison and discrimination without which the term "intelligence" would be a mere solecism. They discern between evil and good; between good and better; they possess will or freedom—within certain limits at least.... [Intelligences possess the] power, among others, to determine upon a given course of conduct as against any other course of conduct. The individual intelligence can think his own thoughts, act wisely or foolishly; do right or wrong. To accredit an intelligence with fewer or less important powers than these would be to deny him intelligence altogether.[2]

Although Widtsoe agreed, he was encouraged not to include in his book *A Rational Theology* his opinion that intelligences were self-cognizant entities capable of choice before they were begotten spirits, a point around which a controversy had arisen at the time. This was because some other prominent Mormon theologians took issue with the notion and preferred to believe that the idea of self did not begin until spirit birth. For example, a contemporary of Roberts, Joseph Fielding Smith did not agree that "intelligences" were self-cognizant. Bruce R. McConkie reflected Joseph Fielding Smith's view when he said that "intelligence or spirit element became intelligences after the spirits were born as individual entities."[3] McConkie also went on to say that "as far as I know there is no official pronouncement on the subject at hand.... In my judgment there was no agency prior to spirit birth and we did not exist as entities until that time."[4] However, both camps agreed that Joseph spoke of intelligences that had always existed. "The ... intelligence which man possesses is co-equal with God himself."[5] By way of explanation Roberts said that "there

---

1. Widtsoe, *A Rational Theology* (1915), 245–25.
2. See Roberts, The Truth, The Way, The Life (BYU Studies edition, 1994), 255.
3. McConkie, *Mormon Doctrine* (1966), 387.
4. For an excellent discussion on various views on intelligences, see Ostler, "The Idea of Pre-Existence in the Development of Mormon Thought," 1.
5. Smith, *Teachings of the Prophet Joseph Smith*, 353.

can be no question, but what this 'co-equal' is an error. From the whole tenor of the discourse, the word used must have been 'coeternal' with God, not 'co-equal.'"[1]

A strict reading of section 93 implies that intelligence is something more than just an inert mass. The section mentions the attributes of intelligence and describes it as "independent" and able to "act for itself"—agency. (See verse 30.) Based upon this assertion the next verse, verse 31, concludes, "Behold here is the agency of man, and here is the condemnation of man; because that which was from the beginning is plainly manifest unto them, and they receive not the light." Crediting "intelligences" with a "will" and "agency" is important because if *intelligences* have always existed (uncreated) and are able to act for themselves (autonomous) then this fact absolves God from being the creator of a life form capable of evil and therefore being the original source of evil, a problem traditional Christianity struggles to explain because of their doctrine that God created all things *ex nihilo*.

Finally, the view that *intelligences* are self-existent with God and subject to evolutionary development prior to the time they are incorporated into spirit entities is entirely consistent with Joseph's idea that God institutes laws for the advancement of *intelligences*. In the King Follett discourse Joseph said:

> The first principles of man are self-existent with God. God himself, finding he was in the midst of spirits and glory, because he was more intelligent, saw proper to institute laws whereby the rest could have a privilege to advance like himself. The relationship we have with God places us in a situation to advance in knowledge. He has power to institute laws to instruct the weaker intelligences, that they may be exalted with himself, so that they might have one glory upon another, and all that knowledge, power, glory, and intelligence, which is requisite in order to save them in the world of spirits.[2]

Joseph Fielding Smith and others take[3] the position that the term *intelligence* in this context refers to a spirit child born of God and therefore would not allow for its use in support of the idea that intelligences have independent wills. Nevertheless, as Widtsoe pointed out, in either case "the progress of intelligent beings is a mutual affair."[4] God is not a lone

---

1. See Roberts, *The Truth, The Way, The Life* (BYU Studies edition, 1994), 254.
2. See Smith, Teachings of the Prophet Joseph Smith, 354; emphasis added.
3. Orson Pratt also took the position that *intelligences* are not self-cognizant entities. This idea is sometimes referred to as the "soup theory" of *intelligences*, meaning that *intelligences* are fungible. This premise presumes that all *intelligences* are alike (in the same soup bowl). At spirit birth, this so-called *intelligent* matter is incorporated. However, the very term *intelligence* seems to imply that *intelligences* are more than this.
4. Widtsoe, *Rational Theology* (1937), 27.

being in the universe but accomplishes his purposes only when the whole universe advances. It is this law of progression that gives purpose to life.[1]

The glory of God is intelligence

"The glory of God is intelligence" (verse 36) is one of the best-known phrases in the Doctrine and Covenants and is often used to communicate the idea that God's glory is manifested by his intellect and knowledge of all the laws of the universe. As Elder Widtsoe expressed it, it is by knowledge and the use of that knowledge that God "became greater until he attained at last a conquest over the universe, which to our finite understanding seems absolutely complete."[2] Certainly, this idea is consistent with Mormon theology.

Nevertheless, in context, the expression, "The glory of God is intelligence" should be more narrowly defined. *Intelligence* or light of truth may very well refer to the *intelligences* spoken of in the preceding verses (29–31), or that material which has always existed and is coeternal with God. After all, the intelligence spoken about has "agency" and the capacity to "forsake that evil one." (See verse 37.) Taken this way, "The glory of God is intelligence" means that God is glorified when *intelligences* (which ultimately may progress and become spirit children of God and eventually resurrected personages) shun evil and turn to God. It is reminiscent of the view expressed by the Lord to Moses that "this is my work and my glory—to bring to pass the immortality and eternal life of man." (Moses 1:39.)

Truth cannot be comprehended in isolation but only in context

The definition of "truth" in section 93 is comprehensive and embodies two ideas. First, truth is an accurate understanding of the facts in the past, present, and future. "And truth is knowledge of things as they are, and as they were, and as they are to come." (Verse 24.) Second, truth is all three (past, present, future) taken together—or in other words, context and perspective.

The notion that truth involves a complete understanding is an admission that "truth" is more than simply a recitation of the facts. It embraces far more. Truth includes knowing the relationship of the facts to each other so that the meaning of any given situation may be discerned. As N. T. Wright, a prominent New Testament scholar, explained, it is knowing the

---

1. "The only purposeless life is the one that does not use its faculties. It matters little what tasks men perform in life, if only they do them well and with all their strength.... Upon that will growth depends." (Widtsoe, *Rational Theology* [1937], 22.)

2. Widtsoe, *Rational Theology*, 25.

"outside" as well as the "inside" part of the story. In Wright's analogy, the "outside" refers to the particulars of an event and the "inside" refers to an understanding of what the particulars mean.

He compares his approach to a vase that was broken when it fell onto a hard floor and shattered. The fact that the vase was broken tells us very little. The situation, however, becomes "meaningful" when context is filled out. The vase, for example, was part of an overall aim to live in a beautiful house and therefore encourage children to decorate with flowers. The intent was to hand one of the daughters in the household a vase to put flowers in. When the mother handed her daughter the vase, the daughter did not expect it. Therefore, her daughter dropped it and the vase fell to the floor and broke. The "outside" is that the vase broke. The "inside" story is about human aims, intentions, motivations, and consequent actions. Therefore, truth not only involves a marshalling of the facts but an understanding of their deeper meaning.[1]

Finally, the meaning individuals may give to any set of facts depends on the lens through which the facts are interpreted or one's "worldview." Stated another way, the facts (story) only become meaningful when understood in the context of a person's grand narrative or big story, the larger blueprint. The view always includes the viewer. In Mormonism, this idea is referred to as the "key of knowledge" or correct vantage point. It means that Mormons interpret events in life as part of an overall story that begins in a premortal existence, continues on in mortality, and ends when men and women die and enter into the presence of God. This grand narrative is explained in Mormon temples.

The Mormon "story" explains that each individual *intelligence* or *ego* has always existed. At some point in time, *intelligences* were incorporated into *spirit bodies* (a type of refined matter), a process that involves being "born" of heavenly parents (God the Father and God the Mother). Therefore, God's spirit children are connected to their parents just as biological parents are genetically related to their earthly parents. In this premortal life, God's spirit children lived with God and their spirit brothers and sisters. The aim of existence was to become like their Father and Mother in Heaven. This involved being born into mortality, obtaining a physical body, acquiring solitary experience away from the presence of God, learning to love humankind, dying, and ultimately clothing their spirit body with a new physical body, just like the one God has (resurrection).

The earth was created by God for this purpose and is therefore good and beautiful. The predicament is that humanity rebelled against God and therefore they are out of tune with God's intentions. The solution is God's

---

1. See Wright, *The New Testament and the People of God*, 110.

intervention. He sent prophets to warn and impart God's counsel and love for his children. However, men and women continually changed, ignored, and muddled what God intended. Ultimately, God sent his Son (parable of the vineyard–Matthew 21:33–41) to atone and provide an example and a way for men and women to come back into his presence and to progress and become like their Heavenly Parents.

Since all mankind is not made acquainted with the plans and intents of God in this life, those who die without the key of knowledge and the ordinances associated with God's plans (baptism, the endowment, eternal marriage) are given an opportunity after death to participate. Therefore, after this life humankind will continue to have opportunities to progress and become more and more like God.

This grand narrative is the Mormon worldview and is the lens through which events in life become significant. It is the "key of knowledge" that helps Mormons make sense out of the sum of existence. It expresses the fundamental aim of God—to bring to pass the immortality and eternal life of men and women. This is what motivates God and what should motivate man. It is the expression of God's ultimate compassion for his children, to give them everything that he has. Jesus expressed it: "I am praying not only for these disciples but also for all who will ever believe in me because of their testimony. My prayer for all of them is that they will be one, just as you and I are one, Father. . . . I have given them the glory you gave me, so that they may be one as we are. . . . *Then the world will know that you sent me and will understand that you love them as much as you love me.*" (NLT John 17:20–23; emphasis added.)

In a post-modern age, it is important to recognize that the grand narrative of Mormonism and for that matter the grand narratives of the Old and New Testaments stand in stark contrast to our Western image of reality; that image sees the universe as ultimately indifferent to mankind and sees us as separate and apart from God. As Marcus Borg, a New Testament scholar, points out, "According to the worldview that emerged in the Enlightenment, reality is made up of tiny bits of stuff, of atoms and subatomic particles in constant motion, of matter and energy in interaction with each other. . . . As such, it is indifferent to human purposes and hopes—it simply is."[1] This non-reassuring, impersonal, cosmic loneliness is at the center of our culture's art, music, dance, movies, and literature. By way of contrast, the gospel message is that God is not absent, does intervene, and is concerned about the well-being of his children.

---

1. See Borg, *Jesus: Uncovering the Life, Teachings, and Relevance of a Religious Revolutionary*, 168.

Men and women become like God by keeping the commandments

Verses 27–28 teach that there is a connection between keeping the commandments and learning "truth and light." The idea that a person must be worthy of inspiration and revelation to supplement the normal processes of learning is not only taught here but also in Doctrine and Covenants 88:118: "Teach one another words of wisdom; yea, seek ye out of the best books words of wisdom; seek learning, even by study and *also by faith*." (Emphasis added.)

Men and women can receive a "fulness of joy" only when resurrected

Section 93 not only addresses the eternality of matter,[1] but also the concept that some substances are more proficient and capable than other forms of matter. In other words, all matter is not created equal when it comes to *intelligences*, spirits,[2] mortal bodies, and resurrected bodies.[3] While all varieties of life are made out of particles—stuff—the difference involves what stuff? Spirits, for example, are more refined, pure, and elastic. Mortal bodies have better sensors and are more capable of advancement. Resurrected bodies are more proficient and durable—free from death and disease. Joseph's premise is that each form of intelligent life, starting with *intelligences* and moving through spirits, mortal bodies, and resurrected bodies are each an improvement on the former. (See D&C 93:33–34; 138:17.) The definitive life form is a celestial body—the type and kind of a body that gods enjoy.

---

1. Mormons assume that matter is not created *ex nihilo* or out of nothing. In the King Follett discourse Joseph Smith teaches that matter is eternal and that "God had materials to organize the world out of chaos—chaotic matter." (Smith, *Teachings of the Prophet Joseph Smith*, 351.) Matter cannot be destroyed but matter "may be organized and re-organized." (See Smith, *Teachings of the Prophet Joseph Smith*, 352.)

2. See Smith, *Teachings of the Prophet Joseph Smith*, 207. "We shall find a very material difference between the body and the spirit; the body is supposed to be organized matter, and the spirit, by many, is thought to be immaterial, without substance. With this latter statement we should beg leave to differ, and state the spirit is a substance; that it is material, but that it is more pure, elastic and refined matter than the body; that it existed before the body, can exist in the body; and will exist separate from the body, when the body will be mouldering in the dust; and will in the resurrection, be again united with it."

3. In connection with spirits in the spirit world, D&C 138:50 teaches, "For the dead had looked upon the long absence of their spirits from their bodies as a bondage."

If you teach the principles and grand narrative in section 93 to your children, the world of evil will not have power over them

Section 93 was received about the same time the school of the prophets was organized. Undoubtedly, this revelation was considered by the school. Nonetheless, section 93 was not explicitly designated to be a curriculum for the school but rather a course of study to be taught in the Mormon homes. Each member of the First Presidency—Joseph Smith, Sidney Rigdon and Frederick G. Williams—was singled out and chastised, along with Bishop Newel K. Whitney, for not teaching the concepts in this section—as well as truth in general—to family members. "You have not taught your children light and truth." It is for this reason that the "wicked one hath power, as yet, over you, and this is the cause of your affliction." (Verse 42.) By analogy, section 93 is a reminder to parents to teach their children the gospel so that the evil one will not have power over them. And, judging from the core curriculum set out in section 93, the Lord is speaking about a challenging and demanding course of study.

SECTION 94: WHITNEY STORE, KIRTLAND, OHIO, MAY 6, 1833[1]

Heading

The Saints instructed to build Zion after the pattern of ancient Israel. Administrative offices and a printing house initiated.

The big question

Question: What is the structure of the Church?
Answer: A Church administration building should be constructed for use by the First Presidency, as well as a printing house to publish Church literature.

Introduction

Revelation given through Joseph Smith the Prophet, in the Whitney store, at Kirtland, Ohio.[2] Hyrum Smith, Reynolds Cahoon, and Jared Carter are appointed to a Church building committee to construct a Church administration building to provide offices for the First Presidency and a printing house with a press to print Church publications.

---

1. The date of reception should be August 2, 1833. (See Woodford, "Discoveries from the Joseph Smith Papers Project," 32.)
2. Smith, *History of the Church*, 1:346–47.

Background

During the 1830s missionaries were called to preach the gospel in nearby communities. Missionary assignments were often of short duration—a few months. The Elders would preach until their resources ran out and then return to their homes to work and replenish their coffers before going out into the mission field again. Convert baptisms were on the rise and missionary efforts were reinforced in January 1833 when Joseph announced that a school of the prophets would be opened in Kirtland to train missionaries and make them even more effective. In 1837, just four years after this revelation was given, an estimated twenty thousand persons were baptized.[1]

The Whitney store in Kirtland had by default become Church headquarters. On the second floor a small room about 11 feet by 14 feet served as a classroom for the school of the prophets, and another small room provided space for the Prophet Joseph and his associates to conduct Church business; this was called the "revelation room." As Church membership increased, the Whitney store was no longer a suitable place to administer Church affairs and train missionaries. In March 1833, Levi Hancock commented on the general state of affairs: "We had no place to worship in."[2]

Church growth and less than adequate space in the Whitney store prompted the need for the Church to build new facilities. In December 1832 and again in March 1833, the Lord commanded that a temple be built. (See D&C 88:119; 90:7–9.) At a conference held on March 23, 1833, Church leaders met in the school of the prophets in the Whitney store and arranged to purchase lands for future Church buildings. Another conference was held on May 4, 1833, and appointed Hyrum Smith, Jared Carter, and Reynolds Cahoon to form a building committee in Ohio. They were to raise money and supervise Church construction. Section 94 most probably came in connection with this conference.[3]

The command to build a separate administration building and a second structure for printing Church literature as set out in verses 4–5 and 10–12 never came about;[4] the Saints were instructed not to build "until I give unto you a commandment concerning them." (Verse 16.) Ultimately, lack of resources prevented the Saints from building two buildings, and a single structure was completed, which served as administrative offices, a

---

1. See Allen and Leonard, *Story of the Latter-day Saints*, 73.
2. Woodford, *The Historical Development of the Doctrine and Covenants*, 1222.
3. See Robinson and Garrett, *Doctrine and Covenants Commentary*, 3:198.
4. In connection with the command to build an administration and printing house, the Lord specified the size of the structures and the activities associated with each. For example, the Lord instructs that "this house shall be *wholly* dedicated . . . for the work of the printing." (Verse 12; emphasis added. See also verse 7.)

publishing house, and the new location for the school of the prophets. The first story was used for the school of the elders (prophets) and the second story for the printing press. Other rooms on each level, as well as the attic, were used as offices for the presidency of the Church and for a variety of other meetings.[1] Heber C. Kimball described the dire state of affairs that made construction difficult: "The Church was in a state of poverty and distress in consequence of which it appeared almost impossible that the command [to build the Kirtland Temple] could be fulfilled, at the same time our enemies were raging and threatening destruction upon us."[2]

A planned community after the Israelites in the wilderness

Section 94 speaks about a planned community "done according to the pattern which I have given unto you," with the temple situated in the center of the town. (See verse 2.) The city was to be laid out by lots north, south, east, and west of the temple. The two lots immediately south of the temple were for the administration building and a publishing house. On the first and second lots on the north, Reynolds Cahoon and Jared Carter were to receive their lots or "inheritances" as remuneration for their work performed on the building committee. (See verses 14–15.) The physical layout of the town and the giving of inheritances followed the pattern adhered to in ancient Israel. Land was distributed by lot, or in other words, by chance. The inheritances were to be situated by tribe (families) north, south, east, and west of the tabernacle (temple). (See Numbers 1:52–53; 2:1–4, 10, 18, 25; 26:52–55. Compare D&C 94:1–2.)

The pattern to be followed in Kirtland was similar to the pattern of the city of Zion in Jackson County, Missouri. According to Joseph, such cities would center on a fifteen-acre block containing twenty-four buildings for worship and education. The structures were to be called "temples," and each was to be of identical dimensions and two stories high. There were to be ten-acre blocks, with twenty equal lots for homes. Growth of the city would be curtailed once its dimensions reached one mile square or contained fifteen to twenty thousand people. Lands on the north and south of the city were for barns and stables. The idea was to concentrate the people in the city so that all could enjoy the benefits provided at the city center—worship, education, entertainment, and so forth.[3]

The concept of Zion emphasized the importance of community and

---

1. See Cook, *Revelations of the Prophet Joseph Smith*, 196–97. The administration/printing house was later attached to satisfy a judgment in late 1837. On January 16, 1838, it burned to the ground.
2. Woodford, *The Historical Development of the Doctrine and Covenants*, 1223.
3. See Roberts, *Comprehensive History of the Church*, 1:311–12.

concentrated people in close proximity to one another. The design of the city expressed the social and communitarian values of the Saints. Members of the community would all enjoy a more equal distribution of the world's goods and live in homes of about the same size. There would be no rich or poor. Private forms of recreation, sports, music, and entertainment would be replaced by public facilities that all could enjoy. In the main, the ideal community envisioned by the Mormons is often set aside today in favor of a society that values the individual over the needs of the community. People often live alone and are isolated from one another by housing, incomes, education, employment, race, ethnicity, religion, and freeways. Individuals tend to know very little about their neighbors and do not interact with them. Groups tend to cluster together in similar socioeconomic factions. The values expressed diverge sharply from the egalitarian ideals embodied in the city of Zion.

Section 95: Whitney Store, Kirtland, Ohio, June 1, 1833[1]

Heading

Start building the Kirtland Temple.

The big question

Question: How do we live together and build a community now that we have gathered?

Answer: Build temples so that the Saints may be endowed with power from on high, taught, and prepared to preach the gospel.

Introduction

Revelation given through Joseph Smith the Prophet in the "revelation room" located in the Whitney store at Kirtland, Ohio, on June 1, 1833.[2] This revelation is a continuation of divine direction to build houses for worship and instruction, especially the House of the Lord or Kirtland Temple. The purpose of the temple is to endow the Saints with "power from on high."[3]

---

1. "We now accept June 3, 1833, as the correct date." (Woodford, "Discoveries from the Joseph Smith Papers Project," 32.)

2. Smith, *History of the Church*, 1:350–52.

3. It should be remembered that a covenant-making temple similar to the modern temples of today had not been revealed. The endowment as we know it was first revealed to the Prophet Joseph in May 1842. The purpose for the construction of the Kirtland Temple was to

Background

Just one year after Joseph organized the Church in the summer of 1831, the Lord commanded that a temple be built in Independence, Missouri. (See D&C 57:3.) The site for this sanctuary was dedicated in August 1831. About a year and a half later, in December 1832, Joseph learned that a temple should also be built in Kirtland. (See D&C 88:119.) By the time section 95 was received in the summer of 1833, a full two years had passed and temple construction in Independence or Kirtland had not started.

Even though Joseph had organized a conference to talk about purchasing land for the Kirtland Temple just three months before (March 23, 1833),[1] and had reconvened a second conference two months later (May 4, 1833),[2] section 95 makes it clear that the Lord was not pleased with the rate of progress. "For ye have sinned against me a very grievous sin, in that ye have not considered the great commandment in all things, that I have given unto you concerning the building of mine house." (Verses 3 and 10.) The brethren took the rebuke seriously, and just four days after section 95 was received they started work on the temple, not knowing where the money to do so was going to come from. "Hyrum Smith and Reynolds Cahoon started digging by hand the trench for the foundation, and George A. Smith hauled the first wagon of stone."[3]

The command to build a temple was complicated by the fact that the Saints were poverty stricken. Benjamin F. Johnson remarked in his diary that "there was not a scraper and hardly a plow that could be found among the saints" to dig out the foundation of the building.[4] Based on their dire lack of resources, some members thought it appropriate to build a house of logs. Lucy Mack Smith said of this suggestion that Joseph sharply rejected it. "And shall we, brethren, build a house for our God of logs? No, I have a better plan than that. I have the plan of the house of the Lord, given

---

endow missionaries with "power from on high" and provide a place for "the school of mine apostles." (See verses 8 and 17.)

1. The conference that took place in March 1833 was organized by Joseph in the school of the prophets at the Whitney store in Kirtland, Ohio, to discuss purchasing land for the construction of a temple. (See Robinson and Garrett, *Doctrine and Covenants Commentary*, 3:204–5.) A month later, in April 1833, the Church purchased 103 acres from Peter French for $5,000. "It was eventually decided to locate the temple on the southeast corner of this property on a wooded plateau overlooking the beautiful Chagrin River valley." (Preece, *Learning to Love the Doctrine and Covenants*, 231.)

2. The conference in May 1833 was comprised of high priests and elders gathered to establish a building committee. (See Robinson and Garrett, *Doctrine and Covenants Commentary*, 3:204–5.)

3. Preece, *Learning to Love the Doctrine and Covenants*, 230–31.

4. See Preece, *Learning to Love the Doctrine and Covenants*, 231.

by himself. You will see by this the difference between our calculations and his idea of things."[1]

With no money, construction materials, provisions, and shelter for workers, Joseph moved ahead even though detailed architectural plans were not available. Truman O. Angell[2] said that the Prophet informed his counselors, Sidney Rigdon and Frederick G. Williams, that the Lord would show them in vision how to construct the temple.[3] Frederick G. Williams described the experience some time later:

> Joseph received the word of the Lord for him to his two counselors Williams and Rigdon and come before the Lord, and he would show them the plan or model of the House to be built. We went upon our knees, called on the Lord, and the building appeared within viewing distance: I being the first to discover it. Then all of us viewed it together. After we had taken a good look at the exterior, the building seemed to come right over us, and the makeup of this hall seems to coincide with what I there saw to a minutia.[4]

Section 95 supplements this vision by giving the actual size and function of the primary rooms. The first story is to consist of an assembly hall for general meetings and the second story a school, referred to as a "school of mine apostles" or school of the prophets, as it is referred to elsewhere. (See verses 14–17 and D&C 88:117–41.)

The Lord chastens his Saints

When the Saints fail to live the commandments, the Lord sends chastisement upon them as a corrective to encourage them to change course. In this way God prepares "a way for their deliverance in all things out of temptation." (See verses 1–2.) The idea is that we experience the painful effects of sin and therefore repent. Through adversity and "chastisement" we are better able to see the errors of our ways and be perfected.

Many are called but few are chosen

The "grievous sin" that delayed the construction of the Kirtland Temple was in part the inability of the Saints to comprehend and act upon the principles of the gospel revealed to them. It was difficult for them to see

---

1. Robinson and Garrett, *Doctrine and Covenants Commentary*, 3:205.
2. Truman O. Angell moved to Kirtland in 1835 and helped build the Kirtland Temple. Later in his life he would become the architect for the Salt Lake Temple and design the Lion House, Beehive House, the Utah Territorial State House, and the St. George Temple.
3. See Preece, *Learning to Love the Doctrine and Covenants*, 231.
4. Cook, Revelations of the Prophet Joseph Smith, 198.

the implications of what they had been given, and therefore they did not conduct themselves accordingly. "I say unto you, that there are many who have been ordained among you, whom I have called but few of them are chosen. They who are not chosen have sinned a very grievous sin, in that they are walking in darkness at noon-day." (See verses 5–6; see also D&C 121:34.)

Section 96: Whitney Store, Kirtland, Ohio, June 4, 1833

Heading

Lands purchased for the construction of a Church administration building and temple.

The big question

Question: What is the structure of the Church?
Answer: United orders should be established in conjunction with the law of consecration to accomplish various specific economic objectives of the Church.

Introduction

Revelation given to Joseph Smith the Prophet in the "revelation room" at the Whitney store, at Kirtland, Ohio. The occasion was a conference of high priests, and the chief subject of consideration was the purchase and management by the Church of the French farm, which was to be divided into lots and become a model city of Zion. (See D&C 95.) The conference could not agree on who should take charge of the farm once purchased, and all agreed to inquire of the Lord concerning the matter. Newel K. Whitney was appointed to take charge.

Background

On March 23, 1833, a council of high priests and elders had been convened in Kirtland in the school of the prophets to discuss the matter of purchasing the Pete French farm and brick tavern located thereon, as well as other properties that would provide real estate for a Church administration building and a temple. Brethren were dispatched during the meeting to ascertain the terms of a possible purchase of the French farm. Word came back that French would sell his 103 acres to the Church.[1] The Church council voted to buy and authorized Ezra Thayre and Joseph Coe to negotiate the purchase.[2]

On June 4, 1833, the day on which this revelation was received, a group of high priests met in the Prophet's translating room, or what was sometimes called the "revelation room," at the Whitney store in Kirtland, Ohio. Section 96 made known that Bishop Newel K. Whitney should oversee the newly acquired properties.

The minutes of the meeting on June 4, 1833, indicate:

> A conference of High Priests met in Kirtland . . . [to decide] how the French farm should be disposed of. The council could not agree who should take the charge of it, but all agreed to enquire of the Lord. Accordin[g]ly we received a revelation which decided that Broth N. K. Whitney should take the charge thereof and also that brother John Johnson be admitted as a member of the United Firm. Accordingly he was ordained unto the High Priesthood and admitted.[3]

Members of this order comprised some of the leading elders who had been given the responsibility to oversee Church-owned properties. This United Order (1832–1834), sometimes called the United Firm, and others like it were somewhat different from the social structures referred to in connection with the law of consecration and stewardship. The latter were cooperative enterprises that were set up to bring about relative income equality, group self-sufficiency, and the elimination of poverty. Church members would consecrate or give title to all their real and personal property to the Church. In return, the Church would lease back a portion (stewardship or inheritance). "Thereafter, Church members would consecrate annually any surplus production from their stewardships to the bishop's storehouse" for the use of the Church generally.[4] By way of contrast, united orders or firms were partnerships set up to accomplish a specific economic objective, as was the case in this instance—to manage and supervise Church properties. Any income generated was for its members and any excess surplus for the benefit of the Church. Later, under the leadership of Brigham Young, the term united order was used more

---

1. See Robinson and Garrett, *Doctrine and Covenants Commentary*, 3:204–5.

2. Convening an ad hoc "council" or "conference" was a typical decision-making process Joseph employed to govern the affairs of the Church. The decision to buy the property and build the Kirtland Temple on it caused the Church to go deeply into debt. (See Preece, *Learning to Love the Doctrine and Covenants*, 234.)

3. Collier and Harwell, Kirtland Council Minute Book, 15.

4. See *Encyclopedia of Mormonism*, 4:1493.

loosely to refer to any Church-sponsored organization set up to institute greater economic equality among a group of Saints.

The united order instituted to oversee the French farm properties was different from the "order" referred to in verse 4. This reference alluded to the Literary Firm, another united order set up to publish Joseph's revelations. As stated, this order was "for the purpose of bringing forth my word to the children of men." (See verse 4 and also D&C 70:3.) John Johnson was commanded to join this order.

Section 97: Whitney Store, Kirtland, Ohio, August 2, 1833

Heading

The Saints living in Zion, Jackson County, Missouri, warned that if they do not live the commandments they will not be protected.

The big question

Question: How do we live together and build a community now that we have gathered?
Answer: Repent

Introduction

Revelation given through Joseph Smith the Prophet, received in the "revelation room" in the Whitney store, at Kirtland, Ohio, on August 2, 1833.[1] This revelation deals particularly with the affairs of the Saints in Zion, Jackson County, Missouri, in response to the Prophet's inquiry of the Lord for information. Members of the Church in Missouri were at this time subjected to severe persecution, and on July 23, 1833, had been forced to sign an agreement to leave Jackson County. Zion is told that she will escape only if "she observe to do all things whatsoever I have commanded her." If not, Zion would be visited with "sore affliction, with pestilence, with plague, with sword, with vengeance, with devouring fire." (Verses 26–27.)

Background

In early May 1833, Independence, Missouri, was experiencing an influx of Mormons. In May 1833 there were about a thousand Mormons in the area and more coming every day. Comparatively speaking, there were

---

1. Smith, *History of the Church*, 1:400–402.

more Mormons in Jackson County than there were in the Kirtland area. Independence in Jackson County had been singled out as Zion, the New Jerusalem, to which Christ would come as part of his Second Coming. Missourians were concerned that the Mormons would soon make up a majority and displace the original settlers.

At first relations between the Mormons and non-Mormons were reasonably peaceful. However, the relative calm in Independence was tested when W. W. Phelps wrote an article entitled "Free People of Color," which was interpreted by non-Mormons as an endorsement of bringing free slaves into the area, an idea vehemently opposed by the Missourians, who were generally proslavery. Under pressure from their non-Mormon neighbors, Phelps printed a retraction on July 16, 1833. Nevertheless, distrust and friction between the Mormons and non-Mormons continued to mount. On July 20, 1833, a mob numbering from three hundred to five hundred people gathered to decide what action should be taken against the Saints. The Mormon printing house and home of W. W. Phelps in Independence was ransacked, and the earliest edition of the Book of Commandments (Doctrine and Covenants) was destroyed except for a few copies. The local Mormon general store (Gilbert and Whitney) was marauded and its goods strewn on the street. Bishop Edward Partridge and Charles Allen were tarred and feathered. (For a more complete discussion on the causes of the unrest between Mormons and non-Mormons in Missouri, see commentary on D&C 98.)

By July 23, 1833, violence erupted and the Mormons, at the point of a gun, were forced to sign an agreement in which they pledged to leave the area by January 1, 1844. Oliver Cowdery signed the agreement on behalf of the Saints. On July 25 or 26, Oliver Cowdery left Independence, Missouri, and headed for Kirtland to inform the Prophet Joseph of their predicament. Kirtland was some nine hundred miles away. Most healthy horses of suitable breeds are capable of traveling about twenty miles a day without ill effects. Therefore, the time it would normally take to cover this distance would be about forty-five days. Considering the fact that this was an emergency, Cowdery must have doubled his efforts, because the *Painesville Telegraph* reported that he arrived in Kirtland on August 16, just twenty-nine days after he left Independence, Missouri.[1]

The fact that Joseph could not possibly have known that violence had erupted in Independence and the Saints were being driven out before August 16, when Cowdery arrived, is important because of two revelations the prophets received in early August—section 97 on August 2 and section 98 on August 6. Both contained very relevant information for the Saints in

---

1. See Robinson and Garrett, *Doctrine and Covenants Commentary*, 3:218.

Missouri. Section 97 warned the Saints there that if they did not repent they would be driven out of the area, and section 98 commanded the Saints not to respond in kind if their enemies visited violence upon their heads.

> There are those that must needs be chastened, and their works shall be made known.
> The ax is laid at the root of the trees; and every tree that bringeth not forth good fruit shall be hewn down and cast into the fire. I, the Lord have spoken it.
> Verily I say unto you, all among them who know their hearts are honest, and are broken, and their spirits contrite, and are willing to observe their covenants by sacrifice—yea, every sacrifice which I, the Lord, shall command—they are accepted of me. . . .
> But if she [Zion] observe not to do whatsoever I have commanded her, I will visit her according to all her works, with sore affliction, with pestilence, with plague, with sword, with vengeance, with devouring fire.
> Nevertheless, let it be read this once to her ears, that I, the Lord, have accepted of her offering; and if she sin no more none of these things shall come upon her;
> And I will bless her with blessings, and multiply a multiplicity of blessings upon her, and upon her generations forever and ever, saith the Lord your God. (Section 97 verses 6–8, 26–28.)

Within weeks, Zion would prove unfaithful and be driven out of the land of Zion. The promised judgments would come to pass.

A few months prior to receiving section 97 Joseph Smith wrote:

> The Lord will have a place whence His word will go forth, in these last days, in purity; for if Zion will not purify herself, so as to be approved of in all things, in His sight, He will seek another people; for His work will go on until Israel is gathered, and they who will not hear His voice, must expect to feel His wrath. Let me say unto you, seek to purify yourselves, and also the inhabitants of Zion, lest the Lord's anger be kindled to fierceness.
> Repent, repent, is the voice of God to Zion; and strange as it may appear, yet it is true, mankind will persist in self-justification until all their iniquity is exposed, and their character past being redeemed, and that which is treasured up in their hearts be exposed to the gaze of mankind. I say to you (and what I say to you I say to all), hear the warning voice of God, lest Zion fall, and the Lord swear in His wrath the inhabitants of Zion shall not enter into His rest.
> The brethren in Kirtland pray for you unceasingly, for, knowing the terrors of the Lord, they greatly fear for you. . . . Our hearts are greatly grieved at the spirit which is breathed both in your letter and that of Brother Gilbert's, the very spirit which is wasting the strength of Zion like a pestilence; and if it is not detected and driven from you, it will ripen Zion for the threatened judgments of God. Remember God sees the secret springs of human action, and knows the hearts of all living.[1]

---

1. See Smith, Teachings of the Prophet Joseph Smith, 18–19.

As Joseph McConkie and Craig Ostler said when considering the implications of why Zion would not receive her reward, "God's designs always honor the agency of his children. Although the Lord foreordained that Zion in all her beauty should fill the earth, he has not predestined such to be the course for any particular set of people."[1] Obedience is the prerequisite because the Lord "cannot look upon sin with the least degree of allowance." (D&C 1:31.) Although merciful, the Lord is not able to save those who will not follow him. This sobering realization is one of the important lessons to be learned in Missouri.[2]

Section 98: Whitney Store, Kirtland, Ohio, August 6, 1833

Heading

Counsel to the Saints on violence, the constitutional law of the land, elected officials, and church and civil authority.

Introduction

Revelation given through Joseph Smith in the "revelation room" of the Whitney store at Kirtland, Ohio, on August 6, 1833.[3] This revelation came in consequence of the persecution the Saints were suffering in Missouri. It was natural that the Saints in Missouri, having suffered physically and also having lost property, should feel an inclination toward retaliation and revenge. Although some news of the problems in Missouri had undoubtedly reached the ears of the Prophet in Kirtland (nine hundred miles

---

1. McConkie and Ostler, *Revelations of the Restoration*, 706.
2. Bruce R. McConkie explains in connection with this era in Church history, "Time and time again the early saints in this dispensation were offered the precious privilege of building up Zion.... But always the promises were conditional. Always the divine provisos set forth the need for faith, obedience, righteousness, and complete conformity to the high, holy, and heavenly law. Sad to say, the Lord's people failed to gain the promised blessing. Obeying only in part, they received only a partial reward. Failing to live the fulness of the divine law, they were denied an inheritance in the Holy City in the days of their mortal probation.... It was with the Latter-day Saints as it had been with their ancestors in the days of Moses.... A few in Israel gained wondrous gifts and powers, but the generality of the people obeying only in part, rose no higher in spiritual stature than provided for in the lesser law.... And so it has been among us. Though the newly called saints of the nineteenth century failed to build their promised Zion, yet they retained the glorious gospel, with all its hopes and promises. They were left in that state which now exists among us. What we now have is a schoolmaster to prepare us for that which is yet to be. We are now seeking to build Zion in our hearts by faith and personal righteousness as we prepare for the day when we will have power to build the city whence the law will go forth when He rules whose right is." (*A New Witness for the Articles of Faith*, 610–11.)
3. Smith, *History of the Church*, 1:403–6.

away), the seriousness of the situation could not have been known by him on this date—at least by mortal means. The Lord reveals that in affliction the Saints shall be strengthened. Even if attacked by their enemies, the Saints are to renounce war, proclaim peace, and forgive their enemies.

The big question

Question: How do we live together and build a community now that we have gathered?

Answer: Love our enemies, support constitutional principles, and elect good and wise people to public office.

Anchor section

Memorize: Renounce war and proclaim peace

Background

A few days after this revelation was received, Oliver Cowdery arrived in Kirtland with the news that the citizens of Jackson County were demanding that the Mormons leave. (See commentary on D&C 97.) Within six months the Saints would be driven from Jackson County under horrifying circumstances. Conflict and distrust between the Mormons and the residents of Jackson County had been brewing for over a year. Violence had broken out. Non-Mormons had thrown rocks and bricks through the windows of Mormon homes and had set fire to their haystacks. Mobs milled about and jeered as Mormons went by.

The Missourians' suspicions about the Mormons had been fueled by the rapid growth of the Mormons in the area and what it would mean politically. By the summer of 1833, there were a thousand Mormons in the county, a full third of the total population. Mormons were still moving in at alarming rates. In a short time, it became evident that the  Mormons would soon make up a majority and control most if not all of the political offices in the area.

Mormons flocked to the Jackson County, Missouri, area because of its extraordinary spiritual significance. It was the place where the Saints would build Zion—a place founded on the laws of God. It was such an important place that at the beginning of the Millennium Jesus would appear there. Furthermore, members of the Church thought that the Second Coming was imminent and so it was important to stake out a spot there before the "great and dreadful day of the Lord" arrived. Building a city for such lofty and significant purposes caused some of the Saints to believe that they ought to have exclusive use of the area. Josiah Gregg, a non-Mormon merchant doing business in Independence, said the Mormons grew bolder in their predictions as more settled the area. "At last they became so emboldened by impunity, as openly to boast of their determination to be the sole proprietors of the 'Land of Zion.' The frontiersman and rough hewn settlers who had first claimed Jackson County as their home believed that such religious fanaticism would see the ruin of their community."[1]

Tensions rose in July 1833 when William Phelps published an article in the *Evening and Morning Star* about the legal requirements of bringing free Negroes into the state. Missourians interpreted this as a summons for African Americans to come and settle the area. This outraged the local population, who favored slavery and were concerned about Negro uprisings, which they knew had occurred in other communities elsewhere. Subsequently, when Phelps was accused by the Missourians of inviting free African Americans to inhabit the area, he quickly disavowed any such intention. But the residents of Jackson County were not convinced. A meeting of locals was called on July 15, 1833, and a manifesto was signed by three hundred residents calling for a mass meeting on July 20. At that meeting a committee of twelve was commissioned to inform the Mormons that their printing press must close and every Mormon must leave the county. When Phelps and Partridge asked for ten days to consider the order, violence broke out. The Mormon printing press and the part of it that served as Phelps's home was destroyed. Bishop Partridge and Charles Allen were tarred and feathered, and Sidney Gilbert's store was looted and the store's goods scattered in the street.

Although it is not always apparent for people living in the twenty-first century to understand why a community might feel justified in taking the law into their own hands to carry out mob violence, Bushman points out that at this time in American history the practice was not uncommon. If a majority of citizens believed there was a dire threat in their community, it was considered a "time-honored American tradition" that citizens could resort to "vigilante action." The practice went back to the Stamp Tax distributors in 1765 and the closing of courts to prevent debt collection during Shays' Rebellion in 1786–87. Following such precedents, citizens of Jackson County believed they could act legally to put the Mormons in their place. From the Missourians' point of view, this was not mob action but "people in action." Accordingly, the Missourians involved were not the dregs of society, but rather the jailor, county clerk, Indian agent, post-

---

1. See Bushman, *Joseph Smith: Rough Stone Rolling*, 223.

master, judge, attorneys-at-law, justice of the peace, and other notable and respectable people in the community. They met on the courthouse steps and pledged their "lives, fortunes and sacred honors," borrowing familiar language from the famous last line of the Declaration of Independence.[1]

There were other socio-cultural issues that divided the Mormons from the non-Mormons. Church members felt themselves superior to the local population. Joseph Smith said he found the Missourians to be "lean in intellect and degraded," living in a great wilderness, a century behind the times. Although Missouri had been a state for ten years, it was still underdeveloped for its time, and the people were generally crude and rough around the edges. Missourians said "I reckon" and "tote" instead of carry. They did not say "bucket" or "pail" but "piggin." Their clothes were not "washed" but "battled." Women and children wore skins, and money was scarce. Their cabins were crude, with mud chimneys and dirt floors, and their open windows were covered in cold weather by a slab of wood or a blanket.[2] By comparison, the Mormons were from the Northeast and were more urbane and sophisticated. Their homes were comely and their children better cared for.

Ultimately in July the committee demanded that half the Mormons leave the county within six months, the rest following by April. This gave the leaders time to consult Joseph. When Joseph heard the news, it rapidly spread throughout Kirtland. The city was in an uproar. People were devastated by the news. On August 18, 1833, Joseph wrote an anguished letter to the leaders in Independence and Jackson County. In it he said that the situation could drive him to "madness and desperation." The Saints were supposed to build a temple in Independence, establish Zion, and await the Savior's return. Could such grand and God-revealed plans fail? What now?[3]

As a last resort, Joseph raised an army, Zion's Camp, to march to Missouri (Zion) and save the Saints and their plans for the Second Coming. The Mormons driven out of Independence and the surrounding area had gathered a few miles to the north with the thought in mind that once Mormon troops arrived they would be able to return to their homes. The march did not accomplish its ostensible objective, and Joseph's militaristic response was tempered no doubt by the language in section 98 about renouncing war and proclaiming peace. (See verse 16; see also commentary on D&C 97.) Even though Joseph and his armed men were just miles from

---

1. See Bushman, *Joseph Smith: Rough Stone Rolling*, 223.
2. See Hill, *Joseph Smith, the First Mormon*.
3. See Bushman, *Joseph Smith: Rough Stone Rolling*, 225.

Joseph Smith letter of August 18, 1833

By August 18, 1833, word had arrived from Independence about the dire situation in Independence, Missouri, and Joseph was distraught. His distress and anxiety were expressed in a letter he wrote to William Phelps, John Whitmer, Edward Partridge, Isaac Morley, John Corrill, and Sidney Gilbert about forsaking Independence and Jackson County. He begins by petitioning God for help and thereafter expressing his feelings and emotions. Unlike his revelations, his language is at times confusing and runs together in a long run-on sentence.[1] His spelling was atrocious (and has been corrected here), but there were no clear spelling guides at the time.[2]

> O thou dispenser of all good! In the name of Jesus Christ I ask thee to inspire my heart . . . Oh Lord what more dost thou require at their hands before thou wilt come and save them may I not say thou wilt . . . Oh Lord . . . thy will be done and not mine
>
> . . . with a broken heart and a contrite spirit I take the pen to address you but I know not what to say to you . . . there is no safety only in the arm of Jehovah none else can deliver and he will not deliver unless we do prove ourselves faithful to him in the severest trouble for he that will have his robes washed in the blood of the Lamb must come up through great tribulation even the greatest of all affliction . . . I verily know that he will speedily deliver Zion for I have his immutable covenant that this shall be the case but god is pleased to keep it hid from mine eyes the means how exactly the thing will be done . . . never at any time have I felt as I now feel that pure love and for you my brethren the warmth and zeal for your safety . . . I trust will keep us from madness and desperation and the power of the gospel will enable us to stand . . . and bear with patience the great affliction that is falling upon us on all sides . . . we like the children of Israel with the Red Sea before them and the Egyptians ready to fall upon them to destroy them and no arm could deliver but the arm of God and this is the case with us we must wait on God to be gracious and call on him without ceasing . . . I know that if God shall spare my life that he will permit me to settle on an inheritance on the land of Zion

---

1. It is instructive to compare this letter to some of Joseph's revelations. The difference is astonishing. When one considers that Joseph's revelations were slowly dictated to a clerk, with very few changes and no opportunity to edit and refine the language, it is a study in contrast. Compare this language to section 88 or section 93, for example. In each of these revelations the content is complex and the ideas difficult to express. Yet, each of these revelations is lucid, logical, coherent, and well reasoned. The remarkable influence of the Spirit of the Lord on Joseph as he dictated the mind and will of the Lord is evident and lifts the Prophet to a level of expression beyond his normal capacities.

2. There were no universally accepted spelling standards during this period of time. In any case, some of Joseph's spellings are almost incomprehensible.

in due time but what I do not know but this I do know that I have been kept from going up as yet for your sakes and the day will come that Zion will be kept for our sakes therefore be of good cheer and the cloud shall pass over . . . cursed shall every man be that lifts his arm to hinder this great work and god is my witness of this truth . . . we must wait patently until the Lord comes and restores unto us all things and build the waste places again for he will do it in his time and now what shall I say to comfort . . . you are not speculating with them for lucre but you are willing to die for the cause you have espoused you know that the church have treated lightly the commandments of the Lord . . . God . . . might prepare you for a greater work that you might be prepared for the endowment from on high [Kirtland Temple in 1836] . . . we are all friends of the Constitution . . . in the mean time God will send ambassadors to the authorities of the government and sue for protection and redress . . . O how unsearchable are the depths of his mysteries and his ways past finding out . . . all things shall work together for good to them who are willing to lay down their lives for Christ sake we are suffering great persecution on account of one man by the name of Dr. Hurlburt who has been expelled from the Church . . . you shall be delivered from your anger and shall again flourish in site of hell this God has communicated to me by the gift of the Holy Ghost that this should be the case after much prayer and supplication and also that an other printing office must be build the Lord knows how and also it is the will of the Lord that the store would be kept and that no one foot of land purchased should be given to the enemies of God or sold to them but if any is sold let it be sold to the Church we cannot get the consent of the Lord that we shall give the ground to the enemies yet let those who are bound to deliver a word to the wise is sufficient therefore Judge what I say for know assuredly that every foot of ground that fall into the hand of the enemies with consent is not easy to be obtained again Oh be wise and not let the knowledge I give unto you be known abroad for your sakes . . . I conclude by telling you that we wait the command of God to do whatever he pleases and if he shall say go up to Zion and defend thy brethren by the sword we fly and we count not our lives dear to us I am your brother in Christ . . . Joseph Smith, Jr.[1]

The law of the land, civil disobedience, the kingdom of God, and civil authority

Section 98 informs the Saints that support for the laws of the land is not unconditional. Civil law need be sustained only if consistent with the "principle[s] of freedom in maintaining [the] rights and privileges" that belong "to all mankind." (See verses 4–7.) From the writings of Joseph Smith, these principles included civil and religious liberties, tolerance for all religious persuasions, and a guarantee that all men and women of

---

1. Jessee, Personal Writings of Joseph Smith, 285–88.

every nation, without regard to race, be protected.[1] "Whatsoever is more or less than this, cometh of evil." (Verse 7.) The unmistakable implication of section 98 is that in certain situations God's laws take precedence over civil laws promulgated by the state.[2]

The supremacy of God's laws on earth was not just an academic consideration for the Mormons, primarily because Joseph was not interested in just building churches, but rather communities. His vision encompassed the establishment around the earth of communities just like the one he was trying to build in Independence—Mormon communities where Church and state were inseparable, communities where nonmembers of the Church and minorities could easily feel disenfranchised and threatened. This is why Joseph's emphasis on individual agency, free speech, religious tolerance for all (those in and out of the Church), and civil rights are important considerations. On the one hand, he intended to establish a government governed by religious authority. On the other hand, that government was intended to be benign by emphasizing the individual rights and liberties of all.

Some of Joseph Smith's final thoughts on this matter were expressed in an unpublished revelation he received in 1844, the year of his death.

> Thus saith the Lord God who rules in the heavens above and in the earth beneath, I have introduced my Kingdom and my Government, even the Kingdom of God, that my servants have heretofore prophesied of and that I taught my disciples to pray for, saying "Thy Kingdom come, thy will be done on earth as it is in heaven," for the protections of my Church, and for the maintenance, promulgation and protection of civil and religious liberty in this nation and throughout the world; and all men of every nation, color and creed shall yet be protected and shielded thereby; and every nation and kindred, and people, and tongue shall yet bow the knee to me, and acknowledge me to be Ahman Christ, to the glory of God the Father.[3]

Furthermore, in a subsequent revelation, the Lord also clarified that

---

1. In an unpublished revelation given in 1844 concerning the establishment of the kingdom of God on earth, the Lord said that the laws should be made for the "protection of my Church, and for the maintenance, promulgation and protection of civil and religious liberty in this nation and throughout the world; and all men of every nation, color and creed shall yet be protected and shielded thereby." (Quinn, *Origins of Power*, 122.)

2. Such reasoning accounts for periods in Mormon history when the Saints engaged in civil disobedience, a prime example of which is their response to the U.S. federal government's campaign against polygamy. In B. Carmon Hardy's book, *Doing the Works of Abraham*, he described the Saints' fierce and extended resistance against the federal governments' attempts to outlaw polygamy and said that the Mormons engaged in "one of the longest campaigns of civil disobedience in American history. It is a reminiscence abundant with character and sacrifice, forever tempting our gaze." (Page 392.)

3. See Quinn, *Origins of Power*, 122.

the Government of God would not be made up solely of members of the Church but those outside the faith as well. "And because ... the free agency of man should be guaranteed to all men, I moved upon him [Joseph Smith] to introduce into my Kingdom certain parties not in my Church ... [having] the rights of representation ... and ... a full and free opportunity of presenting their views, interests and principles."[1] In retrospect, whether or not this ideal, like the ideal of economic equality, could have ever been effectively realized during the time of Joseph Smith is at best uncertain.

Even the suggestion that the Church intended to govern civilly as well as religiously was enough to seriously alarm non-Mormons. Therefore, as a matter of good public relations, Joseph emphasized that at least until Jesus came to rule and reign, civil governments were important and should be honored without revealing what he might do if the two came into conflict. In order to survive, some of the more radical implications of kingdom building were deemphasized and the Church agreed to "render unto Caesar the things which are Caesar's." (Matthew 22:21.) In preparing a statement of Mormon beliefs which he intended the world to see, he said in 1842, "We believe in being subject to kings, presidents, rulers, and magistrates, in obeying, honoring, and sustaining the law." (A of F 12.)[2]

Love your neighbor and laws against violence

While civil disobedience may be acceptable, violence is not. Jesus set the standard, "Love your enemies, bless them that curse you, do good to them that hate you, and pray for them which despitefully use you." (Matthew 5:44.) "Whosoever shall smite thee on thy right cheek, turn to him the other also." (Matthew 5:39.) Physical harm, on a personal or societal level (war) is forbidden. In the words of section 98, "Renounce war and proclaim peace, and seek diligently to turn the hearts of the children to their fathers, and the hearts of the fathers to the children." (Verse 16.) The Saints are to bear evil "patiently and revile not ..., neither seek revenge." (Verse 23.)

While self-defense is acceptable, it is not preferred and is only "justified." (Verse 31.) Note that is it not "approved" of or recommended. And then, self-defense is only "justified" after your enemy has smitten you at least three times. (Verse 29.) On the fourth the Saints were given permission to protect themselves, but if they would "spare him [enemy] [they would] be rewarded for ... righteousness. (Verse 30.) Even then, before the Saints could go into battle, they must "lift a standard of peace unto that people, nation or tongue" and thereafter seek God's permission to defend them-

---

1. See Quinn, *Origins of Power*, 127.
2. See Smith, *History of the Church*, 4:535–41.

selves. (See verses 34–36.) To make the point, and to avoid alternative interpretations of section 98 based on other parts of the canon, the Lord cautions, "Behold, this is the law I gave unto my servant Nephi, and thy fathers, Joseph, and Jacob, and Isaac, and Abraham, and all mine ancient prophets and apostles." (Verse 32.)

When the "wicked rule the people mourn"

Although political ideology may be a consideration when it comes to choosing our leaders, basic honesty, virtue, uprightness, and good judgment (wisdom) are traits that should be sought after in those whom we elect to office. Unfortunately, many who seek public office do so to advantage themselves—"to gratify [their] pride, [their] vain ambition" and "to exercise control or dominion or compulsion upon the souls of the children of men." (D&C 121:37.) Those who are wicked, self-centered, lack good judgment, and dishonest not only abuse power, but are often times less compassionate; they therefore do not act upon the legitimate needs of the less fortunate who petition their governments for redress. As a result, "When the wicked rule the people mourn." (Verse 9.) Consequently, "honest men [and women] and wise men [and women] should be sought for diligently." (Verse 10.) Furthermore, such office holders should be upheld and supported in office. (See verse 10.)

SECTION 101: WHITNEY STORE, KIRTLAND, OHIO, DECEMBER 16, 1833[1]

Heading

The Lord explains why the Saints were forced out of Zion, Jackson County, Missouri, and addresses the issue of when the Saints will be able to return and redeem the land of Zion.

Introduction

Revelation given to Joseph Smith the Prophet in the "revelation room" in the Whitney store, at Kirtland, Ohio, on December 16, 1833.[2] At this time the Saints who had gathered in Missouri were suffering great persecution. Mobs had driven them from their homes in Jackson County, and

---

1. "This revelation was written on December 16 and 17, 1833." (Woodford, "Discoveries from the Joseph Smith Papers Project," 32.)
2. Smith, *History of the Church*, 1:458–64.

some of them had tried to establish themselves in Van Buren County, but persecution followed them. The main body of the Saints was at that time in Clay County, Missouri. Threats of death against individuals and the destruction of the Saints' homes, crops, and livestock were widespread. The Lord explains that the Saints are chastened and afflicted because of their transgressions. The Saints are to importune the government for the redress of their grievances.

The big question

Question: How do we deal with disappointment and unrealized promises?
Answer: Live the commandments.

Background

By December 16, 1833, what has been referred to as the Mormon War was well underway in Missouri. Mobs attacked the Saints' homes, destroyed their crops, and beat up and killed men, women, and children. Contrary to the Lord's command in section 98 not to retaliate, Mormon bands roamed the countryside looking for caches of weapons they feared might be turned on them. By mid-November, well over a thousand Saints were scattered on the prairies or on the far side of the Missouri River in Clay and Van Buren counties. There were casualties on both sides.[1]

To some degree this sudden burst of persecution against the Mormons in Missouri during the summer months of 1833 was fueled by the Saints themselves. Mormons were true believers and spoke boldly about God's plans for the region, the destruction of the wicked, and the imminent return of Jesus Christ, who would inaugurate a thousand years of peace. Jackson County was to play a central role in all of this. The land was to be redeemed as a gathering place for the Mormons and become one of two world headquarters during the Millennium. In fact, some bragged of a complete takeover of the area prior to Jesus' Second Coming. The *Evening and Morning Star* talked about 'taking possession of this country." Josiah Gregg, a non-Mormon merchant, said the Mormons grew more vocal and bolder as their numbers increased. "At last they became so emboldened by impunity, as openly to boast of their determination to be the sole proprietors of the 'Land of Zion.'"[2] All of this stirred up negative sentiments by the non-Mormons, who felt they had a right to

---

1. See Robinson and Garrett, *Doctrine and Covenants Commentary*, 3:259.
2. Bushman, *Joseph Smith: Rough Stone Rolling*, 223.

control this area of the country which they had settled first, long before the Mormons arrived.

When Joseph Smith became aware that a deadline had been set for the Mormons to leave Jackson County, and that the Saints were being physically evicted from the area by force of arms and bloodshed, he was distraught. On December 10, 1833, just after he had received the latest information on the crisis from Orson Hyde and John Gould, Joseph exclaimed, "Oh my brethren! My brethren.... [W]ould that I had been with you, to have shared your fate. Oh my God, what shall I do in such a trial as this!"[1] The feelings Joseph felt were shared by the other members of the Church in Kirtland, where panic and anguish were apparent everywhere. Kirtland was in an uproar, and families and friends in Kirtland worried about the fate of their loved ones in Missouri.[2]

Typical of the violence was the attack on the Whitmer Settlement on the Big Blue River, west of Independence. Thirteen Mormon houses were unroofed and several men were whipped nearly to death, including Hiram Page, one of the Eight Witnesses to the Book of Mormon. Men were beaten, and women and children terrorized. By November 4, 1833, on a day known as the "bloody day," several Missourian mob members captured a Mormon ferry on the Big Blue River. Thirty or forty armed men from each side confronted each other in the corn fields over the incident. Brother Philo Dibble was shot in the stomach but was miraculously healed by Newel Knight. Andrew Barber was mortally wounded. At least two Missourians and a few of their horses were killed. On the same day several Church leaders were arrested in Independence and scheduled for trial. A crowd threatened to kill the prisoners. At the instigation of Lieutenant Governor Boggs, some of the state militia was called into action, ostensibly to disarm both sides, but in fact they ended up helping the anti-Mormons drive the Saints out of Missouri.[3]

The winter of 1833-34 was a deplorable time for the Mormons. As the violence continued and the Saints were driven from their homes, both shores of the Missouri River near the ferry were lined with refugees. Parley P. Pratt described the situation:

> When night again closed upon us the cottonwood bottom had much the appearance of a camp meeting. Hundreds of people were seen in every direction, some in tents and some in the open air around their fires, while the rain descended in torrents. Husbands were inquiring for their wives, wives for their husbands; parents for children, and children for parents.... The

---

1. Robinson and Garrett, *Doctrine and Covenants Commentary*, 3:259.
2. See Robinson and Garrett, *Doctrine and Covenants Commentary*, 3:260.
3. *Church History in the Fulness of Times*, 135–36.

scene was indescribable, and, I am sure, would have melted the hearts of any people on the earth, except our blind oppressors.[1]

Scenes such as this continued until all of the Mormons were driven out of Jackson County. Lyman Wight said: "I saw one hundred and ninety women and children driven thirty miles across the prairie, with three decrepit men only in their company, in the month of November, the ground thinly crusted with sleet; and I could easily follow on their trail by the blood that flowed from their lacerated feet on the stubble of the burnt prairie!"[2]

When Joseph and the Saints realized that it was doubtful the Mormons would be able to stay and establish Zion, two questions loomed. First, why would the Lord allow the wicked to drive the Saints out of Zion, thus thwarting plans for the Second Coming? Second, when would the Saints be able to return and retake Zion and prepare for the second coming? Sections 101, 103, 104, and 105 all address these crucial concerns.

The Saints driven out of Zion on account of their collective unrighteousness

The answer to the first question, why were the Saints driven from Zion, was an issue Joseph had worried about ten months before. On January 11, 1833, he wrote to W. W. Phelps:

> [I]f Zion will not purify herself, so as to be approved of in all things, in His sight, He will seek another people . . . and they who will not hear His voice, must expect to feel His wrath. Let me say to you, seek to purify yourselves, and also all the inhabitants of Zion, lest the Lord's anger be kindled to fierceness. Repent, repent, is the voice of God to Zion . . . hear the warning voice of God, lest Zion fall, and the Lord sware in His wrath the inhabitants of Zion shall not enter into His rest. . . . This from your brother who trembles for Zion and for the wrath of heaven, which awaits her if she repent not.[3]

Joseph's concerns were also expressed in a revelation he received on August 2, 1833, before he knew about the extent of the violence against the Mormons in and around Jackson County, Missouri. "But if she [Zion] observe not to do whatsoever I have commanded her, I will visit her according to all her works, with sore affliction, with pestilence, with plague, with sword, with vengeance, and with devouring fire." (D&C 97:26.)

The revelation recorded in section 101 confirmed Joseph's worries. Transgression was the cause of the Saints' expulsion from Zion. "I, the Lord,

---

1. Church History in the Fulness of Times, 137.
2. *Church History in the Fulness of Times*, 137.
3. See Robinson and Garrett, Doctrine and Covenants Commentary, 3:260.

have suffered the affliction to come upon them, wherewith they have been afflicted in consequence of their transgressions." (Verse 2.) However, the Lord would not completely forsake his people. He would yet make them "my jewels" (verse 3), and comfort his people. (See verses 12–14.) Those who gave their lives for Zion would be "crowned" with glory. (See verse 15.) At a future day Zion would be redeemed. In the meantime the Saints were to "be still and know that I am God." (Verse 16.)

It will be "many days" before the Saints will be permitted to return to the land of Zion

Although the promise was given that Zion would be redeemed at some point, the question remained: When? First-generation Mormons believed it would be within their lifetimes, but this was not to be. They based their hope in part on this revelation which said that Zion would "not be moved out of her place, notwithstanding her children are scattered." (Verse 17.) But other parts of the revelation cautioned that Zion would not be redeemed again until "after many days."[1] (See verse 62.) In the meantime, section 101 advised that there were two immediate concerns. First, the Saints were to organize and gather in other places (stakes). (See verses 63–68.) Second, they were to petition the governor and the president of the United States and do all that could be done to reclaim Zion. (See verses 86–87.)

As the Latter-day Saints await the building of Zion once again, there are many lessons to be learned from this tragic episode in Church history. It is a reminder that Zion cannot be built up except upon the principles of righteousness. And it is not enough that this "righteousness" and "purity" be found among a few. It must be collective and extend throughout the Church in general. God's people must be worthy, tried and tested as gold is purified by fire. (See Revelation 3:18–21; see also D&C 101:1–23, 35–42, 97–101.) The Saints are not to be like other men and women but "are accounted as the salt of the earth and the savor of men," and if the "salt" loses its "savor, behold it is thenceforth good for nothing only to be cast out and trodden under the feet of men." (Verses 39–42.)

The expulsion from Missouri also illustrates the need to petition God and take his commandments seriously "in the day of . . . peace," as well as in the "day of . . . trouble." For "in the day of their peace they esteemed lightly my counsel; but in the day of their trouble, of necessity they feel after me." (Verse 8.) If not, then "they must needs be chastened and tried,

---

1. For further information on this subject, see commentary on section 103, where the parable of the vineyard, which appears in this section, is more fully analyzed. (See verses 43–62.)

even as Abraham, who was commanded to offer up his only son. For all those who will not endure chastening, but deny me, cannot be sanctified." (Verses 4–5.) This testing entails not only patience in persecution, but also in dealing, as Abraham did, with the uncertainty of wondering whether God will bring about his promised blessings or whether, through our own agency, we are no longer entitled to them.

Slavery condemned

For the most part, the Saints were northerners and not in favor of slavery. Northern attitudes were reflected in an article written by W. W. Phelps when he published a controversial editorial in the *Evening and Morning Star* titled "Free People of Color." In it Phelps outlined the procedures for the migration of free blacks to Missouri. The locals did not feel disposed to allow free blacks into the state and often beat those who came. Needless to say, the Missourians were highly critical of Phelps's point of view. It was one of a number of reasons why the Missourians decided it was time to force the Mormons out of Jackson County, Missouri.[1]

Section 101 did not calm the fears of the Missourians on this subject but declared that slavery was morally wrong. "It is not right that any man should be in bondage one to another." (Verse 79.) In addition, the section makes it plain that even though slavery may have been allowed by the U.S. Constitution, it should not have been. "And for this purpose have I established the Constitution of this land, by the hands of wise men whom I raised up unto this very purpose." (Verse 80.) Those purposes would more fully come about after the Civil War, when amendments to the Constitution were added that ended the practice of slavery. Clearly,

---

1. The local Missourians responded by printing a rebuttal ("The Manifesto of the Mob") which called for the "removal" of the Mormons from the state. Among other things it said: "In a late number of the Star, published in Independence by the leaders of the sect, there is an article inviting free Negroes and mulattoes from other states to become 'Mormons,' and remove and settle among us. This exhibits them in still more odious colors. It manifests a desire on the part of their society, to inflict on our society an injury that they know would be to us entirely insupportable, and one of the surest means of driving us from the country; for it would require none of the supernatural gifts that they pretend to, to see that the introduction of such a caste among us would corrupt our blacks, and instigate them to bloodshed. . . . We believe it a duty we owe to ourselves, our wives, and children, to the cause of public morals, to remove them from among us, as we are not prepared to give up our pleasant places and goodly possessions to them or to receive into the bosom of our families, as fit companions for wives and daughters, the degraded and corrupted free Negroes and mulattos that are now invited to settle among us. . . . We agree to use such means as may be sufficient to remove them, and to that end we each pledge to each other our bodily powers, our lives, fortunes and sacred honors." (http://www.blacklds.org/mob)

the Lord intended that "all flesh" should be protected in their rights. (See verse 77.)

Chapter 27

Joseph Smith Home: Kirtland, Ohio, February 1834–December 1835

Section 102: Joseph Smith Home, Kirtland, Ohio, February 17, 1834

Heading

First high council established.

The big question

Question: What is the structure of the Church?
Answer: Establish formal Church councils.

Introduction

Minutes of the organization of the first high council of the Church at the home of Joseph Smith at Kirtland, Ohio, on February 17, 1834.[1] The original minutes were recorded by Elders Oliver Cowdery and Orson Hyde. Two days later, the minutes were corrected by the Prophet, read to the high council, and accepted by the council. When the 1835 addition of the Doctrine and Covenants was published, verses 30–32, which make reference to the Council of the Twelve Apostles, were added by the Prophet Joseph Smith to reflect changes that were made in the organization of the Church after section 102 was received.[2]

---

1. Smith, *History of the Church,* 2:28–31.
2. In 1835 Twelve were called to do missionary work and preside over areas of the Church in which a stake was not organized. Later this changed and the Prophet Joseph explained that the Twelve should stand next to the First Presidency to help govern the entire Church. Section 107 does not reflect this change, which came later in 1841. (See *Encyclopedia of Mormonism,* 1186.)

Anchor section

Memorize: High council

Background

As the Church continued to grow, the organization of the Church changed to accommodate new circumstances. On February 12, 1834, Joseph met with a group of high priests and elders at his home in Kirtland to discuss the function of Church councils. Joseph said that governing councils to administer the affairs of the Church had been "shown to him by vision."[1] In reference to the importance of this new development, Joseph said that "in ancient days councils were conducted with such strict propriety, that no one was allowed to whisper, be weary, leave the room, or get uneasy in the least, until [a decision had been reached].[2]

Prior to this time Joseph had on many occasions convened ad hoc councils of high priests and or elders to help him make decisions that affected the Church. Such councils were often times referred to as a "conference" of the Church. The establishment of standing councils pursuant to section 102 was an important step toward the establishment of governing committees to regulate the affairs of the Church and its members. Section 102 authorizes the *high council* to make policy, receive revelation, and sit as a court. Due process is emphasized and procedures set in place to protect the rights of the members of the council and those who appeared before the council when it was acting in a judicial capacity. An appellate procedure is also set forth. During the following year Joseph would receive another revelation, section 107, which would expand the Saint's understanding of the organization of the Church and give further instruction on how councils were to be established and operate. (See D&C 107:27–31.)

The primary thrust of section 102 concerns the council's judicial function. The procedure recognizes that some cases are more difficult to adjudicate than others. (See verses 13–19.) Therefore, a preliminary finding on whether or not the case is complex or simple must be reached before the council adjudicates a particular matter. If the case was considered simple or complex, a different set of procedures was followed. An appellate procedure involving a review of the record (informal record at best) and a trial de novo was provided for. (See verses 19–21, 27.) The accused had the right or "privilege" to speak for himself or herself before the council. (See verse 18.) The accused also had the right to be represented by at least "one-half of the council." (See verse 15.) In the spirit of evenhandedness Joseph

---

1. See Cook, *Revelations of the Prophet Joseph Smith*, 207.
2. See Cook, *Revelations of the Prophet Joseph Smith*, 206–7.

also said that the brethren were to "speak precisely according to evidence" and not speculate.[1] In addition, each member of the high council must have pure motives. Joseph said "no man was capable of judging a matter in council" unless his "own heart was pure."[2] A variety of Church and civil matters were heard. However, criminal cases were rarely convened.[3]

A most important function of the council and its president was to receive revelation, especially in cases where there is not "a sufficiency written to make the case clear to the minds of the council." (Verse 23.) In such instances, the "president may inquire and obtain the mind of the Lord by revelation." (Verse 23.) Although the president of the council may receive a revelation on doctrinal matters, the revelation would not be generally binding for the Church. "No one shall be appointed to receive commandments and revelations in this church excepting my servant Joseph Smith, Jun." (D&C 28:2; 43:3–6.) Ultimately, in order for a revelation to be authoritative it would have to have the unanimous assent of the leading quorums (First Presidency, Quorum of the Twelve, and Seventy) and then accepted by vote in a representative body of the Church, such as general conference. (See commentaries on section 107 and on Declaration 2.) When section 102 was received, it should be noted that Joseph Smith was the president of the Church and the president of this newly established high council. Therefore, if Joseph had received a revelation under the system in operation at this time, the revelation would have been obligatory.[4]

The formal organization of the Kirtland high council occurred on February 17, 1834. After the high council in Kirtland was created, the First Presidency acted as its head. A second high council was organized in Clay County, Missouri, on July 7, 1834. Similar councils were established in Far West and in Nauvoo. An incident out of Church history illustrates the function of councils and the approach and way in which Joseph related to such proceedings. On April 8, 1842, a high council was convened to hear the case of Pelitiah Brown. The defendant had been summoned before the court for teaching false doctrines about the Book of Revelation. Joseph Smith appeared and testified on behalf of the defendant and criticized the tenor of the proceedings. Joseph said, "I did not like the old man being called up for erring in doctrine. It looks too much like the Methodist, and not like the Latter-day Saints. Methodists have creeds which a man must believe or be asked out of their church. I want the liberty of thinking and believing as I please. It feels so good not to be trammelled. It does not

---

1. See Cook, *Revelations of the Prophet Joseph Smith*, 207.
2. See Cook, *Revelations of the Prophet Joseph Smith*, 206.
3. See Cook, *Revelations of the Prophet Joseph Smith*, 207.
4. See Smith, *History of the Church*, 2:25–26.

prove that a man is not a good man because he errs in doctrine."[1] The charges were dropped.

Section 103: Joseph Smith Home, Kirtland, Ohio, February 24, 1834

Heading

Joseph raises an army (Zion's Camp) to save the Saints in Missouri from destruction and to redeem Zion.

The big question

Question: How do we deal with disappointment and unrealized promises?
Answer: Live the commandments.

Introduction

Revelation given through Joseph Smith the Prophet in his home at Kirtland, Ohio, February 24, 1834.[2] This revelation was received after the arrival in Kirtland, Ohio, of Parley P. Pratt and Lyman Wight, who had come from Missouri to counsel with the Prophet as to the relief and restoration of the Saints to their lands in Jackson County. The Lord reiterates why he permitted the Saints to be persecuted and driven out of Jackson County. The Saints are promised that ultimately Zion will be established in Jackson County, Missouri. Joseph is commanded to raise an army (Zion's Camp) and march to Zion, presumably to restore the Saints to their rightful lands and property.

Background

When it became apparent that enemies of the Church were driving the Saints out of Zion (Jackson County, Missouri), at Joseph's bidding the Kirtland high council made plans to organize an army to help the Missouri Saints retake their real and personal property from their enemies. Members were recruited between March through May 1834 and the army, known as Zion's Camp, began its march in May. The camp reached its maximum numerical strength of 207 on June 8.

---

1. Smith, *History of the Church*, 5:340–41.
2. Smith, *History of the Church*, 2:36–39.

Joseph Smith Home: Kirtland, Ohio, February 1834-December 1835

Even though their mission seemed straightforward, Joseph was never entirely sure what his ragtag volunteer army would ultimately accomplish. Certainly, at a minimum, it was anticipated that the army would assist the Saints. But would they do it by force and if necessary retake their lands in Jackson County? Although section 103 said that  "the redemption of Zion must needs come by power," Bushman suggests that this did not necessarily mean physical force. After all, Zion's Camp was not a well-trained military unit and, based upon Joseph's actions, he was not particularly interested in schooling his soldiers in military strategy and drills. Along the way, only one sham battle was attended to while the army waited for one of its members to buy a horse. Nothing about fighting is mentioned in section 103, and apparently Joseph felt the mission was peaceful enough to admit woman and children on the march.

Most importantly, Joseph Smith probably thought he would never have to use force in the first place. Initially he had envisioned that the governor of Missouri, Governor Dunklin, would escort the Saints back to their lands. When this failed, Zion's Camp was disbanded before a shot was fired.[1]

No doubt this band of Saints hoped and intended to return the Missouri Saints to their homes in Jackson County. Since they were unable to do so, outsiders certainly saw it as a failure. As a result, some members of the camp apostatized. Yet, as Bushman points out, others "felt more loyal to Joseph Smith than ever, bonded by their hardships."[2] What's more, Bushman continues, "The future leadership of the Church came from this group. Nine of the Church's original Twelve Apostles, all seven presidents of the Seventy, and sixty-three other members of the Seventy marched in Zion's Camp."[3]

The fact that there were not more defectors bears record of the reality that regardless of the outcome, many were still convinced that Joseph was a prophet because while on the march they experienced the reassuring power of God, which had been made manifest in marvelous ways amongst all the hardship. For example, on June 18, 1834, when Zion's Camp arrived within a mile of Richmond, Joseph had premonitions of danger. He prayed and was assured that the Lord would protect them.

The details of the story are remarkable. That night the company had camped just inside Clay County on a hill between two branches of the Fishing River. Joseph had learned that when those in Jackson County were

---

1. See Bushman, *Joseph Smith: Rough Stone Rolling*, 326.
2. Bushman, *Joseph Smith: Rough Stone Rolling*, 147.
3. Bushman, *Joseph Smith: Rough Stone Rolling*, 147.

informed that a Mormon army was approaching, they panicked and sent an army twice the size of Joseph's (four hundred-plus men) to exterminate Zion's Camp. Joseph prayed for divine protection. Sounds of gunfire were heard and some of the Mormons wanted to fight, but the Prophet promised that the Lord would protect them. "Stand still and see the salvation of God," Joseph said.[1]

Sure enough, a ferry load of Clay County mobbers crossed the Missouri River to the south, intending to engage the Mormons, as a small black cloud appeared in the clear western sky. It moved eastward, unrolling like a scroll. In a moment a squall made it nearly impossible for the boat to return to pick up another load. As the storm progressed, Zion's Camp abandoned their tents and found shelter in the old Baptist meetinghouse nearby. Joseph said, "Boys, there is some meaning to this. God is in this storm."[2] It was not possible for anyone to sleep, and therefore the group sang hymns and rested on the benches.[3]

The mobbers still tried to approach, but they eventually were forced to seek refuge from the furious storm. Eyewitnesses described what happened:

> The storm was tremendous; wind and rain, hail and thunder met [the mob] in great wrath, and soon softened their direful courage, and frustrated all their designs to "kill Joe Smith and his army." . . . [The mob] crawled under wagons, into hollow trees, and filled one old shanty, till the storm was over, when their ammunition was soaked. . . . [The mob] experienced the pitiless pelting of the storm all night; and as soon as arrangements could be made, this "forlorn hope" took the "back track" for Independence, to join the main body of the mob. . . . Very little hail fell in our camp, but from half a mile to a mile around, the stones or lumps of ice cut down the crops of corn and vegetation generally, even cutting limbs from trees, while the trees, themselves were twisted into withes by the wind. The lightning flashed incessantly which caused it to be so light in our camp through the night, that we could discern the most minute objects; and the roaring of the thunder was tremendous. The earth trembled and quaked, the rain fell in torrents, and, united, it seemed as if the mandate of vengeance had gone forth from the God of battles, to protect His warrants from the destruction of their enemies. . . . Many of my little band sheltered in an old meetinghouse through this night, and in the morning the water in Big Fishing river was about forty feet deep, where, the previous evening, it was no more than to our ankles.[4]

---

1. See *Church History in the Fulness of Times*, 148.
2. *Church History in the Fulness of Times*, 148.
3. *Church History in the Fulness of Times*, 148.
4. Smith, History of the Church, 2:104–5.

Joseph and his faithful band had been saved.[1]

Others in the camp witnessed the power of healing. Just after Joseph decided to abandon the march, some of the men that were angry and disappointed, turned their backs on Joseph, and never returned. Joseph warned the camp that the Lord would send a devastating scourge upon them as a consequence of their unrighteousness. Immediately thereafter, two men contracted cholera. The epidemic spread to sixty-eight. When Joseph tried to heal one of the sick men, he was immediately stricken with the disease himself. Fourteen members of the camp died, one of whom was a woman by the name of Betsy Parrish. On July 2, Joseph told the camp that "if they would humble themselves before the Lord and covenant to keep His commandments and obey my counsel, the plague would be stayed from that hour, and there should not be another case of the cholera among them. The brethren covenanted to that effect with uplifted hands, and the plague was stayed."[2]

The details of the story are found in the *History of the Church*. The brethren reported that the cholera "burst forth among us and about midnight it was manifested in its most virulent form."[3] Joseph reported:

> At the commencement, I attempted to lay on hands for their recovery, but I quickly learned by painful experience, that when the great Jehovah decrees destruction upon any people, and makes known His determination, man must not attempt to stay His hand. The moment I attempted to rebuke the disease I was attacked, and had I not desisted in my attempt to save the life of a brother, I would have sacrificed my own. The disease seized upon me like the talons of a hawk, and I said to the brethren: "If my work were done, you would have to put me in the ground without a coffin."[4]

The horrid disease continued to take its toll.

> We were not able to obtain boards to make coffins for those who died but were under the necessity of rolling them up in their blankets, and burying them in that manner. So we placed them in a little bluff by the side of a small stream that emptied into Rush creek. This we accomplished by dark, and returned. Our hopes were that no more would die, but while we were uniting in a covenant to pray once more with uplifted hands to God, we looked at our beloved brother, Elder Wilcox, and he was gasping his last. At this scene my feelings were beyond expression. . . . We felt to sit and weep over our brethren, and so great was our sorrow that we could have washed them with our tears.

---

1. *Church History in the Fulness of Times*, 148.
2. *Church History in the Fulness of Times*, 149.
3. Smith, *History of the Church*, 2:114.
4. Smith, History of the Church, 2:114.

Finally the sickness abated. Joseph said, "I told them if they would humble themselves before the Lord and covenant to keep His commandments . . . the plague should be stayed from that hour."[1] The disease was stayed.

Even though Joseph had failed to reclaim Zion, he was not defeated. His motto became "next year in Zion." Joseph continued to predict a return within two years.[2] The Jackson County Saints moved north and waited patiently for the Prophet to give them the signal that it was time to return. Ultimately, Joseph never gave the order to try to retake Zion. Rather, persecution increased. By 1838 the Saints were surrounded in Far West and driven out of the state. It was clear that Joseph never envisioned a bloody battle. He said, "It is not our intention to commit hostilities against any man, or set of men; it is not our intention to injure any man's person or property . . . we have every reason to put ourselves in an attitude of self defense, considering the abuse we have suffered."[3] Almost certainly, Joseph's attitudes were fashioned by the revelation received before he even knew that the Saints would be forcibly evicted from Independence, Missouri, which said "renounce war and proclaim peace." (D&C 98:16.)

Joseph commanded to raise an army

The command to raise an army was specific. Joseph was told that he should try to raise a force of five hundred. (See verse 30.) Recognizing that "men do not always do my will" the Lord said he would be satisfied with three hundred or as little as one hundred. (See verses 32–34.) If Joseph could not get the minimum number, presumably the march would have been cancelled. It took time to raise the two hundred or so men that ultimately marched, as well as to gather together the supplies necessary. The Saints were poor, and Joseph sent representatives around the country asking the Saints to contribute.

Zion will be restored

Zion was not established because the Saints in Zion (Jackson County, Missouri), did not obey the commandments and were not unified in their desire to live the law of consecration. The Lord warned, "But inasmuch as they keep not my commandments, and hearken not to observe all my words, the kingdoms of the world shall prevail against them." (Verses 5–8,

---

1. Smith, *History of the Church*, 2:120.
2. Bushman, *Joseph Smith: Rough Stone Rolling*, 247.
3. Bushman, *Joseph Smith: Rough Stone Rolling*, 244.

14.) Therefore, the Lord observed that Zion would not be redeemed until after much tribulation. (See verses 12–14.) And when Zion is restored, it "must needs come by power" at a time when the Lord will "raise up unto my people a man, who shall lead them like as Moses led the children of Israel." (Verses 16–18.) In the meantime, the Saints were to follow Joseph, who was the servant mentioned in the parable of the vineyard in section 101.

The parable of the vineyard summarizes the Lord's thoughts on this matter. A certain "nobleman had a spot of land" that was "very choice" (Zion). God's people were commanded to go and settle there and plant "twelve olive trees." (See D&C 101:44.) The Lord commanded that "watchmen" be posted and that a "tower" be built so that an enemy could be seen from afar off. The servants of the Lord started the project, but because they were "slothful" and not unified on the need for such a structure, they stopped short of building the tower. After all, some said, it was a time of peace. (See verses 46–50.) Therefore, when the enemy arrived the servants of the Lord were overtaken and the Lord said to his people, "Ought ye not to have done even as I commanded you." (Verse 53.) The Lord gathered the "residue" of his people together and told them to "redeem my vineyard" and to "avenge me of mine enemies." (Verses 55–58.)

The servants then asked, "When shall these things be?" (Verse 59.) The Lord replies to his servant, Joseph Smith Jr., "When I will." (See verse 60; see also D&C 103:21.) In the meantime, Joseph is commanded to "go ye straightway, and do all things whatsoever I have commanded you." (Verse 60.) At some point the Lord promises, "a faithful and wise steward in the midst of mine house, a ruler in my kingdom," will appear on the scene and "after many days all things were fulfilled." (See verses 61–62.)

The Lord then turns his attention to the "churches" and reminds the Saints that he will continue to gather together the "wheat" and the "tares" until the "time of harvest is come, and my word must needs be fulfilled." (See verses 63–69.) Therefore, continue to purchase land in Zion. (See verses 70–74.)

Finally the Lord comments that "there is even now already in store sufficient, yea, even an abundance, to redeem Zion, and establish her waste places, no more to be thrown down, were the churches, who call themselves after my name, willing to hearken to my voice." (Verse 75.)

Section 105

Section 101 begins the discussion on why Zion failed, and section 105 completes the Lord's commentary on the events that occurred when the Saints were driven out of Zion. In section 105 the Lord reiterates once more that Zion will be deferred for a little season and that the Saints should continue to buy land in Zion.

SECTION 104: JOSEPH SMITH HOME, KIRTLAND, OHIO, APRIL 23, 1834

Heading

Zion criticized for not living by the principles of the law of consecration. United orders or firms based on the law of common consent. Underlying principles of the law of consecration explained. Property belongs to the Lord, and therefore it is not for man to decide how the resources of the world are to be used.

The big question

Question: What is the structure of the Church?
Answer: Organize united orders or firms based on the law of common consent.

Introduction

Revelation given to Joseph Smith concerning the united order, and the order of the Church for the benefit of the poor, received in his home at Kirtland, Ohio, on April 23, 1834.[1] The occasion was that of a council meeting of the First Presidency and other high priests, in which the pressing temporal needs of the people had been given consideration. The united order at Kirtland was to be temporarily dissolved and reorganized, and the properties as stewardships were to be divided among members of the order. The united order is to operate by common consent.

---

1. Smith, *History of the Church,* 2:54–60.

Joseph Smith Home: Kirtland, Ohio, February 1834-December 1835

Background

In the spring of 1834 the Church was deeply in debt. Two years earlier, in April 1832, the united order or united firm[1] had secured a five-year loan for $15,000, a significant amount of money in Joseph's time. The loan was used primarily to purchase goods and property in Missouri. When the Saints were driven out of Jackson County, the order lost its collateral on this loan, as well as its means of paying back the debt. At the same time, other financial demands were pressing. Joseph was also trying to raise money for Zion's Camp. Debtors, recognizing the precarious finances of the Church, brought lawsuits against Church leaders.[2]

On April 10, 1834, Joseph met with members of the United Firm in Kirtland and agreed that the firm should be dissolved and each member of the firm have his stewardship allotted to him individually as private property.[3] As Max H. Parkin has explained, after Joseph Smith organized the Church in 1832, he put together a management team to direct the early business affairs of the Church. This team operated the Lord's storehouses, printed the 1833 edition of the Book of Commandments (the first Doctrine and Covenants), planned for the new city of Zion in Jackson County, Missouri, and its temples, as it also had done in Kirtland. Most of the revelations about the United Firm were published in the 1835 edition of the Doctrine and Covenants. As explained, financial problems brought an end to the enterprise. The United Firm's responsibilities soon shifted to the high councils.[4]

In this revelation the term "United Order" was substituted for "United Firms," which can be confusing. Orson Pratt called it a "fictitious title." Confusing things further, Joseph renamed the revelation that terminated the firm "Revelation given to Enoch." Undoubtedly, these changes were made to protect those involved from those outside the faith who were critical of the Church, its leaders, and its finances, and to shield them from "peering creditors."[5] Fifty-four changes to the names of officers, business

---

1. The united orders or united firms were businesses, the profits of which were dedicated for the use of the Church.
2. See Robinson and Garrett, *Doctrine and Covenants Commentary*, 3:295.
3. United orders differed from the more common economic orders referred to as living the law of consecration. The law of consecration entailed giving all real and personal property to the bishop in fee simple absolute, to be used for the general good. The bishop would then lease back what individuals (stewards) needed to farm and otherwise make a living. At the end of the year, any surplus was given over to the bishop's storehouse for the general use of the Church and for the poor and needy. Section 104 is about united orders or united firms, a more specialized form of the order. United orders were given specialized functions to perform for the community at large, such as the establishment of a printing house, as is the case in section 104.
4. See Parkin, "Joseph Smith and the United Firm," *BYU Studies* 46:3:33.
5. Ibid., 58.

properties, and places were made in the original revelation.[1] In the 1981 edition of the Doctrine and Covenants, all original names were restored except for the term "United Order" in place of "United Firm."[2] When Brigham Young reached the Great Basin, he borrowed the term "United Order" to describe his new effort to institute the principles associated with the law of consecration in Utah.[3]

The Saints criticized for not living the law of consecration as the Lord had commanded

The Saints' inability to live the law of consecration and implement the principles of Zion was the reason given by the Lord for Jackson County's demise. In rather explicit terms, section 104 details the Lord's complaint against his people. The people were "not faithful"; therefore, they were "nigh unto cursing." (See verse 3.) "Some of my servants have not kept the commandment [law of consecration], but have broken the covenant through covetousness and with feigned words, I have cursed them with a very sore and grievous curse." (See verses 4, 52, 86.) "For I, the Lord, have decreed in my heart, that inasmuch as any man belonging to the order shall be found a transgressor, or, in other words, shall break the covenant with which ye are bound, he shall be cursed in his life, and shall be trodden down by whom I will." (Verse 5.) An equal distribution of the world's goods is a principle about which the Lord feels strongly. He was not pleased that Joseph's followers had not wholeheartedly embraced it and implemented it.

All the things of the earth belong to the Lord

The idea that some can accumulate wealth while others go without is contrary to the ways of the Lord. Since all things in the earth belong to God, he holds title to everything he created. "I the Lord stretched out the heavens, and built the earth, my very handiwork; and all things therein are mine." (Verses 14, 55–56.) Gods plan is to "provide for my saints . . . in mine own way." (Verses 15–16.) And what is that way? The "poor shall be exalted, in that the rich are made low." (Verse 16.) "Therefore, if any man shall take of the abundance which I have made, and impart not his portion, according to the law of my gospel, unto the poor and the needy, he shall, with the wicked, lift up his eyes in hell, being in torment." (Verse 18.)

---

1. Ibid.
2. Ibid., 59.
3. Ibid., 5–6.

The united order and by extension, the law of consecration, operates upon the principle of "common consent"

Control of economic resources was not concentrated in the hands of a few, but rather distribution of resources was to be decided by the "united consent or voice of the order." (See verses 21, 64, 70–72.)

Section 106: Joseph Smith Home, Kirtland, Ohio, November 25, 1834

Heading

Predictions about the Second Coming—it will not overtake the Saints like a thief in the night.

Introduction

Revelation given through Joseph Smith the Prophet in his home at Kirtland, Ohio.[1] This revelation is directed to Warren A. Cowdery, an older brother of Oliver Cowdery, when he was called as a local presiding officer in the Church.

Background

November was a busy month for the Prophet Joseph. He was making preparations for the school of the elders.[2] He described his feelings when he said that "no month ever found me more busily engaged than November; but as my life consisted of activity and unyielding exertions, I made this my rule: When the Lord commands, do it."[3] Prior to this time, in July of the same year, Joseph and others traveled through western New York state to preach and solicit donations to finance Zion's Camp. When the Prophet returned to Kirtland in August, he received the revelation that Warren A. Cowdery should be appointed to preside over the branch of the Church in Freedom, Cattaraugus County, New York. The revelation instructs that Cowdery should be "ordained a presiding high priest."

---

1. Smith, *History of the Church*, 2:170–71.
2. It was in this school of the elders, or, as it was also called, the school of the prophets, that the Lectures on Faith were first given.
3. Cook, *Revelations of the Prophet Joseph Smith*, 214.

Spirits in the spirit world are aware of men's and women's activities on earth

When Warren Cowdery "separated himself from the crafts of men" and accepted his call to head up the Church in Freedom, New York, there "was joy in heaven." (See verse 6.) Based on Cowdery's acceptance of his new calling, the Lord promised that "I will have mercy on him . . . notwithstanding the vanity of his heart." (Verse 7.)

The Second Coming will not overtake the Saints as a thief

The early 1830s occurred at a time when predictions about the Second Coming of Jesus and ushering in of a millennial era permeated people's thinking. Speculation on the timing of these events was common. Both the French and American revolutions were seen as signs of the coming new age. As Bushman points out, "Expectations had not dimmed a generation later. Eighteen thirty-one was a signal year for millenarian activity."[1] In the case of the Mormons, the revelations about Zion and the Second Coming only heightened expectations.

Pinpointing the exact date or time of this cataclysmic event was a point of real interest. In Southampton County, Virginia, Nat Turner "the slave visionary, was awaiting a moment for his people to rise against their masters. In February 1831, he interpreted a solar eclipse as the signal. Five months later, moved by further signs, Turner acted. In August, while Joseph returned from Missouri, fifty slaves armed with knives and clubs slew fifty-seven whites before the outbreak was stopped. Over a hundred slaves were executed in retribution."[2] It was also at this time that "William Miller, later famed for predicting an exact date in 1843 for the Second Coming, began preaching his chronology of millennial events, matching historical occurrences with scriptural predictions."[3] The Latter-day Saints also searched the signs of the times, waiting for Jesus to establish his kingdom in their midst. (See D&C 68:11.)

It was in this context that the Lord confirmed that "the coming of the Lord draweth nigh, and it overtaketh the world as a thief in the night." (Verse 4.) However, the Saints would have a general idea when Jesus would return again. "You may be the children of light, and that day shall not overtake you as a thief." (Verse 5; see also 1 Thessalonians 5:2–4.)

A decade later, after Zion had failed to come about, the Prophet Joseph was pondering the time of the Second Coming. He said, "Were I going to

---

1. Bushman, *Joseph Smith: Rough Stone Rolling*, 165–66.
2. See Bushman, *Joseph Smith: Rough Stone Rolling*, 166.
3. Bushman, *Joseph Smith: Rough Stone Rolling*, 166.

prophesy, I would say the end [of the world] would not come in 1844, 5, or 6, or in forty years. There are those of the rising generation who shall not taste death till Christ comes."[1] (See commentary on D&C 130.) However, despite praying earnestly on the subject, Joseph was unable to understand even the general timing of the second coming. (See D&C 130:14–16.)

Whatever the case may be, Joseph was convinced that there was much that must transpire before Jesus would come again. "It is not the design of the Almighty to come upon the earth and crush it and grind it to powder but he will reveal it to His servants the prophets. Judah must return, Jerusalem must be rebuilt, and the temple, and water come out from under the temple, and the waters of the Dead Sea be healed. It will take some time to rebuild the walls of the city and the temple . . . and all this must be done before the Son of Man will make His appearance."[2]

SECTION 108: JOSEPH SMITH HOME, KIRTLAND, OHIO, DECEMBER 26, 1835

Heading

Lyman Sherman to be one of the "first of mine elders" to be spiritually endowed in the Kirtland Temple. He is to "strengthen" others in all his "conversation, . . . prayers . . . exhortations, and . . . doings."

The big question

Question: How do we live together and build a community now that we have gathered?

Answer: Be spiritually endowed with power from on high and set a good example.

Introduction

Revelation given through Joseph Smith the Prophet in his home at Kirtland, Ohio, on December 26, 1835.[3] This section was received at the

---

1. Smith, *Teachings of the Prophet Joseph Smith*, 286.
2. Smith, *Teachings of the Prophet Joseph Smith*, 286–87. Joseph continued, "There will be wars and rumors of wars, signs in the heavens above and on the earth beneath, the sun turned into darkness and the moon to blood, earthquakes in divers places, the seas heaving behold their bounds; then will appear one grand sign of the Son of Man in heaven. But what will the world do? They will say it is a planet, a comet, etc. But the Son of Man will come as the sign of the coming of the Son of Man, which will be as the light of the morning cometh out of the east." (Smith, *Teachings of the Prophet Joseph Smith*, 286–87.)
3. Smith, *History of the Church*, 2:345.

request of Lyman Sherman, who had previously been ordained a high priest and a seventy, and who had come to the Prophet with a request for a revelation to make known his duty.

Background

Brother Sherman had been with Joseph on Zion's Camp and thereafter was called to be a member of the First Quorum of Seventy on February 28, 1835. He was set apart as one of the seven presidents of this quorum.[1] Just after Christmas he came to the Prophet Joseph and asked for a revelation. The Lord promised that Sherman would receive an ordination in conjunction with the "first of mine elders," a term that referred to a chosen few who were to receive an "endowment" of the Spirit in the Kirtland Temple. (See verse 4.) Brethren who were selected to participate in this important event met regularly in the Kirtland Temple even before it was finished. In this way it was intended that each of the participants would sanctify himself by confessing his sins and asking for forgiveness; covenanting with God to be faithful; having one's body washed and bathed with cinnamon-perfumed whiskey; washing one's own body with pure water and perfume; having one's head anointed with holy oil; having the anointing blessing sealed with uplifted hands;[2] washing of faces and feet; and partaking of the Lord's Supper.[3]

It was not unusual for Joseph Smith to make use of rituals to invite the power of God into the lives of men and women. An interesting example was told by Lorenzo Dow Young, who became very ill and was nigh unto death. Lorenzo's father went to Joseph and asked if there was anything Joseph could do. Joseph explained that he had an appointment he must go to but suggested that Lorenzo get Joseph's brother, Hyrum, and about twelve or fifteen other men. He told them to go to his son's home and all join in prayer, one being the mouth and the others repeating back the words of the prayer. After the prayer, Joseph instructed, they divide into groups of three. "Let the first quorum . . . anoint with oil; then lay hands on him, one being mouth and the other two repeating in unison with him. When all the quorums have in succession, laid their hands on [him] and

---

1. He was released as a member of the Quorum of Seventy in April 1837 because he had previously been ordained a high priest. (See Smith, *Teachings of the Prophet Joseph Smith*, 112.) In a revelation given to Joseph while incarcerated in Liberty Jail, Lyman Sherman was called to become a member of the Quorum of Twelve. He died of an illness at age thirty-five without ever learning of the call. (See McConkie and Ostler, *Revelations of the Restoration*, 860.)

2. The sealing blessing consisted of three parts: a solemn prayer, a sealing prayer, and the hosanna shout. (See Cook, *Revelations of the Prophet Joseph Smith*, 217.)

3. See Cook, *Revelations of the Prophet Joseph Smith*, 216–17.

prayed for him, begin again with the first quorum, by anointing with oil as before [and] continuing the administration in this way until you receive a testimony that he will be restored."[1] Brother Young reported that the administrations continued until it came the turn of the first quorum the third time, when his son was healed.

---

1. See *Lorenzo Dow Young Narrative*, 44.

Chapter 28

Printing House: Kirtland, Ohio, March 1835–August 1835

SECTION 107: PRINTING HOUSE, KIRTLAND, OHIO, MARCH 28, 1835

Heading

Church government, presiding quorums, and offices of the Aaronic and Melchizedek priesthoods described.

Introduction

Revelation on Church government, presiding quorums, and offices of the Aaronic and Melchizedek priesthoods revealed through Joseph Smith the Prophet in the printing house at Kirtland, Ohio, on March 28, 1835.[1] The general powers of the Aaronic and Melchizedek priesthoods are defined. The Twelve met in council, confessed their individual weaknesses and shortcomings, repented, and sought further guidance of the Lord. They were about to separate on missions to districts assigned. Although portions of this section were received on the date named, the historical records affirm that various parts were received at sundry times, some as early as November 1831.[2]

---

1. Smith, *History of the Church*, 2:209–17.
2. The first 52 verses and verses 56–58 were given in response to the request of newly ordained apostles. Verses 53–55 were extracted from the blessing given to Joseph Smith Sr. when he was ordained Church patriarch by Joseph on December 18, 1833. (See Smith, *Teachings of the Prophet Joseph Smith*, 30–34.) Verses 59–100, with the exception of verses 61, 70, 73, 76–77, 88, 90, and 93–98, were given in November 1831 (*Kirtland Record Book*). The verses in the latter part were not received in 1831 and were added in the 1835 edition of the Doctrine and Covenants. (See McConkie and Ostler, *Revelations of the Restoration*, 785.)

The big question

Question: What is the structure of the Church?
Answer: The Church will be administered by presiding priesthood quorums through priesthood offices that govern upon the principle of unanimity.

Anchor section

Memorize: Melchizedek Priesthood

Background

When members of the Church left New York to gather in Ohio, the organization of the Church consisted of elders, priests, teachers, and deacons, led by its First and Second Elders, Joseph Smith and Oliver Cowdery. Over the ensuing years the Church organization evolved and matured, and new quorums and offices were added. By March 1835, the general outlines of Church governance had developed and are reflected in section 107.

About one month prior to the receipt of section 107, the Quorum of the Twelve had been organized (February 14, 1835). They were about to separate on assignments and desired guidance from Joseph. In response, the first 58 verses, excluding verses 53–55, were received.[1] Years earlier, in February 1831, the office of bishop was created when Edward Partridge was appointed. He was responsible for operating a storehouse, helping the poor, and administering property transactions connected with the law of consecration. (See D&C 42:30–39; 58:17.) As the Church continued to grow it was necessary to appoint additional bishops to help administer its business. In December 1831 Newel K. Whitney was the second individual

---

1. On March 12, 1835, the Twelve were called on their first missions. In preparation for their departure, they met in the afternoon of March 28, 1835. Orson Hyde and William E. McLellin recorded the minutes. "On reviewing our past course we are satisfied, and feel to confess also, that we have not realized the importance of our calling to that degree that we ought; we have been light-minded and vain, and in many things have done wrong. For all these things we have asked the forgiveness of our heavenly Father; and wherein we have grieved or wounded the feelings of the Presidency, we ask their forgiveness. The time when we are about to separate is near; and when we shall meet again, God only knows; we therefore feel to ask of him whom we have acknowledged to be our Prophet and Seer, that he inquire of God for us, and obtain a revelation, . . . that we may look upon it when we are separated, that our hearts may be comforted. Our worthiness has not inspired us to make this request, but our unworthiness. We have unitedly asked God our heavenly Father to grant unto us through His Seer, a revelation of His mind and will concerning our duty [in] the coming season, even a great revelation, that will enlarge our hearts, comfort us in adversity, and brighten our hopes amidst the powers of darkness." (Smith, *History of the Church*, 2:209.)

to be appointed to the office of bishop. (See D&C 72; 20:66.)[1] Soon the bishop was recognized as the chief local ecclesiastical office; as time passed the duties of bishops expanded and they presided in Church meetings. For example, when conferences of elders were convened every three months, Bishop Partridge generally "moderated" the session. By 1832 the role of the office of elder in the Church was replaced by a council of high priests, but the bishop continued to be recognized as the local head of the Church. This pattern of governance continued until stakes were organized.

On February 17, 1834, the first stake of the Church was organized in Kirtland, Ohio, along with a high council that replaced the council of high priests and bishops as the local governing body. The First Presidency, which had general jurisdiction over the entire Church, also functioned as the presidency of the Kirtland Stake, "but after Kirtland was abandoned, these functions were separated."[2] In July a separate stake presidency and high council was organized in Clay County, Missouri.

On a general Church level, Joseph had organized a First Presidency, Quorum of Twelve, Quorum of Seventy, and patriarch. At first, the Quorum of Twelve had limited jurisdiction. They presided only in areas where stakes had not been organized. (See D&C 107:33.) Later, in 1841, this would change and the Quorum of the Twelve would be given general jurisdiction over the entire Church.[3] The role of the Seventy during this period of Church history involved special assignments. For example, in 1838 the First Quorum of Seventy organized and led the Kirtland Camp, consisting of 529 people, in their march from Kirtland to Far West.[4]

---

1. Whitney served in Ohio, and Edward Partridge was later called as the bishop in Missouri. Partridge was the first bishop in the Church. He and his family were Campbellites when his wife, Lydia Clisbee, was converted by Oliver Cowdery. He was baptized by the Prophet Joseph and within two months called to be the bishop. Four months after his call he and Joseph went to Zion (Independence, Missouri), where he remained as bishop of Zion. (See Garr, Cannon, and Cowan, *Encyclopedia of LDS History*, 897.) Whitney's call to the bishopric would require him to open his home to the members of the Church. One account states: "Newel K Whitney, staggering under the weight of the responsibility that was about to be placed upon him, said to the Prophet: 'Brother Joseph, I can't see a Bishop in myself.' . . . The Prophet answered: 'Go and ask the Lord about it.' And Newel did ask the Lord, and he heard a voice from heaven say, 'Thy strength is in me.'" (Black, *Who's Who in the Doctrine and Covenants*, 340.)

2. Allen and Leonard, *Story of the Latter-day Saints*, 79.

3. See *Encyclopedia of Mormonism*, 3:1186; Allen and Leonard, *Story of the Latter-day Saints*, 80.

4. See *Encyclopedia of Mormonism*, 3:1301.

General powers and offices associated with the Melchizedek and Aaronic priesthoods

Section 107 explains that there are at least "two divisions" of priesthood, Melchizedek and Aaronic. (See verse 6.) Each of these priesthoods had general powers and responsibilities and each was divided into various offices. The Melchizedek was greater than the Aaronic.

The general powers of the Melchizedek Priesthood were to administer the affairs of the Church, such as presiding at various meetings (see verse 8), and to exercise the "keys of all the spiritual blessings." (See verse 18.) Foremost among these spiritual blessings was the right "to enjoy the communion and presence of God the Father, and Jesus." (See verse 19.) The general powers of the lesser or Aaronic Priesthood were to administer the first principles and ordinances of the gospel (faith, repentance, and baptism) and commune with angels. (See verse 20.)

The offices of the Melchizedek Priesthood include apostles, patriarch, bishop, high priest, seventy, and elder. At first the office of elder was not associated with the Aaronic or Melchizedek Priesthoods. (See D&C 20:38.)[1] Later this office became associated with the Melchizedek Priesthood. The offices of the Aaronic Priesthood include bishop, priests, teachers, and deacons.

Responsibility of the Quorum of Twelve limited at first

Just after the Quorum of Twelve was organized, their duties were confined to the scattered branches of the Church abroad, or places were there were no stakes. "The Twelve are a Traveling Presiding High Council, to officiate . . . to build up the church and regulate all the affairs of the same in all nations." (Verse 33.) Later the Lord sent them on proselytizing missions to foreign lands (1840–41). Upon their return, their duties and

---

1. Just after John the Baptist restored the Aaronic Priesthood (May 15, 1829), he indicated that at some point in the future the Melchizedek Priesthood would be restored. On April 6, 1830, the Church was formally organized. There is a split of opinion among historians as to whether or not the Melchizedek Priesthood had been restored by this time. In any case, at the commencement of the Church, Joseph and Oliver were referred to as the First and Second Elder of the Church. (See D&C 21:18.) In D&C 21:18 and in D&C 18:9, 27–38 (given prior to the time the Church was organized) Oliver Cowdery was likened unto the Apostle Paul. Since this was long before the organization of the Quorum of Twelve on February 14, 1835, it is likely that the term apostle in this context did not refer to a particular office in the Church but was rather used to denote a special witness for Christ. In reference to how members of the Church viewed elders in and around the time the Church was organized, Quinn points out that Joseph Smith and Oliver Cowdery ordained the first elders in mid-1829, shortly after the date John the Baptist restored the Aaronic Priesthood. "In 1829–30 this new 'Church of Christ' reflected the Old Testament model of teachers, priests, elders, seers, and prophets, rather than the offices and callings of the New Testament." (Quinn, *Origins of Power*, 27–28.)

responsibilities were expanded to include regulation of the affairs of stakes. Ultimately, in 1844, Joseph conferred on the Twelve all of the authority, keys, and ordinances that he possessed.[1]

Checks and balances and the principle of unanimity

In the early days of the Church Joseph Smith held a position of pre-eminence. He alone would give commandments to the Church. (See D&C 28:2–4.) However, this changed as the governing quorums or councils of the Church evolved. Once the government of God was established more fully, the focus shifted from one man to the governing quorums, the First Presidency being chief among them. The Lord explained that three persons constitute the First Presidency and "constitute a quorum . . . to receive the oracles for the whole church." (D&C 124:126; see also D&C 112:20.) Furthermore, those constituting the First Presidency "are accounted as equal with thee [Joseph] in holding the keys of this last kingdom." (D&C 90:6.)

This diffusion of power from one person, Joseph Smith, to a quorum of three, acts as a check and a balance because any priesthood quorum or council, whether it be the First Presidency or the Quorum of the Twelve, may not make a decision unless all of the members of the quorum are of one mind. "And every decision made . . . must be by the unanimous voice of the same; that is, every member . . . must be agreed to its decisions." (D&C 107:27.) This system of governance guards against error by making it far less likely that one person will be able to impose his will upon the others.

The establishment of the First Presidency was just the first step in decentralizing power and the decision-making functions. Significant power and authority was also dispersed among the other four governing quorums of Church government, the Twelve Apostles, the Seventy, the standing high councils, and the high council in Zion.[2] Each of these quorums formed a

---

1. See *Journal of Discourses*, 13:164; *Encyclopedia of Mormonism*, 3:1186.
2. At the time this revelation was given there were two high councils. The one in Kirtland was presided over by the First Presidency or Joseph Smith, Sidney Rigdon, and Frederick G. Williams. The other high council in Missouri was presided over by what was called "the Presidency of the Church in Zion," consisting of David Whitmer, William W. Phelps, and John Whitmer. These two groups governed the affairs of the two main bodies of Saints, while the Twelve and the Seventy focused on the preaching of the gospel to the world. (See Robinson and Garrett, *Doctrine and Covenants Commentary*, 4:24.) However, a literal reading of verse 37 indicated that the high council in Zion was to have a special place in the affairs of the kingdom and was equal to all of the other councils in the other stakes of Zion. As a practical matter, when the Saints reached the Great Basin Kingdom, the center stake in Salt Lake and its high council played a central role in governing and training stake leadership in the regions round about. As the Church grew, this function was taken over by the Quorum of the Twelve and other General Authorities of the Church.

body "equal in authority" to one another, although it is clear that the lesser councils were to work "under the direction of the higher councils of the Church," the First Presidency being the highest governing body and the last resort of appeal. (See verses 24, 26, 33–34, 37, 39, 58, 64–67, 91–97.)[1]

The idea that many, not one, would govern the Mormon kingdom was manifest not only at the highest levels of the Church government, but the same principles extended downward into the local organizations. While the highest quorums had ultimate authority and could intervene and give explicit direction to local congregations, such interference was rare. Since all male members were ordained priests, many were co-opted into some local leadership role. By the time the Church established itself it Nauvoo, Joseph would also organize women along priesthood lines. As a result, local governance was left up to local leaders and congregations. Almost all members were expected to play some kind of official role within the local organizations of the Church. They, too, would operate like the highest leaders in the Church, sitting "in council" with each other, setting policy, receiving revelation, teaching the gospel, and administering local affairs. From the First Presidency to the Relief Society to the deacon's quorums, all had tasks to perform and a role to play. (See verses 85–89.) "Wherefore, now let every man learn his duty, and to act in the office in which he is appointed, in all diligence." (Verse 99.)

Bushman points out that "Mormonism succeeded when other charismatic movements foundered on disputes and irreconcilable ill feelings partly because of the governing mechanisms Joseph put in place early in the Church's history."[2] From the beginning Joseph had made it a practice to meet in councils of seven or eight men to decide on mission calls, transact general business, and handle transgressors. Leaders were trained to consult with others and express their views and opinions.[3] As section 107 illus-

---

1. Some commentators have been uncomfortable with the idea that the quorums are in any substantive way equal in authority. Hyrum M. Smith and Janne M. Sjodahl explained, "There can never be two or three quorums of equal authority at the same time; therefore in the revelation where it reads that the Twelve Apostles form a quorum equal in authority with the First Presidency, and that the Seventies form a quorum equal in authority with the Twelve, it should be understood that this condition of equality could prevail only when the ranking quorum is no longer in existence." (McConkie and Ostler, *Revelations of the Restoration*, 792.) However, such a reading of the text misses the import of its clear meaning. There have been times in Church history when the quorums have deadlocked and decisions were put on hold. For example, between 1932 and 1942 the First Presidency and Quorum of Twelve deadlocked over the appointment of an official Church patriarch. The Twelve ultimately relented. Some felt that if one quorum was unified and the other was not, the quorum that was unified should prevail. If both quorums were unified, then this resulted in deadlock. (See Quinn, *Extensions of Power*.)

2. Bushman, *Joseph Smith: Rough Stone Rolling*, 251.

3. In the early days of the Church these councils were often times referred to as "conferences."

trates, priesthood councils became the backbone of Church governance.[1] Based on this observation, Bushman concluded:

> The characterization of Joseph Smith as the prophet with no gift for administration, whose inchoate movement was saved by the genius of Brigham Young, misses the mark. Joseph did not attend to details the way Young did, but he could certainly organize. Almost all of his major theological innovations involved the creation of institutions—the Church, the City of Zion, the School of the Prophets, the priesthood, the temple. Joseph thought institutionally more than any other visionary of his time, and the survival of his movement can largely be attributed to this gift.[2]

That Joseph intended these councils to operate independently of himself is illustrated by the fact that he was not always in charge of the councils he attended. The group itself sometimes chose the moderator, shifting the responsibility from one to another of the more experienced men like Sidney Rigdon or Oliver Cowdery, but sometimes employing new converts like William E. McLellin. Therefore, Joseph could be absent from these meetings without crippling business. It was on this basis that the men in Missouri managed their affairs along with Joseph.[3]

The relationship between the governing principle of unanimity and receiving revelation

Section 107 requires that any decisions made by priesthood quorums in the Church "must be by the unanimous voice of the same." (Verse 27.) In practice this means that a decision made by the priesthood should not reflect the desires or will of one person but rather the wishes of a group made up of persons with diverse interests. This system works best when all of the members of the group are accorded equal privilege and are willing to operate upon principles of righteousness. Consequently, the attitude of mind when making a decision is spelled out:

"The decisions . . . are to be made in all righteousness, in holiness, and lowliness of heart, meekness and long suffering, and in faith, and virtue, and knowledge, temperance, patience, godliness, brotherly kindness and charity." (Verse 30.)

---

1. See Bushman, *Joseph Smith: Rough Stone Rolling*, 251.
2. See Bushman, *Joseph Smith: Rough Stone Rolling*, 251.
3. See Bushman, *Joseph Smith: Rough Stone Rolling*, 252. Bushman makes an interesting observation: "How could an authoritarian religion distribute so much power to individual members? Just as every member was expected to speak scripture by the Holy Ghost, so individual priesthood holders were allowed a voice in church governance, giving them ownership of the kingdom to which they had subjected themselves." (Bushman, *Joseph Smith: Rough Stone Rolling*, 252.)

If this attitude of heart is achieved, then the Lord promises that the spirit of revelation will attend the decision-making process, for "if these things abound in them they shall not be unfruitful in the knowledge of the Lord." (Verse 31.)

None are exempted from the justice and the laws of God

Section 107 sets out an excommunication procedure for all leaders in the Church, including members of the First Presidency.[1] "There is not any person belonging to the church who is exempt from this council of the church." (Verse 81.) Therefore, if a member of the First Presidency "transgress, he shall be had in remembrance before the common council of the church . . . ; and their decision upon his head shall be an end of controversy concerning him." (Verses 82–83.)[2] For that reason, no one is "exempted from the justice and laws of God, that all things may be done in order and in solemnity." (Verse 84.) In other words, all members of the Church are under the same obligation to live the commandments, for God is not partial.

The Aaronic Priesthood reorganized for young men

Prior to the turn of the century, members of the Aaronic Priesthood were generally adults. Therefore, it was common for older men to perform Aaronic Priesthood functions. Furthermore, some wards had no deacons and many no priests. In situations where younger men were asked to participate in the Aaronic Priesthood, some bishops "would not ordain their young men to a particular office until there were sufficient numbers to make a quorum."[3] Quorums held meetings at different times—some weekly, some biweekly, some monthly. Meetings were frequently held on Monday through Saturday. Most quorums were adjourned during the

---

1. When as a member of the First Presidency Sidney Rigdon tried to establish a rival leadership in September 1844, he was excommunicated from the Church. He left with a few followers for Pennsylvania and organized a short-lived Church of Christ. In 1863 he made another attempt, founding the Church of Jesus Christ of the Children of Zion, which failed in the 1880s. (See Garr, Cannon, Cowan, *Encyclopedia of LDS History*, 1032–33.)

2. After the martyrdom of Joseph and Hyrum Smith, Sidney Rigdon tried to assert himself as the leader of the Church. He argued that he had a right to preside over the Church by virtue of his office as first counselor in the presidency of the Church. He presented his claim before the people on August 8, 1844, but was rejected. He returned to Pennsylvania, where he endeavored to establish himself with a following. He was tried for apostasy on September 8, 1844. As a result of this proceeding he was excommunicated.

3. See Hartley, "The Priesthood Reform Movement, 1908–1922," 138.

summer months. Lesson manual materials were selected by the local quorums.[1]

Under the direction of President Joseph F. Smith, priesthood organization was changed and improved. The Aaronic Priesthood was placed in the hands of young men under the age of twenty, and specific age groupings were established for the Aaronic Priesthood.[2] Specific duties were identified for deacons, teachers, and priests. Bishops assumed presidency over the lesser priesthood. Year-round quorum meetings were required. Lesson manuals were provided.[3]

Adam and the life of Adam and Eve

Section 107 recounts a short history of the priesthood, starting with Adam. The history records that just prior to his death, he gathered together Seth, Enos, Cainan, Mahalaleel, Jared, Enoch, and Methuselah (all high priests), along with the residue of his posterity into the Valley of Adam-ondi-Ahman. There he "bestowed upon them his last blessing" and prophesied what would befall future generations. (See verses 53, 56.) The account concludes by informing us that "these things were all written in the book of Enoch, and are to be testified of in due time." (Verse 57.)

This description of Adam's gathering with his family at his death is not mentioned in the Bible (Genesis) account but is mentioned in at least one noncanonical book, *The Life of Adam and Eve*, a pseudepigraphic work. This extra-canonical work informs us that Adam lived 930 years, and "knew his days were at an end and therefore said, Let my sons be gathered to me, that I may bless them before I die, and speak with them."[4] His sons assembled at a place where they "used to worship God," and Adam spoke with them about the experience of death.[5] *The Life of Adam and Eve* was first published in English in 1886 and therefore was not available to Joseph Smith.

The verses dealing with Adam and his posterity (verses 53–55) were taken from a blessing that Joseph Smith Jr. gave his father Joseph Smith Sr. when the Prophet Joseph ordained him a patriarch. He was promised that like Adam, when he was old, he would be given the privilege of assembling his posterity.

---

1. See Hartley, "The Priesthood Reform Movement, 1908–1922," 138.
2. Deacons are ordained at age twelve, teachers at age fourteen, and priests at sixteen. By age twenty most active Aaronic Priesthood members matriculate into the Melchizedek Priesthood and are ordained elders.
3. See Hartley, "The Priesthood Reform Movement, 1908–1922," 154–55.
4. Charlesworth, *The Old Testament Pseudepigrapha*, 2:227.
5. Charlesworth, *The Old Testament Pseudepigrapha*, 2:227.

Two priesthoods or one

Section 107 describes two priesthoods, the Melchizedek and the Aaronic, which includes the Levitical. (See verse 2.) However, Joseph Smith taught that the Melchizedek Priesthood "comprehends the Aaronic or Levitical Priesthood, and is the grand head, and holds the highest authority which pertains to the priesthood, and the keys of the Kingdom of God in all ages of the world."[1]

Appendages to the priesthood

All offices in the Church are "appendages" or helps to the Melchizedek Priesthood to help redeem people and bring about the designs, objectives, and purposes of God. (See verse 5.) It is in this sense that "bishops" are referred to as appendages to the priesthood in Doctrine and Covenants 84:29–30. This idea illustrates that the priesthood is greater than any of its offices, which "derive their rights, prerogative, graces, and powers from the priesthood."[2]

The office of a seventy

The office of a seventy is to preach the gospel throughout the earth. Section 107 implies that the seventy are to help the Quorum of the Twelve and therefore are directly under their supervision. This was not always the case. For many years the seventy worked under the direction of local stake presidents. John Taylor inquired of the Lord about the organization of the seventy on April 14, 1883. President Taylor said that no answer came, but that "everything that shall be necessary for the future development and perfection of my Church" will be revealed through the "channels that I have appointed."[3] This occurred on October 3, 1974, when President Spencer W. Kimball reorganized the seventy. President Kimball discontinued local seventies quorums and established a quorum of Seventy that was given general jurisdiction over the entire Church more along the lines that Joseph Smith had originally envisioned.[4]

---

1. See Smith, *Teachings of the Prophet Joseph Smith*, 166.
2. See Bruce R. McConkie as quoted by McConkie and Ostler, *Revelations of the Restoration*, 786–87.
3. See Collier, *Unpublished Revelations*, 140.
4. See *Encyclopedia of Mormonism*, 3:1302.

The First Presidency chosen by "the body"

Section 107 describes the organization of the "three Presiding High Priests" or the First Presidency and states that they are "appointed by the body," a reference to the Quorum of Twelve. Joseph F. McConkie points out that "Precedence accords that at the death of the president of the Church, his counselors are released and the quorum of the First Presidency dissolved."[1] The body that is responsible to form the new presidency is the Quorum of Twelve. As a matter of tradition the senior member of the Twelve is appointed president and chooses his counselors, generally from among the Twelve. In this system of governance, "No room exists for contention, aspirations of the unworthy, or uncertainty. Nor is the Church left without inspired leadership for so much as a moment, for with his last breath one prophet bequeaths the office to another according to a system instituted by the God of heaven himself."[2] This was not always the case and after the death of the Prophet Joseph Smith, several factions sought to wrest control of the Church.

SECTION 134: PRINTING OFFICE, KIRTLAND, OHIO, AUGUST 17, 1835

Heading

A declaration of belief on the role of governments.

The big question

Question: How do we live together and build a community now that we have gathered?
Answer: Keep the government from exercising its influence over the kingdom of God.

Introduction

A declaration of belief regarding governments and laws in general, adopted by unanimous vote at a general assembly of the Church.[3] The occasion was a meeting of Church leaders brought together to consider the proposed contents of the first edition of the Doctrine and Covenants. At that time this declaration was given the following preamble: "That our

---

1. McConkie and Ostler, *Revelations of the Restoration*, 790.
2. McConkie and Ostler, *Revelations of the Restoration*, 791.
3. Smith, *History of the Church*, 2:247–49.

belief with regard to earthly governments and laws in general may not be misinterpreted nor misunderstood, we have thought proper to present at the close of this volume our opinion concerning the same."

Anchor section

Memorize: On government

Historical background

In August 1835 the Saints assembled in Kirtland, Ohio, and voted to approve the new and revised edition of the Book of Commandments,[1] originally printed in 1833. The book was renamed the Doctrine and Covenants. New revelations were added and some of the revelations originally published in the Book of Commandments were revised, expanded, and corrected.[2] The minutes reflect that Brother Gates spoke, expressed his satisfaction with the book, and "called a vote of all the members present, both male and female."[3] Afterward, William W. Phelps rose and read a chapter on the rules of marriage (monogamous).[4] Then President Oliver Cowdery of the First Presidency rose and read a statement on the role and scope of governments (which became D&C 134). Both documents were voted on and added to the new book of scripture in the appendix.[5]

---

1. The *Book of Commandments* was the first compilation of Joseph Smith's revelations; its complete title was *A Book of Commandments, for the Government of the Church of Christ*. It contained sixty-five chapters. During the publication of this book, the printing office of the Church in Independence, Missouri, was destroyed by a mob in July 1833 and only a few copies survived. A copy may be found in the New York Library, special collections.

2. Joseph and others went back and made corrections in some of the earlier revelations. Most of the revisions are minor and involve changes in grammar and sentence structure. In other instances, Joseph and other members of the committee wrote information back into the text of earlier revelations reflecting their increased understanding at the time of publication. For instance, Melchizedek Priesthood information was inserted into the text of section 20, which originally contained information only about the Aaronic Priesthood. (See D&C 20.) Section 8 on the "gift of Aaron" was the only section that was changed significantly. (See D&C 8.) Another very important change was the addition of the *Lectures of Faith*.

3. Woodford, *The Historical Development of the Doctrine and Covenants*, 1784.

4. By this time Joseph Smith had received a revelation on and was secretly involved in the practice of polygamy. Consequently, questions arose. Was Joseph was morally justified? Was he a fallen prophet? Should others in the Church follow Joseph's example? To help keep the practice secret and discourage others from asking about polygamy, this statement on marriage was drafted. "Inasmuch as the Church of Christ has been reproached with the crime of fornication, and polygamy: we declare that we believe, that one man should have one wife; and one woman, but one husband." The statement also said that a wife and children should not be baptized "contrary to the will of her husband." (Wood, *Joseph Smith Begins His Work*, 2:251.)

5. The appendix contained three statements, the first on the imminent Second Coming of Christ, the second on marriage, and the third on governments (section 134).

Later, the statement on marriage would be removed from the Doctrine and Covenants and replaced by section 132 on celestial marriage for time and eternity or polygamy.

Section 134, and for that matter the statement on monogamous marriage, were not presented as "revelations" but rather statements of "belief" or "opinions." (See preface to D&C 134.) In this respect section 134 is unique. It was adopted at a meeting where Joseph was not present at the time because he was "visiting Saints and preaching in Michigan."[1]

Proselyting to slaves

Section 134 was written to call attention to the Mormon belief in freedom of religion and religious tolerance. It was also written with an eye to dispel concerns the general population in Jackson County, Missouri, had that Mormons were against slavery. In 1833, W. W. Phelps published an antislavery statement in *The Evening and Morning Star* in Independence, Missouri, that played a part in precipitating bloodshed and persecution against the Mormons. In this regard, section 134 assures non-Mormons that Latter-day Saints do not intend "to interfere with bond-servants, neither preach the gospel to, nor baptize them contrary to the will and wish of their masters, nor to meddle with or influence them in the least to cause them to be dissatisfied with their situations in this life" (verse 12). This statement did not reflect the feelings of the Mormons generally and undoubtedly was placed in this section for political reasons. This point is underscored by the fact that in February 1831, Joseph was commanded

---

The statement on the Second Coming was originally written as a conclusion to the *Book of Commandments* and is now section 133. The statement said that the "Lord" was about to come to his "temple" in Zion (Jackson County, Missouri). Therefore, the Saints should "prepare" and gather in Zion. Missionaries should be sent forth to all the nations to invite them come to Zion. All were told to "watch, therefore, for ye know neither the day nor the hour." Jesus will speak from Zion and from Jerusalem in Israel. Land masses will reunite into one single land mass, as it was in the beginning, before the time of Peleg. The Lost Tribes will come down from the north with their prophets to be blessed at the hand of the servants of Ephraim. The tribe of Judah will also be reunited. The Lord will come dressed in red robes, and the "sun shall hide his face in shame; the moon shall withhold its light; and the stars shall be hurled from their places; and his voice shall be heard." All the ancient prophets will join with Christ and the "graves of the saints shall be opened." It was for this reason that the "fulness of his gospel" and the "everlasting covenant" has been restored. When Jesus came to his own, the Jews, he was rejected and therefore they "were delivered over unto darkness ... where there is weeping, and wailing, and gnashing of teeth. Behold the Lord your God hath spoken it. Amen."

By contemporary sensibilities, the tone is somewhat anti-Semitic. On the other hand, the Saints were pro-Jewish and honored the Jews as the descendants of Abraham and heirs to the Abrahamic Covenant. Statements about the Second Coming accurately reflect the expectations of the Missouri Mormons. (See Wood, *Joseph Smith Begins His Work*, 2:247–50.)

1. Smith, *History of the Church*, 2:246.

to preach to "both bond and free" (D&C 43:20), an injunction entirely in harmony with the statement in the Book of Mormon that God "denieth none that come unto him, black and white, bond and free, male and female" (2 Nephi 26:33). And in December 1833, Joseph received a revelation that spoke out unambiguously against slavery: "It is not right that any man should be in bondage one to another. And for this purpose have I established the Constitution of this land" (D&C 101:79–80).

All of this political maneuvering came about in the context of the Saints' pending fear of violence that was predicted in Joseph's revelation on war given in December 1832 (section 87). Concerns were heightened as well because Ohio had "become a hotbed of turmoil . . . [and] inconsequential issues seemed to set off a firestorm that could quickly threaten lives."[1] For example, a thirty-three-year-old Kentucky printer named James Birney started an abolitionist newspaper, the *Philanthropist*, in Cincinnati, Ohio, in January 1836. In no time, circulation reached twelve thousand. In the summer of 1836 a mob destroyed the press by throwing it into the river and scattering Birney's newspapers into the streets. During the same year the Missourians who had suppressed Phelps's paper ran Presbyterian printer Elijah Lovejoy out of the state for publishing articles urging gradual abolitionism.[2]

Not surprisingly, Joseph feared that if Latter-day Saint views on slavery became better known, the Saints might become the subjects of violence themselves. At this point "Joseph Smith . . . recapitulated scriptures showing that righteous individuals such as Shem and Abraham had bond servants, nor did the New Testament apostles condemn slavery among early members."[3] Joseph, however, said he did not know why God allowed slavery among these ancient worshippers. He concluded, "This people [anciently] were led and governed by revelation and if such a law [allowing slavery] was wrong God only is to be blamed, and abolitionists are not responsible."[4] Based upon this reasoning, Joseph determined that Mormons would not preach to slaves without the consent of their masters, but it would be better if "[all] men are to be taught to repent; but we have no right to interfere with slaves contrary to the mind and will of their masters. In fact, it would be much better and more prudent, not to preach at all to slaves, until after their masters are converted."[5]

---

1. Staker, *Hearken, O Ye People*, Kindle locations 6325–29.
2. Ibid., 6325–32.
3. Ibid., 6345–47.
4. Ibid., 6347–49.
5. Ibid., 6350–53.

Separation of church and state and the right to oppose governments

Although section 134 speaks positively about government's role in organizing the affairs of the people, it is not an unconditional endorsement. Governments were ordained of God to govern, but it was not intended that the government have unlimited powers. The government had no business interfering with the free exercise of religion. The Saints believed in strict separation of church and state, as reflected in the statement that "we do not believe that human law has a right to interfere in prescribing rules of worship to bind the consciences of men, nor dictate forms for public or private devotion."[1] (Verse 4.) Section 134 warned:

> We believe that rulers ... have a right, and are bound to enact laws for the protection of all citizens in the free exercise of their religious beliefs; but we do not believe that they have a right in justice to deprive citizens of this privilege, or proscribe them in their opinions, so long as a regard and reverence are shown to the laws and such religious opinions do not justify sedition nor conspiracy. (Verse 7.)

The plain implication was that if government did limit religious worship, resistance by the Saints and Church was justifiable. The issue of whether the laws of God ultimately took precedence over the laws of the state had also been addressed in 1833. The Saints were expected to observe only "that law of the land which is constitutional, supporting that principle of freedom in maintaining rights and privileges." (D&C 98:5.) "Whatsoever is more or less than this, cometh of evil." (D&C 98:7.)

Joseph Smith's campaign for president of the United States

In 1843 and 1844 Joseph ran for the presidency of the United States, in part because there was no candidate the Saints could fully endorse. The Twelve met in January 1844 and unanimously endorsed Joseph's candidacy. His platform reflected many of the same concerns that section 134 addresses—freedom of religion and conscience, and separation of church

---

1. Strict separation of church and state was an ideal to be followed in situations where the Saints were under the governance of non-Mormons. "We do not believe it is just to mingle religious influence with civil government." (Verse 9.) Later, Joseph Smith would begin to establish a theocratic form of government under a legislative body known as the Council of Fifty. Under this system the President of the Church sat as the president of the Council, presiding over approximately fifty legislators, who were seated according to age, beginning with the oldest. Operational procedure required that all decisions be unanimous. Joseph envisioned that nonmembers would sit on this council, recognizing to some extent, at least, the need to include views outside the Mormon community. (See *Encyclopedia of Mormonism*, 1:326–27.) The Council of Fifty would help plan the trek west and serve as the beginnings of a state legislature once the Saints reached the Great Basin.

and state. Of his own run Joseph said, "If I ever get into the presidential chair, I will protect the people in their rights and liberties."[1]

Joseph's concern for religious freedom and equal rights brought him into sharp conflict with the doctrine of "states' rights." The prophet had antipathy for those who asserted that the notion of a separate national and state government prohibited the federal government from intervening and protecting the rights of persecuted peoples, namely the Mormons. The memory of the mobs in Missouri and his pleas in vain for help from the federal government remained vivid. In his journal he noted, "The state rights doctrines are what feed mobs. They are a dead carcass—a stink, and they shall ascend up as a stink offering in the nose of the Almighty."[2]

In reference to the slave question he proposed the abolition of slavery by compensating slave owners for the loss of their slaves and sending them back to Africa, a solution that had been proposed by others as well. Consequently, official Church neutrality on the slave issue, as articulated in section 134, was not adhered to. Joseph called for calm and criticized some of the abolitionists who he said were "fanning the fires of civil conflict."[3] In support of his anti-slavery sentiments, he spoke about "unalienable rights: that among these are life, liberty, and the pursuit of happiness, but at the same time, some two or three millions of people are held as slaves for life, because the spirit in them is covered with a darker skin than ours." On whether the white race was superior to the African American, a view that would be adopted by the United States Supreme Court in the Dred Scott decision in 1857, Joseph said, "They [the negro] came into the world slaves. . . . Change their situation with the whites, and they would be like them. They have souls [a notion not universally accepted in Joseph's day], and are subjects of salvation. Go into Cincinnati or any city, and find an educated negro . . . and you will see a man who has risen by the powers of his own mind to his exalted state of respectability."[4]

---

1. *Church History in the Fulness of Times*, 269.
2. Smith, *History of the Church*, 6:95.
3. *Dialogue*, 3:3:24.
4. Smith, *Teachings of the Prophet Joseph Smith*, 269.

Chapter 29

Kirtland Temple: Kirtland, Ohio, March 1836–July 1837

Section 109: Kirtland Temple, Kirtland, Ohio, March 27, 1836

Heading

Kirtland Temple dedication.

The big question

Question: How do we live together and build a community now that we have gathered?

Answer: Build a temple or sacred place to endow the Saints with spiritual power.

Introduction

Prayer offered at the dedication of the temple.[1] According to the Prophet's written statement, this prayer was given to him by revelation.

Anchor section

Memorize: Kirtland Temple

Historical background

By 1831 most members had started to take steps to gather in Kirtland, Ohio. (See D&C 37:3.) As early as January 1831 Joseph was commanded

---

1. See Smith, *History of the Church*, 2:420–26.

to build the Kirtland Temple and promised that in it his followers would be endowed "with power from on high." (See D&C 88:119; 95:3, 8, 11; 105:33.) At this time the Church was small, a few hundred members in the Kirtland area, and did not have the resources to start a small, let alone a large building project. Under these circumstances, some felt it would be sufficient to build the temple out of logs, but Joseph had other plans, which had been revealed to the First Presidency in a vision, where each saw together what the exterior and interior of the Kirtland Temple should look like. The first floor was to contain a lower court or gathering place "for your sacrament offering, and for your preaching, and your fasting, and your praying, and the offering up of your most holy desires unto me, saith your Lord." The second floor or "higher part" of the "inner court" was to be "dedicated unto me for the school of mine apostles." (See D&C 95:13–17.) The third or attic story would be used for meeting rooms, classrooms, and offices.

The edifice was finished and dedicated on March 27, 1836. Saints from far and near came to witness the event. A repeat dedication ceremony was held on March 31, 1836. Hymns were sung, including the "Spirit of God Like a Fire Is Burning," which was written for this occasion. The sacrament was administered. After the dedicatory prayer was read, the various priesthood quorums, as well as the entire congregation, voted in turn to unanimously accept the building as a holy place.[1] Joseph intended to repeat this process and duplicate the Kirtland Temple in Independence and Far West, Missouri, but his plans were upset by increased persecution. In just two years (1838) the Saints would be forcefully evicted from Kirtland and would abandon their temple. Today this edifice is owned by the Community of Christ Church, formerly known as the Reorganized Church of Jesus Christ of Latter Day Saints.[2]

The temple built in a time of poverty and persecution

Adversity appreciably slowed down construction of the temple. The dedicatory prayer acknowledged that the completion of the temple had come at great cost and sacrifice for the poverty-stricken Latter-day Saints. "For thou knowest that we have done this work through great tribulation; and out of our poverty we have given of our substance to build a house to thy name." (Verse 5.) George A. Smith hauled the first load of stone

---

1. See Cook, *Revelations of the Prophet Joseph Smith*, 218.
2. The Reorganized Church of Jesus Christ of Latter Day Saints was organized after the death of the Prophet Joseph and split off from the main body of the Mormons, who moved west under the leadership of Brigham Young. Emma Smith was a member of this group and Joseph Smith III, Joseph's son, eventually assumed leadership.

to the site. Hyrum Smith and Reynolds Cahoon dug a trench for the foundation. Work continued until the cornerstone was laid and Joel Hill began making bricks. In September 1833 Joseph expressed his hope that the temple would be completed by the spring of 1834, but it was not to be. The members were so poor that "there was not a scraper and hardly a plow that could be found among the saints" to dig the foundation, and at times work was discontinued for lack of materials.

The building of the temple was also complicated during the winter and spring of 1833–34, when circumstances dictated that men stand guard at night to protect the temple walls from destruction by mobs. On May 7, 1834, the project was interrupted when Zion's Camp, an emergency militia, departed for Missouri to help restore the Saints in Missouri to their homes, from which they had been driven by enemies of the Church. This left only a few men to work in Kirtland on the temple. Yet, even though times were hard, the Lord prodded the Saints to keep working on the temple. "Verily I say unto you, it is expedient in me that the first elders of my church should receive their endowment[1] from on high in my house, which I have commanded to be built unto my name in the land of Kirtland." (D&C 105:33.) In early September 1834, when Zion's Camp returned, work continued in earnest. By February 1835 walls were "to the square," and the roof was being put on. By the spring of 1835, "Many of the first elders of Missouri" reciprocated for the help and assistance they had received from the Kirtland Saints and traveled to Kirtland to help build the temple. Yet, still pressed for the means to complete the project, the Twelve Apostles traveled to the East on missions to "solicit donations" to facilitate the completion of the structure.

Joseph was anxious to use the building, and activities were conducted in the temple before its completion. On July 26, 1835, almost a full year before the building was dedicated, Sabbath-day services were held there. Later, its use was interrupted when Truman Angell moved to Kirtland and was given the assignment to supervise and put the finishing touches on the building—interior plaster, hard finish work, stucco, and so forth. In January 1836, three months before the temple dedication, a Hebrew school was held in the "translating room" on the third floor, where Joseph Smith and Sidney Rigdon had been working on Bible revisions.

Finally, after years of hardship and sacrifice, the temple was ready for public use. Rules of behavior were drafted. On March 26, 1836, the dedicatory prayer was written and on March 27, 1836, the temple dedicated.

---

1. The "endowment" spoken of refers to a spiritual endowment or outpouring, not the modern temple ceremony participated in by Latter-day Saints in Mormon temples. Section 124 is the only part of the Doctrine and Covenants were the term *endowment* is used to refer to the temple ceremony.

On March 29–30, 1836, all-day and all-night fast meetings were held. On March 31, 1836, a second dedicatory service was observed. On April 3, 1836, Jesus appeared at the pulpits on the main floor of the temple and formally accepted the edifice. His visitation was followed by the appearance of Moses, Elias, and Elijah who restored the authority (keys) necessary to perform marriages for time as well as eternity and to begin the salvific process of doing vicarious work for the dead. These keys and authorities would soon be relied upon to fashion an "endowment" or ritual that is performed in modern temples to this day.

Content of the dedicatory prayer

The dedicatory prayer was written by Joseph Smith, Oliver Cowdery, and several others.[1] It was filled with Hebraic overtones. In it the Prophet pleaded with the Lord for the visible manifestation of God's presence (the *Shekhinah*), as in the Tabernacle of Moses, at Solomon's temple, and on the day of Pentecost.[2] "And let thy house be filled as with a rushing mighty wind, with thy glory." (D&C 109:37; see also Exodus 29:43; 33:9–10; 2 Chronicles 7:1–3; Acts 2:1–4.)[3] The content of the dedicatory prayer also reflected the ever-present concerns of the Latter-day Saints who were living in Kirtland and Missouri: missionary work (see verses 23, 38–41), persecution (see verses 24–34, 45–53), the establishment of Zion (see verses 58–67), and the events associated with the Second Coming of Jesus Christ (see verses 73–77).

A time of spiritual endowment

The pleas in the dedicatory prayer for a Pentecostal outpouring were granted in astonishing measure, as recorded in the diaries of the Saints. Eliza R. Snow wrote, "The ceremonies of that dedication may be rehearsed, but no mortal language can describe the heavenly manifestations of that

---

1. See Woodford, *The Historical Development of the Doctrine and Covenants*, 1440. Oliver Cowdery wrote in his journal concerning the composition of the prayer: "Attended Heb [Hebrew] school up to Saturday the 26. Nothing of note transpiring. This day our school did not keep. We prepared for the dedication of the Lord's house. I met in the president's room [with] Pres. J. Smith, Jr., Sidney Rigdon, my brother W. A. Cowdery and Elder E. Parrish, and united in writing a prayer for the dedication of the house." (Oliver Cowdery Journal, 21.)

2. Givens points out that there were other indications that Joseph tied this temple to other ancient temples like Solomon's. For example, Joseph "evoked in the very name, house of God" a term that "was used anciently" in reference to the "Tabernacle and later the Temple of Solomon's." He also points out that Joseph's references to "the main chambers of the temple as 'lower court' and 'upper court' further established a connection with Solomon's great Temple with its two courts (2 Kings 21, 23)." (*People of Paradox*, 108.)

3. *Encyclopedia of Mormonism*, 798.

memorable day. Angels appeared to some, while a sense of divine presence was realized by all present, and each heart was filled with 'joy inexpressible and full of glory.'"[1] The high point, of course, occurred on April 3, 1836, when Jesus, Moses, Elias, and Elijah appeared. (See D&C 110.)

The proceedings of the dedicatory and spiritual events were recorded in the official history of the Church.

> The congregation began to assemble at the Temple, at about seven o'clock, an hour earlier than the doors were to be opened. Many brethren had come in from the regions round about, to witness the dedication of the Lord's House and share in His blessings; and such was the anxiety on this occasion that some hundreds (probably five or six) assembled before the doors were opened. The presidents entered with the doorkeepers, and stationed the latter at the inner and outer doors; also placed our stewards to receive donations from those who should feel disposed to contribute something to defray the expense of building the House of the Lord. We also dedicated the pulpits, and consecrated them to the Lord.
>
> The doors were then opened. Presidents Rigdon, Cowdery and myself seated the congregation as they came in, and, according to the best calculation we could make, we received between nine and ten hundred, which were as many as could be comfortably seated. We then informed the doorkeepers that we could receive no more, and a multitude were deprived of the benefits of the meeting on account of the house not being sufficiently capacious to receive them; and I felt to regret that any of my brethren and sisters should be deprived of the meeting, and I recommended them to repair to the schoolhouse and hold a meeting, which they did, and filled that house also, and yet many were left out . . .
>
> At nine o'clock A.M. President Sidney Rigdon commenced the services of the day by reading the 96th and 24th Psalms."[2]

This was followed by prayer, hymns, sermons, the administration of the sacrament, and the sustaining of Church officers. In the afternoon Joseph read the dedicatory prayer. These services were repeated and concluded on the following Sunday, when Jesus visited the temple. (See D&C 110.)

It is fair to say that at no other time in Church history have the gifts of the Spirit been so generally participated in by so many at one time. Many attested to the events that took place, including Lorenzo Snow.

> There we had the gift of prophecy—the gift of tongues—the interpretation of tongues—visions and marvelous dreams were related—singing of heavenly choirs was heard, and wonderful manifestations of the healing power, through the administrations of the Elders, were witnessed. The sick were healed—the deaf made to hear—the blind to see and the lame to walk, in very

---

1. See *Encyclopedia of Mormonism*, 799.
2. See Smith, History of the Church, 2:410–11.

many instances. It was plainly manifest that a sacred and divine influence—a spiritual atmosphere pervaded that holy edifice.[1]

Karl Anderson records in *Joseph Smith's Kirtland* that the Savior appeared not only once but many times in various rooms of the temple. Visions included an appearance of the Father and the Son, multiple appearances of Jesus, and the visitation of angels.[2] Orson Pratt recalled that the "veil was taken off from the minds of many; they saw the heavens opened; they beheld the angels of God."[3] Prescindia Huntington recorded that the "whole half of the congregation were on their knees, praying vocally." Apparently this was the custom when Father Smith presided. Yet there was no confusion: "the voices of the congregation mingled softly together."[4] She also saw "on the temple angels clothed in white covering the roof from end to end,"[5] noting, "They seemed to be walking to and fro; they appeared and disappeared. The third time they appeared and disappeared before I realized that they were not mortal men. Each time in a moment they vanished, and their reappearance was the same. This was in broad daylight, in the afternoon. A number of the children in Kirtland saw the same."[6]

In summary, section 110 records these remarkable services. "Yea the hearts of thousands and tens of thousands shall greatly rejoice in consequence of the blessings which shall be poured out, and the endowment with which my servants have been endowed in this house." (D&C 110:9.) "And the fame of this house shall spread to foreign lands." (D&C 110:10.)[7] The spiritual power displayed was a primary reason so many stayed faithful in the dark and demanding days ahead.

The function and purpose of the Kirtland Temple

The purpose of the Kirtland Temple included the promise of a spiritual endowment, as well as a place for public meetings, school classes, and office space. It became the headquarters of the Church. The main floor functioned as a traditional chapel, with a table for the administration

---

1. See Anderson, Joseph Smith's Kirtland, 170.
2. See Anderson, *Joseph Smith's Kirtland*, 170.
3. Anderson, *Joseph Smith's Kirtland*, 175.
4. Anderson, *Joseph Smith's Kirtland*, 176.
5. Anderson, *Joseph Smith's Kirtland*, 177.
6. Anderson, *Joseph Smith's Kirtland*, 177.
7. Even before the temple dedication, on January 21, 1836, Joseph Smith and his friends had a vision of the Father and Son at a meeting in the west end of the temple's upper story, where the First Presidency had its offices. Present were Joseph Smith Sr., the First Presidency, the presidency of the Church in Missouri, the bishoprics in Kirtland and Missouri, and Warren Parrish, the Prophet's scribe. A partial account is recorded in section 137. (Anderson, *Joseph Smith's Kirtland*, 170.)

of the Lord's Supper. The second floor served as a school room. It was almost identical to the meeting place on the main floor, but it did not have a sacrament table, and there were small fold-down desktops for taking notes. (See D&C 95:13–17.)

On the main floor, canvas dividers came down from the ceiling to separate the assembly room into four compartments so simultaneous meetings could be held. During the middle of the week, when it was customary to hold fast and testimony meetings, it was not uncommon to divide the hall in four sections so more people could participate. There were also canvas dividers to separate the three sets of pulpits at each end of the hall into private rooms. Wilford Woodruff said he would occasionally go to the temple to pray in one of these areas. On both the first and second floor, multiple pulpits were built at each end—nine altogether, with three rows of three each. In the book *Nauvoo*, Glen Leonard describes the function of the pulpits at each end of the hall.

> A single pulpit in most churches of the times lifted the minister above his congregation to symbolize his role as God's representative. Joseph Smith lowered the pulpit and added pews to place the emphasis on priesthood quorums. Behind the single pulpit at each end of the main floor hall were four rising pews. He placed the officers of the higher, or Melchizedek Priesthood at the [west] end, with the First Presidency seated at the top pew, inscribed with the letters P.H.P. (Presidency of the High Priesthood). The presidency of the local stake of Zion sat one tier down, in a pew labeled P.S.Z., and the presidencies of the high priests (P.H.Q.) and the elders (P.E.Q) sat on the two lower tiers. The Aaronic Priesthood officers had seats behind a pulpit at the hall's [east] end, from the bishop and his counselors at the top (P.A.P. or Presidency of the Aaronic Priesthood), to the presidencies of the priests (P.P.Q), teachers (P.T.Q.), and deacons quorums (P.D.Q.) below them.[1]

When the meeting was presided over by the Melchizedek Priesthood, members of the congregation would face the Melchizedek Priesthood pulpits. When the Aaronic Priesthood presided, the seating could be turned around so that the audience faced the Aaronic Priesthood pulpits.

Rituals performed in the Kirtland Temple

One of the distinguishing features of the Restoration was the inspiration Joseph received to employ rituals. He came to understand that a concept is made more real if it is "visibly supported in some way—lived, external, compelling."[2] Therefore, Joseph often instituted rituals that made abstract

---

1. See Leonard, Nauvoo, 243–44.
2. Becker, *The Denial of Death*, 200.

spiritual ideas more concrete and brought people into closer proximity with God. Pageants, crowds, consecrated space, sacred ordinances, and ceremonial dress were employed by Joseph to drive home and memorialize the essence of God's teachings. During the Kirtland Temple era, rituals of washings and anointings were instituted and later modified during the Nauvoo Temple period. At the Kirtland Temple school of the prophets, a specific liturgy was employed to welcome students to class. (See D&C 88:129–37.) A washing of feet rite was also observed. (See D&C 88:138–41.)

In January 1836, three months before the Kirtland Temple was formally dedicated, Joseph described some of the practices he initiated.

> At about 3 o'clock P.M. I dismissed the School [of the Prophets]. The presidency retired to the loft of the printing office, where we attended to the ordinance of washing our bodies in pure water. We also perfumed our bodies and our heads in the name of the Lord.
>
> At early candlelight, I met with the Presidency at the west school room in the Chapel [Kirtland Temple] to attend to the ordinance of anointing our heads with holy oil. Also the Councils of Kirtland and Zion met in the two adjoining rooms, who waited in prayer while we attended to the ordinance.
>
> I took the oil in my left hand, Father Smith being seated before me and the rest of the Presidency encircled him roundabout. We then stretched our right hands to heaven and blessed the oil and consecrated it in the name of Jesus Christ. We then laid our hands on our aged Father Smith and invoked the blessings of heaven. I then anointed his head with the consecrated oil and sealed many blessings upon him.
>
> The Presidency then in turn laid their hands upon his head, beginning at the eldest, until they had all laid their hands on him and pronounced such blessings upon his head as the Lord put into their hearts. All blessing him to be our patriarch to anoint our heads and attend to all duties that pertain to that office.
>
> I then took the seat and my father anointed my head and sealed upon me the blessing of Moses to lead Israel in the latter days. . . .

As often occurred, the ritual preceded a spiritual manifestation.

> The heavens were opened upon us and I beheld the Celestial Kingdom of God and the glory thereof, whether in the body or out I cannot tell. I saw the transcendent beauty of the gate through which the heirs of that will enter, which was like unto circling flames of fire. Also the blazing throne of God whereon was seated the Father and the Son. I saw the beautiful streets of that kingdom which had the appearance of being paved with gold.

Joseph went on to record the appearance of Adam (Michael) and Abraham. He saw his brother Alvin in the celestial kingdom, who had died prior to baptism, and wondered how he could have arrived at this state without having been baptized. The Lord revealed that "all that shall die

The Kirtland Temple, used for worship, a school, and washings and anointings.

... without a knowledge of [the gospel], who would have received it, if they had been permitted to tarry, shall be heirs of the Celestial Kingdom of God."[1] Part of this vision is now recorded as section 137.

In early March 1836, just before the temple was dedicated, Joseph met there with the priesthood. He spent the first part of the meeting in solemn prayer, "without any talking or confusion and the conclusion with a sealing prayer by President Sidney Rigdon when all the quorums are to shout with one accord a solemn hosanna to God and the Lamb with an amen, amen, and amen."[2] Joseph then had the brethren take their seats and lift their hearts in silent prayer to God, noting that if any obtained a "prophecy or vision to rise and speak that all may be edified and rejoice together."[3] Joseph then mentioned in frustration that he had difficulty convincing all the quorums to participate in the prescribed order. He went from room to room "repeatedly and charged each separately, assuring them that it was according to the mind of God." Yet some participated in the recommended procedure and others did not. Joseph felt something was wrong in the elders' room. When he joined them he found that they had not observed the order, causing the "spirit of the Lord to withdraw."[4]

---

1. Faulring, *An American Prophet's Record*, 118–19.
2. Faulring, *An American Prophet's Record*, 129.
3. Faulring, *An American Prophet's Record*, 129.
4. Faulring, *An American Prophet's Record*, 129.

Section 110: Kirtland Temple, Kirtland, Ohio, April 3, 1836

Heading

Jesus, Moses, Elias, and Elijah appear to Joseph Smith and Oliver Cowdery in the Kirtland Temple and restore the keys and authority to perform temple ordinances for the living and the dead.

Introduction

Visions were given to Joseph and Oliver Cowdery in the Kirtland Temple on April 3, 1836,[1] during a Sabbath-day meeting. The Prophet wrote, "In the afternoon, I assisted the other Presidents in distributing the Lord's Supper to the Church, receiving it from the Twelve, whose privilege it was to officiate at the sacred desk this day. After having performed this service to my brethren, I retired to the pulpit, the veils being dropped, and bowed myself, with Oliver Cowdery, in solemn and silent prayer. After rising from prayer, the following vision was opened to both of us."

This revelation was not published until 1852 in the *Deseret News* but was recorded just after it in the Prophet's diary in the hand of his clerk, Warren A. Cowdery, Oliver Cowdery's brother.[2] Later in his life, Joseph acknowledged that persecution forced him to keep secret the circumstances surrounding the restoration of the priesthood from heavenly messengers.[3] Revelations about the priesthood, therefore, were not included in the Book of Commandments. The first printing of section 110 appeared in the 1876 edition of the Doctrine and Covenants.[4]

The big question

Question: What is the structure of the Church?

Answer: Keys and authorities must be restored for the salvation of the human family.

Anchor section

Memorize: Restoration of priesthood keys

---

1. Smith, *History of the Church*, 2:435–36.
2. See Cook, *The Revelations of Joseph Smith*, 220.
3. Starker, *Hearken, O Ye People*, Kindle locations 5238–40.
4. Ibid., 5240–45.

Historical background

On Easter Sunday, April 3, 1836, just one week after the dedication of the Kirtland Temple, members of the Church gathered at their new edifice to worship. About a thousand attended the morning service and then returned in the afternoon for the sacrament.[1] At the conclusion of the meeting, Joseph and Oliver secluded themselves from the congregation by lowering the curtain partition (referred to as a veil) that cordoned off the Melchizedek Priesthood pulpits on the west end of the main assembly room on the first floor. Both men prayed silently, after which they saw a series of visions wherein Jesus, Moses, Elias, and Elijah appeared. Jesus accepted the temple as his house; Moses restored the "keys of the gathering of Israel"; and Elias and Elijah restored the authority or keys to perform temple ordinances for the living and the dead.[2]

As Joseph Fielding Smith pointed out, Elijah's appearance in the temple came on the same day that Jews were celebrating the feast of the Passover, leaving their doors open and setting a place at the table for Elijah. "On that day Elijah came, but not to the Jewish family homes, but to the Temple in the village of Kirtland near the banks of Lake Erie, to two humble servants of the Lord who were appointed by divine decree to receive them."[3]

Joseph did not speak about this revelation to the Saints in Kirtland, and no contemporary explanation was given of what the keys meant. Certainly the keys concerning Moses were not new. Yet the full meaning of what the gospel of Abraham meant would be sorted out later in the endowment and marriage ceremonies practiced in the Nauvoo Temple. After the Kirtland Temple dedication and appearance of Jesus, Moses, Elias, and Elijah, Joseph said that he had completed the organization of the Church and that Zion could now be built. Indeed, he had. All of the governing councils of the Church had been introduced. (See D&C 107.) Yet, as Bushman points out, "The revelation behind the veil suggested that Joseph was moving ahead of his followers. He began to speak of revelations they could not bear."[4] During the next few years Joseph would introduce a higher dimension of priesthood to his followers; Joseph later referred to it as the "fulness of the priesthood." (See D&C 124:28.) Polygamy, the temple endowment, and other higher ordinances and principles would be fleshed out.

---

1. See Bushman, *Joseph Smith: Rough Stone Rolling*, 319.
2. See Cook, *Revelations of the Prophet Joseph Smith*, 220.
3. Woodford, *The Historical Development of the Doctrine and Covenants*, 1458.
4. Bushman, *Joseph Smith: Rough Stone Rolling*, 320–21.

The appearance of Jesus and his acceptance of the Kirtland Temple as his house

The appearance of Jesus to Joseph Smith and Oliver Cowdery can be seen as an answer to the prayer Joseph offered at the dedication of the Kirtland Temple. "O Lord . . . accept of this house . . . thou didst command us to build." (D&C 109:4.) When Jesus stood over the breastwork of the pulpit, he announced in a "voice" like the "sound of the rushing of great waters, even the voice of Jehovah, saying: . . . I have accepted this house and my name shall be here." (D&C 110:3, 7.)

Jesus' appearance was grand, reassuring, and magnificent. "His eyes were as a flame of fire; the hair of his head was white like the pure snow; his countenance shone above the brightness of the sun." (Verse 3.) Joseph and Oliver Cowdery were forgiven of their sins and told, "you are clean before me; therefore lift up your heads and rejoice." (Verse 5.) Christ promised his people that if they would keep his commandments, he would "appear unto my servants, and speak unto them with mine own voice." (Verse 8.) Furthermore, he would not limit his appearances to a select group: "I will manifest myself to my people in mercy in this house." (Verse 7.)

Moses restores the keys of the gathering of Israel

Moses appeared and restored the "keys of the gathering" to bring together the twelve tribes of Israel, which have been scattered to the "four parts of the earth." (See 2 Nephi 10:8.) The lost tribes are gathered by missionaries who invite people to be baptized and become members of the Church. (See D&C 137:6; 3 Nephi 5:20; 21:6.)

Moses also restored the keys or authority to lead the "ten tribes from the land of the north." (See verse 11 and A of F 10.) Bruce R. McConkie explained that the Ten Tribes were first taken as a body to Assyria and then northward, where they were "splintered" and "scattered into all places among all peoples. These Ten Tribes, no matter where they are located, are in nations and places known in the days of Isaiah and Jeremiah and the ancient prophets as the north countries. Hence, their return to Palestine at least will be from the land of the north."[1]

In explaining why the Ten Tribes will return to Palestine, McConkie said that they are "destined to return (at least in large and representative numbers) to the same soil where the feet of their forebears walked during the days of their mortal pilgrimage. They are to return to Palestine. At least a constituent assembly will congregate there in the very land given

---

1. See McConkie, *Millennial Messiah*, 319–21.

of God to Abraham their father. Others will, of course, be in America and in all lands, but the formal return, the return from the north countries, will be to the land of their ancient inheritance."[1]

Elias restores the blessings of Abraham

The term *Elias* is used in a number of different contexts. First, Elias is the Greek form of Elijah, the Old Testament prophet whose ministry is described in 1st and 2nd Kings. Second, "an Elias" refers to any prophet who acts as a forerunner to prepare the way for something greater. (See JST Matthew 17:11, 13.) Third, Elias is sometimes used to refer to a *restoration* of something rather than a *preparation* for something. For instance, the scripture speaks of John the Baptist as an Elias of preparation (Luke 1:16–17; JST John 1:21–22) and Christ as an Elias of restoration (JST John 1:26–28). Fourth, Elias can also be a title for a prophet who restores something. John the Revelator is referred to as an Elias in Doctrine and Covenants 77:9, 14.

This brings us to section 110. In this text the term *Elias* is used to refer to a prophet restoring the keys of the blessings of Abraham. Who this prophet may specifically be is not entirely certain. It could be Abraham himself or perhaps Melchizedek. Some think it was Noah because he is identified as an Elias in Doctrine and Covenants 27:5–6.

What, then, did this Elias spoken of in the context of section 110 restore? The fulness of the Abrahamic Covenant, which included all of the blessings of the gospel, and more particularly the blessings of eternal or celestial marriage. (See Genesis 15:5; Abraham 2:9–11; D&C 130; 132.) As Joseph would explain later in reference to this patriarchal priesthood of Abraham, "Go to and finish the temple . . . and you will then receive more knowledge concerning this priesthood."[2]

Elijah restores the sealing keys

The prophet Malachi foretells that Elijah the prophet will visit the earth prior to the "great and dreadful day of the Lord." (See Malachi 4:5.) At that time he will "turn heart of the fathers to the children, and the heart of the children to their fathers." Joseph interpreted this to mean that the power to bind, seal, or connect family members to each other for eternity would be restored to God's authorized servants on earth. This sealing power, of course, is the basis for eternal marriage covenants and underlies

---

1. McConkie, *Millennial Messiah*, 319–21.
2. Smith, *Teachings of the Prophet Joseph Smith*, 323.

vicarious work for the dead in Mormon temples. The sealing power is the authorization by which ordinances performed on earth are recognized in heaven. (See D&C 127; 128; 138.)

Elias and Elijah restore temple authority or keys

The restoration of authority (keys) by Elias and Elijah is the beginning of the modern temple endowment. The power transferred to Joseph in this vision by these heavenly couriers permitted him to reinstate a set of ordinances and liturgy that would encapsulate the ideas, doctrines, and teachings of Mormonism and what it means to be saved. It would put at the center of Joseph's theology a Mormon understanding of the Abrahamic covenant, which features eternal family relationships, eternal procreation, embodied gods, resurrected personages, the eternal development of God's children, and a concern for the advancement and deliverance of the whole human family from the curse of death and ultimate destruction.

SECTION 112: KIRTLAND TEMPLE, KIRTLAND, OHIO, JULY 23, 1837

Heading

Thomas B. Marsh, the president of the Quorum of the Twelve, calls a meeting of his quorum.

Introduction

Revelation given through Joseph Smith to Thomas B. Marsh concerning the Twelve Apostles of the Lamb in the Kirtland Temple on July 23, 1837.[1] The Prophet records that this revelation was received on the day on which the gospel was first preached in England. Thomas B. Marsh was at this time president of the Quorum of the Twelve.

The big question

Question: What is the structure of the Church?
Answer: The Quorum of the Twelve should take counsel from the First Presidency.

---

1. Smith, *History of the Church*, 2:499–501.

Background

Although section 107 (1835) identified which councils would govern the Church, the revelation did not go into detail on how each of the quorums would be administered and to what degree each would be autonomous. By July 1837, Thomas B. Marsh had been appointed president of the Quorum of the Twelve and was concerned about the cohesiveness of the quorum he had been asked to head. Marsh lamented that his quorum had not maintained close contact since their missions to the eastern states in 1835. Of even more concern was news that some of the members of the Twelve had fallen into apostasy and others (Parley P. Pratt) were planning missions to foreign lands without his knowledge or approval.[1]

Marsh decided to take matters into his own hands and called for a quorum meeting in Kirtland to be held on July 24, 1837. At that time, Marsh undoubtedly intended to bring up the matter of Parley P. Pratt's mission call without Marsh's knowledge or approval. However, unbeknownst to Marsh, Pratt's mission was just the tip of the iceberg. Joseph and the First Presidency had already called other members of the Twelve to serve missions in England, set them apart, and witnessed their departure. In fact, Heber C. Kimball, one of the Twelve, had been set apart and called to preside over the first foreign mission of the Church, in England. And apostles Orson Hyde and Willard Richards, along with Joseph Fielding, a priest, and others had already been assigned to serve under Kimball.

Justifiably, Marsh was somewhat frustrated and distraught over the situation. He went directly to Joseph, spoke with him about it, did not feel that Joseph was sympathetic, and got into an altercation over it. Wilford Woodruff recorded in his journal that Brigham Young remembered that "as soon as they came I got Marsh to go to Joseph. . . . He got his mind prejudiced and when he went to see Joseph. Thomas insulted Joseph and Joseph slapped him in the face and kicked him out of the yard this done Thomas good."[2]

Section 112 was received after Joseph and Marsh came to blows and one day before the scheduled meeting of the Quorum of the Twelve. Marsh served as scribe and Joseph dictated section 112.[3] The revelation rebuked Marsh and pointedly admonished him to "rebel not against my servant Joseph" and clarified that the Quorum of the Twelve should take direction from the First Presidency. (See verses 15–19.)

---

1. See Cook, *Revelations of the Prophet Joseph Smith*, 222.
2. Cook, *Revelations of the Prophet Joseph Smith*, 223–24.
3. See Cook, *Revelations of the Prophet Joseph Smith*, 224.

Thomas B. Marsh eventually falls away from the Church but returns to fellowship

Section 112 emphasized that Marsh should be humble and that if he would the "Lord thy God shall lead thee by the hand, and give thee answer to thy prayers." (Verse 10.) He was specifically admonished not to "exalt" himself, but rather work with the First Presidency and take instruction from them. (See verse 15 and D&C 107:33.) He was reminded, "how great is your calling." (See verse 33.) Therefore, "be faithful." (See verse 34.) Even though Marsh was the president of the Quorum of the Twelve and had seniority over Brigham Young, he would eventually apostatize and leave the Church, thus leaving Brigham Young to stand in his place and become the second President of the Church after Joseph's assassination.

In August 1838 Marsh got crosswise with the Prophet Joseph again, this time over an incident with Marsh's wife, Elizabeth. Elizabeth had gotten into a disagreement with Lucinda Harris over "cream strippings." Lucinda desired to make cheese, and as George A Smith explained, "neither of them possessing the requisite number of cows, they agreed to exchange milk. . . . It was agreed that they should not save the strippings, but that the milk and strippings should all go together. . . . Mrs. Marsh, wishing to make some extra good cheese, save[d] a pint of strippings from each cow and sent Mrs. Harris the milk without the strippings."[1]

What should have been a passing incident escalated into a full-blown Church trial. The bishop decided that Elizabeth had defrauded Lucinda. Thomas Marsh appealed to the First Presidency, who affirmed the lower court's decision. George A. Smith said that "Thomas B. Marsh then declared that he would sustain the character of his wife, even if he had to go to hell."[2] Marsh, embarrassed and dejected, went off to Richmond, Missouri, where he spoke evil of the leaders of the Church and signed an affidavit that helped convince Governor Boggs, the governor of Missouri, to send troops to Far West to exterminate the Mormons. For all of this Marsh was excommunicated from the Church on March 17, 1839.

During the next eighteen years Marsh moved from state to state, sustaining himself as a teacher of biblical geography. Finally he decided to reassociate with the Saints and, in the summer of 1857, Marsh joined the Walker company and migrated to the Rockies.[3] He arrived in Salt Lake City on September 4, 1857, and the very next day visited Brigham Young. Brigham said, "He came into my office and wished to know whether I

---

1. Black, *Who's Who in the Doctrine and Covenants*, 187.
2. Black, *Who's Who in the Doctrine and Covenants*, 188.
3. See Black, *Who's Who in the Doctrine and Covenants*, 188.

could be reconciled to him, and whether there could be reconciliation between himself and the Church of the living God."[1]

Young invited Marsh to speak on Temple Square, where he made peace with the Church and those in the Twelve that he had offended so many years ago. He said:

> My voice never was very strong, but it has been very much weakened of late years by the afflicting rod of Jehovah. He loved me too much to let me go without a whipping . . . for if he had not cared anything about me, he would not have taken me by the arm and given me such a shaking. . . .
>
> . . . I know that I was a very stiffnecked man . . . I want your fellowship; I want your God to be my God . . . I have learned to understand what David said when he exclaimed, "I would rather be a doorkeeper in the house of God than to dwell in the tents of wickedness."[2]

As part of his remarks, he acknowledged his controversy with the First Presidency of the Church. "I have now got a better understanding of the Presidency of the Church than I formerly had. . . . God is at the head of this kingdom."[3]

At the conclusion of his remarks Brigham Young said, "Brother Marsh now wishes to be received into full fellowship, and to be again baptized here . . . I shall call for a vote." The vote was unanimous and Thomas said, "I thank God for it." Marsh was rebaptized. He moved to Ogden. He died in January 1866, a pauper and an invalid.[4]

---

1. Black, *Who's Who in the Doctrine and Covenants*, 188.
2. Black, Who's Who in the Doctrine and Covenants, 188–89.
3. *Journal of Discourses*, 5:208.
4. See Black, *Who's Who in the Doctrine and Covenants*, 189. After the vote that Marsh be admitted to fellowship, Brigham Young commented: "I considered Brother Marsh a great man; but as soon as I became acquainted with him, I saw that the weakness of the flesh was visibly manifest in him. I saw that he was ignorant and shattered in his understanding, if ever he had good understanding. He manifests the same weakness today. Has he the stability of a sound mind? No, and never had. And if he had good sense and judgment, he would not have spoken as he has. He has just said, "I will be faithful, and I will be true to you." He has not wisdom enough to see that he has betrayed us once, and don't know but what he will again. He has told me that he would be faithful, and that he would do this and the other; but he don't know what he will do next week or next year." (*Journal of Discourses*, 5:212.)

Section 137: Kirtland Temple, Kirtland, Ohio, January 21, 1836

Heading

All who have died without a knowledge of this gospel, who would have received if they had been permitted to tarry, shall be heirs of the celestial kingdom of God.

Introduction

A vision given to Joseph Smith in the Kirtland Temple on January 21, 1836.[1] The occasion was a meeting in the Kirtland Temple prior to its dedication. (See D&C 109.)

Background

Section 137 was received at the west "pulpits" of the chapel in the Kirtland Temple. It was first published in the Doctrine and Covenants in the 1981 edition. However, the vision had been earlier published in the *Deseret News* on September 4, 1852. The vision was received on an occasion when Church leaders from Kirtland and Missouri met in the Kirtland Temple prior to its dedication. The brethren participated in anointing ordinances.[2]

Two separate meetings were held during the evening hours, one of which continued into the early morning hours. Visions and spiritual manifestations were witnessed in both meetings.[3] In addition to the revelation recorded in the Doctrine and Covenants, Joseph also recorded on this occasion:

> I saw the 12 Apostles of the Lamb, who are now upon the earth who hold the keys of this last ministry in foreign lands, standing together in a circle much fatigued, with their clothes tattered and feet swollen, with their eyes cast downward, and Jesus standing in their midst and they did not behold him. The Savior looked upon them and wept. . . . I also saw Brigham Young standing in a strange land, in the far southwest, in a desert place, upon a rock in the midst of about a dozen men of color, who appeared hostile. He was preaching to them in their own tongue, and the angel of God standing above his head with a drawn sword in his hand protecting him, but he did not see it. And I finally saw the 12 in the Celestial Kingdom of God. I also beheld

---

1. Smith, *History of the Church*, 2:380–81.
2. See Cook, *Revelations of the Prophet Joseph Smith*, 303.
3. See Cook, *Revelations of the Prophet Joseph Smith*, 303.

the redemption of Zion, and many things which the tongue of man cannot describe in full. Many of my brethren who received this ordinance with me, saw glorious visions also. Angels ministered unto them, as well as myself, and the power of the highest rested upon us. The house was filled with the glory of God and we shouted Hosanna to God and the Lamb.[1]

Oliver Cowdery mentioned this meeting in his journal and said that the visions described came in conjunction with the brethren washing their bodies with pure water preparatory to the anointing with holy oil. He said that after the brethrens' bodies were washed, they were perfumed. He compared the practice to that found in the book of Exodus and said that it was "the same kind of oil and in the manner that were Moses and Aaron, and those who stood before the Lord in ancient days."[2]

The part of the vision included in section 137 sets forth part of the doctrinal premise for vicarious work for the dead: "All who have died without a knowledge of this gospel who would have received it if they had been permitted to tarry, shall be heirs of the celestial kingdom of God." (Verse 7.) The vision then exempts little children who die before the age of accountability from this general principle by stating that "all children who die before the age of accountability are saved in the celestial kingdom of heaven." (Verse 10.)

This doctrine of what happens when a person on earth dies without a knowledge of the gospel raises the question of whether or not it is fair for all children who die before the age of accountability to be universally saved regardless of how they would have accepted or rejected the gospel had they been given the opportunity. Accordingly, a person may be justified in taking the position that "all children will be saved"—but only if they would have received the gospel with all their hearts had they been given an opportunity to receive it. The problem with this position is that, on its face, the statement about little children seems to be placed in the text to modify the general principle—namely, all are saved if they would have accepted the gospel, with the exception of pre-accountable children, who are always saved, regardless. Assuming that all pre-accountable children are saved regardless, does this mean that there is a group of God's children who do not need this earthly experience to be saved in the first place, a group that made enough progress in their pre-earth life that they do not need to be tested in mortality but need only receive a body? Perhaps a limited understanding of a larger context makes it difficult to understand how these two principles (saving adults versus pre-accountable children) interconnect.

---

1. See Cook, Revelations of the Prophet Joseph Smith, 304.
2. McConkie and Ostler, *Revelations of the Restoration*, 1138.

Kirtland Temple: Kirtland, Ohio, March 1836–July 1837

Section 51: Thompson, Ohio, May 1831[1]

Heading

The Lord commands the Colesville Saints arriving in Kirtland, Ohio, to live the law of consecration.

The big question

Question: How do we live together and build a community now that we have gathered?
Answer: Enter into and live the law of consecration.

Introduction

Revelation to Joseph Smith the Prophet at Thompson, Ohio, in May 1831.[2] At this time the Saints migrating from the eastern states began to arrive in Ohio, and it became necessary to make definite arrangement for their settlement. As this undertaking belonged particularly to the bishop's office, Bishop Edward Partridge sought instruction on the matter, and the Prophet inquired of the Lord. Bishop Partridge was appointed to regulate stewardships and property, and establish a bishop's storehouse. Ohio is not to be a permanent gathering place.

Historical background

Five months before Joseph received section 51, the Saints in the East had been commanded to gather in Ohio. (See D&C 37:3.) By May 1831 the easterners began to arrive. The Saints from the East consisted primarily of the Colesville, New York, branch, comprised largely of Joseph Knight Sr. and his extended family.[3] Bishop Partridge was the only bishop in the Church at the time and was the person responsible for providing for the needs of incoming members. Those moving to Ohio had been promised that when they arrived there the brethren would, as the Lord had commanded, divide their land with them. (See D&C 48:1–2.) In addition,

---

1. "We can now show that this revelation is dated May 20, 1831." (Woodford, "Discoveries from the Joseph Smith Papers Project," 30.)
2. Smith, *History of the Church*, 1:173–74.
3. Joseph Knight Sr. was a close friend of the Prophet Joseph. Joseph Smith at one time was an employee of Joseph Knight, and when Joseph was translating the Book of Mormon in Harmony, Pennsylvania, Knight brought much-needed provisions to Joseph and Emma so that Joseph Smith could continue to translate the Book of Mormon.

they were promised that they would receive the law of the Lord[1] and be endowed with power from on high.[2] (See D&C 38:32.)

Leman Copley, a good member of the Church, owned land in Thompson and offered to share it with the incoming Saints. (See D&C 49.) Bishop Partridge made the arrangements and sought guidance from the Prophet Joseph. Joseph went to Thompson and there received section 51. Many years later, in 1874, Orson Pratt said that he was present on this occasion. He said, "No great noise or physical manifestation was made; Joseph was as calm as the morning sun."[3] Still, Pratt noticed a change in Joseph's countenance. "His face was exceedingly white, and seemed to shine."[4]

When the Colesville Saints arrived they immediately began making improvements on Copley's property, a 759-acre plot. They fenced acreage and planted crops. In the meantime, Leman Copley, a former Shaker, had been called to preach the gospel to his old Shaker congregation and lost his faith over it. (See D&C 49.) He returned to Kirtland, broke his agreement with the Colesville Saints, and evicted them from his land. Thereafter, the Colesville Saints were commanded to move to Zion, in Jackson County, Missouri, and live the law of consecration there. (See D&C 54.)

Principles associated with the law of consecration

The law of consecration was originally given in Doctrine and Covenants 42:30–39. Thereafter, other revelations explained in greater detail how the order would function. (See D&C 48, 51, 56, 57, 70, 78, 82, 83, 85, 90, 92, 96, 101, 104, and 105.) Section 51 was written by way of an example (see verse 18) to others who would also be called to live in a communal order. The principles set forth in section 51 were that:

1. Each member of the communal order would be "equal according to his family, according to his circumstances and his wants and needs." (Verse 3.) The principle was that those who needed more than others (larger families, for example) would be given more. In addition, the "wants" of those entering the order would also be taken into consideration.

2. A bishop, in this case, Bishop Partridge, would be appointed to administer the order. (See verse 4.)

---

1. The law of the Lord is contained in section 42 and is a reiteration of the Ten Commandments in a modern day and the command to live the law of Consecration.

2. The "endowment" spoken of in this context refers to the promise of a spiritual outpouring at the time of the dedication of the Kirtland Temple. A covenant-making endowment is not introduced until the Saints settle in Nauvoo and build the Nauvoo Temple. (See D&C 124:27–48.)

3. Cook, *Revelations of the Prophet Joseph Smith*, 69.

4. Cook, *Revelations of the Prophet Joseph Smith*, 69.

3. An agent would be appointed to assist the bishop. The following month Sidney Gilbert was called as the "agent." (See D&C 53:4.)

4. Excess profits or goods would be retuned to the bishop and his agent and be placed in the bishop's storehouse "to provide food and raiment, according to the wants of this people." (See verses 8, 13.)

5. Those in the order should strive to "deal honestly and be alike among this people, and receive alike, that ye may be one." (Verse 9.)

6. The bishop as a full-time Church worker would be remunerated for his services. (See verse 14.)

By comparing the original revelation with the first version published in the Book of Commandments, it is evident that a verse was deleted in the 1835 edition and a substitute verse added.[1] The change was instituted because a Missouri court in March 1833 held that a member of the law of consecration who wished to leave the order could force the Church to give back title to any real property he or she may have gifted to the Church. However, under this ruling the Church was not obligated to return any personal property.

The case in question involved a brother by the name of Bates who apostatized and then demanded the return of the property he had contributed to the economic order. As practiced originally, the property deeded to the Church at the outset was not returned to an individual who wished to abandon his or her commitment.[2] In upholding Bates's position, the court relied on the idea of equity (fundamental fairness) and principles of British common law.[3] The court case caused Joseph, when he was preparing the second edition of the Doctrine and Covenants, to make sure that the printed instructions comported with the court case. "And if he shall transgress and is not accounted worthy to belong to the church, he shall not have power to claim that portion which he has consecrated unto the bishop . . . but shall only have claim on that portion that is deeded unto him." (Verses 5–6.)

---

1. See Woodford, *The Historical Development of the Doctrine and Covenants*, 666. In the 1835 edition verse 2 is deleted and verse 5 is added.

2. See D&C 42:30–32: "And behold, thou wilt remember the poor, and consecrate of thy properties for their support that which thou hast to impart unto them, *with a covenant and a deed which cannot be broken*. And inasmuch as ye impart of your substance unto the poor ye will do it unto me; and they shall be laid before the bishop of my church. . . . And . . . after they are laid before the bishop . . . they *cannot be taken from the church*." (Emphasis added.)

3. See Robinson and Garrett, *Doctrine and Covenants Commentary*, 2:111.

Chapter 30

John Johnson Home: Hiram, Ohio, October 1831–August 1832

The Move to Hiram, Ohio

During Joseph's first two years in the Kirtland, Ohio, area he struggled to set up a regular household. In September 1831, just two weeks after Joseph returned from his travels to Missouri, he moved his family from Kirtland to Hiram, about thirty miles southeast of Kirtland. The move became necessary when Joseph told his followers to sell the Morley farm, the place he and his family were living. The Morley farm was the site of a communal living order. The sale was part of a plan to have Morley, his family, and others relocate to Zion in Jackson County, Missouri.[1] For this reason, Joseph accepted an invitation to stay with the John Johnson family for about six months.[2] Prior to this time Joseph had instantly healed John Johnson's wife's partially paralyzed arm from rheumatism, and it was with a sense of gratefulness that the family welcomed the Smiths as honored guests in their home.[3]

On September 12, 1831, Joseph and his family made the move. Joseph felt Johnson's hospitality as an answer to prayer. A month earlier, he had been commanded to "seek them a home, as they are taught through prayer by the Spirit." (D&C 63:65.) The Johnsons invited Joseph and Emma to reside in a main-floor bedroom with a double bed and a trundle bed tucked

---

1. See Robinson and Garrett, *Doctrine and Covenants Commentary*, 2:201.
2. In 1818 John Johnson and his family had moved to Hiram, Ohio, where Father Johnson, as he was called, purchased 100 acres. Over the years he bought additional land and by 1830 owned 304 acres and a newly constructed farmhouse.
3. *Church History in the Fulness of Times*, 90. After the Prophet arrived in Kirtland, Ohio, Johnson, fifty-three years old at the time, went with his wife, Elsa, and Methodist minister Ezra Booth to Kirtland to investigate Mormonism. While discussing Mormon beliefs, Joseph healed her of chronic rheumatism. The healing led to the conversions of both Elsa and her husband. (See Black, *Who's Who in the Doctrine and Covenants*, 152.)

underneath for their two adopted children. Joseph was allowed to use an upstairs room for an office, which became the headquarters of the Church during the time he stayed there.

The Inspired Version of the Bible

During Joseph's time in Hiram he enjoyed, for the most part, uninterrupted time to study and revise the Bible, with Sidney Rigdon as his scribe.[1] Those who observed the process said that Smith and Rigdon would discuss various passages, and Joseph would dictate changes in the Bible text to Rigdon. Although this process has been referred to as Joseph "translating" the Bible, to speak about it in this way is misleading. Joseph did not purport to be "translating" in the way in which the term is usually used—looking at one language and changing it into another. Joseph never claimed to be using the original Greek texts to come up with a more perfect rendition of the New Testament text. Rather, he made inspired interpolations, additions, and deletions in the King James Version of the Bible by the spirit of revelation.

The process of revising the Bible began in June 1830 when Joseph received "the words of God, which he spake unto Moses at the time when Moses was caught up in to an exceedingly high mountain, and he saw God face to face, and he talked with him," which he used as a preface to the book of Genesis. (See Moses 1:1.) From that time forward, the Lord repeatedly prompted Joseph to continue making changes in the Bible text. Although his later revisions would not introduce whole chapters, entire verses were added, and existing verses were changed. Between June 1830 and March 1831 he worked on Genesis. He probably intended to translate the entire Old and New Testaments, starting with the beginning and working to the end. However, on March 7, 1831, he was instructed by the Lord to stop working on the Old Testament and move to the New. (See D&C 45:60–62.) He began with the gospel of Matthew in March 1831 and continued making revisions throughout the entire New Testament until July 1832. Thereafter, Joseph went back again to the Old Testament and worked on revisions starting in Genesis 24 and completing Malachi in July 1833.

Just prior to Joseph's move to the Johnson farm, he had spent most of the summer of 1831 in Independence, Missouri, exploring and dedicating the land of Zion. Once he settled into his new environs on the Johnson farm,

---

1. At this time the Rigdon family included at least six and possibly seven children. A son, George, was born and died sometime in 1831. The Rigdons settled in the old log cabin where Sidney and his wife, Phebe, had lived a year earlier.

he did little else besides correct and improve the Bible. However, instead of recommencing the translation at the end of Matthew 26:71, where he had left off prior to his departure to Missouri, he started at the beginning of chapter 26 instead. During the process he revised earlier alterations. Some have suggested that the double revision was an oversight, suggesting he simply forgot or did not check where he left off. Another explanation might be that he was not completely satisfied with the changes made just prior to his trip to Missouri. Whatever the reason, it is clear that Joseph did not consider his revisions a finished product cast in stone. We know this because Joseph went back and made double revisions in other places in the New Testament as well. For example, he changed for a second time the text in 2 Peter 3:4–6 about scoffers in the last days.[1] Regardless, the reediting of Matthew did not result in a text that was markedly different from what Joseph did the first time around.[2]

Section 1: John Johnson Home, Hiram, Ohio, November 1, 1831[3]

Heading

Preface to the Doctrine and Covenants.

The big question

Question: How do we live together and build a community now that we have gathered?

---

1. See Jackson and Jasinski, "The Process of Inspired Translation," 36, 39. Those who make the argument that Joseph simply forgot, point to the fact that the "translation" was interrupted for at least three months by the Prophet's first trip to Missouri and all of the events associated with it. (See Jackson and Jasinski, "The Process of Inspired Translation," 41.)

2. The differences in the two translations of the same text are not substantive and give us insight into the translation process. In both instances Joseph reworded language to improve clarity, modernized the archaic King James language, and introduced new content. (See Jackson and Jasinski, "The Process of Inspired Translation," 58.) Kent P. Jackson and Peter M. Jasinski point out that "we see that in both translations the Prophet added the same thought, yet he rarely expressed that thought in the same words, and sometimes it was not even inserted at the same location." (Jackson and Jasinski, "The Process of Inspired Translation," 59.) By observing Joseph's modus operandi, it appears that he was left to clothe his spiritual insights and impressions as best he could in his own language. This puts forward the idea that scriptural language is loosely constructed and need not be strictly interpreted. The focus should not be on the meaning of a particular word or the placement of a comma, but rather on the general idea expressed.

3. This section was received November 1, 1831. (See Woodford, "Discoveries from the Joseph Smith Papers Project," 31.)

Answer: Canonize and act upon the revelations of Joseph Smith.

Introduction

Revelation given through Joseph Smith at the John Johnson home in Hiram, Ohio, during a special conference of elders of the Church in the John Johnson home on November 1, 1831.[1] Many revelations had been received from the Lord prior to this time, and the compilation of these for publication in book form was one of the principal subjects passed upon at the conference. This section constitutes the Lord's Preface to the doctrines, covenants, and commandments given in this dispensation.

Anchor section

Memorize: Preface

Historical background

Section 1 is referred to as the "Lord's Preface" because it serves as an introduction to the Doctrine and Covenants. The section summarizes many of the major doctrines of the restoration and refutes a number of doctrines commonly taught by traditional Christianity during the time of Joseph. The preface makes it clear that God approves of the compilation of this new book of scripture. The revelation touches on missionary work, the apostasy, the Second Coming, the restoration of the gospel, salvation by works, the idea that all men and woman may receive revelation, the importance of the Book of Mormon, forgiveness, and the value of studying the scriptures.

Joseph and Emma had been invited to live in the John Johnson home located about thirty miles southeast of Kirtland. The Smiths arrived on September 12, 1831, and left on April 1, 1832, about seven months later. The Johnsons were particularly grateful to Joseph because he had miraculously healed John Johnson's wife, Elsa. In the spring of 1831 Ezra Booth brought the Johnsons and others to Kirtland. Elsa's arm was partially paralyzed from rheumatism, and she could not lift her arm above her head. While a group of people were visiting with the Prophet Joseph, the discussion turned to whether or not anyone could heal Elsa's arm. Joseph approached Elsa and took her by the hand and calmly said, "Woman in the name of the Lord Jesus Christ I command thee to be whole." Elsa was immediately healed.[2] Those present were speechless as Joseph left. For

---

1. Smith, *History of the Church*, 1:221–24.
2. See *Church History in the Fulness of Times*, 94.

years thereafter Elsa could raise her arm and could hang the wash on the clothesline with ease. Ezra Booth and the Johnsons joined the Church as a result of this miraculous incident.

It must have been with a willing heart and a debt of gratitude that the Johnsons welcomed Joseph and Emma to live with them. Sidney Rigdon also moved to Hiram to assist Joseph as his scribe. Joseph and Emma slept in a bedroom on the main floor of the Johnson home. Sidney lived in a log home located on the farm. Joseph was offered space on the second floor of the Johnson home as temporary office headquarters of the Church while he resided there.

During the time that Joseph resided at the Johnson farm, the Prophet received seventeen sections of the Doctrine and Covenants—1, 65, (66), 67, 68, 69, 71, 73, 74, 76, 77, (78), 79, 80, 81, 99, and 133. (The sections in parenthesis indicate that the revelation probably came at the Johnson farm location, but historians are not entirely sure.) Joseph also continued to work on the Inspired Version of the Old and New Testament.

The need for a new book of scripture

Members of the Church knew that Joseph had received and was receiving many revelations from God. The Saints took comfort in the knowledge that God was making his will known and referred to Joseph's revelations as "commandments." While they enjoyed listening to the Prophet Joseph's sermons, they preferred and often implored Joseph to receive a commandment from the Lord so that it could be written down for future reference.

Some members of the Church convinced Joseph to let them copy some of his revelations, which they carried around on their person for reference purposes. These copies were known as "pocket revelations." One can just imagine new converts conversing on a point of doctrine and reaching into their grubby overalls to consult an authoritative statement from the Prophet of God. Joseph also made some copies of his revelations available to the members in *The Evening and the Morning Star*, an official Church publication.

As more revelations came and interest in them intensified, Joseph decided to call a special conference of high priests of the Church beginning on November 1, 1831, to consider whether or not some of his revelations ought to be compiled in a book of scripture like the Bible or Book of Mormon.[1] Conference sessions were held over a twelve-day period in five

---

1. Here, again, we see the Prophet's modus operandi when making major Church decisions. He would convene a special council or conference and proceed to discuss the matter with them. This procedure was eventually canonized in D&C 107:27–31.

separate meetings. Questions were raised about how many and which of the revelations should or should not be published. Between sessions, section 1 was written down. As stated, its purpose was to serve as an introduction or preface to this newly proposed book of scripture.

There must have been a sense of excitement at the conference. Christians generally believed that the canon of scripture was closed and that God had revealed all that was necessary for a modern world to know about him in the Bible. The very idea of producing a new book of scripture by a living prophet was a startling proposition and brought into sharp focus the idea that God was now speaking to the world as directly as he did through earlier prophets like Peter, Paul, Moses, and Abraham.

As might be expected, some questioned the idea of a modern scripture and expressed skeptical criticism. William E. McLellin and some others made derogatory comments about some of Joseph's revelations because some contained a few grammatical errors and sentence construction was sometimes awkward. In response to the doubters and specifically in response to McLellin, Joseph received section 67, which confirmed the genuineness of Joseph's revelations and challenged any who thought they could do better to try to duplicate what Joseph had done.

McLellin failed miserably when he put the challenge to the test and attempted to write a revelation on his own.[1] His letdown was noted by those present at the conference and by the fact that McLellin dropped the matter. Joseph remarked of McLellin that "he endeavored to write a commandment like unto one of the least of the Lord's, but failed."[2] In 1836 McLellin apostatized from the Church but never lost his testimony of the Book of Mormon. He was heard to say just three years before his death, "I have set my seal that the Book of Mormon is a true, divine record and it will require more evidence than I have ever seen to ever shake me relative to its purity."[3]

Inherent in McLellin's condemnation of Joseph's revelations was the assumption that revelations from God are dictated to the recipient word for word. McLellin did not understand what Orson Pratt, another devoted follower of Joseph, did. Pratt observed that on occasion "Joseph the Prophet in writing the Doctrine and Covenants, received ideas from God, but clothed those ideas with such words as came to mind."[4] Orson was not

---

1. McLellin had been a member of the Church for only a few months, having joined the Church in the summer of 1831. He was an experienced teacher and undoubtedly more educated than the Prophet. In McLellin's mind, he was justly critical of what he considered to be substandard revelatory language. This view may have contributed to his later apostasy.
2. Smith, *History of the Church*, 1:226.
3. Black, *Who's Who in the Doctrine and Covenants*, 192.
4. Woodford, *The Historical Development of the Doctrine and Covenants*, 9.

alone in this understanding. Such things were openly talked about during the conference sessions.

In the meeting held on November 8, 1831, Sidney Rigdon spoke concerning the mistakes and errors in the revelations to be published and called for a vote of the conference to make corrections. It was "Resolved, by this conference that Brother Joseph Smith, Jr. correct those errors or mistakes which he may discover by the Holy Spirit."[1] The preface itself makes reference to the problem of writing down revelations from God. "These commandments are of me, and were given unto my servants in their weakness, after the manner of their language, that they might come to understanding." (Verse 24.)

The idea that it was necessary to correct the revelations of Joseph was extended to the Bible as well. It was also resolved that Joseph should make corrections in the "fulness of the scripture," which he did as he continued to work on revisions of portions of the Bible.[2] Joseph referred to this process of clarifying points in the Bible as a "translation." However, the use of this word is misleading, since Joseph did not have original Greek manuscripts in front of him and never claimed to be a "translator" in the traditional sense of the word. Understood correctly, "translation" of the Bible in Joseph Smith's mind meant writing into the text inspired interpolations and clarifications.

The method by which the Prophet received section 1

William Kelley, one of the persons present when this revelation was given, describes the circumstances. "A committee had been appointed to draft a preface, consisting of O. Cowdery and, I think Sidney Rigdon, but when they made their report ... the conference then requested Joseph to enquire of the Lord about it, and he said that he would if the people would bow in prayer with him. This they did and Joseph prayed."

After the prayer Joseph dictated "by the spirit" the preface while he sat by a window during a conference session with everyone present. Sidney Rigdon wrote the revelation down. "Joseph would deliver a few sentences and Sidney would write them down, then read them aloud, and if correct, Joseph would proceed and deliver more, and by this process the preface was given."[3]

At the end of the conference a new book of scripture was approved and it was voted that ten thousand copies be printed. However, due to the

---

1. Woodford, *The Historical Development of the Doctrine and Covenants*, 24.
2. See Woodford, *The Historical Development of the Doctrine and Covenants*, 24.
3. William Kelly quoted in Backman, *Joseph Smith and the Doctrine and Covenants*, 2.

circumstances of the Saints, this number was later reduced significantly. The first printing began but was halted on July 10, 1833, when a mob in Independence, Missouri, destroyed the printing press along with all but a few unbound sheets of what was titled the Book of Commandments.[1]

Section 65: John Johnson Home, Hiram, Ohio, October 1831[2]

Heading

A prayer that God's kingdom might be established on the earth—a stone cut out of the mountain.

Introduction

Revelation given through Joseph Smith, received in October 1831 at the John Johnson home located in Hiram, Ohio.[3] The Prophet designates this revelation as a prayer.

Historical background

Joseph Smith remembered this revelation coming in early October 1831. However, the *Kirtland Revelation Book*, *The Evening and the Morning Star*, and William McLellin's manuscript all date it later in the month, on October 30, 1831. The McLellin manuscript also adds that Joseph received this revelation when studying Matthew 6:10, "Thy kingdom come. Thy will be done in earth, as it is in heaven."[4]

---

1. See Cook, *Revelations of the Prophet Joseph Smith*, 4.
2. "We can now establish this date as October 30, 1831." (Woodford, "Discoveries from the Joseph Smith Papers Project," 30.)
3. Smith, *History of the Church*, 1:218.
4. Robinson and Garrett, *Doctrine and Covenants Commentary*, 2:221.

The prayer for the kingdom to be established on earth as it is in heaven

The prayer portion of the revelation comes in the concluding verse: "Wherefore, may the kingdom of God go forth, that the kingdom of heaven may come, that thou, O God mayest be glorified in heaven so on earth, that thine enemies may be subdued; for thine is the honor, power and glory, forever and ever, Amen." (Verse 6.)

The prayer comes in response to two invitations to pray: "Pray unto the Lord" and "Call upon the Lord."[1] (See verses 4 and 5.)

The idea of the kingdom of heaven being established on earth plays a central role in Mormon theology, as it does in the New Testament. Joseph understood that this earth was to become a celestial kingdom, completely transformed and dedicated to God's purposes. The idea was expressed in the notion that not only would there be a "new heaven" but also a "new earth" that would epitomize the kingdom of God. In this kingdom the Saints would continue to advance and live together in a society patterned after God's society. To live in this social unit, our promised resurrection was necessary that we might live in this "new and gloriously embodied reality."[2]

This vision of the future of mankind is quite different from the vision shared by most Protestant and other Christians, who think about a future life in terms of being rescued from death, "going to heaven," singing praises to God, and resting from the cares and troubles of this world. As long as salvation is seen in these terms—going to heaven—"the main work of the church is bound to be seen in terms of saving souls for that future. But when we see salvation, as the New Testament sees it"[3] (and as Joseph did)—in terms of a righteous society ever advancing the human race—then we understand what Joseph's kingdom building is all about in the Doctrine and Covenants and what Jesus prayed for. "Thy Kingdom come. Thy will be done in earth, as it is in heaven." (Matthew 6:10.)

The stone cut out of the mountain that rolls forth

Section 65 refers to a "stone which is cut out of the mountain without hands" which "shall roll forth, until it has filled the earth. The "stone" is a reference to Daniel's interpretation of King Nebuchadnezzar's dream. (See Daniel 2.) The Prophet Joseph understood this prophetic night vision to be a reference to the establishment and growth of the kingdom of God,

---

1. Verse 4 admonishes, "Pray unto the Lord," and verse 5 refrains, "Call upon the Lord."
2. See Wright, *Surprised by Hope*, 197.
3. Wright, *Surprised by Hope*, 197.

or the restored Church. In this vision the king of Babylon saw a large statue in the shape of a man constructed of various substances. The head was of gold, the breast of silver, the belly and thighs of brass, the legs of iron, and the feet of a mixture of iron and clay. (See Daniel 2:32–33.) A stone which was "cut out without hands" struck the image on its feet and broke it into tiny pieces. Meanwhile the stone that smashed the image rolled forward until it became as large as a mountain and filled the whole earth. (See Daniel 2:34–35.)

Daniel stated that the "statue" represented a succession of world monarchies and the "stone" represented the kingdom of God. Scholars have surmised that the statue represents a historical timeline and explains a succession of kingdoms in and around the time Daniel lived. The gold head represented Nebuchadnezzar's kingdom and the Babylonian Empire (610 B.C. to 539 B.C.). The breast and arms of silver stand for the Persian Empire under Cyrus (539 B.C. to 63 B.C.). The belly and thighs of brass correspond to the Mesopotamian Empire established by Alexander the Great (330 B.C. to 63 B.C.). The legs of iron signify the Roman Empire (63 B.C. to A.D. 636). Students of the Bible have suggested that the "part of iron, and part of clay" represent the nations of the earth after the fall of the Roman empire.

The "stone" described in Daniel's dream was unlike the statue or kingdoms of this world built with "human hands," where each succeeding domain depended upon the ruin and collapse of previous empires. Rather, the "stone" was "cut out without hands" or in other words, it was of divine creation. According to Joseph, it was the restored Church that would continue to grow and expand until it filled the earth and ushered in the Millennium. For that reason, this "stone" of God's making would thrive, "roll forth," fill the earth, and never be destroyed or broken in pieces.[1] That Joseph associated himself with the establishment of this kingdom there is no doubt. "I [Joseph] calculate to be one of the instruments of setting up the kingdom of Daniel by the word of the Lord, and I intend to lay a foundation that will revolutionize the whole world."[2]

Section 66: Hiram, Ohio, October 25, 1831[3]

Heading

A revelation to William E. McLellin.

---

1. See Preece, *Learning to Love the Doctrine and Covenants*, 125–26.
2. Smith, *Teachings of the Prophet Joseph Smith*, 366.
3. "We now know the date to be October 29, 1831." (Woodford, "Discoveries from the Joseph Smith Papers Project," 30.)

Introduction

Revelation given through Joseph Smith in Hiram, Ohio, on October 25, 1831.[1] This was the first day of an important conference. In prefacing this revelation, the Prophet wrote, "At the request of William E. McLellin, I inquired of the Lord, and received the following."

Revelation received in Hiram, not Orange, Ohio

The heading to section 66 indicates that it was received in Orange, Ohio. This is not the case. The revelation was received in the upper room of the Johnson home located in Hiram, Ohio. The revelation was directed to William E. McLellin, who also acted as scribe. In his journal he notes that Joseph had been in Orange for a conference but returned to his residence in Hiram before receiving this revelation.[2]

Historical background

In July 1831 David Whitmer and Harvey Whitlock were on their way to Zion, located in Jackson County, Missouri. (See D&C 52:25.) En route they stopped in Paris, Illinois, where they became acquainted with William E. McLellin, who expressed an interest in the gospel. McLellin decided to travel to Zion in company with Whitmer and Whitlock because he understood that the Prophet Joseph was there. However, by the time McLellin arrived, the Prophet had left for Kirtland, Ohio, and the two could not meet. Regardless, McLellin decided to be baptized in Jackson County and soon thereafter was ordained an elder.[3]

McLellin eventually made his way to Ohio to meet the Prophet Joseph. He arrived at the time a special conference was being held in Orange, Ohio, which Joseph had convened to consider the publications of his revelations. McLellin met the Prophet and was ordained to the high priesthood, along with sixteen others.[4] While in company with Joseph, he requested a revelation or "commandment" on his behalf and section 66 was received.[5]

Two years later, in 1833, McLellin wrote to his relatives about the circumstances under which section 66 was given. He said that he had attended the Orange conference with about forty elders. After the conference, McLellin went with Joseph to the Prophet's residence in Hiram, Ohio, and lived

---

1. Smith, *History of the Church*, 1:219–21.
2. See Robinson and Garrett, *Doctrine and Covenants Commentary*, 2:226.
3. See *Journals of William E. McLellin*, 33–34.
4. See Cook, *Revelations of the Prophet Joseph Smith*, 105.
5. See Woodford, *The Historical Development of the Doctrine and Covenants*, 838.

with him for about three weeks. Of the experience McLellin said, "From my acquaintance then and until now I can truly say I believe him to be a man of God. A Prophet, a Seer and Revelator to the Church of Christ."[1]

In 1835 McLellin was chosen to be one of the Twelve Apostles at the organization of that quorum. He went east on a mission and baptized five converts. While serving his mission, for some reason he became disaffected and wrote a letter to the First Presidency in Kirtland, criticizing them. Thereafter, he was disfellowshipped. A few months later he confessed the error of his thinking and returned to full fellowship.[2]

About three years later, in May 1838, he again lost confidence in the First Presidency and was tried before a bishop's court in Far West and excommunicated for his "sinful lusts"; this was a problem that must have plagued McLellin for some time because it was mentioned in section 66. ("Seek not to be cumbered. Forsake all unrighteousness. Commit not adultery—a temptation with which thou hast been troubled."—Verse 10.) Heber C. Kimball and others were also aware of McLellin's propensities. Kimball recorded a conversation in his journal with McLellin in which McLellin queried, "Brother Heber, what do you think of Joseph Smith the fallen prophet, now, has he not led you blindfolded long enough; look and see yourself poor, your family fix, are you satisfied with Joseph?" Heber replied that he was "more satisfied with . . . [Joseph] a hundred fold, than ever I was before."[3] In Kimball's diary he then records a conversation with the Prophet wherein Joseph had made mention to Kimball that he had warned McLellin that he would "be a Judas to betray your brethren, if you did not forsake your adultery, fornication, lying and abominations."[4]

After McLellin's excommunication, he became a bitter enemy to the Church and tried to establish his own church without success. He even actively participated in persecuting the Saints by joining with the mobs in Missouri. While Joseph and others were imprisoned in Richmond, Missouri, McLellin attended the Prophet's trial and asked for permission to flog Joseph. Although McLellin was a large man, he wanted to use a club in the beating and limit Joseph to defending himself with his fists. Joseph agreed, but the sheriff did not allow the spectacle to take place unless the odds were even.[5] McLellin backed down.

---

1. Woodford, *The Historical Development of the Doctrine and Covenants*, 839.
2. See Preece, *Learning to Love the Doctrine and Covenants*, 129.
3. Woodford, *The Historical Development of the Doctrine and Covenants*, 839.
4. Woodford, *The Historical Development of the Doctrine and Covenants*, 839.
5. See Preece, *Learning to Love the Doctrine and Covenants*, 129.

Five questions

McLellin's initial respect and esteem for the Prophet Joseph grew out of his contact with Joseph at the time this revelation was received on his behalf. He wrote in his journal that the revelation came after he had made a special request of the Lord. "I went before the Lord in secret, and on my knees asked him to reveal the answer to five questions through his Prophet, and that too without his having any knowledge of my having made such a request."[1] McLellin acknowledged in his journal that section 66 did answer each of his five questions. McLellin copied section 66 into his journal and then ended his entry for the day by commenting that "this revelation gives great joy to my heart because some important questions were answered which had dwelt upon my mind with anxiety yet with uncertainty."[2] McLellin repeated this same sentiment ten years after his disaffection from the Church in an article published in the *Ensign of Liberty*.

"I now testify in the fear of God, that every question which I thus lodged in the ears of the Lord of Sabbath, were answered to my full and entire satisfaction. I desired for a testimony of Joseph's inspiration. And I to this day considered it to me an evidence which I cannot refute."[3]

Although McLellin never left a list of the questions he had in mind, the editors of McLellin's journal, Jan Shipps and John W. Welch, put forward what they believe the questions were based on McLellin's diary and section 66.

Question 1: How does this little church that I have just joined, organized by Joseph Smith, fit into the religions of the world?

Answer: It represents mine everlasting covenant, even the fulness of my gospel, sent forth unto the children of men, that they might have life and be made partakers of glories which are to be revealed in the last days, as it was written by the prophets and apostles of old. (D&C 66:2.)

Question 2: What is my spiritual standing?

Answer: You are clean, but not all; repent therefore of those things which are not pleasing in my sight, saith the Lord, for the Lord will show them unto you. (D&C 66:3.)

Question 3: What is my role in the Church? I have closed my school and settled my affairs in Illinois. What am I to do now?

Answer: It is my will that you should proclaim my gospel, from land to land and from city to city . . . Tarry not many days in this place [Ohio]; go not up unto the land of Zion [Missouri] as yet; but inasmuch as you can send, send; otherwise think not of property. . . . Go unto the eastern lands,

---

1. *Journals of William E. McLellin*, 248.
2. *Journals of William E. McLellin*, 249.
3. See *Journals of William E. McLellin*, 249.

bear testimony in every place . . . reasoning with the people. . . . Let my servant Samuel H. Smith go with you, and forsake him not. (D&C 66:5–8.)

Question 4: I have seen and personally experienced the power to heal by both Joseph and Hyrum Smith. Will I be able to have this power?

Answer: Lay your hands upon the sick, and they shall recover. (D&C 66:9.)

Question 5: How can I escape the temptations of adultery and other sins which have burdened me, especially since the recent death of my wife?[1]

Answer: Be patient in affliction. Ask, and ye shall receive; knock and it shall be opened unto you. Seek not to be cumbered. Forsake all unrighteousness. Commit not adultery, a temptation with which thou hast been troubled. . . . Continue in these things even unto the end, and you shall have a crown of eternal life at the right hand of my Father who is full of grace and truth. (D&C 66:9, 10, 12.)[2]

McLellin's commission to preach in the East revoked

McLellin's commission in verse 7 to preach the gospel "unto the eastern lands" was revoked on January 25, 1832. By that time, he had lost the confidence of the Prophet Joseph.[3]

SECTION 67: JOHN JOHNSON HOME, HIRAM, OHIO, NOVEMBER 1831[4]

Heading

Conference held to discuss the publication of Joseph's revelations. Some critical of his revelations challenged to do better. William E. McLellin makes the attempt.

---

1. McLellin was married twice—first to Cinthia Ann in 1829 and next to Emeline Miller in 1832. Cinthia and an infant child died and were buried near Charleston, Illinois, before the summer of 1831, suggesting that she may have died in childbirth. McLellin had tender feelings for his first wife, Cinthia, and his temptation to commit adultery came after her death and not from any dissatisfaction in their marriage. Whatever his problem, the Lord promised him a "crown of eternal life" if he repented. (See D&C 66:12.) This must have given him comfort. (See *Journals of William E. McLellin*, 251.)

2. See *The Journals of William E. McLellin*, 249–50.

3. See Cook, *Revelations of the Prophet Joseph Smith*, 106.

4. This revelation was received on November 2, 1831. (See Woodford, "Discoveries from the Joseph Smith Papers Project," 31.)

The big questions

Question: How do we live together and build a community now that we have gathered?

Answer: Canonize and act upon the revelations of Joseph Smith. Seek the face of the Lord.

Introduction

Revelation given through Joseph Smith at the Johnson home in November 1831.[1] The occasion was a special conference called to discuss the publication of the revelations already received from the Lord through the Prophet. (See D&C 1.) It was decided that Oliver Cowdery and John Whitmer should take the manuscripts of the revelations to Independence, where W. W. Phelps would publish them as the Book of Commandments. Many of the brethren bore solemn testimony that the revelations to be published were true. The Prophet records that after the revelation known as section 1 (Preface), had been received, some of the brethren had some negative conversations concerning the imperfections of the language used in the revelations. This revelation followed. The revelation challenges the wisest person to duplicate the least of Joseph's revelations and encourages his followers to press forward without being fearful of failure until they have seen the face of God for themselves.

Historical background

The decision to collect Joseph's revelations and have them published is illustrative of the procedure the Prophet followed when making decisions that affected his followers prior to the time that the organization of the Church was fully established. Typically, Joseph would call together a special conference or council of some of the leading elders of the Church to vote and make decisions. As Preece points out, it must be remembered that at this point in Church history there was no First Presidency, Quorum of Twelve, Quorum of Seventy, or even any stakes, for that matter.[2] Church organization at this time consisted of Joseph Smith and Oliver Cowdery as the first and second elder, respectively.[3]

---

1. Smith, *History of the Church*, 1:224–25.
2. See Preece, *Learning to Love the Doctrine and Covenants*, 130.
3. In November 1831, Joseph Smith was appointed President of the High Priesthood of the Church. However, as Bushman points out, this "revelation had surprisingly little effect. The office of president remained in the background for more than a year. Joseph was running the Church through his informal councils, each chaired by a moderator chosen for the occasion. He did not preside in these councils in any formal sense, although his influence

When Joseph called these impromptu conferences, a moderator would be chosen and business conducted. Although Joseph Smith played a pivotal role at each conference or council, he was not always appointed to be the moderator. However, when Joseph was present he was ultimately in charge. In this particular instance, Joseph called upon Sidney Rigdon, Oliver Cowdery, William E. McLellin, David Whitmer, Orson Hyde, John Whitmer, Luke Johnson, Peter Whitmer Jr., Lyman Johnson, Peter Whitmer, Christian Whitmer, and Reynolds Cahoon to counsel with him.[1] It appears as though Oliver Cowdery was the moderator for the first session. The record is not entirely clear on who moderated the second session, but we do know that William E. McLellin was the moderator for the third and final session.[2] Each session of the conference lasted a day or two, and the three sessions in question took place over a twelve-day period beginning in early November.[3]

The first session was convened on November 1, 1831. The decision to publish was assumed[4] and the number of books to be published was discussed. Oliver Cowdery called for a vote on the matter, and it was decided that ten thousand copies should be printed.[5] During a noon break in the meeting, section 1, the Lord's Preface, was received. The group reconvened in the afternoon, and Joseph suggested that a testimony be placed at the beginning of the compilation. This seemed to raise questions about mistakes and grammatical errors in the sacred writings and exactly how inspired the revelations really were. Some undoubtedly felt that if the revelations were from God there should be no errors and mistakes. (See verse 5.) It was at this juncture that section 67 was received, which invited anyone who wished to write a revelation equal to the least of the revelations Joseph had received. The conference closed for the day, and William E. McLellin took up the challenge, attempting to write his own

---

was paramount. The 1831 revelation calling for a President of the High Priesthood was not even included in the first batch of revelations prepared for publication that fall." (Bushman, *Joseph Smith: Rough Stone Rolling*, 259.)

1. See Woodford, *The Historical Development of the Doctrine and Covenants*, 22.

2. See Woodford, *The Historical Development of the Doctrine and Covenants*, 24.

3. By 1835 the decision-making process involving conferences or councils was formalized in D&C 107:27–31.

4. The purpose of the conference was to discuss the plan to publish the revelations and take action as a group. (See Woodford, *The Historical Development of the Doctrine and Covenants*, 21.)

5. Eventually it was decided that only 3,000 copies would be printed. On April 30, 1832, in Independence, Missouri, Joseph Smith met with the publishers, the Literary Firm, and the following was entered in the minutes: "Ordered by the council that three thousand copies of the *Book of Commandments* be printed the first edition." (Woodford, *The Historical Development of the Doctrine and Covenants*, 27.)

revelation before the conference reconvened on the following morning. (See verses 6–9.)

McLellin, according to Joseph Smith, had a high opinion of himself and thought that he was a wise man. However, in the eyes of his brethren, his attempt to write revelations failed miserably and silenced any doubters. McLellin had retired to an adjacent room for some period of time and tried to write something. When he returned, he stood in the doorway and wept, with nothing written on his note paper. Shortly thereafter, the brethren met and a "Pentecostal-type outpouring of the Spirits followed, as all bore testimony of the truthfulness of the revelations."[1] In connection with McLellin's failure, Joseph commented that "it was an awful responsibility to write in the name of the Lord."[2]

The next day the conference reconvened. Oliver Cowdery read section 67 to those assembled, and "the brethren then arose in turn and bore witness to the truth of the *Book of Commandments*."[3] As all were willing to attest to the truthfulness of the revelations, Joseph Smith received the following language, which has been placed in the introduction of every edition of the Doctrine and Covenants since:

"We, therefore, feel willing to bear testimony to all the world of mankind, to every creature upon the face of the earth, that the Lord has borne record to our souls, through the Holy Ghost shed forth upon us, that these commandments were given by inspiration of God, and are profitable for all men and are verily true."[4]

It was probably intended that those present sign the declaration of testimony. However, when the book was published, it was signed only by the first Quorum of Twelve, William E. McLellin among them.

The second session of the conference convened on November 8, 1831, and the issue of errors in the revelations was raised by Sidney Rigdon and others. It was resolved that Joseph correct the errors or mistakes, along with Oliver Cowdery, a school teacher.[5] It should be noted that the errors in question were primarily grammatical in nature, and therefore, in most instances, the changes were relatively minor. It was left to Oliver Cowdery to select the revelations that should be included in the first Book of Commandments, later renamed the Doctrine and Covenants.[6]

At the final session of the conference, held on November 12, 1831, William E. McLellin was moderator. The meetings lasted over two days,

---

1. Preece, *Learning to Love the Doctrine and Covenants*, 131.
2. Woodford, *The Historical Development of the Doctrine and Covenants*, 23.
3. Woodford, *The Historical Development of the Doctrine and Covenants*, 23.
4. See Woodford, *The Historical Development of the Doctrine and Covenants*, 23.
5. Woodford, *The Historical Development of the Doctrine and Covenants*, 24.
6. Woodford, *The Historical Development of the Doctrine and Covenants*, 24.

and on each day the meetings went on into the evening. On this occasion it was voted that Joseph "dedicate and consecrate" those brethren assigned to take the manuscript to Zion, where it was to be published.[1] The brethren also voted that these writings be "prized by this conference to be worth to the Church the riches of the whole earth."[2] Joseph commented at the close of the conference that this book would benefit the Church and the world and serve as "the foundation of the Church in these last days." (Verse 4.)[3] Joseph then received section 70, appointing "stewards" to publish the Book of Commandments.

Press on until you see God

Those associated with the Prophet Joseph knew that it was possible to part the veil and see spirits, angels, and gods. However, sins, weaknesses of the flesh, doubts, jealousy, pride, and fear of failure often times prevailed and prevented many from obtaining such spiritual experience. In a verse reminiscent of the plea in the New Testament, "I believe; help thou my unbelief" (see Mark 9:24),[4] this revelation encouraged men and woman not to lose hope.

> Ye endeavored to believe that ye should receive the blessing which was offered unto you; but behold verily I say unto you there were fears in your hearts, and verily this is the reason that ye did not receive. . . .
> . . . it is your privilege, and a promise I give unto you . . . that inasmuch as you strip yourselves from jealousies and fears, and humble yourselves before me, for ye are not sufficiently humble, the veil shall be rent and you shall see me and know that I am—not with the carnal neither natural mind, but with the spiritual.
> For no man has seen God at any time in the flesh; except quickened by the Spirit of God.
> Neither can any natural man abide the presence of God, neither after the carnal mind.
> Ye are not able to abide the presence of God now, neither the ministering of angels; wherefore, continue in patience until ye are perfected.
> Let not your minds turn back; and when ye are worthy, in mine own due time, ye shall see and know that which was conferred upon you by the hands of my servant Joseph Smith, Jun. Amen. (Verses 3, 10–14.)

Many Latter-day Saints, in addition to the Prophet Joseph, can attest

---

1. Woodford, *The Historical Development of the Doctrine and Covenants*, 25.
2. Woodford, *The Historical Development of the Doctrine and Covenants*, 26.
3. See Woodford, *The Historical Development of the Doctrine and Covenants*, 26.
4. See also New Living Translation: "I do believe, but help me not to doubt!"

that they have pierced the veil. The Lord's counsel in this regard is to be patient and press on.

Section 68: John Johnson Home, Hiram, Ohio, November 1831[1]

Heading

Revelation to certain members who attended the conference to discuss the publication of some of Joseph's revelations.

The big question

Question: How do we live together and build a community now that we have gathered?
Answer: Seek the spirit of inspiration. Live the law of consecration with a generous heart. Parents, teach your children the gospel.

Introduction

Revelation given through Joseph Smith at the request of Orson Hyde, Luke S. Johnson, Lyman E. Johnson, and William E. McLellin, received in the Johnson home located in Hiram, Ohio, in November 1831.[2] Although this revelation was given in response to supplication that the mind of the Lord be made known concerning the leaders named, much of the content pertains to the whole Church. For example, members are given instruction on inspired utterances being scripture when moved upon by the Holy Ghost, and parents are commanded to teach the gospel to their children, observe the Sabbath day, and pray.

The date when this revelation was given is uncertain. The *History of the Church* indicates that the revelation probably came near the commencement of the conference in Hiram, Ohio, on November 1–3, 1831. (See D&C 67.) Minutes in the "Far West Record" indicate that this section, or at least part of it, was received November 11, 1831. Verses 1–13 seem to have been revealed sometime between November 1 and 3, and verses 22–35 on November 11, 1831.[3] Verses 15–21 were added by the Prophet in the 1835 edition and reflect knowledge about the Melchizedek Priesthood and infor-

---

1. Received November 1, 1831. (See Woodford, "Discoveries from the Joseph Smith Papers Project," 31.)
2. Smith, *History of the Church*, 1:227–29.
3. See Cook, *Revelations of the Prophet Joseph Smith*, 108.

mation about the organization of the First Presidency that was not known in 1831 when the majority of this revelation was given. (See D&C 107.)[1]

Anchor section

Memorize: Parents to teach children the gospel

Historical background

Section 68 originated at the special conference called by the Prophet Joseph to discuss publication of Joseph's revelations. (See D&C 1; 67.) The revelation was received at the request of Orson Hyde, Luke S. Johnson, Lyman E. Johnson, and William E. McLellin, who were all in attendance at the conference. Although this revelation was not the main focus of the conference, it contains information that is particularly useful for parents to understand about their responsibility to teach their children.

Parents should teach their children the gospel

Just as parents in ancient Israel were commanded to teach their children about God at all times and in all places, parents in modern-day Israel are commanded to do likewise. (See Deuteronomy 6:7.) The language used by the Lord in section 68 is direct and unequivocal. Parents are commanded to teach their children "the doctrine of repentance, faith in Christ . . . and . . . baptism and the gift of the Holy Ghost." In addition, they are to teach their children to pray and to walk uprightly before the Lord." (Verses 25, 28.) If parents fail in this responsibility, then "the sin be upon the heads of the parents." (Verse 25.)

The curriculum parents are expected to teach their children is more fully described in section 93, and the subject matter is rigorous. Section 93 advises parents to instruct the family on such topics as deification, man's premortal existence, truth, the coeternality of God and man, intelligences, agency, eternal matter, and the glory of God. (See D&C 93:1–38.) By way of admonition, section 93 warns, "You have not taught your children light and truth" and, accordingly, "that wicked one hath power, as yet, over you, and this is the cause of your affliction." (D&C 93:42.)

The responsibility for parents to teach their children rests first and foremost with the father and mother. While classes outside the home may be helpful, such instruction is at best supplemental. Church educational opportunities are at times outstanding, depending on the training and

---

1. See Woodford, *The Historical Development of the Doctrine and Covenants*, 854.

quality of the instructor and the profundity of the subject matter. However, it is not uncommon for some well-meaning teachers to rely on gimmicks, emotional stories, and overly simplified lesson materials that fail to fairly and adequately evaluate Church history and explain and contextualize the unique aspects and doctrines that are central to a more complete understanding of the restoration of the gospel. A more rigorous approach to gospel study will help fortify children against what at first glance may seem like valid criticism of unique Mormon doctrines and its history.

The Spirit of the law of consecration

It has always been a considerable challenge for the Saints to abide by the spirit of the law of consecration. Sharing material wealth and working hard to provide for others does not come naturally. Sustaining a generous spirit over time is problematic, and ultimately the Saints were not up to the challenge. In the following passages, Oliver Cowdery was commanded to carry a word of admonition to those in Zion, Jackson County, Missouri, who were trying to implement this law.

> Now, I, the Lord, am not well pleased with the inhabitants of Zion, for there are idlers among them; and their children are also growing up in wickedness; they also seek not earnestly the riches of eternity, but their eyes are full of greediness.
> These things ought not to be, and must be done away from among them; wherefore, let my servant Oliver Cowdery carry these sayings unto the land of Zion. (Verses 31–32.)

What is spoken by the Spirit is scripture

Scripture is generally used to refer to the inspired *written word* of God as it is contained in the standard works. However, section 68 uses the word more loosely to refer to the spoken word as well. "Whatsoever they shall speak when moved upon by the Holy Ghost shall be scripture, shall be the will of the Lord, shall be the mind of the Lord, shall be the word of the Lord, shall be the voice of the Lord, and the power of God unto salvation." (Verses 3–4.) However, this does not mean that such spoken statements are authoritative in the sense that they are universally binding on members of the Church. In order for statements to be authoritative church wide, the pronouncement must be unanimously agreed upon by the First Presidency, Quorum of Twelve, and Quorums of Seventy, and then adopted by a vote of a representative body of the members of the Church in a general conference and thereafter included in the canon of LDS scripture.

Note that the language in these verses about speaking under the influence of the Holy Ghost is not reserved solely for those in the governing quorums of the Church but is applicable as "an ensample unto all those who were ordained unto this priesthood, whose mission is appointed unto them to go forth" or, in other words, missionaries.[1] By extension, this principle of uttering inspired statements applies to Latter-day Saint Church officers and both men and women alike.

SECTION 69: JOHN JOHNSON HOME, HIRAM, OHIO, NOVEMBER 1831[2]

Heading

Oliver Cowdery assigned to carry the manuscript containing Joseph's revelations to Independence, Missouri, to be published.

The big question

Question: How do we live together and build a community now that we have gathered?

Answer: Compile and make available to the Saints the revelations of Joseph Smith.

Introduction

Revelation given through Joseph Smith the Prophet at the John Johnson home in Hiram, Ohio, in November 1831.[3] During the special conference of November 1, 1831, those attending had agreed to compile revelations intended for publication (The Book of Commandments). On November 3, section 133 was added and called the Appendix. By action of the conference, Oliver Cowdery was appointed to carry the manuscript of the compiled revelations and commandments to Independence, Missouri, for printing. He was also asked to take with him moneys that had been contributed for the building up of the Church in Zion, Jackson County, Missouri. As the course of travel would lead him through a sparsely settled county to the frontier, a traveling companion, John Whitmer, was assigned to go with him.

---

1. Specifically this verse refers to Orson Hyde as an example of one ordained a high priest and promised the spirit of revelation as a missionary. (See verse 1.)
2. This revelation was received on November 11, 1831. (See Woodford, "Discoveries from the Joseph Smith Papers Project," 31.)
3. Smith, *History of the Church*, 1:234–35.

Historical background

The decision of the Hiram, Ohio, conference was that Oliver Cowdery and John Whitmer should carry the revelations to Independence, Missouri, (Zion) for printing. There, W. W. Phelps had set up a press for this purpose. These two men left Ohio on November 20, 1831, and then stopped in Winchester, Indiana, for about a week (November 29 through December 7, 1831) to regulate some problems in a branch of the Church. The two arrived in Independence, Missouri, on January 5, 1832.[1]

Section 69 also instructs John Whitmer to continue to write a history of all the important things occurring in the Church. (See verse 3.) This was especially important in Jackson County, Missouri, because it was to be a "seat" or place of central importance to the Church. (See verse 6.)

John Whitmer commanded to keep a history

Section 69 commands John Whitmer to make "a history of all the important things which he shall observe and know concerning my church" (verse 3). His commission was a reiteration of a similar command given to him by revelation in March 1831. Section 69 was certainly meant to encourage him in his responsibilities as Church historian.

The sense that keeping a history was important was an extension of the belief of first-generation Mormons that "nineteenth century experiences were as important to the history of God's implementation of his covenant as the events described in the Bible." [2] Therefore, "writing, copying, selecting, and obtaining all things which shall be for the good of the church, and for the rising generations" has always been an essential Church undertaking (verse 8)

John Whitmer, however, was not up to the assignment. His reaction was, "I would rather not do it." He would agree to do it, however, provided Joseph received a revelation that it was the mind and will of the Lord.[3] Whitmer's calling abruptly ended when he was excommunicated in 1838. Thereafter, Joseph Smith and Sidney Rigdon tried to obtain a copy of Whitmer's history, but Whitmer refused to comply, making it necessary for the Church to begin a new record, known today as *History of the Church*. Whitmer's history eventually came into the possession of the Reorganized Church of Jesus Christ of Latter Day Saints, now known as the Community of Christ, which subsequently published it.

---

1. See Cook, *Revelations of the Prophet Joseph Smith*, 112.
2. Staker, *Hearken, O Ye People*, Kindle location 663.
3. See McKiernan and Launius, eds., *An Early Latter Day Saint History*, 56.

John Johnson Home: Hiram, Ohio, October 1831–August 1832

SECTION 71: JOHN JOHNSON HOME, HIRAM, OHIO, DECEMBER 1, 1831

Heading

Joseph Smith and Sidney Rigdon directed to stop work on their inspired revisions of the Bible and defend the Church against its critics.

The big question

Question: How do we live together and build a community now that we have gathered?
Answer: Defend the faith when the Church is criticized by its detractors.

Introduction

Revelation given to Joseph Smith the Prophet and Sidney Rigdon at the Johnson farm in Hiram, Ohio, on December 1, 1831.[1] The Prophet had continued to revise the Bible, with Sidney Rigdon as his scribe, until this revelation was received, at which time it was temporarily laid aside so as to enable them to fulfill the instruction given herein. The brethren were to go forth to preach in order to allay the unfriendly feelings that had developed against the Church as a result of the publication of some newspaper articles by Ezra Booth, who had apostatized.

Historical background

When section 71 was given, some members of the Church had apostatized as a result of outside criticisms of Mormonism. During this time Joseph Smith and Sidney Rigdon were revising the Bible at the Johnson farm; meanwhile, controversy about the Mormons continued to increase in the community. The situation became serious enough that the Lord instructed Joseph and Sidney to stop revising the Bible and openly defend the faith. Accordingly, Joseph and Rigdon left Hiram and traveled the thirty miles or so to Kirtland.

From the outset, the local population in Kirtland was critical of the Mormons. As persecution increased, members of the Church began leaving. Norman Brown quit because his horse had died during Zion's Camp. Joseph Wakefield abandoned the faith because he saw Joseph playing with

---

1. Smith, *History of the Church*, 1:238–39.

children and felt it was beneath a prophet to engage in this kind of frivolity. Others left because they were poor and unable to support themselves.[1]

The most prominent and influential apostate was Ezra Booth, a former Methodist minister and convert to Mormonism. He had become a member in 1831 and went to Hiram on a brief missionary assignment. While there he met Simonds Ryder, a Reformed Baptist minister. Booth asked Ryder if he could speak to Ryder's congregation after Ryder's sermon. Ryder was "deeply affected" but not persuaded. Yet when Ryder thereafter went to Kirtland he heard a young Mormon girl predict the destruction of Peking, China. A month later, when Ryder read of the destruction of that city, he joined the Church and was ordained an elder in June 1831.[2]

When Ryder's name was misspelled on his missionary commission, he began to doubt and compared notes with his associate, Booth. Although they discussed their concerns with Rigdon, they continued to doubt and left the Church. A former associate of Booth, the Reverend Ira Eddly of Nelson, Portage County, asked Booth to publicly voice his concerns. Booth wrote a series of nine letters to Eddly, which appeared in the *Ohio Star* from October 13 to December 8, 1831.[3] The extensive publication of the letters had a dramatic impact. He spoke of the failures of Smith's revelations, Joseph's despotic personality, and Joseph's personal weaknesses. He was so effective that some thought he would stop the Church in its tracks.[4]

Meanwhile, Joseph and Rigdon were told to preach in the area "for the space of a season." (See D&C 71.) The Lord promised that "there is no weapon that is formed against you that shall prosper; and if any man lift his voice against you, he shall be confounded in mine own due time." (D&C 71.) For the next six weeks Joseph and Rigdon traveled the countryside defending Mormonism.

Rigdon was in many ways a more effective apologist than Joseph. Older, trained as a minister, and schooled in Bible history, he was a formidable opponent. As well, he was an eloquent and powerful speaker skilled in a debate. Rigdon challenged both Booth and Ryder to debate, but both avoided him in public.[5] The challenge to the Church subsided, and Joseph and Rigdon resumed revising the Bible again early January 1831. (See D&C 73:3.)

---

1. See *Church History in the Fulness of Times*, 113.
2. Van Wagoner, *Sidney Rigdon: A Portrait of Religious Excess*, 109.
3. Van Wagoner, *Sidney Rigdon: A Portrait of Religious Excess*, 109–10.
4. Van Wagoner, *Sidney Rigdon: A Portrait of Religious Excess*, 110–11.
5. Van Wagoner, *Sidney Rigdon: A Portrait of Religious Excess*, 111.

Section 73: John Johnson Farm, Hiram, Ohio, January 10, 1832

Heading

Joseph and Sidney Rigdon commanded to start revising the Bible once again after a hiatus during which they devoted their energies to a public defense of the Church.

Introduction

Revelation given to Joseph Smith the Prophet and Sidney Rigdon at the Johnson farm in Hiram, Ohio, on January 10, 1832.[1] Since the early part of the preceding December, the Prophet and Sidney Rigdon had been engaged in defending the Church against apostates Ezra Booth, Simonds Ryder, and others. (See commentary on D&C 71.) By this means much was accomplished in diminishing the unfavorable feelings that had arisen against the Church. (See D&C 71.) In order to preach, Joseph and Rigdon had stopped making inspired revisions to the Bible for a season. Section 73 commands them once again to begin to "translate" (make inspired modifications to) the Bible.

Historical background

Section 73 instructs Oliver Cowdery and Joseph to return to the work of making inspired revisions to the Bible after a short hiatus during which they had traveled around the area defending the Church against its critics. The Church was under particular attack at this time because several apostates had joined with other anti-Mormons in the community in criticizing the Church.

Section 73 also makes reference to a conference of elders that was planned for January 4, 1832. Several elders anticipated formal mission calls from the Lord at this conference. (See verse 2.) These men wondered what they should do in the meantime. The Lord instructs that they should continue to preach "the gospel . . . in the regions round about, until conference." (Verse 1.)

---

1. Smith, *History of the Church*, 1:241–42.

THE KIRTLAND, OHIO, PERIOD

SECTION 74: JOHN JOHNSON HOME, HIRAM, OHIO, JANUARY 1832[1]

Heading

Joseph's revisions of Paul's views on marriage as found in 1 Corinthians 7:14.

Introduction

Revelation given to Joseph Smith at the Johnson farm in January 1832.[2]

1 Corinthians 7:14

1 Corinthians 7:14 is about Christians living in a marriage where one was a member and the other was not. Paul exhorted those in such marriages to stay together because the believer's faith will have a spiritual or sanctifying influence on the nonbelieving spouse. Undoubtedly, Paul addressed this subject because some of his followers were experiencing marital conflicts in such situations.

Joseph's revisions to 1 Corinthians 7:14 adds more information about what must have been a contentious issue in some marriages between Christians and non-Christians—namely, a disagreement over whether or not a son ought to be circumcised when eight days old in order to be acceptable to the Lord. By the spirit of revelation, Joseph adds to our understanding of this text by pointing out that it was Paul's opinion, not necessarily the Lord's, that "a believer should not be united to an unbeliever" unless both agreed that their children did not have to be circumcised. (See verse 5.)

1 Corinthians 7 is interesting to Mormons for other reasons as well. In it Paul plays down the importance of marriage—something Joseph would have disagreed with in light of Joseph's teachings about the importance of eternal marriage. (See D&C 130 and 132.) That said, it is interesting to note that Joseph believed that Paul's teachings in this chapter about marriage were out of context and that Paul's remarks advising against marriage were not addressed to the members of the Church in general but rather to missionaries or those "in the ministry" in particular. (See JST 1

---

1. "This is a real surprise to those who thought this revelation was received in connection with the work Joseph Smith was doing in correcting the text of the Bible. This section was actually received sometime in the last part of 1830, and not January 1832 as found in all editions of the Doctrine and Covenants. It probably stemmed from discussions about infant baptism." (Woodford, "Discoveries from the Joseph Smith Papers Project," 31.)
2. Smith, *History of the Church*, 1:242.

Corinthians 7:29.[1]) If indeed Paul was speaking to missionaries who were on assignment to travel from one town to the next, it is not surprising that he advised against marriage and suggested that "if you do not have a wife, do not get married." (NLT 1 Corinthians 7:27.)

Finally, Paul's views on women and marriage, as we have them today in his letters, may not be an accurate reflection of his thoughts on the subject. Bart D. Ehrman and some other New Testament scholars have recently pointed out that at least some of Paul's views on women did not accurately reflect his genuine attitudes and were added after his death to reflect society's outlook.[2] This observation is bolstered by evidence found in some early Christian writings that taught that marriage was the highest sacrament in the Church. In the *Gospel of Philip*, an early Christian gospel that was never canonized, Philip speaks of marriage and eternal offspring as the ultimate Christian rite.[3]

Scriptural inerrancy

Consistent with Joseph Smith's views on biblical inerrancy, Section 74 describes a situation where Joseph thought a prophet/apostle (Paul) gave a commandment (revelation), and the commandment reflected the individual's own views and not necessarily the Lord's. "The apostle wrote unto the church, giving unto them a commandment, not of the Lord, but of himself, that a believer should be united to an unbeliever." (Section 74:5)

SECTION 76: JOHN JOHNSON HOME, HIRAM, OHIO, FEBRUARY 16, 1832

Heading

Joseph and Sidney Rigdon's vision of the three degrees of glory.

Introduction

A vision given to Joseph Smith and Sidney Rigdon in the upper room of the Johnson home in Hiram, Ohio, on February 16, 1832.[4] Prefacing his

---

1. 1 Corinthians 7:29 reads in the JST, "But I speak unto you who are called unto the ministry. For this I say, brethren, the time *remaineth* is *but* short *that ye shall be sent forth unto the ministry. Even* they *who* have wives, *shall* be as though they had none; *for each are called and chosen to do the Lord's work.*
2. See Ehrman, *Misquoting Jesus*, 181–92, on Paul and women.
3. See Wilson, *The Gospel of Philip*, 18, 39, 46.
4. Smith, *History of the Church*, 1:245–52.

record of this vision, the Prophet wrote: "Upon my return from Amherst conference, I resumed the translation of the Scriptures. From sundry revelations that had been received, it was apparent that many important points touching the salvation of man had been taken from the Bible, or lost before it was compiled. It appeared self-evident from what truths were left, that if God rewarded every one according to the deeds done in the body, the term 'Heaven,' as intended for the Saints' eternal home, must include more kingdoms than one. Accordingly, while translating St. John's Gospel, myself and Elder Rigdon saw the following vision." It was after the Prophet revised John 5:29 that this vision was given.

Anchor section

Memorize: Three degrees of glory

Historical background

At the time section 76 was given, Joseph and Sidney Rigdon were living on the Johnson farm, located not far from Kirtland in Hiram, Ohio. Joseph and his family lived in the farmhouse with the Johnsons, and Rigdon was with his family in a log cabin. Johnson gave permission for Joseph and Rigdon to use one of the upper rooms as an office and study, where Joseph and Rigdon could continue to make revisions to the Bible.[1] Seventeen revelations that are now included in the Doctrine and Covenants were received in this workplace and temporary headquarters for the Church.

On the day the revelation was received, February 16, 1832, a number of other people were present. Philo Dibble, an eyewitness to this event, recorded:

> There were other men in the room, perhaps twelve, among who I was one during a part of the time—probably two-thirds of the time—I saw the glory and felt the power, but did not see the vision....
>
> Joseph would, at intervals, say: "What do I see?" as one might say while looking out the window and beholding what all in the room could not see. Then he would relate what he had seen or what he was looking at. Then Sidney replied, "I see the same." Presently Sidney would say "What do I see?" and would repeat what he had seen or was seeing, and Joseph would reply, "I see the same."
>
> This manner of conversation was repeated at short intervals to the end of the vision, and during the whole time not a word was spoken by any other person. Not a sound nor motion made by anyone but Joseph and Sidney, and

---

1. Joseph Smith and Sidney Rigdon had been working on Bible revisions pursuant to the Lord's command since about January 10, 1832. (See D&C 73:2.)

it seemed to me that they never moved a joint or limb during the time I was there, which I think was over an hour, and to the end of the vision.

Joseph sat firmly and calmly all the time in the midst of magnificent glory, but Sidney sat limp and pale, apparently as limber as a rag, observing which, Joseph remarked, smilingly, "Sidney is not used to it as I am."[1]

In Dibble's account, he indicates that not all of what was seen was written down. Joseph later said of the vision that he "could explain a hundred fold more than I ever have or the glories of the kingdoms manifested to me in the vision, were I permitted, and were the people prepared to receive them."[2]

The fact that Dibble and a number of others were present was not unusual. Elders of the Church would come to listen as Joseph and Sidney worked on the Bible revisions. There were often several elders present at any one time.[3] When Joseph and Rigdon came to John 5:28–29, they were prompted to question it. They knelt in prayer for further information and knowledge on the subject. After about two hours the vision ended.

At the close of the vision, Joseph and Rigdon, while still in the Spirit, wrote down those portions of the vision that could be shared with the Church. (See verses 28, 49, 80, 113, 114–15.) Their account was sent to Independence, Missouri, for Church publication and appeared in *The Evening and Morning Star* in July 1832.[4]

About eleven years later, Joseph penned a poetic version at the request of W. W. Phelps, a poet himself.[5] This version apparently came about "when someone wrote a somewhat antagonistic letter to the editor of the *Times and Season* in Nauvoo," which criticized the vision because Joseph had not recorded it in poetic verse like some of the Old Testament prophets' revelations. Based on this observation, the critic claimed that Joseph could not have been a "true prophet."[6] Phelps, the editor of the *Times and Seasons*, gave the letter to Joseph, and Joseph proceeded to pen the vision in a poetic form. In Joseph's poetic version, he added a little material that he had not written down earlier. For example, in the poetic adaptation we find

---

1. Woodford, The Historical Development of the Doctrine and Covenants, 927.
2. Woodford, *The Historical Development of the Doctrine and Covenants*, 928.
3. See Preece, *Learning to Love the Doctrine and Covenants*, 143.
4. Robinson and Garrett, *Doctrine and Covenants Commentary*, 2:288.
5. See Woodford, *The Historical Development of the Doctrine and Covenants*, 933.
6. Preece, *Learning to Love the Doctrine and Covenants*, 145.

a reference to "Kolob."¹ The poetic account was organized into 78 verses while section 76 contains 119 verses.

Although the idea of multiple degrees of glory seems reasonable, this was not the case at the time the vision was given. Even stalwarts like Brigham Young had trouble accepting it. He said that "it was so directly contrary and opposed to my former education, I said, wait a little; I did not reject it, but I could not understand it."² Others left the Church over the revelation. It was controversial enough that Joseph asked the missionaries not to refer to it when preaching to prospective members but rather stick to the basics of faith, repentance, and baptism.³

Mormons in the 21st century may find it difficult to understand why a more inclusive theology about heaven and hell would be such a stumbling block. After all, Calvinistic conceptions of salvation and damnation along with the idea that only a sliver of the human race would be saved constitute a grim way to look at one's prospects for the afterlife. "For centuries, the polarities of heaven and hell, election and reprobation, had informed the contours of Protestant thought. Thus, in the world into which Mormonism was born, it was customary to conceptualize man as either saint or sinner, righteous or wicked, bound for heaven or headed for hell; and this formed an important part of the cultural baggage early converts carried with them into the Church."[4]

As a result, even Joseph Smith and the leading brethren continued to preach as though only Mormons would be saved. In 1838, (six years after Joseph received Section 76) when asked "Will every body be damned but the Mormons?" he replied, "Yes, and a great portion of them, unless they repent and work righteousness."[5] It was not until the last sixteen months or so of the prophets life that he seems to have fully grasped or at least spoken publically about the implications of Section 76 and Section 19, a revelation received before the church was organized that described a "terminable hell."[6] Wilford Woodruff noted that the Prophet Joseph said, "Says one I believe in one hell and one heaven all equally miserable or equally happy, but St. Paul informs us of three glories and three heavens."[7] Nevertheless, by the time he gave his King Follett discourse at the very end of his life Joseph conceptualized hell as a state of mental anguish. "I have no fear of hell fire, that doesn't exist, but the torment and disappointment of the

---

1. In the poetic version see stanza 7: "From the council in Kolob, to time on the earth." (Cook, *Revelations of the Prophet Joseph Smith*, 159.)
2. Woodford, *The Historical Development of the Doctrine and Covenants*, 929.
3. See Woodford, *The Historical Development of the Doctrine and Covenants*, 932.
4. Underwood, "'Saved or Damned,'" *BYU Studies*, 25:3:88.
5. Ibid 86. See also *Elder's Journal of the Church of Latter Day Saints* 1 (July 1838): 42.
6. Ibid 99.
7. Ibid 98. See also Ehat and Cook, eds., *Words of Joseph Smith*, 214.

mind of man is as exquisite as a lake burning with fire and brimstone."[1] By this time only the Sons of Perdition "would be damned in the fullest and most traditional sense ... [Joseph] began to emphasize a pluralized, rather than a polarized picture of eternity. He symbolized hell, diminished damnation's domain, and expanded salvation."[2]

The historical development of ideas within the Doctrine and Covenants provides insight into why concepts change from generation to generation. Grant Underwood explains:

> Absolutely essential to a proper understanding of Mormon thought is that one recognize the line-upon-line principle, that is, the construct that allows for a gradual focusing and refining of doctrine based on both human capacity and divine design.... The more it is studied, the more we realize the naiveté of intersecting our past at any given point in time and expecting to hold the Church accountable for the finality of all views there discovered. Indeed, to pursue Paul's metaphor, the Church is like a body, and all bodies go through successive stages of development from infancy to adulthood. A wise and loving father does not immediately correct all his children's mistaken notions or attempt to teach them all truth at once. Rather, he closely monitors their development, adding, subtracting, and refining until they reach maturity. Would a perfect Father in Heaven be less wise?"[3]

At base, Joseph's view of theology and scripture was that it is an ever-expanding, self-correcting exercise. Theology and the kingdom of God on earth are always a work in progress. Continuing revelation was and is the beacon, the "light that shineth more and more unto the perfect day."[4] (Proverbs 4:18)

The Celestial Kingdom

Those who attain to the celestial kingdom are those who:
1. Receive the testimony of Jesus;
2. Believe;
3. Are baptized by immersion;
4. Keep the commandments;
5. Receive the Holy Ghost by an authorized servant of God;
6. Overcome by faith;

---

1. Ibid 98. See also Stan Larson, "The King Follett Discourse: A Newly Amalgamated Text," *BYU Studies* 18 [Winter 1978]; 205.
2. Ibid 99.
3. Ibid., 102.
4. Ibid.

7. Enter into the "order of Melchizedek" or "order of the only begotten" (temple endowment);[1] and

8. Have their calling and election made sure. (See verses 50–70.)

Attaining the celestial kingdom means that men and woman may become "gods." (See verse 58 and D&C 132:19–20.) This doctrine parallels the understanding expressed in the New Testament by Jesus and Paul that men and woman are perfectible and may become joint heirs with Christ. (See Matthew 5:48; Romans 8:15–17.)

The terrestrial kingdom

It is commonly taught that those who enter into the terrestrial kingdom are those who have had an opportunity to accept the gospel in this life and reject it or were not "valiant" or intrepid in their adherence to the gospel of Jesus Christ. (See verses 74 and 79.) The implications of this teaching are that if a person rejects the gospel truth on earth or is not entirely faithful, he or she will not have an opportunity in the spirit world to reconsider, repent, and thereafter go on to receive the highest blessings.[2] This position should be viewed with some caution in light of section 138, which teaches that even those who "rejected the prophets" are given an opportunity in the next life to be baptized, receive the Holy Ghost, be "judged according to men in the flesh," and become "heirs of salvation," a term that on its face implies becoming a joint heir with Jesus Christ. (See D&C 138:32–34, 58–59.)

The telestial kingdom

Those entering the telestial kingdom "received not the gospel, neither the testimony of Jesus, neither the prophets, neither the everlasting covenant" here or in the next life and are wicked. (See verse 101.) Such are confined to hell in the spirit world until the resurrection. (See verse 106.)

---

1. The "order of Melchizedek" or "order of the only begotten," sometimes referred to as the "order after the only begotten," is a term of art that refers to the temple endowment. (See D&C 128:27–48, 123; Alma 13:1–34.)

2. This interpretation is reinforced in the poetic version.
56. These are they that are hon'rable men of the earth;
Who were blinded and dup'd by the cunning of men:
They receiv'd not the truth of the Savior at first;
But did, when they heard it in prison, again.
57. Not valiant for truth, they obtain'd not the crown,
But are of that glory that's typ'd by the moon;
They are they, that come into the presence of Christ,
But not to the fulness of God, on his throne.

Section 131 explains that in the
celestial kingdom there are three divisions

Section 131 explains that in the celestial kingdom there are three divisions or degrees. In order for a person to enter the highest of the three degrees of the celestial kingdom, he or she must enter into an order of the priesthood called the "new and everlasting covenant of marriage." In other words, a person must be married; and, therefore, this highest degree of glory cannot be obtained separately or singly.

Sons of perdition

The sons of perdition are the only persons not saved. (See verse 40.) Sons of perdition are those who have an unqualified knowledge of Jesus and deny him or "crucify him" as it were afresh and "put him to an open shame." (See verse 35.) Joseph expressed this idea in the King Follett discourse.

> All sins shall be forgiven, except the sin against the Holy Ghost; for Jesus will save all except the sons of perdition. What must a man do to commit the unpardonable sin? He must receive the Holy Ghost, have the heavens opened unto him, and know God.... He has got to say that the sun does not shine while he sees it; he has got to deny Jesus Christ when the heavens have been opened unto him, and to deny the plan of salvation with his eyes open to the truth of it.[1]

Evidently, in Joseph's understanding, to deny the Holy Ghost meant far more than feeling the promptings of the Spirit and thereafter rejecting such communications. Rather it was a term of art used for those singularly blessed to behold Jesus (have the heavens open to them), who thereafter denied that it ever happened.

The final end of the sons of perdition is not known. Joseph advised in response to a letter on this subject from W. W. Phelps in 1833 that anyone who suggested that they knew the final destiny of the sons of perdition were not telling the truth.

> Say to ... brother Hulet and to all others, that the Lord never authorized them to say that the devil, his angels, or the sons of perdition, should ever be restored; for their state of destiny was not revealed to man, is not revealed, nor ever shall be revealed, save to those who are partakers thereof: consequently those who teach this doctrine have not received it of the Spirit of the Lord. Truly Brother Oliver declared it to be the doctrine of devils. We, therefore, command that this doctrine be taught no more in Zion.[2]

---

1. Smith, *Teachings of the Prophet Joseph Smith*, 358.
2. See Smith, *Teachings of the Prophet Joseph Smith*, 24.

The content of Joseph's letter is consistent with section 76 itself, "Wherefore, he saves all except [sons of perdition]. . . . And the end thereof, neither the place thereof, nor their torment, no man knows; neither was it revealed, neither will be revealed unto man, except to them who are made partakers thereof." (Verses 44–48.)

Three degrees of glory: progression from one to the other or not?

Some students of the gospel believe that the language in section 76 implies that there is progression from kingdom to kingdom while others do not. At the turn of the twentieth century the issue became so controversial that the First Presidency asked members of the Church not to debate the matter. The position of the First Presidency on the matter was reflected in a letter written sometime after the issue first became controversial. In a letter dated August 7, 1958, to Mr. Donald R. Snow in Berkeley California from Joseph Anderson, Secretary to the First Presidency, Anderson addresses the "possibility of advancing from one glory to another after the resurrection." Anderson then states that there are two views on the matter, neither of which has ever been adopted by the Church and each of which is held by persons of equal authority in the Church."[1]

On the side of progression, we find statements by Brigham Young and Wilford Woodruff. Woodruff reported Young as saying:

> None would inherit this Earth when it became celestial and translated into the presence of God but those who would be crowned as Gods . . . all others would have to inherit another kingdom . . . [yet] they would eventually have the privilege of proving themselves worthy and advancing to a celestial kingdom but it would be a slow process.[2]

Woodruff himself opined that "if there was a point where man in his

---

[1]. In the letter, Joseph Anderson makes reference to a memorandum from the First Presidency directed to Ward Magleby of Manti as follows:

"March 5, 1952.

"*Question*—Please inform me as to the teaching of the Church regarding the possibility of a person progressing from one kingdom to another after the resurrection.

"*Answer*—The Brethren direct me to say that the Church has never announced a definite doctrine upon this point. Some of the Brethren have held the view that it was possible in the course of progression to advance from one glory to another, invoking the principle of eternal progression; others of the Brethren have taken an opposite view. But, as stated, the Church has never announced a definite doctrine on this point.

"[Signed by Joseph Anderson, Secretary to the First Presidency.]"

[2]. Woodruff Journal, August 5, 1855, 4:333–34.

progression could not proceed any further, the very idea would throw a gloom over every intelligent and reflecting mind."[1]

In the twentieth century, James E. Talmage in *The Articles of Faith* originally wrote that "it is reasonable to believe, in the absence of direct revelation ... that in accordance with God's plan of eternal progression, advancement from grade to grade within any kingdom, and from kingdom to kingdom, will be provided for."[2] However, because of the difference of opinion on this point among the authorities, this sentiment was modified and eventually taken out of *The Articles of Faith* altogether.

On the other side of the divide, Joseph Fielding Smith and Bruce R. McConkie took a strong stance to the contrary. "It has been asked if it is possible for one who inherits the telestial glory to advance in time to the celestial glory? The answer to this question is NO!"[3] McConkie said, "There are those who say that there is progression from one kingdom to another in the eternal world. Or if not that, lower kingdoms eventually progress to where higher kingdoms once were. This is worse than false. It is an evil and pernicious doctrine."[4]

The differences of opinion expressed by both sides was based upon a selective reading of section 76. On the side of advancement from kingdom to kingdom, students point to the language that states that persons in the telestial kingdom may become "heirs of salvation," meaning "joint heirs" with God and Christ. (See verse 88.) Those who reject this interpretation point to language in the text that says of those in the telestial kingdom that "they shall be judged according to their works ... and shall be servants of the Most High; but where God and Christ dwell they cannot come, worlds without end." (Verses 111–12.)

Regardless, Joseph felt that section 76 held out hope for development and advancement after death. At a minimum, he said that the "scope for action" and "the continued duration for completion, in order that the heirs of salvation may confess the Lord and bow the knee" had been expanded "beyond the narrow-mindedness of men."[5] The optimism that he felt about the vision reflected the instruction given as the vision commenced. Only a few, the sons of perdition, would remain beyond God's saving power. "For all the rest shall be brought forth by the resurrection of the dead." (Verses 37–39.) "Wherefore, he saves all except [the sons of perdition]." (Verse 44.) Thus "this is the gospel of glad tidings." (Verse 40.)

---

1. *Journal of Discourses*, 6:120.
2. Talmage, *The Articles of Faith* (1899 edition), 420–21.
3. Smith, *Doctrines of Salvation*, 2:31.
4. McConkie, "Seven Deadly Heresies," June 1, 1980.
5. Robinson and Garrett, *Doctrine and Covenants Commentary*, 2:287.

Three degrees of glory, not one degree of glory and two degrees of damnation

It should be emphasized that section 76 was a message of hope and optimism about the ultimate destiny of mankind. It should not be viewed as one degree of salvation (the celestial kingdom), and two degrees of damnation (the terrestrial and telestial kingdom). To take this point of view is to read back into section 76 a Protestant perspective. It should be emphasized that all three heavens are degrees of "glory." "And thus we saw in the heavenly vision, the glory of the telestial, which surpasses all understanding, and no man knows it except him to whom God has revealed it." (Verses 89–90.)

From Joseph's reaction to the vision, it is clear that he saw it as a manifestation of God's mercy to the children of men. The superlative blessings to come and the opportunity to lay hold upon those blessings was beyond what men and women had conceived of from reading the Bible and Book of Mormon before the vision was made known.

Universal redemption

The early Christian Father Origen thought that man's fall and subsequent alienation from God could not be permanent. In the end, all humankind would reach perfection at different rates and times. Other influential Christian thinkers who followed him, however, disagreed with Origen's ideas on how many would make it to heaven. Emperor Justinian vehemently opposed Origen's ideas and in 543 AD wrote his *Book against Origen*. By 553 AD the Fifth Ecumenical Council anathematized those who favored a plentiful heaven in favor of an endless hell. Therefore, historic Christianity held that hell was almost always a more populous place than heaven.[1] John Calvin in the 1500s agreed and taught that "the greater part of mankind [to] abide in death [would do so] without any possibility of redemption."[2]

By 1738, Wesley and others began to decry the idea of an endless hell and proposed that "God's grace is free to all."[3] The idea that God would save the vast majority of his children became known as the doctrine of universal redemption. This trend toward a more roomy heaven continued into the 19th century. Teryl Givens points out that the "dominant New England school of theology of the era and the New Divinity Movement

---

1. Givens, *Wrestling the Angel*, 240.
2. Ibid., 242.
3. Ibid.

generally held a rather more hopeful estimate of the number of those who would find redemption."[1]

Section 76 sides with Wesley and adopts a more universalistic view of who will be saved. But Joseph, while admitting that God's grace was an essential element of salvation, placed greater emphasis on works and the inherent capabilities of humankind to progress and become like God. Section 76 is all about glories and almost mentions as an aside that there are a few incorrigibles who end up in Perdition. Joseph described a bright future for the human race after death. It was just a matter of time before the vast majority of God's children would of their own free will come back into his presence. Just before the prophet's death, he said in his most famous discourse, the King Follett Sermon, that "when we are ready to come to [God], he is ready to come to us."[2]

SECTION 77: JOHN JOHNSON FARM, HIRAM, OHIO, MARCH 1832

Heading

Interpretation of the book of Revelation.

Introduction

Revelation given to Joseph Smith the Prophet in the upper room of the Johnson farm home in March 1832.[3] The Prophet wrote, "In connection with the translation of the Scriptures, I received the following explanation of the Revelation of St. John."

Historical background

By March 1832 Joseph Smith, with Sidney Rigdon as scribe, had been revising the Bible for about two months in the upper room at the Johnson farm. In January Joseph had a revelation explaining 1 Corinthians 7:14 on marriage in the early church, and in February he received the vision of the three degrees of glory, a revelation clarifying that John 5:29 did not give the full picture on the judgment of mankind, along with rewards and punishments in the afterlife. (See D&C 74; 76.) Section 77 came in March and explained parts of the book of Revelation.

This revelation was not contained in the 1833 Book of Commandments

---

1. Ibid.
2. Smith, *Teachings of the Prophet Joseph Smith*, 350.
3. See Smith, *History of the Church*, 1:253–55.

or in the 1835 edition of the Doctrine and Covenants. It was included in the first edition of the Pearl of Great Price in 1851. It first appeared in the Doctrine and Covenants in 1876.[1]

Interpreting the book of Revelation

The interpretation of the book of Revelation has long been a source of debate and disagreement. Some have held that it is solely a message about the first century. Others take the position that the book is a prophecy about future events. Still others borrow from both these points of view. For example, the first three chapters of the book address the apostate status of the seven churches located in what was then known as Asia (Turkey) as they existed in John's day. On the other hand, future events leading up to the Second Coming are also depicted in the book of Revelation, such as the restoration of the gospel (Revelation 14:7), the building of the New Jerusalem, and God's final triumph over evil. From a Latter-day Saint perspective, the book addresses events in John's day (and shortly thereafter), as well as events that would come about in the distant future. With very few exceptions, Joseph did not believe that parts of the book of Revelation referred to events that preceded John's day.[2]

By its very nature, the metaphorical content of the book of Revelation adds to the problem of interpretation, because the meaning of the beasts and other images in the book are malleable and open to a number of very different explanations, depending upon the vantage point of the reader. In this respect, it is important to recognize that Joseph Smith was not overly concerned that those reading the book of Revelation get it just right but rather encouraged his followers to enjoy studying and thinking about it. In reference to the visions in the book of Revelation, Joseph said that God "always holds Himself responsible to give a revelation or interpretation of the meaning thereof, otherwise we are not responsible or accountable for our belief in it. Don't be afraid of being damned for not knowing the meaning of a vision or figure, if God has not given a revelation or interpretation of the subject."[3]

Unlike the Evangelicals of our day who interpret the images specifically as present-day events and use the book of Revelation as a road map and

---

1. See Robinson and Garrett, *Doctrine and Covenants Commentary*, 2:336.
2. See Smith, *History of the Church*, 5:342. "The things which John saw had no allusion to the scenes of the days of Adam, Enoch, Abraham or Jesus, only so far as is plainly represented by John, and clearly set forth by him." The Prophet said further, "Now, I make this declaration, that those things which John saw in heaven had no allusion to anything that had been on the earth previous to that time." (Smith, *History of the Church*, 5:342.)
3. Smith, *History of the Church*, 5:343.

timetable about the Second Coming, Joseph took a different approach and tended to emphasize various doctrines in the book rather than explicit interpretations. Some of those points of doctrine are a description of the apostasy (Revelation 1–2); the importance of overcoming the world (Revelation 3:21; 21:7); the thought that the faithful are to be kings and priests unto God and will reign on the earth (Revelation 1:6: 5:10; 20:6; 21:7); the idea that animals are resurrected from the dead and that there are animals in heaven redeemed by the blood of Christ (Revelation 5:11–14; D&C 77:3);[1] the explanation that the "woman driven into the wilderness" is the Church and the "man child" the political kingdom of God growing out of the Church (see Revelation 12); the doctrine that all people shall be judged by their works out of the books that are written both on earth and in heaven (Revelation 20:11–13; D&C 128:6–7); and the understanding that Satan went to war with God in the premortal life and was cast down to earth with a third of the hosts of heaven (Revelation 12:3–4). By comparison, Joseph turned to the book of Revelation for a rather short list of future events. Some were the restoration of the gospel by an angel (Revelation 14:6–7); the prophecy about the two prophets who will lie dead in the streets of Jerusalem in the last days and then be raised (Revelation 11:1–11); and the future establishment of the New Jerusalem, the four-square city that will be built in connection with Jesus' Second Coming (Revelation 3:12; 7; 21:1–22; Ether 13:2–10; Moses 7:62–63; 3 Nephi 20:22; 21:23–25).

Section 77 deals with an interpretation of some of the specific symbols found in the book of Revelation. It was never intended to be a complete interpretation of the book of Revelation but rather concerns only the chapters between 4 and 11 of the 22 chapters found in the book. Hyrum M. Smith points out that this section "is a key. A key is a very small part of the house. It unlocks the door through which an entrance may be gained, but after the key has been turned, the searcher for treasure must find it for himself. It is like entering a museum in which the students must find out for themselves what they desire to know."[2]

In Nauvoo in early April 1843, some of the elders were giving competing interpretations of the book of Revelation. Joseph intervened and reminded his coworkers that they should not be critical of each other over differing explanations about what the book meant. Joseph said that such behavior looked "too much like the Methodists, and not like the Latter-day Saints. Methodists have creeds which a man must believe or be asked out of their church. I want the liberty of thinking and believing as I please. It feels so good not to be trammeled. It does not prove that a man is not a

---

1. Smith, *History of the Church*, 5:343.
2. Woodford, *The Historical Development of the Doctrine and Covenants*, 973.

good man because he errs in doctrine."[1] After admonishing his brethren about being tolerant of each other's views and in an effort to settle some of the disputes, Joseph said in reference to the beasts that the "eyes are a representation of light and knowledge, that is, they [the beasts] are full of knowledge." (Verse 4.) "Their wings are a representation of power to move, to act." (Verse 4.) Joseph seems to interpret a symbol by identifying its function and going from there.[2]

SECTION 78: HIRAM, OHIO, WHITNEY STORE, KIRTLAND, OHIO, MARCH 1832[3]

Heading

Plans made for a storehouse in Kirtland, Ohio, and Independence, Missouri.

The big question

Question: How do we live together and build a community now that we have gathered?

Answer: Establish united orders and be equal in temporal things.

---

1. Smith, *History of the Church*, 5:340.
2. See Smith, *History of the Church*, 5:344. When speaking about the book of Revelation, Joseph suggested that the King James Version in some respects was inadequate. "I am now going to take exception to the present translation of the Bible in relation to these matters. Our latitude and longitude can be determined in the original [language] with far greater accuracy than in the English version. There is a grand distinction between the actual meaning of the prophets and the present translation." (Smith, *History of the Church*, 5:342–43.) He went to say, "There is a mistranslation of the word dragon in the second verse. The original word signifies the devil, and not dragon, as translated. In chapter 12, verse 9, it reads, 'That old serpent, called the devil,' and it ought to be translated devil in this case, and not dragon. It is sometimes translated Apollyon." Joseph believed that the beasts that worshiped God were "actually living in heaven, and were actually to have power given to them over the inhabitants of the earth, precisely according to the plain reading of the revelations." (Smith, *History of the Church*, 5:345.) Some of these beasts giving glory to God were "of a thousand forms, that had been saved from ten thousand times ten thousand earths like this,—strange beasts of which we have no conception: all might be seen in heaven. John learned that God glorified Himself by saving all that His hands had made, whether beasts, fowls, fishes or men; and he will glorify Himself with them." In other contexts the beasts referred to powers on earth. "The beasts which John saw had to devour the inhabitants of the earth in days to come." (Smith, *History of the Church*, 5:342.)
3. "We now date this section March 1, 1832." (Woodford, "Discoveries from the Joseph Smith Papers Project.") Joseph and Sidney Rigdon had been commanded to stop their revisions of the Bible in early December 1831 in order to blunt the attacks against the Church of apostates Ezra Booth and Simonds Ryder. Mission accomplished, the Lord commanded that the revisions begin again. While they were engaged in the process, section 74 was given as Joseph and Rigdon studied and revised 1 Corinthians 7:14.

John Johnson Home: Hiram, Ohio, October 1831–August 1832

Introduction

Revelation given through Joseph Smith sometime in March 1832. It is not known whether the revelation was received at the Whitney store or on the Johnson farm in Hiram, Ohio.[1] In it Joseph was instructed to travel to the land Zion (Missouri) to explain more fully to his followers the principles and purposes underlying the law of consecration. Joseph left Hiram for Zion on Sunday, April 1, 1832. After he arrived he "sat in council" with the leaders of Church on April 26, 1832.[2] Section 78 also instructed leaders of the Church to provide for a bishop's storehouse in Ohio and Missouri, a central feature of the law of consecration that had not yet been accomplished.[3]

Anchor section

Memorize: Be equal in temporal things

Background

When the law of consecration was first introduced, a storehouse had been described as a mechanism for redistributing wealth within the community. (See D&C 42:34, 55.) Even though it had been a year since this law was first introduced, no storehouses had been provided for. (See D&C 51:13.) Consequently, Joseph Smith and Sidney Rigdon went to Zion in Jackson County, Missouri, to more fully institute this law. Section 78 is part of this effort and among other things directs that bishops' storehouses be established. This section also instructs Joseph, Sidney Rigdon, and Newel K. Whitney to form a business partnership called a united order or firm to generate revenue for the Church. This business entity was to operate on the same basis as the Literary Firm, which had previously been established to publish Church materials. These "orders" or "firms" were not administered by the bishop, who directed "inheritances" for the general membership. Rather, united orders and firms operated more along the lines of a private business. (See D&C 70.)[4]

---

1. In 1832 Joseph was living on the John Johnson farm in Hiram and reported that he received five revelations during the month of March. However, he did not note in the official history of the Church at what location each revelation was received. Some scholars believe all the March revelations were received in Hiram. However, the Kirtland Revelation Book indicates that Joseph received this revelation while visiting in Kirtland. Therefore, some Mormon historians have suggested that Joseph probably received it in the Whitney store, which was located there.
2. See Woodford, *The Historical Development of the Doctrine and Covenants*, 992.
3. See Smith, *History of the Church*, 1:255–57.
4. See Robinson and Garrett, *Doctrine and Covenants Commentary*, 350–51.

One of the end results of section 78 was to co-opt the Gilbert-Whitney store in Kirtland as a bishop's storehouse. A similar storehouse was set up in Independence, Missouri. Unfortunately, these united orders/firms, as well as the law of consecration, were short-lived. On April 10, 1834, the Gilbert-Whitney firms were dissolved. Thirteen days later, section 104 gave instructions that the two branches of the firm operate privately as separate entities once again.[1]

The Saints must be equal in temporal things in order to be equal in spiritual things

The principles underlying the law of consecration are described in the Book of Moses. "And the Lord called his people ZION, because they were of one heart and one mind, and dwelt in righteousness; and there was no poor among them." (Moses 7:18.) The Doctrine and Covenants makes it clear that the starting point for such a society is an equitable distribution of the world's goods. "It is not given that one man should possess that which is above another, wherefore the whole world lieth in sin." (D&C 49:20.)

Section 78 also gives emphasis to the idea that there should an equitable distribution of the world's goods. Yet it carries the idea further by explaining that the purpose behind such a society is "the obtaining of heavenly things." The Lord continues, "That you may be equal in the bonds of heavenly things, yea, and earthly things also, for the obtaining of heavenly things. For if ye are not equal in earthly things ye can not be equal in obtaining heavenly things." (Verses 5–7.)[2]

This cause-and-effect relationship between economic equality and spiritual blessings is best illustrated by Jesus himself, when he instituted a Zion-like society in the Americas.[3] "And they had all things common

---

1. See Cook, *Revelations of the Prophet Joseph Smith*, 168.

2. Max H. Parkin explains that it was time, as stated in this revelation, that Newel K. Whitney, Joseph Smith, and Sidney Rigdon "sit in council" with the Saints in Missouri. "A crucial but unpublished part of the revelation informed the Prophet as to their specific purpose for going to Missouri. There 'must needs be ... an organization of the literary and mercantile establishments of my church both in this place and in the land of Zion,'" it declared. (Kirtland revelation Book, 16) This new unified enterprice should be 'for a permanent and everlasting establishment and firm unto my Church.' The revelation instructed Joseph Smith and others, including the leaders in Zion, to be 'joined together in this firm' as partners by an 'everlasting covenant' and thereby be equal in both heavenly and earthly things. (Section 78:3-4) Thus they were directed to operate the Church's mercantile and literary interests as a united enterprise to be governed by a single board of managers." See Max H. Parkin, "Joseph Smith and the United Firm: The Growth and Decline of the Church's First Master Plan of Business and Finance, Ohio and Missouri, 1832-1834," *BYU Studies* 46:3:13 (2007).

3. The connection between disproportionate wealth and social breakdown is a theme oft repeated Book of Mormon. "For behold the Lord had blessed them so long with the riches of

among them; therefore there were not rich and poor, bond and free, but they were all partakers of the heavenly gift." (4 Nephi 1:3.) The spiritual gifts were described as "great and marvelous" and were "wrought by the disciples of Jesus, insomuch that they did heal the sick, and raise the dead, and cause the lame to walk, and the blind to receive their sight, and the deaf to hear; and all manner of miracles did they work among the children of men."[1] (4 Nephi 1:5.) In sum, "There were no envyings, nor strifes, nor tumults, nor whoredoms, nor lyings, nor murders, nor any manner of lasciviousness; and surely there could not be a happier people among all the people who had been created by the hand of God." (4 Nephi 1:16.)

In connection with section 78, it should be stressed that the equality spoken about is more than just caring for the poor. It is about the disparity of wealth between individuals. It is about the equitable distribution of economic resources in a society so that all have equal opportunities. The language in the Doctrine and Covenants could not be clearer on this point. "I, the Lord, have decreed to provide for my saints, that the poor shall be exalted, in that the rich are made low." (D&C 104:16.) By elevating the poor and lowering the rich, both are placed on a more equal playing field. Section 78 stresses the principle behind the law of consecration; and the mechanics of how this "oneness and equality" was to be brought about are set out in detail in other sections in the Doctrine and Covenants.

---

the world that they had not been stirred up to anger, to wars, nor to bloodshed; therefore they began to set their hearts upon their riches; yea, they began to seek to get gain that they *might be lifted up one above another;* therefore they began to commit secret murders, and to rob and plunder, that they might get gain." (Helaman 6:17; emphasis added.)

See also 3 Nephi 6:11–16:

"For there were many merchants in the land, and also many lawyers, and many officers. And the people began to be distinguished by ranks, according to their riches and their chances for learning; yea, some were ignorant because of their poverty, and others did receive great learning because of their riches. Some were lifted up in pride, and others were exceedingly humble; some did return railing for railing, while others would receive railing and persecution and all manner of afflictions, and would not turn and revile again, but were humble and penitent before God.

"And thus there became a great *inequality* in all the land, insomuch that the church began to be broken up; yea, insomuch that in the thirtieth year the church was broken up in all the land save it were among a few of the Lamanites who were converted unto the true faith; and they would not depart from it, for they were firm, and steadfast, and immovable, willing with all diligence to keep the commandments of the Lord.

"Now the cause of this *iniquity* of the people was this—Satan had great power, unto the stirring up of the people to do all manner of iniquity, and to the puffing them up with pride, tempting them to seek for power, and authority, and riches, and the vain things of the world. And thus Satan did lead away the hearts of the people to do all manner of iniquity; therefore they had enjoyed peace but a few years." (Emphasis added.)

1. When the people began to reject the principle of economic equality, the spiritual gifts decreased. (See 4 Nephi 1:43.)

The system depended upon each Saint voluntarily consecrating all he or she had to the Lord.

Use of code names

Section 78 is the first of a number of revelations in which code names were employed—fictitious names were substituted for real names. This practice was adopted to protect certain brethren from being identified and thereafter harassed and persecuted by nonmembers.[1] Orson Pratt abandoned the use of code names when he compiled the 1854 edition of the Doctrine and Covenants.[2] Orson Pratt explained: "Joseph was called Baurak Ale, which was a Hebrew word; meaning God bless you. He was also called Gazelam, being a person to whom the Lord had given the Urim and Thummim. He was also called Enoch. Sidney Rigdon was called Baneemy."[3]

Pratt also explained that other words were changed to protect the brethren in other ways as well. He noted that in this revelation, where it read "so many dollars," it was changed to "talents," and the city of New York was changed to "Cainhannoch."[4]

Sitting in council

Prior to the time that Joseph Smith received section 107, which provides that the governing quorums of the Church should "sit in council" and operate upon the principle of unanimity, it was Joseph Smith's custom to informally "sit in council" with his brethren. Section 78 is illustrative of this practice. When Joseph arrived in Zion, he called a conference or council of high priests. John Whitmer, the clerk for the meeting, noted that Sidney Rigdon said the reason he and Joseph made the trip to Zion from Kirtland was so they could "sit in council with the High Priests here, for the particulars which read the commandments."[5] The same idea was repeated in the revelation itself: "Let my servant Newel K. Whitney and my servant Joseph Smith, Jun., and my servant Sidney Rigdon sit in council with the saints which are in Zion." (Verse 9.)

---

1. See Woodford, *The Historical Development of the Doctrine and Covenants*, 993.
2. See Woodford, *The Historical Development of the Doctrine and Covenants*, 994.
3. See Woodford, *The Historical Development of the Doctrine and Covenants*, 994.
4. See Woodford, *The Historical Development of the Doctrine and Covenants*, 994.
5. Woodford, *The Historical Development of the Doctrine and Covenants*, 993.

Property once donated to the consecrated order not returned if the person donating the property decided to leave the order

When Saints were invited to enter the law of consecration, they deeded everything they had over to the Church. In return, the Church leased back to the individual what he or she needed to sustain life. Although as time went on Joseph did return some of the property that had been donated by certain people, this was not what the Lord originally intended. The "bond or everlasting covenant" by which men and women consecrated their properties was binding—"cannot be broken." And if this provision was disregarded, such would lose their standing in the Church. (See verses 11–12.)

The Lord warns of tribulation to come

Section 78 warns of "tribulation which shall descend upon you." (Verse 14.) This phrase proved to be prophetic. Within a few short years the Saints would be pushed out of Kirtland, Jackson County, Clay County, and the city of Far West, Missouri. Persecution, violence, and uncertainty would prevail. Yet the Lord promised that the Saints would receive crowns and "be made rulers of many kingdoms" in a future day. (See verse 15.) The Lord knew that ultimately this group of Saints would not be able to establish Zion because they "cannot bear all things now." (See verse 18.) Nevertheless, the Lord encouraged his Saints to "be of good cheer, for I will lead you along." (Verse 18.) Ultimately, he would lead the body of the Saints to Nauvoo and finally the Great Basin Kingdom.

SECTION 79: JOHN JOHNSON HOME, HIRAM, OHIO, MARCH 1832[1]

Heading

Jared Carter called to do missionary work.

The big question

Question: What is the structure of the Church?
Answer: Missionaries are called to preach the gospel.

---

1. "This section is now dated March 12, 1832." (Woodford, "Discoveries from the Joseph Smith Papers Project," 31.)

Introduction

Revelation given through Joseph Smith the Prophet in the upper room of the Johnson farm home located in Hiram, Ohio, in March 1832. Jared Carter is called to preach the gospel to the "eastern countries" by the Comforter or Holy Ghost.

Historical background

Jared Carter was a part of the community of the Colesville Saints who had joined the Church in New York sometime in February 1831. He moved to Ohio with the body of the Church and settled first in Thompson, Ohio. Thereafter, he moved to Amherst about fifty miles west of Kirtland to be near his brother Simeon. In June he was ordained a priest (see D&C 52:38) and later an elder sometime before September 1832.[1]

In March 1832 Carter went to Hiram, Ohio, to visit the Prophet Joseph and ask him to "inquire the will of the Lord concerning my ministry and the ensuing season." Section 79 came in response.[2] Carter recorded the following in his diary:

> The word of the Lord came forth that showed that it was his will that I should go forth to the Eastern countries in the power of the ordinance wherewith I had been ordained, which was to the high privilege of administering in the name of Jesus Christ even to seal on earth and to build up the Church of Christ and to work miracles in the name of Christ.... Now I have received a revelation of the will of the Lord to me by the mouth of Joseph the Seer, that I should not only preach the gospel from place to place, but from city to city.[3]

Having obtained the word of the Lord through the Prophet, Jared Carter began his ministry with confidence that he was on the Lord's errand. He said, "I was acting according to the will of the Lord for I have received a revelation of the will of the Lord to me by the mouth of Joseph the Seer."[4] Prayerfully, Jared Carter came to the conclusion that his brother Simeon should be his companion and go "where he felt led by the Spirit."[5] Six months later Jared Carter returned home. He made ninety-eight converts and felt that "many others have been convinced of the work that sooner or later I think will" become members.[6]

Carter moved with the Saints to Missouri and in 1838 became associated

---

1. See Robinson and Garrett, *Doctrine and Covenants Commentary*, 2:360.
2. See Cook, *Revelations of the Prophet Joseph Smith*, 169.
3. See Cook, Revelations of the Prophet Joseph Smith, 169.
4. Woodford, *The Historical Development of the Doctrine and Covenants*, 1005.
5. See Woodford, *The Historical Development of the Doctrine and Covenants*, 1005.
6. See Cook, *Revelations of the Prophet Joseph Smith*, 169–70.

with a radical element within the Church known as the Danites, a group of militant members that organized a militia to defend and take offensive action against anti-Mormon mobs and vigilantes.[1] The First Presidency ultimately distanced itself from this group, and Jared Carter and others became disaffected from the Church. During the Nauvoo period, in 1843, he was accused of conspiring with John C. Bennett, Sidney Rigdon, and George W. Robinson in turning against the Prophet Joseph. At one point he was disfellowshipped. Later he repented and regained his standing in the Church. Ultimately, he left Nauvoo and settled in Chicago. He died at age fifty-three. George A. Smith reported that he heard him say, "I have sacrificed all my property once, but I will never do it again."[2]

Jared Carter was typical of others who were called to serve proselytizing missions for the Church during the Kirtland period. Missionaries were called by revelation, went two by two, served as time permitted, were often married and therefore left their families behind, preached in unspecified areas, and did not work under the direction of any particular Church leader. It was not uncommon when married brethren went out on missions for friends and neighbors to help provide financial assistance for their families. Sometimes missionaries went without "purse or scrip." (See D&C 84:78, 86.) Missionaries were instructed to restrict their preaching to the first principles of the gospel (see D&C 19:31), warn the people of the imminent second coming of Jesus Christ (see D&C 133:1–6, 11, 46–53), and testify of the truth of the restored gospel (see D&C 88:81–82). On some occasions missionaries would pronounce a blessing or curse upon homes they visited. (See D&C 75:19–20.)

SECTION 80: JOHN JOHNSON HOME, HIRAM, OHIO, MARCH 1832[3]

Heading

Stephen Burnett and John Murdock called to preach the gospel and teach what they have "heard, . . . believe, . . . and know to be true."

The big question

Question: What is the structure of the Church?
Answer: Missionaries are called to preach the gospel.

---

1. See Black, *Who's Who in the Doctrine and Covenants*, 53. Carter's Danite nickname was "the terrible Brother of Gideon." (See Black, *Who's Who in the Doctrine and Covenants*, 53.)
2. Black, *Who's Who in the Doctrine and Covenants*, 54.
3. "Correct this date to March 17, 1832." (Woodford, "Discoveries from the Joseph Smith Papers Project," 31.)

Introduction

Revelation given through Joseph Smith the Prophet in the upper room of the Johnson home at Hiram, Ohio, in March 1832.[1] Stephen Burnett and Eden Smith are called to preach in whatever place they choose.

Historical background

Stephen Burnett first heard about the gospel when a missionary by the name of John Murdock preached in his hometown of Orange, Ohio. Murdock wrote in his diary that he baptized three in Orange, including Burnett. Both men, full of enthusiasm and "carried away in the spirit" decided to share the gospel good news with Burnett's uncle, but to no avail.[2] Burnett's interest in converting others did not go unnoticed. In January 1832, Burnett was called to serve a mission with Rubles Eames. (See D&C 75:35.) It was either a short mission or Burnett or Eames failed to respond to the call, because just weeks later, in March 1832, Burnett was called to serve a mission with another companion, Eden Smith. (See D&C 80.) Burnett and Smith established a small branch of the Church in Dalton, New Hampshire, which within a short time grew to about fifteen members.[3]

In 1837 Burnett became disaffected with the Church and united with Warren Parrish and others in Kirtland who claimed Joseph was a fallen prophet. The dissidents adopted the name "reformers" and, among other things, insisted that the "regular authorities in Kirtland had departed from the true order of things by calling the Church 'The Church of the Latter-day Saints.'"[4] In addition, the financial collapse of a bank Joseph had established (Kirtland Safety Society Anti-Banking Company) only exacerbated feelings of discontent about Church leaders.[5] Joseph defended himself and called Burnett "a little ignorant blockhead . . . whose heart was . . . set on money . . . who got wearied of the restraints of religion . . . and could not bear to have his purse taxed."[6] It is not known whether or not Burnett ever reassociated himself with the main body of the Church.

Burnett's companion, Eden Smith, had once before served a short mission of just days' duration within five to fifteen miles of his home during 1831–1832. He would preach for a few days and then return home to work

---

1. Smith, *History of the Church*, 1:257.
2. See Black, *Who's Who in the Doctrine and Covenants*, 39.
3. See Black, *Who's Who in the Doctrine and Covenants*, 40.
4. See Black, *Who's Who in the Doctrine and Covenants*, 40; and *Church History in the Fulness of Times*, 176.
5. See *Church History in the Fulness of Times*, 171.
6. See Black, *Who's Who in the Doctrine and Covenants*, 40.

to support his family before going out to preach again. Of his mission experience with Burnett, he said that they served in eastern Ohio and the surrounding countryside, held many meetings, and baptized a few.

Soon after Eden Smith's mission, he also left the Church. However, he returned to the faith a short time later. He moved with the Saints to Missouri, Nauvoo, and finally relocated in the Great Basin. His testimony waned over time and he returned to Kanesville, Nebraska, in 1848. By 1850 he was residing in Pottawattamie County, Iowa, and died on December 7, 1851, at age forty-five.[1]

Missionaries may testify about the things they have "heard . . . believe . . . and know to be true."

Individual conviction about the "truths" of the gospel varies, depending upon an individual's knowledge and spiritual experience. Section 80 makes it clear that missionaries are not expected to overstate what they may or may not know and are free to speak about things they have "heard, . . . believe, . . . and know to be true." (Verse 4.) Each of these three options—what one has heard, believes, or knows—implies a different degree of personal certainty. To speak about something that a person has *heard* acknowledges that the credibility of the statement rests on another individual. To state one's *belief* means that the person has some reservations but is willing to testify that the information is certain enough to be reliable. To state that one has *knowledge* means that the information is based on what that person considers to be undeniable personal experience and implies the highest level of certainty. For example, Joseph's statement that he had seen God, Jesus, and angels fits into this category. Recognition that there are different levels of assurance gave these early missionaries permission to be personally honest with themselves about the message they were declaring. Missionaries were not expected to be disingenuous and vouch for something they did not believe in.[2]

---

1. See Black, *Who's Who in the Doctrine and Covenants*, 271–72.
2. The Book of Mormon teaches that over time faith ripens into certainty. (See Alma 32.)

Section 81: John Johnson Home, Hiram, Ohio, March 15, 1832[1]

Heading

Presidency of the High Priesthood organized.

The big question

Question: What is the structure of the Church?
Answer: The Presidency of the High Priesthood is organized and given the "keys of the kingdom" or right to direct the affairs of the Church.

Introduction

Revelation given through Joseph Smith the Prophet in the upper room of the Johnson home at Hiram, Ohio, on March 15, 1832.[2] Frederick G. Williams is called to be a high priest and a counselor in the Presidency of the High Priesthood, later to become known as the First Presidency. The historical records show that when this revelation was received in March 1832, Jesse Gause, not Frederick G. Williams, was called to the office of counselor to Joseph Smith in the presidency. However, when he failed to continue in a manner consistent with this appointment, the call was subsequently transferred to Frederick G. Williams.[3] The revelation (dated March 1832) should be regarded as a step toward the formal organization of the First Presidency, specifically calling for the office of counselor in that body and explaining the dignity of the appointment.

---

1. This date should be March 15, 1832. (See Woodford, "Discoveries from the Joseph Smith Papers Project," 32.)
2. Smith, *History of the Church*, 1:257–58.
3. Jesse Gause served for a time, but was excommunicated from the Church in December 1832. Frederick G. Williams was ordained to the specified office on March 18, 1833.

Historical background

On January 25, 1832, in Amherst, Ohio, Joseph Smith was ordained and sustained President of the High Priesthood. About two months later two men, Jesse Gause and Sidney Rigdon, were appointed to stand with him in the Presidency of the High Priesthood. At this time in Church history there was only one office in the high priesthood, and that was the office of high priest. The Presidency of the High Priesthood was to preside over all ordained high priests. However, by 1833 or 1834, the Presidency of the High Priesthood became known as the First Presidency.[1]

The Kirtland revelation book for March 8, 1832, states that "brother Jesse Gause and Brother Sidney [Rigdon]" were to be called "to be my councilors of the ministry of the presidency of the High Priesthood."[2] As stated in the introduction, the first recipient of that revelation was Jesse Gause. However, the revelation was later altered to read "my servant Frederick G. Williams."[3] On March 18, 1833, Frederick G. Williams and Sidney Rigdon were ordained by Joseph Smith as his counselors.[4]

Jesse Gause disappears from the pages of Church history in August 1832.[5] The background on Jesse Gause prior to the time he joined the Church and rose to a position of leadership, as well as his subsequent apostasy, are not entirely clear. What little is known is discussed in more detail in the commentary to section 90.

Duties of the members of the Presidency of the High Priesthood

The duties of the Presidency of the High Priesthood, later to become the First Presidency, were to pray always "vocally and in thy heart, in public and in private." (Verse 3.) In addition, they were instructed to "succor the weak, lift up the hands which hang down, and strengthen the feeble knees." (Verse 5.)

Section 81 also clarifies that the administrative duties of the Church are centered in the Presidency of the High Priesthood. "I have given [Joseph Smith] the keys of the kingdom, which belong always unto the Presidency

---

1. See Cook, *Revelations of the Prophet Joseph Smith*, 171; and Robinson and Garrett, *Doctrine and Covenants Commentary*, 3:1.
2. Cook, *Revelations of the Prophet Joseph Smith*, 171.
3. See Cook, *Revelations of the Prophet Joseph Smith*, 171. On March 15, 1832, section 81 was received, according to Woodford. Since Jesse Gause was already a member of the Presidency of the High Priesthood, section 81 does not mark the time Gause was called to this position. Rather, this revelation was only to give Gause further direction in the work to which he had already been called. (See Woodford, *The Historical Development of the Doctrine and Covenants*, 1018.)
4. See Woodford, *The Historical Development of the Doctrine and Covenants*, 1019.
5. Woodford, *The Historical Development of the Doctrine and Covenants*, 1018.

of the High Priesthood." (Verse 2 and D&C 90:2.) Each member of the First Presidency was "accounted as equal with thee [Joseph Smith] in holding the keys of this last kingdom." (D&C 90:6.)

Section 99: John Johnson Home, Hiram, Ohio, August 1832[1]

Heading

John Murdock called as a missionary.

Introduction

Revelation given through Joseph Smith the Prophet to John Murdock in the upper room of the Johnson home at Hiram, Ohio, in August 1832. Although editions of the Doctrine and Covenants beginning with 1876 have listed this revelation as Kirtland, August 1833, earlier editions and other historical records make it clear that this revelation was received in Hiram.

The big question

Question: What is the structure of the Church?
Answer: Send out missionaries.

Historical background

John Murdock always had an interest in finding the "true" religion and finally settled on Mormonism in the winter of 1830, just months after the Church was organized. His conversion was almost immediate. He heard about the Mormons, journeyed to Kirtland, Ohio, and was given a Book of Mormon, which he read that night. The next morning, on November 5, 1830, he was baptized by Parley P. Pratt.[2] Section 99 calls him to be a missionary. He served three missions during his lifetime.

Prior to his membership in the Church he had been a member of the Lutheran Dutch Church, Presbyterian Seceder Church, Baptist Church, Methodist Church, and Campbellite Church. His rapid succession through so many religious organizations occurred because he did not feel any of them conformed to his understanding of the New Testament.

In April 1831 his wife Julia died just six hours after she gave birth to

---

1. "We now accept August 29, 1832, as the correct date." (Woodford, "Discoveries from the Joseph Smith Papers Project," 32.)
2. See Black, *Who's Who in the Doctrine and Covenants*, 202.

twins. Murdock was unable to care for his newborns, and Joseph and Emma Smith offered to rear them. Prior to this time Joseph had become acquainted with the Murdocks and in June 1831 had called John Murdock on a mission to the Missouri area, along with Joseph's brother Hyrum. (See D&C 52:8–9.) Once again, for a second time, Murdock was called to serve and did so between April 1833 through April 1834.[1] He was promised that "you shall have power to declare my word in the demonstration of my Holy Spirit." (Verse 2.) Years later, in 1851, while he was living in the Salt Lake Valley, he was called to serve as a missionary in Australia. During this sojourn that he wrote his mission president and informed him that he was discouraged for "want of Books of Mormon, Doctrine and Covenants, Voice of Warnings, and Hymn Books."[2] On October 14, 1852, in a letter from Brigham Young, Murdock was released and told to "Return in peace."[3]

Murdock served his missions at considerable sacrifice, especially in light of the fact that his wife had died and he had four living children. His daughter Julia was living with Joseph Smith and his family, and so Murdock arranged for his remaining three children to be taken to Missouri to stay with Caleb Baldwin and his family. He importuned Bishop Partridge to help care for them while he was away. (See verse 6.) Murdock recorded in his journal, "Previous to this I had provided for my children and sent them up to the Bishop in Zion according to the revelation by Brother Caleb Baldwin and paid him thirty dollars for carrying them and [other] things. And after making proper preparations according to the revelation I journeyed forth. September 27, 1832, Brother Zebedee Coltrin and myself started on a mission."[4]

In the spring of 1833 the Prophet Joseph promised him in the school of the prophets that he would be blessed spiritually. Murdock records in his journal:

> I saw the form of a man [the Savior], most lovely, the visage of his face was sound and fair as the sun. His hair a bright silver grey, curled in most majestic form, His eyes a keen penetrating blue, and the skin of his neck a most beautiful white and he was covered from the neck to the feet with a loose garment, pure white, whiter than any garment I have ever before seen. His countenance was most penetrating, and yet most lovely.[5]

Murdock volunteered for Zion's Camp, remarried in the summer of

---

1. See Black, *Who's Who in the Doctrine and Covenants*, 202.
2. Black, *Who's Who in the Doctrine and Covenants*, 203.
3. See Black, *Who's Who in the Doctrine and Covenants*, 203.
4. Robinson and Garrett, *Doctrine and Covenants Commentary*, 3:250.
5. Robinson and Garrett, *Doctrine and Covenants Commentary*, 3:248.

1836, and trekked west, where in his later years he became a patriarch in the Church.[1]

Section 133: John Johnson Home, Hiram, Ohio, November 3, 1831

Heading

Information included in the appendix of the 1833 edition of the Doctrine and Covenants. Building up Zion in preparation for Second Coming of Jesus.

Introduction

Revelation through Joseph Smith the Prophet in the upper room of the Johnson home.[2] Prefacing this revelation the Prophet wrote: "At this time there were many things which the Elders desired to know relative to preaching the Gospel to the inhabitants of the earth, and concerning the gathering; and in order to walk by the true light, and be instructed from on high, on the 3rd of November, 1831, I inquired of the Lord and received the following important revelation."

Historical background

Section 133 was originally intended to be made a part of the appendix in the 1833 edition of the Book of Commandments. However, the destruction of the Church printing press in Independence, Missouri, on July 20, 1833, prevented its inclusion. In the 1835 edition it was placed in the appendix and in later editions assigned a section number and included with the main body of revelations.

Section 133 was received and intended to be an appropriate conclusion to a new book of scripture. Prior to its inclusion in the 1835 edition it was published in the *Morning and Evening Star*. In the headnote it said, "Having given, in a previous number, the Preface to the Book of Commandments now in press, we give below, the close or as it has been called, the Appendix. It affords us joy to lay before the saints an article fraught with so much heavenly intelligence."[3] Section 133 was received during the same conference at which the Preface was revealed. (See commentary to D&C 1.)

---

1. See Black, *Who's Who in the Doctrine and Covenants*, 203.
2. Smith, *History of the Church*, 1:229–34.
3. Cook, *Revelations of the Prophet Joseph Smith*, 295.

Section 133 reflects the ideas and concerns most talked about in Kirtland

Section 133 speaks about Millennialism, the Second Coming, the return of the lost tribes, fleeing Babylon, establishing Zion, and the destruction of the wicked. Each of these concerns was front and center during the Kirtland and Missouri periods and slowly declined in importance after the Saints arrived in the Salt Lake Valley. This inevitable shift in focus came about after the Saints were expelled from Missouri and Nauvoo and realized that the establishment of Zion in preparation for the Second Coming of Jesus was not destined to occur in the immediate future.

SECTION 66: HIRAM, OHIO, OCTOBER 25, 1831

Although the heading of section 66 indicates that it was received in Orange, Ohio, this is not the case. The revelation was received in the upper room of the Johnson home located in Hiram, Ohio. The revelation speaks directly to William E. McLellin, who also acted as scribe. In his journal he notes that Joseph had been in Orange for a conference but returned to his residence in Hiram before this revelation was received.[1]

SECTION 75: SIMEON CARTER HOME, AMHERST, OHIO, JANUARY 25, 1832

Heading

Joseph Smith sustained and ordained President of the High Priesthood. Twenty missionaries called.

The big questions

Question: What is the structure of the Church?
Answer: At its head there should be a President of the High Priesthood. Also, the Church sends out missionaries.

Introduction

Revelation given through Joseph Smith the Prophet in Simeon Carter's home located in Amherst, Ohio, on January 25, 1832.[2] The occasion was

---

1. See Robinson and Garrett, *Doctrine and Covenants Commentary*, 2:226.
2. Smith, *History of the Church*, 1:242–45.

that of a conference previously appointed. At this conference Joseph Smith was sustained and ordained President of the High Priesthood. Certain elders, who had encountered difficulty in bringing men to an understanding of their message, desired to learn more in detail as to their immediate duties. This revelation followed.

Historical background

During a conference in June 1831, Joseph Smith and twenty-two other priesthood bearers were ordained "to the high priesthood" for the first time in Church history. (See D&C 44 and 52.) In January 1832 Joseph was ordained and sustained as the president of the high priesthood. Orson Pratt related:

> At this conference the Prophet Joseph was acknowledged President of the High Priesthood, and hands laid on him by Elder Sidney Rigdon. At this conference, by the request of the Priesthood, the Prophet inquired of the Lord, and a revelation was given and written in the presence of the whole assembly, appointing many of the Elders to missions, among whom Elder Lyman E. Johnson and myself were named and appointed on a mission to the Eastern States.[1]

Joseph Smith did not call counselors immediately. However, in March 1832, just three months later, he organized a quorum of three, referred to as the Presidents of the High Priesthood. When the three presidents were organized, the purposes and functions of this council were made known in an unpublished revelation clarifying that the president and his counselors presided over all the concerns of the Church.[2] Information about this "high priesthood" continued to be revealed incrementally through March 1835, when Joseph received section 107, which summarized the relationship between the various priesthood quorums of the Church. The designation of three "presidents of the high priesthood" has since come to be referred to as the First Presidency.

Section 75 concerns itself almost entirely with missionary work. Joseph called about twenty individuals to serve missions. Most were married with children. For this reason, arrangements had to be made to care for missionaries' families in their absence. (See verses 24–26). Missionaries did not serve for a specified period but rather for as long as individual circumstances would permit.[3]

---

1. See Robinson and Garrett, *Doctrine and Covenants Commentary*, 2:280.
2. See Preece, *Learning to Love the Doctrine and Covenants*, 141.
3. See Preece, *Learning to Love the Doctrine and Covenants*, 142.

The pairs of missionaries were called and given instructions on how to accomplish their work. Whenever they were received into a house, they were to leave a blessing. (See verse 19.) If their message was rejected, they were to dust off their feet as a testimony against those who rejected them. (See verse 20.) Orson Hyde describes the process.

> Soon after our return to Kirtland I was sent on another mission in company with Brother Samuel H. Smith, a younger brother of the Prophet, who was a man slow of speech and unlearned, yet a man of good faith and extreme integrity. We journeyed early in the spring of 1832, eastward together without "purse or scrip," going from house to house, teaching and preaching in families, and also in the public conversations of the people. Wherever we were received and entertained, we left our blessing; and wherever we were rejected, we washed our feet in private against those who rejected us, and bore testimony of it unto our Father in Heaven, and went on our way rejoicing, according to the commandment.[1]

Based on Hyde's description, it seems that some of the elders who went out on missions at this time understood that "dusting" of feet could also be accomplished by the "washing" of feet.

SECTION 100: FREEMAN NICKERSON HOME, PERRYSBURG (SOUTH DAYTON), NEW YORK, OCTOBER 12, 1833

Heading

Joseph and Sidney Rigdon, while on a mission to Perrysburg, New York, are assured that their families are well. Rigdon to be a spokesman and Joseph a revelator.

Introduction

Revelation given to Joseph Smith the Prophet and Sidney Rigdon, at Perrysburg, New York.[2] The two brethren, having been absent from their families for several days, felt some concern about them. The Lord reassures them that "their families are well." They are told to peach the gospel for the salvation of souls. Sidney is to be the spokesman and Joseph the revelator.

---

1. See Preece, *Learning to Love the Doctrine and Covenants*, 142.
2. Smith, *History of the Church*, 1:416, 419–21.

Historical background

On October 5, 1833, Joseph Smith, Sidney Rigdon and a convert to the Church by the name of Freeman Nickerson left Kirtland for a short mission to New York and Canada. Nickerson's family lived in Perrysburg, New York, and no doubt he encouraged Joseph and Rigdon stop along the way for a visit and to do some impromptu missionary work. All three stayed at the Nickerson home when they arrived in Perrysburg, where this revelation was received.

Concern for family and for the Saints in Zion

Section 100 assures Joseph and Rigdon that in their absence their families were well. Undoubtedly this was a concern for both men because of the intense persecution they had experienced in March 1832 while living at the Johnson farm, where they were working on Bible revisions. A group of about fifty men dragged both Joseph and Rigdon out of their respective sleeping quarters and tarred and feathered them, severely injuring both of them.[1] During the ensuing months, persecution continued and prominent members of the Church left the faith; among them was Ezra Booth, a convert to the Church and former Methodist minister. Booth published a series of letters in the *Ohio Star*, which were very critical of Joseph. His letters were circulated extensively and later became a major section of the first anti-Mormon book written by Eber D. Howe, *Mormonism Unvailed*, published in 1834. Violence and persecution were also beginning in Jackson County, Missouri. By July 1833 some prominent citizens in the area drafted a "secret constitution" that ultimately led to the expulsion of the Mormons from the area. That same month the printing house was destroyed and a number of Mormons were beaten and harassed.[2]

Sidney Rigdon the speaker and Joseph Smith the revelator

In section 100 Sidney Rigdon is designated by the Lord as a powerful "spokesman . . . mighty in testimony [and in] expounding all scriptures." (Verses 8–9.) Joseph, on the other hand, is described as a "revelator" to make known and "certain" all of the "things of my kingdom on the earth." (Verse 9.)

There is no doubt that Rigdon was an exceptional orator and well qual-

---

1. See *Church History in the Fulness of Times*, 115.
2. Joseph's concerns for the safety of the Saints in Zion are alluded to in verse 13: "And now I give unto you a word concerning Zion. Zion shall be redeemed, although she is chastened for a little season." (See also *Church History in the Fulness of Times*, 127.)

ified as an apologist for the Church. He was a former Baptist minister and one of the founders of the Campbellite movement.[1] Rigdon was an outstanding student of the Bible and its history and mesmerized audiences with his enthusiasm and animated presentations. In his biography, Richard S. Van Wagoner said that Rigdon was "well suited for preaching . . . [and] blessed with a powerful and mellifluous voice, enthusiasm, and a prodigious memory for scripture. His listeners gulped his words in like a gush of cool water. An avatar of eloquence who carried the flame of the visionary tradition, he could sway by the sheer force of his faith, passion, and ideological fervor."[2] He was a mature man, twelve years older than the Prophet Joseph Smith. He had a certain gravitas and bearing that intimidated anti-Mormons and others who wished to debate him. Section 35 compared him to the forerunner of the faith in Jesus' day, John the Baptist. (See D&C 35:4, 20.)

Joseph, on the other hand, was appreciated most for his revelatory powers, rather than his speaking ability. Almost from the very beginning Joseph's followers referred to him not only as a prophet but as a "seer," one who could discern the "mysteries of godliness" and "make hidden things known." He was not the fervent speaker Rigdon was. His more subdued style was described by Matthew Davis, an experienced journalist, in February 1840 when the Prophet was petitioning the federal government in Washington, D.C., for redress. In a letter to his wife, Davis reported of Joseph's speaking style that there was "no levity—no fanaticism—no want of dignity in his deportment."[3] His precepts were spoken in such a way as to "soften the asperities of man toward man . . . [and he] displayed strongly a spirit of charity and forbearance. . . . There was no violence; no fury; no denunciation. His religion appears to be the religion of meekness, lowliness, and mild persuasion."[4] Joseph's appeal was in his ability to receive revelation—to open the heavens.

Having said this, people yearned to listen to the Prophet Joseph for his unusual content and remarkable insights.

---

1. The Campbellites were a prominent religious group in the Kirtland, Ohio, area. When Rigdon left the Campbellite faith and joined with the Mormons, many Campbellites defected with him. The Campbellites were restorationists and believed it was important to follow the teachings and practices of the Christianity as originally set forth at the time of Jesus.

2. Van Wagoner, *Sidney Rigdon: A Portrait of Religious Excess*, viii.

3. Bushman, *Joseph Smith: Rough Stone Rolling*, 394.

4. Bushman, *Joseph Smith: Rough Stone Rolling*, 395. Bushman goes on to point out that "Joseph insisted more than once that 'all who would follow the precepts of the Bible, whether Mormon or not, would assuredly be saved.'" (Bushman, *Joseph Smith: Rough Stone Rolling*, 395.)

Part 7

The Missouri Period

Chapter 31

The Establishment of Zion: The Prophet Joseph's Trip to the Promised Land

ZION, JACKSON COUNTY, INDEPENDENCE, MISSOURI,
JULY AND AUGUST 1831

Historical background

In 1831, locating and establishing Zion, the place for the New Jerusalem (see Moses 7:19–21; Isaiah 33:20; 52:1, 8; Revelation 21:2; Ether 13:2–3; 3 Nephi 20:22), the latter-day land of promise, became one of Joseph's prime objectives. On June 3, one day after the fourth general conference of the Church, he received a revelation directing him to go to Missouri, where "the land of their inheritance" would be revealed.[1] As part of this effort, Joseph called thirteen pairs of missionaries to go to Missouri, or what was then called the "western boundary," and to preach the gospel along the way. (See D&C 52:3–8, 22–33; 56:5–7.)[2] Finally, he instructed the members known as the Colesville Branch, living in the Kirtland area, to pull up stakes and move west to settle Zion once its exact location was made known.[3] (See D&C 28:9; 57:1.)

Joseph also started a journey to the "western boundary" himself. On his arrival, he learned through revelation that Jackson County was the general area where Zion would be established. A lot in Independence was identified as the precise spot where a temple should be built. (See D&C 57:1–3.)

---

1. See *Church History in the Fulness of Time*, 102.
2. See *Church History in the Fulness of Time*, 102.
3. The Colesville Branch was trying to live the law of consecration on the Thompson farm just outside Kirtland, Ohio. For various reasons, this communal order had proved unsuccessful, so it must have seemed reasonable to Joseph that this group of Saints be one of the first assigned to settle in the promised land. Section 54 instructed the Colesville Branch to "take [their] journey into the regions westward, unto the land of Missouri, unto the borders of the Lamanites." (D&C 54:8; *Church History in the Fulness of Time*, 102–3, 106.)

With the land of promise identified, the Saints began to organize. The first order of business was to purchase lands. (See D&C 57:3–5; 58:37, 49–52; 63:27.) Sidney Gilbert was appointed "an agent unto the Church" to receive money from contributors for this purpose. (See D&C 57:6.) Edward Partridge, already living in the area, acted as bishop to administer the law of consecration and divide inheritances. (See D&C 57:7.) The Zion enterprise was to be "done in order." (See D&C 58:55–56.)[1]

Bushman points out that when Joseph first arrived in Independence in mid-July 1831, he "recoiled at the village's ragged collection of settlers."[2] The town had only twenty dwellings and was essentially a way station for the Santa Fe trade and fur traffickers.[3] Yet although Joseph may have been disappointed at first, once Jackson County was revealed to be the land of promise, his attitude changed. "Enveloped in these promises, the land became beautiful in Joseph's eyes."[4] A revelation reflected this change. "The fulness of the earth is yours," and all things are "made for the benefit and use of man, both to please the eye, and to gladden the heart." (D&C 59:16, 18.) Founded on Joseph's vision, the Saints started migrating to "Zion"; by November 1833 the number of Mormons in the area had grown to over a thousand, dwarfing the local population.[5]

Bushman points out that when Joseph first arrived in Independence in mid-July 1831, he "recoiled at the village's ragged collection of settlers."[6] The town had only twenty dwellings and was essentially a way station for the Santa Fe trade and fur traffickers.[7] Although Joseph may have been disappointed at first, once Jackson County was revealed to be the land of promise, his attitude changed. "Enveloped in these promises, the land became beautiful in Joseph's eyes."[8] A revelation reflected this change. "The fulness of the earth is yours," and all things are "made for the benefit and use of man, both to please the eye, and to gladden the heart." (D&C 59:16, 18.) Founded on Joseph's vision, the Saints started migrating to "Zion"; by November 1833 their number in the area had grown to over a thousand, dwarfing the local population.[9]

The land of Zion was not only holy ground but was also designated

---

1. See *Church History in the Fulness of Time*, 107.
2. Bushman, *Joseph Smith: Rough Stone Rolling*, 162.
3. See Bushman, *Joseph Smith: Rough Stone Rolling*, 162.
4. Bushman, *Joseph Smith: Rough Stone Rolling*, 163.
5. See Bushman, *Joseph Smith: Rough Stone Rolling*, 164.
6. Bushman, *Joseph Smith: Rough Stone Rolling*, 162.
7. See Bushman, *Joseph Smith: Rough Stone Rolling*, 162.
8. Bushman, *Joseph Smith: Rough Stone Rolling*, 163.
9. See Bushman, *Joseph Smith: Rough Stone Rolling*, 164.

as the place Jesus would appear as part of his Second Coming. All these reasons combined to fuel the fires of religious enthusiasm. In a moment, Joseph had turned a way station in Missouri into the promised land. Bushman comments on this unique event: "The sacralization of space usually results from a succession of holy events like repeated miracles, or from accumulated layers of worship and veneration over centuries, in the way of Lourdes and Jerusalem. Rather than growing from repeated sacred happenings, Joseph's Zion was created in a stroke. A few words from heaven declaring Independence to be the site of the New Jerusalem inscribed indelible marks on the land—forever."[1]

Jackson County had become in an instant the spot where God could collect the Saints into one safe place during the calamities of the last days. It was to be a "land of peace, a city of refuge, a place of safety for the saints of the most high God." (D&C 45:66, 69.)

---

1. See Bushman, *Joseph Smith: Rough Stone Rolling*, 164.

Chapter 32

The Big Questions: Independence, Jackson County, Missouri

What and Where Is Zion?

Today Zion is defined by Latter-day Saints as any location where members of the Church have established a community. In fact, stakes are often referred to as "stakes of Zion" and are assembling places for instruction, edification, the performance of sacred rituals or ordinances (sacrament and baptism), and other joint enterprises. (See D&C 43:8–11.) During the Missouri period, however, Zion was a designated parcel of land located in Jackson County, Missouri. (See D&C 57:1–3.) It was not just *a* place but *the* place where the main body of Saints would establish their headquarters, build temples, and create a godlike society characterized by righteousness and economic equality. (See D&C 38:24–27; 78:5–6; 97:21; 4 Nephi 1:3.) It was one of two places where Jesus would come to usher in the Millennium. The other was Jerusalem.

The fundamental principles that were to govern Zion were revealed to the Prophet on a trip he made to Jackson County, Missouri, in July and August 1831. First, Zion would be a communal society where the Saints would hold all things in common. Members would deed all of their earthly possessions to the bishop, and the bishop, on behalf of the Church, would lease back to each family what they needed to survive and be economically productive. Excess capital would be centralized in the hands of the Church and used as religious authorities thought best to care for the poor, provide schools, build temples, construct chapels for worship, and provide recreational activities. Second, in such a community there would be no poor among them. To use the scriptural language, the poor would be exalted and the rich made low. All would have the necessities of life. Third, it would be a dedicated place of gathering where the virtuous—the "pure in heart"—dwell, and where the Saints would be unified—of one mind and spirit. Fourth, it would be the place where Jesus would come at the beginning of the Millennium to set up the machinery of government to administer the affairs of North and South America.[1]

How Do We Deal with Disappointment and Unrealized Promises?

The idea that Joseph's flock would build a Zion to usher in the Second Coming and the Millennium was electrifying and highly motivating to his followers.[2] Members of the Church sold their homes, gathered in Kirtland as a holding place, and waited until the Prophet gave the word that they, too, could join the Saints in Zion, Jackson County, Missouri. (See D&C 57 and 58.) Some headed directly to Zion, even though Church authorities advised against it. But this religious enthusiasm was dampened as time went on. Persecution began and the Saints were physically forced out of Zion to Far West, Missouri. Eventually they were driven from Missouri altogether. Under the Lord's direction, Joseph even raised an army (called Zion's Camp) to try to reinstate the Saints in Zion, but the attempt failed. At each step in their history the Saints hoped and prayed that the Lord would make it possible for them to return to their Zion, but such was not to be—they went on to Nauvoo and then to the Great Basin. Finally they realized that Jesus would not be coming as soon as they had expected and this generation of Saints would not be preparing a city for his return. Members of the Church were disheartened and downcast. Even some of Joseph's closest followers were disillusioned and discontent enough to leave the faith.

The expulsion of the Saints from Zion in Missouri was a devastating blow. How could the Lord designate Zion, command the Saints to gather there, and then allow the Saints to fail? Even Joseph was "distraught and

---

1. The eastern continents will be administered from Jerusalem.
2. Bushman placed the situation in the context of Joseph's times. "Dedication of the Missouri site occurred during an upswing in millennial thinking in the transatlantic world. In the late eighteenth century, the American and French revolutions had spurred speculation about the imminent coming of Christ. Millenarians saw the two revolutions as signs of the coming Kingdom. Expectations had not dimmed a generation later. Eighteen thirty-one was a signal year for millenarian activity. Besides Joseph's dedication of *Zion*, William Miller, later famed for predicting an exact date in 1843 for the Second Coming, began preaching his chronology of millennial events.... Mormon Millenarianism was more akin to that of the Shakers ... [where] members collected into communities where they exercised spiritual gifts and established a code of behavior.... Rather than pointing to a date for Christ's return, Shaker millenarianism served more to inject urgency into the sect's reform efforts. Both Shakers and Mormons felt the pressure of the time." (Bushman, *Joseph Smith: Rough Stone Rolling*, 165–66.)

confused" and "began to murmur against the Lord."[1] When he asked how long Zion's tribulation would last he was told to "be still, and know that I am God!"[2] Bushman observed that, considering all of the spiritual experience Joseph had been blessed with, he knew he should not complain. The Prophet said, "I am sensible that I ought not to murmur and do not murmur only in this, that those who are innocent are compelled to suffer for the iniquities of the guilty; and I cannot account for this." Joseph agonized over the bad news from Zion. He said it "weighs us down; we cannot refrain from tears."[3]

By December 1833, however, Joseph received a series of revelations explaining God's purposes. Zion had failed because the Saints had broken God's commandments. Selfishness prevailed and made it impossible for them to "hold all things in common." (See D&C 101.) There were no shortcuts—Zion could not be built up "unless it is by the principles of the law of the celestial kingdom; otherwise I cannot receive her unto myself." (D&C 105:5.) There was some hope, though: Zion would not be "moved out of her place, notwithstanding her children are scattered." (D&C 101:17.) In the meantime, "all they who have mourned shall be comforted. And all they who have given their lives for my name shall be crowned." (D&C 101:14–15.) Still, the Saints constantly pushed Joseph for knowledge of when they could return to Zion and when Jesus would come. The answer was always the same: It is not for man to know.[4] "Joseph gradually regained his footing" after December 1833, but the events in Missouri "cast a long shadow over Mormon history."[5]

---

1. Bushman, *Joseph Smith: Rough Stone Rolling*, 229.
2. Bushman, *Joseph Smith: Rough Stone Rolling*, 229.
3. Bushman, *Joseph Smith: Rough Stone Rolling*, 229.
4. After the Saints had been driven out of Zion, Jackson County, Missouri, and Joseph's attempt to take it back with Zion's army had failed, he again approached the Lord. After prayer and much supplication he said: "I cannot learn from any communication by the Spirit to me, that Zion has forfeited her claim . . . , notwithstanding the Lord has caused her to be thus afflicted. . . . I know that Zion, in the due time of the Lord, will be redeemed; but how many will be the days . . . , the Lord has kept hid from my eyes; and when I inquire concerning this subject, the voice of the Lord is: Be still, and know that I am God!" (Smith, *Teachings of the Prophet Joseph Smith*, 34.) The issue of when that redemption would come was most pressing during the Missouri years, and it came up again in Nauvoo because William Miller had predicted an exact date (April 3, 1843) for the Second Coming, which Joseph was asked about. One day before Miller's date for Jesus' return, the Prophet said it would not be for many years. (See commentary on D&C 130:14–17.)
5. Bushman, *Joseph Smith: Rough Stone Rolling*, 230.

Chapter 33

Joshua Lewis Home: Jackson County, Missouri, July–August 1831

SECTION 57: JOSHUA LEWIS HOME,[1]

Heading

Identifies Jackson County as Zion, the New Jerusalem, and reveals the location for the temple to be constructed. (See verses 1–3.)

The big question

Question: What and where is Zion?
Answer: Zion should be built in Independence, Jackson County, Missouri. A temple will be built there. The Saints are to enter into the law of consecration.

Introduction

Revelation to Joseph Smith, received on July 20, 1831, in Joshua Lewis's home in Jackson County, Missouri.[2] In compliance with the Lord's command in section 52, the elders had journeyed from Kirtland to Missouri. In contemplating the state of the Indians (Lamanites) and the lack of civilization, refinement, and religion among the people generally, the Prophet exclaimed in yearning prayer: "When will the wilderness blossom as the rose?[3] When will Zion be built up in her glory, and where will

---

1. Joshua Lewis was converted by some of the missionaries sent to the convert the Lamanites. The Colesville Branch from New York settled in Kaw Township in 1831. Jackson County, Missouri, July 20, 1831
2. Smith, *History of the Church*, 1:189–90.
3. When Joseph arrived, he was less than impressed with the people in the area. He said, "But our reflections were many, coming as we had from a highly cultivated state of society

thy Temple stand, unto which all nations shall come in the last days?" Subsequently he received this revelation, which renamed Independence, Missouri, the City of Zion and designated the exact location for the temple. Sidney Gilbert is told to establish a store. W. W. Phelps is assigned to be a printer. Oliver Cowdery is called to assist Phelps and edit written materials for publication.

Historical background

Kirtland was never intended to be the final destination for the Saints. Rather, Zion was to be established farther to the west. Although no one knew the exact location, the Saints knew that it was in the "western countries" (D&C 45:64; 54:8), on the "borders by the Lamanites" (D&C 28:9).[1] Obedient to instructions in D&C 28:8, Joseph sent missionaries west to convert the Lamanites, or the Indians. Although the Indians showed no serious interest in the Church, along the way the missionaries did convert many white settlers who later made major contributions to the Church.

During the summer of 1831, Joseph and his companions[2] started traveling west to the same vicinity where the first Mormon missionaries were residing—Jackson County, Missouri. They arrived on July 17, 1831, and were met by Oliver Cowdery and others. Joseph Smith said that this "meeting of our brethren, who had long awaited our arrival, was a glorious one, and moistened with many tears."[3]

While in Jackson County, Joseph received section 57, pinpointing Independence, Missouri, as the place for the City of Zion. The revelation also

---

in the east, and standing now upon the confines or western limits of the United States, and looking into the vast wilderness of those that sat in darkness; how natural it was to observe the degradation, leanness of intellect, ferocity, and jealousy of a people that were nearly a century behind the times, and to feel for those who roamed about without the benefit of civilization, refinement, or religion." (See Robinson and Garrett, *A Commentary on the Doctrine and Covenants*, 2:142.)

1. The term *Lamanite* should be used advisedly in this context. The Saints no doubt believed that most American Indians were Lamanites or descendants of the Book of Mormon peoples. However, this almost certainly is not the case. Today, anthropologist John L. Sorenson has made a convincing case that the descendants of the Lamanites most probably lived in and around Mexico, Honduras, El Salvador, and Guatemala. In this regard, there is no evidence that Moroni's instruction to Joseph Smith included geography, nor did Joseph claim inspiration on the matter. We know that Joseph thought many of the American Indians were Lamanites, but he also came to believe that the inhabitants of South America were also related to Book of Mormon peoples. Frederick G. Williams stated that Joseph said, "Lehi and his company . . . landed on the continent of South America, in Chile, thirty degrees, south latitude." (See Sorenson, *An Ancient American Setting for the Book of Mormon*, 2.)

2. Joseph's companions were Sidney Rigdon, Martin Harris, Edward Partridge, W. W. Phelps, Joseph Coe, and Elizabeth Gilbert.

3. Cook, *Revelations of the Prophet Joseph Smith*, 91.

identified the very spot where the temple should be built (see verse 3), and instructed Joseph to purchase all the lands round about (see verse 4). Sidney Gilbert was enlisted to buy property and to set up a store. (See verses 6, 8–10.) Edward Partridge, the first bishop of the Church, was instructed to establish the law of consecration and designate "inheritances," or parcels of land, to the Saints who would be coming to Zion. W. W. Phelps was told to establish a printing house and to enlist Oliver Cowdery to assist him.

Just three days after Joseph and his company arrived, the Colesville Saints began to settle in. This group were originally a branch of the Church living in Colesville, New York. They had moved en masse to Kirtland, where they were assigned to live the law of consecration on the Thompson farm just outside the city. The group, consisting mainly of Joseph Knight, his family, and some of his friends, tried to live the law of consecration but were unsuccessful, partially because of conditions beyond their control. Joseph therefore asked them to go farther west and help settle Zion. When the Colesville Saints arrived there, they pledged themselves to live the law of consecration once again. Bishop Partridge immediately began the process of giving out inheritances to members of this group to live on and cultivate.

Section 58: Joshua Lewis Home,[1]

Jackson County, Missouri, August 1, 1831

Heading

God commands some of the Saints to gather in Zion. Instructions are given regarding how Zion should proceed and be organized.

The big question

Question: What and where is Zion?

Answer: Zion is compared to a feast where all sup without regard to rank or social distinction. Zion is a place that is dedicated to the Lord where the Saints are to gather for protection from the travails of the last days and to await the Second Coming of Jesus Christ.

---

1. "Joshua Lewis was converted by the early missionaries to the Lamanites. The Colesville Branch from New York settled in Kaw Township in 1831." (See Mortensen, "Doctrine and Covenants Revelations Sites," http://www.dcsites.com/)

Anchor section

Memorize: Zion

Introduction

This revelation was given through Joseph Smith the Prophet on August 1, 1831, in the Joshua Lewis home in Jackson County, Missouri.[1] On the first Sabbath after the arrival of the Prophet and his party in Jackson County, Missouri, a religious service was held, and two members were received by baptism. During that week members of the Colesville branch arrived. Many were eager to learn the will of the Lord for them in this new place of gathering.

Historical background

During July 1831 Joseph Smith and a company of brethren, including Edward Partridge and Sidney Rigdon, arrived in the Independence area of Jackson County, Missouri. A few days later, the Colesville branch of the Church arrived to make a new home in what Joseph had designated as Zion, the place of the New Jerusalem. It was the place where a temple would be built to the Lord and Christ would return to usher in the Millennium. (See D&C 57.)

Section 58 gave explicit instructions on how Zion should be established, which families should settle there, and how it should be organized. Edward Partridge was appointed bishop and instructed to resettle with his family there. (See verses 13–18, 24.) Sidney Rigdon was directed to write a description of the land of Missouri to be used to raise funds for Zion. (See verse 50.) Rigdon was also assigned to dedicate the land of Zion, which he accomplished on August 2, 1831.

Section 58 instructed Joseph to hold a conference in Zion. The Saints gathered for that purpose on August 4, 1831, with thirty-one members present. (See verse 58 and D&C 52:2.) At this meeting Joseph encouraged the Saints to perform "acts of righteousness," and promised a blessing upon all who would keep "the commandments of the Lord."[2]

The idea of Zion or a New Jerusalem

Joseph Smith taught that a New Jerusalem would be built upon the American continent. (See Article of Faith 1:10.) This knowledge may have

---

1. Smith, *History of the Church*, 1:190–95.
2. See Cook, *Revelations of the Prophet Joseph Smith*, 93.

come to him while he was translating the Book of Mormon. (See 3 Nephi 20:22; Ether 13:2–6.) This subject is addressed in Doctrine and Covenants 28; 42:33–36, 62, 67; and 57:3.[1] On July 20, 1831, Joseph announced by way of a revelation (section 57) that the headquarters for the New Jerusalem would be Independence, Missouri.

The rebuilding of the New Jerusalem in Jackson County, Missouri, is linked with the Second Coming and was spoken of in some detail years later in a Proclamation of the Twelve written in 1845.

> He will assemble the Natives, the remnants of Joseph in America; and make them a great, and strong, and powerful nation: and he will civilize and enlighten them, and will establish a holy city, and temple and seat of government among them, which shall be called Zion.
>
> And there shall be his tabernacle, his sanctuary, his throne, and seat of government for the whole continent of North and South America for ever. In short, it will be to the western hemisphere what Jerusalem will be to the eastern....
>
> The city of Zion, with its sanctuary and priesthood, and the glorious fullness of the gospel, will constitute a standard which will put an end to jarring creeds and political wranglings, by uniting the republics, states, provinces, territories, nations, and South America in one great and common bond of brotherhood. Truth and knowledge shall make them free, and love cement their union. The Lord also shall be their king and their lawgiver; while wars shall cease and peace prevail for a thousand years.[2]

Jesus will also make an appearance at the traditional Jerusalem in Israel. Therefore, both Old and New Jerusalem will play important roles in the last days. Latter-day Saints believe that Isaiah makes reference to these two religious capitals, the old Jerusalem in the east and the new Jerusalem to be established by the Saints in the west. "Out of Zion [Missouri] shall go forth the law, and the word of the Lord from Jerusalem." (Isaiah 2:2–3; Micah 4:1–2.) Graham W. Doxey pointed out: "Latter-day Saints believe this refers to the two Zion headquarters in the two hemispheres from which the Messiah, the returned Son of God, will reign triumphantly over the whole earth."[3]

---

1. The book of Revelation also speaks of "the holy city, new Jerusalem, coming down from God out of heaven." (See Revelation 21:2, 10.) This most probably relates to the return of the city of Enoch. (See Moses 7:12–21, 59–64.) Bruce R. McConkie taught that "this New Jerusalem on the American continent will have a dual origin. It will be built by the Saints on earth and it will also come down from heaven, and the cities so originating will be united into one holy city." (*Mormon Doctrine*, 532; see also Ether 13:3–11.)

2. See *Encyclopedia of Mormonism*, 1010.

3. *Encyclopedia of Mormonism*, 1010.

Sidney Rigdon's description of Zion

After Sidney Rigdon arrived in Jackson County, he was commanded to write a description of Zion that would be used to solicit money to purchase lands there. (See verses 50–52.) Instead of a straightforward description, Rigdon wrote an emotion-packed epistle that focused on the "day of tribulation which is coming on the earth."[1] Joseph did not think it was fitting and the Lord commanded that it be written again, "I, the Lord, am not pleased with my servant Sidney Rigdon; he exalted himself in his heart, and received not counsel, but grieved the Spirit; wherefore his writing is not acceptable unto the Lord, and he shall make another." (D&C 63:55–56.) Furthermore, he was told that if he did not do a better job the second time around he would be released as a member of the First Presidency. (See D&C 63:56.)

Rigdon tried again and succeeded. This time the "doomsday rhetoric" was taken out and Rigdon was careful to limit his writing to the task of convincing the Saints to immigrate.[2] This version was accepted as the "will of the Lord" and printed. Oliver Cowdery and Newel K. Whitney used Rigdon's description to solicit money for Zion and to encourage the Saints to immigrate there.[3]

Joseph and Oliver Cowdery returned to Kirtland, Ohio, on September 11, 1831. At that time the Lord explained that the move to Zion would take place over an extended period of time. For that reason, Kirtland was to be retained as a "stronghold . . . for the space of five years." (D&C 64:21.)

Lands dedicated in Zion

At a special service held on August 2, 1831, twelve men (five of them from the Colesville branch) representing the twelve tribes of Israel laid the first log "as a foundation of Zion in Kaw township, twelve miles west of Independence."[4] Sidney Rigdon dedicated the land as he had been instructed. (See verse 57.) As part of the service, he asked those gathered, "Do you pledge yourselves to keep the laws of God on this land, which you never have kept in your own lands? [The audience responded,] we do."[5] "I now pronounce this land consecrated and dedicated to the Lord for a possession and inheritance for the Saints in the name of Jesus Christ

---

1. Van Wagoner, *Sidney Rigdon: A Portrait of Religious Excess*, 103.
2. Van Wagoner, *Sidney Rigdon: A Portrait of Religious Excess*, 103–4.
3. See Van Wagoner, *Sidney Rigdon: A Portrait of Religious Excess*, 105.
4. See *Church History in the Fulness of Time*, 107.
5. *Church History in the Fulness of Time*, 107.

having authority for him. And for all the faithful servants of the Lord to the remotest ages of time. Amen."[1]

Before leaving Zion, Joseph Smith laid the cornerstone of the temple in Independence. Joseph dedicated the temple lot. Sidney Rigdon dedicated the land of Zion for the gathering of the Saints.[2] (See verse 57.)

Zion to be established after much tribulation and after many years

Undoubtedly, first-generation Mormons believed that they would establish Zion in just a few years and that within their lifetime the Second Coming would take place and the Millennium commence. Yet, a careful reading of section 58 does not support this timetable. Rather, the revelation sounds a cautionary note. First, it predicts that the Saints will not be able to discern the meaning of the events that will shortly take place in Zion. "Ye cannot behold with your natural eyes, for the present time, the design of your God concerning those things which shall come hereafter, and the glory which shall follow." (Verse 3.) Second, it predicts that Zion will not be established until "after much tribulation." (See verses 3–4.) And, third, it predicts that Zion will not be established for many years. "And now, verily, I say concerning the residue of the elders of my church, the time has not yet come for many years." (Verse 44.)

Bushman commented on what he describes as this rather "somber revelation" and also interprets it to mean that the Saints who settled in Zion would not "enjoy a triumphant entrance into the promised land." He said the "revelation implied that the enjoyment of Zion lay in the future."[3] The mission of first-generation Mormons was not to bring about Zion in their lifetime but rather to lay the foundation and to bear "record of the land upon which Zion of God shall stand." (Verse 7.) The actual establishment of Zion would be left for future generations to accomplish.

Prefiguring what was about to happen, the Lord warned that the privilege of establishing Zion rested upon strict obedience and that failure to do all that was commanded would result in a revocation of promised blessings.

> I command and men obey not; I revoke and they receive not the blessing.

---

1. *Church History in the Fulness of Time*, 107.
2. See Robinson and Garrett, *A Commentary on the Doctrine and Covenants*, 2:148.
3. "Somewhat incongruously, a somber revelation tempered this enthusiasm. Warning that only 'after much tribulation cometh the blessing,' the revelation implied that the enjoyment of Zion lay in the future. The missionaries had been sent 'that you might be honored of laying the foundation, and of bearing record of the land upon which the Zion of God shall stand,' and no more. They were not to enjoy a triumphant entrance into the promised land." (Bushman, *Joseph Smith: Rough Stone Rolling*, 164.)

Then they say in their hearts: This is not the work of the Lord, for his promises are not fulfilled. But wo unto such, for their reward lurketh beneath, and not from above. (D&C 58:32–33.)

A short time later, promised blessings were lost because of the Saints' unfaithfulness, and they were forced to leave Zion. (See D&C 103; 105.) As predicted, many fell away because they felt that the promises of the Lord had not come to pass.

Zion is compared to a feast for the poor without regard to social rank or distinction

Section 58 explains that the law of consecration and the more equal distribution of the world's goods means more than economic equality. Rather, it is a way to reorder society so that there are no social divisions. To communicate this idea, Zion is compared to a feast in which all are invited to partake and all are treated alike—"a feast of fat things . . . prepared for the poor . . . yea, a supper . . . well prepared . . . unto which all nations shall be invited . . . first the rich and the learned, the wise and the noble . . . then . . . the poor, the lame, and the blind, and the deaf . . . come . . . and partake of the supper of the Lord." (Verses 8–11.)

Comparing Zion and law of consecration to a feast is a New Testament theme found in Jesus' parable of the great wedding feast in Matthew 22:1–13 and Luke 14:15–24.[1] In this parable Jesus teaches what it means to have a share in the kingdom of God. He illustrates by telling the story of a king who prepared a great wedding feast for his son and sent out many invitations to notify guests that it was time for them to come. The invited ones made excuses and justified their absence by explaining that their business responsibilities conflicted with the invitation. They even murdered the king's servants who extended the invitation. The king became furious and "sent out his army to destroy the murderers and burn their city." (NLT Matthew 22:7.) The king declared that the guests he had invited were not worthy and he sent out invitations to everyone else, "good and bad alike." (See NLT Matthew 22:10.) In Luke's version, the poor, the crippled, and the lame were also invited and the banquet hall was filled. (See NLT Luke 14:21.)

---

1. This parable is also found in the Gospel of Thomas, a noncanonical work completely preserved in a papyrus Coptic manuscript discovered in 1945 at Nag Hammadi, Egypt. It is a list of 114 sayings attributed to Jesus. Some of those sayings resemble those found in the four canonical Gospels, but other sayings were unknown until this book was discovered. Unlike the four canonical gospels, which employ narrative accounts of the life of Jesus, *Thomas* is a brief dialogue with Jesus and a collection of sayings which were reported to Judas Thomas, the Twin.

Joshua Lewis Home: Jackson County, Missouri, July–August 1831

John Dominic Crossan has written about Jesus' comparing a person's share in the kingdom of God to a feast and Jesus' eating with sinners (see Mark 2:15–17)—a notion Crossan referred to as "open commensality." It was a way of teaching that God affords all of his children the same standing, social status, and dignity. It illustrated the ideal society where all sup together as intimate acquaintances. Crossan gets to the heart of the matter by describing different dining arrangements in a society.

> Think, for a moment, if beggars came to your door, of the difference between giving them some food to go, of inviting them into your kitchen for a meal, of bringing them into the dining room to eat in the evening with your family, or of having them come back on Saturday night for a supper with a group of your friends. Think, again, if you were a large company's CEO, of the difference between a cocktail party in the office for all the employees, a restaurant lunch for all the middle managers, or a private dinner party for your vice presidents in your own home. Those events are not just ones of eating together, of simple table fellowship, but are what anthropologists call commensality—from mensa, the Latin word for "table." It means the rules of tabling and eating as miniature models for the rules of association and socialization. It means table fellowship as a map of economic discrimination, social hierarchy, and political differentiation.[1]

Crossan concludes, based upon his reading of "The Great Wedding Feast" and other parables and eating situations in Jesus' life, that what Jesus had in mind was "an eating together without using table as a miniature map of society's vertical discriminations and lateral separations."[2] This is an idea described in the book of Revelation where Jesus stands at the door and knocks, in the hope that his friends will invite him to come in and share a meal with them. The meal is described as an invitation to "sit with me on my throne" or share in everything that Jesus has. (See NLT Revelation 3:20–22.)[3] In sum, the feast is "a symbol and embodiment of radical egalitarianism, of an absolute equality of people . . . that denies . . . the necessity of any hierarchy among them."[4]

As section 58 suggests, Joseph's concept of Zion was also based on the idea of a feast, helping him form a mental picture of what a Zion society ought to be like—an occasion where all shared alike without regard to rank or station. Although Joseph did not use the term *open commensality* to describe this ideal, he used the concept of eating together when a "feast

---

1. Crossan, *Jesus, a Revolutionary Biography*, 68.
2. Crossan, *Jesus, a Revolutionary Biography*, 70.
3. As Crossan also points out, "The social challenge of such equal or egalitarian commensality is the parable's most fundamental danger and radical threat." Jesus' intent was not lost on the power elite of Jesus' day. (See Crossan, *Jesus, a Revolutionary Biography*, 70.)
4. Crossan, *Jesus, a Revolutionary Biography*, 71.

after the order of the Son of God" was held. Perhaps Jospeh meant to describe such a feast in his journal. Attended a sumptuous feast at Bishop Newel K. Whitney's. This feast was after the order of the Son of God—the lame, the halt, and the blind were invited, according to the instructions of the Savior. . . . We . . . received a bountiful refreshment, furnished by the liberality of the Bishop. The company was large, and before we partook we had some of the songs of Zion sung; and our hearts were made glad by a foretaste of those joys that will be poured upon the heads of the Saints when they are gathered together on Mount Zion, to enjoy one another's society for evermore, even all the blessings of heaven, when there will be none to molest or make us afraid."[1]

Staker points out that as a Freemason, Bishop Newel K. Whitney was likely familiar with the "sumptuous dinners" that the Masons "hosted for the widows, fatherless, and poor in the area."[2] Whitney said, "We did not feel like using our means and time in a way that would only benefit those who had an abundance of this world's means. According to our Savior's pattern and agreeably to the Prophet Joseph's and our own ideas of true charity and disinterested benevolence, we determined to make a Feast for the Poor, such as we knew could not return the same to us; the lame, the halt, the deaf, the blind, the aged and infirm. The feast lasted three days, during which time all in the vicinity of Kirtland who would come were invited, and entertained as courteously and generously as if they had been able to extend hospitality instead of receiving it."[3]

Repentance involves forsaking sin

W. W. Phelps was admonished for competing with his brethren: "For he seeketh to excel, and he is not sufficiently meek before me." (Verse 41.) Forgiveness was offered: "Behold, he who has repented of his sins, the same is forgiven, and I, the Lord, remember them no more." (Verse 42.) However, the test of his true repentance was that he cease from his evil ways: "By this ye may know if a man repenteth of his sins—behold, he will confess them and forsake them." (Verse 43.)

---

1. Smith, *History of the Church*, 2:362–63.
2. Staker, *Hearken O Ye People*, Kindle locations 7903–09.
3. Ibid., 7909–19.

Men should be anxiously engaged in good causes

In this wilderness on the frontiers of the United States there was much to accomplish. Section 58 admonishes the Saints not to wait to be commanded in all things. Rather they should seize the initiative.

> Verily, I say, men should be anxiously engaged in a good cause, and do many things of their own free will, and bring to pass much righteousness;
> For the power is in them, wherein they are agents unto themselves. And inasmuch as men do good they shall in nowise lose their reward. (Verses 27–28.)

SECTION 59: JOSHUA LEWIS HOME,[1] ZION, JACKSON COUNTY, MISSOURI, AUGUST 7, 1831

Heading

The law of the Sabbath reiterated in a modern day.

The big question

Question: What and where is Zion?
Answer: Zion is a place where the people are holy, sanctified, and keep the Sabbath day holy.

Introduction

This revelation was given through Joseph Smith at the home of Joshua Lewis in Jackson County, Missouri, on Sunday, August 7, 1831.[2] Preceding his record of this revelation, the Prophet writes descriptively of the land of Zion where the people were then assembled. The land was consecrated as the Lord had directed, and the site for the future temple was dedicated. The Lord makes these commandments especially applicable to the Saints in Zion.

Anchor section

Memorize: Sabbath day

---

1. "Joshua Lewis was converted by the early missionaries to the Lamanites. The Colesville Branch from New York settled in Kaw Township in 1831." (See Mortensen, "Doctrine and Covenants Revelations Sites," http://www.dcsites.com/)
2. Smith, *History of the Church*, 1:196–201.

Historical background

On August 6, 1831, one day before this revelation was received, Polly Knight became the first member of the Church to die in Zion. She was the wife of Joseph Knight, a good friend of the Prophet, and the mother of Newel Knight, another prominent member of the Church. Polly and her family were part of the Colesville branch that, at the behest of Joseph Smith, had recently arrived in Jackson County, Missouri, to settle in and build up Zion. On their journey from Kirtland to Jackson County, Polly had become seriously ill. The official history of the Church records:

> She was very ill during her journey from Kirtland to Missouri. "Yet," says her son, "she would not consent to stop traveling.... [H]er greatest desire was to set her feet upon the land of Zion, and to have her body interred in that land. I went on shore and bought lumber to make a coffin in case she should die before we arrived at our destination—so fast did she fail. But the Lord gave her the desire of her heart, and she lived to stand upon that land.[1]

On Sunday, August 7, 1831, Polly Knight died and Joseph Smith preached her funeral sermon.[2] Afterward, Joseph received section 59, restoring anew God's law regarding Sabbath day observance. Section 59 speaks words of consolation most probably directed to members of the Knight family. "Those that live shall inherit the earth, and those that die shall rest from all their labors, and their works shall follow them; and they shall receive a crown in the mansions of my Father, which I have prepared for them." (D&C 59:2.)

This revelation indicated that proper observance of the Sabbath day would, as Woodford put it, "help insure a continued inheritance in Zion."[3] In other words, the members of the Church in Zion had a special duty to be upright, sanctified, and holy, because they were responsible for ordering a Zion society that would welcome Jesus when he came to Zion to usher in the Millennium.

---

1. Smith, History of the Church, 1:199.
2. Polly was buried in the woods near the home of Joshua Lewis, a member of the Church who had been baptized the winter before. Joseph Knight reported in his diary that he "was along by where she was buried a few days after and I found the pigs had begun to root where she was buried. I being very unwell but I took my ax the next day and went and built a pen around it. It was the last I done for her." (See Cook, *Revelations of the Prophet Joseph Smith*, 94.)
3. Woodford, *The Historical Development of the Doctrine and Covenants*, 752.

Joshua Lewis Home: Jackson County, Missouri, July–August 1831

Sabbath day principles, rather than specifics

The stated purpose of living the Sabbath was to keep the Saints "unspotted from the world," so that they might be sanctified and fully prepared to participate in the New Jerusalem. (See verse 9.) The Saints' "righteousness" must consist of "a broken heart and a contrite spirit." (Verse 8.) Personal purity, a contrite spirit, and a broken heart would be encouraged and strengthened by Sabbath day observance.

According to Jesus, the kind of Sabbath day observance God wanted was not slavish adherence to a multiplicity of rules and regulations as the Pharisees taught. Rather, righteousness involved a principle-oriented approach to life in general, and more specifically to Sabbath day worship. Therefore, section 59 sets forth general principles, not specific practices, to be observed. For example, on the Sabbath the Saints were to "fast" from the things of this world, "rest" from their labors, "pay their devotions" to God, "offer up their sacraments," and "do none other thing, only let thy food be prepared with singleness of heart." (Verses 10–13.)

This principle-oriented approach is somewhat flexible and allows each member of the Church, depending upon their upbringing and the culture, as well as their faith and spiritual sensitivity, to decide for themselves what may or may not be appropriate activity on the Sabbath. For example, some Mormon families are comfortable going for a leisurely drive on Sunday while others are not. Some might watch television while others keep their TV set off. Sabbath day practices may also vary as circumstances change. In Brigham Young's day, during the nineteenth century, some members of the Church felt it inappropriate to ride in a buggy on Sunday. Today, members of the Church regularly ride to Church in their automobiles. Unlike the Amish and orthodox Jews, Mormon Sabbath day practices may differ depending upon the situation, time, and place. Practices change over time, and the Mormon approach to the Sabbath is not based upon a static bill of particulars.

Having said this, however, we note that the Church has from time to time given guidelines. In 1978 President Spencer W. Kimball said:

> The Sabbath is not a day for indolent lounging about the house or puttering around in the garden, but is a day for consistent attendance at meetings for the worship of the Lord, drinking at the fountain of knowledge and instruction, enjoying the family, and finding uplift in music and song.
>
> Abstinence from work and recreation is important, but insufficient. The Sabbath calls for constructive thoughts and acts, and if one merely lounges about doing nothing ... he is breaking it. To observe it, one will be on his knees in prayer, preparing lessons, studying the gospel, meditating, visiting the ill and distressed, writing letters to missionaries, taking a nap, reading wholesome material....

It is true that some people must work on the Sabbath. And, in fact, some of the work that is truly necessary—caring for the sick, for example—may actually serve to hallow the Sabbath. However, in such activities our motives are a most important consideration.

When men and women are willing to work on the Sabbath to increase their wealth, they are breaking the commandments; for money taken in on the Sabbath, if the work is unnecessary, is unclean money. . . .

Sabbath-breakers too are those who buy commodities or entertainment on the Sabbath, thus encouraging pleasure palaces and business establishments to remain open—which they otherwise would not do.[1]

Section 59 also recommended that members of the Church confess their sins before the Church and before the Lord. (See verse 12.) This resulted in a practice in some Church meetings[2] before the turn of the century in which members would stand and confess their foibles and wrongdoings as part of the monthly fast and testimony meeting. Today public confession is not felt to be an appropriate practice and is discouraged. However, members of the Church are encouraged to be introspective on the Sabbath and use this day of the week to ponder repentance of their sins and to evaluate their relationship with God.

Promised blessing associated keeping the Sabbath day holy

The Lord promises that those who live the law of the Sabbath will enjoy the "fulness of the earth." (See verses 16–18.) However, hoarding the world's goods, wasting material bounty, or taking material goods by force are specifically condemned. (See verse 20.) Material blessings must be used "with judgment, not to excess, neither by extortion."[3] (Verse 20.) D&C 59 also reflects the notion that physical pleasures are pleasing to God. Taste, smell, touch, hearing, and sight all add joy and satisfaction to life. Material bounty is "for food and for raiment, for taste and for smell, to strengthen the body and to enliven the soul." (Verse 19.)

Finally, the spirit of the Sabbath is observed when men and woman are grateful for their blessings and reflect an attitude of thanks and appreciation to God. "Thou shalt thank the Lord thy God in all things." (Verse 7.) "In nothing doth man offend God, or against none is his wrath kindled, save those who confess not his hand in all things." (Verse 21.)

---

1. See Encyclopedia of Mormonism, 1242.
2. Confession of sin was a regular part of fast and testimony meeting, originally held once a month on a Thursday evening.
3. Extortion in this context means a fraudulent taking of something or taking something by unlawful force.

Zion to be characterized by love of God and neighbor

As Jesus so clearly taught, Christians should be known for their love of neighbor and even of their enemies. This principle is clearly taught in section 59 because it is at the heart of a Zion-like community with its emphasis on the poor, downtrodden, and disadvantaged.

> Wherefore, I give unto them a commandment, saying thus: Thou shalt love the Lord thy God with all thy heart, with all thy might, mind, and strength; and in the name of Jesus Christ thou shalt serve him.
> Thou shalt love thy neighbor as thyself. (Verses 5–6.)

SECTION 60: JOSHUA LEWIS HOME,[1] JACKSON COUNTY, MISSOURI, AUGUST 8, 1831

Heading

Missionaries are to preach the gospel. Do not ask the Lord for revelations on the inconsequential aspects of everyday life.

Introduction

This revelation was given through Joseph Smith the Prophet at the home of Joshua Lewis in Jackson County, Missouri, on August 8, 1831.[2] The elders who had been appointed to return to Kirtland and the East from Zion desired to know how they should proceed and by what route and manner they should travel. They were told to preach the gospel on their way and not idle away their time.

---

1. "Joshua Lewis was converted by the early missionaries to the Lamanites. The Colesville Branch from New York settled in Kaw Township in 1831." (See Mortensen, "Doctrine and Covenants Revelations Sites," http://www.dcsites.com/)

2. Smith, *History of the Church*, 1:201–2.

Historical background

Joseph Smith remained in Independence, Missouri, about three weeks during the late summer of 1831. During this time he located the land of Zion, assisted Sidney Rigdon in dedicating the temple lot and the land of Zion, and welcomed the Colesville Saints. He established a bishopric, a general store, and a bishops' storehouse, and he made plans for a publishing house. In addition, he instructed some of the Saints to begin purchasing lands and building homes.[1]

On August 4, 1831, a conference was convened, during which travel plans were discussed. Before Joseph's party departed on August 8, 1831, the Prophet received this revelation. The Lord said that it had pleased him that this vanguard group had visited Zion. He instructed them not to "hide" their talents, to preach the gospel on their return trip, and not to be afraid to "open their mouths." (See verse 2, 13.) When Joseph inquired about specific travel plans, the Lord said it made no difference to him and that he expected the brethren to handle such details for themselves. (See verse 5.) However, the revelation does specify that the brethren take their journey from "the place which is called St. Louis." (See verse 5.) From St. Louis, Joseph, Sidney Rigdon, and others were told to go to Cincinnati to preach the gospel. (See verse 6.) Finally, the Lord instructed that their time should be used wisely. (See verse 13.)

Some things do not matter to the Lord

Joseph and his assembly were anxious to know by what means they should travel back to Kirtland. On such matters the brethren were informed to make up their own minds:

"But, verily, I will speak unto you concerning your journey. . . . Let there be a craft made, or bought, as seemeth you good, it mattereth not unto me." (Verse 5.)

This approach is reminiscent of section 8: "Remember that without faith you can do nothing; therefore ask in faith. Trifle not with these things; do not ask for that which you ought not." (D&C 8:10.) There is a certain independence that the Lord expects.

---

[1]. Robinson and Garrett, *A Commentary on the Doctrine and Covenants*, 2:169.

Section 61: McIlwaine's Bend, by Missouri River (Near Miami, Missouri), August 12, 1831

Heading

The power of the destroyer on the waters is made manifest as Joseph and his brethren return from a visit to Zion, Jackson County, Missouri.

Introduction

This revelation was given through Joseph Smith on the banks of the Missouri River at McIlwaine's Bend near Miami, Missouri, on August 12, 1831.[1] On their return trip to Kirtland from Independence, Missouri, the Prophet and ten elders had traveled down the Missouri River in canoes. On the third day of the journey, they experienced many dangers. During the day, Elder William W. Phelps saw in vision the destroyer riding in power upon the face of the waters.

Historical background

As instructed in Doctrine and Covenants 60:5, Joseph and ten elders left Independence, Missouri, in canoes and headed down the Missouri River for St. Louis. There are two accounts of what happened on August 11, 1831, the third day of their journey. One account relates that the canoe in which Joseph and Sidney were riding actually hit a "sawyer," or partially submerged tree, and was nearly overturned.[2] In another account, the canoe in which the Prophet and Sidney were riding hit a tree bobbing in the river and turned the canoe over, almost drowning them.[3] Both accounts do agree that Joseph and Sidney found themselves in harm's way, as did some of their fellow travelers. As a result, the bedraggled party stopped at McIlwaine's Bend (or Miami Bend), about forty miles above Chariton, Missouri, to get their bearings and to rest on the banks of the river.

While the brethren were recuperating from these harrowing experiences, William W. Phelps reported that he saw a vision of Satan riding upon the waters of the river. Others present said they heard some peculiar noises but did not see the vision.[4] The next morning, on August 12, 1831, Joseph Smith received section 61, confirming that Phelps's vision was consistent with what could be expected in the turbulent latter days leading up to

---

1. Smith, *History of the Church*, 1:202–5.
2. See Robinson and Garrett, *A Commentary on the Doctrine and Covenants*, 2:174.
3. See Cook, *Revelations of the Prophet Joseph Smith*, 96.
4. See Preece, *Learning to Love the Doctrine and Covenants*, 116.

Jesus' second coming: "Behold, there are many dangers upon the waters, and more especially hereafter." (Verse 4.)

Unfortunately, the somewhat dire circumstances Joseph and his brethren found themselves in resulted in discord between them. In a letter written to Edward Partridge on September 20, 1831, Ezra Booth said:

> The morning after they left Independence, the conduct of some of the elders displeased Oliver who uttered a malediction something like, "As the Lord God liveth, if you do not behave better, some accident will befall you." In the afternoon of the third day while negotiating some treacherous waters, Joseph took command and issued some orders which were resented by the brethren in one of the canoes who refused to obey, and in so doing became tangled in some brush and almost capsized. This frightened Joseph who ordered them all ashore, while some of the brethren felt they should continue. Once on shore, at McIlwaine's bend, tempers flared and words were exchanged. Joseph and Oliver were accused of being "highly imperious and quite dictatorial." Joseph was also called a coward. After much emotional discussion, apologies were made, and a reconciliation of sorts reached.[1]

Since travel by canoe seemed somewhat dangerous, Joseph Smith, Oliver Cowdery, and Sidney Rigdon were given special instructions in section 61 to travel overland to St. Louis and Kirtland. (See verse 23). Most of the remaining brethren continued their journey via the river (verse 27), with the exception of Sidney Gilbert and W. W. Phelps, who traveled over land in search of a press to bring back to Zion. (See verses 9–12.)

Joseph, Sidney, and Oliver arranged to go by stage, but some of the other brethren complained that it was overly expensive. Some even suggested that Joseph chose this means of travel because he was afraid of the river. "Why do we have to beg our passage on foot while they get to travel by stage?" they asked. Joseph, Sidney, and Oliver were instructed to preach in Cincinnati, a command each failed to obey. (See verse 30–31.)[2]

Prohibition on swimming and missionaries

Some have suggested that section 61 is the basis for the Church's policy prohibiting missionaries from swimming. Those supporting this proposition point to the language in verse 5: "For I, the Lord, have decreed in mine anger many destructions upon the waters." Some have reasoned from this statement that all waters are unsafe and therefore missionaries ought to avoid even swimming pools. Such an interpretation is not well founded and ignores the fact that most of the brethren traveling with the prophet,

---

1. Preece, *Learning to Love the Doctrine and Covenants*, 117.
2. See Preece, *Learning to Love the Doctrine and Covenants*, 118.

Joshua Lewis Home: Jackson County, Missouri, July–August 1831

McIlwaines Bend, Missouri. The place where tempers flared between Joseph Smith and his brethren.

even in light of this warning, continued by boat to their destination. (See verses 27–28.) The proscription against missionaries swimming undoubtedly grows out of more practical concerns about exposing missionaries to unnecessary dangers.

SECTION 62: SITE OF THE TOWN OF CHARITON, BY THE MISSOURI RIVER (NEAR CAZZELL, MISSOURI), AUGUST 13, 1831

Heading

Revelation given to bless and encourage the Prophet's brother Hyrum and friends Joseph met on his way back to Kirtland from Missouri. The Lord forgives them of their sins. In the mundane affairs of life, it does not matter to the Lord what men and women do.

Introduction

This revelation was given through Joseph Smith on August 13, 1831, on the banks of the Missouri River at Chariton, Missouri.[1] On this day the Prophet and his group, who were on their way back to Kirtland from

---

1. Smith, *History of the Church,* 1:205–6.

Independence, met several elders who were on their way to the land of Zion. After joyful salutations, Joseph received this revelation.

Historical background

Joseph had been in Independence for about three weeks and was traveling to Kirtland with a handful of brethren. When they reached McIlwaine's Bend, on August 11, 1831, on the banks of the Missouri River (near Miami, Missouri), Joseph and his party stopped for the night. The next day they split up and went in different directions. Joseph, Sidney Rigdon, and Oliver Cowdery crossed the Missouri River at Chariton, Missouri, and encountered Hyrum Smith and John Murdock on their way to Independence, Missouri. It had originally been intended that they would all be in Missouri at the same time, but Hyrum Smith and John Murdock had been instructed to travel via Detroit, which lengthened their journey. In addition, John Murdock became ill and was in bed for a week. Feeling somewhat better, he sold his watch to a William Ivy to secure a wagon to carry him to Chariton, some seventy miles away.[1] After section 62 was received, Joseph and his party traveled on foot to Fayette, Missouri, where they boarded a stagecoach to St. Louis, and then to Kirtland, arriving on August 27, 1831.[2]

The Lord expects men and women to use their own judgment in the common and mundane affairs of life

Apparently there had been quite a bit of discussion on the best mode of transportation and what route the brethren should travel. Section 62 addresses this concern and advises that the Lord was willing to provide but left it up to his children to decide on the means of travel. "I, the Lord, am willing, if any among you desire to ride upon horses, or upon mules, or in chariots." (Verse 7.) "These things remain with you to do according to judgment and the directions of the Spirit." (Verse 8.) Whatever the Lord provides, the recipients should receive with a "thankful heart." (Verse 7.)

---

1. See Robinson and Garrett, *A Commentary on the Doctrine and Covenants*, 2:183–84.
2. See Cook, *Revelations of the Prophet Joseph Smith*, 98.

Joshua Lewis Home: Jackson County, Missouri, July–August 1831

The Lord knows how to succor the weaknesses of men

Section 62 acknowledges that all men have "weakness" but that God knows how to "succor [aid and assist] them who are tempted." (Verse 1.) The Lord is pleased that these brethren have been bearing testimony on their travels and forgives them of their sins. (See verse 3.)

Chapter 34

Setting Zion in Order: Jackson County (Independence), Missouri, April 1832

HISTORICAL BACKGROUND

As the Saints began to gather to their new promised land, millennial excitement dominated their thoughts and conversation. "Zion went forward under the looming shadow of the Second Coming."[1] The designation of the land of Zion was, for them, further evidence that the Second Coming was near. The Saints watched for the signs of the times and warned people to flee to Zion. After all, in Joseph's earlier revelations he had warned of calamities. (See D&C 29:9, 18; 43:18, 21–22.) America was under condemnation for its unabashed materialism. (See 2 Nephi 29; Moses 7:61.) There was a feeling that society was coming apart and that the existence of Zion would put things right by assembling the righteous together in one place to care for each other and for the poor among them. The Saints' resolve was resolute. "The Zion drama overshadowed everything."[2]

In July 1831 Joseph had made his first visit to Independence, Missouri, to establish Zion. Less than a year later, Joseph made a second visit to deal with disputations that had arisen and to set the Church in order. (See D&C 78:9.) Just a few months earlier, in March 1832, Joseph received a revelation warning that some of the Saints in Zion were being tempted by Satan to "turn their hearts away." (D&C 78:10.)[3] When he arrived in July, he found some contention and discontent among the members of his flock. Some were resentful that Joseph lived in comparative comfort in Kirtland instead of with them on the frontier.[4]

---

1. Bushman, *Joseph Smith: Rough Stone Rolling*, 165.
2. Bushman, *Joseph Smith: Rough Stone Rolling*, 168.
3. See *Church History in the Fulness of Time*, 115.
4. See section 78, which alludes to such issues.

Setting Zion in Order: Jackson County, Missouri, April 1832

There were also administrative reasons for Joseph to make this trip. It was necessary to more closely coordinate the operation of the Church's storehouses in Kirtland and Independence.[1] Finally, prior to this time, in Amherst, Ohio, in January 1832 Joseph Smith had been sustained as President of the High Priesthood. It was now appropriate for the Saints in Jackson County to participate in the same sustaining.[2]

Once Joseph arrived in October 1832, his first order of business was to settle a dispute between Sidney Rigdon and Edward Partridge, the bishop in Missouri. Bushman explains that "Rigdon had not forgiven Partridge for questioning Joseph's prediction of a large branch in Jackson County in 1831."[3] Partridge complained that Joseph's prediction had not been fulfilled. Soon differences were settled and they turned to other issues.[4]

As was Joseph's custom, he called a conference of some of the brethren to discuss the problems facing Zion. Most pressing was the fact that the bishop's storehouse did not have enough goods in it to keep pace with population growth.[5] In an effort to solve this problem and better coordinate the affairs of the Church, Joseph turned to the Lord and received section 82, which placed authority for the economic affairs of both Kirtland and Missouri in the hands of one supervising council. This made it possible for Joseph to exert more influence over the affairs in Zion, even though he was residing in Kirtland. (See D&C 82:11–12.)

But the centralization of authority into one council failed to correct the problems. The people were not living the law of consecration correctly and so were not able to sustain themselves; the God-ordained orders of communal living were short-lived. Bushman identified some of the apprehension many of the early Saints struggled with. "Nothing was more sacrosanct in American ideology than the individual's right to the fruits of his labor. Equalizing wealth required each person to be 'seeking the interest of his

---

1. In March 1832 a revelation established two storehouses, one in Kirtland and the other in Independence, Missouri. (See D&C 78.) Everyday management of the storehouse in Kirtland was with Bishop Whitney and Bishop Partridge in Missouri. Overall direction was to come from a higher council, who were "to manage the affairs of the poor, and all things pertaining to the bishopric both in the land of Zion, and in the land of Shinehah [Kirtland]." (See D&C 82:11–12.) This council was sometimes referred to as the United Order. It functioned like a company, managing a tannery, steam sawmill, a printing press, and real estate in hopes of serving the Saints and turning a profit for the bishops' storehouses. (See Bushman, *Joseph Smith: Rough Stone Rolling*, 182.)
2. On April 26, 1832, a "general council" in Missouri sustained Joseph as President of the High Priesthood. (See *Church History in the Fulness of Time*, 115.)
3. Bushman, *Joseph Smith: Rough Stone Rolling*, 181.
4. See Bushman, *Joseph Smith: Rough Stone Rolling*, 181. Partridge and Rigdon knew each other quite well. Partridge had been a member of the Campbellite congregation in Mendon, Ohio, prior to their joining the Church. Rigdon was Mendon's Campbellite minister.
5. See Bushman, *Joseph Smith: Rough Stone Rolling*, 181.

neighbor, and doing all things with an eye single to the glory of God.' Could they? The little band of Saints had no prior experience with equality of property."[1] Furthermore, the scarcity of property to distribute among the "poverty stricken early members hampered the system's effectiveness from the start."[2]

Joseph continued to encourage the living of this divine law, aided by Bishop Partridge and the loyal Colesville Saints. Yet a short time later, Joseph would be forced discontinue Church-sponsored egalitarian communities. After 1833, when the Saints were expelled from Zion, communal orders were never fully reinstituted. A halting attempt was made in Far West to reestablish such orders in a modified form, but by the time the Saints settled in Nauvoo the effort was abandoned. Much later, in Utah, Brigham Young experimented with the principle by organizing several cooperatives; for the most part, these died out by the turn of the twentieth century.[3]

Considering the looming concerns Zion was faced with, Joseph's visit was all too short. Within days he was on his way back to Kirtland. His counsel went largely unheeded, and by the end of the year disagreements within the Zion community were even more intense. Selfishness, jealousies, and the spirit of criticism abounded. Joseph wrote letters from Kirtland to the leaders in Zion to lessen such feelings, all to no avail.[4]

Several issues set the local non-Mormon community on edge. In addition to all the talk of "Zion," the Latter-day Saints displayed sympathies for the Indians and African-Americans.[5] This alarmed the local population, who felt otherwise. Leaders in the non-Mormon community began to organize against the Mormons, led by the Protestant ministers.[6] A few months after Joseph left, violence erupted, and between November and December 1833 the Saints were expelled from Zion. They fled north into Clay County.

Section 82: Edward Partridge Home and Schoolhouse, Independence, Missouri, April 26, 1832

Heading

Saints in Missouri called upon to repent and establish Zion. The Lord is bound when the Saints obey his commandments.

---

1. Bushman, *Joseph Smith: Rough Stone Rolling*, 182.
2. Bushman, *Joseph Smith: Rough Stone Rolling*, 182.
3. See Bushman, *Joseph Smith: Rough Stone Rolling*, 183.
4. See *Church History in the Fulness of Time*, 128.
5. See *Church History in the Fulness of Time*, 131.
6. See *Church History in the Fulness of Time*, 130–31.

Setting Zion in Order: Jackson County, Missouri, April 1832

The big question

Question: What and where is Zion?
Answer: Zion is a place where the Saints are "to be equal," taking into account their "wants and . . . needs."

Introduction

This revelation was given to Joseph Smith the Prophet in the Edward Partridge home and school house in Independence, Missouri, on April 26, 1832.[1] The occasion was a general council of the Church at which Joseph Smith was sustained as the President of the High Priesthood. He had previously been ordained to this office at a conference of high priests, elders, and members, at Amherst, Ohio, January 25, 1832. (See D&C 75.) Originally, unusual names were used in the publication of this revelation to conceal the identity of the persons involved. (See heading to section 78.) These unusual names have now been dropped, except in cases where the identity is not known. (See verse 11.)

Historical background

In early March 1832 the Prophet Joseph, Sidney Rigdon, and Newel K. Whitney, all residing in the Kirtland area, had been commanded to travel to Independence, Missouri, to counsel with the Saints in Zion. (See D&C 78:9.) Over the next few weeks Joseph received several revelations regarding united orders or "firms" to be established in Kirtland and the organization of the Presidency of the High Priesthood.[2]

As they were making preparations to travel to Zion, persecution and violence erupted against the Prophet and Sidney Rigdon, who were then living on the Johnson farm in Hiram, Ohio. Even though Joseph and Sidney had initially been quite successful in blunting criticism in the community, a spirit of hostility had been stirred up. An apostate by the name of Booth had been preaching against Mormonism and publishing anti-Mormon attacks in the local newspaper.

On the night of March 24, 1832, a drunken mob of twenty-five or thirty men attacked the Johnson home where Joseph was staying. At the time Joseph had stayed up late caring for his newly adopted infant son, who was sick with the measles. Just after Joseph fell asleep on a trundle bed the mob burst into his room and dragged him out the door as Emma screamed for help. The Prophet struggled but was overpowered as the mob ridiculed,

---

1. Smith, *History of the Church*, 1:267–69.
2. See Robinson and Garrett, *A Commentary on the Doctrine and Covenants*, 3:7.

pummelled, and choked him and stripped him of his clothing. A member of the mob tried to force a vial of acid into Joseph's mouth, chipping one of his teeth, which caused him thereafter to speak with a slight whistle. One man scratched him with his nails and yelled, "G—d—ye, that's the way the Holy Ghost falls on folks!" Joseph was then tarred and feathered over his whole body.[1] Sidney Rigdon was also dragged from his home and tarred and feathered on the same night.[2] Just days after this mob

---

1. *Church History in the Fulness of Time*, 115. A later account written by Luke Johnson, one of John Johnson's sons who had apostatized from the Church, said that during the attack Joseph was "stretched on a board, and tantalized in the most insulting and brutal manner; they tore off the few night clothes that he had on, for the purpose of emasculating him, and had Dr. Dennison there to perform the operation; but when the Dr. saw the Prophet stripped and stretched on the plank, his heart failed him, and he refused to operate." (See Bushman, *Joseph Smith: Rough Stone Rolling*, 179.) The castration failed. The historian Fawn Brodie speculated that the castration was egged on because one of John Johnson's sons, Eli, meant to punish Joseph for a suspected intimacy with his sister, Nancy Marinda, but her hypothesis failed for lack of evidence. (See Bushman, *Joseph Smith: Rough Stone Rolling*, 179.)

2. Often overlooked was the beating that Sidney Rigdon took on the same night. Sidney Rigdon lived in a log cabin on the Johnson farm so that he could help the Prophet make revisions to the Bible. Rigdon was well known in the area by the inhabitants who were primarily Reformed Baptists or Campbellites. Rigdon had been their former leader and when he left the Campbellites for Mormonism, those left behind viewed him as a charlatan who was out to get their property into a common fund—a reference to communal living orders which Rigdon favored even before he came into the Church. (See Van Wagoner, *Sidney Rigdon: A Portrait of Religious Excess*, 114.) On the same night that Joseph was tarred and feathered, Rigdon was forced from his home by intruders. Rigdon recalled that "they broke into my house, dragged me out of my bed—out of the door my head beating on the floor. They dragged me over the wood pile, and on they went my head thumping on the frozen ground, after which they threw tar and feathers on me—and endeavored to throw aqua fortes [nitric acid] in my face but I turned my face and it missed me." (See Van Wagoner, *Sidney Rigdon: A Portrait of Religious Excess*, 115.) Rigdon's son remembers his 225-pound father being dragged by his heels and recounted how his assailants "pounded him till they thought he was dead and then went to get Joseph Smith." (See Van Wagoner, *Sidney Rigdon: A Portrait of Religious Excess*, 115.) Joseph was carried by the mob to the place where Rigdon lay unconscious and supposed his dear friend dead. Rigdon was badly hurt and lay on the ground for some time before he regained consciousness. When he came to his senses, he "went reeling along the road not knowing where he was; he would have passed his house but my mother was out the door watching for him and went out as he came along and got him in the house." (Van Wagoner, *Sidney Rigdon: A Portrait of Religious Excess*, 116.) Rigdon was slow to recover. Joseph recalled that when he visited his colleague, he "found him crazy, and his head highly inflamed, for they had dragged him by his heels, and those, too, so high from the ground that he could not raise his head from the rough, frozen surface, which lacerated it exceedingly; and when he saw me he called to his wife to bring him his razor. She asked him what he wanted of it; and he replied, to kill me. Sister Rigdon left the room, and he asked me to bring his razor; I asked him what he wanted of it, and he replied he wanted to kill his wife; and he continued delirious some days." (See Van Wagoner, *Sidney Rigdon: A Portrait of Religious Excess*, 116.) This beating was the second head trauma suffered by Rigdon. Sidney's brother Loammi said that his brother had been thrown from a horse when he was seven and got his foot caught in a stirrup and was dragged some distance before he was rescued. (See Van Wagoner, *Sidney Rigdon: A Portrait of Religious Excess*, 116.) No doubt Rigdon suffered a closed head injury that contributed to his manic depression, which plagued

violence, on April 1, 1832, Joseph, Sidney, and Newel K. Whitney began their travels to Missouri, where they arrived on April 24, 1832. The mob followed them all the way to Cincinnati.[1]

In Independence on April 26, 1832, a general council of the Church was organized to set in order the affairs of the Church in Independence. The primary purpose of the conference was to address problems that had arisen in administering the law of consecration. Because this economic order was being lived in both Kirtland and Missouri, it was necessary to try to better coordinate and oversee operations. A central council was organized for this purpose after Joseph received section 82. (See verses 11–12.) During the conference, Joseph was acknowledged as the President of the High Priesthood according to a previous ordination at a conference of high priests, elders, and members in Amherst, Ohio, on January 25, 1832.

Rigdon had accused Partridge of not having faith to accept Joseph's prediction made in 1831 that a large branch would someday exist in Independence.[2] Rigdon and Partridge were able to bridge their differences and everyone came together in the afternoon for a second session of the conference. It was at this time that section 82 was revealed to the Prophet Joseph Smith. The opening verses make reference to the Rigdon-Partridge matter: "Inasmuch as you have forgiven one another your trespasses, even so I, the Lord, forgive you." (Verse 1.)

Saints promised that if they would live the laws of the gospel, the Lord would bless them

Section 82 very directly reminded those Saints in Zion of what was expected of them and promised that God would bless them if they obeyed his commandments. "For of him unto whom much is given much is required; and he who sins against the greater light shall receive the greater condemnation." (Verse 3.) Therefore, "sin no more." Furthermore, "unto that soul who sinneth shall the former sins return." (Verse 7.) Then came the promise: "I, the Lord, am bound when ye do what I say." (Verse 10.)

Then section 82 describes what kind of society the Saints were to establish:

---

him all the days of his life. Manic behavior and depression were little understood at the time, and Rigdon's mood swings damaged his friendship with Joseph. For long periods of time in Nauvoo he was bedridden and reported to have "melancholia." Even so, Rigdon was one of the giants of the Restoration, with an incisive and quick mind. Although he was ultimately excommunicated, he left his mark on Mormonism and made a remarkable contribution to the Mormon movement at its inception.

1. See Bushman, *Joseph Smith: Rough Stone Rolling*, 180.
2. See Bushman, *Joseph Smith: Rough Stone Rolling*, 181.

You are to be equal, ... every man according to his wants and his needs, inasmuch as his wants are just.

... All this for the benefit of the church ... , that every man may improve upon his talent, that every man may gain other talents, yea, even an hundred fold, to be cast into the Lord's storehouse, to become the common property of the whole church—

Every man seeking the interest of his neighbor, and doing all things with an eye single to the glory of God. (Verses 17–19.)

Finally, the Lord once again warns that those who fall short risk Church discipline. "And the soul that sins against this covenant, and hardeneth his heart against it, shall be dealt with according to the laws of my church, and shall be delivered over to the buffetings of Satan until the day of redemption." (Verse 21.)

The Saints encouraged to make friends with their nonmember neighbors

By April 1832 trouble was brewing between the Latter-day Saints and their Missouri neighbors.[1] Many members of the Church had been unwise and made comments about the Saints taking over the land in preparation for the return of the Lord Jesus Christ. It was in this context that the Lord said:

"And now, verily I say unto you, and this is wisdom, make unto yourselves friends with the mammon of unrighteousness, and they will not destroy you." (Verse 2.)

Most of the Saints ignored this counsel and the warning associated with it. Accordingly, unstable relations between the Missourians and the Mormons were exacerbated and finally broke down altogether. Those identified with the "mammon of unrighteousness" confronted the Saints in 1838 and 1839 and forcibly drove them out of Zion.

---

1. During the conference, Joseph was made aware of the festering problems between the Saints and the local Missourians and said that members of the Church "were settling among a ferocious set of mobbers, like lambs among wolves." (See Robinson and Garrett, *A Commentary on the Doctrine and Covenants*, 3:18.)

Section 83: Edward Partridge Home and Schoolhouse, Independence, Missouri, April 30, 1832

Heading

If a husband dies or is killed, his survivors (widow and children) may remain on the family inheritance (land) and the Church must provide for them.

The big question

Question: What and where is Zion?
Answer: Zion is a place where widows and orphans are cared for.

Introduction

This revelation was given through Joseph Smith in the Edward Partridge home and schoolhouse in Independence, Missouri, on April 30, 1832.[1] This revelation was received by the Prophet as he sat in council with his brethren; it concerns family duties. Women and children have claim upon their husbands and fathers for their support. Widows and orphans have claim upon the Church for their support.

Historical background

In accordance with instructions given in Doctrine and Covenants 78:9, Joseph and Sidney left Hiram, Ohio, for Missouri on April 1, 1832, with Newel K. Whitney and Jesse Gause, to "sit in council" with the Missouri Saints. Joseph and his party arrived in Independence on April 24, 1832; and a conference was held on April 26–27, 1832, during which Joseph received section 82. During the conference he talked with the brethren about principles associated with the law of consecration and was sustained as the President of the High Priesthood, having previously been sustained to this position by the Ohio Saints on January 25, 1832. (See commentary on D&C 75.)

After the conference, on April 28 and 29, Joseph visited Kaw township, west of Independence along the Big Blue River. The Saints who had settled there were originally from Colesville, New York. Joseph Knight, a close friend and one of the leaders of the Colesville Saints, was among them. Joseph was given a warm welcome.[2]

---

1. Smith, *History of the Church*, 1:269–70.
2. See Preece, *Learning to Love the Doctrine and Covenants*, 187.

Section 83 was received on April 30, 1832, the day that Joseph returned to Independence to incorporate the Missouri branch of the Gilbert-Whitney store into the United Firm and to coordinate the printing activities of the Literary Firm.[1] It was at this time that the Literary Firm decided to print 3,000 copies of the Book of Commandments instead of the 10,000 originally planned.[2]

Widows and orphans

Section 83 gives instructions regarding whether or not a stewardship should be dissolved in the event a husband and father dies or is killed. Does the family's stewardship revert to the Church or pass on to his wife and children? Section 83 clarifies that the fatherless family "may remain upon their inheritances according to the laws of the land" and that it is the responsibility of the Church to care for the remaining family (the man's widow and children). (See verses 3–4.)

---

1. See Cook, *Revelations of the Prophet Joseph Smith*, 175.
2. See Robinson and Garrett, *A Commentary on the Doctrine and Covenants*, 3:18.

Chapter 35

Zion's Camp: Summer 1834

The forced exodus from Jackson County, Missouri, in 1838–39 was one of the most dispiriting episodes in Church history. The leaders of the Church, including Joseph Smith, could hardly believe that the Lord would allow his people to be displaced. After all, it was the Lord himself who had designated this very spot as Zion, a "gathering place," a sacred land to which he, as part of the Second Coming, would come to usher in his reign on earth. It was unthinkable that such momentous plans could fail. The Saints were convinced that the mass departure from Jackson County must be only a temporary setback. Therefore, when the Lord commanded Joseph to raise an army (Zion's Camp) to take back Zion, the faithful thought that the venture would certainly succeed.

At first, Joseph was encouraged in his plans to march some 900 miles from Kirtland to Independence, Missouri. Several reports had reached him that Missouri Governor Daniel Dunklin was willing to arm the Saints and return them to their lands under military escort if the Saints could provide enough of their own forces to retain their property. So hope ran high when Joseph departed for Zion on May 1, 1834, with a band of 85 militia members. The army's numbers increased along the way as others joined, the group eventually numbering 207 men, 11 women, and 11 children. Each soldier understood that he might be required, if necessary, to give his life to "redeem Zion."[1]

During their journey, some members of the camp grumbled about Joseph's leadership and about the living conditions. In early June, Joseph prophesied that if the camp did not repent, the Lord would bring down a scourge upon them. By June 22, 1834, the army had stopped at Fishing River, just a few days' journey from Zion. Joseph heard from Orson Hyde and Parley P. Pratt that Governor Dunklin had changed his mind and was no longer willing to help the Saints regain their homes in Jackson County.

---

1. See Robinson and Garrett, *A Commentary on the Doctrine and Covenants*, 3:304–5.

The governor reportedly said that while he recognized the Saints' rights had been violated, state help was impractical and could lead to a civil war between Missouri Mormons and non-Mormons.[1]

It was under these circumstances that Joseph received section 105, in which the Lord told the Saints that in consequence of their transgressions, the time was not right for Zion to be established. The revelation said the Lord had accepted his people's sacrifices, and the army should disband. As many of them as possible should stay in the area and the rest should return to their homes. On July 3, two months and two days after the march had begun, the militia was officially dispersed.

Feelings of disappointment and frustration spread throughout the camp. According to Nathan Tanner, some were so upset that they vented their dissatisfaction by attacking bushes with their swords, cutting the plants to shreds. Others simply walked away and apostatized. Then, suddenly and without warning, cholera struck the camp. Some 68 became ill and at least 14 died.[2] Even the Prophet was taken ill when he tried but failed to heal one of his brethren. Joseph went before the Lord and was promised that if the members of the camp would repent, the disease would be stayed. Joseph told the camp to repent of their sins, backbiting, apostasy, and unwillingness to follow the counsel of the Lord. The disease abated and the camp was spared further illness.

As members of the camp started home, many felt demoralized. Some suggested that Joseph was a false prophet. How could he organize an army that failed when the Second Coming depended on it? Even the press made fun of the Mormons. The *Painesville Telegraph* said the event was a wild "goose chase."[3] The Missourians rejoiced. The mobs felt vindicated, and their confidence increased. On the other hand, Joseph told his men that all was not lost. He said that God had not "designed" all their trials and suffering "for nothing." "It was the will of God that those who went to Zion, with a determination to lay down their lives, if necessary, should be ordained to the ministry, and go forth to prune the vineyard."[4] From the remaining faithful, Joseph chose his leaders and filled the newly organized Quorums of the Twelve and the Seventy.

---

1. See Robinson and Garrett, *A Commentary on the Doctrine and Covenants*, 3:305.
2. See Robinson and Garrett, *A Commentary on the Doctrine and Covenants*, 3:305.
3. See Preece, *Learning to Love the Doctrine and Covenants*, 268.
4. Preece, *Learning to Love the Doctrine and Covenants*, 268.

Zion's Camp, East Fork, Fishing River (Lawson), Missouri, near a Baptist church. While storms raged, the brethren met and sang hymns here, dissuading their enemies from attacking them.

Section 105: East Fork, Fishing River (Lawson), Missouri, June 22, 1834

Heading

Zion's camp is disbanded and the hopes to redeem Zion are put on hold.[1]

The big question

Question: How do we deal with disappointment and unrealized promises?
Answer: Repent of sin and be patient!

Introduction

This revelation was given through Joseph Smith at Fishing River, Missouri, on June 22, 1834.[2] Violence against the Saints in Missouri had increased, and mobs from several counties had declared their intent to destroy the Latter-day Saint people. The Saints had been driven out of Zion, Jackson County, Missouri, north into Clay County. The Prophet raised an army in Kirtland, known as Zion's Camp, to rescue the Saints and once again reestablish them in their homes in Zion. While this army was encamped on Fishing River, not far from Jackson County, the Prophet received this revelation, in which he was told to disband the military force and return to Kirtland.

Historical background

On June 20, 1834, Joseph and his army camped at John Cooper's farm, not far from Fishing River. Concerned about their enemies, the open prairie in this area provided a means of escape if they were attacked. Destitute of food, the army was fed at the farm. On the same day Colonel John Scone and two other men from Ray County found Zion's Camp and sought information about Joseph's intentions. On the next day, June 21, additional consultations took place between the leaders of Zion's Camp and Cornelius Gilliam, the sheriff of Clay County. The Mormons declared in writing their

---

1. In D&C 103:29–40 Joseph was commanded to raise an army (Zion's Camp) and march to Zion to restore the Saints who had been expelled from their homes in Zion. He did so, but when his army reached the outskirts of Zion the Prophet disbanded the militia and returned to Kirtland.
2. Smith, *History of the Church*, 2:108–11.

peaceable intentions.[1] On June 22, section 105 was revealed, instructing Joseph to disband his army and send them home.

Why Zion and Zion's Camp failed

Section 105 stated that the establishment of Zion and her redemption by Zion's Camp had failed because the Saints had sinned and were in need of repentance. Zion, the Lord said, "cannot be built up unless it is by the principles of the law of the celestial kingdom." (Verse 5.) The Saints had failed to live the higher law and therefore, the Lord said, "I cannot receive her unto myself." (Verse 5.) The Saints' primary failure had been their inability to fully live the law of consecration.

> But behold, they have not learned to be obedient to the things which I required at their hands, but are full of all manner of evil, and do not impart of their substance, as becometh Saints, to the poor and afflicted among them....
> Therefore, in consequence of the transgressions of my people, it is expedient in me that mine elders should wait for a little season for the redemption of Zion. (Verses 3, 9.)

Accordingly, the early Saints lost their opportunity to institute in its fulness the kingdom of God on earth in preparation for the Second Coming. "I say unto you, were it not for the transgressions of my people, ... they might have been redeemed even now." (Verse 2.) In the meantime, "my people must needs be chastened until they learn obedience, if it must needs be, by the things which they suffer." (Verse 6.) (See also D&C 1:31; Alma 45:16.)

Many will say, "Where is their God?"

So much had been said about the imminent establishment of Zion in preparation for the Second Coming that when it became apparent that the Saints had failed to establish, let alone hold on to, their Zion, some of their enemies saw this as proof that Mormonism could not possibly be God's true religion. In fact, section 105 foresaw this reaction. Many would say under these circumstances, "Where is their God?" (Verse 8.) Faith in the face of resounding defeat and a call to repentance was an important lesson for the Saints to learn. Inevitably, some would walk away from the faith.

---

1. See Berrett, *Sacred Places*, 4:590.

The Saints must not resort to violence to redeem Zion

Even though the Lord had sanctioned the raising of an army to redeem Zion, the principle of "renounce war and proclaim peace" was still in full force. (D&C 98:16.)

> And again I say unto you, sue for peace, not only to the people that have smitten you, but also to all people.
> And lift up an ensign of peace, and make a proclamation of peace unto the ends of the earth;
> And make proposals for peace unto those who have smitten you, according to the voice of the Spirit which is in you, and all things shall work together for your good. (Verses 38–40.)

Zion could not be redeemed by blood but by "purchase" only. "For it is my will that these lands should be purchased; and after they are purchased that my saints should possess them according to the laws of consecration which I have given them." (Verse 29.)

Loving their enemies and lifting up "an ensign of peace" proved difficult. The Mormons in Missouri had experienced severe maltreatment, death, and privation at the hands of their enemies. The spirit of retribution could not be completely contained. As a result, further bloodshed and animosity resulted in the Saints being expelled from the state of Missouri altogether. Some Mormon leaders engaged in threatening rhetoric. Although Joseph declined to resort to violence, other Mormons did. Some went about the countryside on preemptive strikes looking for their enemies' stashes of weapons and ransacking non-Mormon homes for food and supplies. A group known as the Danites organized and threatened those in and out of the Church with death. They stressed loyalty to the leading brethren and engaged in paramilitary actions against their enemies. When confronted with what the Danites were doing, Joseph repudiated their actions as "false and pernicious things which were calculated to lead the saints far astray." Had the presidency known of these things, Joseph insisted, "they would have spurned them and their authors from them as they would the gates of hell."[1]

Be considerate of the Missourians in order to avoid the condemnation of the world

Section 105 cautioned the Saints to be wise in the way they treated their non-Mormon neighbors in Missouri. Prior to this time, some Mormons

---

1. Bushman, *Joseph Smith: Rough Stone Rolling*, 372.

had even gone so far as to say that when Jesus returned the Missourians would no longer be welcome there and would lose their land. As could be expected, the Missourians were furious at such talk.

> And let all my people who dwell in the regions round about be very faithful, and prayerful, and humble before me, and reveal not the things which I have revealed unto them, until it is wisdom in me that they should be revealed.
>
> Talk not of judgments, neither boast of faith nor of mighty works, but carefully gather together, as much in one region as can be, consistently with the feelings of the people. (Verses 23–24.)

If God was to bless the Saints with "favor and grace" in the eyes of their enemies, discretion was necessary so that wrongs could be redressed. (See verse 25.)

The righteous will be endowed with power from on high

Not all those who participated in Zion's Camp had been unfaithful in adversity. The Lord promised that such would be "endowed" with spiritual power. "For behold, I have prepared a great endowment and blessing to be poured out upon them, inasmuch as they are faithful and continue in humility before me." (Verses 11–12.) "For ye receive no witness until after the trial of your faith." (Ether 12:6.) Two years later, many of those tried by fire were blessed with spiritual experiences and "power from on high" at the dedication of the Kirtland temple. (See D&C 105:11; 109.)

Zion will not be established for "many days"

Finally, section 105 advised that enthusiastically predicted timetables for the establishment of Zion and the Second Coming should be put on hold. The people of God must now wait patiently upon the Lord until some future day when God's mighty power would be made manifest. "And inasmuch as they follow the counsel which they receive, they shall have power *after many days* to accomplish all things pertaining to Zion." (Verse 37; emphasis added. See commentary on D&C 82.)

Chapter 36

The Saints Forced Farther Away from Zion to Far West: March–July 1838

REASONS FOR THE MOVE TO FAR WEST

By March 1838 Kirtland had become a cauldron of apostasy, as well as animosity directed at Joseph Smith. On January 2, 1837, the leading brethren had established a bank called the Kirtland Safety Society. Serious problems soon arose. A number of the other banks in the area refused to accept Kirtland Safety Society bank notes as legal tender and the anti-Mormon newspapers called the currency worthless. Furthermore, the society's capital was primarily in the form of land, so the bank was short on hard currency such as gold and silver to satisfy demands made for redemption of its paper currency. Enemies of the Church gathered up notes and intentionally made a run on the bank, forcing it to suspend payment *in specie* to its customers for a few weeks. In this midst of these troubles, Joseph and Sidney Rigdon were brought to trial and charged with violating the banking statutes of Ohio.[1]

In the spring of 1837 the Kirtland Safety Society's problems were compounded by the financial Panic of 1837 that spread west from New York. Many banks were forced to close. At the same time there was a growing spirit of speculation in and out of the Church. People went into debt to purchase land, hoping they would be able to pay off the debt based on the land's appreciation in value. When the economy turned sour and the Kirtland bank was forced to close its doors, 200 individuals who invested in the bank lost nearly everything they had. Seventeen lawsuits were filed against the Prophet.[2] People wondered why God would allow his prophet to lead a doomed financial venture.

---

1. See *Church History in the Fulness of Time*, 172.
2. *Church History in the Fulness of Time*, 172–73.

Although the Saints were desperately poor and could hardly put together the means to build the Kirtland Temple, after its dedication the year before there was a feeling of optimism. Their spirits had been buoyed up by the remarkable pentecostal outpouring of the Spirit leading up to and during the temple's dedicatory services. Before this, the failure of Zion's Camp and the persecution and dislocation of the Missouri Saints were very discouraging, causing defections from the Church. How could Joseph lead an army to redeem Zion, and fail, and still be a true prophet? But the spiritual outpouring in the temple reassured them that regardless of what had happened in Missouri, God was still behind the Saints. How could anyone doubt it? The heavens had been opened and angels—and even Jesus himself—had appeared unto many.

The sense of prosperity at that time was because of high land values and the number of Saints arriving to settle in Kirtland. For a short period of time many of the Saints felt prosperity was right around the corner and unfortunately became "haughty in their spirits, and lifted up in the pride of their hearts."[1] As is often the case when money is to be made, unscrupulous brethren took advantage of newcomers by luring them into shaky investments, taking their money and deserting them.[2] And no one expected the nationwide Panic of 1837 with the resulting deflation.

Other problems beset the Prophet as well. Although it was not widely known or believed at the time, some of the brethren--Oliver Cowdery in particular—accused Joseph of adultery with a woman named Fanny Alger. In April 1838, Cowdery was brought up on charges of "seeking to destroy the character of President Joseph Smith Jr. by falsely insinuating that he was guilty of adultery."[3] The question of Joseph's fidelity was significant enough to warrant placing in the appendix of the 1835 edition of the Doctrine and Covenants an "Article on Marriage" stating that Church members had been "reproached with the crime of fornication and polygamy." The article reaffirmed the Church's position that monogamy was the only appropriate relationship between men and women. Bushman summed up the situation: "The bank failure, suspicions about Joseph's morals, and economic stress combined to bring on the apostasies of 1837."[4]

Complicating matters, Joseph became ill during the summer of 1837

---

1. *Church History in the Fulness of Time*, 173.
2. See *Church History in the Fulness of Time*, 173.
3. See Bushman, *Joseph Smith: Rough Stone Rolling*, 324. Looking back, all agree that Joseph married Fanny Alger as a plural wife. Bushman reports that "Mosiah Hancock wrote in the 1890s about Joseph engaging Levi Hancock, Mosiah's father, to ask Alger's parents for permission to marry their daughter. Levi Hancock was Alger's uncle and an appropriate go-between. He talked with Alger's father, then her mother, and finally to Fanny herself, and all three consented." (See Bushman, *Joseph Smith: Rough Stone Rolling*, 325.)
4. Bushman, *Joseph Smith: Rough Stone Rolling*, 336.

and then was gone from Ohio much of the remainder of the year on a mission to Canada and a trip to establish stakes in Far West, Missouri. By this time, of course, the Saints in Zion, Jackson County, had been forced north to Clay County. With each passing day it became more and more apparent that they would not be able to resettle Zion. Arrangements were made with government officials for the displaced Mormons to move even farther north to settle in Far West in Caldwell County.

By the time Joseph returned to Kirtland after his mission to Canada and Far West, many faithful Saints had already moved to Far West for security and safety. Brigham Young, a staunch supporter of Joseph Smith, had been forced to move on December 22, 1837, and Joseph moved shortly thereafter. On January 12, 1838, he was literally chased out of town. After a hard winter journey he arrived in Far West on March 14, 1838. When he arrived in Far West he was warmly welcomed to a thriving city with thousands of Saints living on tens of thousands of acres of land that had been purchased, cleared, and improved.[1]

Yet, all was not well in Far West either. Shortly before Joseph Smith and Sidney Rigdon arrived, the Church in Missouri had accused and rejected the leadership of the stake presidency, David Whitmer, W. W. Phelps, and John Whitmer. Phelps and John Whitmer[2] were excommunicated and shortly afterwards so were David Whitmer and Oliver Cowdery.[3] Therefore, Joseph came into a situation where he would have to calm troubled waters.[4]

---

1. See Robinson and Garrett, *A Commentary on the Doctrine and Covenants*, 4:95–96.

2. W. W. Phelps, with money collected from the Saints, settled in Far West and purchased the northern half of Far West. John Whitmer purchased the southern half. Their business dealings raised suspicion of self-dealing, and the high council investigated. They were exonerated with an agreement to transfer the land to Bishop Edward Partridge, with all proceeds from land sales going to build up the Church. However, on September 4, 1837, Joseph received a revelation: "John Whitmer and William W. Phelps have done those things which are not pleasing in my sight." (See Smith, *History of the Church*, 2:511.) In March 1839 Phelps and Whitmer were excommunicated. Phelps became a bitter enemy but repented in 1840 and came back into the Church. (See Black, *Who's Who in the Doctrine and Covenants*, 225.) John Whitmer never came back; after 1856 he was the last survivor of the Eight Witnesses. (See Black, *Who's Who in the Doctrine and Covenants*, 333.)

3. David Whitmer had in 1837 associated with apostates in Kirtland. He came to believe that Joseph had "abandoned the primitive faith" and "drifted into error." He was excommunicated in Far West on April 13, 1838 and never came back into membership. As one of the Three Witnesses to the Book of Mormon he remained faithful to his testimony and died at the age of eighty-three. (See Black, *Who's Who in the Doctrine and Covenants*, 329–30.) Oliver Cowdery also became disaffected over polygamy and accused Joseph of adultery. Believing Joseph was a fallen prophet, Oliver was excommunicated at Far West on April 12, 1838.

4. See Robinson and Garrett, *A Commentary on the Doctrine and Covenants*, 4:96.

Missouri

The last days in Kirtland and the experience of the Saints in Missouri is primarily a story of setback and survival. The Saints were expelled from Zion, Jackson County, Missouri, in November and December 1833 and pushed north into Clay County, Missouri. The causes of conflict were religious, political, economic, and social. The Saints had not been wise in the statements they made, speaking about the land being redeemed by its "rightful inheritors."[1] The *Evening and the Morning Star* wrote about "taking possession of this county."[2] Josiah Gregg, a nonmember merchant living in Independence said that the Mormons grew bolder as their numbers increased. "At last they became so emboldened by impunity, as openly to boast of their determination to be the sole proprietors of the 'Land of Zion.'"[3] By the summer of 1833 the Saints held over 2,400 acres of land in the area and threatened complete takeover.[4] Their population had grown to 1,200, with more arriving each month. The political threat was obvious—soon every major office would be held by a Mormon. Surely economic domination would follow as well.

Socially, the Saints were New Englanders and the Missourians a coarse, rough-and-ready group from the mountainous regions of several southern states. This meant that each group viewed the world very differently. Mormons were antislavery. The Missourians were proslavery, a particularly sensitive issue in Missouri. Missouri had come into the Union as a slave state under the famous Compromise of 1820. Slaveholding was limited, however. The old settlers prized their right to hold slaves and strongly opposed abolitionism.[5] In addition, Mormons revered the Indians as descendants of the Book of Mormon people, the Lamanites, referred to in the Book of Mormon as the "remnants of Jacob," who it was believed would join with the Saints and build the New Jerusalem at Zion—another proposition the Missourians thought dangerous to the safety of the community.

The difference in social refinement and customs made it difficult for the more crude and bawdy Missourians to break bread with the Saints. Profanity, Sabbath-breaking, horse-racing, cock-fighting, idleness, drunkenness, gambling, and violence caused a deep divide between the two groups living in the same area.

When the stated mission of Zion's Camp had failed and it became clear that Zion would not be redeemed immediately, the Saints moved to Far

---

1. Bushman, *Joseph Smith: Rough Stone Rolling*, 223.
2. Bushman, *Joseph Smith: Rough Stone Rolling*, 223.
3. Bushman, *Joseph Smith: Rough Stone Rolling*, 223.
4. See Bushman, *Joseph Smith: Rough Stone Rolling*, 223.
5. See *Church History in the Fulness of Time*, 130–32.

West, settling there as early as the summer of 1836. Caldwell and Daviess Counties were created for them by Missouri political leaders. The Prophet arrived and settled there in May 1838. However, by that time the Mormons' relationship with the locals had once again deteriorated badly for many of the same reasons that the Saints could not get along in Independence. War broke out between the Saints and the Missourians. In October 1838 there was a battle at DeWitt, and guerrilla warfare ensued in Daviess County. By the end of October a member of the Twelve, David W. Patten, had been killed at the Battle of Crooked River and Missouri Governor Lilburn W. Boggs issued his famous "extermination order," stating that if the Mormons did not leave the territory they could be shot on sight. An outlying community of Saints were massacred at Haun's Mill. Joseph and other leaders of the Church were jailed in October, and in November Far West was surrounded and attacked. Pushed across the Mississippi River in the dead of winter, the Saints would seek refuge in Illinois.

The Changing Structure of the Doctrine and Covenants

The changing structure of the Church and the circumstances of the people are both reflected in the number of canonized revelations received during various periods of time. In just two years, 1830 through 1832, seventy-four canonized revelations were received. During the next eleven years, 1833 through 1844, forty-six canonized revelations were received. From 1845 to the present, four have been added to the Doctrine and Covenants.

This can be accounted for in a number of ways. First, at the inception of the Church, written instruction to the members was necessary to establish the direction and character of the new religious movement. Second, Bushman makes the point that as Church organization developed, the decision-making apparatus shifted from Joseph to various councils on a general and local level. It was understood that councils were to meet, receive revelation, and set policy for the Church. Finally, I would suggest that during the Missouri period of 1838 through 1839, when only eleven sections were received, the sparse number reflected the fact that the Saints were focused on survival, not on pulling back the curtain of heaven to contemplate new ideas and doctrines. The subject matter of the revelations during this time period supports this. Most of these revelations address financial matters and persecution.

Far West, Missouri, founded by W. W. Phelps and John Whitmer in August 1836. Far West became the headquarters of the Church in 1838 when the Prophet Joseph relocated here.

Section 113: Joseph Smith Jr. Home, Far West Caldwell County, Missouri, March 1838

Heading

An interpretation of Isaiah 11 and 52.

Introduction

Answers to certain questions on the writings of Isaiah are given by Joseph Smith the Prophet in his home in Far West, Caldwell County, Missouri, in March 1838.[1] The revelation sheds light on Isaiah 11 and 52.

Historical background

Just prior to the time section 113 was received, Joseph had been out walking with his brother, Samuel Harrison Smith, and Elias Higbee, a member of the high council in Far West. Various sources indicate that they were probably conversing about and asking Joseph for his interpretation of passages in Isaiah.[2] The last two questions addressed in section 13 were raised by Elias Higbee.[3]

Isaiah 11 and 52

Isaiah 11 speaks of a branch of David's line that will grow a shoot ("rod"), a new branch bearing fruit from the old root referred to as the "stem of Jesse." Section 113 clarified that the "stem of Jesse" mentioned in Isaiah 11 is a reference to the Lord Jesus Christ. (See Isaiah 11:1–2.) This explanation makes sense because Jesse was the father of David, who stands at the head of the royal line through which Jesus was prophesied to come. (See Micah 5:2; Hebrews 7:14.) Therefore, Isaiah 11 should be understood as a Messianic prophecy about Christ's mission during the latter days, when "the wolf . . . shall dwell with the lamb, and the leopard shall lie down with the kid; and the calf and the young lion and the fatling together; and a little child shall lead them." (Isaiah 11:6.)

The "rod" and the "Branch [growing] out of his roots" mentioned in connection with the "stem of Jesse" in Isaiah 11 is depicted as the servant

---

1. Smith, *History of the Church*, 3:9–10.
2. The other two sections in the Doctrine and Covenants that deal directly biblical interpretations are section 74 on 1 Corinthians 7:14 and section 77 on portions of the book of Revelation.
3. See Preece, *Learning to Love the Doctrine and Covenants*, 314; and Cook, *Revelations of the Prophet Joseph Smith*, 224.

of "the stem of Jesse" and therefore may be understood to be a reference to the Prophet Joseph Smith's role in the latter days. In this connection Joseph F. McConkie and Craig Ostler point out that the "root of Jesse" is portrayed as a person like Joseph to "whom rightly belongs the priesthood, and keys of the kingdom" in the last days.[1] (See D&C 86:8–10; see also D&C 27:13; 35:17–18; 65:2; 81:2; 90:3; 112:32.)

Isaiah 52 is about the deliverance of Jerusalem. Section 113 clarifies that it refers to Israel's redemption in the last days, when God will redeem Israel for the last time (see verse 8), when "the scattered remnants are exhorted to return to the Lord from whence they have fallen"—a reference to the gathering of all God's people prior to the second coming. (Verse 10.)

Section 114: Joseph Smith Jr. Home, Far West Caldwell County, Missouri, April 17, 1838

Heading

David W. Patten, a member of the Twelve, is told to prepare for a mission in the spring. Before he could fulfill this mission he was killed in the Battle of Crooked River.

Introduction

This revelation was given through Joseph Smith the Prophet in his home in Far West, Caldwell County, Missouri, on April 17, 1838.[2] Church positions held by those who are not faithful will be given to others.

Historical background

The year 1838 was marked by dissent and apostasy. Many, including well-known leaders such as Oliver Cowdery[3] and David Whitmer,[4] were excommunicated. In addition, during this same period apostles Luke Johnson, Lyman E. Johnson, and John Boynton were excommunicated,

---

1. McConkie and Ostler, *Revelations of the Restoration*, 910–11.
2. Smith, *History of the Church*, 3:23.
3. When the Church was organized, Cowdery was viewed as the authority just after Joseph and was referred to as the Second Elder in the Church. He was a man of tremendous stature and was with the Prophet Joseph when John the Baptist restored the Aaronic Priesthood; when Peter, James, and John restored the Melchizedek Priesthood; and when Jesus, Moses, Elias, and Elijah appeared in the Kirtland Temple to restore keys.
4. David Whitmer was likewise a man of integrity and well respected. He was one of the Three Witnesses to the Book of Mormon.

as was, less than a year later, apostle William E. McLellin.[1] The trend continued, and in 1839 other stalwarts such as John Whitmer, one of the Eight Witnesses to the Book of Mormon, and W. W. Phelps, who helped publish the 1835 edition of the Doctrine and Covenants, would disavow Mormonism. Thomas B. Marsh, David W. Patten, and Brigham Young, three senior members of the Twelve, remained faithful during this period and provided a stabilizing influence. It was under these trying circumstances that the Lord assured Joseph, "For verily thus saith the Lord, that inasmuch as there are those among you who deny my name, others shall be planted in their stead and receive their bishopric."[2] (Verse 2.)

Over time, some who left the Church repented and came back into full fellowship and were fully reinstated. W. W. Phelps was a prime example. He repented of his sins and, after corresponding with Joseph, was forgiven by the Prophet and served as one of his clerks during the Nauvoo period.[3]

Section 114 advises David W. Patten, a member of the Twelve, to "settle up all his business as soon as he possibly can" to enable him to "perform a mission unto me next spring." (Verse 1.) Patten did so; however, this opportunity never materialized. On October 25, 1838, he was shot to death during a confrontation with a Missouri mob at what is referred to as the Battle of Crooked River.

---

1. See Cook, *Revelations of the Prophet Joseph Smith*, 317.

2. The use of the word *bishopric* in this context means a general office in the Church and does not refer to the office of bishop and bishop's counselors.

3. In section 55 W. W. Phelps was "called and chosen" to the ministry. The call included an assignment to assist Oliver Cowdery with "the work of printing, and of selecting and writing books for schools in this church." (See D&C 55:1, 4–5.) In the same revelation Phelps was commanded to go to Jackson County, Zion. Once there he was given the assignment of establishing a publishing house. (See D&C 57:11, 13.) Over the next few years Phelps and his family experienced overwhelming turmoil. In 1836 Phelps helped arrange for the Saints to remove from Clay County to the "Mormon county" in Caldwell County. He founded and laid out the settlement in Far West. "Since Phelps and Whitmer used considerable Church funds in setting up Far West and acted independently of the Missouri High Council, Church leaders felt these men abused their power, so the council released them from their leadership posts in the Church in 1838. Consequently, Phelps joined a growing group of dissidents who tried throughout the remainder of the year to undercut the work . . . in northern Missouri. . . . In the Richmond preliminary hearing in November 1838, Phelps's testimony against Joseph Smith contributed to the Prophet's lengthy incarceration in Liberty Jail. Phelps was officially excommunicated from the Church in March 1839." Phelps moved his family to Dayton, Ohio. He lost complete contact with Church until Orson Hyde and John E. Page of the Twelve went to Dayton to proselyte. Noting that Phelps's heart had softened and finding him in an impoverished condition, these brethren wrote to Joseph on Phelps's behalf and asked that he be received back into full fellowship. Phelps wrote a letter accompanying the one sent by Hyde and Page and said. "I am as the prodigal son, though I never doubt[ed] or disbelieved[d] the fullness of the Gospel, I have been greatly abused and humbled." Joseph wrote back. "Believing your confession to be real and your repentance genuine, I shall be happy once again to give you the right hand of fellowship, and rejoice over the returning prodigal." (See Van Orden, "William W. Phelps's Service in Nauvoo as Joseph Smith's Political Clerk," 3–4.)

Patten was the first Mormon leader to suffer martyrdom and is legendary for his courage in the face of adversity. He was an impressive figure, standing six feet one inch tall and weighing over 200 pounds. The Prophet Joseph said that Patten had confided to him sometime early in the summer of 1838 that while he had been praying he "had asked the Lord to let him die the death of a martyr."[1]

An anti-Mormon by the name of Samuel Bogart, along with others, had been assigned to patrol the border between Caldwell and Ray counties, which separated the Mormons from the non-Mormons, allegedly to prevent a Mormon attack. Bogart and his men twice went on the offensive without cause and entered Caldwell County where the Saints were living, attacking Latter-day Saint homes and taking prisoners. This prompted the Mormons to retaliate. Elias Higbee, a Caldwell County judge and the highest civil authority in the area, raised a militia to counter the mob and rescue the prisoners. David W. Patten and Charles C. Rich assumed leadership of the Mormon militia.

As dawn approached, Patten and his troops drew close to a ford on the Crooked River twenty miles from Far West, unaware that Bogart had concealed himself and his band along the banks of the river. Bogart and his gang opened fire. Patten ordered his men forward; Patten was wounded by gunfire and died not long after. The militia was able to free the Mormon prisoners. At Patten's funeral the Prophet said, "There lies a man that has done just as he said he would—he has laid down his life for his friends."[2]

The fact that Patten was called as a missionary by revelation but died before he could enter the mission field raises a thought-provoking question. Why would God inspire the Prophet Joseph to extend the call to Patten if it would never come about? Did Patten disqualify himself in some way? Or did Patten's desire to be a martyr cause him to foolishly place himself in harm's way?

One explanation involves understanding the role of a prophet. Unlike during Old Testament times, where a prophet's role was generally limited to being an oracle and social critic rather than running a church, prophets in the latter days are charged with being the "chief executive" of an organization—the Church—and of establishing the kingdom of God on earth. This involves calling people to the ministry to administer the affairs of the organization. Therefore, in this context, when a prophet says, "thus saith the Lord," he or she may not be speaking prophetically but rather may be indicating by what authority he or she acts.[3]

---

1. Cook, *Revelations of the Prophet Joseph Smith*, 317.
2. *Church History in the Fulness of Time*, 200.
3. Another possibility is that in this particular instance Joseph got the inspiration wrong in

Section 115: Joseph Smith Jr. Home, Far West Caldwell County, Missouri, April 26, 1838

Heading

The Saints in Kirtland are commanded to resettle in Far West. The official name of the Church is revealed. Under trying circumstances, Brigham Young and his associates lay the cornerstone for a temple.

The big questions

Question: What and where is Zion?
Answer: Zion is a place where the Saints gather and build a temple.
Question: How do we deal with disappointment and unrealized promises?
Answer: We do all that is humanly possible to follow the commands of the Lord.

Introduction

This revelation was given through Joseph Smith at his home in Far West, Missouri, on April 26, 1838. The Saints are commanded to leave Kirtland and build a temple.[1] This revelation is addressed to the presiding officers of the Church. The name by which the Church should be known is revealed.

Section 115 originally part of a longer revelation

Thomas B. Marsh, then president of the Quorum of the Twelve, disclosed in a letter to Wilford Woodruff that section 115 was a "lengthy revelation in which many important items are shown forth." Since the section as we know it is only nineteen verses long, it is fair to assume that it is not the entire revelation.[2]

---

the first place. As Joseph freely admitted, prophets are not infallible guides nor are prophets always able to discern the mind and will of the Lord. Joseph taught a principle that relates to the few occasions when it appears as though his predictions did not come to fruition; he admonished the brethren that "some revelations are of God; some revelations are of men; and some revelations are of the devil." (See Roberts, *Comprehensive History of the Church*, 1:165.) The issue of whether such circumstances should vitiate prophetic leadership is discussed in the commentary on section 111.

1. Smith, *History of the Church*, 3:23–25.
2. Woodford, *The Historical Development of the Doctrine and Covenants*, 1506–7.

Historical background

During the years 1837 and 1838 the Saints were leaving Kirtland, Ohio, for Far West, Missouri. Apostasy and discontent were rife, and comments criticizing Joseph Smith were common.[1] Men who held positions of trust and responsibility in the Church rejected Joseph's leadership and claimed he was no longer a "true prophet."[2] Even such stalwarts as Parley P. Pratt were temporarily caught up in apostasy.[3] Most of the disgruntlement grew out of the closing of the Kirtland Bank, a financial institution set up by Joseph and his associates in early January 1837. Just eleven months after it opened its doors, it was forced into bankruptcy in November 1837. By January the situation was serious enough that the Prophet was forced to leave Kirtland on the run in the dead of night.

Far West designated as a Zion

When Joseph arrived in Far West in March 1838, he received section 115, designating this new gathering place as a new Zion, a place of "refuge from the storm." (Verse 6.) In addition, all those left behind in Kirtland were commanded to pack up their belongings, sell their property, settle their debts, and gather with the main body of Saints.

> And that the gathering together upon the land of Zion, and upon her stakes, may be for a defense, and for a refuge from the storm, and from wrath when it shall be poured out without mixture upon the whole earth.[4]
>
> Let the city, Far West, be a holy and consecrated land unto me; and it shall be called most holy, for the ground upon which thou standest is holy. (Verses 6–7.)

Most of the Saints followed the command to relocate. By September 1838 it was estimated that only a few members of the Church were living in Kirtland and over twelve thousand in the Far West area.[5]

Just before the exodus to Far West some Latter-day Saints lived a few miles south in Clay County. This group was comprised of the Colesville Saints and others who had been compelled to leave Independence, Mis-

---

1. See *Church History in the Fulness of Time*, 173.
2. *Church History in the Fulness of Time*, 173.
3. See *Church History in the Fulness of Time*, 173.
4. Far West was not only to be a place of refuge for the moment but also a place of "refuge . . . from wrath when it shall be poured out without mixture upon the whole earth" (D&C 115:6), a reference to the commotions and pestilence that will take place just prior to the Second Coming. This prediction is yet to be fulfilled and most probably will take place when the Saints return to the Zion in Jackson County, Missouri, in preparation for the return of Jesus.
5. See Preece, *Learning to Love the Doctrine and Covenants*, 323, 320.

souri, under dire circumstances in 1833–34. At first, members of the Church had been accepted in Clay County. However, as time passed and more and more Mormons moved into the area the same pattern that occurred in Independence was repeated. On June 29, 1836, a mass meeting comprised of some of the leading non-Mormon citizens in the area was held at the courthouse to discuss their objections to the Mormons remaining in the area.[1]

This time the Saints did not resist the invitation to leave and did everything they could to avoid any more bloodshed. They hired a lawyer, Alexander W. Doniphan, to represent them. Doniphan was a well-known legal advocate and a member of the state legislature. The Mormons paid him to introduce a bill creating Caldwell and Daviess Counties to recompense for Mormon losses in Jackson County. Shortly after the creation of Caldwell County, Far West was designated the county seat and became the headquarters for the Church.[2] This area was sparsely populated and was not considered well suited for settlement because a lack of timber made it more difficult to build homes. For these reasons, the bill passed. To keep the Mormons separate and isolated from the non-Mormons, a six-mile-wide buffer—three miles on each side of the dividing line between the newly created Mormon counties and non-Mormon counties—was designated a "no-man's land" where neither Mormon nor non-Mormon could settle. This done, the Clay County Saints pulled up stakes and relocated in Far West, along with their bedraggled brothers and sisters coming from Kirtland, Ohio. Joseph arrived from Kirtland on March 14, 1838.[3]

The Saints commanded to build a temple in Far West

With Far West secured, there was no time to delay. Section 115 instructed that a temple and a new Zion be built.

---

1. See *Church History in the Fulness of Time*, 181. The list of Clay County citizen complaints paralleled the objections raised in Jackson County during 1833–34. The locals were concerned that: (1) the Saints were poor, (2) religious differences stirred up prejudice, (3) the Saints' Eastern customs and dialect were alien to Missourians, (4) the Saints opposed slavery, (5) the Saints believed the Indians were God's chosen people destined to inherit the land of Missouri with them, and (6) the Saints would stay in Clay Country, despite their promises to leave. (See *Church History in the Fulness of Time*, 181–82.)
2. See *Church History in the Fulness of Time*, 183–84.
3. As more and more Saints gathered in Missouri, it became more and more difficult for Joseph Smith to provide guidance to the main body of Saints. A stake had been organized without his permission and in his absence. Therefore, on January 12, 1838, he received a revelation that only the First Presidency could form a stake. (See *Church History in the Fulness of Time*, 186.) Section 115 reinforces the leadership role of Joseph Smith: "For behold, I will be with him, and I will sanctify him before the people; for unto him have I given the keys of this kingdom and ministry." (See verse 19.)

> Therefore, I command you to build a house unto me, for the gathering together of my saints, that they may worship me....
>
> And again, verily I say unto you, it is my will that the city of Far West should be built up speedily by the gathering of my saints;
>
> And also that other places should be appointed for stakes in the regions round about, as they shall be manifested unto my servant Joseph, from time to time. (Verses 8, 17–18.)

The command to build a temple, let alone other stakes, would never come about. By October 27, 1838, the governor of Missouri, Lilburn Boggs, would issue his infamous extermination order, Far West would be surrounded by an army, blood would be spilt, and the Mormons would be compelled to leave once again. This time they crossed the Mississippi River into Illinois, where they would build Nauvoo.

Laying the cornerstone

Doctrine and Covenants 115:11 specifically instructed the Saints to lay the foundation of the temple "one year from this day," or April 26, 1839. What seemed like a simple instruction to follow at the time became complicated. The Saints were driven from their homes in Far West by the end of 1838, which made the laying of the cornerstones in April 1839 very dangerous.[1] Also, the Twelve were appointed to "take leave of my saints in the city of Far West, on the twenty-sixth day of April next, on the building-spot of my house, saith the Lord." (D&C 118:5.) From that spot the Twelve were to depart for missions.

Even though the Saints' hopes of building Zion once again in Far West had been thwarted, Brigham Young urged his colleagues to return to Far West as sections 114 and 118 had directed. On that day Brigham, Heber C. Kimball, Orson Pratt, John E. Page, John Taylor, Wilford Woodruff, and George A. Smith arrived in Far West in the dead of night. Under the light of the moon they rolled up a large stone near the southeast corner of the temple lot, laying the foundation of the temple. (See verse 11.)[2] Brigham Young said, "Thus was this revelation fulfilled, concerning which our enemies said, if all other revelations of Joseph Smith were fulfilled that one should not, as it had day and date to it."[3]

---

1. See *Church History in the Fulness of Time*, 226.
2. See *Church History in the Fulness of Time*, 226.
3. *Church History in the Fulness of Time*, 226.

Zion

At first the Saints thought about Zion in terms of a specific geographical space, meaning the city of the New Jerusalem that was to be built in Jackson County. By commanding that another Zion be built, section 115 shifted the Saints' thinking somewhat. Zion in Jackson County, Missouri, would be built someday, but in the meantime the Saints would build other cities dedicated to God. From this point forward, the term *Zion* was used more broadly to signify any place where a group of God's followers were gathered, any location where the "pure in heart" dwell (D&C 97:21), or any land appointed for gathering.[1] (D&C 101:16–22; 3 Nephi 20–22.) At one time Joseph referred to "the whole of America" as "Zion itself from north to south."[2]

The name of the Church

Section 115 is best known as the revelation that makes known the formal, complete name of the Church—The Church of Jesus Christ of Latter-day Saints. Prior to this revelation the Church had been referred to as "The Church of Christ"[3] (April 6, 1830, to May 3, 1834), "The Church of the Latter Day Saints" (May 3, 1834, to to March 1838),[4] as well as the "Church of Jesus Christ," or simply "The Church of God." Nonmembers called members of the Church "Mormons" or "Mormonites"[5] as terms of disrespect.

The Community of Christ (formerly the Reorganized Church of Jesus Christ of Latter Day Saints) claim that the name placed on the Kirtland Temple in 1834 or 1835 was "The Church of Jesus Christ of Latter-day Saints." If this is the case, then the name had already been in use before Joseph received this revelation in 1838.[6]

---

1. Other uses of the term *Zion* also reference a place where people serve God in righteousness (D&C 100:13, 16), gather in stakes (D&C 43:8–11), establish a city of holiness (Moses 7:19), or a place where people have all things in common (4 Nephi 1:3; D&C 82:17–18; 51:3, 9; Moses 7:18).

2. See Smith, *Teachings of the Prophet Joseph Smith*, 362. Joseph also used the term *Zion* to refer to a place where the Saints would build a temple that would be located in the "center of the land." (See Smith, *Teachings of the Prophet Joseph Smith*, 362.)

3. The Savior in the Book of Mormon instructed the Nephites to call his Church after his name. (See 3 Nephi 27:8–9.)

4. See Cook, *Revelations of the Prophet Joseph Smith*, 227.

5. See Woodford, *The Historical Development of the Doctrine and Covenants*, 1507.

6. See Woodford, *The Historical Development of the Doctrine and Covenants*, 1507.

Section 117: Joseph Smith Jr. Home, Far West (Caldwell County), Missouri, July 8, 1838

Heading

The Lord's gives his perspective on property. William Marks and Newel K. Whitney are told to close their financial interests in Kirtland and immediately move to Far West.

The big question

Question: What and where is Zion?
Answer: Zion is a place where the Saints should not be focused on personal wealth or take advantage of their neighbors in any way.

Introduction

This revelation was given through Joseph Smith at Joseph's home in Far West, Missouri, on July 8, 1838. Concerning the immediate duties of William Marks, Newel K. Whitney, and Oliver Granger, Marks and Whitney are commanded to leave Kirtland and move to the new Zion in Far West, Missouri.[1] The Lord's servants should not covet temporal things and must forsake "littleness of soul."

Historical background

In section 115 the Saints had been commanded to move to Far West. Consequently, the leaders in Kirtland began making preparation for Church members, especially the poor among them, to move. The exodus was supervised by the Seventy, one of whose presidents, James Foster, was spurred on in this effort when he saw a vision of the orderly march of about five hundred Saints from Kirtland to Far West. Encouraged by what he had seen, he drew up plans and formed a camp of those willing to take the journey.[2]

On July 6, 1838, under Foster's leadership, a group of Saints known as the Kirtland Camp left for Far West. The trip was not without incident or insult from non-Mormons along the way. Eggs were thrown at the Saints, threats of violence were made, and in one instance Missouri citizens placed artillery in the street to prevent the camp from passing through their town.

---

1. Smith, *History of the Church*, 3:45–46.
2. See *Church History in the Fulness of Time*, 178–79.

Several of the camp's leaders were jailed overnight.[1] Besides persecution, accidents and illness afflicted the company. Some were crushed under wagon wheels and others died of disease. The Saints turned to God and many were instantly healed. The camp arrived in Far West in September, only to be greeted by the grim news that war had broken out between the Mormons and their enemies.[2]

The Kirtland Camp was one of the last groups of Saints to leave Kirtland and head for Missouri. Unbeknownst to Joseph, however, two of his key leaders, William Marks and Newel K. Whitney, had not followed instructions in section 115 to come to Far West themselves. Rather, they decided to stay behind to take advantage of various financial opportunities. Section 117 commands them to immediately wrap up their affairs and come west.

> Verily thus saith the Lord unto my servant William Marks, and also unto my servant Newel K. Whitney, let them settle up their business speedily and journey from the land of Kirtland, before I, the Lord, send again the snows upon the earth.
>
> Let them awake, and arise and come forth, and not tarry, for I, the Lord, command it.
>
> Therefore, if they tarry it shall not be well with them. (Verses 1–3.)

Marks's and Whitney's hesitancy to leave quickly for Far West was motivated by a spirit of financial speculation that had overtaken Kirtland and was partially responsible for the collapse of the Kirtland Bank. The lure of making money had afflicted many. Section 117 rebukes Marks and Whitney for their "covetous desires before me." (Verse 4.) They are told to "let the properties of Kirtland be turned out for debts . . . and whatsoever remaineth, let it remain in your hands, saith the Lord." (Verse 5.)

"What is property unto me? saith the Lord."

At a time when many of the Saints had lost everything and were on the move again, the Lord expressed his perspective on property and wealth and commanded the Saints not to hesitate to leave their possessions behind and go to Far West. He said:

> For have I not the fowls of heaven, and also the fish of the sea, and the beasts of the mountains? Have I not made the earth? Do I not hold the destinies of all the armies of the nations of the earth?
>
> Therefore, will I not make solitary places to bud and to blossom, and to bring forth in abundance? saith the Lord.

---

1. See *Church History in the Fulness of Time*, 179.
2. See *Church History in the Fulness of Time*, 179.

Is there not room enough on the mountains of Adam-ondi-Ahman, and on the plains of Olaha Shinehah, or the land where Adam dwelt, that you should covet that which is but the drop, and neglect the more weighty matters? (Verses 6–8.)

With this assurance, section 117 issued the invitation, "Therefore, come up hither unto the land of my people, even Zion." (Verse 9.)

Nicolaitane band

Section 117 warns of a renegade group known as the "Nicolaitane band." (Verse 11.) Apparently Newel K. Whitney was associated with its "secret abominations" because of "his littleness of soul before me." (Verse 11.) Therefore, he was commanded to repent, come to Far West, and "be a bishop unto my people . . . not in name but in deed, saith the Lord." (Verse 11.)

The reference to a Nicolaitane band is from the New Testament. Nicolas was one of seven men appointed by Christ's apostles to collect and distribute property when the early Christians held "all things in common," as described in the book of Acts. (See Acts 2:44; 6:5.) Nicolas was believed to have apostatized and became the founder of a subversive group known as the "Nicolaitans." (Revelation 2:6.) There is some evidence that the Nicolaitans misused the "commonly held" property of the body of the Church for their own benefit and purposes. Marks and Whitney were dangerously close to doing the same thing, and both were in a position to do so. Whitney was the bishop in charge of distributing goods under the law of consecration in Kirtland, and Marks was his agent or assistant. Perhaps Whitney and Marks were abusing their financial privileges and were trying to capitalize on the economic turmoil that resulted when the Saints left en masse for Far West, and were forced to sell their goods for far less than the market price.[1]

---

1. See Preece, *Learning to Love the Doctrine and Covenants*, 325.

Oliver Granger

In contrast to Marks and Whitney, Oliver Granger is described in section 117 as a person who was entirely reliable in the tumultuous times in Kirtland. He is said to be one whose name should be held in "sacred remembrance" for his faithfulness. (Verse 12.) He was commissioned as the Prophet's attorney-in-fact to "settle up . . . business affairs" in Kirtland.[1] He carried out his assignment to the satisfaction of both the First Presidency and their creditors, one of whom said, "Oliver Granger's management in the arrangement of the unfinished business of people that have moved to the Far West, in redeeming their pledges and thereby sustaining their integrity, has been truly praiseworthy, and has entitled him to my highest esteem, and ever grateful recollection."[2]

Granger had been given a letter and a copy of section 117, which he was instructed to hand deliver to Marks and Whitney in Kirtland. Granger had moved to Far West in June 1838 and only a month later left on this assignment. He arrived in Kirtland in August and stayed until October.[3] He was described by the First Presidency as "a man of the most strict integrity and moral virtue; and in fine, . . . a man of God"[4] and was entrusted with the financial affairs of the Church.

SECTION 118: JOSEPH SMITH JR. HOME, FAR WEST (CALDWELL COUNTY), MISSOURI, JULY 8, 1838

Heading

The Twelve are rebuked; some are dropped from the quorum. Specific instructions are given regarding how to reconstitute the quorum. Certain members of the Twelve are called on missions and leave for Great Britain.

---

1. See Cook, *Revelations of the Prophet Joseph Smith*, 229. Granger's mission was necessitated by the fact that Joseph left Kirtland on the run, pursued by a mob. He made mention of this in a statement he made sometime later. "As I was driven from Kirtland without the privilege of settling up my business, I had employed Colonel Oliver Granger as my agent, to close all my affairs in the east." (See Cook, *Revelations of the Prophet Joseph Smith*, 229.)

2. Black, *Who's Who in the Doctrine and Covenants*, 108.

3. See Cook, *Revelations of the Prophet Joseph Smith*, 230. Granger was born in 1794 in Ontario County, New York. He married Lydia Dibble and had three known children. He lost much of his sight at age thirty-three from overexposure to the cold in 1827. He was the sheriff of Ontario County, New York. He was baptized and ordained an elder in Wayne County, New York, by Brigham and Joseph Young. He moved to Kirtland in 1833. He served a number of missions. In 1840 he was asked to once again return to Kirtland to make land exchanges for Church members. He died there in 1841. (See Cook, *Revelations of the Prophet Joseph Smith*, 230.)

4. Black, *Who's Who in the Doctrine and Covenants*, 108.

The big question

Question: How do we deal with disappointment and unrealized promises?

Answer: Follow the instructions of the Lord to the best of your ability under the circumstances.

Introduction

This revelation was given through Joseph Smith in his home in Far West, Missouri, on July 8, 1838.[1] Four of the original Twelve had apostatized, and the quorum was in disarray. This revelation came in response to the supplication, "Show us thy will, O Lord, concerning the Twelve."

Historical background

The years 1837 to 1838 were a time of disruption on every front. Following their expulsion from Jackson County in late 1833, the Missouri Saints were in a holding pattern in Clay County. They consistently petitioned government authorities for permission and protection to reestablish their homes in Jackson County. But as each day passed it became more and more clear that their hopes would never be realized. At first, the Missouri Saints lived in peace with their neighbors in Clay County, but when it became apparent that the Mormon settlers were there to stay, local residents began to complain.[2] In June 1836 the non-Mormons held a mass meeting in the Clay County courthouse in Liberty to discuss their grievances against the Mormons. The divisions were deep enough that some feared civil war.

The list of complaints about the Mormons in Clay County was similar to those raised earlier by their neighbors in Jackson County. Many Mormons were poor, so non-Mormons believed that they were a drain on the community. The Mormon religion was unconventional and challenged the standing of other faiths. Their Eastern manners and dialect were offensive to the locals. Finally, their opposition to slavery and their belief that the American Indians were a chosen people were in fundamental opposition to the sentiments of the Missourians, who felt threatened by both of these groups.[3] With all of these factors against them, the Saints decided not to resist and made arrangements to move farther north to "Far West."[4]

In Kirtland, Ohio, things were no better. The failure of the Kirtland

---

1. Smith, *History of the Church*, 3:46–47.
2. See *Church History in the Fulness of Time*, 181.
3. See *Church History in the Fulness of Time*, 180–82.
4. See *Church History in the Fulness of Time*, 181.

Bank due to financial speculation on the part of the Saints and rumors that Joseph might be an adulterer[1] fueled hard feelings. Bushman captures the spirit of the times in Kirtland during 1837 and 1838. He describes the tensions that occurred between two members of the Twelve, Parley and Orson Pratt, and Joseph Smith.

> The bank failure, suspicions about Joseph's morals, and economic stress combined to bring on the apostasies of 1837. When Joseph, battered by creditors, tried to collect payment for three city lots he had sold to Parley Pratt in the inflationary delirium a few months earlier, Pratt exploded in rage and frustration. "If you are still determined to pursue this wicked course, until yourself and the Church shall sink down to hell, I beseech you at least, to have mercy on me and my family." His brother Orson and Lyman Johnson brought charges against Joseph for lying, extortion, and "speaking disrespectfully, against his brethren behind their backs." It took months for the Pratts to recover their composure and return to the fold.[2]

In response to those who criticized Joseph, Church courts were convened. For example, on May 29, 1837, the high council met and considered the injurious conduct of Parley P. Pratt, David Whitmer, Frederick G. Williams, Lyman Johnson, and William G. Parrish, all prominent Church leaders. The council was unable to ferret out the truth or falsity of the allegations made against Joseph and dispersed in confusion.[3]

By July 1838 four members of the original Quorum of Twelve had fallen into apostasy and were excommunicated—William E. McLellin, Lyman E. Johnson, Luke Johnson, and John F. Boynton. Of these four only one, Luke Johnson, was rebaptized, in 1846.[4] It was in these trying circumstances that Joseph approached the Lord for guidance on what he should do and received section 118.

The revelation advised that the vacancies in the Twelve should be filled (verse 1), and named replacements for the brethren who fell away—John Taylor, John E. Page, Wilford Woodruff, and Willard Richards. (See verse 6.) Once the quorum was replenished, members of the Twelve were instructed to serve missions "over the great waters." (Verse 4.) Specific instructions were given regarding when and from where they should depart on their new assignments. "Let them take leave of my saints in the city of Far West, on the twenty-sixth day of April next, on the building-spot of my house, saith the Lord." (Verse 5.)

---

1. By this time Joseph had secretly entered into the practice of polygamy, which started rumors that Joseph had transgressed the high moral standards expected within the Mormon community.
2. Bushman, Joseph Smith: Rough Stone Rolling, 337.
3. See Bushman, *Joseph Smith: Rough Stone Rolling*, 337.
4. See Preece, *Learning to Love the Doctrine and Covenants*, 327–28.

Following the instructions contained in the revelation

The command for the Twelve to leave on their missions from the temple site in Far West proved to be problematic. Section 118 was given in July 1838. By the time designated for the Twelve's departure—April 26, 1839—the Saints had been forcefully ousted from Far West and the vicinity.

The Brethren must have felt disappointment at being expelled from Far West. And there was great danger associated with a return visit—enemies of the Church knew about the particular day and place the Twelve were commanded to meet, and they had vowed to keep any such meeting from taking place. Nevertheless, undaunted, and determined to fulfill the exact terms and conditions of the revelation, the departing missionaries and others journeyed to Far West the next spring. On the precise day designated in section 118, the men arrived in Far West. During the early morning hours, while it was still dark, the brethren held a meeting on the temple site. Brigham Young, Parley P. Pratt, Orson Pratt, John Taylor, and Wilford Woodruff[1] took formal leave for their missions.[2]

SECTION 119: JOSEPH SMITH JR. HOME, FAR WEST (CALDWELL COUNTY), MISSOURI, JULY 8, 1838

Heading

The law of tithing is introduced.

Introduction

This revelation was given through Joseph Smith at his home in Far West, Missouri, on July 8, 1838. It came in answer to his supplication, "O Lord, show unto thy servants how much thou requirest of the properties of thy people for a tithing."[3] The law of tithing, as understood today, had not been given to the Church previous to this revelation. The term "tithing" in Joseph's prayer and in previous revelations (D&C 64:23; 85:3; 97:11) was not a reference to giving a tenth of one's income to the Church

---

1. It was at this spot and time that Wilford Woodruff was set apart and ordained a member of the Quorum of the Twelve by Brigham Young.

2. Although it seemed counterintuitive to send top leaders to England to preach the gospel at a time when the Church was struggling for its very existence, many converts joined the Church and immigrated to America. The new stream of converts replenished the Church in Nauvoo. Between 1840 and 1850, over 5,000 converts from the British Isles journeyed to the Nauvoo area to bolster the Church. (See Preece, *Learning to Love the Doctrine and Covenants*, 330.)

3. Smith, *History of the Church*, 3:44.

but rather was a term used more generally to mean any contribution or free-will offering.

Before this time the Lord had revealed the law of consecration and stewardship. When section 119 was received, tithing was not viewed as a replacement for the law of consecration but as an amendment to or clarification of it. The law of tithing at that time required the members of the Church to give all they had to the Church ("all their surplus property") and thereafter "one-tenth of all their interest annually." (Verses 1, 4.) Today, of course, the law of tithing does not require members to give all of their surplus property to the Church but rather requires them to give one-tenth of their income or "interest" annually.

Anchor section

Memorize: Tithing

Historical background

By 1838 the Church was overwhelmed with financial difficulties. The construction of the Kirtland Temple had drained scarce resources, and the collapse of the Kirtland Bank had devastated members of the Church. In addition, the Saints, both in Kirtland and Missouri, had largely failed to live the law of consecration, first revealed in section 42 in February 1831. Caught up in financial trouble, in December 1837 Joseph Smith had organized a committee to address the financial shortages facing the Church. A committee was organized and recommended that a voluntary tithing program, based on assets and income, be adopted. This plan recommended that each member present a yearly inventory to the bishop. The plan was never instituted.[1]

About six months later, on May 12, 1838—at the height of the financial crisis—the issue of financial support for the Church came to a head. On that day, Joseph and Sidney Rigdon attended the Kirtland high council meeting. Joseph, Sidney, and some others were spending most, if not all, of their time tending to Church business, and as a result they were penniless. At this meeting they explained their dire financial need to their brethren. A committee of the high council was formed to consider the matter of supporting Joseph's and Sidney's families. The committee recommended that both of them receive $1,100 as just remuneration for

---

1. See Preece, *Learning to Love the Doctrine and Covenants*, 331.

their past services. They then turned the matter over to a subcommittee for further consideration.[1]

When the subcommittee reported back to the high council at a subsequent meeting, the question of payment to Joseph and Sidney was "warmly discussed by the members of the council until near sundown."[2] Understandably, some bitterly opposed the idea. The Church had never had a salaried ministry and in hard economic times it did not seem reasonable to some of the members of the high council to change the policy. Nevertheless, they voted 12 to 1 in Joseph's and Sidney's favor. When members of the Church heard about the decision to give payment to Joseph and Sidney they "lifted their voices against it."[3] Consequently, at the next high council meeting the body rescinded the authorization for payment. Less than a month later, Joseph received section 119 on the law of tithing.

Living the law of tithing in Joseph's day

The law as originally given in section 119 required members to first give "all their surplus property" to the bishop. (Verse 1.) "Surplus property" meant anything that the family did not need to meet their basic day-to-day needs. After consecrating this property to the Church, the law required members to pay "one-tenth of all their interest annually." Because members could decide for themselves how much was and was not "surplus," there were problems from the beginning. As Orson Pratt commented, "Who in the world among all the Latter-day Saints would have any surplus property if it is left to his own judgment?"[4] Not surprisingly, more specific instructions on what constituted a surplus were given later. By 1841, however, the Twelve wrote to the Saints that "surplus" could be defined as a tenth of what one possessed upon entering into the law.[5]

Over the years, the law of tithing was modified further. In May 1899, President Lorenzo Snow received a revelation defining tithing as members of the Church understand it today. This change came at a time when the Church was once again beleaguered by financial troubles. President Snow said that members should pay a tenth of their income annually to the

---

1. See Woodford, *The Historical Development of the Doctrine and Covenants*, 1551.
2. Woodford, *The Historical Development of the Doctrine and Covenants*, 1552.
3. Woodford, *The Historical Development of the Doctrine and Covenants*, 1552.
4. Preece, *Learning to Love the Doctrine and Covenants*, 332; and *Journal of Discourses*, 16:157; 17:110.
5. See Preece, *Learning to Love the Doctrine and Covenants*, 333; Smith, *History of the Church*, 4:473. In 1854 the First Presidency also stated that tithing meant that all should initially pay one-tenth of their entire property and thereafter pay one-tenth of all their increase. (See Preece, *Learning to Love the Doctrine and Covenants*, 333.)

Church. The notion of donating a "surplus" when a person commenced living the law was discontinued.

Understandably, defining "income" has always been a point of debate even among some members of the Church. On March 19, 1970, the First Presidency published a letter on the subject, stating that "every member of the Church is entitled to make his [or her] own decision as to what he thinks he owes the Lord and to make payment accordingly."[1] This leaves with the individual the issue of determining tithing amounts before or after taxes (on "gross" or on "net" income).

Section 120: Joseph Smith Jr. Home, Far West (Caldwell County), Missouri, July 8, 1838

Heading

A council headed by the First Presidency is organized to decide how tithing funds should be used.

Introduction

This revelation was given through Joseph Smith the Prophet in his home in Far West, Missouri, on July 8, 1838, making known the disposition of the properties tithed pursuant to section 119.[2]

Historical background

On the very same day the law of tithing was given (D&C 119), Joseph also received section 120, giving instructions on how to administer and dispose of these funds. The Lord instructed that a council for this purpose be established, consisting of the First Presidency, the bishop (later the Presiding Bishop), and the high council (later the Twelve). Much like today, tithing funds were used primarily to purchase property and to construct and maintain meetinghouses, temples, and other Church buildings, and to administer educational programs. These funds were also used for the support of the poor, the First Presidency, and other key leaders in need of sustenance.

Before this revelation, the bishop was the primary financial officer of the Church. The donation of all surplus property and the distribution of it back to the Saints as stewardships were primarily under his management

---

1. *Encyclopedia of Mormonism*, 1481.
2. Smith, *History of the Church*, 3:44.

and control. At times the local high councils played a role as well, and sometimes the bishop and high council disagreed on how funds should be allocated. Section 120 established how divisions in opinion would be decided by the First Presidency, in conjunction with "the bishop and his council, and by my high council." (Verse 1.)

Shortly after this council was formed, they met and decided that the First Presidency should "keep all their properties that they could dispose of to advantage."[1] It was mentioned specifically that they could use the proceeds for "their support,"[2] a point of controversy between Joseph and the high council. (See commentary on section 119.) The remainder was to be placed in the hands of the bishop for distribution as he saw fit.[3] This procedure legitimized the expenditure of Church funds and gave all parties an opportunity to compete for scarce resources. This was especially important at a time in Church history when the needs of the Church exceeded the available resources.

Section 116: Spring Hill, Adam-Ondi-Ahman, Daviess County, Missouri, May 19, 1838

Heading

Adam-ondi-Ahman is the place where Adam dwelt.

Introduction

This revelation was given to Joseph Smith near Wight's Ferry, at a place called Spring Hill, Daviess County, Missouri, on May 19, 1838, explaining that this area is named Adam-ondi-Ahman by the Lord because it is the place where Adam will come to visit his people prior to the Second Coming of Christ.[4]

---

1. See Woodford, *The Historical Development of the Doctrine and Covenants*, 1559. It should be remembered that the Saints were leaving Kirtland and their property behind to move to Far West with the body of the Church. The Church had substantial assets in Kirtland that were being sold at a loss to pay debts and fund the Church. Much if not all of this property came from members who faithfully consecrated their surplus to the bishop in Zion.
2. See Smith, *History of the Church*, 3:47, as quoted in Woodford, *The Historical Development of the Doctrine and Covenants*, 1559.
3. See Woodford, *The Historical Development of the Doctrine and Covenants*, 1559.
4. Smith, *History of the Church*, 3:35.

Historical background

Adam-ondi-Ahman was a Mormon settlement located in Daviess County, Missouri.[1] In May 1838, Joseph Smith "led surveyors to a horseshoe bend of the Grand River, seventy miles north of present-day Kansas City, and proclaimed [it] a new community . . . because, said he, 'it is the place where Adam shall come to visit his people, or the Ancient of Days shall sit, as spoken of by Daniel the Prophet'" (D&C 116:1.)[2]

Joseph explained that this future gathering of the Lord's people is preparatory to the second coming of Christ. It is here that Adam "will call his children together and hold a council with them to prepare them for the coming of the Son of Man."[3] At this meeting the prophetic heads of other dispensations will give an accounting to the Father of the human race. Joseph elaborated: "He (Adam) is the father of the human family, and presides over the spirits of all men, and all that have had the keys must stand before him in this grand council. This may take place before some of us leave this stage of action."[4] Joseph taught that during this council that "the Son of Man will stand before Adam, "and there is given him glory and dominion. Adam delivers up his stewardship to Christ, that which was delivered to him as holding the keys of the universe, but retains his standing as head of the human family."[5]

In addition, Joseph taught that Adam-ondi-Ahman and the surrounding area were rich in religious history. He said:

1. The Garden of Eden was located nearby in Jackson County, Missouri;[6]
2. After Adam was expelled from the garden he went north to live in Adam-ondi-Adam;
3. Three years before Adam's death he gathered his family around

---

1. Orson Pratt said that the name meant "Valley of God, where Adam dwelt." (See *Journal of Discourses*, 18:343; *Encyclopedia of Mormonism*, 1:19.)
2. *Encyclopedia of Mormonism*, 1:19.
3. Smith, *Teachings of the Prophet Joseph Smith*, 157.
4. Smith, *Teachings of the Prophet Joseph Smith*, 157.
5. Smith, *Teachings of the Prophet Joseph Smith*, 157. Joseph's statement references Daniel's apocalyptic vision. (See Daniel 7:9–10.) Based on what Joseph teaches, it is clear that the "Ancient of Days" mentioned in that vision is Adam. The "Son of Man" is Jesus. At this meeting, the sacrament of the Lord's Supper will be administered. (See JST Matthew 1:23; 26:23–26; D&C 27:5–14; 45:43–52.) For a good discussion on these points of doctrine see McConkie and Ostler, *Revelations of the Restoration*, 925–26.
6. "Again President Young said Joseph the Prophet told me that the garden of Eden was in Jackson Co Missouri, & when Adam was driven out of the garden of Eden He went about 40 miles to the Place which we Named Adam Ondi Ahman, & there built an Altar of Stone & offered Sacrifice. That Altar remains to this day. I saw it as Adam left it as did many others, & through all the revolutions of the world that Altar had not been disturbed. Joseph also said that when the City of Enoch fled & was translated it was where the gulf of Mexico now is. It left that gulf a body of water." (Staker, *Waiting for World's End: The Diaries of Wilford Woodruff*, 305.)

him at this spot and blessed them and prophesied of future events (D&C 107:53–57);[1]

4. Adam built altars in Adam-ondi-Ahman for the worship of God;[2] and

5. Tower Hill near Adam-ondi-Ahman commemorated a place where a Nephite altar or tower stood.[3]

Bushman pointed out that "Joseph invested the place with a history, partly from the Book of Mormon, partly from the Bible."[4]

As for the future, during the Millennium Jackson County will become Zion or the New Jerusalem, the center place of the kingdom of God on the western hemisphere. A temple will be erected there, and it will operate concurrent with the temple in Old Jerusalem in the eastern hemisphere. (D&C 57:1–3; Isaiah 2:3; Micah 4:2.)[5]

With millennial hopes centered in this historic spot, Latter-day Saints flocked to the area in 1838. Settlements sprang up and by May there were 150 houses in Far West. In June Joseph organized a stake at Adam-ondi-Ahman. By October 200 houses had been built.[6]

John A. Widtsoe on Jackson County, Missouri, as the spot where the Garden of Eden was located

There is no doubt that most people of the world believe the Garden of Eden was located in the eastern hemisphere, by the Tigris and Euphrates rivers. Joseph Smith's views on this subject are unique and deserve com-

---

1. See *Encyclopedia of Mormonism*, 1:21.

2. Heber C. Kimball recalled: "The Prophet Joseph called upon Brother Brigham, myself and others, saying, 'Brethren, come, go along with me, and I will show you something.' He led us a short distance to a place where were the ruins of three altars built of stone, one above the other, and one standing a little back of the other, like unto the pulpits in the Kirtland Temple, representing the order of three grades of Priesthood. 'There,' said Joseph, 'is the place where Adam offered up sacrifice after he was cast out of the garden.' The altar stood at the highest point of the bluff. I went and examined the place several times while I remained there." (See *Life of Heber C. Kimball*, 209–10, as quoted in Preece, *Learning to Love the Doctrine and Covenants*, 322.)

3. Joseph said, "We pursued our course up the river, mostly through timber, for about eighteen miles, when we arrived at Colonel Lyman Wight's home. He lives at the foot of Tower Hill (a name I gave the place in consequence of the remains of an old Nephite altar or tower that stood there), where we camped for the Sabbath." (Smith, *History of the Church*, 3:34–35, as quoted in McConkie and Ostler, *Revelations of the Restoration*, 923–24.)

4. Bushman, *Joseph Smith: Rough Stone Rolling*, 345. Some religious scholars have argued that Mormonism became the most significant American religion because Joseph Smith, by claiming that the Garden of Eden was in the new world, that a branch of Israel inhabited the Americas, and that the post-resurrected Jesus appeared in the Americas, made the New World as important to God as the Old World. It endowed America with an ancient sacred history and a concrete connection to the God of Israel.

5. See Smith, *History of the Church*, 1:188; Widtsoe, *Evidences and Reconciliations*, 395.

6. See Bushman, *Joseph Smith: Rough Stone Rolling*, 346.

ment. In reference to this subject, John A. Widtsoe, an apostle during the first half of the twentieth century, remarked on a conversation between Orson Hyde and Brigham Young on March 15, 1857. President Young said:

> You have been both to Jerusalem and Zion, and seen both. I have not seen either, for I have never been in Jackson County. Now it is a pleasant thing to think of and to know where the Garden of Eden was. Did you ever think of it? I do not think many do, for in Jackson County was the Garden of Eden. Joseph has declared this, and I am as much bound to believe that as to believe that Joseph was a prophet of God.[1] (See Section 107:53–56; 116:1; 117:8.)

Widtsoe observed on this subject:

> [This] is the position of the Latter-day Saints today, with respect to the much-discussed location of the Garden of Eden. Adam, after his expulsion from the Garden of Eden, lived in the vicinity of the great Missouri and Mississippi rivers. As his descendants multiplied, they would naturally settle along the fertile and climatically acceptable river valleys. When the flood came in the days of Noah, the Mississippi drainage must have increased to a tremendous volume, quite in harmony with the Biblical account. Noah's ark would be floated on the mighty, rushing waters, towards the Gulf of Mexico. With favorable winds, it would cross the Atlantic to the Eastern continents. There the human race, in its second start on earth, began to multiply and fill the earth.
>
> The location of the Garden of Eden in America, and at Independence, Missouri, clears up many a problem which the Bible account of Eden and its garden has left in the minds of students.[2]

The *Encyclopedia of Mormonism* points out that "neither biblical records nor secular history and archaeological research identify the dimensions or the location of the garden in terms of the present-day surface of the earth."[3]

The topic of just where the Garden of Eden was located is not new, and the exact location of the Garden of Eden has been a subject of speculation within Christianity and Judaism. For example, Martin Luther commented that "we ask in vain today where and what that garden was."[4] In 1691 Bishop Pierre-Daniel Huet, a member of the French Academy, summarized the thinking on this subject in his day.[5]

---

1. See Journal History, March 15, 1857; see also Journal of Discourses, 10:235; 11:336–37; Smith, Doctrines of Salvation, 3:74.
2. Widtsoe, Evidences and Reconciliations, 395–97.
3. *Encyclopedia of Mormonism*, 2:534.
4. Delumeau, *History of Paradise*, 155.
5. See http://en.fairmormon.org/Garden_of_Eden_in_Missouri%3F (November 2, 2008). I am indebted to FAIR for the information mentioned in the discussion about various views on the Garden of Eden and how Mormons approach the subject of the actual location of the Garden of Eden.

[The earthly paradise] has been located in the third heaven, in the fourth, in the heaven of the moon, on the moon itself, on a mountain close to the heaven of the moon, in the middle region of the air, outside the earth, on the earth, under the earth, and in a hidden place far removed from human knowledge. It has been placed under the Arctic pole.... Some have located it ... either on the banks of the Ganges or on the island of Ceylon, and have even derived the name "India" from the word "Eden." ... Others have located it in the Americas, others in Africa below the equator, others in the equinoctial East, others on the mountain of the moon, from which they believed the Nile to flow. Most have located it in Asia: some in Greater Armenia, others in Mesopotamia or Assyria or Persia or Babylonia or Arabia or Syria or Palestine. There have even been those who wished to honor our Europe and, in a move that strays into complete irrelevance, have located it in Hedin, a town in Artois, their reason being the similarity between the words "Hedin" and "Eden."[1]

The Bible seems to locate the Garden of Eden at the center of the world. (See Genesis 2:10–14.) Four great rivers are described and yet none matches any known modern location. This has led some to take the position that the description of Eden must be symbolic of Eden being at the "center" of all that was known. However, it is commonly thought that the location of the Garden of Eden is at the headwaters of the Tigris and Euphrates rivers in Mesopotamia (modern Iraq), or in Eastern Africa and the Persian Gulf, among other hypotheses. Most put the Garden of Eden in the Middle East. Yet some literalists argue that the world of Eden was destroyed during Noah's flood and therefore it is impossible to place the Garden anywhere in post-Flood geography. Taking the Flood into account, there has been an attempt to connect the Garden of Eden with the mysterious sunken land of Atlantis referred to by Plato. As it is described, most place the Garden somewhere in the Middle East, but some strands of the Scottish Gaelic tradition place it in Mointeach Bharbhais (Barvas Moor) on the Isle of Lewis in the Outer Hebrides.

A Jewish tradition holds that the Garden of Eden was in Jerusalem. It is believed that a spring of water there known as Gihon was one of the unidentified rivers of Paradise. Ezekiel says that "thou hast been in Eden the garden of God" and seems in the next verse to locate it on the "holy mountain." (Ezekiel 28:13–14.) Since the "holy mountain" is often understood to be the Temple Mount, Jewish tradition suggests that the Garden of Eden may have been on the Temple Mount in Jerusalem.[2] The most striking thing about all of these theories is that they have virtually no reliable ties to the text about the Garden in the book of Genesis.

Since Joseph took the position that the Garden of Eden was in the

---

1. Delumeau, History of Paradise, 162.
2. Delumeau, *History of Paradise*, 162.

Jackson County, Missouri, area, it is fair to ask how Abraham, Moses, and other biblical figures ended up in the Old World if it all started in the Americas. The Foundation for Apologetic Information and Research (FAIR) has suggested a number of different approaches:

1. Some have conceptualized the earth as originally having only one land mass (e.g., Pangaea), even into historical time, which was not separated until the days of Peleg. (See Genesis 10:25.) Therefore, the idea of Eden in a world with continents separated by an ocean is not a factor in the analysis.

2. Those who accept a universal Noachian flood simply see Noah floating from a New World site to Ararat in the Old.

3. Those who accept a "limited flood" theory see a similar process occurring whereby Noah traveled down rivers or from sea coasts with the flood's arrival. (This would, in effect, be a reversal of the Book of Mormon's Old World to New World migrations.)

4. Since there is evidence for human migration over the Siberia-Alaska land bridge from Old World to New World, some have postulated travel in the opposite direction.

5. It has been suggested that the Lord gave a *second* site the name of Adam-ondi-Ahman in the Americas, while the original site was located elsewhere, in the Old World. In this model, early Church leaders assumed that there was only one Adam-ondi-Ahman, when there were (in fact) two.

6. Some have seen the concept of Eden as a symbolic idea that "sacralized" the Americas for a new gospel dispensation, without having reference to actual geographic realities. Early members then made this concept more literal than intended.

7. Some see Eden as a place that was always "separate" from the fallen world around it, and so regard questions about the present "location" of Eden as nonsensical.

8. Many, perhaps most, members consider the matter of relatively little importance, and have no strong feelings about the issue at all.[1]

Since there is no official position on these matters and little scriptural or scientific evidence in support of any of these hypotheses, Mormon attitudes on this subject are not fixed and depend upon how an individual approaches such subjects as death before the fall of Adam, evolution, pre-Adamite men and women, the nature and scope of Noah's flood, and the extent to which the scriptures should be interpreted literally or metaphorically.

---

1. Delumeau, *History of Paradise*, 162.

Church purchased lands in Jackson County, Missouri

In light of the fact that the Jackson County, Missouri, area is of such great interest to the Latter-day Saints, it is not surprising that the Church has in modern times authorized the purchase of land in this area. In 1944 Wilford C. Wood bought thirty-eight acres at Adam-ondi-Ahman for the Church, and additional acreage has since been acquired.[1]

SECTION 111: UNION STREET BOARDING HOUSE, SALEM, MASSACHUSETTS, AUGUST 6, 1836

Heading

Finding buried treasure, and the accuracy of prophetic utterances.

Introduction

This revelation was given through Joseph Smith at Salem, Massachusetts, August 6, 1836.[2] Due to their labors in the ministry, the leaders of the Church were heavily in debt at this time. Hearing that a large amount of money had been abandoned and hidden away in a cellar in Salem, the Prophet, Sidney Rigdon, Hyrum Smith, and Oliver Cowdery traveled there from Kirtland, Ohio, to investigate this claim and to preach the gospel. The brethren transacted several items of Church business and did some preaching in the city. When it became apparent that they could not lay hold upon any treasure, they returned to Kirtland.

Historical background

Section 111 came at a time of financial hardship for the Church. Between 1833 and 1836, the Church had incurred significant debt. The Saints in Jackson County, Missouri, had been driven out of their homes by mobs and were in dire financial need, and the Church was making an effort to help return these Saints to their homes and retake possession of Church property there. To accomplish this objective the Prophet organized a small army called Zion's Camp, which required more funds.[3] Believing their

---

1. See *Encyclopedia of Mormonism*, 1:20.
2. Smith, *History of the Church*, 2:465–66.
3. In Kirtland the Church had incurred a $13,000 debt for the construction of the Kirtland Temple, and at this time the Church faced the additional expense of trying to establish a new stake of the Church in Clay County, Missouri, the place where the Saints living in the Independence area had gathered after their expulsion. (See Bushman, *Joseph Smith: Rough Stone Rolling*, 329.)

Adam-ondi-Ahman located in Daviess County, Missouri. Joseph taught that this was the location of the Garden of Eden. It was also the site of a small Mormon settlement in 1838.

efforts to retake Zion would soon bear fruit and provide a gathering place for the Saints, the Church continued to buy property according to the revelations of God. (See D&C 105:29.) Frederick G. Williams summed up the situation: "The church [is] poor, Zion [is] to be built and we have no means to do it unless the rich assist, and because the rich have not assisted, the heads of the church have to suffer and are now suffering under severe embarrassments and are much in debt."[1]

The need to borrow money to operate the Church had been addressed in section 104. Loans were secured against land owned by Church members, and rising land values in the Kirtland area increased the amount that could be borrowed using land to secure the land. "And pledge the properties which I have put into your hands, this once, by giving your names by common consent or otherwise, as it shall seem good unto you." (D&C 104:85.) Joseph believed that in this way the Church would "be delivered this once out of your bondage." (D&C 104:83.) The need for capital caused Joseph Smith to consider how the Saints might establish their own bank.[2] Money matters were a huge concern, and Joseph and his brethren were constantly seeking funds to finance Church programs.

It was under these circumstances that a member of the Church by the name of Jonathan Burgess of Barnstable, Massachusetts, said that a "large amount of money had been secreted in the cellar of a certain house in Salem, Massachusetts."[3] In great need of funds, Joseph decided to act on this information. On July 25, 1836, Joseph left Kirtland with Hyrum Smith, Oliver Cowdery, and Sidney Rigdon.[4] They boarded a steamer, the *Charles Townsend*, at nearby Fairport and made their way east by boat and rail. In New York City on the last day of July, the brethren met with creditors, made business contacts, and inquired about plates and dies for printing notes for a Church bank.[5] They left New York City on August 3 and arrived in Salem on the following day. The brethren stayed in Salem about three weeks and departed for Kirtland about August 25, 1836.[6]

---

1. Bushman, *Joseph Smith: Rough Stone Rolling*, 329.
2. See Robinson and Garrett, *A Commentary on the Doctrine and Covenants*, 4:72.
3. Cook, *Revelations of the Prophet Joseph Smith*, 221. It was not uncommon in Joseph Smith's day for people to secure their valuables by hiding them in the ground.
4. It is of note that the entire First Presidency, consisting of Joseph Smith, Sidney Rigdon, and Oliver Cowdery, went on this journey together.
5. See Robinson and Garrett, *A Commentary on the Doctrine and Covenants*, 4:72. A Church financial institution, the Kirtland Safety Society, was opened for business on January 2, 1837, just five months later.
6. See Cook, *Revelations of the Prophet Joseph Smith*, 221; Van Wagoner, *Sidney Rigdon: A Portrait of Religious Excess*, 180–81.

Upon their arrival in Salem, Brother Burgess had difficulty locating the house where it was presumed the money was hidden. They rented a house on Union Street, where, on Sunday, August 6, 1836, section 111 was received. Joseph's traveling companions had gone to visit the famous East India Marine Society museum,[1] but the Prophet had stayed behind. He was visited by Brigham Young and Lyman E. Johnson, who were engaged as missionaries in the area, and were present when section 111 was given.

Apparently Joseph believed, at least momentarily, that he had found the place where the treasure was hidden. He wrote to his wife, Emma, on August 19, 1836, "We have found the house since Brother Burgess left us, very luckily and providentially, as we had [during] one spell been most discouraged. The house is occupied, and it will require much care and patience to rent or buy it. We think we shall be able to effect it; if not now, within the course of a few months."[2]

What happened shortly after this letter was written is not clear. Hyrum left Salem the same day that Joseph wrote the letter to Emma, and by week's end Joseph, Oliver Cowdery, and Sidney Rigdon also departed. Perhaps Joseph realized he could not linger in the area waiting for an opportunity to occupy the house. Maybe he intended to send others back at a later time to take possession of the house when it became available. Perhaps he came across information that he had the wrong house and felt he would never be able to locate funds for the Church in Salem. Whatever the case may be, the home was never purchased and the money never found.

Missionary work in Salem, Massachusetts

Section 111 predicts that "many people in this city" will be gathered "in due time for the benefit of Zion, through your instrumentality." (See verse 2.) In this regard, Erastus Snow was called on a mission to Salem, Massachusetts, in 1841. He departed for the mission field with a handwritten copy of section 111.[3] In 1841 Snow recorded the following in his diary:

> Until this time I had been calculating to spend the summer in the country and return home to Nauvoo late in the fall in compliance with advice given by President Joseph Smith when I left in November last. But President Hyrum Smith and William Law who had been east as far as Salem, Massachusetts and just returned through Philadelphia on their way home again counseled that I should not return to Nauvoo in the fall but that I should go immediately

---

1. See Bushman, *Joseph Smith: Rough Stone Rolling*, 329.
2. Van Wagoner, *Sidney Rigdon: A Portrait of Religious Excess*, 181.
3. See Robinson and Garrett, *A Commentary on the Doctrine and Covenants*, 4:73.

with Brother Winchester to Salem, Massachusetts and try to establish the kingdom in that city. They left with us a copy of a revelation given about that people in 1836 which said the Lord had much people there whom he would gather into his kingdom in his own due time and they thought the due time of the Lord had come.

Though I felt anxious to go home in the fall and thought it would involve what little property I had in the west in a difficulty to stay I felt willing to do the will of the Lord. I prayed earnestly to know his will and his spirit continually whispered to go to Salem. I also thought of the Apostles who cast lots to see which should take the place of Judas. I therefore, after writing on one ballot Nauvoo and on the other Salem prayed earnestly that God would show by the ballot which way I should go and I drawed the ballot that had Salem on it twice in succession and I then resolved as soon as I had filled the appointments I had out I would go to Salem.[1] The conference also voted that I should go and promised their prayers in my behalf that God might open an effectual door for the word.[2]

Erastus Snow preached in Salem and baptized more than one hundred converts.[3] He returned to Nauvoo in April 1843.[4]

On buried treasure

Section 111 not only promised converts but "much treasure in this city for you, for the benefit of Zion." (Verses 2, 4–5.) Based upon Jonathan Burgess's assertions, Joseph expected to find money in a home in Salem; this was his primary reason for going there. The idea that treasures were hidden away in homes was not uncommon at the time. Safety deposit boxes were not in ordinary use, and hiding valuables in a home or under the ground was a way of securing one's wealth. In fact, "in Salem itself the treasure-quest was sufficiently common that in 1838 local resident Nathaniel Hawthorne published a story about a Salem man's effort to locate treasure that was concealed in a house."[5]

The heading to section 111 acknowledges—and there is no evidence to suggest otherwise—that Joseph and his associates did not find any money or treasure while in Salem, Massachusetts. In an effort to explain this incident, some students of the scriptures have focused on the part of the revelation that mentions the brethren's "follies" (verse 1), suggesting that

---

1. Drawing lots was consistent with the scriptures and the magic world view of Joseph Smith's time. It was a perfectly logical way to proceed, provided you believed that God was behind which ballot or lot was chosen. (See Quinn, Early Mormonism and the Magic World View [rev. ed.], 3, 325, 363n55.)
2. Woodford, The Historical Development of the Doctrine and Covenants, 1468–69.
3. See Cook, *Revelations of the Prophet Joseph Smith*, 221.
4. See Woodford, *The Historical Development of the Doctrine and Covenants*, 1469.
5. Quinn, *Early Mormonism and the Magic World View* (rev. ed.), 263.

going after hidden treasure fits into this category. Indeed, BYU professor Donald Q. Cannon has written: "In August 1836, however, they had relied on the arm of flesh, even to the extent of looking for hidden treasure in Salem." He then went on to say, "It is no wonder that the Lord used the term 'follies.'"[1] However, this explanation is not entirely satisfactory because the context and plain meaning of the language in section 111 suggest that hidden treasure *is* to be found: "And it shall come to pass in due time that I will give this city into your hands, that you shall have power over it, insomuch that they shall not discover your secret parts; and its wealth pertaining to gold and silver shall be yours." (Verse 4.) "Concern not yourselves about your debts, for I will give you power to pay them." (Verse 5.)

The prediction in section 111 that in "due time" converts would join the Church in Salem was fulfilled, but the words about finding a hidden treasure that would help pay the Church's debt was not fulfilled. Perhaps Joseph's strong and righteous personal desires to save the Church financially became intertwined with the revealed word. Joseph himself taught that once he "visited with a brother and sister from Michigan, who thought that 'a prophet is always a prophet;' but I told them that a prophet was a prophet only when he was acting as such."[2] Paul explained that prophets "are men of like passions with you." (Acts 14:15.) And Joseph said, "Although I was called of my Heavenly Father to lay the foundation of this great work . . . , I am subject to like passions as other men, like the prophets of olden times."[3] In other words, even an exceptionally gifted prophet like Joseph Smith can make mistakes.

Section 111 can be interpreted as a lesson in how prophets' righteous desires may become interwoven with an inspired utterance. The Apostle Paul said he taught certain of his own personal views "by permission, and not of commandment" (1 Corinthians 7:6); a Book of Mormon prophet expressed his "opinion" concerning doctrines only partially revealed to him concerning the resurrection (Alma 40:20); and Joseph gave his opinion about the meaning of a revelation he had received from God but did not understand (D&C 130:14–17).

Brigham Young was also aware that even the best God has to offer are men with feet of clay: "I do not . . . believe that there is a single revelation, among the many God has given to the Church, that is perfect in its fullness. The revelations of God contain correct doctrine and principles so far as they go; but it is impossible for the poor, weak, low, groveling sinful

---

1. Quinn, *Early Mormonism and the Magic World View* (rev. ed.), 263.
2. Smith, *Teachings of the Prophet Joseph Smith*, 278.
3. Smith, *History of the Church*, 5:516.

inhabitants of the earth to receive a revelation from the Almighty in all its perfections."[1]

In our day, J. Reuben Clark Jr., while a member of the First Presidency said in the April 1940 session of the general conference of the Church that "we [the First Presidency] are not infallible in our judgment, and we err, but our constant prayer is that the Lord will guide us in our decisions and we are trying so to live that our minds will be open to His inspiration."[2]

In discussing this subject, it is important to recognize that the accuracy of any given revelation depends in part on the method God uses to convey the message. Some revelations of a less direct nature are more prone to misinterpretation and error than others. For example, section 134 claims to be only an inspired "declaration of belief" and is not even referred to as a revelation. Other revelations claim inspiration regarding administrative matters that could be accomplished in a number of alternative ways, such as who should serve a particular mission. On the other hand, some revelations are far more direct, such as the visitation of an angel (D&C 13 or 110), or a vision (D&C 76), or an actual voice from heaven (D&C 130:14). In such instances human error is less likely. On the spectrum from simple "inspiration" to an appearance of a heavenly being, section 111 seems to be more along the lines of "inspiration"—a category of revelation that is open to greater interpretation. Perhaps this is partly why Joseph cautioned that the more important the subject, the more direct the revelation will be.

> We may look for angels and receive their ministrations, but we are to try the spirits and prove them, for it is often the case that men make a mistake in regard to these things. God has so ordained that when he has communicated, no vision is to be taken but what you see by the seeing of the eye, or what you hear by the hearing of the ear. When you see a vision, pray for the interpretation; if you get not this, shut it up; there must be certainty in this matter. An open vision will manifest that which is more important. Lying spirits are going forth in the earth. There will be great manifestations of spirits, both false and true.[3]

Joseph warned, "Nothing is a greater injury to the children of men than to be under the influence of a false spirit when they think they have the Spirit of God. Thousands have felt the influence of its terrible power and baneful effects."[4]

All of this places a sobering responsibility on each member of the Church to decide for himself or herself what is or is not from God. Taking the words

---

1. *Journal of Discourses*, 2:314.
2. Conference Report, April 4, 1940, 14.
3. Smith, Teachings of the Prophet Joseph Smith, 161.
4. Smith, *Teachings of the Prophet Joseph Smith*, 205.

of the prophets at face value without any evaluation in most instances may not be troublesome, but the Lord does not intend his Saints to be mere automatons. Brigham Young expressed the thought in this way:

> I am more afraid that this people have so much confidence in their leaders that they will not inquire for themselves of God whether they are led by Him. I am fearful they settle down in a state of blind self-security, trusting their eternal destiny in the hands of their leaders with a reckless confidence that in itself would thwart the purposes of God in their salvation, and weaken that influence they could give to their leaders, did they know for themselves, by the revelations of Jesus, that they are led in the right way. Let every man and woman know, by the whispering of the Spirit of God to themselves whether their leaders are walking in the path the Lord dictates, or not.[1]

The realization that each of us has an individual responsibility to know for ourselves what is or is not from God means that we must avoid two possible errors. The first error is noncritically accepting anything a Church leader may say, which may turn to our detriment. The second is to falsely judge the things of God to be of man. Either of these two mistakes is injurious to our spiritual well-being. As Paul said, "Wherefore, my beloved, as ye have always obeyed, not as in my presence only, but now much more in my absence, work out your own salvation with fear and trembling." (Philippians 2:12.)

If this is the case, then what should a member of the Church do if he or she cannot accept what seems like an authoritative statement from a prophet-leader in the hierarchy of the Church? If after earnest study and prayer, a member of the Church cannot agree with an authoritative statement of the prophet or his representatives, he or she has two choices. First, he or she can trust in a personal testimony that the President of the Church is God's living prophet, even though he or she does not have a spiritual confirmation of the specific statement or action of the prophet. Second, he or she may choose faithfully to continue to sustain the President of the Church in his office and calling, but not subscribe personally to the statement or action of the Prophet.[2] In this case, a Church member is in error only if he or she has not sought the Lord's guidance, or if he or she publicly challenges the authority of the President of the Church. Forced uniformity of thought is not required to be a member of the Church.

---

1. Journal of Discourses, 9:150.
2. Quinn, *Living Prophets*, unpublished statement in the possession of the author.

The Toronto incident

Another well-known instance where Joseph prophesied something that seemed not to come to pass is the so-called Toronto incident. The details for this situation rest on David Whitmer's account, given many years after the fact. However, it is well enough attested that B. H. Roberts addressed it in his *Comprehensive History of the Church*. Joseph received a revelation through the seerstone, advising Joseph and his brethren to go to Canada, where the revelation predicted they would sell the copyright of the Book of Mormon. The brethren made the trip, but they failed to sell the copyright. Roberts's analysis follows:

> The revelation respecting the Toronto journey was not of God, surely; else it would not have failed; but the Prophet, overwrought in his deep anxiety for the progress of the work, saw reflected in the "Seer Stone" his own thought, or that suggested to him by his brother Hyrum, rather than the thought of God.[1]

When Joseph was confronted with the failure of his revelation to come to pass he reportedly said, "Some revelations are of God; some revelations are of men; and some revelations are of the devil." Roberts then goes on to address the subject of "Does that circumstance vitiate his claim as a prophet?" His answer follows:

> No; the fact remains that despite this circumstance there exists a long list of events to be dealt with which will establish the fact of divine inspiration operating upon the mind of this man Joseph Smith. The wisdom frequently displayed, the knowledge revealed, the predicted events and the fulfillment thereof, are explicable upon no other theory than of divine inspiration giving guidance to him.[2]

This statement speaks for itself. When one considers the life of the Prophet Joseph, one sees that it is filled with otherwise inexplicable events, fulfilled prophecies, and manifestations of God's power.

B. H. Roberts explains that there are three lessons to be learned from the Toronto incident. First, it is important to realize that not every impression men and women receive is from God. Second, we can expect certainty only in the fundamentals, not in more peripheral matters such as certain aspects of the administration of the Church. Third, walking by faith is an essential part of our religious education in this life.

As to the thought that not every impression is from God, Roberts said:

---

1. Roberts, Comprehensive History of the Church, 1:165.
2. Roberts, Comprehensive History of the Church, 1:165.

How important for the Prophet's disciples to know that not every voice heard by the spirit of man is the voice of God; that not every impression made upon the mind is an impression from a divine source. . . . It was important that these disciples be made aware of these facts, that they may not stumble in matters of grave concerns. . . . The matter of the journey itself, and its object, were of small importance, but the lesson that came out of the experience was of great moment. . . . It is to the Prophet's credit that he submitted the matter to God for the solution. It is doubly to his credit that he boldly gave the answer received to his disciples, though it involved humiliation to him.[1]

Regarding the thought that we can expect certainty only in the fundamental matters of religion, Roberts said:

But one will say, what becomes of certainty even in matters of revelation and divine inspiration if such views as these are to obtain? The answer is that absolute certainty, except as to fundamental things, the great things that concern man's salvation, may not be expected. Here, indeed, that is, in things fundamental, we have the right to expect the solid rock, not shifting sands, and God gives that certainty. But in matters that do not involve fundamentals, in matters that involve only questions of administration and policy, the way in which God's servants go about things; in all such matters we may expect more or less of uncertainty, even errors; manifestations of unwisdom, growing out of human limitations.[2]

Certainly such limitations on our facility to apprehend the "whisperings of the Spirit" require humility on our part and a willingness to walk by faith. In fact, as Roberts points out, walking by faith "is the very means of our education."[3]

Unfortunately, Robert probably did not have the original revelation at hand when he made his defense of the Toronto incident. This revelation was only recently located and became available in the *Joseph Smith Papers*. The underlying assumption that the revelation which Joseph received to secure the copyright was not fulfilled is tempered by a careful reading of it. The language is not absolute but depends upon a number of preconditions.

Wherefore I say unto you that ye shall go to [Kingston] seeking me continually through my only Begotten & if ye do this ye shall have my spirit to go with you & ye shall have an addition of all things which is expedient in me. & I grant unto my servant a privilege that he may sell a copyright through you . . . if the people harden not their hearts against the enticings

---

1. Roberts, Comprehensive History of the Church, 1:166.
2. Roberts, Comprehensive History of the Church, 1:166.
3. Roberts, *Comprehensive History of the Church*, 1:166.

of my spirit.... Behold my way is before you & the means I will prepare ... if you are faithful.[1]

It should be observed that even though David Whitmer recalled many years later that this revelation was false, the revelation was not addressed to him and he was not one of the brethren sent to Canada to sell the copyright. Those undertaking this assignment were Oliver Cowdery, Hiram Page, and Josiah Stowell. As far as we know, none of these brethren ever raised an objection to the revelation.

I have taken the time to address the subject of seemingly unfulfilled revelation in some detail because it is troubling to all members of the Church when the subject is squarely faced for the first time. The spiritual maturity to know about and understand such matters is an essential part of our religious development if we expect to come to a fuller understanding of the way in which God deals with men and women in this life.

Where Joseph and his associates resided in Salem

The revelation indicates that Joseph and his associates would know where they should stay. "And the place where it is my will that you should tarry, for the main, shall be signalized unto you by the peace and power of my Spirit, that shall flow unto you." (Verse 8.) They are further told that they will be able to rent the space while they "inquire diligently concerning the more ancient inhabitants and founders of this city; for there are more treasures than one for you in this city." (Verses 9–10.)

The visit to the East India Marine Society and additional treasure

At the time Joseph received section 111, his traveling companions, Hyrum Smith, Oliver Cowdery, and Sidney Rigdon went to the East India Marine Society museum to "inquire ... concerning the ... ancient inhabitants and founders of this city." (Verse 9.) This particular museum was founded in 1799 and contained a hodgepodge of items ranging from the tail of an Indian elephant to "a model of a dog, made of shells, by Miss Bell of Nantucket, when only 6 years old."[2] In the context of seeking out treasures, Cowdery and Rigdon may have been interested in finding information that might lead them to additional hidden treasures in the

---

1. Joseph Smith Papers, 2:31–32.
2. Cotter, "Art Review: A Bounty from Salem's Globe Trotter," *New York Times*, August 1, 2003.

Union Street, in Salem, Massachusetts, where Joseph Smith stayed in search of treasure.

area.[1] In this regard section 111 advises, "For there are more treasures than one for you in this city." (Verse 10.) Some interpreters of this section have suggested that this sentence does not refer to additional monetary treasures but rather future converts from Salem.

Nonmembers of the Church will not discover Joseph's plan to find treasure in Salem while he is there

Joseph is also reassured that the inhabitants of the city will not discover his clandestine plans to buy or rent the house with the money in it, thus making it possible for him to find and secure the money without outside interference. "I will give this city into your hands, that you shall have power over it, insomuch that they shall not discover your secret parts; and its wealth pertaining to gold and silver shall be yours." (Verse 4.)

---

1. Rigdon may not have been as prone to the idea of looking for treasures. "He was the only member of the First Presidency at Salem for whom there is no evidence of affinity toward folk magic. Rigdon had previously been an ordained minister, and the Protestant clergy usually led the opposition to folk magic." (See Quinn, *Early Mormonism and the Magic World View* [rev. ed.], 264.)

Chapter 37

Lessons Learned about the Nature of God in Missouri: Joseph Smith Incarcerated, Liberty Jail, Missouri, March 1839

Sections 121–123 were written in Liberty Jail, Liberty, Missouri, in March 1839, a tumultuous and difficult period of time for the Church. A year earlier, Joseph had fled Kirtland for Far West, Missouri, where the Saints were gathering as a body. During the summer of 1838, because of deteriorating relations between them and their neighbors in Clay County, the Saints were moving farther north, pouring into a Mormon town called Adam-ondi-Ahman ("Diahman" for short), just four miles north of Gallatin, the county seat. Eighteen thirty-eight was an election year and as the Saints' numbers continued to grow as part of the gathering, non-Mormons were concerned about their political clout. In an effort to maintain political control, local residents formed mobs determined to prevent the Saints from voting. When the Saints arrived at the polls, violence broke out. Soon thereafter, Judge Austin A. King falsely accused Joseph Smith of raising an army of five hundred men, saying that if the Mormons did not change their ways they would be killed.[1]

By September 1838 enemies of the Church, including many from outside of Daviess County, prepared to attack the Saints who had settled in Adam-ondi-Ahman. Both Mormons and mobbers sent scouts throughout the area and occasionally took prisoners. During these conflicts, hostile events occurred on both sides between the Saints who had settled in DeWitt County and the non-Mormons in Carroll County. By October, fighting between the two groups broke out. Anti-Mormon forces marched toward Daviess County to remove the Saints, with eight hundred advancing toward Adam-ondi-Ahman.

To advance their interests and to protect themselves, the Saints orga-

---

1. See *Church History in the Fulness of Time*, 193–95.

nized and armed themselves into a militia. Guerrilla warfare raged between Mormon and anti-Mormon forces as both sides plundered and burned each other's property. David W. Patten, a member of the Twelve, was shot and killed in a skirmish at Crooked River.[1] By the last week of October 1838, Lilburn W. Boggs, the governor of Missouri, issued his infamous extermination order stating that the Mormons must be killed if they refused to leave the state. Three days later William O. Jennings led an attack on a small Mormon settlement known as Haun's Mill, murdering seventeen and wounding many others.[2]

Under these circumstances, on October 31, 1838, a Mormon colonel by the name of Hinkle invited Joseph to attend a peace conference with members of the state militia, ostensibly as a way of avoiding further conflict. Joseph Smith, Sidney Rigdon, Parley P. Pratt, Lyman Wight, and George W. Robinson arrived at the meeting place and, much to their shock, were taken as prisoners of war and treated with contempt. The next day Hyrum Smith and Amasa Lyman were also taken prisoner and taken to the camp. A court martial was held and all of the Mormon prisoners were sentenced to be shot.[3] The lives of Joseph and his captive brethren were spared only when General Alexander Doniphan, a friend of the Saints, refused to carry out the order. The prisoners were taken instead to Richmond, Missouri, for trial. The judge bound Joseph and five others over for trial and sent them to Liberty Jail. Joseph and his colleagues were incarcerated in a cold, small basement dungeon for the next four months.[4]

The conditions at Liberty Jail were deplorable. The 22-square-foot basement holding cell was in reality a dungeon. *Church History in the Fulness of Times* describes the situation well: "Small, barred windows opened into the upper level, and there was little heat. A hole in the floor was the only access to the lower level, where a man could not stand upright. For four winter months the Prophet and his companions suffered from cold, filthy conditions, smoke inhalation, loneliness, and filthy food. Perhaps worst

---

1. *Church History in the Fulness of Time*, 195–200.
2. *Church History in the Fulness of Time*, 201–4. Feelings against the Mormons were certainly exacerbated by what the Missourians perceived as Mormon aggression. Sidney Rigdon at the Independence Day celebration on July 4, 1838, in Far West delivered an emotional oration in which he said, "From this day and this hour we will suffer it no more . . . the man, or set of men who attempt it, do it at the expense of their lives. And that mob that comes on us to disturb us, it shall be between us and them a war of extermination; for we will follow them until the last drop of their blood is spilled; or else they will have to exterminate us, for we will carry the seat of war to their own houses and their own families, and one party or the other shall be utterly destroyed." (See Preece, *Learning to Love the Doctrine and Covenants*, 335–36.) He did add that the Saints should not be the aggressor or infringe upon other rights but such modifying language was lost on the Missourians as well as some of the Saints.
3. See Smith, *History of the Church*, 3:188–90.
4. See *Church History in the Fulness of Time*, 204–7.

of all, they were unable to accompany the faithful Saints, who were being driven from the state."[1]

It was during Joseph's incarceration that he wrote letters to the body of the Church, letters which now appear as sections 121, 122, and 123.

Finally, on April 15, 1839, just after a grand jury had issued a bill or statement against the prisoners for "murder, treason, burglary, arson, larceny, theft, and stealing,"[2] Joseph and his friends escaped en route to Daviess County for trial. The prisoners escaped across the Mississippi River into Quincy, Illinois. Some believe the escape was the result of a $6,000 bribe to a guard, a huge sum of money in the 1830s. Other Mormon prisoners in the Richmond Jail also escaped and made their way to Nauvoo. King Follett, one of the prisoners, was recaptured but finally released in October 1839.[3]

It was during the Missouri period that Joseph and the Saints learned some difficult and some reassuring lessons about God's perspective and how he relates to his children.

1. *God allows men and women to misinterpret events.* The revelation on Zion cautioned that Zion would be established "after much tribulation" and "many years." (D&C 58:3, 44.) Yet Joseph and the Saints sincerely believed that the Zion in Jackson County would be established in their lifetime. The potential for the Saints' misapprehension of forthcoming events[4] was commented on in the revelation itself, "Ye cannot behold with your natural eyes, for the present time, the design of your God concerning those things which shall come hereafter." (D&C 58:3.)

2. *God does not always disclose information his people desperately want to know.* Once the Saints were forced out of Zion, the burning question was, When would members of the Church be allowed to return to Zion to prepare for Christ's second coming? Until the end of his life Joseph repeatedly inquired regarding this issue, but the information was never forthcoming. Rather, after much prayer the Lord said to Joseph, in effect, "Be still and know that I am God!" (D&C 101:16; see also D&C 130:14–17; commentary on D&C 130.)

3. *God may revoke commandments.* At the time Zion was founded the Saints were warned that if they did not obey his commandments, God

---

1. *Church History in the Fulness of Time*, 208.
2. Smith, *History of the Church*, 3:315.
3. See *Church History in the Fulness of Time*, 209.
4. People's misperception of events and the designs and purposes of God often occur because it is difficult for men and women to separate themselves from the cultural assumptions of their day. During this period of American history, Millennialism was in the air and it was no wonder that the Saints took the view that Jesus would be returning within their lifetime. Today, in our secular culture, the opposite assumption could be easily made, when in truth and in fact the Second Coming might be closer at hand than we think.

would "revoke and they [would] receive not the blessing." (D&C 58:32.) In Nauvoo this same principle of revocation would be utilized but not because of a lack of obedience. "When I give a commandment to any of the sons of men to do a work unto my name, and those sons of men go with all their might and with all they have to perform that work . . . and their enemies come upon them and hinder them from performing that work, behold, it behooveth me to require that work no more at the hands of those sons of men, but to accept of their offerings." (D&C 124:49.)

4. *God is not concerned about property.* When the Saints were being asked to leave their homes and temporal belongings and move from Kirtland to Far West, the Lord cared little about their temporal belongings. "For what is property unto me? saith the Lord. . . . [H]ave I not the fowls of heaven . . . ? Have I not made the earth? . . . Is there not room enough . . . that you should covet that which is but the drop, and neglect the more weighty matters?" (D&C 117:4, 6, 8.)

5. *God desires that people use their own judgment in the daily affairs of their lives.* When the Saints asked trivial questions, questions about where and how they should travel, the Lord said, "It mattereth not unto me." (D&C 60:5.) Furthermore, he explained, "I, the Lord, am willing, if any among you desire to ride upon horses, or upon mules, or in chariots, he shall receive this blessing, if he receive it from the hand of the Lord, with a thankful heart in all things. These things remain with you to do according to judgment and the directions of the Spirit." (D&C 62:7–8.) As noted, it is always appropriate seek the directions of the Spirit.

6. *God is pleased when his children are anxiously engaged in good causes.* God does not like to compel his children. Rather, men and women have the power to do much good on their own and should do so. (See D&C 58:26–29.)

7. *God at times does intervene in the affairs of his people.* Although the Saints were not always certain what the Lord wanted, it was clear to them that he could intervene in their daily affairs. Many saw miraculous healings and experienced visions and dreams. When Zion's Camp was about to be destroyed, God defeated their enemies by summoning a storm.

8. *God allows all men and women to suffer.* Suffering and disappointment are part of life. This principle applies to everyone. It matters not whether a person is a prophet or a nonmember of the Church; no one leaves this life unscathed. Such experience is part of what this life is all about. Ultimately, what we are called to pass through in this life will be for our benefit. "All these things shall give thee experience, and shall be for thy good." (D&C 122:7.)

Section 121: Liberty Jail, Liberty, Missouri, March 20, 1839

Heading

Priesthood power can be exercised only upon the principles of righteousness—acting with no hypocrisy, no self-aggrandizement, no coercion of others.

The big question

Question: What and where is Zion?
Answer: Zion is a place where power and authority are based on gentle persuasion.

Introduction

This prayer and these prophecies were written by Joseph Smith while he was incarcerated in Liberty Jail, Liberty, Missouri, on March 20, 1839.[1] The Prophet and several companions had been in prison for months. Their petitions and appeals to the executive officers and the judiciary had failed to bring them relief.

Anchor section

Memorize: Proper use of the priesthood

Historical background

In October 1838, Joseph Smith and other Church leaders were betrayed into the hands of their enemies in Missouri. After a month of mock trials Joseph and several others were incarcerated in Liberty Jail from December 1, 1838 to April 6, 1839.[2] Even though none of these men were convicted of any crimes, they were held in custody for many months. During that time a few visitors were allowed to see them, and they were permitted to write and receive letters.

---

1. Smith, *History of the Church*, 3:289–300.
2. Approximately fifty men were arrested and charged with breaking the law. However, almost all were released within about three weeks of their arrest or were out on bail. (See Cook, *Revelations of the Prophet Joseph Smith*, 239.) The others incarcerated with the Prophet were Hyrum Smith, Lyman Wight, Caleb Baldwin, Alexander McRae, and Sidney Rigdon (later released).

Toward the end of March 1839 Joseph dictated a letter to the Saints, and to Edward Partridge in particular, which has now been canonized as section 121. Alexander McRae was scribe, and it was signed by all the prisoners. This letter was followed a short time later by a second, also in the hand of McRae. Sections 121–123 consist of extracts from these two letters.[1] Joseph and his brethren escaped from prison on April 6, 1839.

From the period of Joseph's incarceration, there are eight surviving letters. Four were addressed to Emma Smith, his wife, and "all of them display the sterling character of the Prophet Joseph under trials of the most extreme conditions imaginable."[2] Alexander McRae and Caleb Baldwin acted as scribes. Segments of letters were included in the Doctrine and Covenants for the first time in 1876, but the texts were reported earlier in the *Times and Seasons*, in May and July 1840, and were slightly reworded.[3]

Joseph Smith as prisoner

After Joseph's arrest he was first transferred to Richmond, where he and his brethren were chained together and held prisoner in an old vacant house for over two weeks. In the middle of November Joseph was taken before circuit judge Austin A. King, who presided over the prisoners' thirteen-day trial. When the prisoners submitted their list of witnesses, those witnesses were methodically run out of the county or put in jail themselves. Alexander Doniphan, Joseph's attorney, said, "If a cohort of angels were to come down, and declare we were innocent, it would all be the same; for he (King) had determined from the beginning to cast us into prison."[4] As expected, at the end of the judicial proceedings Judge King ordered Joseph and five others incarcerated in Liberty Jail in Clay County.

While being held prisoner in the Richmond jail, Parley P. Pratt records that for several hours Joseph and his brethren had listened to "obscene jests . . . , horrid oaths . . . , blasphemies and filthy language" as their captors rehearsed the atrocities they had inflicted on the Saints. Parley lay next to the Prophet and said that he could hardly refrain from speaking out. Suddenly Joseph arose to his feet, in shackles and unarmed. Parley recalls that Joseph spoke with a thunderous voice:

---

1. See Woodford, *The Historical Development of the Doctrine and Covenants*, 1566–67.
2. Jessee and Welch, "Revelations in Context," *BYU Studies* 30:3:125.
3. Ibid., 130.
4. Smith, *History of the Church*, 3:213.

"SILENCE, ye fiends of the infernal pit. In the name of Jesus Christ I rebuke you, and command you to be still; I will not live another minute and hear such language. Cease such talk, or you or I die THIS INSTANT!"

He ceased to speak. He stood erect in terrible majesty. Chained, and without a weapon; calm, unruffled and dignified as an angel, he looked upon the quailing guards, whose weapons were lowered or dropped to the ground; whose knees smote together, and who, shrinking into a corner, or crouching at his feet, begged his pardon, and remained quiet till a change of guards.[1]

This scene was one which was never forgotten by those imprisoned with the Prophet.

Joseph's incarceration in Liberty Jail turned out to be one of the most dreadful times in his life. It was during this painful time that even Joseph wondered about the survival of the Church. Finally, after he had languished in prison four months under dire and horrid circumstances, his patience failed him. On March 10, 1839, ill-fed, cold, uncomfortable, weary, and exhausted, the Prophet cried out to God in prayer: "O God, where art thou? And where is the pavilion that covereth thy hiding place? How long shall thy hand be stayed, and thine eye . . . behold . . . the wrongs of thy people . . . and thine ear be penetrated with their cries?" (D&C 121:1–4.)

Section 121 records the Lord's response:

> My son, peace be unto thy soul; thine adversity and thine afflictions shall be but a small moment;
>
> And then, if thou endure it well, God shall exalt thee on high; thou shalt triumph over all thy foes.
>
> Thy friends do stand by thee, and they shall hail thee again with warm hearts and friendly hands.
>
> Thou art not yet as Job; thy friends do not contend against thee, neither charge thee with transgression, as they did Job. (Verses 7–10.)

While these words were reassuring, Joseph was still left to languish in prison for another three and a half weeks before he and his brethren escaped when they were being transferred to another jurisdiction for trial.

The part of the letter that appears in section 121 was preceded by a list of particulars that showed how the Saints had been the victims of mobocracy and extermination, having been driven from their homes and families. It expressed their revulsion at being imprisoned and subjected to a hell filled with demons, with no choice but to listen to them blaspheme sacred things, including the name of God. Joseph writes about the drunken guards' murders and their unrelenting inhumanity toward the Saints, which was enough to "shock all nature" and was "too much for contemplation." At the

---

1. Pratt, Autobiography of Parley P. Pratt, 180.

same time he and the other prisoners felt that they were "left to perish with their helpless offspring clinging around their necks."[1] Joseph's despair follows: "O God, where art thou? And where is the pavilion that covereth thy hiding place?" (verse 1).

Use of priesthood power

Section 121 reinforces Jesus' teaching on the appropriate use of religious authority. During his lifetime, one of his abiding frustrations was the abuse of power by some of the Pharisees and Sadducees. There are numerous examples in the Gospels where Jesus accused these ruling elite of hypocrisy and condemned them for using religion to safeguard their privileged positions. Many times Jesus could hardly contain his contempt for these charlatans, whom he referred to as "vipers" and "snakes." (Luke 3:27.) In contrast, section 121 teaches the appropriate use of religious authority, pointing out that Church governance should be based on gentle persuasion and a genuine concern for others (see verses 41–43):

> ... there are many called, but few are chosen. And why are they not chosen?
> Because their hearts are set so much upon the things of this world, and aspire to the honors of men, that they do not learn this one lesson—
> That the rights of the priesthood are inseparably connected with the powers of heaven, and that the powers of heaven cannot be controlled nor handled only upon the principles of righteousness.
> That they may be conferred upon us, it is true; but when we undertake to cover our sins, or to gratify our pride, our vain ambition, or to exercise control or dominion or compulsion upon the souls of the children of men, in any degree of unrighteousness, behold, the heavens withdraw themselves; the Spirit of the Lord is grieved; and when it is withdrawn, Amen to the priesthood or the authority of that man. ...
> We have learned by sad experience that it is the nature and disposition of almost all men, as soon as they get a little authority, as they suppose, they will immediately begin to exercise unrighteous dominion. ...
> No power or influence can or ought to be maintained by virtue of the priesthood, only by persuasion, by long-suffering, by gentleness and meekness, and by love unfeigned;
> By kindness, and pure knowledge, which shall greatly enlarge the soul without hypocrisy, and without guile—
> Reproving betimes with sharpness, when moved upon by the Holy Ghost; and then showing forth afterwards an increase of love toward him whom thou hast reproved, lest he esteem thee to be his enemy;
> That he may know that thy faithfulness is stronger than the cords of death.

---

1. Jessee and Welch, "Revelations in Context," *BYU Studies* 39:3:132–33; Doctrine and Covenants 122:6.

Let thy bowels . . . be full of charity towards all men. (Verses 34–45.)

The meaning of the phrase "reproving *betimes* with sharpness" (Verse 42, emphasis added) is better understood by a sense of context. The word "betimes" in contemporary use implies only an occasional rebuke of someone in "sharpness". However, the meaning of "betimes" in the Webster's 1828 Dictionary means "before it is too late". Therefore, the better interpretation of verse 42 is not that a person may occasionally admonish someone sternly. Rather, it is appropriate to reproach someone in a timely way – before it is too late to turn back from sinful behavior.

A time to come when "nothing shall be withheld"

Latter-day Saints generally talk about the "restoration of all things" in the context of the restoration of various doctrines, rituals, and practices observed by Jesus Christ and his followers in the primitive Church. Section 121 broadens this perspective to include secular as well as religious knowledge.

> God shall give unto you knowledge by his Holy Spirit . . . that has not been revealed since the world was until now;
> Which our forefathers have awaited with anxious expectation to be revealed in the last times . . .
> A time to come in . . . which nothing shall be withheld, whether there be one God or many gods, they shall be manifest. . . .
> And also, if there be bounds set to the heavens or to the seas, or to the dry land, or to the sun, moon, or stars—
> All the times of their revolutions, all the appointed days, months, and years, and all the days of their days, months, and years, and all their glories, laws, and set times, shall be revealed in the days of the dispensation of the fulness of times—
> According to that which was ordained in the midst of the Council of the Eternal God of all other gods before this world was, that should be reserved unto the finishing and the end thereof, when every man shall enter into his eternal presence and into his immortal rest. (Verses 26–32.)

In keeping with this more expansive understanding, Parley P. Pratt's definition of "theology" included what are usually thought of as secular subjects, such as science, philosophy, history, and more.[1]

---

1. See Pratt, *Key to the Science of Theology*, 12.

Plurality of Gods

Section 121 teaches plainly the idea that there are many Gods and that there is an "Eternal God" above other gods.

> According to that which was ordained in the midst of the Council of the Eternal God of all other gods before this world was, that should be reserved unto the finishing and the end thereof, when every man shall enter into his eternal presence and into his immortal rest. (Verse 32; emphasis added.)

For Joseph, the notion of the plurality of Gods meant that God's children would someday attain godly station for themselves. (See D&C 76:57–60; 132:19–20.)

Section 122: Liberty Jail, Liberty, Missouri, March 1839

Heading

The importance of gaining experience in this life.

The big question

Question: How do we deal with disappointment and unrealized promises?

Answer: Understand that disappointment, sorrow, and unrealized promises are experiences that may be consecrated for our good and our self-development.

Introduction

This revelation is the word of the Lord to Joseph Smith the Prophet, while he was a prisoner in Liberty Jail.[1]

Historical background

Section 122 is also taken from the letters Joseph wrote while incarcerated in Liberty Jail in March 1839. (See historical introduction to D&C 121.) Doctrine and Covenants 122:6 describes the circumstances of the Prophet's arrest in Far West, Missouri, in November 1838. Lyman Wight was present on that day and recorded what happened.

---

1. See Smith, *History of the Church,* 3:300.

Model of Liberty Jail, in Liberty, Missouri, where Joseph and his associates were imprisoned from December 1, 1838, to April 6, 1839.

About the hour the prisoners were to have been shot on the public square in Far West, they were exhibited in a wagon in the town, all of them having families there, but myself; and it would have broken the heart of any person possessing an ordinary share of humanity, to have seen the separation. The aged father and mother of Joseph Smith were not permitted to see his face, but to reach their hand through the curtains of the wagon, and thus take leave of him. When passing his own house, he was taken out of the wagon and permitted to go into the house, but not without a strong guard, and not permitted to speak with his family but in the presence of his guard and his eldest son, Joseph, about six or eight years old, hanging to the tail of his coat, crying father, is the mob going to kill you? The guard said to him, "you damned little brat, go back, you will see your father no more."[1]

The spirit of prophecy

In retrospect, the statements in section 122 that the people of the Church would "never be turned against" the Prophet and that the "ends of the earth" would inquire after him proved to have been written under the spirit of prophecy. (See verses 1 and 3.) Of course, Joseph has always held a place of preeminence in Mormonism as its founder; and as missionary work progresses, people all over the globe inquire after the name of Joseph Smith.

The hardships and difficulties men and women experience in this life will ultimately be for their good

In the face of relentless persecution the Lord comforted the Prophet by assuring him that, ultimately, even though his circumstances were dire, "all these things shall give thee experience, and shall be for thy good." (Verse 7.) Like the Son of God, he also would not be spared hardship. "The Son of Man hath descended below them all. Art thou greater than he?" (Verse 8.) With these thoughts the Lord encouraged Joseph to "hold on thy way" and to "fear not what man can do, for God shall be with you forever and ever." (Verse 9.) After this inspired letter was written, Joseph was not delivered from his enemies immediately and soldiered on for almost another month before he was finally released. Based on these verses, and likening all scriptures unto ourselves (1 Nephi 19:23), we may understand that the same principle—difficult circumstances being consecrated for one's good—applies to all of God's children.

---

1. Lyman Wight statement before the Municipal Court of Nauvoo, July 1, 1843, "Nauvoo Municipal Court Docket Book," under date, Church Archives; quoted in Cook, Revelations of the Prophet Joseph Smith, 240. See also Times and Seasons 4 (15 July 1843): 268.

Section 123: Liberty Jail, Liberty, Missouri, March 1839

Heading

Petition the government for the redress of wrongs perpetrated on the Mormons in Missouri.

The big question

Question: How do we deal with disappointment and unrealized promises?

Answer: Make an effort to change the situation.

Introduction

The duty of the Saints in relation to their persecutors is set forth.[1]

Historical background

Section 123 was also taken from one of the letters Joseph wrote while incarcerated in Liberty Jail. (See historical introduction to D&C 121.) In this particular epistle Joseph recommended that a committee be organized to collect various accounts describing the persecution the Saints suffered in Missouri. Shortly thereafter, a conference was held wherein Almon W. Babbit, Erastus Snow, and Robert B. Thompson were appointed as a "traveling committee" to collect eyewitness accounts documenting the personal injury and property loss the Saints had endured. To give credence to the Mormons' claims, sworn affidavits were prepared and lists of the names of some of the perpetrators were recorded. Libelous newspaper articles were also collected.[2]

The spirit of the creeds

Section 123 ties some of the tyranny and oppressions to the influence of "the creeds of the fathers, who have inherited lies, upon the hearts of the children, and filled the world with confusion, and has been growing stronger and stronger, and is now the very mainspring of all corruption." (Verse 7.) The creeds mentioned here are formal statements of religious belief or confessions of faith adhered to by apostate Christianity. The word derives from the Latin *credo* for "I believe." During the time of the apostasy,

---

1. Smith, *History of the Church*, 3:302–3.
2. See Preece, *Learning to Love the Doctrine and Covenants*, 351.

the creeds of traditional Christianity were adopted at various councils to authoritatively settle doctrinal disputes. One of the oldest and most celebrated creeds is the Nicene Creed, written in the fourth century A.D. in an attempt to explain the Trinity and to unify the Christian church under Emperor Constantine.[1] Such creeds are considered to be the expression of God's will, to be "set in stone," and they are required confessions of faith for members of almost all traditional Christian denominations.

From the time of the First Vision Joseph Smith understood that he "must join none of" the established religious denominations and "that all their creeds were an abomination in [God's] sight." He made a point of teaching that Latter-day Saints did not have such creeds and that God had told him that the "professors" of religion who relied upon creeds "were all corrupt; that: 'they draw near to me with their lips, but their hearts are far from me, they teach for doctrines the commandments of men.'" (JS–H 1:19.) Therefore, it is not surprising that in section 123 Joseph implored his followers to "waste and wear out [their] lives in bringing to light all the hidden things of darkness, wherein we know them; and they are truly manifest from heaven." (Verse 13.) He believed that by comparing the differences between the false ideas embedded in traditional Christianity with the true ideas revealed in Mormonism that many would join the Church: "For there are many yet on the earth . . . who are only kept from the truth because they know not where to find it." (Verse 12.)

Joseph Smith's aversion to creeds was also based on the Christian tradition that, once compiled, such creedal declarations were rigid and inflexible expressions. That belief was inconsistent with the spirit of continuing revelation that expands and increases men and women's understanding of the eternal nature of God. Bushman expressed Joseph's views well:

> The flow of revelations prevented him from ever saying the work was finished. Even at the end of his career, he resisted any attempt to stanch the springs of inspiration. "The most prominent point of difference in sentiment between the Latter Day Saints & sectarians," a clerk later recorded him saying, "was, that the latter were all circumscribed by some peculiar creed, which deprived its members the privilege of believing anything not contained therein; where the L.D. Saints had no creed, but are ready to believe all true principles that exist, as they are made manifest from time to time." Creeds fixed limits. They seemed to say "thus far and no further," while for Joseph the way was always open to additional truth.[2]

---

1. From a Mormon standpoint, the Trinity as it is explained in the creeds is at the root of the great apostasy and completely ignores the corporality and separate identity of God the Father and his son Jesus Christ.
2. Bushman, Joseph Smith: Rough Stone Rolling, 285.

Because of this, Joseph felt it perfectly acceptable for him to revise his own revelations. He wanted the "door left ajar for truth from every source."[1] And, as section 123 points out, the creeds were so highly esteemed and cherished that such authoritative statements of doctrine prejudiced the minds of men and women against the spirit of the restored gospel.

Do not count what you are doing as insignificant, for there is much that lies in futurity

Section 123 encouraged members of the Church to understand that what they were doing to build the kingdom was vitally important. Little did they know, nor could they apprehend, how significant even their smallest deeds and sacrifices might become to future generations.

> Let no man count them as small things; for there is much which lieth in futurity, pertaining to the Saints, which depends upon these things.
> You know, brethren, that a very large ship is benefited very much by a very small helm in the time of a storm, by being kept workways with the wind and the waves.
> Therefore, dearly beloved brethren, let us cheerfully do all things that lie in our power; and then may we stand still with the utmost assurance, to see the salvation of God, and for his arm to be revealed. (Verses 15–17.)

This same idea was expressed in some of Joseph's earlier revelations. In September 1831, seven and a half years before section 123 was revealed, and about a year and a half after the Church was organized, the Lord said, "Wherefore, be not weary in well-doing, for ye are laying the foundation of a great work. And out of small things proceedeth that which is great." (D&C 64:33.) An encouraging word here, a convert there, the resolve to withstand persecution and stay with the main body of the Saints, Church assignments fulfilled, a willingness to conform our lives to the gospel, a child born and raised in the faith—each of these seemingly inconsequential (in the grand scheme of things) performances may be vitally important for the future success of the Church.

---

1. Bushman, *Joseph Smith: Rough Stone Rolling*, 285.

Part 8

The Nauvoo Period

Chapter 38

At the Point of a Gun: Nauvoo, Illinois, January 1841–June 1844

The Move to Nauvoo

The Saints' stay in Missouri disintegrated quickly between the summer of 1838 and the beginning of 1839. On August 6, 1838, violence broke out when Latter-day Saints went to cast their votes in a local election in Gallatin. The Missourians tried to keep the Mormons from voting. On September 7, 1838, Joseph Smith and Lyman Wight were brought up on charges before Judge Austin King. By early October the so-called Missouri Mormon War had begun. The Mormons organized and began to defend themselves. Violence again broke out in DeWitt County, and some Mormons went on the offensive and waged a type of guerrilla warfare in Daviess County. In late October, Elder David W. Patten, a member of the Quorum of the Twelve Apostles, was killed in a skirmish at Crooked River. Two days later Governor Lilburn Boggs issued the infamous extermination order stating that the Mormons must be treated as enemies and "exterminated" or driven from the State of Missouri. On October 30, 1838 a Mormon settlement at Haun's Mill was massacred,[1] and on the same day an army of 2,500 Missourians gathered a mile and a half south of Far West, under the temporary command of Samuel Lucas of Jackson County.[2]

Cornered and outgunned, Joseph sued for peace. Lucas presented terms to George Hinckle, one of three men chosen by Joseph to negotiate with their enemies. Displaying Governor Boggs's extermination order, Lucas threatened to reduce Far West to ashes. He gave the Mormons an hour to decide

---

1. See *Church History in the Fulness of Times*, 193.
2. Bushman, *Joseph Smith: Rough Stone Rolling*, 366.

whether or not they would leave the State. Betrayed by Hickle, Joseph and other Church leaders were taken as prisoners.[1] Mormon property in Missouri was confiscated to reimburse the Daviess County citizens for their property damage. Bushman stated, "The Mormons were to give up everything except their lives."[2] On November 1, soldiers searched the city for firearms, threatening and ridiculing the Saints. A few days later the Mormon settlement at Adam-ondi-Ahman surrendered as well. "The Mormon men came one by one to a table where they signed away their property to the state of Missouri while militia men stood by and struck anyone who protested. Meanwhile, marauders were attacking outlying farms, molesting women, whipping men, and killing animals."[3] The circumstances had become serious enough that the Mormons were willing to leave Missouri.

In January 1839, with Joseph in Liberty Jail, Brigham Young organized a Committee on Removal to systematically move the Saints out of the area. "Some people saw the flight from Missouri as evidence that the Lord had forsaken the Saints. The Prophet Joseph was in Liberty Jail with no prospects of release. Whatever hope the Saints had of regaining political rights and property in Missouri or establishing the city of Zion was dimmed."[4] This description is at best an understatement. The Church was in chaos.

By mid-spring 1839 Church leaders still had not determined where the Saints should resettle. Some even suggested that gathering large numbers of Saints in any one place was counterproductive because it alarmed non-Mormon neighbors. But, from prison, Joseph had advised the Saints to gather again. Word reached Brigham Young and others that the citizens of Illinois were sympathetic and would welcome the Mormons. The citizens of Quincy, in particular, with a population of 1,200, were "generous and sympathetic to the plight of the exiles."[5] Many Mormon refugees were given shelter. Money was collected and food and clothing gathered to help the Saints. Meanwhile, Joseph, Hyrum, and their fellow prisoners were finally allowed to escape and arrived in Quincy on April 22, 1839. After exploring their options, plans were made to settle in Commerce, Illinois, later renamed Nauvoo.[6] Within months, eight to ten thousand Saints migrated to western Illinois.[7]

---

1. See Bushman, *Joseph Smith: Rough Stone Rolling*, 366.
2. Bushman, *Joseph Smith: Rough Stone Rolling*, 367.
3. Bushman, *Joseph Smith: Rough Stone Rolling*, 367.
4. *Church History in the Fulness of Times*, 211.
5. *Church History in the Fulness of Times*, 213.
6. See *Church History in the Fulness of Times*, 215–16.
7. See *Church History in the Fulness of Times*, 215.

Chapter 39

The Big Question: Nauvoo, Illinois

How Shall We Be Saved?[1]

Before the Nauvoo period, the doctrinal emphasis in the Church had been on faith, repentance, baptism, the gift of the Holy Ghost, and missionary work—practices and beliefs clearly explained in Joseph's early revelations and in the Book of Mormon. (See D&C 6:9; 11:9; 15:6; 19:31; 20:71; 39:36; 2 Nephi 31:17.) Joseph taught these concepts in a new context: the restoration of the primitive gospel that Jesus taught, new and continuing revelation, and through the introduction of additional scripture—the Book of Mormon. However, except for the introduction of the Book of Mormon, none of these ideas was totally new or foreign to traditional Christianity in the early 1800s or, for that matter, even today. With some variation, most, if not all, Christian denominations taught the need for faith in the Lord Jesus Christ, repentance, and baptism, accompanied by an outpouring of the Holy Spirit. The concept of revelation was an essential part of the idea that God answered prayers. Likewise, other denominations also had a missionary agenda. Given this background, what made the Nauvoo era doctrinally unique was the further explanation by Joseph that certain beliefs, rituals, practices, and doctrines were absolutely necessary if his followers were to receive the highest rewards God had in store for his people in this life and in the next.[2]

The distinctive doctrinal teachings of the Nauvoo period are easily

---

1. See D&C 124, 127, 128, 129, 130, 131, 132.
2. It should be noted that some of the ideas that seemed to suddenly come onto the scene during the Nauvoo period were in fact contained in some of Joseph's earlier revelations. For example, section 76 (1832) speaks about multiple heavens and the idea that men and women may become gods and goddesses. The Book of Moses in the Pearl of Great Price (1830) introduces the idea of multiple worlds and the eternality of matter. Section 93 (1833) talks about the premortal life and "intelligences." But, these ideas were never publically preached or expanded upon until the Nauvoo period, when Joseph seemed to fix his attention on the implications of such ideas and receive more revelation concerning such matters.

illustrated by listing some of the concepts Joseph expanded upon and introduced during this time—concepts that would unalterably pit Mormonism against mainstream Christianity.

1. God is an exalted man with a body of flesh and bones.

2. Spirits are made of a material substance which is more refined or pure than that comprising mortal bodies.

3. God is married. Therefore, there is a Heavenly Mother as well as a Heavenly Father. From this union spiritual offspring were sired and lived with their Heavenly Parents in a premortal life.

4. Premortal spirits were clothed with an earthly body when born into this life, and they came without a recollection of their premortal existence, so that they might be tested, developed, and gain experience.

5. The purpose of this existence is to help men and women advance and become more like their Heavenly Father and Mother—gods and goddesses.

6. When men and women become gods and goddesses, they will produce spiritual offspring just like their Heavenly Parents do.

7. Since men and women may become gods and goddesses, it follows that there are multiple gods who work cooperatively with one another to nurture and move forward their heavenly offspring.

8. The highest form of marriage—celestial marriage—encompasses plural marriage, which may, if God commands, be practiced on earth and in heaven.

9. There are an infinite number of other planets in the universe populated by male and female spirits, men and women, gods and goddesses, who are related to one another in one great family organization as well as other life.

10. Matter, or the elements, is eternal and has always existed. Therefore, there is no such thing as an *ex nihilo* creation. God created the earth by organizing matter into its various forms.

11. Men and women are co-eternal and have always existed. In the beginning, or at first, life forms were less advanced and consisted of some kind of "intelligence" or "ego."

12. In order to be saved, men and women must enter into covenants with God, signified by ordinances that are part of the Mormon "temple endowment."

13. Saving ordinances in this life are not valid unless ratified by the Holy Ghost.

14. Men and women, in this life or in the next, may know that they have passed the test and will be saved in the highest heaven—a concept that is referred to as having one's "calling and election made sure."

15. All saving ordinances or sacraments, beginning with baptism and extending through the temple endowment and marriage sealing, may be

performed vicariously for those who are dead so that they may also be saved and exalted.

16. Men and women are saved by knowledge.

This list, although not exhaustive, is a sampling of knowledge Joseph Smith received through revelation during this period in Church history.

Many of the ideas listed above are only briefly touched upon in the revelations contained in the Doctrine and Covenants during the Nauvoo period. However, this is not an indication that such teachings were not considered important. During the Nauvoo period of Joseph's ministry, he did not formally record his revelations as often as he had during the New York, Pennsylvania, Kirtland, and Missouri periods. This was due in part to the fact that Joseph was no longer giving day-to-day instructions to members of the Church. Responsibility had shifted more and more to the governing quorums of the Church to receive their own revelation and direction from God for their stewardships. During the Nauvoo period, Joseph often communicated with members by speaking to them in large and small assemblies. Therefore, information about his revelations, dreams, and visitations by heavenly beings were disclosed in his public speeches, privately to close friends, or in letters. Bushman concurs: "After the completion of the council system in 1835 [D&C 107], the number of written revelations opening with lines like 'verily thus saith the Lord' diminished. Instead of formal, dictated revelations, the later teachings were delivered in sermons, conversations, or letters."[1]

Sections 130 and 131 illustrate the shift in the way Joseph communicated with his followers during the Nauvoo period. The teachings in section 130 on the nature of the Father and the Son, intelligence, and obedience were redactions from a speech the Prophet gave at Ramus, Illinois, on April 2, 1843. Likewise, the expression in section 131 that marriage is an order of the priesthood was taken from a sermon Joseph gave in Ramus on May 16 and 17, 1843. Sections 127 and 128 on baptism for the dead were epistles written in September 1842. Consequently, Bushman points out, some of the most significant ideas the Prophet taught are "delineated only in ragged, compacted listeners' notes."[2]

---

1. Bushman, *Joseph Smith: Rough Stone Rolling*, 419.

2. See Bushman, *Joseph Smith: Rough Stone Rolling*, 419. Bushman, notes that "Occasionally, he [Joseph] mentioned 'the visions that roll like an overflowing surge before my mind.'" (See Bushman, *Joseph Smith: Rough Stone Rolling*, 419.)

Chapter 40

Nauvoo, Illinois: January 19, 1841–July 12, 1843

SECTION 124: JOSEPH SMITH JR. HOMESTEAD, NAUVOO, ILLINOIS, JANUARY 19, 1841

Heading
The fulness of the priesthood and the temple endowment.

The big question
Question: How shall we be saved?
Answer: By entering into temple covenants.

Introduction
This revelation was given to Joseph Smith the Prophet in his home at Nauvoo, Illinois, January 19, 1841.[1] Joseph is commanded to build both a house "for the entertainment of strangers"—i.e., a boarding house or hotel—and a temple in Nauvoo. Baptisms for the dead and the modern endowment are described. Hyrum Smith and others are called to various positions in the Church.

Anchor section

Memorize: Fulness of the priesthood/temple endowment

---

1. Smith, *History of the Church*, 4:274–86.

Nauvoo, Illinois: January 19, 1841–July 12, 1843

Historical background

There seems to have been a hiatus between the revelations Joseph wrote while he was imprisoned in Liberty Jail (D&C 121–123) and section 124, which was received almost two years later in January 1841.[1] There may be at least two reasons for this interruption. First, this was a period of tremendous upheaval for Joseph and for the Church. The fall of Far West forced the Saints to flee to Quincy, Illinois, and when Joseph finally escaped from Liberty Jail and joined the Saints in Quincy on April 22, 1839, his focus was finding and purchasing land where the main body of the Saints could gather. Second, Joseph turned his attention to redressing the wrongs committed against the Saints while they lived in Missouri. Armed with affidavits and other information about the ill treatment, Joseph and a few of his brethren traveled to Washington, D.C., where they spoke with President Martin Van Buren. Realizing that their pleas fell on deaf ears, Joseph returned to Nauvoo, where his time was spent in planning and building a new city.

The scant number of written revelations during this time period can also be accounted for by the fact that the leadership role of Joseph was changing as the organization of the Church developed. Bushman pointed out that the need for almost daily, formal, written revelations from Joseph to guide the Church diminished as an apparatus of councils or governing quorums was put in place. Revelation for the day-to-day operation of the Church now rested on those appointed to administer Church affairs in various geographical locations. (See D&C 107.) Particularly during the Nauvoo period, information concerning Joseph's revelations was contained in his speeches, in which he spoke about his spiritual impressions, dreams, visions, angelic visitations, and revelations. Perhaps the most well known of this "revelatory" type of speeches is the King Follett discourse, given shortly before Joseph's death in June 1844.

The revelatory letter known as section 124 is best known for its instruction regarding temple ordinances and its concurrent command to build the

---

1. We do know of one revelation given Oliver Granger on May 13, 1839, concerning his assignment to help the First Presidency with some of the financial affairs of the Church. (See D&C 117.) The May 14, 1839, revelation is short and commends Granger. "I will lift up my servant Oliver Granger, and beget him a great name on the earth, and among my people, because of the integrity of his soul." The revelation also instructs the Saints to cooperate with Granger in his Church assignment. "Therefore, let all my saints abound unto him, with all liberality and long suffering, and it shall be a blessing on their heads." (See Collier, *Unpublished Revelations of the Prophets and Presidents of The Church of Jesus Christ of Latter-day Saints*, 1:90.

Nauvoo Temple, where the Saints could participate in these ordinances. In addition, it includes seemingly mundane instructions on raising money for a reception center and on other Church appointments. Most importantly, however, section 124 is the only place in scripture where the contemporary temple endowment is publicly discussed in any detail.

The first endowments were performed on May 4, 1842, about a year and a half after section 124 was received and before the completion of the Nauvoo Temple. The Prophet initiated nine men into the ritual in the upper room of the red brick store in Nauvoo, a ritual patterned after what he called an "ancient order." The first persons to receive this rite, later referred to as the endowment, met regularly and were known as the Quorum of the Anointed. By June 1844 the Prophet had selected twenty-five additional men and thirty-two women to become part of this select group.

On December 10, 1845, endowment work started on a broader scale in the attic story of the Nauvoo Temple. During the next eight weeks, nearly 5,600 members (males and females) participated in these ceremonies. The Saints took upon themselves solemn covenants to live a life patterned after the Savior and entered into an expanded marriage covenant lasting not only for time but also for eternity.[1]

Nauvoo Temple

The Nauvoo Temple faced west on a bluff that looks out over the Mississippi River. It was made of grayish-white limestone mined in a local quarry, its tower standing 158 feet above the ground.[2] The exterior of the building was faced with symbols, sunstones, star stones, and moonstones, reminding the Saints of the afterlife and the three degrees of glory depicted in section 76.[3] William Weeks was the architect of the building, but the design was guided by Joseph, who had seen what it should look like in vision prior to its construction.[4]

The inside of the building as well as the exterior were patterned after the Kirtland Temple. The most significant departure was a basement-level area with a white limestone laver or font, used for baptisms for the dead, resting on the backs of twelve life-sized statues of oxen. Like its Kirtland counterpart, the first and second floors of the temple consisted of meeting

---

1. Some also received their second endowments. (See commentary on section 132.) Also during this period at least 15,626 proxy baptisms were performed in Nauvoo, either in the baptistery of the temple or in rivers or streams.

2. Some British converts contributed a bell weighing over 1,500 pounds which is now featured on Temple Square in Salt Lake City, Utah.

3. See also Paul's vision in 1 Corinthians 15:41.

4. See Smith, *History of the Church*, 6:196–97; see also *Encyclopedia of Mormonism*, 3:1001.

rooms with elaborate pulpit areas, each graded into four tiers of seats. The Aaronic Priesthood pulpits were at one end of the hall and the Melchizedek Priesthood pulpits at the other. The seats used by the congregation could be reversed, allowing the congregation to face either direction, depending on the purpose of the meeting.[1]

The half-story on the west end was used for the endowment. The main attic under the pitched roof was plastered, painted, and carpeted,[2] and used for marriages and sealings. Regular Sunday services and some general conferences of the Church were held in the meeting rooms on the first and second floors.[3]

When the Saints were forced out of Nauvoo due to mob violence in early February 1846, a special crew stayed behind to complete the temple. This was a serious undertaking—the Lord had made it clear that if the Saints were to continue to receive the blessing of heaven, completion of the temple was not optional. He warned that if the building was not finished "ye shall be rejected as a church." (Verses 31–32.) So for three months after many of the Saints had started west, a band worked diligently to finish the building. Finally, beginning on May 1, 1846, the building was dedicated over a three-day period. Thousands witnessed the event; visitors paid one dollar to be admitted. The money was used to help the workmen who had stayed behind move west.[4]

By September 1846 the temple was completely abandoned—and mobs desecrated it. In October 1848 the temple was consumed by a deliberate arson fire. Only the bare walls were left standing. A few years later it was struck by a tornado, which knocked down some of the walls and damaged others so severely that the building was razed. Some of the stone was reused in other buildings nearby.[5]

Nauvoo House

Section 124 also commanded the people to build the Nauvoo House, a reception center and hotel that would be "a delightful habitation for man, and a resting-place for the weary traveler." (Verses 60; see also verse 23.) Joseph owned the land and donated it for this purpose. A committee was formed to raise money for its construction by selling stock in the enterprise. The building was to be made out of brick and stand three stories high. Construction began in the spring of 1841 and continued until 1845, but it

---

1. See *Encyclopedia of Mormonism*, 3:1001–2.
2. See *Encyclopedia of Mormonism*, 3:1002.
3. See *Encyclopedia of Mormonism*, 3:1002.
4. See *Encyclopedia of Mormonism*, 3:1002.
5. See *Encyclopedia of Mormonism*, 3:1002–3.

was discontinued when it became necessary for all of the Saints' resources to be used to complete the Nauvoo Temple.[1]

What remained of the structure was eventually torn down so that Emma Smith's second husband, Lewis C. Bidamon, could use the bricks to complete a smaller hotel known as the Bidamon House and the Riverside Mansion. Emma and Lewis lived there from 1871 until they died.[2]

The Endowment

"The word 'to endow' (from the Greek *enduein*), as used in the New Testament, means to dress, clothe, put on garments, put on attributes, or receive virtue."[3] The modern Mormon endowment fits squarely within this tradition and is a continuation of or an "unfolding or culmination of the covenants made at baptism."[4] Its connection to early Christianity will be considered under the heading "Early Christian versions of the endowment," below. The temple endowment is a process of drawing oneself into close proximity with God. It enables men and women to receive or to be "endued with power from on high." (Luke 24:49; D&C 95:8–9.)

The endowment procedure includes four aspects that are described by Alma P. Burton, in *The Encyclopedia of Mormonism*.

> First is the preparatory ordinance, a ceremonial washing and anointing, after which the temple patron dons the sacred clothing of the temple.
>
> Second is a course of instruction by lectures and representations. These include a recital of the most prominent events of the Creation, a figurative depiction of the advent of Adam and Eve and of every man and every woman, the entry of Adam and Eve into the Garden of Eden, the consequent expulsion from the garden, their condition in the world, and their receiving of the plan of salvation leading to the return to the presence of God. The endowment instructions utilize every human faculty so that the meaning of the gospel may be clarified through art, drama, and symbols. All participants wear white temple robes symbolizing purity and the equality of all persons before God the Father and his Son Jesus Christ. . . .
>
> Third is making covenants. The temple endowment is seen as the unfolding or culmination of the covenants made at baptism. . . . They include the "covenant and promise to observe the law of strict virtue and chastity, to be charitable, benevolent, tolerant and pure; to devote both talent and material means to the spread of truth and the uplifting of the [human] race; to maintain devotion to the cause of truth; and to seek in every way to contribute to

---

1. See *Encyclopedia of Mormonism*, 3:997.
2. See *Encyclopedia of Mormonism*, 3:997.
3. *Encyclopedia of Mormonism*, 2:454.
4. *Encyclopedia of Mormonism*, 2:455.

the great preparation that the earth may be made ready to receive ... Jesus Christ. . . ."

Fourth is a sense of divine presence. In the dedicatory prayer of the temple at Kirtland, Ohio, the Prophet Joseph Smith pleaded "that all people who shall enter upon the threshold of the Lord's house may feel thy power, and feel constrained to acknowledge that thou hast sanctified it, and that it is thy house, a place of thy holiness" (D&C 109:13). . . . Through the temple endowment, one may seek "a fullness of the Holy Ghost" (D&C 109:15).[1]

Throughout the temple ceremonies, the participants are reminded expressly and symbolically of the atonement and the central place of Jesus Christ in God's plan. The promise to those who participate in the endowment is that "my name shall be here; and I will manifest myself to my people in mercy in this holy house."[2] (See D&C 110:7.)

In Nauvoo Joseph taught that the endowment was not only for the living but also a means by which the dead may qualify to come into the presence of God. Thus, Latter-day Saints return to the temple often to participate in the endowment ceremony as proxies on behalf of deceased persons. Alma P. Burton pointed out that, "consistent with the law of agency, it is believed that those so served have complete freedom in the spirit world to accept or reject the spiritual blessings thus proffered them."[3]

---

1. Encyclopedia of Mormonism, 2:455.

2. *Encyclopedia of Mormonism*, 2:455. Just as in ancient Israel, since God dwells in the temple, those worthy to do so may see the face of God in these holy precincts. A grandchild of President Snow reported that "one evening when I was visiting Grandpa Snow in his room in the Salt Lake Temple, I remained until the doorkeepers had gone and the night watchman had not yet come in, so grandpa said he would take me to the main, front entrance and let me out that way. He got his bunch of keys from his dresser. After we left his room and while we were still in the large corridor, leading into the celestial room, I was walking several steps ahead of grandpa when he stopped me, saying: 'Wait a moment, Allie. I want to tell you something. It was right here that the Lord Jesus Christ appeared to me at the time of the death of President Woodruff. He instructed me to go right ahead and reorganize the First Presidency of the Church at once and not wait as had been done after the death of the previous presidents, and that I was to succeed President Woodruff.' Then Grandpa came to a step nearer and held out his left hand and said: 'He stood right here, about three feet above the floor. It looked as though he stood on a plate of solid gold. Grandpa told me what a glorious personage the Savior is and described His hands, feet, countenance and beautiful white robes, all of which were of such a glory of whiteness and brightness that he could hardly gaze upon Him. Then Grandpa came another step nearer me and put his right hand on my head and said: 'Now, granddaughter, I want you to remember that this is the testimony of your grandfather, that he told you with his own lips that he actually saw the Savior here in the Temple and talked with Him face to face.' Then we went on and Grandpa let me out of the main front door of the Temple." (Snow, "Remarkable Manifestation to Lorenzo Snow," 3, 6. See also Lundwall, *Temples of the Most High*, 139–41. Such blessings are not limited to the President of the Church. See D&C 93:1.)

3. *Encyclopedia of Mormonism*, 2:455.

The relationship of Masonry to the endowment

One of the more provocative aspects of Mormon temple sacraments is the relationship between the endowment and the rituals of Freemasonry, a secret society for men that declares itself to be based on "brotherly love, faith, and charity." Masons participate in ceremonies, some of which are extended allegories based on Old Testament themes and anecdotes. The rituals are highly symbolic and demand a vow of secrecy and a belief in God, who is referred to as "the great architect of the universe." At the time of the beginnings of Mormon temple worship, Masonic lodges were fairly common in rural America. Lodges in the United States during the nineteenth century generally traced their beginnings to the English Grand Lodge, established in 1717, although recent scholarship tentatively fixes the development of the societies to medieval stonemasons' guilds.[1]

Joseph and other members of the Quorum of the Anointed were Masons.[2] Joseph's brother Hyrum had been a Mason since the days when the Smith family had lived in New York. Joseph became a Mason in the spring of 1842. The number of Masons in Nauvoo was larger than those in all the rest of Illinois combined. The Nauvoo Lodge had burgeoned as Mormon males enthusiastically joined. No doubt the brethren's experience with Masonry influenced the presentation of the endowment ceremony. Those familiar with both recognize certain similarities. But it is also apparent that the covenants and the theological context of the endowment are very different from Masonry.[3] Thus, any similarities between the Mormon temple endowment and Masonry cannot be explained as wholesale borrowing from Masonry; neither can it be explained as completely unrelated to Masonry.[4]

Most Latter-day Saints believe that the similarities between the two ceremonies stem from common ancient origins dating back to Solomon's temple.[5] The idea that the Mormon endowment is of ancient origin is supported by current and ongoing scholarship. It is now widely recog-

---

1. See *Webster's Universal Encyclopedia*, 377.

2. See Buerger, "The Development of the Mormon Temple Endowment Ceremony," 43–46.

3. According to Joseph, any similarities between the Mormon temple endowment and Masonry are based on his belief that the Masonic ceremony was an aberrant version of the ancient priesthood rites performed in Solomon's temple. While parts of the two rituals are very similar, other parts, such as the emphasis on the Garden story, the fall, the content of the covenants, and washings and anointings, have no parallel in Masonry.

4. See Buerger, "The Development of the Mormon Temple Ceremony," 45. See also Duncan, *Duncan's Masonic Ritual and Monitor*, and Hannah, *Darkness Visible*, where the Masonic ritual and some of its many variations are described.

5. Another legitimate position on the relationship of Mormonism and Masonry is a variation on the first. It can be argued that the Mormon endowment may have been influenced by Masonry. Certainly some of the mechanics of the ceremony, the methods chosen to convey the unique ideas encountered in the temple, are similar to Masonry. However, this is where

nized that parts of the endowment ceremony seem closely aligned with concepts expressed in the Nag Hammadi Qumran, pseudepigraphic literature (books bridging the gap between the Old and New Testament), the Dead Sea Scrolls, gnostic writings, and the Forty-Day Documents (books describing the acts and teachings of the resurrected Christ during his forty-day visit to his followers after his death). In these writings are found references to purification rites,[1] Gods,[2] creations of order out of matter in chaos,[3] premortal existence of spirits or souls,[4] stories about Adam and Eve,[5] altars, prayer circles for healing[6] and an emphasis on the forces of good and evil, represented by light and darkness.[7] Additionally, ancient texts such as the Dead Sea Scrolls, the Nag Hammadi codices, the pseudepigrapha, and Rabbinic and early Christian literature speak of ideas

---

the likeness ends. The Mormon covenants, their emphasis on the creation, multiple Gods, and premortal existence do not have their counterparts in Masonry. The theological context of the Endowment is most conspicuously Mormon, except to the extent that the two rituals share an emphasis on the importance of ethical conduct. Those who take this approach point out that Joseph's brother Hyrum and a number of other prominent Mormons were long-time Masons and thus were familiar with the Masons' ceremonies.

1. Nibley, *The Message of the Joseph Smith Papyri*, 273–75. Compare, for example, ritual purification ceremonies set out in the "Pistis Sophia," an early Coptic work from Thebes in upper Egypt, which is dated in about the third century. The opening paragraphs identify the sayings as statements of Jesus made to his disciples "after he had risen from the dead." On page 279 of the same work, Nibley reproduces some of the text of what is known as "Cyril of Jerusalem's Lectures on the Ordinances," written in Jerusalem and dated about A.D. 347, as follows: "Upon emerging from the tank of holy running water, you were given an anointing the antitype of which was the anointing of Christ. . . . He was anointed with . . . what is called the olive oil of exaltation . . . while you were anointed with myrrh, making you companions and co-partners with Christ. You were anointed on your brow and your other sense-organs, and so while the body is anointed in outward appearance with myrrh, the soul is sanctified by the life-bestowing Holy Spirit. First of all you were anointed on the brow, forehead and eyes to free you from the shame which completely involved the First Man when he fell, and that you might clearly perceive the glory of the Lord with wide-open mind. Then your ears that you might receive the hearing ears of the mysteries of God. . . . Next come the nostrils, that upon receiving the holy ordinance you may say: 'We are the sweet odor of Christ to God among the saved.'"

2. See, for example, Gaster, *The Dead Sea Scriptures*, 174, 418.

3. See, for example, Madsen, *Nibley on the Timely and the Timeless*, 49–84.

4. See, for example, Winston, "Pre-existence in Hellenic, Judaic and Mormon Sources," 13–36; see also Gaster, *The Dead Sea Scriptures*, 144; McConkie, "Premortal Existence, Foreordination, and Heavenly Councils," *Apocryphal Writings and the Latter-day-Saints*, 173–98; Nibley, *The Message of the Joseph Smith Papyri*, 170, 260 (Dead Sea Scrolls–Serek or Manual of Discipline), 264 (Odes of Solomon), 267–68 (The Pearl), 276 (Pistis Sophia); Nibley, "The Expanding Gospel," 7, no. 1.

5. See, for example, Charlesworth, *The Old Testament Pseudepigrapha*, 1:707–20 (Apocalypse of Adam), 989–95 (The Testament of Adam). See also Charlesworth, *The Old Testament Pseudepigrapha*, 2:249–95 (Life of Adam and Eve).

6. See, for example, Nibley, *Mormonism and Early Christianity*, 45–99.

7. See, for example, Wilson, *The Gospel of Philip*; Robinson, *The Nag Hammadi Library*, 399–403 (Melchizedek).

familiar to temple-attending Latter-day Saints, such as sacred garments,[1] passwords that enable one to pass by the angels who guard the gate of God's domain,[2] and ideas about multiple heavens that differ in glory.[3] Most interesting to Mormons is the emphasis on rituals in addition to baptism that are considered essential for a person to return to the presence of God and the idea that the living can perform such ordinances on behalf of the dead. The Apocryphon of John, for example, speaks of those not receiving ordinances in this life receiving them beyond the grave.[4]

The early Christians and temple worship

An early Christian connection to temple rituals has been written about extensively by Margaret Barker.[5] In her writings she asserts that Jesus restored an ancient temple tradition practiced by Melchizedek and Abraham that existed in a corrupted form at the time of Jesus. Evidence that some of the early Christians had a temple ritual that was different from the temple tradition practiced by the Jews in Jesus' day can be found in *Cyril of Jerusalem's Lectures on the Ordinances*,[6] written in about 386 A.D. Cyril was a bishop in Jerusalem who gave instructions to early Christian initiates on the "mysteries," a term that biblical scholar Morton Smith points out was often used by the first Christians to refer to an ordinance.[7] Such "mysteries" were considered secret, and participants were limited to an inner circle in the early Church.

Cyril's so-called "mysteries" are of considerable interest to Latter-day Saints who participate in the modern-day temple ritual briefly described in section 124. Of particular interest are the purification rites, prayer circles, concern for saving the dead, symbolic gestures, and a liturgy that connects early Christians to their first parents, Adam and Eve, who established a pattern that was intended to save all of their descendants.

---

1. See, for example, Nibley, *The Message of the Joseph Smith Papyri*, 268–71 (The Pearl), 284 (Gospel of Philip), 247, 278, 280 (Cyril of Jerusalem's Lectures on the Ordinances); see also Ostler, "Clothed Upon: A Unique Aspect of Christian Antiquity," n.p.; Nibley, "Sacred Vestments," n.p.

2. Nibley, *The Message of the Joseph Smith Papyri*, 275. See also Ostler, "Clothed Upon: A Unique Aspect of Christian Antiquity," n.p.; Nibley, "Teachings from the Dead Sea Scrolls," n.p.

3. See, for example, Charlesworth, *The Old Testament Pseudepigrapha*, 2:266 (footnote 25a), 164–70 (Martyrdom and Ascension of Isaiah).

4. Ostler, "Clothed Upon: A Unique Aspect of Christian Antiquity," 32.

5. See, for example, Barker, *Temple Theology*; Barker, *An Introduction*, and *The Gate of Heaven: The History and Symbolism of the Temple in Jerusalem*.

6. See the appendix in Nibley, *The Message of the Joseph Smith Papyri* (first edition). Cyril became one of the bishops of the early church.

7. Smith, *The Secret Gospel*.

Cyril explains that, upon entering into a holy place, initiates should remove their street clothes, be washed and anointed, and put on sacred clothing.

> You were anointed on your brow and your other sense organs. . . . First of all you were anointed on the brow to free you from the shame which completely involved the First Man when he fell, and that you might clearly perceive. . . . Then your ears that you might receive the hearing ears of the mysteries of God. Next come the nostrils. . . . After that on the breast. . . . It is because you are worthy of this holy anointing that you are called Christians . . . after washing him with water he anointed him.
> You now celebrate as you put on the garment of the Lord Jesus Christ.[1]

The initiate was then told about the creation, the Garden of Eden, and how a person may find his way back to God. That path involves imitating the first parents, Adam and Eve. Proxy work for the dead is mentioned. A prayer circle is described, in which the initiates form a circle and repeat back in unison a prayer that includes a petition for the healing of the sick. An "exchange of signs" is called for.[2] The ceremony ends with an admonition to "keep these traditions inviolate, and see that you do not stumble."[3]

The temple and the "fulness of priesthood"

Section 124 connects the Mormon temple endowment to the priesthood, explaining that the authority given up to this time (1841) to perform ordinances and to administer the organization of the Church was only a part of what the concept of priesthood entailed. There was more—"even the fulness of the priesthood," which embodied the temple endowment. (See verse 28.) This must have come as somewhat of a surprise to the Saints at that time. Five years earlier, in section 107, the Lord had set out in detail the priesthood organization of the Church, and put the fundamentals of Church government in place: the First Presidency, the Quorum of the Twelve, the Quorum of Seventy, stake presidencies, high councils, bishoprics, high priests quorums, elders quorums, priests quorums, teachers quorums, and deacons quorums. The idea that the priesthood was more than a way to administer a church organization was certainly a new concept for Joseph's followers.

To more fully grasp the evolving understanding of priesthood in the early Church, it is important to realize that the concept expanded as the

---

1. See the appendix in Nibley, The Message of the Joseph Smith Papyri (first edition), 280.
2. See the appendix in Nibley, *The Message of the Joseph Smith Papyri*, (first edition), 282.
3. See the appendix in Nibley, *The Message of the Joseph Smith Papyri* (first edition), 283.

Church matured. Bushman points out that when the Church was first organized in 1830, the idea of priesthood was not comprehensively defined but rather "would grow into one of the defining principles of Mormonism."[1] At first, the focus was on individual offices, quite apart from priesthood itself. It was not until the first high priests were ordained in June 1831 on the Morley farm that it was suggested that priesthood was not only the authority to officiate in an office but also a way of accessing spiritual power as well. This development was later canonized in section 84, which explained that priesthood is not only the "authority" to officiate but also the authority to perform certain ordinances that unlock "the power of godliness." (See D&C 84:20–21.)[2] The exercise of these added priesthood powers made it possible for men and women to come into the presence of God. (See D&C 84:21–22.)

By 1841, what Joseph was hinting at in the summer of 1831 and spring of 1832, when section 84 was given, had come into full view. What was referred to as the "ordinances" through which "the power of godliness is manifest" was now a set of rituals and ordinances defined as the "fulness of priesthood," or the endowment, as introduced in section 124. It was by participating in this priesthood ritual that men and women would receive the instruction and tools necessary to ultimately come into the presence of God.[3]

Speaking about this subject, Joseph Smith explained: "If a man gets a fulness of the priesthood of God, he has to get it in the same way that Jesus Christ obtained it, and that was by keeping all the commandments and obeying all the ordinances of the house of the Lord."[4] Joseph Fielding Smith interpreted this to mean that it makes no difference what office you hold in this Church (apostle or otherwise) "you cannot receive the fulness of the Priesthood unless you go into the temple of the Lord and receive these ordinances of which the Prophet speaks."[5] Brigham Young understood the relationship between the priesthood and the temple ordinances when he said, "When we give the brethren their endowments, we ... confer upon them the Melchizedek Priesthood; but I expect to see

---

1. Bushman, *Joseph Smith: Rough Stone Rolling*, 159.
2. Bushman, *Joseph Smith: Rough Stone Rolling*, 159.
3. As section 84 explained, offices were "appendages" to the priesthood, a means of governing the Church. (See D&C 84:29–30.) Therefore, priesthood office was necessary but part of the periphery. At the center was the "fulness of the priesthood" or temple ritual, which endowed men and women with spiritual power.
4. Smith, *Teachings of the Prophet Joseph Smith*, 308.
5. Doctrine and Covenants Student Manual, 306–7. The term "fulness of priesthood" can have more than one meaning, depending on context. Sometimes it refers to the second endowment, calling and election, or the godhood. (See Ehat and Cook, *The Words of Joseph Smith*, 303–4.)

the day, when we shall . . . say to a company of brethren, you can go and receive the [endowment] ordinances pertaining to the Aaronic order of Priesthood. . . . Now we pass them through the [temple] ordinances of both Priesthoods in one day."[1]

With this view in mind, the "keys of the priesthood" in the context of temple worship do not refer to the authority to perform certain tasks and rituals. Rather, they comprise the rituals themselves. As Joseph Smith explained, the "keys of the holy priesthood" are the signs and tokens exchanged in the endowment. (See verse 34.)[2] He said: "I spent the day in the upper part of the store, that is in my private office [with my brethren] . . . in council. . . . [I instructed] them in the principles and order of the Priesthood, attending to washings, anointings, endowments and the communication of keys [signs and tokens] pertaining to the Aaronic Priesthood . . . to the highest order pertaining to the Ancient of Days, [so that the Saints might] come up and abide in the presence of the Eloheim in the eternal worlds."[3]

Although there is no question that the first generation of Mormons reflected the chauvinistic attitudes of the general culture, the temple endowment sends a different message. Both men and women are clothed in the robes of the priesthood, take upon themselves the same covenants, have a symbolic interview with God himself, and are welcomed into the celestial realms, all on the same basis. Furthermore, both men and women perform priesthood ordinances in the temple. In all respects, in the temple women are given the very same "fulness of the priesthood." By nineteenth-century standards this is remarkable. The import of it was not lost on Bathsheba W. Smith, a member of the Quorum of the Anointed and the fourth general president of the Relief Society. "I have always been pleased that I had my endowments when the Prophet lived. He taught us the true order of prayer. I never like to hear a sermon without hearing something of the Prophet, for he gave us everything, every order of the priesthood."[4] She went on to say that Joseph "said he had given the sisters instructions

---

1. Ehat and Cook, *The Words of Joseph Smith*, 303–4; *Journal of Discourses*, 10:309.
2. Smith, *Teachings of the Prophet Joseph Smith*, 119, 237, 363.
3. Smith, *History of the Church*, 5:1–2; Smith, *Teachings of the Prophet Joseph Smith*, 237.
4. Quinn, "Mormon Women Have Had the Priesthood Since 1843." On September 28, the demographics of the Quorum of the Anointed began to change. For the first time, women were initiated as regular members, beginning with Emma, who received her endowment on or just before that date. The previous year, Joseph had organized the all-female Relief Society. At that time he said that he would "make of this Society a kingdom of priests as in Enoch's day." (See Nauvoo Female Relief Society, Minutes, March 17, 1842, quoted in Buerger, *Mysteries of Godliness*, 51.)

that they . . . [would be as the] women were in Paul's day, 'A kingdom of priestesses.'"[1] (See Exodus 19:6.)

In summary, priesthood in the context of Church office is received by the laying on of hands. Priesthood in the context of the temple is received when the initiate is "ordained by the ordinance of my holy house." (Verse 39.) Unquestionably, section 124 opens our minds to an entirely different way of understanding and talking about priesthood.[2]

In late October 2015 the Church published on its official website (LDS.org) an essay called "Joseph Smith's Teachings about Priesthood, Temple, and Women." In it the restoration of the fulness of the priesthood is explained. The essay points out that priesthood restoration was accomplished in connection with the establishment of the Relief Society so that "men and women could receive and administer sacred priesthood ordinances in holy temples." In this way, women were to be organized "in the Order of the Priesthood." The essay goes on to explain that "Joseph spoke of 'ordain[ing]' women and said that Relief Society officers would 'preside over the Society.' He also declared, 'I now turn the key to you in the name of God.' These statements indicate that *Joseph Smith delegated priesthood authority to women* in the Relief Society" (emphasis added).

Therefore, Joseph Smith organized the Relief Society as part of the priesthood and "structure of the Church." The Relief Society was never meant to be an auxiliary organization. The essay explains that this aspect of the fulness of the priesthood and of women's use of priesthood in the temple "remains largely unrecognized by people outside the Church and is sometimes misunderstood or overlooked by those within. Latter-day Saints and others often mistakenly equate priesthood with religious office and the men who hold it, which obscures the broader Latter-day Saint concept of priesthood." Unlike the Catholic and Protestant traditions, priesthood in the Mormon faith never has been limited to one gender but is a shared prerogative and responsibility.

---

1. Quinn, "Mormon Women Have Had the Priesthood Since 1843," n.p.
2. Section 124 also provides a key to more fully understanding Alma 13, where Alma talks about "being called . . . and ordained unto the high priesthood of the holy order of God." In describing how a person enters this "holy order," Alma uses the same kind of language that we find in D&C 124:39: ". . . ordained with a holy ordinance, and taking upon them the high priesthood of the holy order, which calling, and ordinance, and high priesthood, is without beginning or end." Further reference is made to Melchizedek, "who was also a high priest after this same order." The order is described: " . . . these ordinances were given after this manner, that thereby the people might look forward on the Son of God, it being a type of his order, or it being his order, and this that they might look forward to him for a remission of their sins." (Alma 13:6, 8, 14, 16.)

The endowment as it is defined in Doctrine and Covenants 124

Defined broadly in section 124, the endowment included the practice of baptisms for the dead, washings, anointings, solemn assemblies, "memorials for your sacrifices by the sons of Levi," "oracles in your most holy places wherein you receive conversations, and your statutes and judgments." (Verse 39.) The "sacrifices by the sons of Levi" refer to the last blood sacrifice that will be performed in the temple to be built in Independence, Missouri, as part of the restitution of all things. (See D&C 13:1; 84:31.)[1] "Oracles in your most holy places" is probably a reference to conversations at the veil. (See verse 39.) The term "statutes and judgments" in this context is a reference to the laws of the gospel as expressed in the binding covenants entered into by qualified members of the Church in the temple. (See verse 39.)

The Abrahamic Covenant and the temple

Latter-day Saints teach that Abraham was baptized, had conferred upon him the Holy Ghost and Melchizedek Priesthood, entered into celestial marriage, participated in an ancient endowment ceremony, was given certain promises by God, and received an assurance that all of these blessings would be offered his posterity and others by adoption or covenant. (See Abraham 2:6–11; D&C 132:29–50.) These promises are referred to as the Abrahamic covenant, named after Abraham because of his exceptional faith. The idea that people are saved by covenanting like Abraham is not unique to Mormonism but was taught by Paul as well, "Through the work of Christ Jesus, God has blessed the Gentiles with the same blessings he promised to Abraham." (NLT Galatians 3:14).[2]

Modern-day Saints enter into the Abrahamic covenant in the temple. In rooms set aside for this purpose, they renew their baptismal covenant of obedience, promise to sacrifice for the gospel's sake, live the principles of the gospel as they are taught in the canon, love their fellow men and women, share their material wealth, and marry for time and eternity. In return, the Saints are promised that they will receive the blessings of Abraham. The Abrahamic covenant and blessings are discussed in more detail in the commentary to section 132.

---

1. Smith, *Teachings of the Prophet Joseph Smith*, 171–73.
2. Mormons believe that Abraham received the Melchizedek Priesthood and temple endowment under the hands of Melchizedek. (See Genesis 14:17–24 and JST Genesis 14:25–40.)

Prayer and the temple

Prayer is an important part of temple worship and is referred to in section 124. Hyrum Smith is told that he will be shown the "keys whereby he may ask and receive," a reference to the manner in which prayers are offered in temples. (See verses 95, 97.) In the 1879 edition of the Doctrine and Covenants, Orson Pratt indicates in the heading to section 124 that these keys were "the order of God for receiving revelations."

Ritualization of ideas and doctrines revealed to Joseph Smith

A ritual is a set of repeated actions within a group or a culture that bind the members together and strengthen social bonds. It is a way of signifying one's affiliation and of obtaining social acceptance and approval. The temple ritual serves all of these ends and is in addition a way of preserving and transmitting from one generation to the next the core values and ideas agreed upon by a particular society or religion. The temple ceremony preserves and transmits the fundamental values and doctrines taught by the Prophet Joseph during his lifetime, and especially those that were developed during the Nauvoo period.

Many of the key concepts and revelations that distinguish Mormonism as a religion were received by Joseph during the later part of his life and are personified in the temple liturgy and practices. For example, the temple speaks of the preeminence of eternal law, the negation of a belief in an *ex nihilo* creation in favor of the idea that matter is eternal (the earth was not created by God out of nothing but rather by organizing matter), the idea of an anthropomorphic God who is married, eternal procreation by God, and the belief that men and women may become gods and goddesses—deification. The temple also epitomizes the long-sought-after Zion-like community, a place where there is social and economic equality. All wear the same clothing and during the endowment are not separated according to rank and station. In fact, the ideal of living in a Zion community is part of a specific covenant made in the temple about consecrating one's time and material wealth. Hence, the temple is a place where Mormons learn about Mormon ideas and doctrines and envision the purpose of life and death from a Mormon perspective.[1]

Finally, ritualizing Mormon theology as part of the temple endowment connects modern Mormons with their founding fathers and freezes Mormonism in a particular setting or time almost like a snapshot. This is

---

1. The concept of Zion as a community of equals is also depicted in the temple. All participants dress in the same clothing, without any indication of rank or station, indicating that "all are alike unto God." (2 Nephi 26:33.)

true because the temple ceremony is considered important and sacred, and therefore it is not changed without much thought, prayer, revelation, and consensus among the highest leaders in the Church. It makes it more difficult for Mormonism to stray from its central tenets as each generation passes and as each generation is influenced by their own culture and way of looking at things. It helps keep the faith centered on its fundamental doctrines when the Church was first organized. It is a way of assuring that over time the essential understanding of Mormonism will not gradually and imperceptibly change, thus altering the fundamental intent and original understanding.

Proclamation to the kings of the earth

Section 124 commands that a proclamation be written and sent to the kings of the earth, the president-elect, and the governors of the United States. (See verses 2–16, 107.) In the revelation certain brethren were commissioned to assist in the preparation of the proclamation. However, the command was not fulfilled in Joseph's lifetime because other pressures took precedence. In 1863, William W. Phelps reported that he had been asked in May 1844 to write the "great Proclamation" under Joseph's direction, lamenting that after the martyrdom the project was temporally dropped until, in 1845, the Quorum of the Twelve fulfilled the command by publishing their proclamation to the rulers of the nations.[1]

The reorganization of priesthood quorums

Apostasy, death of Church leaders, and other situations called for the reorganization of various quorums. Church patriarch Joseph Smith Sr. died and left a vacancy in his office. Hyrum Smith was designated to take his father's place. (See verse 124.) The Lord told Hyrum that he would also receive the "same blessing, and glory, and honor, and priesthood" that Oliver Cowdery had held before his excommunication in 1838. Thus he became assistant president of the Church to support his brother in the work. (See verse 95.) Brigham Young was appointed president of the Quorum of the Twelve, and the Twelve was reorganized, along with the Nauvoo high council and the Nauvoo stake presidency, with William Marks as its president.

---

1. See Cook, *Revelations of the Prophet Joseph Smith*, 243.

God revokes the command to build the temple at Independence

Section 124 teaches that God may revoke his commands—a notion that is not new to the canon of scripture. When Moses went up on the mount the first time, he received the higher law. When he returned to the people, the Israelites had "hardened their hearts" (D&C 84:24), so the Lord gave them a lesser law instead. He eventually "took Moses out of their midst, and the Holy Priesthood also" (D&C 84:25) and only the lesser law and the "lesser priesthood continued" (D&C 84:26). When Jesus reintroduced the higher law, he discontinued, for example, the Levitical prohibitions against various foods, such as pork, shellfish, and so forth. (See Leviticus 11; Mark 7:1–23.) Other examples include the suspension of the law against murder when Nephi was commanded to kill Laban and the intermittent approval of the practice of polygamy.

The more difficult consideration is not that God, from time to time, revokes what he has commanded, but rather why? This requires a more subtle analysis and depends upon the historical context. Sometimes God is displeased because of the weaknesses displayed by his children: "Were it not for the transgressions of my people, . . . they might have been redeemed even now." (D&C 105:2.) "But behold, they have not learned to be obedient." (D&C 105:3.) "And Zion cannot be built up unless it is by the principles of the law of the celestial kingdom; otherwise I cannot receive her unto myself." (D&C 105:5.) But, in section 124, the revocation of the command to build the temple in Far West does not seem to fit in this category. The historical context shows that sometimes, when God's people have done all they can but are unable to obey, God revokes his command because circumstances have made their obedience impossible:

"Verily, verily, I say unto you, that when I give a commandment to any of the sons of men to do a work unto my name, and those sons of men go with all their might and with all they have to perform that work, and cease not their diligence, and their enemies come upon them and hinder them from performing that work, behold, it behooveth me to require the work no more at [their] hands."

In such circumstances God will "accept of their offerings."[1] (D&C 124:49.)

---

1. It should be noted that in light of section 124, Nephi's observation that "I know that the Lord giveth no commandments unto the children of men, save he shall prepare a way for them that they may accomplish the thing which he commandeth them" (1 Nephi 3:7) does not always apply. Clearly some commandments are revoked before they are accomplished. For example, it is certainly the expectation that prior to the Second Coming God's people will found Zion in Jackson County, Missouri, a command presently on hold.

Temple recommends

Today a member of the Church may not enter a temple without a recommend signed by a member of his local bishopric and stake presidency. Members are asked questions individually to ascertain their basic faith in the Godhead and the restored gospel. Worthiness requirements include being honest, refraining from sexual relations outside of marriage, paying a full tithe, obedience to the Word of Wisdom (D&C 89), fulfilling family obligations, and avoiding affiliation with apostate or anti-Mormon groups.

Worthiness as a prerequisite for temple admission grows out of an acknowledgment that temples are holy sanctuaries where only the pure in heart and those seeking after righteousness should be admitted. The policy is of ancient origins and was in place in Jesus' time for those who wished to enter certain sacred precincts of Herod's temple. In the Old Testament Ezekiel says, "Thus saith the Lord GOD; No stranger, uncircumcised in heart, nor uncircumcised in flesh, shall enter into my sanctuary." (Ezekiel 44:9.) In the dedicatory prayer for the Kirtland Temple the Prophet Joseph prayed that the temple "may be sanctified and consecrated to be holy, and that thy holy presence may be continually in this house; . . . and that no unclean thing shall be permitted to come into thy house to pollute it." (D&C 109:12, 20.)[1]

The temple recommends that are so familiar to members of the Church today were not always required to enter a Mormon temple. During the Nauvoo period the Saints simply had to be invited by Church leaders to enter and receive their endowments. Once they were settled in the Great Basin, local leaders relied on broad categories of worthiness and recommended members to the Church president, who issued approval.

Letters of recommendation from the local leaders had to be counter-signed by the Church president until 1891—that year Wilford Woodruff signed over 3,000 such letters. Thereafter, authority to determine who should or should not enter temples was delegated to bishops and stake presidents. The first standard set of questions was issued about 1922 and asked about matters of belief in God and Jesus Christ, whether Mormonism was the restoration of pure Christianity, loyalty to Church leaders, and a willingness to live gospel principles.[2]

"Payment of tithing was always important for a temple recommend, but adherence to the faith's prohibition against coffee, tea, alcohol and tobacco varied in strictness."[3] The 1940 and 1944 temple recommend questions called for a "willingness to undertake" to observe the Word of

---

1. See *Encyclopedia of Mormonism*, 4:1446.
2. See Kimball, *Journal of Mormon History*, Spring 1998.
3. Stack, "New Era Dawns for LDS Temple Recommends."

Wisdom. The 1968 version specified that keeping the Word of Wisdom meant abstaining from "alcoholic beverages" rather than "liquor" to "make sure that even light beer and wine were included."[1] Cola drinks have never been included.

For the past twenty years a question about supporting or affiliating with "opposition groups," meaning polygamists, has been asked. Concern about involvement in the thrift-and-loan scandals of the 1970s caused a question about being honest with your fellowmen to be added. In 1979 a question on domestic and sexual abuse was added, asking the member to consider whether or not there was anything in his or her conduct with the family that was "not in harmony with the teachings of the Church." The Church began asking about child support in the 1980s, and in 1999 began asking specifically if divorced recommend applicants were up-to-date with any court-ordered financial obligations to their children and former spouses.

Sexual sin, adultery, and fornication

Adultery or fornication is discussed in section 42 in no fewer than eight verses. (See verses 22–26, 74–75 and 80.) Provision is made for repentance, but repeated and continued instances of adultery merit excommunication. (See verses 23–26, 74–75, 80.) Such sins are serious and are entirely inconsistent with the ideal of reserving sexual relationships for marriage partners only. "Thou shalt love thy wife with all thy heart, and shalt cleave unto her and none else." (Verse 22; see also verse 23.)[2]

The seriousness of adultery in Mormon theology stems from the belief that family relationships are the well-spring of happiness, around which social life revolves in this life and the next. Since infidelity is often the most destructive event that can occur in marriage, it often leads to divorce. In 1886, the First Presidency said:

"To a people who believe, as we do, that true marriage was divinely instituted for the multiplication of mankind, and is not a union for time alone, but reaches into the eternities, the disruption of families by divorce is an evil of not ordinary character, not only bearing a harvest of sorrow and suffering in this life, but also having a far-reaching influence into the

---

1. See Kimball, *Journal of Mormon History,* Spring 1998.
2. "And he that looketh upon a woman to lust after her shall deny the faith, and shall not have the Spirit; and if he repents not he shall be cast out." As Robinson and Garrett point out, this involves more than the occasional stray thought but rather acts intended to bring about an illicit relationship. (See Robinson and Garrett, *A Commentary on the Doctrine and Covenants,* 2:20.)

world beyond the grave, and possibly involving others in ruin who had no voice in the separation or power to avert its occurrence."[1]

Consequently, the Church has always looked with strong disfavor upon anything, especially sexual transgression, that weakens the bonds of family life.

On the other hand, the Church has always been cautious not to define what is sexually appropriate or inappropriate between partners in marriage and recognizes that sexual intimacy is not only for producing offspring but is also a way for spouses to express "love for one another—to bind husband and wife together in loyalty, fidelity, consideration, and common purpose."[2]

Since bishops and stake presidents are authorized to ask Latter-day Saint couples if they have been sexually loyal to their spouse prior to giving permission for members to enter the temple, the First Presidency cautioned that such interviews should be narrowly construed:

"In conducting worthiness interviews . . . you should never inquire into personal, intimate matters involving marital relations between a man and his wife. You should never deviate from or go beyond the specific questions contained in the temple recommend book."[3]

The statement goes on to explain that if in the course of an interview a spouse should ask about the "propriety" of "specific conduct, you should not pursue the matter but should merely suggest that if the member has enough anxiety about the propriety of the conduct to ask about it, the best course would be to discontinue it."[4]

Almon Babbitt rebuked

Almon Babbitt was born in October 1812, and died in September 1856 when he was killed by Cheyenne Indians near Ash Hollow, about one hundred miles northeast of Fort Kearny, Nebraska. Although he stayed with the Church throughout his life and went with the body of the Saints to the Great Basin, he was a mercurial and sometimes disloyal member who struggled to comply with instructions given him by Church leaders.[5]

---

1. *Statements of the LDS First Presidency*, 118.
2. *Statements of the LDS First Presidency*, 418.
3. *Statements of the First Presidency*, 420.
4. *Statements of the First Presidency*, 420.
5. At various times during his life he held important positions in the Church. In February 1835 he was ordained to the First Quorum of Seventy. In 1840 he was the president of the Kirtland Stake. In March 1843 he was the presiding officer in the Ramus Illinois Branch. In May 1844 he was called on a mission to France but did not fulfill the assignment. He rendered legal services to the Church and served as a delegate to Congress. (See Black, *Who's Who in the Doctrine and Covenants*, 2–5.)

At times he supported Joseph and other leaders of the Church and at other times he did not.[1]

In 1838 Babbitt was rebuked by the Prophet for leading a group of Canadian Saints to Missouri to settle on the forks of the Grand River, contrary to counsel. Prior to this revelation Joseph complained in a letter written in July 1840 to Oliver Granger that Babbitt and some of the other brethren were making attempts to "reform the Church."[2] By September 1840 Babbitt was accused of criticizing the Prophet for dressing too extravagantly. Joseph had purchased three suits of clothes while in Washington, D.C., to ask for redress for the wrongs committed against the Saints while they lived in Missouri. Babbitt was also accused of holding secret councils in the Kirtland Temple to undermine Joseph.[3]

Based on this background, it is not surprising that Babbitt was rebuked in section 124:

"And with my servant Almon Babbitt, there are many things with which I am not pleased; behold, he aspireth to establish his counsel instead of the counsel which I have ordained, even that of the Presidency of my Church; and he setteth up a golden calf for the worship of my people." (D&C 124:84.)

Babbitt's reaction to section 124 was predictable. Benjamin F. Johnson recorded that Babbitt "felt hurt by the rebuke in the revelation, and he was in great temptation to complain, and to turn his heel upon the Prophet."[4]

SECTION 125: JOSEPH SMITH JR. HOMESTEAD, NAUVOO, ILLINOIS, MARCH 1841

Heading

The Saints who have emigrated to the Iowa side of the Mississippi should remain there.

The big question

Question: What should we do to be saved?
Answer: Gather to various geographical areas and build up Zion.

---

1. See Black, *Who's Who in the Doctrine and Covenants*, 2–5.
2. See Jesse, *Personal Writings of Joseph Smith*, 511–14.
3. See Black, *Who's Who in the Doctrine and Covenants*, 3.
4. Black, *Who's Who in the Doctrine and Covenants*, 4.

Nauvoo, Illinois: January 19, 1841–July 12, 1843

Nauvoo Temple, Nauvoo, Illinois. Rebuilt and completed in June 2002. The original edifice was the second temple built by the Church. The First temple built in Kirtland was not used for the endowment as we know it today.

The Red Brick Store, in Nauvoo, Illinois, was constructed and owned by Joseph Smith in 1841. It was the center of economic, political, social, and religious activity. It served as the headquarters of the Church. The Relief Society was organized in the meeting hall on its second floor on March 17, 1842, and the first endowment ordinances were performed here on May 4, 1842.

Introduction

This revelation was given through the Prophet Joseph in his home in Nauvoo, Illinois, in March 1841, regarding whether or not the Saints on the Iowa side of the Mississippi River should cross over the river and settle in Nauvoo.[1] The Saints are instructed to remain on the Iowa side and build up Zion there.

Historical background

When the Saints were driven out of Missouri in 1838–39, they were scattered in communities up and down the Mississippi River. By March 1841, as Mormon immigration continued at a fast pace, most of the Missouri Saints had relocated in Nauvoo. New converts were coming from as far away as Great Britain and Canada, as well as from all over the United States. Some settled on the Iowa side of the Mississippi River in Lee County, across from Nauvoo. Before the Mormons started to arrive in Lee County,

---

1. Smith, *History of the Church*, 4:322–23.

Joseph Smith homestead, in Nauvoo, Illinois, on the eastern bank of the Mississippi River. The home served as Church headquarters for about two years. In 1843 the Prophet moved across the street to the Mansion House.

there were just under 3,000 residents in the area. By 1846 there would be over 12,000, most of whom were Latter-day Saints.[1]

Based on the information available, Joseph did not oppose the Iowa settlements. He was particularly interested in having some of the Saints settle in a community named after the Book of Mormon city Zarahemla. In March 1841, John Smith, the Prophet's uncle, recorded in his diary a conversation with Alanson Ripley, a bishop on the Iowa side of the river, who said that he had personally spoken with Joseph and had been instructed that "it was the will of the Lord the brethren in Ambrosia [Iowa] should move in and about the city of Zarahemla [Iowa] with all convenient speed."[2] "Let them build up a city unto my name upon the land opposite the city of Nauvoo, and let the name of Zarahemla be named upon it." (Verse 3.) Zarahemla, however, was by no means the only official site mentioned on the Iowa side of the river. "And let all those who come from the east, and the west, and the north, and the south, that have desires to dwell therein, take up their inheritance in the same [Zarahemla], as well as in the city of Nashville [Iowa], or in the city of Nauvoo, and in all the stakes which I have appointed, saith the Lord." (Verse 4.)

---

1. See Woodford, *The Historical Development of the Doctrine and Covenants*, 1657.
2. Woodford, *The Historical Development of the Doctrine and Covenants*, 1658.

Section 126: Brigham Young Home, Nauvoo, Illinois, July 9, 1841

Heading

Brigham Young is instructed that it is no longer necessary for him to be called away from his family to serve missions.

The big question

Question: How shall we be saved?
Answer: Nurture family relationships.

Introduction

This revelation was given through Joseph Smith the Prophet in Brigham Young's home in Nauvoo, Illinois, on July 9, 1841.[1] At this time Brigham Young was the president of the Quorum of the Twelve (see D&C 124:127) and had just returned from a mission in Great Britain. The Lord revealed that it was no longer necessary for him to be called away from his family. (See verse 1.)

Historical background

Brigham Young had been called on a number of missions that required him to leave his family for long periods of time. Between December 1832 and February 1833, he preached the gospel on a mission in Canada. Six months later he was called to return to the same mission field from April through August 1833. In 1834 he was asked to join Zion's Camp, marching from Kirtland to Missouri to rescue the Saints there and reestablish them in their homes in Jackson County. In 1835 he served a mission to the eastern states, and in 1837 he went on two more missions in the east, with a break in between. Then, between September 1839 and July 1, 1841, he served a mission in Great Britain. Section 126 was received just eight days after he returned home.[2]

Clearly, Brigham Young, at great personal sacrifice[3] had spent a consid-

---

1. Smith, *History of the Church*, 4:382.
2. See Preece, *Learning to Love the Doctrine and Covenants*, 366.
3. The sacrifices experienced by early missionaries is well attested to. In this instance it is interesting to note that Joseph Smith saw the Twelve's deprivations when they were serving in England in 1839–41. In 1836 Joseph had a vision in the Kirtland Temple of the sacrifices Brigham Young and the other apostles would suffer in their lifetime. "I saw the Twelve Apostles of the Lamb, who are now upon the earth, who hold the keys of this last

erable amount of time away from his family as a missionary for the Church. Section 126 must have brought him great relief to know that "it is no more required at your hand to leave your family." (Verse 1.) It is noteworthy that after this section was received, Brigham never served another proselytizing mission for the Church, although he did travel numerous times on Church business throughout the rest of his lifetime.[1]

When this revelation was received, Brigham Young was president of the Quorum of the Twelve. During this time in Church history, the Twelve's function was limited to supervising the missionary efforts of the Church. The Twelve had not yet been given authority to direct the affairs of the Church where stakes had been organized. (See D&C 107:33.) All of this changed within days after section 126 was given. On August 6, 1841, Joseph received a revelation in which the Twelve were instructed that they stood next to the First Presidency and had general jurisdiction over the entire Church, including stakes:

"The time has come when the Twelve should be called upon to stand in their place next to the First Presidency, and attend to the settling of emigrants and the business of the Church at the Stakes, and to assist to bear off the kingdom victoriously to the nations."[2]

From this point forward, members of the Twelve had authority over stake presidents, members of stake high councils, and other local officers of the Church.[3]

In retrospect, this revelation to Brigham Young (D&C 126) not only allowed him more time to nurture his family, but it also kept him at the side of Joseph Smith and prepared him to become the second President of the Church after Joseph was killed. (See verse 3.) Young's eventual rise to leadership had been foreseen much earlier. He recorded that upon first meeting the Prophet, Joseph prophesied that the time would come when Young would preside over the Church. The following account is found in the *Manuscript History of the Church*:

> We immediately repaired to the woods where the Prophet, and two or three of his brothers, [were] chopping and hauling wood. Here my joy was

---

ministry, in foreign lands, standing together in a circle, much fatigued, with their clothes tattered and feet swollen, with their eyes cast downward, and Jesus standing in their midst, and they did not behold Him. The Savior looked upon them and wept.... Also, I saw Elder Brigham Young standing in a strange land, in the far south and west, in a desert place, upon a rock in the midst of about a dozen men of color, who appeared hostile. He was preaching to them in their own tongue, and the angel of God as standing above his head, with a drawn sword in his hand, protecting him, but he did not see it." (See Smith, *History of the Church*, 2:381.)

1. See Preece, *Learning to Love the Doctrine and Covenants*, 367.
2. Smith, *History of the Church*, 4:403.
3. See Woodford, *The Historical Development of the Doctrine and Covenants*, 1663.

full at the privilege of shaking the hand of the Prophet of God, and received the sure testimony, by the spirit of prophecy, that he was all that any man could believe him to be, as a true prophet. . . . In the evening a few of the brethren came in, and we conversed together upon the things of the kingdom. He called upon me to pray. In my prayer I spoke in tongues. As soon as we arose from our knees the brethren flocked around him, and asked his opinion concerning the gift of tongues that was upon me. He told them it was the pure Adamic language. Some said to him they expected he would condemn the gift brother Brigham had, but he said, "No, it is of God, and the time will come when brother Brigham will preside over this Church." The latter part of the conversation was in my absence.[1]

Family relationships

Section 126 advises Brigham Young to "take especial care of your family from this time, henceforth and forever." (Verse 3.) To more fully fulfill this responsibility, it was "no more required at your hand to leave your family as in times past." (Verse 1.) Implicit in this instruction is the notion that time and proximity to family are essential if one is to truly nurture family relationships. There are no shortcuts.

It should not be assumed, however, that Brigham Young's view of the ideal family situation was similar to our own. In large measure the ideal family envisioned by modern Mormons is a product of the 1950s.[2] During this halcyon era in American life, family was defined as a married couple and their minor children living together under the same roof.[3] The father was considered the head of the household and the sole provider of income. The mother's primary responsibility was to serve her husband's needs and be the primary facilitator of their children's education and development. She was content to stay at home to devote herself to child raising and homemaking.[4]

Brigham Young and the founding generation of Latter-day Saints would have nurtured their families with the perspective of the early 1830s. At that time the idea of "separate spheres" of responsibility within a family was common. But, in this rural agrarian environment, it was also not

---

1. Manuscript History, 1 (Sept. 1832): 4.
2. The 1950s family model of the ideal family within the Church is slowly changing to accommodate changing times. Within the last ten to fifteen years there has been greater tolerance for women who work outside the home, and the Church has placed more emphasis on the idea that men and women form an equal partnership in marriage, deemphasizing the more subservient role women have played in the past.
3. It should be acknowledged that this certainly was not the case for the many members of the Church who practiced polygamy in the latter half of the nineteenth century.
4. See Mintz and Kellogg, *Domestic Revolutions*, xiii.

Nauvoo, Illinois: January 19, 1841–July 12, 1843

Brigham Young home, in Nauvoo, Illinois. While Brigham Young was serving a mission, his second wife, Mary Ann, purchased property and built this house.

uncommon for husbands, mothers, and children alike to work to sustain the family. Indeed, this was the case with Joseph Smith's birth family. In Manchester, New York, Joseph's mother, Lucy Mack Smith, made birch brooms, black ash baskets, and painted oil cloth coverings for sale. Joseph peddled these goods and refreshments from a cart that he rolled around Palmyra and to religious camp meetings. Relations within the family were less formal and hierarchical than they had been in the eighteenth century. During Joseph Smith's time husbands and wives were growing increasingly affectionate and egalitarian, both devoting increased care and attention to their offspring.[1]

Sections 127–128: Father Taylor's Home, Nauvoo, Illinois, September 1 and 6, 1842

Heading

General instructions on baptisms for the dead and vicarious work for the dead.

---

1. See Mintz and Kellogg, *Domestic Revolutions*, xv.

The Nauvoo Period

The big question

Question: What should we do to be saved?
Answer: Perform vicarious temple ordinances for the dead.

Introduction

These sections are letters from Joseph Smith the Prophet to Latter-day Saints at Nauvoo, Illinois, containing directions on baptisms for the dead, written at Father Taylor's home (meaning the home of John Taylor's father) on September 1 and 6, 1842.[1]

Anchor section

Memorize: Baptism for the dead (D&C 128)

Historical background

Sections 127 and 128 comprise two letters written just days apart that were dictated by Joseph Smith to William Clayton. They concern baptisms for the dead, "the proxy performance of the ordinance of baptism for one deceased."[2] The letters were addressed to "all the Saints at Nauvoo" and were composed at a time when the Prophet was hiding from law enforcement officials who sought to arrest him as a conspirator in the attempted murder of the ex-governor of Missouri, Lilburn W. Boggs.[3] Since Boggs had issued the infamous Missouri Executive Order 44 on October 27, 1838, better known as the "extermination order," nonmembers of the Church believed that Joseph had revenge in his heart for this notorious anti-Mormon.[4] It was rumored that Joseph had ordered his bodyguard, Orrin Porter Rockwell, to assassinate Boggs. At the direction of law enforcement officials, an arrest warrant had been issued for Rockwell as "principal"

---

1. Smith, *History of the Church*, 5:142–44; 148–53.
2. *Encyclopedia of Mormonism*, 1:95. The necessity to perform posthumous baptisms is based on the premise that certain rites and ordinances must be performed in this life to qualify a person for higher blessings in the next. Therefore, if a person dies without receiving a rite necessary for salvation, it must be done by proxy by someone in this life.
3. See Cook, *Revelations of the Prophet Joseph Smith*, 284. On May 6, 1842, an unsuccessful attempt had been made on Boggs's life when he was seated in his home. The would-be assassin fired a pistol full of buckshot through the window and hit Boggs in the head. (See Preece, *Learning to Love the Doctrine and Covenants*, 368.)
4. The order came in response to what Boggs termed "open and avowed defiance of the laws, and of having made war upon the people of this State . . . the Mormons must be treated as enemies, and must be exterminated or driven from the State if necessary for the public peace—their outrages are beyond all description." The order was formally rescinded in 1976. (See http://en.wikipedia.org/wiki/Extermination_Order_(Mormonism).)

and Joseph as an "accessory before the fact." Rockwell and Joseph were captured on August 8, 1842. They were left in the custody of the Nauvoo City marshal and shortly thereafter freed by friends who realized that Joseph and Rockwell could never receive a fair trial in Missouri. It was shortly after this escape that sections 127 and 128 were written. (See D&C 127:1.)[1]

Section 127 makes repeated reference to Joseph's dire situation. "I have thought it expedient and wisdom in me to leave the place [Nauvoo] for a short season, for my own safety and the safety of this people." (Verse 1.) "As for the perils which I am called to pass through, they seem but a small thing to me, as the envy and wrath of man have been my common lot. . . . I was ordained from before the foundation of the world for some good end, or bad, as you may choose to call it. . . . But nevertheless, deep water is what I am wont to swim in. . . . I feel like Paul, to glory in tribulation." (Verse 2; see also verses 3–4, 11.)

Details on the specific circumstances surrounding sections 127 and 128

Joseph first spoke publicly about baptisms for the dead on August 10, 1840, at the funeral of Colonel Seymour Brunson.[2] Joseph's teaching of the doctrine was accepted by many without delay. Not long after the initial teaching, Jane Nyman remembered rejoicing over the principle when she heard Joseph explain the doctrine during a Sabbath-day meeting. She had lost her husband about a week before, and prior to his death she and her husband had wondered about the spiritual status of their son, who had predeceased both of them and had never been baptized. She was so enthusiastic when she heard about this new doctrine that she convinced Harvey Olmstead to baptize her for her son. Crossing genders when baptizing for the dead was not uncommon at this time. Many others were just as eager to adopt the practice. Within a short time, several hundred persons were baptized for their deceased relatives and friends, some as many as forty times.[3]

Joseph continued to speak on the subject, and both he and Sidney Rigdon

---

1. To avoid capture Joseph and Rockwell frequently moved from place to place and traveled back and forth across the Mississippi River, which divided Illinois from Iowa. (See Preece, *Learning to Love the Doctrine and Covenants*, 368–69.)

2. See Woodford, *The Historical Development of the Doctrine and Covenants*, 1669.

3. See Woodford, *The Historical Development of the Doctrine and Covenants*, 1672. Also, in November 1840, Erastus Snow reported that a recent convert, Judge Adams of Springfield, was baptized in Nauvoo for four of his deceased friends.

addressed it in the April 1841 general conference.[1] At first there was no uniform procedure for keeping track of names of those for whom baptisms had been performed. Undoubtedly, Joseph was concerned about the lack of record keeping. Six months later, in the October 1841 general conference, he instructed the Saints that "there shall be no more baptisms for the dead, until the ordinance can be attended to in the Lord's House."[2] The practice was discontinued but only for a month. On November 21, 1841, a temporary wooden font was dedicated in the basement of the Nauvoo Temple for the first baptisms for the dead in that building.[3]

Restricting baptisms for the dead to one place—the font in the basement of the temple—somewhat lessened the confusion surrounding record keeping for proxy baptisms. But further instructions on the subject were needed. On August 31, 1842, Joseph spoke to the Relief Society and mentioned the necessity of having at least two witnesses present at all proxy baptisms. The following day, most probably in Father Taylor's home,[4] Joseph wrote the first of two letters on baptism for the dead establishing strict record keeping measures. (See D&C 127:6–9; 128:2–8, 14; Revelation 20:12.)

Sections 127 and 128—a report on a lost revelation that Joseph received at an earlier time

Sections 127 and 128 do not claim to be the actual revelation that Joseph received on the subject. Rather, they are Joseph's summary of a principle revealed to him sometime earlier. That there was an actual revelation that had been written down on the subject of vicarious baptisms was attested to by Wilford Woodruff. Woodruff said he "read the revelation given through the Prophet Joseph concerning the redemption of the dead."[5] He further recalled that it was "one of the most glorious principles I had ever become acquainted with on earth."[6] Unfortunately, the original revelation or a copy of it is not available and was probably lost.

---

1. See Woodford, *The Historical Development of the Doctrine and Covenants*, 1674
2. Smith, *History of the Church*, 4:426; Woodford, *The Historical Development of the Doctrine and Covenants*, 1673–74.
3. See Woodford, *The Historical Development of the Doctrine and Covenants*, 1674.
4. Father Taylor, as he was called, was the father of President John Taylor the third President of the Church.
5. Woodford, *The Historical Development of the Doctrine and Covenants*, 1675.
6. *Millennial Star*, June 29, 1891, 404–5, as quoted in Woodford, *The Historical Development of the Doctrine and Covenants*, 1676.

Nauvoo, Illinois: January 19, 1841–July 12, 1843

The doctrine of baptism for the dead was practiced in Jesus' day

In speaking about baptism for the dead, Joseph Smith taught that it was initiated by Jesus[1] and observed by the first Christian communities. In a letter to members of the Quorum of Twelve Apostles Joseph wrote, "It [baptism for the dead] was certainly practiced by the ancient churches, and St. Paul endeavors to prove the doctrine of the resurrection from the same, and says, 'else what shall they do who are baptized for the dead.'"[2]

Although the idea of posthumous baptisms was not well accepted in Joseph's time, this early Christian practice is confirmed by modern biblical scholars today. For example, as basic and well accepted a source as *The Anchor Bible Dictionary* informs its readers that "a belief that baptism ensured life in an almost magic way may also explain the practice of being baptized on behalf of dead people, mentioned in 1 Corinthians 15:29."[3] The Mormon apologist Hugh Nibley also wrote authoritatively on the subject. He reported that in a number of early Christian sources baptism for the dead is spoken about.[4] Quoting the well-known Christian St. Ambrose,[5] one of the most influential ecclesiastical figures of the fourth century, Nibley pointed out that this doctor of the early Church recalled, but did not approve of the practice. "Fearing that a dead person who had never been baptized would be resurrected badly [*male*] or not at all, a living person would be baptized in the name of the dead one. Hence he [Paul] adds: 'Else why are they baptized for them?' According to this he does not approve of what is done but shows the firm faith in the resurrection [that it implies]."[6]

The Gates of Hell

In section 128, Joseph refers to Matthew 16:18–19 and interprets it in connection with baptisms for the dead.

"And again, for the precedent, Matthew 16:18, 19: *And I say also unto thee, That thou art Peter, and upon this rock I will build my church; and the gates of hell shall not prevail against it. And I will give unto thee the keys of the kingdom of heaven; and whatsoever thou shalt bind on earth shall be bound in heaven; and whatsoever thou shalt loose on earth shall be loosed in heaven.*" (Verse 10.)

---

1. Smith, *Teachings of the Prophet Joseph Smith*, 310.
2. Woodford, *The Historical Development of the Doctrine and Covenants*, 1669.
3. *The Anchor Bible Dictionary*, 1:589.
4. See Nibley, "Baptism for the Dead in Ancient Times."
5. Saint Ambrose was a Frankish bishop of Milan who lived about A.D. 338. He was considered to be one of the four most influential church fathers.
6. Nibley, "Baptism for the Dead in Ancient Times," 126.

By way of interpretation Joseph proposed that the "keys" referred to in this verse correspond to the right to perform proxy ordinances on earth that have the effect of unlocking the gates of hell or what Latter-day Saints refer to as the "spirit prison," where the dead await performance of the ordinances on their behalf so that they can move ahead or progress. (See verses 10–13.) Hugh Nibley explains further: "To the Jews 'the gates of hell' meant something very specific. Both Jews and Christians thought of the world of the dead as a prison—*carcer, phylake, phroura*—in which the dead were detained but not necessarily made to suffer any other discomfort. In the Jewish tradition the righteous dead are described as sitting impatiently in their place of detention awaiting their final release and reunion with their resurrected bodies and asking, 'How much longer must we stay here?' The Christians talked of 'the prison of death' to which baptism held the key of release."[1]

Baptism by immersion as a symbol for proxy baptisms

Section 128 reiterates what the Apostle Paul taught, namely, that baptism is not only a symbol of new birth (being born into the kingdom of God) but also of the resurrection—what men and women may become. However, section 128 goes further, tying immersion in water to proxy baptisms: "The ordinance of baptism by water, to be immersed therein in order to answer to the likeness of the dead, that one principle might accord with the other; to be immersed in the water and come forth out of the water is in the likeness of the resurrection of the dead in coming forth out of their graves; hence, this ordinance was instituted to form a relationship with the ordinance of baptism for the dead, being in likeness of the dead." (Verse 12.)

This tie between baptisms for the living and baptisms for the dead is further reinforced by the directive that baptisms for the dead are to be performed in an area below ground level. "The baptismal font was instituted as a similitude of the grave, and was commanded to be in a place underneath where the living are wont to assemble, to show forth the living and the dead, and that all things may have their likeness." (Verse 13.)

The reciprocal nature of ordinances performed by the living for the dead

The premise of Joseph's letter as contained in section 128 is based not only on the proposition that the living can assist the dead but also on the

---

1. Nibley, "Baptism for the Dead in Ancient Times," 105–6.

proposition that the dead can assist the living. "They [the dead] without us cannot be made perfect—neither can we without our dead be made perfect." (Verse 15.) Just how the dead make us perfect is not entirely apparent. Nonetheless, it opens up new avenues of thought about mutually supportive relationships through the veil and the forging of "welding links" (see D&C 128:18) between all the generations of mankind. Referring to Malachi 4:5–6—"And he shall turn the heart of the fathers to the children, and the heart of the children to their fathers, lest I come and smite the earth with a curse"—Joseph explains:

"I might have rendered a plainer translation to this, but it is sufficiently plain to suit my purpose as it stands. It is sufficient to know . . . that the earth will be smitten with a curse unless there is a welding link of some kind or other between the fathers and the children, upon some subject or other—and behold what is that subject? It is the baptism for the dead. For we without them cannot be made perfect; neither can they without us be made perfect." (Verse 18.)

Finally, there is an additional level of cooperation necessary in this blueprint for extraterrestrial aid and assistance. "Neither can they [the dead] nor we be made perfect without those who have died in the gospel also." (Verse 18.) Apparently, those who receive the gospel on earth and now live in the spirit world have special indispensable duties involving "the ushering in of the dispensation of the fulness of times, which dispensation is now beginning to usher in, that a whole and complete and perfect union, and welding together of dispensations, and keys, and powers, and glories should take place, and be revealed from the days of Adam even to the present time. And not only this, but those things which never have been revealed from the foundation of the world, but have been kept hid from the wise and prudent, shall be revealed unto babes and sucklings in this, the dispensation of the fulness of times." (Verse 18.)

The person for whom the baptism is performed may reject it

The doctrine of man's agency to accept or reject the gospel message is so well established that, without doubt, those served by proxy have the right to accept or decline the ordinance performed on their behalf. We have no information, of course, as to numbers of those who accept or reject this work. However, we are assured that most, if not all, of God's children will at some point in the future accept baptism.[1] Otherwise, God's plan would be ineffectual and the time spent doing vicarious work in temples would likewise be ineffectual.

---

1. See, for example, Wilford Woodruff as quoted in Packer, *The Holy Temple*, 203, 206.

The broader implications of the doctrine of baptism for the dead

In Joseph's letters on baptism for the dead (D&C 127 and 128) he introduced a principle that would be extended to include other saving rites and ordinances of the gospel, including the endowment and eternal marriage. In fact, section 127 explicitly stated that the Lord was "about to restore many things to the earth, pertaining to the priesthood." (D&C 127:8.)

The full scope of what the Lord intended had been revealed a few months earlier in May 1842, when portions of the temple endowment were introduced to a few of Joseph's trusted followers. (See D&C 124:27–48.) However, it would not be until the Nauvoo Temple was well underway that it would be revealed to Church members in general. Woodford commented that Joseph recognized that the principle of vicarious work for the dead "presents the gospel in probably a more enlarged scale than some have imagined it."[1]

The building of temples in which proxy ordinances, or "work for the dead," is carried out would become one of the distinguishing features of Mormonism. The act of baptizing living persons on behalf of dead persons was an outward expression of Joseph's comprehension that life after death is a reality, that beneficial rites and ordinances must be performed for everyone, even for those who have died, and that the efficacy of proxy rites depends upon priesthood authority (authority to "seal" a decree on earth and have it recognized in heaven) and upon the willingness of the person to accept the saving ordinance performed on his or her behalf. From this point forward, collaboration would be assumed between persons in this life and the next.

SECTION 129: RED BRICK STORE, NAUVOO, ILLINOIS, FEBRUARY 9, 1843

Heading

Keys are given whereby messengers from beyond the veil may be identified.

---

1. Woodford, *The Historical Development of the Doctrine and Covenants*, 1669–70.

Nauvoo, Illinois: January 19, 1841–July 12, 1843

The big question

Question: What should we do to be saved?
Answer: Learn to detect false from true revelation.

Introduction

These instructions were given by Joseph Smith the Prophet on February 9, 1843, in the Red Brick Store, at Nauvoo, Illinois, making known a means whereby a person might know whether an angel or spirit is from God or from Satan. There are both resurrected and spirit bodies in heaven. Keys are given whereby messengers from beyond the veil may be identified.[1] Section 129 is based upon directions Joseph gave to Parley P. Pratt soon after Parley returned from his mission in 1843.[2] This may not have been the first time that Joseph had spoken on this subject;[3] he may have also spoken about an incident that happened as early as 1830, when Adam (also called Michael) came to Joseph on the banks of the Susquehanna River to assist him in detecting Satan, who had tried to deceive the Prophet by appearing as an angel of light.[4] (See D&C 128:20.) In 1839 Joseph spoke to Wilford Woodruff about discerning other-worldly messengers,[5] and later the same information was recorded in a pamphlet printed in Nauvoo in 1841.[6]

---

1. See Smith, *History of the Church*, 5:267.
2. Parley P. Pratt and other members of the Twelve served a mission in Great Britain. Pratt had remained over a year and a half longer than the rest to preside over the Church there and to serve as editor of the *Millennial Star*. (See Preece, *Learning to Love the Doctrine and Covenants*, 374.)
3. Parley P. Pratt was probably not present on the prior occasions when Joseph addressed this subject with other members of the Twelve.
4. Compare Moses 1:8–24, where Satan appears to Moses as an angel of light and tries to deceive him.
5. On June 27, 1839, Woodruff recorded in his journal that he had "spent the day in Commerce in council with the Presidency and Twelve. . . . Brother Orson Hyde was restored to the Church and the quorum of Twelve in full fellowship by a full vote. . . . Joseph presented the following. . . . In order to detect the devil when he transforms himself nigh unto an angel of light . . . when an angel of God appears unto man face to face in person and reaches out his hand unto the man and he takes hold of the angels hand and feels a substance the same as would in shaking hands with another he may then know that it is an angel of God and he should place all confidence in him . . . but if a personage appears unto man and offers him his hand and the man takes hold of it and he feels nothing . . . he may know it is the devil . . . for when a saint whose body is not resurrected appears unto man . . . he will not offer him his hand for this is against the law given him and in keeping in mind these things we may detect the devil that he deceived us not." (See *Wilford Woodruff Journal*, 1:341.)
6. See Woodford, *The Historical Development of the Doctrine and Covenants*, 1703. "The devil may appear as an angel of light; ask God to reveal it; if it be of the devil he will flee from you, if of God he will manifest himself or make it manifest. If an angel or spirit appears, offer him your hand; if he is a spirit from God he will stand still and not offer you hand . . . etc." In reference to the appearance of spirits and angels the pamphlet states that "a spirit cannot

Historical background

For Joseph Smith, the existence of God, Jesus Christ, angels, and spirits were a given. Therefore, his concern was not so much whether or not extraterrestrial beings existed, but rather how to know the source from which each was sent—God or the devil. Throughout his life Joseph cautioned the Saints about false spirits, false visitations, false visions, and false revelations in general. For example, in 1842 he spoke about the difference between feeling emotion and experiencing the Spirit of God. Emotions, he said, could be manufactured and come from many sources, good or ill. On the other hand, spiritual communications are always accompanied by instructions, information, or knowledge. He put it this way, "Is there any intelligence communicated? Are the curtains of heaven withdrawn, or the purposes of God developed?"[1] A second part of the equation was equally important. The knowledge given must square with prior revelations on the subject and must be consistent with what is already known about God from other reliable sources.[2] Joseph cautioned the people that "nothing is a greater injury to the children of men than to be under the influence of a false spirit when they think they have the Spirit of God."[3]

Section 129 speaks about tests that can be employed to discern a true or false messenger. If an angel is a resurrected messenger from God, he or she will put forth a hand, and when the person beholding the angel clasps the hand he will feel solid flesh. (See Luke 24:35–43.) This "touch" test or assessment through personal contact is reliable because we know that so far only the righteous have been resurrected. Therefore, it must

---

come but in glory; an angel has flesh and bones, we see not their glory." (See also Smith, *Teachings of the Prophet Joseph Smith*, 162.) Clearly, this statement is incomplete and does not accord with some of the appearances Joseph experienced where angels appeared in a glorious light. For example, when the angel Moroni appeared to Joseph and the Three Witnesses a glorious light was present. On other occasions, when righteous spirits have appeared they have not been surrounded by light or appeared in glory. (See Preece, *Learning to Love the Doctrine and Covenants*, 374.)

1. Smith, *Teachings of the Prophet Joseph Smith*, 204. Joseph's teachings about communications from the Holy Ghost are also consistent with his notion that when a revelation is received, so also is knowledge. "No man can receive the Holy Ghost without receiving revelations. The Holy Ghost is a revelator." (See Smith, *Teachings of the Prophet Joseph Smith*, 328.)

2. See Smith, *Teachings of the Prophet Joseph Smith*, 202–14. In the prophet's case, this rule of thumb was not always followed. For example, when he was studying John (John 5:26) and came upon a scripture that talked as if there was only a heaven and a hell, he received a revelation that spoke about gradations of glory. (See D&C 76.) Joseph also reversed the meaning of eternal punishment to mean God's punishment, even though in some contexts the Book of Mormon seems to use the term to refer to the length of the punishment. (See commentary for section 19.)

3. Smith, *Teachings of the Prophet Joseph Smith*, 205.

follow that if a corporeal heavenly messenger makes a visit, it must be from God. (Matthew 27:52–53.)[1]

Revelations from noncorporeal beings, or spirits made of refined matter, are more problematic; it is more difficult to discern whether a spirit comes from God or the devil. Whether our inspiration comes through a voice in the mind, an audible voice, a dream, a vision, or the visitation by a spirit, correct discernment is essential if we are not to be misled. We might appropriately divide spirits into three categories—"just men made perfect" (i.e., those who have had their calling and election made sure—verse 3); spirits in the spirit world who may someday, upon acceptance of the terms and conditions of the gospel, enter the celestial kingdom;[2] and spirits who follow the devil. Joseph taught that "just men made perfect" appear "in . . . glory; for that is the only way he can appear." (Verse 6.) Spirits who have not reached this state of perfection may appear but not in glory.

If the spirit of a "just man made perfect" appears, the recipient is to "ask him to shake hands." (Verses 6–7.) He or she will not move—will not extend the hand—because that would be deceptive, since a spirit hand cannot be felt. "Because it is contrary to the order of Heaven for a just man to deceive," he or she will simply deliver the message. (Verse 7.) If the spirit be of the third sort, a spirit of the devil imitating an angel of light, "he will offer you his hand, and you will not feel anything; you may therefore detect him." (Verse 8.) Since it is likely that a spirit of the devil is knowledgeable about this test, it follows that an evil spirit in an effort to deceive might not put forth his or her hand. Therefore, the efficacy of this test depends upon an absolute assurance that a devil is bound by certain rules that would not allow him to withhold his hand in such a situation.[3] It is also advisable to follow the counsel in section 50, which advises that it is appropriate to pray and ask God if a "spirit manifested" be from God or some other source. "Wherefore, it shall come to pass, that if you behold a spirit manifested that you cannot understand, and you receive not that spirit, ye shall ask of the Father in the name of Jesus; and if he give not unto you that spirit, then you may know that it is not of God." (Verse 31.)[4]

---

1. One might put forward the suggestion that there are substantive beings that are not the product of the resurrection that we are not aware of. However, this thought is countermanded by a revelation Joseph received stating that only angels or personages "who do belong or have belonged" to this earth are allowed to minister here. (See D&C 130:5.)

2. A spirit of a just man made perfect is a righteous person who has died but not been resurrected who has had his calling and election made sure. Because of their righteousness they appear in glory. (See Preece, *Learning to Love the Doctrine and Covenants*, 374.) Not all spirits appear in glory, depending on the degree of their perfection and whether or not the person is actually beholding the spirit or experiencing a night (dream) or day vision.

3. See McConkie and Ostler, *Revelations of the Restoration*, 1038–43; Preece, *Learning to Love the Doctrine and Covenants*, 375.

4. Section 46 was also given in response to a situation where spiritual gifts were being

Joseph referred to the methods of detection mentioned in section 129 as "grand keys." (See verse 9.) It is clear that by the time the temple endowment was revealed during the Nauvoo period there were other "keys" that could also be employed to discern spirits. On Sunday May 1, 1842, Joseph spoke in one of the groves of trees around Nauvoo, saying that there were "keys" or "certain signs and words by which false spirits and personages may be detected from true, which cannot be revealed to the Elders till the Temple is completed.... There are signs in heaven, earth and hell; the Elders must know them all, to be endowed with power, to finish their work and prevent imposition."[1] About a month earlier, on April 28, 1842, he told the Relief Society sisters that they would also receive "keys" in the temple by which they could "detect everything false."[2]

Since Section 129 assures us that a message from a resurrected being is reliably from God, it should be noted that most of the seminal events of the restoration occurred when resurrected messengers appeared to Joseph and/or Oliver Cowdery. Moroni; John the Baptist; and Peter, James, and John were all resurrected or, in the case of John, translated beings, another classification of being with a semi-resurrected body.[3] Further, we know that the "touch" test applied when the Aaronic Priesthood was restored because Joseph and Oliver Cowdery felt hands on their heads when priesthood authority was conferred.[4] This observation is consisten with Joseph's teaching that the more important a revelation is, the more likely it is that it will be communicated by the appearance of an angel or by an open vision.[5]

---

abused, which is instructive in this regard. "But ye are commanded in all things to ask of God, who giveth liberally; and that which the Spirit testifies unto you even so I would that ye should do in all holiness of heart, walking uprightly before me, considering the end of your salvation, doing all things with prayer and thanksgiving, that ye may not be seduced by evil spirits, or doctrines of devils, or the commandments of men; for some are of men, and others of devils." (Verse 7.)

1. Smith, *History of the Church*, 4:608.
2. Smith, *History of the Church*, 4:605; McConkie and Ostler, *Revelations of the Restoration*, 1041.
3. The same logic that applies to resurrected beings being righteous also applies to translated beings as well.
4. Oliver described the experience. "But, dear brother, think, further think for a moment, what joy filled our hearts, and with what surprise we must have bowed, . . . when we received under his hand the Holy Priesthood." (See JS–H 1:71, footnote.)
5. See Smith, *Teachings of the Prophet Joseph Smith*, 161.

Nauvoo, Illinois: January 19, 1841–July 12, 1843

Section 132: Red Brick Store, Nauvoo, Illinois, July 12, 1843

Heading

Covenants must be performed by proper priesthood authority and must be ratified by the Holy Ghost in order to be valid. Plural marriages are explained.

The big question

Question: What should we do to be saved?

Answer: Live worthy of having our saving ordinances ratified by the Holy Ghost (sealed by the Holy Spirit of promise). Enter into the new and everlasting covenant of marriage.

Introduction

This revelation was given through Joseph Smith the Prophet, in the Red Brick Store at Nauvoo, Illinois, July 12, 1843, relating to the new and everlasting covenant, including the eternity of the marriage covenant and the plurality of wives, or polygamy. Although the revelation was recorded in 1843, it is evident from the historical records that the doctrines and principles involved had been known by the Prophet since about 1831. The practice of plural marriage was discontinued at the end of the nineteenth century (see Declaration 1), but the requirement that in order to be saved in the highest kingdom a man and a women must enter into an eternal marriage covenant still stands. (See D&C 131:1–3.)

Anchor section

Memorize: Eternal marriage/Holy Spirit of Promise

Doctrine and Covenants 132 in a modern-day context

In historical context section 132 is a declaration about polygamy, a marriage arrangement that seems distant and anomalous to Mormons living in the twenty-first century. Although it is a well-known fact about Mormon history, it was a system of marriage that was openly practiced for less than fifty years. Yet, once in progress, it became a tenet of the faith around which the faithful, both male and female, rallied, despite excruciating pressure from the federal government to abandon it and society at large to change it. The principle was reluctantly abandoned after the federal government threatened to seize the assets of the Church, including its most sacred buildings, and disenfranchise its members for even expressing a belief in the principle. Nonetheless, later generations of Mormons who did not experience for themselves what it was like to defend the practice are as uncomfortable with the idea as most nonmembers of the Church are, at least in Western society.

Why, then, does section 132 remain in the modern canon, even though some of what it stood for was officially abandoned in 1890 when the Church adopted what is known as Official Declaration—1? Perhaps because when a revelation is "official" or has been "canonized," it remains in the scriptures even though it is no longer practiced. For example,  when Jesus taught that various parts of Leviticus prohibiting the ingestion of various foods no longer applied, the early Christians made no attempt to excise what they no longer observed from their Old Testament. They simply understood that that part of the canon was no longer applicable. (See Leviticus 11; Mark 7:1–23.) But, more important, many of the verses in section 132 are still applicable today. The idea that covenants must be ratified by the Holy Ghost and performed by proper authority is an important concept that applies across the board to all covenants and not just the plural marriage covenant. Such is also the case with the verses in section 132 that explain that marriage is eternal and that men and women can become Gods only by joining together in an eternal union. (See verse 19.) Finally, in consideration of the sacrifices made to live the "principle," as it was called, it serves an important historical purpose in reminding us of what the Lord required in our founding years. To take it out may be seen by outsiders as an attempt to erase the idea from the collective memory of Church members, something which in any case is impossible to accomplish in light of the historical interest in the subject and its ongoing and unauthorized practice by Mormon offshoots. For many outside of the Church, it is the only tenet they are familiar with about the Mormons.

Historical background on when section 132 was received and written down

Latter-day Saints have been reluctant to write about polygamy because of its controversial nature. However, the doctrine was at the core of much of Joseph Smith's thinking, especially during the Nauvoo period. Bushman got it right when he said that "nothing Joseph had done put the Church and his own reputation in greater jeopardy. The doctrine shocked the faithful followers, while Emma vacillated between acceptance and rejection. Yet, Joseph would not and felt that he could not stop. He saw himself in the tradition of Abraham and Solomon, Old Testament patriarchs commanded by God to marry plurally."[1] Joseph viewed it as part of what God required to be restored in the last great dispensation prior to the Second Coming.

Although the *recording* of section 132 bears the date of July 12, 1843, Joseph Smith probably *received* this or a revelation very much like it in approximately 1831.[2] Robert Woodford said that the eternal marriage covenant and polygamy were taught in Kirtland as early as 1835 and acknowledges that Orson Pratt said Joseph talked about the idea in 1831 and 1832.[3] By 1841 Joseph had married three wives and by 1842 he had at least eleven. When section 132 was recorded in 1843, he had at least fourteen.[4]

Plural marriage was practiced secretly in 1843 and was participated in on a clandestine basis until well after Joseph's martyrdom.[5] The doctrine was not openly announced until 1852, when Orson Pratt spoke on the subject at a general conference of the Church in Salt Lake City, Utah. During Joseph's lifetime, he publicly denied that he advocated polygamy. He taught the idea only to a small, trusted group of individuals and told the Twelve about it in the summer of 1841 after their return from their missions in Great Britain.[6]

The specific circumstances that prompted the recording of section 132 revolved around Emma. Emma believed that Joseph was a prophet but had grave reservations about polygamy and during her lifetime was only momentarily convinced of its divine origin. She believed Joseph was a true

---

1. Bushman, *Joseph Smith: Rough Stone Rolling*, 490.
2. See Compton, *Sacred Loneliness*, 2.
3. See Woodford, *The Historical Development of the Doctrine and Covenants*, 1731.
4. See Compton, *Sacred Loneliness*, 2. By the end of Joseph's life a number of the leading brethren and sisters were practicing polygamy. We know of at least eighty-four women who were sealed to Joseph, but most of them after Joseph was martyred. (See Compton, *Sacred Loneliness*, "Acknowledgments.") There are thirty-three well-documented wives of Joseph Smith, which he married while he was living. Some scholars say as many as forty. (See Compton, *Sacred Loneliness*, 1.)
5. See Bushman, *Joseph Smith: Rough Stone Rolling*, 491.
6. See Bushman, *Joseph Smith: Rough Stone Rolling*, 491.

prophet in large measure because she had witnessed the translation of the Book of Mormon and had seen the power of God manifested through him on many occasions.

Hyrum knew that Emma was a faithful believer in the Book of Mormon and convinced Joseph that if he would write the revelation down and allow him to speak to Emma about it, she would be convinced. Hyrum recommended Joseph use the seer stone, or Urim and Thummim, as seer stones were sometimes called, but the Prophet said he knew the content of the revelation perfectly.[1] It took him three hours to dictate the revelation, sentence by sentence, to William Clayton, who also was present at that time in Joseph's office located on the second floor of the Red Brick Store.[2] After it was written down, the revelation was read back to Joseph to make sure it was right.[3]

Emma's skepticism could not be overcome. When Hyrum presented the revelation to her she was adamantly against it. He returned to Joseph, unable to accomplish his mission, and said that he "never received a more severe talking to in his life."[4]

Historical background on polygamy generally

Most LDS historians believe that Joseph asked the Lord about polygamy when he was making inspired changes in the Old Testament. Such an interpretation seems consistent with the opening verses of section 132. Joseph acknowledges that he had questions on the subject—why was it allowed in Old Testament times?—and brought up the issue with the Lord. (See verse 1.) The language that follows was prophetic, because Joseph was indeed reluctant to live the principle once he was commanded to do so. "Prepare thy heart to receive and obey the instructions which I am about to give unto you; for all those who have this law revealed unto them must obey the same." (Verse 3.)

Lorenzo Snow remembered an 1843 conversation during which the Prophet disclosed to him the feelings he had for the repugnant idea.[5] In fact, Joseph did not begin its practice until he received divine warning of the consequences if he did not. There are a number of reports that an

---

1. See Bushman, *Joseph Smith: Rough Stone Rolling*, 496.
2. See Bushman, *Joseph Smith: Rough Stone Rolling*, 496.
3. See Woodford, *The Historical Development of the Doctrine and Covenants*, 1734; Roberts, *Comprehensive History of the Church*, 2:106.
4. Woodford, *The Historical Development of the Doctrine and Covenants*, 1734.
5. See *Encyclopedia of Mormonism*, 1093.

angel of the Lord on three occasions threatened Joseph with his life if he continued to refuse to implement the practice.[1]

Joseph's aversion to polygamy was shared by Brigham Young, Hyrum Smith, and (as noted) Joseph's wife Emma. Brigham said that when he first learned about plural marriage he felt to envy the corpse in a funeral cortege.[2] Their conversion to the principle came after remarkable spiritual experiences confirming the will of the Lord in the matter.

As section 132 emphasized, plural marriage was a highly regulated practice. Elder Parley P. Pratt wrote in 1845 that "these holy and sacred ordinances have nothing to do with whoredoms. . . . They have laws, limits, and bounds of the strictest kind."[3] Plural marriages were generally authorized by the President of the Church. Section 132 instructed that the first wife must give her consent, but this was not always carried out in practice, especially in Joseph's situation. (See verse 61.) For further information on polygamy generally, see Declaration 1.

Once polygamy was abandoned, it became a taboo subject in Church manuals and was dropped from the LDS curriculum. It became a subject of scholarly study, but it also became a topic used by detractors of the faith to criticize the Church. The Internet flourished with accurate and inaccurate information on the subject. The Church, therefore, introduced a series of essays on this topic that are now on the Church's official website. These essays accurately deal with the practice of polygamy as implemented by Joseph Smith and continued by Brigham Young when the Saints arrived in the Great Basin. These essays deal with many of the most controversial aspects of the practice and are a good reference point for Latter-day Saints who wish to learn more about, and find accurate information on, the subject.

---

1. Woodford, *The Historical Development of the Doctrine and Covenants*, 1732; see also Compton, *Sacred Loneliness*, 205–29. George D. Smith reports in *Nauvoo Polygamy* that "according to Eliza, 'Joseph unbosomed his heart' to her brother 'and described the trying mental ordeal he experienced in overcoming the repugnance of his feelings, the natural result of the force of education and social custom, relative to the introduction of plural marriage.' He knew that by violating societal norms, the 'whole Christian world stared him in the face' in disapproval but also that a 'commandment' had to be 'obeyed.' According to Eliza, the prophet 'hesitated and deferred' until 'an angel of God stood by him with a drawn sword, and told him that, unless he moved forward and established plural marriage, his Priesthood would be taken from him and he should be destroyed! This testimony he not only bore to my brother, but also to others—a testimony that cannot be gainsayed." (See p. 255.) Lorenzo Snow's account follows on pages 255–56.
2. See *Journal of Discourses*, 3:266; *Encyclopedia of Mormonism*, 1093.
3. Pratt, *The Prophet*, May 24, 1845; *Encyclopedia of Mormonism*, 1094.

The principles involved in section 132

There are two general principles around which the discussion on plural marriage and eternal marriage revolves. The first is that blessings in the next life are predicated upon obedience to the new and everlasting covenant of the gospel. (See verse 5.) The second involves what makes covenants binding or of full force and effect in the next life.

The first principle is straightforward. Obedience to God's law brings about certain blessings in a cause-and-effect relationship. In the context of section 132, obedience to the laws of marriage in this life makes it possible for the marriage union to continue in the next and for the couple to receive all of the blessings from God that are possible to receive.

The second idea—what makes covenants binding—needs more explanation. First, covenants are binding only if performed by a person with proper priesthood authority. (See verse 7.) Second, the person with authority may act only if authorized to do so. In the case of plural marriage, the President of the Church is the only person who can authorize its practice. "I have appointed unto my servant Joseph to hold this power in the last days, and there is never but one on the earth at a time on whom this power and the keys of this priesthood are conferred." (Verse 7.)[1] This is particularly interesting in light of the fact that all other keys are shared equally by the First Presidency. (See D&C 81:2; 90:6.)[2]

Finally, priesthood authority and keys are important, but not sufficient, to make covenants binding. In addition, the persons entering into the covenants must be worthy. Worthiness depends on whether or not a person is making an effort to live the commandments and is doing so for the right reasons. If the person is worthy, the Holy Ghost ratifies the covenant, a process discussed in more detail below.

Use of the term "new and everlasting covenant"

Section 132 refers to celestial marriage as "a new and an everlasting covenant." (See verses 4, 6, 19, 26–27, 41–42; see also D&C 131:2.) It should be noted that in other contexts "the new and everlasting covenant" is used more broadly and most often refers to the "sum total of all gospel covenants and obligations."[3] (D&C 66:2; see also verses 4–7.)

---

1. Smith, *Teachings of the Prophet Joseph Smith*, 324.
2. "And again, verily I say unto thy brethren, Sidney Rigdon and Frederick G. Williams, . . . they are accounted as equal with thee in holding the keys of this last kingdom." (See D&C 90:6.)
3. McConkie and Ostler, *Revelations of the Restoration*, 1054.

Nauvoo, Illinois: January 19, 1841–July 12, 1843

The Holy Spirit of Promise or ratification by the Holy Ghost

The expression "Holy Spirit of promise" is to be understood differently depending upon the context. (See commentary on D&C 130 and 88.) In section 132 it is used to express the idea that God will recognize as binding or eternally valid only those observances that are ratified or approved by Holy Ghost, and that the Holy Ghost will ratify our observance only if we live righteously and keep our covenants faithfully:[1]

"All covenants, contracts, bonds, obligations, oaths, vows, performances, connections, associations, or expectations, that are not made and entered into and sealed by the Holy Spirit of promise . . . are of no efficacy, virtue, or force in and after the resurrection from the dead; for all contracts that are not made unto this end have an end when men are dead." (Verse 7.)

The intention of this doctrine is to make it clear that doing things for the right reasons is indispensable, and that a person must be worthy for a covenant to be binding. In other contexts, the expression "Holy Spirit of promise" is used as a synonym for having one's calling and election made sure. (See commentary on D&C 84:3–5.)

God's house a house of order

Section 132 teaches that God's house "is a house of order." (Verse 8.) In the context of plural marriage, this means that such marriages were strictly regulated by the Church according to the laws of God. For example, only Joseph could authorize a plural marriage (verse 7), it was required that the first wife give permission for her husband to take another wife (verse 61),[2] and strict fidelity was required within the marriage arrangement (verse 41).

Rules and regulations governing plural marriage were no doubt necessary because of the potential for abuse. For example, when John C. Bennett, a friend and counselor of Joseph Smith and one-time mayor of Nauvoo, found out about plural marriage, he immediately used it to justify his bad behavior, enticing women into illicit relations not authorized by proper priesthood authority. [3]Therefore, when persons who were unauthorized to

---

1. Sometimes the word "justification" is used to express the same idea. For example, it is appropriate to say that a person has been justified by the Spirit. (See Moses 6:60.)

2. It should be noted that prior permission was not always obtained, especially in the case of Joseph when he began the practice. Joseph got the "tentative support of his own first wife, Emma, who gave tacit approval to the radical restructuring of their family, even though it was under some duress and with reluctance." (See Smith, *Nauvoo Polygamy*, 50.) Consent by the first wife became more common as the practice became more established, and the first wife was most often present when her husband married another woman. (See Pratt, *The Seer*, 31–32.)

3. Bushman, *Joseph Smith: Rough Stone Rolling*, 491.

take plural wives did so, it was without the explicit permission of Joseph and was condemned.

Marriage scenarios

Section 132 outlines four different marriage scenarios.

The first involves a man and wife not married by benefit of priesthood authority. In such circumstances the marriage is valid for time, during this life only, and "not of force when they are dead." (Verse 15.)

The second scenario involves a man and woman who make a covenant with one another to be married "for time and for all eternity" but "that covenant is not by me or by my word." In this case their marriage is for time only because it was not done by proper authority and has not been "sealed by the Holy Spirit of promise," or in other words ratified by the Holy Ghost. (See verse 18.)

The third situation involves a man and a woman who are married by priesthood authority, who sincerely live the commandments, and who have their calling and election made sure, either in this life or the next. In this instance their marriage is enduring and is in full force and effect in the next life. They become god and goddess. (See verses 19–25.)

The fourth scenario contemplates individuals who are married by priesthood authority, have their calling and election made sure, and then commit the "unpardonable sin."[1] They are damned and become sons and daughters of perdition. If they commit serious transgression short of the "unpardonable sin," they pay for their own sins before they are saved. (See verses 26–28.) Joseph Fielding McConkie and Craig Ostler point out that these verses speak "simultaneously of eternal marriage and having one's calling and election made sure. The promised blessings require both."[2] They went on to say:

> The chain of thought is as follows: a man and woman must be married according to the law of the Lord, meaning they must enter into the eternal covenant of marriage. They must then go forth and so live that they can receive the promise through the Lord's anointed that they will come forth in the first resurrection to inherit thrones and kingdoms. Having received that promise, which is certainly not given to them at the time of their marriage,

---

1. The unpardonable sin is to deny the truth of the gospel after having seen the Savior and viewing the visions of eternity. It is sometimes referred to as "shedding innocent blood," "blasphemy against the Holy Ghost" or "denying the Holy Ghost." (See Smith, *Teachings of the Prophet Joseph Smith*, 358.)

2. McConkie and Ostler, *Revelations of the Restoration*, 1062.

their salvation is sure, unless they so transgress that they become perdition (v. 26).[1]

McConkie and Ostler conclude by saying, "With that promise they have received all that is necessary to their exaltation as long as they do not commit the unpardonable sin (v. 26)."

Because these verses can be somewhat confusing regarding when and how a person or a couple may be sealed by the Holy Spirit of promise, it is helpful to see the historical context that Bushman illustrates for them. Between September 28, 1842, and February 26, 1843, Joseph established a ritual to be participated in after the marriage ceremony, which is referred to as the "second anointing" or "second endowment." Bushman said:

> This ceremony, given to eighteen men and their wives, was Joseph's attempt to deal with the theological problem of assurance. How did a Christian, in the words of the first chapter of 2 Peter, "give diligence to make your calling and election sure"? Calvinist theologians had argued over the question of certain knowledge for centuries. Was it possible to end doubt about one's standing with the Lord? Preaching from 2 Peter in May 1843, at the time he was reviving the endowment, Joseph had taught that the "more sure word of prophecy" meant "a man's knowing that he was sealed up unto eternal life by revelation and the spirit of prophecy through the power of the Holy priesthood." A few months later, the revelation on priesthood marriage had promised those who married eternally that they would surely enter into exaltation, even if they sinned, if once their bond had been "sealed by the Holy Spirit of Promise." Characteristically, Joseph embodied this process of certification in a ritual whose details were never described but that involved ordination as king and priest, words found in Revelation of St. John: Christ "hath made us kings and priests unto God and his Father."[2]

The couples who participated in this ritual were "noticeably quiet about the proceedings."[3] Bushman's reference to this certification ritual after marriage, which gave a person assurance of eternal life through an "anointed" "servant" with "keys of this priesthood,"[4] places Doctrine and Covenants

---

1. McConkie and Ostler, Revelations of the Restoration, 1062.
2. Bushman, Joseph Smith: Rough Stone Rolling, 498.
3. Bushman, *Joseph Smith: Rough Stone Rolling*, 498.
4. William Clayton referred to this practice when he recorded the details of a marriage ceremony performed for William G. Young and Adelia C. Clark by Brigham Young on January 1, 1846, in the Nauvoo Temple. "He [Brigham Young] requested them to stand up, and they did so, and by his direction joined their right hands together. He then said nearly as follows, William G. Young, you take Adelia C. Clark by the right hand to be your lawful wedded wife, and promise, in the presence of God and Angels, and these witnesses to observe all the laws and obligations and duties pertaining or belonging to this order of the Priesthood, do you? To which the Groom answered Yes Sir. He then asked the same question or nearly so of the Bride, and received a like answer. He then pronounced them husband and wife, *and*

132:19 and 26 in historical context. It should be observed that by the very terms of section 132, the certification ceremony Joseph introduced would be binding only if it were ratified by the Holy Ghost, the Holy Spirit of Promise.[1] (See verse 7.)

Persons may be married for time and eternity only in this life

Like baptisms, marriage ordinances must be performed in mortality. "Therefore, when they are out of the world they neither marry nor are given in marriage." (Verse 16.) Consequently, it is necessary to vicariously marry couples who died without the benefit of eternal marriage. Like baptism, this ordinance is performed in Latter-day Saint temples. This idea that marriages cannot take place in the next life is a reference to an observation made by Jesus to the Sadducees: "For in the resurrection they neither marry, nor are given in marriage, but are as the angels of God in heaven."[2] (Matthew 22:30.)

It is fair to note that the four Gospels do not speak of marriage as an ordinance necessary for men and women to be saved in the highest heaven. Traditional Christianity therefore makes the argument that such an idea was not an essential part of early Christianity, nor do they view it as necessary today. They view eternal marriage as an innovation of Joseph Smith. There is evidence, however, that marriage did play a much larger role in early Christianity than scholars initially assumed. In fact, there is some

---

sealed them together as such for time and for all eternity, and also sealed them up to eternal life, against all sins, except the sin of the Holy Ghost, which is the shedding of innocent blood, and pronounced various blessings upon them, and when he had done [so], told William to kiss his wife." (See Smith, ed., *An Intimate Chronicle: The Journals of William Clayton,* 247; emphasis added) In this instance there are two ceremonies described—eternal marriage, followed by a certification ritual, also described in verse 19 and 26.

1. The "second anointing" or "second endowment" in essence seems to be a ritual which, if ratified by the Holy Ghost, results in a man or woman having their calling and election made sure. However, this is not the only means of obtaining this promise. Joseph taught that this promise of eternal life could be obtained from the Lord Jesus Christ himself. (Smith, *Teachings of the Prophet Joseph Smith,* 358.)

2. A plain reading of Jesus' statement on no marriages after death has been rendered in some of the modern translations to mean that people do not live in a married state in heaven but are separate and single. "For when the dead rise, they won't be married. They will be like the angels in heaven." (See NLT Matthew 22:30). However, other translations seem to leave open the idea that there may be people in marriage relationships in heaven but that marriages cannot be performed there. The Centenary Translation (see the New Testament in Modern English), like the King James Version, leaves open the latter option. " . . . men do not marry, nor are women given in marriage [in the hereafter], but they are like the angels in heaven." (See Matthew 22:30.) In any case, section 132 makes it clear that people do live in marriage relationships in the afterlife and that in order to do so they must be married for time and eternity on earth or have the marriage ordinance authorizing eternal marriage done by proxy on this earth.

evidence that marriage was the highest rite or ordinance in the Church and bestowed upon the worthy participant "all things." Although never canonized, *The Gospel of Philip*, first published in an English translation in 1959, was found along with the more well-known *Gospel of Thomas* at Nag Hammadi in Egypt, even before the discovery of the Dead Sea Scrolls. Dating back to at least A.D. 400, and probably to the second century, it gives information about a tradition independent of what is contained in the canonical Gospels."[1] In *The Gospel of Philip*, five rites are described in ascending order: baptism, chrism (the Spirit), Eucharist, redemption, and *bridal chamber* (marriage). Associated with this bridal chamber ritual is a promise that the "anointed possesses all things—and that the Father gave him this in the bridal chamber."[2]

---

1. *Gospel of Philip*, 2.

2. *Gospel of Philip*, 20. The *Gospel of Philip* does not just stop at simply mentioning the importance of marriage as a Church sacrament. It informs us that: (1) Marriages on earth have their counterpart in heaven, and (2) Jesus was married to Mary Magdalene. "And the consort of [Jesus] is Mary Magdalene." (*Gospel of Philip*, 39:3.) Jesus had a conjugal relationship with Mary Magdalene. "[The Lord loved Mary] more than [all] the disciples, and kissed her on her [mouth] often." (*Gospel of Philip*, 39:4.) Jesus came to prepare a way to unite men and women who had died separate and apart. "Christ came, in order that he might remove the separation . . . and unite the two; and that he might give life to those who died in separation, and unite them." (*Gospel of Philip*, 46:5.) There is a special place for marriages to be solemnized. "But the woman is united to her husband in the bridal chamber." (*Gospel of Philip*, 46:6.) Those married in the "bridal chamber" will no longer be separate. "But those who have united in the bridal chamber will no longer be separated." (*Gospel of Philip*, 46:7.) God the Father united with a virgin to produce a body, presumably his Son. "If I may utter a mystery, the Father of all united with the virgin who came down. . . . He revealed the great bridal chamber. Because of this his body which came into being on that day out of the bridal chamber, in the manner of him who came into being from the bridegroom and the bride." (*Gospel of Philip*, 47; see also 1 Nephi 11:14–24 about the condescension of God.)

Those who have been anointed and received marriage in the "bridal chamber" will be resurrected, and it will presumably be a better resurrection. "He who is anointed possesses the All. He possesses the resurrection. . . . The Father gave him this in the bridal chamber." (*Gospel of Philip*, 50:9.) Gods procreate. "A god begets god. So it is with the bridegroom and the bride. [Their children] originate from the bridal chamber." (*Gospel of Philip*, 57:1.) The Son of Man received the power to beget children from God. "The Son of Man received from God the power to create. He has also the ability to beget. He who has received the ability to create is a creature." (*Gospel of Philip*, 57:11.) Persons who have been given the power to beget children are the offspring of God. "He who has received begetting is an offspring." (*Gospel of Philip*, 57:12.) To receive the blessings of the "bridal chamber," the ritual must be performed on earth. "If anyone becomes a son of the bridal chamber he will receive the light. If anyone does not receive it in this world, he will not receive it in the other place." (*Gospel of Philip*, 62.) Admittedly, I have placed these passages in a Mormon context. However, the point should not be lost that there are some early Christian documents that put great importance on marriage.

On becoming gods and goddesses

Men and women who live the gospel and sincerely enter into the saving ordinances, including the eternal marriage covenant, are promised that they may become gods or goddesses. (See verse 19–20.) Section 132 describes the core of what this means.

1. Gods live eternally and have no end. Implicit in this description is the idea that gods are not subject to death and disease. (See verse 20.)

2. Gods have all power and rule over all things. (See verse 20.)

3. Gods produce spirit offspring, referred to as a "continuation of the lives." (See verse 22.) Contrast this with the description of those who are not able to procreate in the next life: "Broad is the gate, and wide the way that leadeth to the deaths." (Verse 25.)

Therefore, deification is at the heart of Mormon theology and cannot be separated from eternal marriages and procreation. (See also D&C 76:55–70.)

The idea that marriage is an essential part of deification means that a man cannot be exalted or saved without a woman nor can a woman without a man. (See verse 19.) This premise explains the belief in a Mother in Heaven. Godhood is Parenthood and therefore requires a male and a female. In the *Encyclopedia of Mormonism*, Elaine Cannon explains:

> Elohim, the name-title for God, suggests the plural of Caananite El or the Hebrew Eloah. It is used in various Hebrew combinations to describe the highest God. It is the majestic title of the ultimate deity. Genesis 1:27 reads, "So God created man in his own image, in the image of God created he him; male and female created he them" (emphasis added), which may be read to mean that "God" is plural.[1]

In 1901, the First Presidency under Joseph F. Smith commented on the need for gods to be both male and female and said that "man, as a spirit, was begotten and born of heavenly parents, and reared to maturity in the eternal mansions of the Father," as an "offspring of celestial parentage." The statement goes on to explain that "all men and women are in the similitude of the universal Father and Mother, and are literally the sons and daughters of Deity."[2]

Although this idea that there are gods and goddesses may seem strange

---

1. Encyclopedia of Mormonism, 2:961.

2. *Encyclopedia of Mormonism*, 961. John A. Widtsoe said, "It has been said that sex is an eternal principle. The equivalent of sex, dimly understood by man, has always existed and will continue forever. Since sex, then, represents an eternal condition, the begetting of children is coincidentally an eternal necessity. We were begotten into the spirit by God the Father, and have been born into the world which we now possess." (Widtsoe, *Rational Theology*, 155.)

to traditional Christianity, it is not foreign to early Judaism prior to the reign of King Josiah. Margaret Barker, a well-known biblical scholar, has written:

> The earlier religion had known of God Most High—the deity worshipped by Melchizedek (Gen. 14:19)—El Shaddai, the deity of the patriarchs (Exod. 6:3), and Yahweh, who appeared in human form, for example to shut Noah safely into the ark (Gen. 7:16). There is no proof that these were one and the same deity. Only later were all these ancient forms said to be identical. It was the prophet of the exile who declared that Yahweh was El, and that there was no other God (Isa. 43:12–13; 45:22). In the more ancient names for the deities, however, we glimpse the Father (God Most High), the Son (Yahweh, the One who appeared in human form), and the Mother (El Shaddai, whose name means the God with breasts).[1]

Mormon theology harks back to this ancient tradition and teaches that the early Christians knew about and accepted it as well.

---

1. Barker, Temple Theology, 7.

Chapter 41

Among Friends at Ramus: Ramus, Illinois, April and May 1843

April 1843 was a relatively peaceful time for the Prophet Joseph. He had been living in seclusion for the previous two years in order to avoid being brought up on charges of complicity in the attempted assassination of Missouri ex-governor Lilburn W. Boggs. With that crisis over, he left the Nauvoo area in the spring of 1843 for one of his favorite and most often visited outlying settlements, Ramus, Illinois,[1] where members of the Church had taken up residence. This little town was not far from Nauvoo.[2]

Ramus had been founded in 1839 by a Kirtland friend of the Prophet, Joel H. Johnson, and Latter-day Saints comprised the vast majority of the population. A stake had been organized on July 5, 1840, with Joel Johnson appointed by Hyrum Smith as stake president.[3] The city had one of the few meetinghouses built by the Saints; members of the Church usually met in each other's homes or out-of-doors.[4]

In March 1843, Brigham Young wrote to the Church in Ramus, asking them to donate money to support Joseph Smith so that the Prophet could spend more time on Church-related matters. Ramus members gave generously. During April and May 1843, Joseph visited and taught them, as re-

---

1. Ramus in Latin means "branch" and was laid out in September 1840 on the same plan as Nauvoo. The town was later renamed Macedonia by the Saints. (See Cook, *Revelations of the Prophet Joseph Smith*, 287.) After the Saints were pushed out to go west with the body of the Saints, the town was named Webster, after Daniel Webster. (See Rugh, "Conflict in the Countryside," 2:148 [1992].)

2. See Preece, *Learning to Love the Doctrine and Covenants*, 376; Cook, *Revelations of the Prophet Joseph Smith*, 287. Ramus is eight miles northeast of Carthage.

3. See Cook, *Revelations of the Prophet Joseph Smith*, 287; Preece, *Learning to Love the Doctrine and Covenants*, 377.

4. See Berrett, Cannon, and Perkins, *Sacred Places*, 3:202–3. This building was one of the first meetinghouses built by the Mormons. Today the Webster Community Church sits on the site. It was constructed in 1897. (See Berrett, Cannon, and Perkins, *Sacred Places*, 3:203.)

flected in section 130.[1] When Joseph visited Ramus he stayed with his good friend and confidant, Benjamin F. Johnson, whom he called "Bennie."[2]

Section 130: Ramus (Webster), Illinois, April 2, 1843

Heading

The Father and the Son have bodies of flesh and bones. The time of the Second Coming is withheld. Intelligence gained in this life rises with us in the resurrection. All blessings are predicated upon obedience to law.

Introduction

This section is a composite of doctrinal instructions taught by Joseph Smith.[3] The Father and the Son have bodies of flesh and bones and may appear personally to men and women. The time of the Second Coming is withheld from the Prophet. Intelligence gained in this life rises with us in the resurrection. All blessings come by obedience to law.

Anchor section

Memorize: God the Father and the Son have bodies of flesh and bones

Historical background

On April 2, 1843, Joseph visited Ramus, an outlying settlement not far from Nauvoo. Upon his arrival, Joseph participated in a conference that extended throughout the day and into the evening.[4] During the morning

---

1. The community had been unified until late 1841 but began to divide over a heated dispute involving the collection of payments for lots. The situation continued to degenerate, and four persons were accused of impropriety and jailed in a nearby county on charges of stealing. In a spontaneous reaction, citizens gathered at the town square to uncover and find out if there were thieves among them. Joseph and the Twelve took action and sent a letter to Ramus condemning stealing; they also excommunicated the offenders from the Church. Church leaders went to Ramus to heal the rifts that had occurred among the leadership of the Church there. The acrimony was so intense that the stake was disbanded. (See Rugh, "Conflict in the Countryside" [1992], 32:1; 2:148.)

2. Ben Johnson was the son of Ezekiel Johnson. Bennie was twenty-four years old at the time. On April 1, 1843, the Prophet introduced Bennie to the principle of plural marriage. Joseph told him that he wanted to take Bennie's sister, Almera Johnson, as one of his plural wives. (See Johnson, *My Life's Review*, 85–93, as quoted in Preece, *Learning to Love the Doctrine and Covenants*, 377.)

3. Smith, *History of the Church*, 5:323–25.

4. Joseph frequently visited Ramus, stopping there to visit family and friends on his way to various destinations. Ramus citizens remember the Prophet wrestling and pulling sticks

session Orson Hyde spoke on John 14:23 and 1 John 3:2. During his remarks he said that it was his belief that the Father and the Son could dwell in people's hearts. At the lunch break Joseph, Orson, and Hyrum ate with Joseph's sister, Sophronia McLeary.[1] Joseph told Orson that during the afternoon session he would like to offer some corrections to his speech. Hyde graciously responded that the corrections would be "thankfully received."[2] Doctrine and Covenants 130:1–17 and 22 are responses to Hyde's remarks about God. Thirty-three years later, Orson Pratt, under the direction of the First Presidency, extracted this portion of what Joseph said on this occasion and included it in the 1876 edition of the Doctrine and Covenants.[3]

Summarizing the main points of some of Joseph's sermons or redacting parts of his letters for inclusion in the Doctrine and Covenants became necessary because, during the latter part of Joseph's ministry, his revelations were not written down word for word as they had been in earlier years. As the Church grew and became more self-governing it was less necessary for Joseph to give written revelatory instructions. Many precedents had already been published in the 1835 edition of the Doctrine and Covenants and were being referred to and relied upon by Church leaders. This is not to say that the number of Joseph's revelations diminished. He still wrote inspired letters on occasion and referred in his sermons to his visions, dreams, and angelic visitors. Bushman made reference to this change in procedure when he explained that "after the completion of the council system in 1835 [D&C 107], the number of written revelations opening with lines like 'verily thus saith the Lord' diminished. Instead of formal, dictated revelations, the later teachings were delivered in sermons, conversations, or letters."[4]

---

with Justus A. Morse, the strongest man in Ramus. Joseph beat him with only one hand. It is also recorded that he wrestled William Wall, the most expert wrestler in Ramus, and threw him. (Berrett, Cannon, and Perkins, *Sacred Places*, 3:203–4.)

1. Sophronia and Catherine, two of Joseph's sisters, lived in Ramus. Catherine married Wilkins J. Salisbury, a young lawyer and blacksmith in Ramus. He had joined the Church in Kirtland but was excommunicated in 1834. Catherine lived in Ramus until her death in 1900 at age 87. Her gravestone is in the small Ramus Cemetery. During her sojourn in Ramus, Brigham Young sent her $600 to help her. (See Berrett, Cannon, and Perkins, *Sacred Places*, 3:204.)

2. See Preece, *Learning to Love the Doctrine and Covenants*, 377.

3. See Preece, *Learning to Love the Doctrine and Covenants*, 377.

4. Bushman, *Joseph Smith: Rough Stone Rolling*, 419. Sections 127 and 128 are letters about baptism for the dead. Sections 130 and 131 are extracts from speeches. Section 132 on polygamy was written down by special request. With the exception of Joseph's handwritten letters, this meant that many of Joseph's most important insights are found "only in ragged, compacted listeners' notes." (See Bushman, *Joseph Smith: Rough Stone Rolling*, 419.)

God and Jesus have bodies of flesh and bones

Joseph taught that the starting point of any faith is its views of God; what God "is" or is not affects every other aspect of the religion. If the views about God are correct, that which follows is more likely to be correct. If the views about God are wrong, the ideas and doctrines that follow are more likely to be off course.[1] It is for this reason that Mormonism is so fundamentally different from traditional Christianity, which worships a very different God. Latter-day Saints reverence a Godhead of three distinct individuals, two—God the Father and his Son Jesus Christ—with bodies of flesh and bones, and a third—God the Holy Ghost—who has a body of spirit (still consisting of matter but a "more refined" type of physical element). The first two are exalted Men and the third an exalted Spirit personage. Each of these Gods exists materially in time and space.

Traditional Christianity, on the other hand, worships "one God" who is not made of physical elements, exists beyond time and space, and is not anthropomorphic, although this God may manifest itself in at least two other ways, as Jesus Christ or as the Holy Spirit. This conventional doctrine, referred to as the Holy Trinity, was formulated at the Council of Nicaea over three hundred years after the death of Jesus and is adhered to in one form or another by virtually all Christians except the Mormons.

Joseph Smith was very clear on this matter of what God is or is not. He said, "The Father has a body of flesh and bones as tangible as man's; the Son also." (Verse 22.) Therefore, God is "an exalted man," and is called Man of Holiness. This was "the great secret. If the veil were rent today, and the great God who holds this world in its orbit, and who upholds all worlds and all things by his power, was to make himself visible,—I say, if you were to see him today, you would see him like a man in form—like yourselves in all the person, image, and very form as a man."[2]

It is no wonder, then, that Joseph found it necessary to correct Orson Hyde in Ramus when he seemed to speak approvingly of the traditional Protestant and Catholic conception of God. Hyde's suggestion that God could somehow dwell in a man's or woman's heart[3] was not consistent with the idea that God and Jesus are two separate material personages. Doctrine and Covenants 130:1–17, 22 are a rejection of Hyde's characterization of an indwelling God. By way of correction, section 130 begins: "When the Savior shall appear we shall see him as he is. We shall see that he is a

---

1. Joseph said, "It is the first principle of the Gospel to know for a certainty the character of God." (See Smith, *Teachings of the Prophet Joseph Smith*, 345.)

2. Smith, *Teachings of the Prophet Joseph Smith*, 345.

3. In support of his position, Hyde had referred to John 14:23, which says God may "make an abode" with men and women. Orson evidently gave this verse a traditional Christian interpretation, namely that God and Jesus may literally dwell in a person's heart.

man like ourselves," a direct reference to 1 John 3:2. (See D&C 130:1.)[1] To add emphasis, Joseph explained, "The appearing of the Father and the Son, in that verse, is a personal appearance; and the idea that the Father and the Son dwell in a man's heart is an old sectarian notion, and is false."[2] (Verse 3.)

This fundamental premise that God is a corporeal being or an Exalted Man led Joseph to a very different theology about man's relationship to God and the destiny of men and women. Whereas Catholics and Protestants conceived of men and women blissfully, but passively, residing with God in some future existence, Joseph revealed that in the next life God's children would be engaged in a far more momentous and active endeavor. Joseph learned that since God was an Exalted Man, then there must also be Exalted Women. A "God the Father" meant that there was a "God the Mother," and if this were the case, then Gods are married and capable of producing offspring—spirit children who lived with God in a premortal life before coming to this earth. By definition, these offspring may become like their Heavenly Parents—gods and goddesses in their own right. Therefore, in the next life God's children may also be married and produce spiritual offspring in an ongoing creative process that links the entire human race together as brothers and sisters in a mutually supportive enterprise.

While this idea that men and women may become gods and goddesses may seem grandiose, the concept naturally leads to an appreciation of one's own intrinsic worth and the worth of others. James Talmage summed it up this way: "What is man in this boundless setting of sublime splendor? I answer you: Potentially now, actually to be, he is greater and grander, more precious in the arithmetic of God, than all the planets and suns of space. For him were they created; they are the handiwork of God; man is his son. In this world man is given dominion over a few things. It is his privilege to achieve supremacy over many things. . . . 'For behold, this is my work and my glory—to bring to pass the immortality and eternal life of man.'"[3]

---

1. See Preece, *Learning to Love the Doctrine and Covenants*, 377; Smith, *History of the Church*, 5:323.

2. Smith, *Teachings of the Prophet Joseph Smith*, 150–51. In reference to John 14:23 Joseph said, in response to the question, what is the Second Comforter: "It is no more nor less than the Lord Jesus Christ Himself; and this is the sum and substance of the whole matter; that when any man obtains this last Comforter, he will have the personage of Jesus Christ to attend him, or appear unto him from time to time, and even He will manifest the Father unto him, and they will take up their abode with him, and the visions of the heavens will be opened unto him, and the Lord will teach him face to face, and he may have a perfect knowledge of the mysteries of the Kingdom of God; and this is the state and place the ancient Saints arrived at when they had such glorious visions—Isaiah, Ezekiel, John upon the Isle of Patmos, St. Paul in the three heavens, and all the Saints who held communion with the general assembly and Church of the Firstborn."

3. Brown, *Continuing the Quest*, 209.

In Joseph's theology the idea of a personal God also meant that men and women are social beings. "That same sociality which exists among us here will exist among us there, only it will be coupled with eternal glory, which glory we do not now enjoy." (D&C 130:2.) As such, mankind's happiness is based on the degree to which they form mutually supportive relationships and live in a just society based on an equality of station and wealth. "It is not given that one man should possess that which is above another, wherefore the world lieth in sin." (D&C 49:20.)

Finally, the idea that God is a concrete living being, and not just an abstraction or metaphysical principle, makes God more comprehensible. We are akin to him, and his personality is revealed in the divine personality of his Son, Jesus Christ. The distance between God and man is lessened and our relationship to him more clearly understood. There is a greater sense of proximity, familiarity, and intimacy with Deity. It is a doctrine that invites a child to prayerfully become acquainted with a Divine Parent who is comprehensible, loving, and concerned about his offspring.

Historical notes on the Trinity

As stated briefly above, traditional Christianity believes in a Trinity (God the Father, Jesus Christ, and the Holy Ghost), and yet these three are viewed as one God—a God without body, parts, or passions. Today it is almost universally agreed that this idea was not taught at the time of Jesus and became part of traditional Christianity at the Council of Nicaea in the early part of the fourth century A.D. As David H. Wright points out in the *Encyclopedia of Early Christianity:* "It was during the patristic centuries that the church's Trinitarian faith assumed the shape it has largely retained throughout its history."[1]

Another well-known biblical scholar, also by the name of Wright, G. Ernest Wright, concurred, publishing an entry entitled "The Faith of Israel" in the well-respected *Interpreter's Bible,* a commentary used by most, if not all, United States Protestants. With no apologies, G. Ernest Wright explained that throughout the Old Testament God is spoken of as a person by means of "a free and frank use of anthropomorphic language" and is "depicted as possessing practically all the characteristics of a human being, including bodily form and personality."[2] Further, he states that "nowhere in the Bible can there be said to be a doctrine of God's spirituality, unless one were to except John 4:24."[3] God, he says, is "conceived in personal,

---

1. Wright, *Encyclopedia of Early Christianity,* 1142.
2. *Interpreter's Bible,* 1:362.
3. In reference to John 4:24, "God is a Spirit: and they that worship him must worship him

even corporeal terms, and perhaps the most vivid example and the climax of this anthropomorphism is to be found in the doctrine of the Incarnation."[1] God "is not conceived as an abstract idea or principle" but rather as a "forceful personality whom men can meet, know, and worship."[2] Certainly this description captures the God that Joseph Smith knew.

The movement away from "God as Exalted Man" is well documented and needs little comment here other than to touch on a few points. By A.D. 324, debates regarding the nature of God and the differences between Jesus (the Son) and God (the Father) were common. Some early church fathers were more inclined to argue that Jesus was separate from God, namely Arius and Eusebius of Nicomedia. Both believed that Jesus was an individual personality apart from God, a personage whose "moral progress provided the example."[3] This view was opposed by those more friendly to a Platonic conception of God as a nonmaterial, metaphysical "essence" and Jesus as a manifestation of this essence.

When Constantine, emperor of Rome at the beginning of the fourth century, legitimized Christianity and used it as a tool to unify the empire, he entered the debate. He invited the bishops to Nicaea, a city near his imperial palace at Nicomedia with a room large enough to entertain the clergy. Although he was not a Christian at the time, he listened to both sides and settled the controversy by employing Greek philosophy to try to satisfy the divergent points of view. The end result reads like a political compromise, declaring God to be "three yet one."[4]

Phillip Cary, a professor from Yale, succinctly summarizes the situation.

---

in spirit and in truth," Wright states that "the spirit of God is not to be identified with God himself." (*Interpreter's Bible*, 1:362.) According to Bart D. Ehrman, a contemporary scholar on the early Christian church, the only verse in the entire New Testament that provides explicit affirmation on the traditional doctrine of the Trinity—that three divine beings are one (1 John 5:7–8)—is not found in the text of any Greek manuscript until around the time of the invention of printing in the fifteenth century. (See Erhman, *The New Testament*, 66.) Another passage often used to imply the Trinity is John 1:18: "No man hath seen God at any time; the only begotten Son, which is in the bosom of the Father, he hath declared him." Of course, this passage is contradicted by the prophets in the Old Testament who saw God "face to face." Therefore, it is not surprising that Ehrman points out that this passage has been corrupted. He states that all of this was to help the scriptures comport with a Greek understanding of God as disembodied and to lessen the difference between God and Jesus so that it could be argued that God and Jesus are one and the same. (See Ehrman, *The Orthodox Corruption of Scripture*, 264–65.)

1. Ehrman, *The Orthodox Corruption of Scripture*, 264–65.
2. Ehrman, *The Orthodox Corruption of Scripture*, 363.
3. See *Encyclopedia of Early Christianity*, 810.
4. "We worship one God in trinity, and trinity in unity, neither confounding the persons nor dividing the substance. . . . There are not three incomprehensibles, but one incomprehensible. . . . So the Father is God, the Son is God, and the Holy Ghost is God. Yet they are not three gods but one god. So the Father is Lord, The Son is Lord, and the Holy Ghost is Lord, and yet not three Lords but one Lord. . . . For like as we are compelled by Christian verity to

As Christianity gathered converts during the first few centuries after Jesus died, Christian thinkers "wanted to combine both the story of the God of Israel" and the thinking and "categories that they learned from the Greeks, categories of metaphysics."[1] The early church father Tertullian opposed the adoption of Greek thought into Christian theology and believed that Plato was the "source of all great heresies."[2] Tertullian aligned with the Stoics, who were materialists and believed both "God and the soul were made of material stuff."

Other great Christian thinkers, however, rejected the materialist view in place of a nonmaterialist view of both God and the soul as posed by Plato. This approach formulated the idea of the Trinity: the Father, the Son, and the Holy Spirit. As Cary puts it, "To do that, they had to end up stealing language from the Greek metaphysical tradition. They talked about the Son of God—that's Christ—being of one essence with the father. That's a peak piece of metaphysical language that you don't find in the Bible that the church fathers found useful for defining who God was."[3] Therefore, Cary concludes, the discussion about three Gods is from the Bible and discussion about "three in one" or the others being "one essence" with the Father is from the Greeks.[4]

Civil War prophecy

Joseph predicted the American Civil War about sixty years prior to its occurrence. (See D&C 87.) Section 130 gives more detail about this future event and notes that the conflict would begin in South Carolina, which it did. (See D&C 130:12–13.)

The timing of the Second Coming

One of the most perplexing questions for Joseph Smith and first-generation Saints was, When will the Second Coming of Jesus happen? In 1831 Joseph taught that Jesus would appear in the sanctuary to be built on the temple site in Independence, Missouri, where Zion was to be established. The early Saints expected that this event would take place within their lifetime. When it became clear that the Saints would not be able to build the New Jerusalem at that time in the place predicted, this

---

acknowledge every person by himself to be God and Lord, so we are forbidden to say there be three Gods or three Lords." (See Nibley, *The World and the Prophets*, 55.)

1. *Great Minds of the Western Intellectual Tradition*, 2:19.
2. *Great Minds of the Western Intellectual Tradition*, 2:19.
3. *Great Minds of the Western Intellectual Tradition*, 2:20.
4. *Great Minds of the Western Intellectual Tradition*, 2:20.

recognition was deeply troubling. In the anguish of his soul, Joseph took the matter up with the Lord with little success.

"I cannot learn from any communication by the Spirit to me, that Zion has forfeited her claim . . . , notwithstanding the Lord has caused her to be thus afflicted. . . . I know that Zion, in the due time of the Lord, will be redeemed; but how many days . . . the Lord has kept hid from my eyes; and when I inquire concerning this subject, the voice of the Lord is: Be still, and know that I am God!"[1]

Section 130 records yet another effort on the part of the Prophet Joseph to receive a revelation from God on the timing of the Second Coming. This section was received during a time when there was considerable speculation about when this event would commence. Willard Miller, a religious leader contemporary with Joseph, had predicted Jesus' return on April 3, 1843, just one day before Joseph received section 130. Joseph assured the Church that Miller's prophecy would fail. On the timing of this cataclysmic event, he divulged that he had "earnestly" approached the Lord in prayer on December 25, 1832. Joseph explained, however, that the answer he received was ambiguous and he was left "without being able to decide" when the "Son of Man" would make his triumphal appearance. (See verses 14–17.)[2]

Saved by knowledge

One of the unique aspects of the theology taught by Joseph Smith was that in addition to faith, repentance, and baptism, people are saved by knowledge. Whereas all Christian religions speak of the first principles in one form or another, this added obligation was entirely unique to Mormonism. Joseph explained, "If a person gains more knowledge and intelligence in this life through his diligence and obedience than another, he will have so much the advantage in the world to come." (Verse 19.) About a year later, at a general conference of the Church in April 1844, he explained further: "In the world of spirits no man can be exalted but by knowledge. So long as a man will not give heed to the commandments, he must abide without salvation. . . . [But] although [a person] has been

---

1. Smith, *Teachings of the Prophet Joseph Smith*, 34.
2. That Joseph was unable to get information on the exact timing of the Second Coming is not surprising. Matthew and Mark both attest, "But of that day and hour knoweth no man, no, not the angels of heaven, but my Father only." Since only the Father knows the day and hour, Matthew seems to imply that not even Jesus knows when he is coming again. (See Matthew 24:36.) However, Joseph in his inspired rendition of the same passage in Mark made a change that suggests that Jesus also knows the time of his coming. (See JST Mark 14:32.)

guilty of great sins, ... when he consents to obey the Gospel, whether here or in the world of spirits, he is saved."[1]

"Knowledge" meant that having a broad education was part of what it meant to be Mormon. Knowledge in 1828 was defined as "a clear and certain perception of that which exists, or of truth and fact; the perception of the connection and agreement, or disagreement and repugnancy of our ideas."[2] This meant that learning and illumination of the mind must be promoted if God's children were to become more like Him. It was with these ideas in mind that Joseph, according to the Lord's instruction, established the School of the Prophets and the University of Nauvoo. An expansive curriculum was offered Latter-day Saint students, ranging from languages, geography, and literature to math, science, and theology.[3]

Irrevocable law

In Mormonism God is not the author of law; rather, God is subject to it. "But there is a law given, and a punishment affixed ... and the law inflicteth the punishment; if not so, the works of justice would be destroyed, and God would cease to be God." (Alma 42:22, 25.) In June 1844, in his most well-known sermon, the King Follett Discourse, Joseph taught that God makes known to his children the laws necessary for them to progress and become like Himself.

> The first principles of man [laws of the universe] are self-existent with God. God himself, finding he was in the midst of spirits and glory, because he was more intelligent, saw proper to institute laws whereby the rest could have a privilege to advance like himself. The relationship we have with God places us in a situation to advance in knowledge. He has power to institute laws to instruct the weaker intelligences, that they may be exalted with himself, so that they might have one glory upon another, and all that knowledge, power, glory, and intelligence, which is requisite in order to save them in the world of spirits. (Emphasis added.)[4]

The idea is summed up in section 130: "There is a law irrevocably decreed in heaven before the foundations of this world, upon which all blessings are predicated." (Verse 20.)

Since God is subject to the same laws his children are, God cannot arbitrarily bestow gifts and powers on his children any more than he can arbitrarily bestow such gifts and powers on himself. The only way that

---

1. Smith, *Teachings of the Prophet Joseph Smith*, 357.
2. *Webster's Dictionary*, 1828 edition.
3. See commentary on section 88 regarding the School of the Prophets.
4. Smith, Teachings of the Prophet Joseph Smith, 354.

intelligent beings can advance and progress and become Godlike is to obey the same laws that God obeys. Obedience to these eternal laws are the very underpinnings of God's power and of man's eternal progression. Therefore, we are blessed based on the principle of cause and effect: "And when we obtain any blessing from God, it is by obedience to that law upon which it is predicated." (Verse 21.)

Section 131: Ramus, Illinois, May 16, 17, 1843

Heading

Celestial marriage qualifies men and women to enter the highest degree of the celestial kingdom. "The more sure word of prophecy" is explained. Spirits are composed of refined matter.

Introduction

This section is a composite of doctrinal instructions taught by Joseph Smith the Prophet on the three gradations of glory in the celestial kingdom, calling and election, and the material properties of spirits.[1]

Anchor section

Memorize: Marriage is an order of the priesthood

Historical background

The Prophet stopped in Ramus on a number of occasions to visit relatives and friends there. His two most noted visits occurred in April and May 1843, when he spoke about doctrinal subjects that were later summarized in sections 130 and 131. For further background, see section 130.

On May 16, 1843, the Prophet and his company arrived in Ramus in the middle of the afternoon. The Prophet visited at the home of William G. Perkins and then spent the night at the home of his good friend Benjamin F. Johnson ("Bennie"). His scribe, William Clayton, accompanied him.[2] Before retiring at the Johnson home, Joseph put his hand on the knee of William Clayton and said, "Your life is hid with Christ in God, and so [are] many others." Joseph addressed Bennie and said, "Nothing but the unpardonable sin can prevent him [Clayton] from inheriting eternal

---

1. See Smith, *History of the Church*, 5:392–93.
2. See Woodford, *The Historical Development of the Doctrine and Covenants*, 1723.

glory for he is sealed up by the power of the priesthood unto eternal life having taken the step which is necessary for that purpose."[1] In doing this, the Prophet, in essence, announced that William Clayton's calling and election had been made sure.

Joseph then turned his attention to the topic of marriage. On his previous visit to Ramus in April, Joseph had spoken with Benjamin F. Johnson about plural marriage. At that time he had told Johnson that plural marriage had been revealed to him by God and, further, that he (Joseph) had been commanded to live it. He explained that when this an-  cient order had been revealed to him in Kirtland, he had thought he might ask Julia Johnson, Bennie's sister, to marry him. He explained that now he was once again required by God to take more wives, so he had come to ask for Bennie's sister, Almera.[2]

Benjamin's initial response to the whole matter was one of disgust and severe depression. Nevertheless, he arranged a meeting between Almera and the Prophet. He said, "I stood before her trembling, my knees shaking." However, "Just so soon as I found power to open my mouth it was filled for the light of the Lord shone upon my understanding and the subject that had seemed so dark, now appeared of all subjects pertaining to our gospel the most lucid and plain and so my sister and myself were converted together."[3] Joseph and Almera were sealed in marriage not long afterwards.[4] Now, in May, Joseph returned to the subject of marriage and taught Clayton and Johnson that in order to receive all of the blessings of God it is necessary to "enter into this order of the priesthood [meaning the new and everlasting covenant of marriage]."[5] (Verse 2.)

---

1. Cook, *Revelations of the Prophet Joseph Smith*, 291.
2. Johnson said that the Prophet's words "astonished me and almost took my breath—I sat for a time amazed and finally almost ready to burst with emotion." (See Compton, *Sacred Loneliness*, 295–96.) Joseph then told Johnson that he would preach a sermon that night that only he would understand. Joseph spoke on the parable of the talents and explained that to him who had (talents), more would be given; but if a man had only one, that one would be taken away from him, a radical critique on monogamy. (See Compton, *Sacred Loneliness*, 296.)
3. Compton, *Sacred Loneliness*, 297.
4. See Compton, *Sacred Loneliness*, 297–98.
5. He explained further that marriage must be done in this life, "while in this probation by the power and authority of the Holy priesthood." (See Cook, *Revelations of the Prophet Joseph Smith*, 291.) If this were not the case, he explained, then in the next life they would not have the power to procreate "children in the resurrection," while those who were married in this holy order "would continue to increase and have children in the celestial glory." (See Cook, *Revelations of the Prophet Joseph Smith*, 291.) That Joseph was speaking about plural marriage on this occasion is probable. William Clayton, his scribe and companion in Nauvoo, said that the prophet spoke of little else in private during the last year of his life. As Compton points out, "As he developed the principle of sealing ordinances that connected families for eternity,

Calling and election made sure

On the following morning, May 17, 1843, the Prophet took up the subject of "the more sure word of prophecy," saying that this meant that a person's calling and election had been made sure. He explained that a man or woman may know that they have been "sealed up unto eternal life, by revelation and the spirit of prophecy, through the power of the Holy Priesthood."[1] (Verse 5.) Just a few days earlier, the Prophet, speaking on this subject, explained:

> Though they might hear the voice of God and know that Jesus was the Son of God, this would be no evidence that their election and calling was made sure, that they had part with Christ, and were joint heirs with Him. They then would want that more sure word of prophecy, that they were sealed in the heavens and had the promise of eternal life in the kingdom of God. [2]

Joseph explained that a person could know that their calling and election was made sure through personal revelation and exhorted the members to "continue to call upon God" until they had done so.[3]

As Bushman explained, Joseph's teaching about the concept of calling and election dealt "with the theological problem of assurance. How did a Christian, in the words of the first chapter of 2 Peter, 'give diligence to make your calling and election sure'? Calvinist theologians had argued over the question of certain knowledge for centuries. Was it possible to end doubt about one's standing with the Lord?"[4] For Joseph, the answer was yes, but only after a person's faith had been thoroughly tested by life's experiences.

Further, in connection with having one's calling and election made sure, Joseph taught that if a person denied God and Jesus after having been given certain knowledge, that person could not be forgiven. He described this action as blasphemy against the Holy Spirit, repeatedly spoken of in the four Gospels as an unpardonable sin. He said that after seeing Jesus and knowing with a certainty that he is the Son of God, denying that truth

---

this doctrine was inextricably bound up with plural marriage. Later nineteenth-century Mormons taught that a monogamist could not gain complete salvation, a belief that was clearly based on Smith's teachings." (See Compton, *Sacred Loneliness*, 10.) This is not the doctrine today. After the Lord revealed it was no longer necessary to practice polygamy, leaders of the Church have taught that eternal monogamous marriages qualify for salvation.

1. The reference to "Holy Priesthood" is probably a reference to the second endowment. "Joseph introduced a more advanced ordinance called the 'second anointing,' between September 28 and February 26 [1843–44]. This ceremony . . . [was] given to eighteen men and their wives." (See Bushman, *Joseph Smith: Rough Stone Rolling*, 497.)
2. Smith, History of the Church, 5:388.
3. See Smith, *History of the Church*, 5:389.
4. Bushman, *Joseph Smith: Rough Stone Rolling*, 497.

is akin to shedding "innocent blood." Joseph expressed it this way: "All sins shall be forgiven, except the sin against the Holy Ghost" and said that this meant that a person must "deny Jesus Christ" after a having seen him and after "the heavens have been opened unto him, and . . . deny the plan of salvation with his eyes open to the truth of it."[1]

A person may not be saved in ignorance

Section 131 informs us that "it is impossible for a man to be saved in ignorance." (Verse 6.) The knowledge referred to here is probably an awareness of the certainty an individual may have of his or her salvation, or of having his or her calling and election made sure.[2] In this regard Joseph said:

> After a person has faith in Christ, repents of his sins, and is baptized for the remission of his sins and receives the Holy Ghost, (by the laying on of hands), which is the first Comforter, then let him continue to humble himself before God, hungering and thirsting after righteousness, and living by every word of God, and the Lord will soon say unto him, Son, thou shalt be exalted. When the Lord has thoroughly proved him, and finds that the man is determined to serve Him at all hazards, then the man will find his calling and his election made sure, then it will be his privilege to receive the other Comforter.[3]

To receive this other Comforter is to have Jesus appear and to see the visions of eternity.[4] It is this very specific understanding of a person's standing with God that is "an anchor to the soul, sure and steadfast."[5]

The material nature of spirits

During the latter part of the day on May 17, 1843, after listening to a Methodist preacher's lecture, Joseph spoke on the material nature of God and spirits. Upon the conclusion of the minister's remarks, which seem to have asserted that spirits were immaterial, Joseph offered some corrections. He explained that "there is no such thing as immaterial matter. All spirit

---

1. Smith, *Teachings of the Prophet Joseph Smith*, 358.
2. Smith, *History of the Church*, 5:387. In D&C 130:18–19, the knowledge referred to is of a much broader nature.
3. Smith, Teachings of the Prophet Joseph Smith, 150.
4. See Smith, *Teachings of the Prophet Joseph Smith*, 149–51.
5. Smith, *History of the Church*, 5:388. The Prophet also taught that those who have their callings and elections made sure will be saved unless they blaspheme against the Holy Ghost, a term of art meaning that they know for a surety that God lives because the heavens have been opened to them and they then deny it (see Smith, *Teachings of the Prophet Joseph Smith*, 358), which qualifies them as a Son of Perdition (see D&C 76:25–49; 132:26). Joseph had his calling and election made sure. (See D&C 132:49.)

is matter, but it is more fine or pure, and can only be discerned by purer eyes; we cannot see it; but when our bodies are purified we shall see that it is all matter." (See verses 7–8.)[1] This idea that spirits have material substance goes hand in hand with the idea that God is material and has a body. It strikes at the root of the traditional Christian notion that there is a dimension that is wholly nonmaterial or metaphysical. For Joseph, if it was not made of something it did not exist.

The idea that spirits are material has important implications in Mormon theology. It is a product of Joseph's revealing that matter is eternal, just as God is eternal. The inferences of this teaching are (1) that God did not create matter out of nothing (*ex nihilo*). Rather, when God formed the earth he "organized" matter.[2] And (2) that spirits, being made of matter, have always existed in some configuration. "There never was a time when there were not spirits; for they are co-equal [co-eternal] with our Father in heaven."[3] It is from the premise that God is not outside matter but rather part and parcel with it that Mormon theology proceeds.

There are three gradations of glory in the celestial kingdom

Section 131 refines our understanding of section 76, which teaches that there are three degrees of glory. Section 131 adds that not only are there three primary divisions in the hereafter but that the celestial or highest degree of glory is also divided. "In the celestial glory there are three heavens or degrees." (Verse 1.) The most advanced living arrangement involves marriage, family ties, and eternal progeny. (See D&C 132:19–25.)

Marriage is an order of the priesthood

Section 131 describes marriage as an order of the priesthood. (See verse 2.) It follows therefore that the laws governing the priesthood also apply in the marriage covenant, analogous to the leading quorums of the priesthood. The decision-making authority is vested in those quorums and is based on the governing principle of unanimity. "And every decision made . . . must be by the unanimous voice of the same; that is, every member . . . must be agreed to its decisions." (D&C 107:27.) Although this idea was counter-cultural in Joseph's day and therefore not applied to marriages of the time, it is consistent with the teaching of modern-day prophets who emphasize that marriage is an equal partnership.

---

1. See Woodford, *The Historical Development of the Doctrine and Covenants*, 1723.
2. See Smith, *Teachings of the Prophet Joseph Smith*, 350–51.
3. Smith, *Teachings of the Prophet Joseph Smith*, 353; see also 352–54.

This "order of the priesthood" called marriage also involves receipt of the "patriarchal priesthood." Joseph talked about priesthood from three perspectives—the Aaronic, Melchizedek, and patriarchal—described by him as "three grand orders."[1] The Aaronic or Levitical had to do with the "outward ordinances," such as baptism.[2] The Melchizedek had to do with the "keys of power and blessings" and "administering" the kingdom.[3] The patriarchal had to do with "endless life" and the sealing of "fathers [and mothers] to children."[4] This priesthood, he said, encompassed the promise of endless progeny, one of the promises given to Abraham as part of the Abrahamic covenant. Joseph taught that the patriarchal priesthood was received in connection with marriage in the temple: "Go to and finish the temple . . . and you will then receive more knowledge concerning this priesthood."[5]

Section 135: John Taylor home, Nauvoo, Illinois, June 27, 1844

Heading

John Taylor's eulogy to Joseph Smith, the martyr.

Introduction

This document concerning the martyrdom of Joseph Smith the Prophet and his brother, Hyrum Smith the Patriarch, at Carthage Jail, Illinois, on June 27, 1844,[6] was written by Elder John Taylor of the Council of the Twelve, who was a witness to the events. The exact location where the statement was written is not known. Some have suggested Carthage Jail or the 1844 *Times and Seasons* office in Nauvoo.

---

1. See Smith, *Teachings of the Prophet Joseph Smith*, 322–23.
2. See Smith, *Teachings of the Prophet Joseph Smith*, 323.
3. See Smith, *Teachings of the Prophet Joseph Smith*, 322.
4. Smith, *Teachings of the Prophet Joseph Smith*, 322–23.
5. Smith, *Teachings of the Prophet Joseph Smith*, 322–23.
6. See Smith, *History of the Church*, 6:629–31.

Historical background

The last six months of Joseph's life were filled with anxiety and pressure. He was the mayor and chief magistrate of the municipal court and running as a candidate for the Presidency of the United States.[1] He had recently organized the political kingdom of God and had begun weekly meetings with the Council of Fifty.[2] He was also battling dissent from within the Church from those who were upset that some were practicing plural marriage and troubled by Joseph's radical new doctrines concerning deification and the plurality of gods.

In response, some members of the Church formed a so-called reformed church and claimed that Joseph Smith was a fallen prophet.[3] William Law was one of the ringleaders of those who challenged Joseph's leadership. Law arrived in Nauvoo in 1839, an immigrant from Northern Ireland who had been converted in Canada and then traveled south to join the main body of the Saints. Joseph invited Law to become a member of the First Presidency when Joseph's brother Hyrum vacated the position to assume the responsibilities of Church patriarch after their father died. Law

---

1. "After President Martin Van Buren and the federal government refused to act on the Mormon Petitions for Redress concerning the Missouri persecutions, Joseph Smith lost confidence" that the Mormons would receive redress from the government of the United States. Consequently, the Prophet met in the Nauvoo mayor's office with the Twelve and announced that he would run for president. Thereafter "he met with William W. Phelps, who helped him write a platform that was published" under the name *General Smith's Views of the Powers and Policy of the Government of the United States*. In it he "advocated giving power to the president to suppress mobs, . . . reforming the prison system, eliminating courts martial for desertion, forming a national bank, . . . annexing Oregon and Texas," and doing away with slavery. "On April 9, during a regular session of general conference, Brigham Young called for volunteers to serve political . . . missions and 244 stepped forward. During the next few days" more were called, until the number reached about 600. Sidney Rigdon ran as Joseph's vice-president. (See Barr, Cannon, and Cowan, *Encyclopedia of Latter-day Saint History*, 944–45.)

2. "On 7 April 1842, Joseph Smith received a revelation titled 'The Kingdom of God and His Laws With the Keys and Power Thereof, and Judgement in the Hands of His Servants, Ahman Christ,' which called for the organization of a special [political] council . . . known as the Council of Fifty." It was organized on March 11, 1844, to prepare the world for the Second Coming by bringing about a political transformation of the world." A few non-Mormons were members of this group. The Lord said of the organization, "Ye are my Constitution and I am your God and ye are my spokesmen." Decisions were to be unanimous, a pattern followed in the leading priesthood quorums. (See D&C 107:27–31.) Joseph Smith taught the group about how the Constitution of the United States would be applied during the Millennium. Members were involved in Joseph Smith's presidential campaign. "Following the murder of Joseph Smith, Brigham Young presided over the Council of Fifty and used it [to govern the Church] as the Saints moved west." During John Taylor's administration (1880–87), he "revitalized the Fifty, and they met annually during his administration so members could receive instruction regarding political matters. Since that time the Council of Fifty has not [functioned]." (See Barr, Cannon, and Cowan, *Encyclopedia of Latter-day Saint History*, 256–57.)

3. See Bushman, *Joseph Smith: Rough Stone Rolling*, 526.

enthusiastically accepted most of the teachings of the Church. However, when he learned that Joseph had adopted the idea of polygamy he wrote in his journal that it "paralyzes the nerves, chills the currents of the heart and drives the brain almost to madness."[1] Ultimately, Law could not go along with the doctrine of plurality of wives and was excommunicated in April 1844. He then became the leader of those who believed that Joseph, though once a prophet, had lost his prophetic mantle and had fallen into error. By mid-May, at least 300 other individuals had joined Law's secessionist movement.[2]

As criticism from within the Church mounted, so did censure from the non-Mormon community, who feared Joseph's growing political and military power and what they considered to be his grandiose ideas and unorthodox religious teachings. The distinction between Joseph practicing plural marriage and committing adultery was lost on many Church members and was the crux of the difficulties with William Law. As the two sides parted ways, enemies of the Church, including the reform movement, obtained the use of the *Nauvoo Expositor*, a local newspaper, and decided to use it to "expose" what they regarded as the evil doings of Joseph and his group in Nauvoo. The tone of the articles indicated that Law and his followers were hoping to sway converts of the Church. The paper accused Joseph Smith of whoredoms and, along with polygamy, condemned his teaching "that there are innumerable Gods as much above the God that presides over this universe, as he is above us."[3]

Joseph and the city council were outraged by the accusations set forth in the *Expositor*. They met in a long session on Saturday, June 8, 1844, and again on the following Monday. Using Blackstone[4] as their guide, the council reasoned that if nothing were done mob violence could erupt. Consequently, acting in his office as mayor, Joseph "ordered the city marshal, John Greene, to destroy the press, scatter the type, and burn any remaining newspapers."[5] In the legal context of the times, the city council probably acted lawfully to abate a public nuisance by destroying issues of the offending paper. However, the demolition of the press was a violation of property rights.[6] Over and above this legal analysis, outsiders were

---

1. Bushman, *Joseph Smith: Rough Stone Rolling*, 528.
2. See Bushman, *Joseph Smith: Rough Stone Rolling*, 538.
3. Bushman, *Joseph Smith: Rough Stone Rolling*, 539.
4. William Blackstone was an English jurist who lived during the eighteenth century. He produced a commentary on the law that is still used as a reference today.
5. *Church History in the Fulness of Times*, 275.
6. See *Church History in the Fulness of Times*, 275; Bushman, *Joseph Smith: Rough Stone Rolling*, 540.

outraged because Joseph Smith had "trespassed freedom of the press, which had become nearly a sacred right in the United States."[1]

As the situation deteriorated in Nauvoo, Thomas Sharp, editor of the *Warsaw Signal*, the local newspaper in Warsaw (a few miles from Nauvoo), levied pointed attacks against Joseph Smith and the Mormons and called for Joseph's removal from his position, by force if necessary. A well-known anti-Mormon, Sharp said that he had founded the *Warsaw Signal* for the purpose of "either correcting the unhallowed usurpation [of] power of that band of villains, at Nauvoo, or their extermination from civilized society."[2] Bushman points out that "in advocating force,[3] Sharp appealed to the primitive law of communal self-defense that had authorized mob actions from the Revolution to the killing of the abolitionist printer Elijah Lovejoy in Alton, Illinois, in 1837, ironically the same principle underlying the wrecking of the *Expositor*. The theory that a community had the right to enforce its will against impending danger had authorized vigilantism and lynchings in one community after another in every section of the nation. Relying on it to make his case, Sharp was sure of support when on June 12 he called for Joseph's assassination and the extermination of the Mormons."[4]

The situation had grown dangerous, and Joseph had few options. His wife, Emma, and his brother Hyrum believed that Joseph should rely upon the governor and the state's claims that Joseph should submit to the legal process. Joseph believed this would lead to his assassination. Therefore, he left Nauvoo and crossed the Mississippi River. Joseph remained on the Iowa side of the river less than twelve hours. Pressure from those who felt Joseph should trust in the legal process and those in Nauvoo who felt he was deserting them caused him to return to Nauvoo on June 23.[5]

Joseph decided to submit to the legal process; on Monday morning, June 24, 1844, he left for Carthage to give himself up to the legal authorities, charged with multiple crimes for his part in closing down the *Expositor*. Four miles from Carthage his band was met by sixty mounted state militia men "with orders from [Governor] Ford to collect state-issued arms in

---

1. Bushman, *Joseph Smith: Rough Stone Rolling*, 541.
2. Bushman, *Joseph Smith: Rough Stone Rolling*, 542.
3. "These actions prompted citizens' groups in Hancock County to call for the removal of the Saints from Illinois. Thomas Sharp vehemently expressed the feelings of many of the enemies of the Church when he editorialized in the *Warsaw Signal*: 'War and extermination is inevitable! *Citizens* ARISE, ONE and ALL!!!–Can you *stand* by, and suffer such INFERNAL DEVILS! to ROB men of their property and RIGHTS, without avenging them. We have no time for comment, every man will make his own. LET IT BE MADE WITH POWDER AND BALL!!!'" (*Church History in the Fulness of Times*, 275.)
4. Bushman, *Joseph Smith: Rough Stone Rolling*, 543.
5. Bushman, *Joseph Smith: Rough Stone Rolling*, 546.

Nauvoo. Joseph countersigned the order and then returned to Nauvoo ... to aid in the collection."[1] Joseph saw Emma and his family for one last time, then headed for Carthage once more.[2]

In Carthage he was arrested and charged with treason. When he was incarcerated, along with Hyrum, and accompanied by Willard Richards and John Taylor, a friendly jailer allowed the prisoners to move into his own upstairs bedroom. On June 27, 1844, shortly after five o'clock in the afternoon, those intent on assassinating Joseph Smith stormed the jail and, in a barrage of bullets, killed the Prophet and his brother Hyrum, and seriously wounded John Taylor.

The John Taylor account

After the martyrdom, John Taylor wrote section 135, an inspired eulogy to the Prophet. As an eyewitness to the final events in Joseph's life, no one was in a better position to write such a document. Because he was suffering from his wounds, the printing was delayed until October 1844; the eulogy was published in the new edition of the Doctrine and Covenants.[3] The statement speaks for itself and is a loving tribute from a true disciple.

---

1. Bushman, *Joseph Smith: Rough Stone Rolling*, 546.
2. See Bushman, *Joseph Smith: Rough Stone Rolling*, 546.
3. See Preece, *Learning to Love the Doctrine and Covenants*, 398.

Carthage Jail, in Carthage, Illinois, where Joseph and his brother Hyrum were murdered by a mob of approximately 150 men.

Part 9

Winter Quarters and Beyond

Chapter 42

The Big Question: Winter Quarters and Salt Lake City, Utah

How Shall the Church Survive?

By the time the Saints were expelled from Nauvoo in 1846, it had become axiomatic that the kingdom of God and Babylon did not mix. After all, the track record was dismal. The Mormons had, within the space of about seven years, been evicted at gunpoint from Kirtland, Ohio; Independence, Missouri (as well as the rest of Jackson County); Clay County, Missouri; Far West, Missouri; and Nauvoo, Illinois. That the Mormons survived in the face of such fierce resistance is extraordinary. This survival involved establishing a colony in a remote location over a thousand miles to the west. The Mormon exodus is now legendary and begins with a vanguard company that left Winter Quarters, Nebraska, on April 5, 1847, and forged the way for thousands upon thousands who would come by land and by sea from as far away as England and continental Europe to join the Saints in the Great Basin kingdom.

The survival strategy would ultimately entail far more than simply moving out of the way. It would also require a wrenching process of making Mormons more acceptable to the society at large. First and foremost, the Saints would be compelled to abandon the practice of polygamy and, ninety years later, a policy that banned African-Americans from full Church participation, a policy that developed over time once the Saints settled in Utah. (See Official Declaration—1 and Official Declaration—2.) There would be other far-reaching changes as well. Efforts to live in communal orders would be abandoned in favor of a capitalistic distribution of goods and services. An effort to find a more pluralistic and less theocratic political system would be haltingly embraced.

At first the changes would be radical and fundamental. Reorienting marriage practices and embracing an economic system that Orson Pratt, a leading LDS apostle at the time, described as "a plan of the Devil"[1] would not come without some convincing that it was truly necessary. However, as time went on and as the Church entered the twentieth century, the pace of change would become more unhurried and more measured. This evolution is still in progress as the Church makes decisions on how to deal with societies in transition and what parts of the gospel are considered essential in an organization that is becoming a worldwide presence.

Two of the foremost writers on the subject of changes within the Mormon tradition are Thomas G. Alexander in *Mormonism in Transition*, and Jan Shipps in *Mormonism*. In addition to polygamy, politics, and communal living, Alexander explores the adaptation of various doctrines, new direction in Church administrative practices, and intentional strategies to reshape the Mormon image. Shipps captures the sense of disorientation Mormons felt as alterations and adjustments were made. Her description of how nineteenth-century Latter-day Saints might react in a twentieth- or twenty-first-century setting illustrates the point.

> The hypothetical Saints . . . from the twentieth century [visiting the nineteenth] in a time machine would have been astonished to find so few Saints at Sacrament Meeting, because the twentieth-century Sacrament Meeting is a visible worship sign, whereas in the pioneer era more expressive worship signs were irrigation canals, or neatly built and nicely decorated houses, or crops of sugar beets. More significantly, living in the kingdom in the nineteenth century was the sign of citizenship in God's elect nation. Gentiles there were, but the community was a separated one, made special through the institution of the patriarchal order of marriage. While the Word of Wisdom was usually observed in the Mormon community, the Latter-day Saint perception of being special, of being a part of the chosen people, did not depend on abstaining from tobacco and coffee and on universally negative decisions about whether or not to drink the Valley Tea or wine the Saints manufactured in Dixie.[2] Identity was maintained corporately, not individually, which explains why

---

1. Pratt, "Equality and Oneness of the Saints," in *The Essential Orson Pratt*.
2. At the turn of the twentieth century the Church began to emphasize the importance of living the Word of Wisdom and attending meetings. This change came at a time when it was necessary to redraw boundaries because the Church had jettisoned some of its most distinctive features, including communal living orders and plural marriage. The Church's initial commitment to social equality spoke volumes about what its members really valued and was an expression of how to love one's neighbor. After these practices were stopped, attending meetings and strictly living the Word of Wisdom became markers of faithfulness. The problem that has arisen, however, is that this focus on outward performance sometimes encourages Pharisaical attitudes within the Church.

all citizens of the kingdom—those who were involved in plural marriage and those who were not—were willing to defend to the last possible moment the practice of polygamy that kept them set apart.[1]

Maintaining a sense of uniqueness as Mormons while at the same time continuing a trend toward assimilation into the society at large is an issue of importance and it does not come without peril. A balance between adherence to past traditions and changing to accommodate the present is essential if Mormonism is to retain its vitality. Too much of an accommodation could dampen the spiritual power and energy of the religion.[2] Too little change could make Mormonism brittle and irrelevant. Some of the unique aspects of Mormon worship that give it a sense of being apart from the world are found in its temple practices. Maintaining a distinctive identity and deciding how to do it is the challenge of our generation.[3]

Another reason the Church survived is that the hardships and privations experienced by the pioneers compelled them to cooperate with each other. The adversity in Winter Quarters and during the trek to the hostile desert environment of Utah molded the Mormon people into a sturdy and highly supportive community. Jan Shipps explains that it was in this way that the Mormon movement was transformed into something more than a Church to which people belonged, becoming instead much like an ethnic nation.

> The parallel between the Mormon trek and the biblical Exodus needs to be remembered here, for it is the key to the pioneer experience. Just as the original designation of the Saints as chosen was a repetition of God's paradigmatic act in choosing Abraham's seed, so the Mormon trek renewed the force of God's election of the Mormons in precisely the same way that the miraculous departure from Egypt and the journey through the wilderness and into the Promised Land renewed the identity of the Hebraic tribes as citizens of His elect nation. [In this way Mormons] were formed not into a culture whose perpetuation depended not on the preservation of a particular polis, but into an ethnic body, a chosen race. Once they had been no people; now, in truth, they were God's People. . . . Like the children of Israel, the Saints

---

1. See Shipps, Mormonism, 125.
2. Accommodation has not only been accomplished by giving up various practices, such as polygamy, but also by emphasizing others. For example, the emphasis on "happy families" and family home evenings are the kind of themes that are nonthreatening and present Mormonism with a soft edge. Emphasizing the good life and upright living rather than controversial doctrines such as deification gives outsiders less to criticize and makes Mormonism appear like just another brand of Protestantism. While all of this drives Mormonism in the direction of social acceptability, it also gives outsiders little reason to want to become members of the Mormon Church when their own religious traditions seem to offer some of the very same things. In order for a group to be attractive to outsiders, it has to create a certain amount of social tension against the "outside" forces.
3. See Mauss, "Refuge and Retrenchment: The Mormon Quest for Identity."

made their way through the wilderness to claim their "inheritances," and in so doing conjoined the experience and scripture to take possession of that special relationship to God which once had been the sole property of the Jews.[1]

Even to this day, those outside the Church are struck by the sense of family loyalty that exists in Mormon congregations and the degree to which Mormons regularly join together in cooperative enterprises that aid people in need in and out of the Church.[2]

---

1. See Shipps, Mormonism, 122.
2. The Church welfare system, humanitarian aid projects, and education funds for members in third-world countries are just a few examples of the spirit of cooperation that exists in the Church.

Chapter 43

Winter Quarters: January 14, 1847

SECTION 136: SITE OF BRIGHAM YOUNG, HEBER C. KIMBALL, AND EZRA T. BENSON HOMES, WINTER QUARTERS (FLORENCE), NEBRASKA, JANUARY 14, 1847

Heading

Instruction on how to organize for the exodus to the Great Basin kingdom.

The big question

Question: How will the Saints survive?
Answer: Organize and cooperate.

Introduction

The word and will of the Lord, given through President Brigham Young at Winter Quarters of the Camp of Israel, Omaha Nation, West Bank of the Missouri River, near Council Bluffs, Iowa, concerning the Mormon exodus to the Great Basin kingdom.[1]

---

1. See Journal History of the Church, January 14, 1847.

Historical background

After the martyrdom of Joseph Smith on June 27, 1844, a deep gloom fell over the city of Nauvoo. The Twelve, except for John Taylor and Willard Richards, were on missions in the eastern United States and made their way back to Nauvoo as expeditiously as possible. The potential for reprisal by the Mormons against their enemies was real.[1] Yet John Taylor and Willard Richards were able to keep the peace and avoid a massive Mormon retaliation. Elder Taylor wrote to the Saints in Great Britain that "the action of the saints has been of the most pacifistic kind, remembering that God has said, 'Vengeance is mine, I will repay.'"[2]

After a succession crisis in which Sidney Rigdon, Joseph's first counselor in the First Presidency, and others tried to assume leadership of the Church, the mantle fell upon Brigham Young. On Thursday, August 8, 1844, in a meeting held to discuss who should lead the Church, Brigham Young was transfigured before the people. Many of those in attendance reported that when he addressed the Saints, he sounded and looked like the Prophet Joseph. Benjamin F. Johnson, a close friend of the Prophet, reported at the time that "as soon as he [Brigham Young] spoke I jumped upon my feet, for in every possible degree it was Joseph's voice, and his person, in look, attitude, dress and appearance was Joseph himself, personified; and I knew in a moment the spirit and mantle of Joseph was upon him."[3]

The succession crisis resolved, Brigham Young began to assert himself as the leader of the Mormon people. Wilford Woodruff was sent on a mission to England to preside over the Church in Europe. Parley P. Pratt was called to New York to head up the immigration effort. The quorums of seventy were expanded to focus on missionary work. Nauvoo in 1844 began to flourish again. Brigham Young renamed Nauvoo "The City of Joseph," and the city continued to grow.[4]

When it became evident that the death of Joseph Smith had not diminished the vibrancy of the Church, its enemies were infuriated. Persecution again began in earnest. As early as September 1844, Colonel Levi Williams of Warsaw, who had been part of the murderous gang at Carthage, organized a militia to drive the Saints out of Nauvoo. If not for the intervention of troops sent by Governor Ford to keep the peace, he might have been successful.[5] However, peace between the Saints and their neighbors was

---

1. Johnson, *My Life's Review*. Benjamin F. Johnson describes going to a gentile home and seizing weapons and supplies.
2. *Church History in the Fulness of Times*, 287.
3. *Church History in the Fulness of Times*, 291.
4. *Church History in the Fulness of Times*, 300.
5. *Church History in the Fulness of Times*, 300–301.

fleeting, and Brigham Young and his associates decided that it would be best to move the Church out of Nauvoo into the West.

Prior to his death, Joseph Smith had prophesied in 1842 that the Saints would suffer and, at some point, would "go and assist in making settlements and build cities and see the Saints become a mighty people in the midst of the Rocky Mountains."[1] In the spring of 1844, he had instigated plans for colonizing the West. After his martyrdom and the subsequent persecution, the original evacuation of Nauvoo was planned for April 1846, but new threats prompted a hasty exit. The decision to leave was made on February 2, 1846, and the first group left on February 4.

The Saints gathered on the Iowa side of the Mississippi in Sugar Creek. They waited until March 1, 1846, to leave that camp, with Brigham Young at their head. The Iowa trek proved to be the hardest part of the journey. The main group took 131 days to cover three hundred miles. The Pioneer Company a year later took only 111 days to travel just over a thousand miles from Winter Quarters to the Great Basin.[2]

The Saints had not originally planned to stop in Winter Quarters, a small settlement located on the west bank of the Missouri River in Nebraska. Nevertheless, bad weather, inadequate provisions, and overcrowded wagon trains slowed progress considerably. Beginning in October 1846, Winter Quarters sprang up overnight and spilled over the east bank of the Missouri River at Council Bluffs, Iowa. By December about five thousand Mormons had gathered there. The settlement was organized under the leadership of twenty-two bishops, with jurisdiction over wards. High councils were established on both sides of the river. The Saints hunkered down for the winter.[3]

Winter Quarters will be remembered as yet another trial of faith experienced by the Saints. Many were malnourished, had inadequate shelter against the cold winter, and were struck with malaria and scurvy. Between October 1846 and May 1848, as many as a thousand perished and many were buried in unmarked graves. By early spring 1847, the vanguard of pioneers had left for the Great Basin.[4] Prophetic instruction on how they were to organize for the journey west came in January 1847 to the prophet Brigham Young and now appears as section 136.

---

1. *Church History in the Fulness of Times*, 305.
2. See *Church History in the Fulness of Times*, 309.
3. See Garr, Cannon, and Cowan, *Encyclopedia of Latter-day Saint History*, 1349.
4. See Garr, Cannon, and Cowan, *Encyclopedia of Latter-day Saint History*, 1349.

Memorial statue "Tragedy at Winter Quarters" by Avard T. Fairbanks, sculpted in tribute to the Mormon pioneers who died in Winter Quarters, Nebraska, on their way to the Great Basin kingdom.

Specific background relating to Doctrine and Covenants 136

One year after the Saints departed Nauvoo, most of them were temporarily located in and around Winter Quarters waiting for a break in the weather to continue on to the Salt Lake Valley.[1] As preparations were made, Brigham Young followed the same pattern that Joseph did.[2] He held several council meetings to consider the best way to organize the emigration. For example, on January 11, 1847, he "called on Dr. Richards who accompanied him to Elder Ezra T. Benson's . . . where they met in council."[3]

On Thursday, January 14, 1847, Brigham Young and others met in council at the Heber C. Kimball home in the early afternoon. The topic of discussion centered around the best way to organize companies for emigration. "Brigham Young commenced to give the word and will of God concerning

---

1. See Woodford, *The Historical Development of the Doctrine and Covenants*, 1802.
2. From the Church's inception, when Joseph made decisions he called various brethren together to a council. This method of decision making was later formalized in D&C 107:27–31 and is the operating procedure for the leading priesthood quorums in the Church.
3. Journal History of the Church, January 11, 1847, as quoted in Woodford, *The Historical Development of the Doctrine and Covenants*, 1802. At this meeting Brigham Young mentioned that he met and talked with the Prophet Joseph in a dream. (See Woodford, *The Historical Development of the Doctrine and Covenants*, 1802.)

the emigration of the saints and those who journey with them."[1] In the late afternoon the brethren adjourned and later reconvened at Brother Ezra T. Benson's home, where Brigham Young continued to write down parts of section 136. In the early evening, those in council left the Benson home and met in Willard Richards's home, where the process continued. At ten in the evening the meeting closed.[2]

Once Doctrine and Covenants 136 was received, the various quorums of the Church voted to accept it, beginning with the Quorum of Twelve and continuing with the seventies and high priests. The revelation was warmly received as the mind and will of God.

Companies, captains of hundreds, fifties, and tens

Section 136 called for pioneer companies to be organized, with captains over one hundred people, captains over fifty, and captains over ten. (See verse 3.) Each company was to take with them on their journey an equal portion of the widows and poor among them. (See verse 8.) All were to share their property with each other to make it possible for all to survive. (See verse 10.) Specific companies were organized, with a president and two counselors at the head. (See verses 3, 12–16.) The Saints were admonished be honest with each other, shun evil, not contend with each other, cease from drunkenness, and return items borrowed to their owner. (See verses 20–26.) Recreation along the journey (dance and song) was recommended. (See verse 28.) Joseph is mentioned along with some of the other great prophets. (See verse 37.) The Saints are admonished to "be diligent in keeping all my commandments . . . lest . . . your faith fail you, and your enemies triumph over you." (Verse 42.)

Early in April, Brigham Young led the first company of just under 150 Saints on the thousand-mile journey to the Salt Lake Valley. The group arrived on July 24, 1847.

---

1. Journal History of the Church, January 11, 1847, as quoted in Woodford, *The Historical Development of the Doctrine and Covenants*, 1802.
2. Woodford, *The Historical Development of the Doctrine and Covenants*, 1803.

Chapter 44

Salt Lake City, Utah: October 6, 1890–June 1978

OFFICIAL DECLARATION—1: WILFORD WOODRUFF HOME AND OFFICE, OCTOBER 6, 1890

Introduction

President Wilford Woodruff announces the cessation of the practice of plural marriage or polygamy.

The big question

Question: How shall we survive?
Answer: Cease the practice of polygamy.

Historical background

In about 1831 Joseph Smith received a revelation that approved the practice of plural marriage. (See D&C 132 and commentary.) At first, the practice was confined to a very few individuals. However, once the Saints arrived in the Great Basin kingdom, the practice was expanded. A precise number of those participating in plural marriage is not available, but studies suggest that about 20 to 25 percent of LDS adults were members of polygamous households. The Church did not publicly announce the practice until August 29, 1852, five years after the first pioneers entered the valley.

Persecution and outrage over polygamy intensified over the years, and the United States Congress passed anti-polygamy legislation that stripped Church members of their right to vote and disincorporated the Church, which permitted the seizure of Church property by the government. As out-

side pressure against the Mormons for engaging
in polygamy increased, the Church resisted. Woodford described the situation: "Pressure was put upon President Wilford Woodruff by the United States government until it appeared the destruction of the whole Church was imminent if a decision to end polygamy was not soon made. As early as 1888, President Woodruff approached the Quorum of Twelve on the subject of abolishing plural marriages."[1]

The following reflects the decision that was made after some discussion: "I held a meeting with the Twelve till near midnight.... [W]e had an address or document made up for us to accept to do away with polygamy. But, not one of the Apostles would accept of it. All rejected it."[2]

The practice continued.

Finally, on September 24, 1890, President Woodruff met with his counselors and three of the apostles and on the same day wrote Official Declaration—1 or what was known as the Manifesto. President Woodruff worked on a draft that was 510 words long. The statement was edited by George Q. Cannon and reduced to 356 words.

On October 6, 1890, the Manifesto was presented at a general conference of the Church and was approved by the congregation. Some were reluctant to give up the practice, and as a result a limited number of plural marriages were sanctioned after the Manifesto. For this reason, the First Presidency issued a "second manifesto" in April 1904, completely ending polygamy in the Church. Some broke away from the main body of the faith so that they could continue the practice. Such persons were excommunicated.

Wilford Woodruff said on one occasion that he had seen in vision the dire consequences of practicing polygamy if it continued.

> The Lord showed me by vision and revelation exactly what would take place if we did not stop this practice.... I saw exactly what would come to pass if there was not something done. I have had this spirit upon me for a long time. But I want to say this: I should have let all the temples go out of our hands; I should have gone to prison myself, and let every other man go there, had not the God of heaven commanded me to do what I did do; and when the hour came that I was commanded to do that, it was all clear to me. I went before the Lord, and I wrote what the Lord told me to write.[3]

---

1. Woodford, *The Historical Development of the Doctrine and Covenants*, 1825.
2. Wilford Woodruff journal, December 20, 1888, as quoted in Woodford, *The Historical Development of the Doctrine and Covenants*, 1825.
3. See Woodford, The Historical Development of the Doctrine and Covenants, 1827.

Polygamy during the Utah period

Plural marriage usually involved two to three wives. The larger polygamist families like Brigham Young and Heber C. Kimball were an exception to this general rule. As stated above, it is estimated that about 20 to 25 percent of LDS adults were members of polygamous households, which reflects the fact that plural marriages were required to be authorized at the highest levels of Church leadership.[1] The divorce rate was about the same for polygamist marriages as the national average at the time.[2] The practice gave flexibility to pioneer women, who were encouraged by Brigham Young to pursue careers in medicine, accounting, law, and politics. Some insiders felt the practice to be repressive, but many of the women involved were strongly in favor of plural marriage. Non-Mormon women in the East who saw polygamy as repressive were shocked when Mormon women publicly demonstrated in favor of the practice and their right to live it.[3]

Plural marriage worked better for some families than others. Not surprisingly, the most common complaint of second and third wives was that their husbands did not treat them equally or spent too little time with them. Some marriages failed and, although Brigham Young disliked divorce, when women were unhappy in the practice of plural marriage or felt trapped in an unworkable relationship, divorce was sanctioned. On the positive side, many of the wives developed a deep love for and a sense of cooperation with each other. Children grew up in large, well-adjusted extended families. Many prominent civic and Church leaders throughout the West today are descended from polygamous households.[4]

SECTION 138: BEEHIVE HOUSE, SALT LAKE CITY, UTAH, OCTOBER 3, 1918

Introduction

A vision given to President Joseph F. Smith. In his opening address at the eighty-ninth semi-annual conference of the Church, President Smith said that he had received several divine communications during the previous months. One such revelation came in a vision he had had one day prior to the conference. It concerned a visit of the Savior to the spirits of the dead while his body was in the tomb awaiting the resurrection. This vision was recorded following the close of the conference on October 31, 1918,

---

1. See *Encyclopedia of Mormonism*, 1095.
2. See *Encyclopedia of Mormonism*, 1094.
3. See *Encyclopedia of Mormonism*, 1094.
4. See *Encyclopedia of Mormonism*, 1094–95.

submitted to his counselors in the First Presidency, the Council of the Twelve, and the Patriarch, and was accepted by them unanimously. It was first published as part of the Doctrine and Covenants in the 1978 edition. Before that time it was available in a compilation of President Smith's sermons and writings called *Gospel Doctrine.*

Anchor section

Memorize: Spirit World

Historical background

Section 138, commonly referred to as the vision of the redemption of the dead, was received by Joseph F. Smith, sixth president of the Church, on the day before the 1918 October conference. During the conference President Smith alluded to this and other spiritual manifestations he had recently experienced. He said, "I will not, I dare not, attempt to enter upon many things that are resting upon my mind this morning, and I shall postpone until some future time, the Lord being willing, my attempt to tell you some of the things that are in my mind, and that dwell in my heart."[1]

The subject matter of the revelation, the spirit world, was particularly important to President Smith at this time because he had been ill prior to this conference and undoubtedly was pondering his own death and what would come afterward. President Smith died in his home just weeks after this conference, on November 19, 1918, at the age of eighty.[2]

Joseph F. Smith was well acquainted with death; one reason he may have received this revelation was that he had on so many occasions pondered the subject on a very personal level. In 1844, when he was five years old, his father, Hyrum Smith, was martyred in Carthage Jail along with his uncle, the Prophet Joseph. In 1852, when he was fourteen, he lost his mother, Mary Fielding Smith, a woman of tremendous spiritual stature. "Additionally, two of his wives preceded him in death, Levira Annett Clark Smith in 1888, and Sarah Ellen Richards in 1915. Between 1869 and 1918 Joseph F. Smith buried thirteen of his 45 children, nine of whom were

---

1. Holzapfel and Shupe, *Joseph F. Smith,* 258.
2. See Holzapfel and Shupe, *Joseph F. Smith: Portrait of a Prophet,* 228. His body was placed "in a metal casket in the large room on the southeast corner [of the Beehive House]." Amelia Smith, President Smith's granddaughter, who was two and a half at the time, recalled, "I was so very young.... There was a big box in the room. I remember people going over to the box and crying.... Eventually my father [Joseph Fielding Smith Jr.] picked me up in his arms and asked me, 'Do you want to see your Grandfather?' So he lifted me up and walked over to the box so I could look in.... I thought he was sound asleep." (See Holzapfel and Shupe, *Joseph F. Smith: Portrait of a Prophet,* 230.)

young."[1] Just before he received this revelation, he lost his son, Hyrum Mack Smith, who was also a member of the Quorum of the Twelve.

The account of President Smith's first encounter with the loss of a child, his firstborn, Mercy Josephine, is heart-breaking. In late May 1870, Josephine was very ill. President Smith recorded:

> All night up watching and tending my little girl: symptoms of the measles. . . ."Dodie" [Mercy Josephine] very sick all day. high fever. cough. rattling in the throat.
>
> [June 2, 1870] My little "Dodo" was some better, but far from well. . . .
>
> [June 4, 1870] Joseph[ine] very sick all night. I could not feel to leave her, . . . waited on my little daughter all day, gave her two packs, and put warm corn-meal and hops poultice on her chest. . . . But [she] is very languid & weak. I got her a few Straw-berries which She would eat. She takes but little except cold water, or lemon juice. I left a request at the E[ndowment] House for her to be prayed for, and got bro. Tingy to administer to her.
>
> [June 5, 1870] I slept from 10.30 till 1.30. The remainder of the night attending my little Sick girl. . . . I have no appetite, my sympathy & solicitude for my darling little Josephine, has greatly bowed my spirit. Notwithstanding I think I have received a testimony that she will not die. Still, She is a sensitive, delicate, and tender little creature and loves her "Papa." . . . Reached home about 9 [in the] evening, and found my baby much lower than in the morning. I went for Dr. Lee, who came & fixed her some acid drink. . . .
>
> [June 6, 1870] Sarah and I sat up and watched and attended my little girl all night. She gradually Sank, I became very anxious. Early in the morning sent for Bro. Reed & Tingey who with me anointed and laid hands on her, also sent for Dr. Lee, who came and gave her a cathartic I said to her in the morning "you did not sleep good all night my 'Dodo.'" She replied "I'll sleep today Papa." Oh, how these little words shot thro' my heart. I knew, yet I would not fully believe, that she meant the sleep of death. And she did sleep! O, my "Dodo" my heart is nearly broken for the loss of you. You came to me when my heart was wrung in a time of deep trouble, sorrow and affliction. Like a golden Sun-beam of joy. Thou wert a green oasis in my hitherto desert life, my first born lovely—beautiful as the rose, bright intelligent beyond thy age—and possessed of noble mien & heart. Thou art the priceless Jewel & the brightest gem of earth nearest to my heart. Thou didst live in my thoughts and dwelt ever in my hearts purest & best love. . . . I loved thy innocent prattle, and thy little footsteps echoed in my heart. Thy voice was as the music of an holy angel. . . . I loved thee more than tongue can tell, more than the Soul can

---

1. Holzapfel and Shupe, *Joseph F. Smith: Portrait of a Prophet*, 47. The children included six-day-old Sarah Ella, two-year-old Mercy Josephine, eight-month-old Heber John, one-year-old Alfred Jason, one-year-old Rhoda Ann, one-year-old Albert Jesse, two-year-old Robert, one-year-old John Schwartz, four-year-old Ruth, nineteen-year-old Alice, thirty-six-year-old Leonora, twenty-five-year-old Zina, and forty-six-year-old Hyrum Mack. Hyrum's wife, Ida Elizabeth Bowman Smith, died eight months later, leaving five children, including newly born Hyrum Mack Smith Jr. (See Holzapfel and Shupe, *Joseph F. Smith: Portrait of a Prophet*, 47.)

speak through mortal agency. Thou didst make me a better man, for thy sake I loved humanity, earth—and Heaven—more—Thou didst draw me nearer unto God—and purify my heart—for thy sake I besought God with greater faith and fervor on behalf of all children. . . . O! my darling how I miss thee.[1]

Death had not only stalked President Smith personally throughout his life but was also on the minds of all the Saints and the entire nation. War and disease were plaguing the country. The United States had declared war on April 6, 1917, during general conference. Some thought it would be a short war, but it dragged on as millions went to their graves. By the end of the war, seventy million men had taken up arms. There were over thirty million military casualties, including over nine million dead.[2] The killing was enhanced by new technologies: "the improved machine gun, long-range high-explosive artillery, airplanes, tanks, submarines, and mustard gas."[3] The loss of life was unprecedented.

Compounding the situation was the influenza pandemic of 1918. In October, when this revelation was received, "there would be more deaths than in any other month in the nation's history." In just thirty-one days, 195,000 Americans died. Coffins were scarce, and undertakers had to hire security guards to protect their boxes.[4] Mormon families suffered. Stanford Hinckley, older brother of Gordon B. Hinckley, late president of the Church, died of the flu on October 19 at a training camp in Bordeaux, France. B. H. Roberts, chaplain of the 145th Field Artillery, ministered to him during his final hours.[5]

Utah was devastated. The first reported case of flu was prominently mentioned in the *Deseret News* October 4 edition. By October 9, the number of cases had become so alarming that an order closed all public gatherings.[6] BYU was forced to close in October as well, and classes did not resume until January 1919. In the end, 675,000 Americans died, about the same number who had perished during the Civil War.[7]

Section 138 came at a time when reassurance that there was life after death was desperately needed. George S. Tate, a professor of comparative literature at Brigham Young University, put it this way: "Such a panoply of dying; such pervasive hunger to know the fate of the dead—all these things give a special resonance to Doctrine and Covenants 138, with its great concourses of the dead, its assurance of divine love and of the comfort of the Atonement [and resurrection], the blessings of which extended to all mankind, both the living and the dead. Timely and timeless, the vision spoke directly and compassionately to an agonized world . . . as it still speaks to us today and will continue to speak in future ages."[8]

---

1. See Holzapfel and Shupe, Joseph F. Smith: Portrait of a Prophet, 228; some spellings have been modernized.
2. Tate, "The Great World of the Spirits of the Dead," *BYU Studies* 46:1:19.
3. Ibid., 15.
4. Ibid., 27.
5. Ibid., 29.
6. Ibid., 30.
7. Ibid., 33.
8. Ibid.

Paradise and hell

In section 138, the afterlife is referred to as the spirit world and is divided into two main realms—paradise and hell—separated by a gulf. This gulf marks a boundary that separates the righteous from the wicked (D&C 138:18–20, 22; see also Alma 40:11–14.) President Joseph F. Smith referred to this separation prior to the resurrection of all mankind, and he explained that those who are dispensed to hell will be given an opportunity to repent and thereafter receive the same blessings promised the righteous. [1]

In the four Gospels, Jesus speaks about a similar place in his parable about Lazarus and the rich man (Luke 16:19–31.) Lazarus, a beggar on earth, finds himself in paradise after death. A rich man on earth finds himself in hell, a place of torment, after his death. The rich man calls to Lazarus for help but is prevented from coming into paradise. "Between us and you there is a great gulf fixed: so that they which would pass from hence to you cannot; neither can they pass to us, that would come from thence" (Luke 16:26). William R. Herzog II, a widely respected biblical scholar, explains that this Hades or Sheol spoken about in the New Testament does not equal a hell where wicked individuals are eternally consigned. Rather, it is a shadowy abode to which all people who die go prior to final judgment. It is a "waiting place where righteous and sinners alike are gathered after death but separated from each other" and the wicked are given an opportunity to repent. When they do, Abraham will descend into hell and lead them into paradise.[2]

In Section 138, those in paradise reside with "an innumerable company of the spirits of the just." They are described as those who on earth had "been faithful in the testimony of Jesus." (D&C 136:12–14.) As they await resurrection, they are "filled with joy and gladness." (Verse 15.) It is a place of peace. (See verse 22.) Those in hell reside in a place of darkness and are described as those who were "among the ungodly and the unrepentant who had defiled themselves while in the flesh." (Verses 20–22.)

Section 138 explains that although 1 Peter teaches that after Jesus' death he appeared to the spirits in prison (1 Peter 3:18–20), in truth he appeared only to the spirits in paradise and organized a missionary corps to preach the gospel to the spirits in hell. (See D&C 136:27–31.) By this means, those in hell were given the opportunity to learn "all [of the] principles of the gospel." (Verses 32–34.) "The dead who repent will be redeemed, through obedience to the ordinances of the house of God." (Verse 58.) Presumably this is accomplished through vicarious ordinance work for the dead in

---

1. Joseph F. Smith, Joseph Fielding Smith, and Brigham Young, "Spirit World," *Encyclopedia of Mormonism*, 3:1408.

2. Herzog, *Parables as Subversive Speech*, E-book Kindle location at 2304, 2338.

Latter-day Saint temples. "And after they have paid the penalty of their transgressions, and are washed clean, shall receive a reward according to their works, for they are heirs of salvation." (Verse 59.) Apparently they will have the opportunity to receive all of the blessings of the gospel, including eternal marriage.

In describing those who may receive all of the blessings of the gospel, section 138 teaches that it will be taken "to those who . . . died in their sins, without a knowledge of the truth" and to those who were "in transgression, having rejected the prophets." (Verse 32.) Since most Latter-day Saints believe that those who had an opportunity to receive the gospel here and rejected it are assigned to the terrestrial kingdom, along with those who are "not valiant in the testimony of Jesus" (D&C 76:79), section 138 seems inconsistent with section 76. (See D&C 76:73–79 and commentary.) One way to reconcile the two is to recognize that truly having an opportunity to accept the gospel in this life and then rejecting it involves a much higher degree of understanding than is generally contemplated.

OFFICIAL DECLARATION—2: SALT LAKE TEMPLE, SALT LAKE CITY, UTAH, JUNE 1978

Heading

Authorization for all worthy males to hold the priesthood on an equal basis.

Introduction

Revelation authorizing male black Africans and others of the same descent to receive priesthood office. This revelation also permits male and female black Africans and those of the same descent to receive their endowments.

The big question

Question: How shall we survive?
Answer: Give the priesthood to all worthy males on an equal basis.

Historic background

African-Americans joined the Church during the 1830s, although the numbers were few. Most early members of the Church were Caucasian and came from the Northeast or from England. One of the most prominent African-Americans to join the early Church was Elijah Abel, baptized in 1832. In March 1836 he was ordained an elder by Joseph Smith and received his patriarchal blessing.[1] In December 1836 Abel was ordained a seventy and was sent on a mission to Ohio. In 1843 he served another mission for the Church, and in Nauvoo he participated in baptisms for the dead.[2]

Abel's acceptance by the Mormon community reflected Joseph Smith's attitudes. While living in Nauvoo, Abel had close contact with the Joseph Smith family. According to one account he was "intimately acquainted" with the Prophet and lived in his home.[3] He was among six other Nauvoo Saints who attempted to rescue Joseph after his arrest for earlier difficulties in Missouri.[4] Joseph's obvious acceptance of Abel was also reflected in his stated views about African-Americans in general: "Go to Cincinnati . . . and find an educated negro, who rides in his carriage, and you will see a man who has risen by the powers of his own mind to his exalted state of respectability."[5] This may have been a reference to Elijah Abel, who lived in Cincinnati at this time.[6] Joseph said further: "They [African-Americans] came into the world slaves mentally and physically. Change their situation with the whites, and they would be like them. They have souls, and are subjects of salvation."[7] When he ran for the Presidency of the United States in 1844 he "enunciated his most strident antislavery views when he proposed a system for emancipation."[8] He advocated for a universal human family in which "God hath made of one blood all nations

---

1. Elijah Abel received his patriarchal blessing from Joseph Smith Sr. No lineage was declared. His blessing states that "Thou shalt be made equal to thy brethren, and thy soul be white in eternity and thy robes glittering." (See Tungate, *Chronology Pertaining to Blacks and the Priesthood*, www.tungate.com/chronology.htm.
2. See Tungate, *Chronology Pertaining to Blacks and the Priesthood*, www.tungate.com/chronology.htm.
3. See Bush and Mauss, *Neither White Nor Black*, 3.
4. See Bush and Mauss, *Neither White Nor Black*, 3.
5. Smith, *History of the Church*, 5:217.
6. See Bush and Mauss, *Neither White Nor Black*, 3.
7. Tungate, *Chronology Pertaining to Blacks and the Priesthood*, www.tungate.com/chronology.htm.
8. W. Paul Reeve, *Relition of a Different Color: Race and the Mormon Struggle for Whiteness*, 127.

of men, for to dwell on all the face of the earth." (Acts 17:26) He was for a system where the government would pay slave owners a reasonable fee for their slaves so that the entire nation could be free.[1]

Sometime after the Saints arrived in the Salt Lake Valley, a policy developed under the leadership of Brigham Young to exclude African-Americans from holding the priesthood and marrying in the temple. Consequently, when Elijah Abel petitioned the First Presidency to receive his endowment he was turned down. Typical of this period is a statement by Brigham Young: "The seed of Canaan will inevitably carry the curse which was placed upon them until the same authority which placed it there, shall see proper to have it removed."[2] The curse, Young believed, barred African-Americans from participating in the priesthood.

Paul Reeves, a Mormon historian, wrote a groundbreaking book on early Mormon attitudes about race. He points out that after Joseph was murdered, Young began to set his "own agenda on race" that was a marked "departure from Smith's earlier positions."[3] For Young and the Mormons their practice of welcoming blacks into the fold and seeking out Indian converts became increasingly problematic. Blacks and Indians were viewed more and more as a danger to the community. Slave rebellions and Indian uprising were perceived as a real threat. This situation was compounded by the fact that a number of blacks had joined the church and at least one, Enoch Lewis, had married a white woman.[4] Furthermore, Joseph Smith had encouraged some of the brethren to marry Indian women. Mixing the races was considered abhorrent! Even the most ardent abolitionists drew the line at "amalgamation" or interracial marriages.

Interracial marriage and the inclusion of other races in the Church, among other things, became yet another reason to persecute and expel the Mormons from Missouri. Because "being white equaled access to political, social and economic power," the Missourians used race as a way to isolate Mormons from participation in the broader community.[5] Mormons began to be treated "as if they were 'some savage tribe, or some colored race of foreigners.'"[6] Even after the Saints migrated to the Great Basin, such accusations persisted, especially when Brigham Young decided to publicly admit in 1852 that the Mormons were indeed polygamists. For example, people imagined "'a general lack of color' with 'sallow and cadaverous

---

1. Ibid.
2. Quoted in Bush and Mauss, *Neither White Nor Black*.
3. W. Paul Reeve, *Religions of a Different Color*, 156.
4. Ibid, 107.
5. Ibid., 3.
6. Ibid.

cheeks signaling' an absence of good health'" in the Mormon population.[1] Medical journals concurred and spoke about "a marked physiological inferiority . . . a certain feebleness and emaciation . . . while the countenance of almost all [is] stamped with a mingled air of imbecility and brutal ferocity."'[2]

Brigham Young and the Mormons, who were mostly of European stock, "responded with aspirations toward whiteness."[3] Young approached the Utah Legislature and sponsored a "race-based legalized black 'servitude' . . . clearly designed to elevate white Mormons above their black counterparts."[4] Such attitudes spilled over into the Church, and Young decided that while blacks could be baptized, black males could not participate in the priesthood or be endowed. He and other Mormons justified their position by adopting scriptural interpretations used by Protestants in the South in support of slavery.

Some Mormon leaders like Orson Pratt spoke strongly against the "servant code" and found little to distinguish it from slavery. He called it a great evil.[5] Orson Spencer criticized the policy by pointing out that it would be an obstacle to carrying the gospel to Africa.[6] Nevertheless, Brigham Young, as the highest-ranking Mormon leader, prevailed in his approach. As a result, for the first time blacks were ostracized from full fellowship in the Mormon community. It was a way of making Mormons whiter than white. Young's approach was designed to blunt criticism and assure outsiders that he did not want blacks elevated or intermarrying with whites. Reeves sums it up: "From its beginning, Mormonism found itself on the wrong side of white, a racially suspect religion that outsiders feared not only for it new doctrines but also for its reported violation of racial boundaries."[7]

Commenting on this period in Church history, Elder Jeffrey R. Holland, a member of the governing Quorum of the Twelve, has said that the "folklore" used to justify the position that African Americans should not be given the priesthood "must never be perpetuated."[8] In taking this position, Elder Holland acknowledged that his earlier colleagues were doing the

---

1. Ibid.
2. Ibid., 18.
3. Ibid., 3.
4. Ibid., 142.
5. Ibid., 151.
6. Ibid.
7. Ibid., 138.
8. See www.fairmormon.org/Blacks_and_the_priesthood. Elder Holland said, "One clear-cut position is that the folklore must never be perpetuated. . . . I have to concede to my earlier colleagues . . . They . . . were doing the best they knew . . . All I can say is however well intended the explanations were, I think almost all of them were inadequate and/or wrong."

best they could without further light and knowledge from heaven.[1] In this regard, Elder Dallin H. Oaks, also a member of the Quorum of Twelve, has pointed out that some leaders and members ill-advisedly offered various justifications for this policy.[2] By 2015 the LDS the LDS Church on its website "officially renounced the philosophical foundations of its former priesthood restriction, and contextualized the restriction within the cultural norms of the nineteenth century."[3]

Unfortunately, the leaders of the Church found it difficult to change its policy on blacks that had morphed over the years into what some thought was a doctrine making it particularly difficult to deal with. As the Church entered the 20th century it found itself on the wrong side of the moral question and on the wrong side of history. The issue caused ferment within the faith and justifiable criticism from without. Changing the policy was considered from time to time but the momentum for change was slow and halting. Over time, the reality of growing the Church in Africa and in South American where blacks had intermarried many times over augured for change.

Changing social mores and attitudes in the late 1940s and 1950s caused Mormon leaders to begin to reassess the priesthood ban on blacks. After World War II a cascading change of attitudes occurred about race. Black military units had shown themselves to be courageous and competent. On their arrival home they expected to share in postwar prosperity and the G.I. Bill. Blacks began to speak out and demand greater acceptance by the white community. The 1950s marked the beginning of the civil rights movement, which would eventually lead to federal legislation banning discrimination and the end of segregated schools, water fountains, eating establishments, restrooms, and hotel accommodations. Some of these more progressive attitudes about race spilled over into the Church.

In response to the times, the First Presidency allowed Church authorities in the Philippines to ordain "Negrito" men to the priesthood. They were natives with black skin but no known African ancestry. "Decent from black Africans only—not skin color or other racial characteristics—became the disqualifying factor."[4] In 1954, President David O. McKay appointed a committee to study the issue and concluded that the priesthood ban did not have a basis in scripture but that Church members were not ready for change. However, by administrative action he continued to relax the policy banning those of African decent from the priesthood, and he discontinued

---

1. See www.fairmormon.org/Blacks_and_the_priesthood.
2. See www.fairmormon.org/Blacks_and_the_priesthood.
3. Blair Young and Darius Aidan Gray, "Mormons and Race." Found in Terryl L. Givens and Philip L. Barlow (eds.), *The Oxford Handbook of Mormonism*, 380.
4. Kimball, "Spencer W. Kimball and the Revelation on Priesthood," *BYU Studies* 47:2:19.

the practice in South Africa of "requiring converts to trace all line of their ancestry out of Africa as a way of establishing they had no Negroid forebears."[1] In 1965 in Brazil, where some estimate that 80 percent of the population has African ancestry, the "principle of assuming a male convert qualified to receive the priesthood unless there was evidence to the contrary was applied and . . . soon afterward applied generally. Candidates were no longer required to provide pedigrees."[2] President McKay made it clear that the ban on priesthood was not a "doctrine" but rather a "policy." Nevertheless, he still maintained that the policy was inspired and would require "divine intervention."[3]

During the 1960s, fifteen thousand Nigerians affiliated themselves with the Church as unbaptized converts who were waiting for the Church to come to them. The Church decided to begin to organize and provide white priesthood leadership, but in March 1963 the *Nigerian Outlook* condemned the Church as "racist and the government denied visas to missionaries."[4] In 1964 the Civil Rights Bill passed, and pressure to change the policy of banning blacks from the priesthood intensified. Church leaders and members came under attack. BYU basketball games were boycotted, and in some cases violence broke out. The Salt Lake NAACP made plans to picket Temple Square during general conference in the fall of 1963. NAACP chapters announced plans to picket local Mormon mission headquarters as well. The demonstrations were averted when Elder Hugh B. Brown of the First Presidency released a statement in favor of civil rights.

During the 1970s external pressure to change diminished but did not disappear. In 1974 the NAACP sued the Boy Scouts of America over the policy of appointing deacon quorum presidents as patrol leaders. The Church changed the policy.[5] Undoubtedly this caused members and leaders of the Church to question the position of their Church on race. General Authorities and independent scholars began to challenge the generally accepted idea that Joseph Smith taught that blacks should be excluded. Lester E. Bush Jr. wrote an article for *Dialogue*, a Mormon intellectual journal, in which he disputed the historical underpinnings of the priesthood ban. His article had enormous influence within the Mormon community.

During this same period of time, then President of the Church, Spencer W. Kimball sought counsel from the Brethren on the subject over an extended period of time. He asked for opinions and solicited memoranda on the subject. As early as June 1977 he invited at least three General

---

1. Ibid., 19.
2. Ibid., 20.
3. Ibid., 22.
4. Ibid., 24.
5. Ibid., 40.

Authorities to write memos about the doctrinal basis of the policy. Elder Bruce R. McConkie, for example, wrote a long treatise, concluding that no scriptural barrier existed that prevented black Africans and others of the same descent to hold the priesthood.[1] President Kimball also spent time reflecting and praying about the matter. On March 23 he reported to his counselors that he had spent much of the previous night considering the subject.[2] On May 4, at the end of a joint meeting of the First Presidency and the Twelve in the Salt Lake Temple, the policy was discussed in detail. Elder LeGrand Richards, a member of the Twelve, asked permission to speak in this meeting and reported, "I saw during the meeting a man seated in a chair above the organ, bearded and dressed in white, having the appearance of Wilford Woodruff.... I am not a visionary man.... This was not imagination.... It might be that I was privileged to see him because I am the only one here who had seen President Woodruff in person."[3]

Finally, on June 9, 1978, the policy changed when President Spencer W. Kimball announced that he and his brethren had received a revelation allowing those of black African descent to receive the priesthood and participate in all temple rites. He said that he had spent many hours in the temple asking the Lord for clarification on this subject. The actual revelation is not included in the Doctrine and Covenants. Official Declaration—2 is simply a statement reporting that the First Presidency and Quorum of the Twelve received a revelation on the subject. The revelation was welcomed almost universally among Church members.

The revelation to the First Presidency and the Twelve collectively came on June 1, 1978, in the Salt Lake Temple, in a meeting of the First Presidency and the Twelve as they prayed in a circle around one of the altars of the temple. During the prayer, those present experienced spiritual gifts and revelations. Much like the events on the ancient day of Pentecost, and the Kirtland Temple's dedication, all did not have the same kinds of encounters with the divine—but they did all participate in a variety of gifts at the same time. Bruce R. McConkie reported:

> It was as though another day of Pentecost came. On the day of Pentecost in the Old World it is recorded that cloven tongues of fire rested upon the people. They were trying to put into words what is impossible to express directly. There are no words to describe the sensation, but simultaneously the Twelve and the three members of the First Presidency had the Holy Ghost descend upon them and they knew that God had manifested his will.... I had

---

1. See Kimball, *Lengthen Your Stride*, 216.
2. See Kimball, *Lengthen Your Stride*, 218.
3. Kimball, *Lengthen Your Stride*, 219.

had some remarkable spiritual experiences before, particularly in connection with my call as an apostle, but nothing of this magnitude.[1]

The magnitude of the experience completely changed McConkie's views on the subject. McConkie said that he repented of everything he had ever said, taught, written or thought on the subject prior to the revelation.[2]

In 2014 the Church put an official statement on its website recounting its history on this subject. The Church frankly admitted the "highly contentious racial culture" in which the Church had grown up and how Brigham Young instituted a "policy restricting men of black African descent from priesthood ordination."[3] It explained that the "justification for this restriction echoed the widespread ideas about racial inferiority that had been used to argue for the legalization of black 'servitude' in the Territory of Utah."[4] The fact that it took the Church years to change its course and admit blacks into full fellowship is one of the saddest chapters in Mormon history. It is a reminder of how important it is for all of us to measure all that we do against the inclusive teachings of the Lord Jesus Christ.

Darius Gray, one of the best known and influential black members of the Church during the 20th and 21st centuries, summed up this period in Mormon history by reminding his fellow Saints that "Mormons rarely understand the price of the restriction for all members who let their hearts be trained to accept intolerance and racial division." He spells out the costs: "the loss of all black pioneers' descendants from Church," the "mistreatment of many black Latter-day Saints," and, most important, the "disastrous self-deception of any who justified their prejudices by suggesting that God had approved them." In light of Joseph Smith's progressive views on the subject, he concludes, "It is sad and ironic that a church that could have had the strongest reputation in America for egalitarianism, given the hopeful signs in its beginnings, followed trajectories which led to its being perceived as racially intolerant."[5]

---

1. Kimball, Lengthen Your Stride, 222.
2. Bruce McConkie made these remarks at an extended family home evening just after the revelation was received at which I was personally present. He expressed similar sentiments in other settings as well.
3. LDS.org (May 12, 2015)
4. Ibid
5. Young and Gray, "Mormons and Race," in *The Oxford Handbook of Mormonism*, 381.

Conclusion

I remember receiving my first Doctrine and Covenants when I was twelve years old. It was part of a triple combination, but for some reason I was not drawn to read the Book of Mormon or Pearl of Great Price. I seemed to have a natural fascination with the revelations given to Joseph Smith in the Doctrine and Covenants and the declaration in many of the revelations that identified its ultimate author, "Thus saith the Lord." I remember studying and marking my edition with a red pencil and making notes in the margin as I had observed other members of my family do. I remember talking over the meaning of the various sections with my mother, sometimes for a rather extended period of time for a young boy. It was not until I was an adult, during my middle years, that I would fall in love with the five Gospels (Matthew, Mark, Luke, John, and 3 Nephi). Prior to that time, if anyone were to ask me to identify my favorite book of scripture, I would reply, "The Doctrine and Covenants."

In any case, my study of the Doctrine and Covenants gave me an assurance early in life that there was a God and that Joseph Smith fit well within the tradition of being a prophet. Although over the years my understanding of what it meant to say "Thus saith the Lord" would change, mature, and grow, I became convinced that despite all of the questions that can be legitimately asked, at its base The Church of Jesus Christ of Latter-day Saints is a creation of the Lord Jesus Christ, and for this I am grateful. My understanding of this indispensable tenet has given me more peace and confidence than has any alternative way of looking at our frail existence on this planet of ours.

Even though my reading of the Doctrine and Covenants as a young man led me to believe that there was a God, as I matured I wondered whether or not my youthful inclinations were justified. Consequently, I felt that in order for me to have a well-founded testimony I would have to deconstruct my faith to the extent that any person with limited intelligence can. Therefore, I was not relieved from the hard work of asking the perplexing and difficult questions, beginning with "Is there a God?" And even then, assuming God's existence, was Joseph Smith a true prophet and what was the nature of his calling. Lastly, was there anything to fear in the detractors of the Church and its beliefs that should give me pause?

I probably was more concerned than most about knowing for myself that the gospel was "true," as people in the Mormon community are fond of saying. I think this was the case for a number of reasons. First and foremost, I was a "McConkie," which meant I came from a well-known Mormon family of believers. I was concerned that I might say I believed just because my family did, without ever really finding out for myself.

Second, I did not find a simple declaration by others that the "gospel was true" as convincing as those individuals who in addition offered reasons for the hope that they have in the Lord Jesus Christ. (See 1 Peter 3:15.) While sincere testimony bearing almost always touched my heart, it was not enough for me. In addition, my mind also had to be persuaded that Joseph Smith was a messenger from God. And so the testimony I ultimately received is based on what I know and have studied and dissected, as well as confirming spiritual experiences that have spoken peace to my mind concerning these matters (D&C 6:23) and "maketh my bones to quake" (D&C 85:6). And in addition, I can honestly say that my assurance that there is a God and that Joseph Smith is a true witness of the Lord Jesus Christ is based on the fact that over the years I have seen the power of God made manifest in my life and in the lives of others. I have personally experienced the gift of healing, prophecy, and miracles—inexplicable gifts that draw one into close proximity with God. In this regard, the Doctrine and Covenants is a continuing invitation to me, and others who take it seriously, to experience more and more of the Gifts of the Spirit described on so many of its pages.

This study guide for my family is part of the exercise that I have gone through to personally think about and test the proposition that Joseph Smith is a prophet and to assure myself that the revelations contained in the Doctrine and Covenants are "messages, warnings, and exhortations for all mankind," which "contain an invitation to all people everywhere to hear the voice of the Lord Jesus Christ, speaking to them for their temporal well-being and their everlasting salvation." (See D&C Explanatory Introduction.) Its pages are filled with meaning, challenging lessons, and sometimes perplexing questions. Its passages provoke, speak peace to the mind and heart, and are a graduate course in how the God of Israel deigns to speak to and lead his people.

To my children and grandchildren, I say, if you have time to read some of these pages and find something useful herein, please know how much I love your mother and grandmother. I am grateful for her contribution to my gospel thinking. Her fingerprints are all over this manuscript. The idea to organize it around major themes and questions is hers alone. In

Conclusion

my judgment, each suggestion of hers made it just so much better than it would have been otherwise. I wish she had had the time to write most of it, as she did our book on Mormonism, which we will at some future time make available to members of the family. While I was working on this project, she was shouldering heavy responsibility as the curator of the Utah State Capitol during its restoration and writing her book about it, which has been published. Had she been more involved in this project, this effort would have been far more eloquent and stirring. Finally, I also hope that this volume may also be useful to other students of the gospel who are seeking after the truth.

It is your mother's (grandmother's) and my fondest hope that each of you, our beloved children, grandchildren, and great-grandchildren, will find reassurance in this study guide that Joseph Smith is a prophet of God and that when e're we meet, you will be found "walking in truth, as we have received a commandment from the Father." (2 John 1:4.)

Bibliography

Allen, James B., and Glen M. Leonard. *Story of the Latter-day Saints.* Salt Lake City: Deseret Book, 1976.

Allison, Dale C., et al. *The Apocalyptic Jesus: A Debate.* Santa Rosa, CA: Polebridge, 2001.

Anderson, Karl Ricks. *Joseph Smith's Kirtland: Eyewitness Accounts.* Salt Lake City: Deseret Book, 1989.

Anderson, Lavina Fielding. Lucy's Book: *A Critical Edition of Lucy Mack Smith's Family Memoir.* Salt Lake City: Signature Books, 2001.

Anderson, Richard L. *Investigating the Book of Mormon Witnesses.* Salt Lake City: Deseret Book, 1981.

Andrews, Dee E. *The Methodists and Revolutionary America, 1760–1800.* Princeton, NJ: Princeton University Press, 2000.

Arrington, Leonard J. *Adventures of a Church Historian.* Champaign, IL.: University of Illinois Press, 1998.

———. *Great Basin Kingdom: An Economic History of the Latter-day Saints, 1830–1900.* Cambridge, MA: Harvard University Press, 1958.

Arrington, Leonard J., Feramorz Y. Fox, and Dean L. May. *Building the City of God: Community and Cooperation Among the Mormons.* Salt Lake City: Deseret Book, 1976.

Backman, Milton V., Jr., and Richard O. Cowan. *Joseph Smith and the Doctrine and Covenants.* Salt Lake City: Deseret Book, 1992.

Barker, Margaret. *The Gate of Heaven: The History and Symbolism of the Temple in Jerusalem.* London: SPCK, 1991.

———. *Temple Theology: An Introduction.* London: SPCK, 2004.

Becker, Ernest. *The Denial of Death.* New York: Free Press, 1997.

Benz, Ernst W. "Imago Dei: Man in the Image of God." In *Reflections on Mormonism: Judaeo-Christian Parallels.* Edited by Truman G. Madsen. Salt Lake City, UT: Bookcraft and BYU Religious Studies Center, 1978.

Bergera, Gary James. *Statements of the LDS First Presidency: A Topical Compendium.* Salt Lake City: Signature Books, 2007.

Berrett, Lamar C., and Max H Parkin. *Sacred Places: Missouri.* Salt Lake City: Deseret Book, 2004.

Berrett, LaMar C., Keith W. Perkins, and Donald Q. Cannon. *Sacred Places: Ohio and Illinois.* Salt Lake City: Deseret Book, 2001.

Birch, A. Jane, "Question the Comma in Verse 13 of the Word of Wisdom," *Interpreter: A Journal of Mormon Scripture* 10 (2014): 133-149.

Bibliography

Black, Susan Easton. *Who's Who in the Doctrine and Covenants*. Salt Lake City: Bookcraft, 1997.

"Book Notes." In *BYU Studies* 6 (Spring–Summer 1965): 191.

Borg, Marcus J. *Jesus: Uncovering the Life, Teachings, and Relevance of a Religious Revolutionary*. San Francisco: HarperCollins, 2006.

———. *Reading the Bible Again for the First Time: Taking the Bible Seriously But Not Literally*. San Francisco: HarperSanFrancisco, 2001.

Brown, Hugh B. *Continuing the Quest*. Salt Lake City: Deseret Book, 1961.

Brown, Matthew B. *Plates of Gold*. American Fork, UT: Covenant, 2005.

Buerger, David John. "The Development of the Mormon Temple Endowment Ceremony." In *Dialogue: A Journal of Mormon Thought* 20 (Winter 1987): 33–76.

———. *Mysteries of Godliness: A History of Mormon Temple Worship*. San Francisco: Smith Research Associates, 1994.

Bush, Lester E., Jr., and Armand L. Mauss. *Neither White nor Black*. Salt Lake City: Signature Books, 1984.

Bushman, Richard L. *Believing History: Latter-day Saint Essays*. New York: Columbia University Press, 2004.

———. *Joseph Smith and the Beginnings of Mormonism*. Champaign, IL.: University of Illinois Press, 1984.

———. *Joseph Smith: Rough Stone Rolling*. New York: Alfred A. Knopf, 2005.

Cannon, Donald Q., and Lyndon W. Cook. *Far West Record: Minutes of The Church of Jesus Christ of Latter-day Saints, 1830–1844*. Salt Lake City: Deseret Book, 1983.

Charlesworth, James H., ed. *The Old Testament Pseudepigrapha*. 2 vols. Garden City, NY: Doubleday & Company, 1983, 1985.

The Church of Jesus Christ of Latter-day Saints, *Juvenile Instructor*, Salt Lake City, UT, 1827-1901.

Church History in the Fulness of Times—Student Manual: Religion 341–343. Salt Lake City: The Church of Jesus Christ of Latter-day Saints, 1992.

Clark, J. Reuben, Jr. In Conference Report, April 4, 1940, 14.

Clark, James R., comp. *Messages of the First Presidency of The Church of Jesus Christ of Latter-day Saints*. 6 vols. Salt Lake City: Bookcraft, 1965–75.

Collier, Fred. C. *Unpublished Revelations of the Prophets and Presidents of The Church of Jesus Christ of Latter-day Saints*. 2 vols. 2d ed. Salt Lake City: Collier's Publishing, 1981.

Collier, Fred C., and William S. Harwell, eds. *Kirtland Council Minute Book*. Salt Lake City: Collier's Publishing, 1996, 2002.

Compton, Todd. *In Sacred Loneliness: The Plural Wives of Joseph Smith*. Salt Lake City: Signature Books, 1997.

Cook, Lyndon W. *The Revelations of Joseph Smith: A Historical and Biographical Commentary of the Doctrine and Covenants*. Salt Lake City: Deseret Book, 1985.

Cotter, Holland. "Art Review: A Bounty from Salem's Globe Trotter." *New York Times*, August 1, 2003.

Cowdery, Oliver. Journal (March 1836). LDS Church Archives.

Crossan, John Dominic. *Jesus, a Revolutionary Biography*. San Francisco: HarperSanFrancisco, 1995.

Dalton, Dennis, et al. *Great Minds of the Western Intellectual Tradition*. Part II: The Christian Age. DVD. Dubuque, IA: The Teaching Co., 1992.

Bibliography

Delumeau, Jean. *History of Paradise: The Garden of Eden in Myth and Tradition*. New York: Continuum, 1995.

Doctrine and Covenants Student Manual: Religion 324–325. Salt Lake City: The Church of Jesus Christ of Latter-day Saints, 2001.

Duncan, Malcolm C. *Duncan's Masonic Ritual and Monitor*. New York: David McKay Company, 1866.

Easton, Matthew George. *The Illustrated Bible Dictionary*. Thomas Nelson, 1897.

Ehat, Andrew F., and Lyndon W. Cook. *The Words of Joseph Smith*. Provo, UT: BYU Religious Studies Center, 1980.

Ehrman, Bart D. *Misquoting Jesus*. San Francisco: HarperSanFrancisco, 2005.

———. *New Testament. A Historical Introduction to the Early Christian Writings: A Reader*. New York and Oxford: Oxford University Press, 1998.

———. *The Orthodox Corruption of Scripture: The Effect of Early Christological Controversies on the Text of the New Testament*. Oxford: Oxford University Press, 1993.

Faulring, Scott H., ed. *An American Prophet's Record: The Diaries & Journals of Joseph Smith*. 2d ed. Salt Lake City: Signature Books, 1989.

Feldman, Noah. "What Is It About Mormonism?" *New York Times Magazine*, January 6, 2008.

Ferguson, Everett, ed. *Encyclopedia of Early Christianity*. 2d ed. 2 vols. New York: Garland Publishing, 1997.

Frederickson, Kristine Wardle. "D&C 25: Empowering Women in the Nineteenth Century in the Church of Jesus Christ of Latter-day Saints." Paper prepared for the Sperry Symposium at Brigham Young University, October 25, 2008.

Freedman, David Noel, ed. *Anchor Bible Dictionary*. 6 vols. New York: Bantam Doubleday Dell, 1992.

Garr, Arnold K., Donald Q. Cannon, and Richard O. Cowan. *Encyclopedia of Latter-day Saint History*. Salt Lake City: Deseret Book, 2000.

Gaster, Theodor H., ed. *The Dead Sea Scriptures*. Garden City, NY: Anchor Books, 1976.

Givens, Terryl L. *People of Paradox: A History of Mormon Culture*. Oxford: Oxford University Press, 2007.

Givens, Terryl L. and Philip L. Barlow (eds.), *The Oxford Handbook of Mormonism*, New York City, NY: Oxford University Press, 2015.

Givens, Terryl L., *Wrestling the Angel: The Foundations of Mormon Thought*, NYC, NY: Oxford University Press, 2015.

The Gospel of Philip: Annotated & Explained. Translated by Andrew Phillip Smith. Woodstock, VT: Skylight Paths, 2005.

Hardy, B. Carmon, ed. *Doing the Works of Abraham: Mormon Polygamy, Its Origin, Practice, and Demise*. Norman, OK: Clark, 2007.

Hardy, Grant. *The Book of Mormon: A Reader's Edition*. Urbana, IL: University of Illinois Press, 2003.

Hartley, William G. "The Priesthood Reform Movement, 1908–1922." In *BYU Studies* 13 (Winter 1973): 137–56.

Hickman, Martin B. "The Political Legacy of Joseph Smith." In *Dialogue: A Journal of Mormon Thought*, 3 (Autumn 1968): 22–27.

Hill, Donna. *Joseph Smith, the First Mormon*. Garden City, NY: Doubleday and Company, 1977.

Bibliography

Holzapfel, Richard Neitzel, and R. Q. Shupe. *Joseph F. Smith: Portrait of a Prophet.* Salt Lake City: Deseret Book, 2000.
http://en.fairmormon.org/Garden_of_Eden_in_Missouri%3F (November 2, 2008).
http://en.wikipedia.org/wiki/Extermination_Order_(Mormonism).
http://en.wikipedia.org/wiki/Light_of_Christ.
Hyde, Myrtle Stevens. *Orson Hyde: The Olive Branch of Israel.* Scottsdale, AZ: Agreka Books, 2000.
Interpreter's Bible. 12 vols. Nashville, TN: Abingdon-Cokesbury, 1952.
Jackson, Kent P., and Peter M. Jasinski. "The Process of Inspired Translation: Two Passages Translated Twice in the Joseph Smith Translation of the Bible." In *BYU Studies* 42:2 (2003): 36–59.
Jessee, Dean C. "The Early Accounts of Joseph Smith's First Vision." In *BYU Studies* 9 (Spring 1969): 275–96.
———, comp. and ed. *Personal Writings of Joseph Smith.* Salt Lake City: Deseret Book, 1984.
Journal of Discourses. 26 vols. London: Latter-day Saints' Book Depot, 1855–86.
Keener, Craig S. *The IVP Bible Background Commentary.* Downers Grove, IL: InterVarsity Press, 1993.
Kimball, Edward L. "The History of LDS Temple Admission Standards." In *Journal of Mormon History* 24 (Spring 1998): 135–75.
———. *Lengthen Your Stride.* Salt Lake City: Deseret Book, 2005.
Kirtland Record Book. LDS Church Archives.
Knight, Newel. "Labors in the Vineyard." In *Classic Experiences and Adventures.* Salt Lake City: Bookcraft, 1969.
Largey, Dennis L. *Book of Mormon Reference Companion.* Salt Lake City: Deseret Book, 2003.
Latter-day Saints' Messenger and Advocate. Kirtland, Ohio, 1834–37.
Latter-day Saints' Millennial Star. Manchester, England, 1840–1970.
Leonard, Glen M. *Nauvoo: A Place of Peace, a People of Promise.* Salt Lake City: Deseret Book, 2002.
Ludlow, Daniel H., ed. *Encyclopedia of Mormonism.* 4 vols. New York: Macmillan Publishing, 1992; Salt Lake City: Deseret Book, 1995.
Lundwall, N. B. *Temples of the Most High.* Rev. ed. Salt Lake City: Bookcraft, 1968.
Manuscript History. 1839–82. LDS Church Archives.
MacKay, Michael Hubbard, Gerrit J. Dirkmaat, *From Darkness into Light: Joseph Smith's Translation and Publication of the Book of Mormon*, Provo, UT: Brigham Young University and Deseret Book, 2015.
Mauss, Armand L. "Refuge and Retrenchment: The Mormon Quest for Identity." In *Contemporary Mormonism: Social Science Perspectives.* Edited by Marie Cornwall, Tim B. Heaton, and Lawrence A. Young. Urbana, IL: University of Illinois Press, 2001.
McConkie, Bruce R. *A New Witness for the Articles of Faith*, Salt Lake City: Deseret Book, 1985.
———. *Doctrinal New Testament Commentary.* 3 vols. Salt Lake City: Bookcraft, 1970–73.
———. *Millennial Messiah.* Salt Lake City: Deseret Book, 1982.
———. *Mormon Doctrine.* 1st and 2d eds. Salt Lake City: Bookcraft, 1958, 1966.

———. "Seven Deadly Heresies." Fireside address at Brigham Young University, Provo, Utah, June 1, 1980.
McConkie, Joseph Fielding. "Premortal Existence, Foreordination, and Heavenly Councils." In *Apocryphal Writings and the Latter-day-Saints*. Edited by C. Wilfred Griggs. Salt Lake City: Bookcraft, 1986.
McConkie, Joseph Fielding, and Craig J. Ostler. *Revelations of the Restoration*. Salt Lake City: Deseret Book, 2000.
McCune, George M. *Personalities in the Doctrine and Covenants, and Joseph Smith—History*. Salt Lake City: Hawkes Publishing, 1991.
McKiernan, Mark F. and Roger D. Launius, eds., *An Early Latter Day Saint History: The Book of John Whitmer, Kept by Commandment*, Independence, MO: Herald Publishing House, 1980.
Meldrum, D. Jeffrey, and Trent D. Stephens. "Who Are the Children of Lehi?" In *Journal of Book of Mormon Studies* 12, no. 1 (2003): 38–51.
Merrill, Timothy G., and Stephen C. Harper. It Maketh My Bones to Quake': Teaching Doctrine and Covenants 85." In *The Religious Educator* 6, no. 2 (2005).
Middlemiss, Clair. *Cherished Experiences*, Salt Lake City: Deseret Book, 1955.
Mintz, Steven, and Susan Kellogg. *Domestic Revolutions: A Social History of American Family Life*. New York: The Free Press, 1989.
Newell, Linda King, and Valeen Tippetts Avery. *Mormon Enigma: Emma Hale Smith*. Champaign, IL: University of Illinois Press, 1984.
Nibley, Charles. "Logan Temple Lectures." In *The Contributor* 7 (January 1886): 423–29.
Nibley, Hugh. "The Expanding Gospel." In *BYU Studies* 7 (Autumn 1965): 3–27.
———. *The Message of the Joseph Smith Papyri: An Egyptian Endowment*. Salt Lake City: Deseret Book, 1975.
———. *Mormonism and Early Christianity*. Edited by Todd M. Compton and Stephen D. Ricks. Vol. 4 of The Collected Works of Hugh Nibley. Salt Lake City: Deseret Book and Foundation for Ancient Research and Mormon Studies, 1987.
———. *Nibley on the Timely and the Timeless*. Edited by Truman G. Madsen. Salt Lake City: Publisher's Press, 1978.
———. "Sacred Vestments." In Hugh Nibley. *Temple and Cosmos: Beyond This Ignorant Present*. Edited by Don E. Norton. Vol. 12 of The Collected Works of Hugh Nibley. Salt Lake City: Deseret Book and Foundation for Ancient Research and Mormon Studies, 1992.
———. "Teachings from the Dead Sea Scrolls." Typescript of talk given at Long Beach, CA, 1967.
———. *The World and the Prophets*. Edited by John W. Welch, Gary P. Gillum, and Don E. Norton. Vol. 3 of The Collected Works of Hugh Nibley. Salt Lake City: Deseret Book and Foundation for Ancient Research and Mormon Studies, 1987.
O'Dea, Thomas. *The Mormons*. Chicago: University of Chicago Press, 1957.
Ostler, Blake. "Clothed Upon: A Unique Aspect of Christian Antiquity." In *BYU Studies* 22 (Winter 1982): 31–45.
———. "The Idea of Pre-Existence in the Development of Mormon Thought." In *Dialogue: A Journal of Mormon Thought* 15 (Spring 1982): 59–78.
Packer, Boyd K. *The Holy Temple*. Salt Lake City: Bookcraft, 1980.

Bibliography

Peterson, Paul H. "An Historical Analysis of the Word of Wisdom." Master's thesis. Provo, UT: Brigham Young University, 1972.

Phelps, W. W. Letter from W. W. Phelps to President Brigham Young, Great Salt Lake City, May 6, 1867. LDS Church Archives and www.mormon-fundamentalism.com/NEWFILES/One-Mighty-And-Strong.-htm.

Potok, Chaim. *Wanderings: Chaim Potok's History of the Jews.* New York: Knopf, 1978.

Pratt, Orson. "Equality and Oneness of the Saints." In *The Essential Orson Pratt.* Salt Lake City: Signature Books, 1990.

———. *New Jerusalem and Equality and Oneness of the Saints.* Salt Lake City: Parker P. Robinson, c. 1945.

———. *The Seer.* Washington, D.C., 1853–54

Pratt, Parley P. *Autobiography of Parley P. Pratt.* Salt Lake City: Deseret Book, 1938, 1972.

———. *Key to the Science of Theology.* Liverpool and London: F.D. Richards and L.D. Saints' Book Depot, 1855.

———. *The Prophet.* New York City, May 24, 1845.

Preece, Michael J. *Learning to Love the Doctrine and Covenants.* Salt Lake City: MJP Publishing, 1988.

Quinn, D. Michael. *Early Mormonism and the Magic World View.* 1st ed. and rev. ed. Salt Lake City: Signature Books, 1987, 1998.

———. *Living Prophets.* Unpublished statement in the possession of the author.

———. *The Mormon Hierarchy: Extensions of Power.* Salt Lake City: Signature Books, 1997.

———. *The Mormon Hierarchy: Origins of Power.* Salt Lake City: Signature Books, 1994.

———. "Mormon Women Have Had the Priesthood Since 1843." In *Women and Authority.* Edited by Maxine Hanks. Salt Lake City: Signature Books, 1992.

Reeve, W. Paul, *Religion of a Different Color: Race and the Mormon Struggle for Whiteness*, New York, N.Y.: Oxford University Press, 2015

Roberts, B. H. *A Comprehensive History of the Church of Jesus Christ of Latter-day Saints.* 6 vols. Provo, UT: Brigham Young University Press, 1965.

———. *New Witnesses for God.* 3 vols. Salt Lake City: Deseret News, 1909.

———. *The Seventies Course in Theology, Fourth Year: The Atonement.* Salt Lake City: Deseret News, 1911.

———. *The Truth the Way, the Life: An Elementary Treatise on Theology.* Provo, UT: BYU Studies, 1994.

Robinson, James M. *The Nag Hammadi Library.* San Francisco: Harper and Row Publishers, 1978.

Robinson, Stephen E., and H. Dean Garrett. *A Commentary on the Doctrine and Covenants.* 4 vols. Salt Lake City: Deseret Book, 2005.

Rugh, Susan Sessions. Conflict in the Countryside': The Mormon Settlement at Macedonia, Illinois." In *BYU Studies* 32 (Winter–Spring 1992): 149–74.

Staker, Mark Lyman, *Hearken, O Ye People: The Historical Setting of Joseph Smith's Ohio Revelations*, Salt Lake City: Greg Kofford Books, 2009.

Shipps, Jan. *Mormonism: The Story of a New Religious Tradition.* Urbana, IL: University of Illinois Press, 1985.

Bibliography

Shipps, Jan, and John W. Welch, eds. *The Journals of William E. McLellin, 1831–1836*. Urbana, IL: University of Illinois Press and BYU Studies, 1994.

Smith, George D. *Nauvoo Polygamy: "But We Called It Celestial Marriage."* Salt Lake City: Signature Books, 2008.

———, ed., *An Intimate Chronicle: The Journals of William Clayton*. Salt Lake City: Signature Books, 1992.

Smith, Hyrum M., and Janne M. Sjodahl. *Doctrine and Covenants Commentary*. Salt Lake City: Deseret Book, 1974.

Smith, Joseph. *History of the Church of Jesus Christ of Latter-day Saints*. 7 vols. Salt Lake City: Deseret Book, 1978.

———. *Teachings of the Prophet Joseph Smith*. Salt Lake City: Deseret Book, 1972.

Smith, Joseph F. *Gospel Doctrine*. Salt Lake City: Deseret Book, 1939.

Smith, Joseph Fielding. *Doctrines of Salvation*. 3 vols. Salt Lake City: Bookcraft, 1956.

Smith, Lucy Mack. *History of Joseph Smith by His Mother*. Edited by Preston Nibley. Salt Lake City: Bookcraft, 1958.

———. *History of Joseph Smith by His Mother*. Edited by Scot Facer Proctor and Maurine Jensen Proctor. Rev. and enhanced ed. Salt Lake City: Deseret Book, 1996.

Smith, Morton. *The Secret Gospel*. New York: Harper & Row, 1972.

Snow, LeRoi C. "Remarkable Manifestation to Lorenzo Snow." *Deseret News* (Church Section), April 2, 1938, 3, 8.

Sorenson, John L. *An Ancient American Setting for the Book of Mormon*. Salt Lake City: Deseret Book and Foundation for Ancient Research and Mormon Studies, 1985, 1996.

Stack, Peggy Fletcher. "New Era Dawns for LDS Temple Recommends." *Salt Lake Tribune*, August 24, 2007.

Staker, Susan. *Waiting for World's End: The Diaries of Wilford Woodruff*. Salt Lake City: Signature Books, 1993.

Talmage, James E. *The Articles of Faith*. London: The Church of Jesus Christ of Latter-day Saints, 1962.

Taylor, John. *Mediation and Atonement of Our Lord and Savior Jesus Christ*. Salt Lake City: Deseret News Company, 1882.

Times and Seasons. Nauvoo, Illinois, 1839–46.

Tungate, Mel. *Chronology Pertaining to Blacks and the Priesthood*. www.tungate.com/chronology.htm.

Turner, J. B. *Mormonism in All Ages: or the Rise, Progress, and Causes of Mormonism*. New York: Platt and Peters, 1842.

Underwood, Grant R. "Book of Mormon Usage in Early LDS Theology." In *Dialogue: A Journal of Mormon Thought* 17 (1984): 53–59.

Unger, Merrill F., and William White Jr., eds. *Nelson's Expository Dictionary of the Old Testament*. Nashville: Thomas Nelson, 1980.

Van Orden, Bruce A. "William W. Phelps's Service in Nauvoo as Joseph Smith's Political Clerk." In *BYU Studies* 32 (Winter–Spring 1992): 81–92.

Van Wagoner, Richard S. *Sidney Rigdon: A Portrait of Religious Excess*. Salt Lake City: Signature Books, 2006.

Vogel, Dan, *Early Mormon Documents*, 5 vols. Salt Lake City: Signature Books, 1996–2003.

Bibliography

Walker, Steven C., "Doctrine and Covenants As Literature," htt://byu.edu/index.php/Doctrine_and_Coveanats_As_Literature, August 17, 2015.
Walton, Hannah. *Darkness Visible: A Revelation and Interpretation of Freemasonry.* London, England: London Augustine Press, 1952.
Watson, Elden J., ed. *Manuscript History of Brigham Young (1846–1847).* Salt Lake City, 1971.
Webster, Noah. *American Dictionary of the English Language.* 1828.
Webster's Universal Encyclopedia. New York: Bonanza Books, 1987.
Welch, John W., ed., with Erick B. Carlson. *Opening the Heavens: Accounts of Divine Manifestations, 1820–1844.* Provo, UT: Brigham Young University Press, 2005.
Whitney, Orson F. *Life of Heber C. Kimball.* Salt Lake City: Stevens and Wallis, 1945.
Widtsoe, John A. *Evidences And Reconciliations.* Salt Lake City: Bookcraft, 1943.
———. *Rational Theology, As Taught by The Church of Jesus Christ of Latter-day Saints.* Salt Lake City: Deseret Book, 1937.
Wilson, R. M. *The Gospel of Philip.* London: A.R. Mowbray and Co., 1962.
Winston, David. "Pre-existence in Hellenic, Judaic and Mormon Sources." In *Reflections on Mormonism: Judaeo–Christian Parallels.* Edited by Truman G. Madsen. Provo, UT: BYU Religious Studies Center, 1978.
Wood, Wilford C. *Joseph Smith Begins His Work.* Salt Lake City: Wilford C. Wood, 1962.
Woodford, Robert J. "Discoveries from the Joseph Smith Papers Project: The Early Manuscripts." In *The Doctrine and Covenants, Revelations in Context.* Salt Lake City: Deseret Book, 2008.
———. *The Historical Development of the Doctrine and Covenants.* Ph.D. dissertation. 3 vols. Provo, UT: Brigham Young University, 1974.
Woodruff, Wilford. *Wilford Woodruff's Journal, 1833–1898: Typescript.* Salt Lake City: Signature Books, 1984.
Wright, David H., Sinclair B. Fergusen, and J. I. Packer, eds. *Encyclopedia of Early Christianity,* New York: Garland Publishing, 1990.
Wright, N. T. *The New Testament and the People of God.* Minneapolis: Fortress Press, 1992.
———. *Surprised by Hope: Rethinking Heaven, the Resurrection, and the Mission of the Church.* New York: HarperOne, 2008.
Young, Blair and Darius Aidan Gray, "Mormons and Race." Found in Terryl L. Givens and Philip L. Barlow (eds.), *The Oxford Handbook of Mormonism,* New York City, NY: Oxford University Press, (2015), 381.
www.answers.com/topic/carding.
www.blacklds.org/mob.
www.dcsites.com
www.fairmormon.org/Blacks_and_the_priesthood
www.google.com/search?hl=en&lr=&q=plaster+of+paris+definition.
www.mormonfundamentalism.com/NEWFILES/OneMightyAndStrong.htm.
Young, Lorenzo Dow. "Lorenzo Dow Young's Narrative." In *Fragments of Experience: Sixth Book of the Faith Promoting Series.* Salt Lake City: Juvenile Instructor Office, 1882.

Index

Aaron, gift of, 41, 148
Aaronic Priesthood: restoration of, 14, 178–79, 433n1; organization of, 15, 196–200; powers and blessings of, 180, 433, 707; temple work and, 180–82; increased understanding on, 206; information on, 331; reorganization of, 437–38
Abel, Elijah, 732
Abraham, 330, 441–42n5, 457–58
Abrahamic covenant, 653
accountability, of children, 115–16, 219, 464
Adam: and Original Sin, 115–16; baptism and, 120; priesthood and, 438; Adam-ondi-Ahman and, 599–605
Adam-ondi-Ahman, 177, 599–605, 635
addiction, 366
"administration, differences of," 287
adultery, 262–63, 479, 481, 575, 658–59
African Americans, 731–38
agency: of intelligences, 382; to reject baptism, 673
alcohol, 364–65
Alexander, Thomas G., 45, 716
Alexander the Great, 477
Alger, Fanny, 575
Allen, Charles, 396, 400
Allen, James B., 374
Alma, 116–17
Ambrose, Saint, 671
Amos, 63
Amulek, 117n1
ancestral sin, 115–16
anchor sections, xvi, 4–5, 8–9

ancient records, 139–40
Anderson, Joseph, 502
Anderson, Karl, 451
Anderson, Richard L., 149
Angell, Truman O., 392, 448
anointing, 453, 464
The Apocalyptic Jesus: A Debate (Crossan), 56
Apocrypha, 20, 372–74
Apocryphon of John, 648
apostasy, 314–15, 516, 581–82, 585
apostles, 200, 201, 213
Apostles' Creed, 206
April 6, 207
army, commandment to raise, 420
Arrington, Leonard, 56, 74
atonement: overview of, 11; law of, 80–81; punishments and, 113–16; Alma's explanation of, 116–17. *See also* blood atonement

Babbit, Almon, 630, 659–60
Baldwin, Caleb, 521, 622n2
banking, 574, 585
baptism: salvation and, 11, 117–20; age of accountability and, 115–16, 219; authority for, 129; persecution at services for, 176; of Joseph Smith and Oliver Cowdery, 178–82; symbolism of, 672; rejecting, 673; of African Americans, 734
baptisms for the dead, 30, 667–74
Barber, Andrew, 408
Barker, Margaret, 648, 691
Bassett, Heman, 250–51, 297
Bates, Brother, 467
Battle of Crooked River, 583

Index

beasts, in book of Revelation, 508
Beckwith, George, 112
Believing History (Bushman), 70
Bennett, John C., 515, 685
Benson, Ezra T., 722
Benz, Ernst W., 379
"betimes," 626
Bible: revision of, 24, 109, 128, 154–56, 229–32, 277–78, 318–19, 344–45, 469–70, 474; quoted by Doctrine and Covenants, 73; Brigham Young on, 114–15; Urim and Thummim and, 149–50; translation stopped on, 233, 493–94; teaching from JST, 263–64; usage of, 338; King James Bible, 372–73. *See also* Apocrypha
Bickerstaff, H. George, 288
Bidamon, Lewis C., 644
Billings, Titus, 316
Birch, A. Jane, 367
Birney, James, 443
bishops: responsibilities of, 18, 253–54; agents for, 19; consecration and, 273–75, 466; creation and responsibilities of, 431–32; tithing and, 598–99
bishop's storehouse, 508–13, 559
Black Pete, 284
blessings: in oath making, 335–36; of obedience, 395–98, 420–21, 543, 563, 571; of keeping Sabbath day, 549–50
blood atonement, 262
blood sacrifice, 180–81
body/bodies: spiritual gifts compared to, 288–89; matter and types of, 386; of God and Jesus Christ, 693–99
Bogart, Samuel, 583
Boggs, Lilburn W., 305, 321n4, 408, 461, 578, 587, 619, 635, 668, 692
The Book of Commandments: revelations in, 68–69, 121; publication of, 71, 272, 481–86, 489–90, 566; changes made to, 205–6; approval of revised, 441–42
Book of Lehi, 157
Book of Mormon: witnesses of, 10, 90–91, 99–104, 193–96; translation of, 12–13, 46n1, 125–26, 137, 144–47, 186–87; systemic injustice in, 61; lost pages of, 73, 130–34, 157–61; publication of, 110–13;

Martin Harris as witness of, 136–37; Oliver Cowdery as scribe for, 137–39; Emma Smith and, 171n1; Campbell's criticism of, 332–33; commandment to remember, 338; equality of wealth in, 510–11n3; Toronto incident and, 613. *See also* gold plates
book of remembrance, 340–41n4
Booth, Ezra: conversion and apostasy of, 314–15; on conflict with Joseph and brethren, 319–20; apostasy of, 320, 491–92, 526; moves to Hiram, Ohio, 468n3, 471; on Missouri River accident, 554
Borg, Marcus, 39, 60, 62–63, 385
Boynton, John, 581, 594
breastplate, 149–50, 193–96
Brodie, Fawn, 562n1
Brown, Hugh B., 365n1, 736
Brown, Norman, 320, 491
Brown, Pelitiah, 415–16
Brunson, Seymour, 669
Burgess, Jonathan, 607, 609
Burnett, Stephen, 25, 516
Burton, Alma P., 644–45
Bush, Lester E., 736
Bushman, Richard: on Mormonism's split image, 48–53; on Joseph's writing skills, 70; on Jesus' voice in D&C, 75; on religion and Smith family, 89–90; on Joseph as seer, 152; on early Church, 187n3; on Church clergy, 189–90; on organization of Church, 190n1; on priesthood, 198, 303, 456, 650; on Israel and Gentiles, 221; on New Jerusalem, 241n2; on high priesthood ordination, 302; on Zion's Camp, 417; on Second Coming expectations, 426; on Church government, 435; on Joseph as Church leader, 482n3; on Joseph as revelator, 527n4; on Independence, Missouri, 532; on Millenarianism, 535n2; on disappointment over Zion, 536; on Zion, 543; on consecration, 559–60; on apostasies of 1837, 575; on difficulties in Kirtland, 594; on Garden of Eden, 601n4; on creeds and continuing revelation, 631;

on Mormons leaving Missouri, 636; on diminishing revelations, 638; on plural marriage, 681; on second endowment, 687; on recording revelations, 694; on calling and election, 704
businesses, consecration and, 273

caffeine, 365
Cahoon, Reynolds: Church building committee and, 387, 388; Kirtland Temple and, 391, 448; Book of Commandments and, 483
calling and election, 338, 353, 357n3, 686–87, 704–5
callings, common consent and, 173–74
Calvin, John, 504
Campbell, Alexander, 232, 332–33
Campbellites, 99, 331–33, 527n1
Cannon, Angus, 103
Cannon, Donald Q., 610
Cannon, Elaine, 690
Cannon, George Q., 725
canoeing, 319
capitalism, 259n1
carding, 175n3
Carter, Jared, 25, 387, 388, 513–15
Carter, Simeon, 25, 514
Carthage Jail, 710–11
Cary, Phillip, 698–99
castration, 562n1
celestial kingdom: heirs of, 23, 463–64; vision of, 454; on earth, 476; requirements for, 499–500; three divisions in, 501, 706
celibacy, 295
certificates, 209–10
Chase, Sally, 146n5
chastisement, 392
children: teaching gospel to, xv–xvii, 24, 387, 486–88; study methods for, 5–7; to be supported by fathers, 27, 565; accountability of, 219, 464; of Emma and Joseph Smith, 277. *See also* orphans
children of God, 78–79
cholera, 265, 279, 419–20, 568
Christianity: temple worship in early, 648–49; marriage in early, 688–89
chronology, of Doctrine & Covenants, 33–35

Church administration building, 387–89
Church building committee, 387–89
Church leaders: weaknesses of, 74; counsel for, 139; Brigham Young on, 612
Church meetings, 282, 289
Church of Jesus Christ of Latter-day Saints, The: organization of, 14–15, 121, 185–88, 196–213; purpose of, 14–16, 189–90, 217–19; structure of, 17–26, 189–90, 201–10; criticism of, 24, 491–93; Joseph Smith as leader of, 24, 212, 267–69; to provide for widows and orphans, 27, 565; survival of, 31–32; evolution of, 44–53, 715–18; beliefs of, 208–9; internal affairs of, 209–10; revelations for, 213–16; conference for, 234–36; in Kirtland, Ohio, 241–43; civil government and, 404–5; government for, 430–40; growth of, 476–77; John Whitmer commanded to keep history of, 490; name of, 588; financial difficulties of, 607; inclusion of non-whites in, 733–34. *See also* Church leaders; gospel
circumcision, 494
civic idealism, 49–50, 54–59
civil disobedience, 403–5
civil governments, 22, 403–5, 440–45
civil rights, 735, 736
Civil War, 20, 280, 345–49, 699
Clark, Adelia C., 687n4
Clark, J. Reuben Jr., 611
Clark, Levira Annett, 727
Clark, William, 222
Clark, Wycom, 227
Clay County, Missouri, 585, 593, 618–19
Clayton, William, 668, 682, 687n4, 702
code names, 512, 561
Coe, Joseph, 274, 394, 538n3
coffee, 365
Colesville, New York, 165
Colesville Branch: commanded to leave Kirtland, 307–9; consecration and, 465–67, 531n3; settles in Jackson County, 538
A Collection of Sacred Hymns for the Church of the Latter Day Saints, 169–70

752

Index

Coltrin, Zebedee: on school of the prophets, 357; on Word of Wisdom, 363; Jesse Gause and, 368–69; John Murdock and, 521

commandments: reiterated to modern Israel, 261–62; revoked, 312–13, 620–21, 656; obedience to, 386

Committee on Removal, 636

common consent, 173–74, 422–25

communal orders, 249–52, 295. *See also* consecration

community: building, 17–26; Zion as, 389–90

Community of Christ Church, 447

conference(s): revelations given at, 234–36; timing for, 271; of early Saints, 304; to discuss Book of Commandments, 481–85; revelation on, 512; to organize Zion, 560–63

consecration: building community and, 17–26; commandment to practice, 23, 271–72, 465–67; civic idealism and, 50; in Kirtland, Ohio, 236; implementation of, 254–57; dealing with offenses in, 257–58; failure of, 258–59, 559; attitudes on wealth following, 260–61; businesses and, 273; administering, 273–75; Colesville Branch and, 307–9, 465–67, 531n3; Ezra Thayre and, 311–12; forgiveness and, 319–20; dividing inheritances and, 339–44; Saints criticized for not living, 422–25, 488, 571; united orders versus, 423n3; storehouse and, 508–13; donated property under, 513; compared to feast, 544–46. *See also* communal orders; united orders

Constantine, Emperor, 206n3, 631, 698

Constitution, 50

context, in scripture study, 39–43

continuing revelation, 68–69, 631

Cooper, John, 570

Copley, Leman: farm of, 23; Shaker missionary work and, 292–94; possession of, 301; consecration and, 307–8, 320, 466

Corianton, 116

Corrill, John, 268, 402–3

council, sitting in, 512

Council of Fifty, 708n2

Council of Nicaea, 695, 697

covenants: oath and covenant of priesthood and, 333–37; binding, 684. *See also* new and everlasting covenant

Covill, James, 16, 236n3

Cowdery, Elizabeth Ann Whitmer, 191

Cowdery, Oliver: as Book of Mormon scribe, 12, 125–26, 137–39; as worthy vessel, 13; priesthood and, 14, 455–59; as witness, 14, 90–91, 101, 193–96; as Second Elder, 15, 431; Kirtland Temple and, 23, 449; carries manuscript, 24; divining rod of, 41; Literary Firm and, 71, 273; revelation for, 121, 165–67; Bible revision and, 147–48, 493–94; Book of Mormon translation and, 152–56; Samuel H. Smith and, 162n2; revelation given to, 173–74; baptism of, 178–82; moves to Fayette, 185–88; organization of Church and, 189–90; Peter Whitmer Sr. and, 192; Quorum of the Twelve and, 196–200; mission call of, 199; ordained as elder, 210; as apostle, 213, 368; false revelation and, 215–16, 242; as Church historian, 289; William W. Phelps and, 310; fundraising efforts and, 314, 542; communicates with John Whitmer, 340n4; united orders and, 375; leaves Missouri, 396, 399; high council and, 413; Doctrine and Covenants and, 441; on washings and anointings, 464; Book of Commandments and, 482, 483–84, 490; consecration and, 488; called as editor, 538; involved in Missouri River accident, 554; accuses Joseph of adultery, 575; excommunication of, 576, 581; treasure hunting and, 605–8; Toronto incident and, 615

Cowdery, Warren A., 425–27, 449n1

creation: of earth, 79, 706; temporal and spiritual, 219

creeds, 206–7, 630–32

Crooked River, Battle of, 583

Crossan, John Dominic, 56, 545

culture, metanarratives and, 76–82

Cumorah, 106

curses, in oath making, 335–36

753

Index

"Cyril of Jerusalem's Lectures on the Ordinances," 647n1
Cyril of Jerusalem's Lectures on the Ordinances, 648

Daniel, 476
Danites, 515, 572
Daviess County, Missouri, 578, 599, 618, 620, 635–36
Davis, Matthew, 527
Day of Atonement, 61–62
dead: baptisms for, 30, 667–74; temple work for, 180–82, 455–59, 464, 648; help from, 672–73; marriage ordinance for, 688–89
Dead Sea Scrolls, 140, 373, 647
death: life after, 81, 729; Millennium and, 317; of Polly Knight, 548; of Joseph F. Smith, 727n2; of Mercy Josephine Smith, 728–29. *See also* martyrdom, of Joseph and Hyrum Smith
debt, 423
decision-making, independence in, 552, 556, 621
degrees of glory, 24, 495–504
deification, 378–80, 690–91, 696
demands, in oath making, 335, 336
Dennison, Dr., 562n1
desolation of abomination, 339
devils, casting out, 165, 167–68
DeWitt County, Missouri, 578, 618, 635
Dibble, Philo, 408, 496
"differences of administration," 287
digging in the field parable, 356
Dirkmaat, Gerrit, 112
disappointment: dealing with, 26–29, 535–36; as part of life, 621; purpose of, 629
discernment, of false spirits, 128, 295–300, 305
divine nature, 378–80, 627, 690–91
divine witness, in oath making, 335, 336
divining rods, 147–48
divorce, plural marriage and, 726
Doctrine and Covenants: context and, 39–43; as reflection of Mormon history, 44–53; systemic injustice and, 60–65; major editions of, 72; publication of, 72, 441–42; Bible quoted by, 73; structure of, 73; Church leaders in, 74; Jesus Christ and, 75; as metanarrative, 76–82; changes made to, 205–6; preface to, 470–75; changing structure of, 578
Doniphan, Alexander W., 586, 619, 623
Doxey, Graham, 541
Dunklin, Daniel, 417, 567–68
dusting of feet, 525

Eames, Rubles, 516
early Christians, 648–49, 688
earth: plan of salvation and, 79; laws governing, 80; kingdom of God on, 475–77
Eddly, Ira, 492
edify/edification, 299
Edmunds Act (1882), 55
Edmunds-Tucker Act (1887), 55
education, 361–62
Ehrman, Bart D., 495
Eight Witnesses, 101–2
elders, 196–200, 201, 204, 210
election of grace, 338
Elias, 455–59
Elijah, 106–7, 455–59
Ellsworth, George, 209
emotions, versus revelations, 676
endowment: priesthood and, 30, 109–10, 649–52; restoration of keys for, 106–8; in Kirtland Temple, 390–91n3; of Lyman Sherman, 427–28; restoration of authority and, 459; promise of, 573; performed, 642; overview of modern, 644–45; Masonry and, 646–48; early Christians and, 648–49; defined in D&C, 653; ritualizing, 654–55; discernment of spirits and, 678; second endowment, 687, 704n1
enemies, commandment to love, 405
engagement, anxious, 547, 621
Ephraim, stick of, 177
equality, among Church members, 510–12
eternal laws, 354–56, 701–2
eulogy, to Joseph Smith, 707–12
events, misinterpretation of, 620
excommunication: procedure for, 437; of William McLellin, 479; of Missouri Church leaders, 576, 581–82

Index

exodus, Mormon, 719–23
Expositor (newspaper), 709–10
extermination order, 321n4, 578, 587, 619, 635, 668
Ezekiel, 170

FAIR (Foundation for Apologetic Information and Research), 604
Fall, Original Sin and, 115–16
false revelation, 144, 213–16, 267–68, 295–300, 613–15
false spirits: Joseph Smith on, 67n1; discernment of, 68, 128, 295–300, 305, 674–78; spiritual gifts and, 283–86; interpretation of visions and, 611
family: size of, 41, 371; importance of, 664–66
Far West, Missouri, 28, 574–79, 584–92
Far West Temple, 586–87, 656
Fayette, New York, 14–16, 185–88
fear, of God, 161
feast, Zion compared to, 544–46
feet: washing, 338, 351, 357, 357n3; dusting, 525
Feldman, Noah, 46–47
Fielding, Joseph, 460
financial difficulties, of Church, 607
First Presidency: organization of, 20, 368–72; on wealth and community, 260–61; on adultery, 262–63, 658–59; Church government and, 434–35; excommunication and, 437; choosing, 440; Quorum of the Twelve and, 459–60; spirit world progression and, 502; tithing and, 598; on deification, 690–91. *See also* high priesthood
First Vision, 10, 86, 93–98, 127, 202
Flood, 602, 603
flu pandemic, 729
Follett, King, 620
forgiveness, 19, 261–62, 317–23
fornication, 262–63
Forty Day Documents, 140, 372–73, 647
Foster, James, 589
Foundation for Apologetic Information and Research (FAIR), 604
Fox, George, 293
Freemasonry, 546, 646–48

French, Peter, 391n1, 393
Fuller, Edson, 297
fulness of the gospel, 208
futurity, 632

Garden of Eden, 600–604
Garrett, H. Dean: on restoration of priesthood, 109, 198, 199n2, 208; on receiving revelations, 154; on organization of Church, 211n1; on temple in New Jerusalem, 329n2; on "one mighty and strong," 343
gathering: in Kirtland, 16, 232–33, 241–43; building community after, 17–26; in Jackson County, 19, 26, 274, 313–17; obedience and, 395–98; in Adam-ondi-Ahman, 600
Gause, Jesse, 368–69, 519
Gause, Minerva, 368
generation, 328–29
"gift of Aaron," 41, 148
gifts of the spirit, 18, 282–89
Gilbert, Elizabeth, 274, 538n3
Gilbert, Sidney: ordained as elder, 19, 306–7; moves to Jackson County, 274, 318; Joseph and Emma stay with, 277; Civil War revelation and, 346; persecution of, 400; letter from Joseph Smith to, 402–3; collects money for land, 532; commanded to establish store, 538; Missouri River accident and, 554
Gilliam, Cornelius, 570
Givens, Terryl L., 170, 360–61, 504–5
God: body of, 31, 58, 693–99; revelation from, 41, 67–68; Mormon views on, 78–79; communication with, 89–90, 94, 127–28; prophets' understanding of intents and purposes of, 114; tempting, 160–61, 167–68, 315; fearing, 161; eternal laws and, 354–56, 701–2; appears at school of the prophets, 359; nature of, 377, 620–21, 705–6; becoming like, 378–80, 386; intelligence as glory of, 383; seeing, 485; love for, 551
Godhead, 58, 206n3, 354
gods: becoming, 378–80, 690–91, 696; plurality of, 627

755

Index

gold plates: overview of, 86–88, 105–8; given to Joseph Smith, 88; witnesses of, 99–104, 193–96; restored to Joseph Smith, 159–60
Goodman, A. Harold, 365n1
gospel: teaching, to children, xv–xvii, 24, 387, 486–88; fulness of, 208; teaching, 267. *See also* Church of Jesus Christ of Latter-day Saints, The
The Gospel of Philip, 689, 689n2
governments. *See* civil governments
grace, election of, 338
Grandin, Egbert B., 111
Granger, Oliver, 589, 592, 641n1
Grant, Heber J., 72, 364
Grant, Jedediah M., 351
Gray, Darius, 738
Great Basin, exodus to, 719–23
Great Britain, converts from, 595n2
Green, John P., 103
Greene, John, 709
Gregg, Josiah, 400, 407, 577
Griffin, Selah J., 311

Hale, Alva, 88
Hale, Isaac, 87–88, 135, 185
Halsey, Thankful, 223n4
Hancock, Alva, 296n3
Hancock, Levi: conversion of, 222; on communal orders, 250–51; on false spirits, 296–97; on church meetings, 388; Fanny Alger and, 575n3
Hancock, Mosiah, 575n3
Hardy, B. Carmon, 404n2
Hardy, Grant, 46n1, 155
Harmony, Pennsylvania, 11–14, 88, 125–26, 214
Harris, Lucinda, 461
Harris, Lucy, 132
Harris, Martin: rebuked, 11; as witness, 12, 14, 90–91, 101, 193–96; Literary Firm and, 71, 273; Manchester period and, 88; Book of Mormon and, 110–13, 130–34; mentioned, 125; relationship between Joseph Smith and, 131n3; life of, 132n2; revelation for, 136–37; on Urim and Thummim, 150n1; repentance of, 158–59;

arrives in Jackson County, 274, 538n3; united orders and, 375
Harris, Preserved, 132
Haun's Mill Massacre, 578, 619, 635
Hawthorne, Nathaniel, 609
Hayes, John H., 363
healing: as miracle, 167–68; of sick, 264–66; from cholera, 419; of Lorenzo Young's son, 428–29; of Elsa Johnson, 468n3, 471–72
heathen nations, 280–81
Heavenly Father. *See* God
Heavenly Mother, 691, 696
hell, 498–99, 504, 671–72, 730–31
herbs, 264
Herzog, William R., 730
Higbee, Elias, 580, 583
high council, 22, 413–16, 434–35, 596—97
high priesthood: ordinations to, 19, 300–304; presidency of, 25, 518–20; council of, 351; Joseph ordained as president of, 523–25. *See also* First Presidency
Hill, Joel, 448
Hill Cumorah, 106
Hinckle, George, 635
Hinckley, Stanford, 729
Hiram, Ohio, 468–70
historical context, 39–43
Holland, Jeffrey R., 734–35
Holy Ghost: nature of, 58; revelation and, 128, 143–44; conferring, 231–32; conducting meetings with, 288; ministering of, 337; sinning against, 337, 705; ordinances and, 352–53; Light of Christ and, 354; scripture and, 488–89; denying, 501, 686n1; recognizing promptings from, 676; ratification of covenants through, 685; body of, 695
Holy Spirit of Promise, 685
Holy Trinity, 695
hot drinks, 364–65
house of order, 685–86
Houston, Matthew, 369
Howe, Eber D., 315n2, 526
Hubble, Sister, 268
Huet, Pierre-Daniel, 602
humility, 163–64

756

Index

Hunter, David, 348
Hunter, Edward, 30, 674
Huntington, Prescindia, 451
Hyde, Orson: apostasy of, 320–22n4; school of the prophets and, 357; high council and, 413; Quorum of the Twelve and, 431n1; missionary work and, 460, 525; Book of Commandments and, 483; requests revelation, 486; Zion's Camp and, 567–68; William W. Phelps and, 583n3; on God and Jesus Christ, 694, 695
hymns, 168–71

Imagio Dei, 380
immersion, 672
immorality, 262–63
independence, in decision-making, 552, 556, 621
Independence, Missouri: as Zion, 26, 49, 531–33; kingdom of God and, 57; Saints expelled from, 395–97; persecution in, 406–11; Joseph visits, 558–60
Indian Removal Act (1830), 349
infant baptism, 115–16
influenza pandemic, 729
initiative, taking, 547
intelligence, as glory of God, 383
intelligences, 78–79, 380–83, 384, 386
interracial marriage, 733
Iowa, Saints to stay in, 660–63
Isaiah, revelations interpreting, 580–81
Israel, redemption of, 581
Ivy, William, 556

Jackson, Kent P., 470n2
Jackson County, Missouri: gathering in, 18, 233, 274, 313–17; as Zion, 26, 49, 276–80, 531–33, 537–39; kingdom of God and, 57; building, 327; temples in, 328–29; inheritance in, 339–44; Saints expelled from, 395–97; persecution in, 406–11; Zion's Camp and, 416–22, 567–69; instructions for organizing, 539–46; Joseph visits, 558–60; Garden of Eden and, 600–601; land purchases in, 605
Jacob, remnant of, 295. *See also* Lamanites
Jasinski, Peter M., 470n2
Jennings, William O., 619

Jerusalem, 540–41, 603
Jesse, stem of, 580
Jesus Christ: body of, 31, 58, 693–99; systemic injustice and, 63–65; in D&C, 75; birth of, 207; Lyman Wight sees, 301; as "one mighty and strong," 343; as Comforter, 353, 696n2, 705; appears at school of the prophets, 359; nature of, 377; becoming like, 378–80; accepts Kirtland Temple, 449, 450, 455–59; appears to John Murdock, 521; appears to Lorenzo Snow, 645n2; baptisms for the dead and, 670–71; visits spirits in spirit world, 726–31. *See also* Light of Christ
Jews, 441–42n5
Johnson, Almera, 693n2, 703
Johnson, Benjamin F., 391, 660, 693, 702–3, 720
Johnson, Eli, 562n1
Johnson, Elsa, 314, 319n1, 468n3, 471–72
Johnson, Joel H., 692
Johnson, John, 23–25, 317–23, 395, 468–72
Johnson, Julia, 703
Johnson, Luke: Book of Commandments and, 483; requests revelation, 486; on attack on Joseph Smith, 562n1; excommunication of, 581, 594
Johnson, Lyman: Book of Commandments and, 483; requests revelation, 486; mission call of, 524; excommunication of, 581, 594
Johnson, Nancy Marinda, 562n1
John the Baptist, 14, 129, 178–82, 377n1, 433n1
John the Beloved, 139–40, 141–42, 304
Joseph Smith: Rough Stone Rolling (Bushman), 48–53
jubilee year, 55, 62
Judaism, social policy in, 61–65
judgment, for own sins, 115–16
judicial matters, 414–15
justice, eternal laws and, 354n2
Justinian, 504
"just men made perfect," 677

Kelley, William, 474
"key of knowledge," 384–85

keys: of last dispensation, 370–71; for temple ordinances, 455–59; for proxy ordinances, 672; for discerning spirits, 678. *See also* priesthood

Kimball, Heber C.: forgives Orson Hyde, 322n4; on building construction, 389; mission call of, 460; William McLellin and, 479; lays Far West Temple cornerstone, 587; on Garden of Eden, 601n2; Mormon exodus and, 722; plural marriage and, 726

Kimball, Sarah, 361

Kimball, Spencer W., 439, 549–50, 736–37

King, Austin A., 618–19, 623, 635

King, T. Butler, 348

Kingdom, New York, 16

kingdom of God, 54–59, 64n3, 475–77, 632

King Follett discourse, 377, 378, 382, 386n1, 501, 641, 701

King James Bible, 372–73

kings, proclamation to, 655

Kirtland, Ohio: gathering in, 232–33; building Church in, 241–43; Joseph and Emma Smith move to, 252–53; migration to, 291–92; commandment to leave, 307–9, 574–79, 589–92; apostasy in, 314–15, 516, 593–94; layout and plan for, 389–90; persecution in, 560–63

Kirtland Camp, 589–90

Kirtland high council, 434n2

Kirtland Safety Society, 574, 585

Kirtland School, 360–61

Kirtland Temperance Society, 362

Kirtland Temple: construction of, 21, 49, 446–47; sections on, 23; commandment to build, 390–92; adversity in building, 447–48; dedicatory prayer for, 449; dedication of, 449–51; function and purpose of, 451–52; rituals performed in, 452–54; restoration of priesthood keys and, 455–59

Kitchell, Ashbel, 294

Knight, Joseph Jr., 256

Knight, Joseph Sr.: mission call of, 11, 13; revelation for, 121, 163, 164; on Joseph's difficulties, 135; Joseph Smith visits, 165; conversion of, 175–76; on organization of Church, 212; contributions of, 465n3; settles in Jackson County, 538, 565; on death of Polly Knight, 548n2

Knight, Newel: possession of, 165, 284–85; on sacrament wine, 176; on Hiram Page, 214–15; on gathering in Kirtland, 235; consecration and, 307; heals Philo Dibble, 408

Knight, Polly, 176, 548

knowledge: Joseph Smith on, xvi–xvii, 81n1; restoration of, 626; salvation and, 700–701

Kolob, 498

Laban, sword of, 193–96

Lamanites, 219–26, 242, 295, 349, 538, 538n1

Largey, Dennis L., 131

last days, 351

Law, William, 608, 708–9

laws: over matter, 80; atonement and, 116–17; eternal, 354–56, 701–2; upholding civil, 403–5; against violence, 405–6

Lazarus, 63, 730

learning, faith and, 144

The Lectures on Faith, 72

Lee, Ann, 292, 294–95

Lehi: Book of, 157; Lamanites and, 221n2, 225

Leonard, Glen M., 374, 452

Levi, sons of, 180–81

Lewis, Enoch, 733

Lewis, Joshua, 26–29, 537–46, 548n2

Liahona, 41, 151, 193–96

Liberty Jail, 29, 618–25

licenses, 209–10

life. *See* mortality

The Life of Adam and Eve, 438

light-mindedness, 41–42

Light of Christ, 353–54

Lincoln, Abraham, 53, 348

Literary Firm, 71, 273, 395, 566

lost sheep, parable of, 42

lots, casting, 151, 609n1

love: for neighbors, 405–6; for God and neighbors, 551

Lovejoy, Elijah, 443, 710

Index

Lucas, Samuel, 635
Lund, Anthon H., 342
Luther, Martin, 602
Lyman, Amasa, 619
Lyon, T. Edgar, 366

MacKay, Michael, 112
Manchester, New York, 10–11, 85–92, 187n2
Mann, A. Dudley, 348
Marks, William, 28, 589–92, 655
marriage: priesthood and, 30; of Joseph and Emma Smith, 87–88; adultery and, 262–63; celibacy and, 295; William W. Phelps on, 441; Paul's advice on, 494–95; statement on, 575; temple recommends and, 658–59; eternal, 679–91; scenarios for, 686–88; proxy ordinance for, 688–89; in *Gospel of Philip*, 689n2; salvation and, 703; as order of priesthood, 706–7; interracial, 733. *See also* plural marriage
Marsh, Elizabeth, 461
Marsh, Thomas B.: Quorum of the Twelve and, 23, 460; revelation for, 220; mission call of, 222, 311; Ezra Thayre and, 227n4; on Orson Hyde, 320–22n4; falls away from Church, 461–62; faith of, 582
martyrdom, of Joseph and Hyrum Smith, 711
Mason, James M., 348
Masonry, endowment and, 646–48
Matthews, Robert J., 264
McConkie, Bruce R.: on murder, 262; on desolation of abomination, 339; on John the Baptist, 377n1; on intelligences, 381; on Zion and obedience, 398n2; on Ten Tribes, 457; on progression between kingdoms, 503; on New Jerusalem, 541n1; priesthood for African Americans and, 737–38
McConkie, Joseph F.: on Millennium, 282n1; on revocation of commandments, 312–13; on obedience, 398; on First Presidency, 440; on root of Jesse, 581; on eternal marriage, 686–87
McIlwaine's Bend, 319, 553–55
McKay, David O., 286–87, 365n1, 735–36
McLeary, Sophronia, 694

McLellin, Cinthia Ann, 481n1
McLellin, Emeline Miller, 481n1
McLellin, William E.: revelation for, 24, 477–81, 523; inerrancy and, 69; school of the prophets and, 358; Kirtland School and, 361; Quorum of the Twelve and, 431n1; questions revelations, 473; Book of Commandments and, 483–84; requests revelation, 486; excommunication of, 594
McRae, Alexander, 622n2, 623
meat, 295, 366–67
meetings, conducting, 288. *See also* Church meetings
Melchizedek Priesthood: restoration of, 13, 177, 207–8, 433n1; powers of, defined, 20, 433, 707; information on, 22, 331; organization of Church and, 196–200; increased understanding on, 206; high priesthood and, 303, 439
Meldrum, Jeffery, 225
mercy, eternal laws and, 354n2
Mesopotamian Empire, 477
metanarrative, 76–82
Methodists, 507
Miami Bend, 319
migration, to Kirtland, 291–92
Millenarianism, 535n2
Millennialism, 279, 620n4
Millennium, 270, 280–81, 294–95, 317
Miller, William, 279, 426, 535n2, 536n4
miracles, 160–61, 167–68, 315
misinterpretation of events, 620
missionary work: consecration and, 17, 271–72; revelation on, 26; early disciples called to, 121; financing, 167; organization of Church and, 199; instructions for, 270, 326–27, 515–17, 524–25, 551–52; among Shakers, 292–95; school of the prophets and, 360; Quorum of the Twelve and, 431n1; water and, 553–55; in Salem, Massachusetts, 608–9; Brigham Young released from, 664–66
Missouri: commandment to leave Kirtland for, 307–9; expulsion from, 535–36, 635–36
Missouri high council, 434n2
Missouri River, 319, 553–55

759

Index

Morley, Isaac: farm of, 18–19, 276–78, 317–23, 468; persecution of, 103; conversion of, 222; communal orders and, 250; letter from Joseph Smith to, 402–3
Mormon exodus, 719–23
Mormon history, 44–53
Mormonism in Transition: A History of the Latter-day Saints in 1890-1930 (Alexander), 45
Mormon War, 407–8, 635. *See also* persecution
Moroni, 87–88, 101, 105–9, 202
Morse, Justus A., 693–94n4
mortality: understanding, 76–82; gaining experience in, 627–29
Moses, 166n3, 455–59
Mosiah, 151
Mount of Transfiguration, 316
murder, 261–62
Murdock, John: mission call of, 25, 515, 520–22; false spirits and, 68; conversion of, 222; children of, 277; illness of, 556
Murdock, Julia (daughter of John Murdock), 521
Murdock, Julia (wife of John Murdock), 520
murmuring, 171
mutual edification, 299

NAACP, 736
Nag Hammadi collection, 140, 373, 544n1, 647
Native Americans, 221–22, 538n1, 733. *See also* Lamanites
Nauvoo, Illinois: equality in, 50; Saints move to, 635–36; revelations received in, 637–39; Saints leave, 721
Nauvoo House, 643–44
Nauvoo Temple, 640–48
Nauvoo University, 361
Nebuchadnezzar (King), 476
neighbor(s): commandment to love, 405–6, 551; commandment to befriend, 564, 572–73; difficulties with Missouri, 577–78
new and everlasting covenant, 119–20, 684
New Jerusalem, 540–41. *See also* Zion
New Testament, 20, 61–65
Nibley, Charles, 259n1
Nibley, Hugh, 671

Nicaea, Council of, 695, 697
Nicene Creed, 206n3, 631
Nickerson, Freeman, 26, 525–26
Nicolaitane band, 591
Nyman, Jane, 669

Oaks, Dallin H., 735
oath taking, 334–35
obedience: blessings based on, 395–98, 420–21, 543, 563, 571; to government authority, 398–406; to commandments, 620–21; to eternal laws, 702
objects, revelation and, 144–47, 149–50
oil, anointing with, 453
Old Testament, 61–65
Olmstead, Harvey, 669
"one mighty and strong," 341–43
open commensality, 545
order, house of, 685–86
ordinances: authority for, 119; priesthood, 302–3; ratification of, 680
Origen, 504
Original Sin, 115–16
orphans, 27, 565
Ostler, Craig: on Millennium, 282n1; on revocation of commandments, 312–13; on obedience, 398; on First Presidency, 440; on root of Jesse, 581; on eternal marriage, 686–87

Page, Catherine Whitmer, 192
Page, Hiram: false revelation and, 15, 213–16, 242, 268; as witness, 102; marriage of, 192; suffers persecution, 408; Toronto incident and, 615
Page, John E., 582n3, 587, 594
Palmyra, New York, 86
Panic of 1837, 574–75
parable(s): of sheep and goats, 65n1; of digging in the field, 356; of vineyard, 421; of wedding feast, 544–46; of Lazarus and the rich man, 730
paradise, 730–31
Parker, Doug, 78n1
Parkin, Max H., 423, 510n2
Parrish, Betsy, 419
Parrish, E., 449n1
Parrish, Warren, 451n7, 516

Index

Parrish, William G., 594

Partridge, Edward: mission call of, 16, 229–32; called as bishop, 17, 253–54, 274–75, 432; home of, 27; conversion of, 224; consecration and, 308, 320, 340, 465, 466, 532, 538; moves to Jackson County, 318, 538n3; repentance of, 342–43; persecution of, 396, 400; letter from Joseph Smith to, 402–3, 623; commanded to dedicate Zion, 540; dispute between Sidney Rigdon and, 559, 563; bishop's storehouse and, 559n1

Partridge, Lydia Clisbee, 432n1

patriarchal priesthood, 707

patriarchal privilege, 331n3

Patten, David W., 28, 321n4, 578, 581–83, 619, 635

Paul: spiritual gifts and, 288; advice on marriage, 494–95

Paulsen, David L., 355

peace, 398–406, 572

perfection: of Church leaders, 74–75; of children of God, 378–80

Perkins, William G., 702

Perpetual Emigrating Fund, 55

persecution: under John Taylor, 55; of Joseph Smith, 125; revelation of comfort and, 165–67; Emma Smith and, 169, 172; during baptismal services, 176; in Fayette, New York, 185; in Harmony, Pennsylvania, 214; in Missouri, 305, 395–411, 535–36; warning of, 513; of Joseph Smith and Sidney Rigdon, 526, 560–63; in Clay County, 586, 593, 618; of Kirtland Camp, 589–90; of early Saints, 715; race and, 733–34. *See also* petition for redress

personal revelation, 189, 216, 268–69

Peterson, Ziba, 15, 221–22, 223–26

petition for redress, 630–32, 641, 708n1

Phelps, William W.: called as printer, 19, 309–10, 538; printing and, 71; hymns and, 170; moves to Jackson County, 274, 318, 538n3; on "one mighty and strong," 343; speaks against slavery, 396, 400, 411, 442; letter from Joseph Smith to, 402–3, 409; high council and, 434n2; Doctrine and Covenants and, 441; Book of Commandments and, 482, 490; degrees of glory revelation and, 497; admonishment of, 546; sees Satan on waters, 553; excommunication of, 576, 582; repentance of, 582; presidential campaign and, 708n1

Philanthropist, 443

pioneers, 719–23

"Pistis Sophia," 647n1

plan of salvation, 79, 80

plaster of Paris, 186

Plato, 699

plural marriage: revelation on, 30, 679–91; official declaration on, 32, 724–26; Edmunds Act and, 55; as point of contention, 58; keys to authorize, 370n3; resistance against laws against, 404n2; Joseph Smith practices, 441n4, 575, 703; apostasy and, 708–9

pocket revelations, 70–71, 472

politics, 50–52, 444–45, 708n1

polygamy. *See* plural marriage

Potok, Chaim, 335–36

Pratt, Orson: mission call of, 16, 228–29; publication of D&C and, 72; intelligences and, 78n1, 382n3; on baptism and authority, 119; on translation process, 145; conversion of, 223n4; on temple in New Jerusalem, 329; on "one mighty and strong," 343; Word of Wisdom and, 366; on Kirtland Temple dedication, 451; on receiving revelations, 466, 473; code names and, 512; on Joseph and high priesthood, 524; lays Far West Temple cornerstone, 587; excommunication of, 594; on tithing, 597; temple worship and, 654; on plural marriage, 681; on Church's financial system, 716; on "servant code," 734

Pratt, Parley P.: missionary work and, 15, 221–22, 223–26, 242, 460, 720; on receiving revelation, 68; hymns and, 170; baptisms performed by, 227; on false spirits, 283, 296, 297–98, 301n5; Shaker missionary work and, 292–94; Sidney Gilbert and, 306; forgives Orson Hyde, 322n4; school of the prophets and, 358;

on persecution in Missouri, 408–9; Zion's Camp and, 416, 567–68; John Murdock and, 520; excommunication of, 594; taken prisoner, 619; on Liberty Jail, 623–24; discernment of spirits and, 675; plural marriage and, 683
Pratt, Thankful Halsey, 223n4
prayer, 89–90, 94–95, 475–77, 654
preamble, in oath making, 334–36
predestination, 338
preface, to Doctrine and Covenants, 470–75
premortal existence, 78
presidential campaign, 50–52, 444–45, 708n1
priesthood: restoration of, 11, 13–14, 433n1, 455–59; oath and covenant of, 19–20, 333–37; proper use of, 29; fulness of, 30, 109–10, 330, 649–52; official declaration on, 32, 731–38; authority and, 119, 129; common consent and, 173–74; organization of Church and, 196–200; structure of, 201–10; discernment of spirits and, 299; power and authority of, 302–3, 433; as power of God, 330; Campbellites and development of idea of, 331–33; keys, 370–71; equality among quorums of, 435n1; Adam and, 438; exercising, 622, 625; reorganization of quorums, 655; covenants and, 684; marriage and, 706–7. *See also* Aaronic Priesthood; high priesthood; Melchizedek Priesthood
printing/printing house, 19, 309–10, 387–89
proclamation, to kings, 655
prodigal son, parable of, 42n5
progression: on earth, 80; in spirit world, 81; eternal laws and, 355; between kingdoms, 502–3
property, 590, 621
prophets: change in Church and, 45; universal revelation and, 66–67; understanding of, of God's intents and purposes, 114; seers and, 151–52; Joseph Smith as, 205; revelation for Church and, 213–16; infallibility of, 583–84n3; accuracy of, 610–11

protection, for Zion's Camp, 416–18
Pseudepigrapha, 140, 373
punishments, for sin, 113–16
The Pure Church of Christ, 228

Quincy, Illinois, 636
Quincy, Josiah, 51
Quinn, D. Michael, 146, 200
Quorum of the Anointed, 642
Quorum of the Seventy, 432, 434–35, 439
Quorum of the Twelve: Thomas B. Marsh and, 23, 460; revelation rebuking, 28; establishment of, 196–200; mission call of, 431n1; responsibilities of, 432, 433–34; Church government and, 434–35; chooses First Presidency, 440; instructions for, 592–95; sacrifices of, 664n3

race, and persecution of Mormons, 733–34
radical Mormonism, 48–53
Ramus (Webster), Illinois, 31, 692–93
record keeping, 340n4
redemption, universal, 504–5
redress, petition for, 630–32, 641, 708n1
Reeves, Paul, 733, 734
Relief Society, 172–73
remembrance, book of, 340–41n4
Reorganized Church of Jesus Christ of Latter Day Saints, 447
repentance: punishments and, 113–16; atonement and, 116–17; of Joseph Smith and Martin Harris, 133–34; of Martin Harris, 158–59; murder and, 261–62; digging in the field parable and, 356; persecution and, 395–98; of Quorum of the Twelve, 431n1; forsaking sin and, 546; Zion's Camp called to, 567–68; of William W. Phelps, 582; of those in hell, 730
restoration of all things, 626
resurrection(s), 280–81, 386, 676–77
resurrections, 730
Revelation (book of), 505–8
revelation(s): definition of, 12, 127–28, 142–44, 161; receiving, 12, 13, 128–29, 152–56; Joseph Smith and, 17, 24; objects for receiving, 41, 144–47, 149–50; change in Church and, 45; universal, 66–67, 212, 215–16n5; methods of, 67–68; continuing

revelation, 68–69, 631; errors in, 69–70, 483–84; pocket revelations, 70–71, 472; publication of, 71–72, 481–86, 489–90; and understanding scripture, 114–15; false revelation, 144, 213–16, 267–68, 295–300, 613–15; personal, 189, 216, 268–69; personal revelation, 269; compared to Joseph Smith letter, 402n1; high council and, 415; unanimity and, 436–37; criticism of, 473; for insignificant matters, 552, 556, 621; accuracy of, 610–11; during Nauvoo period, 637–39; concepts received through, 638–39; on baptisms for the dead, 670; versus emotions, 676; abandoning, 680; recording, 694. *See also* false revelation

Rich, Charles C., 583

rich, Jesus' warning to, 63–64n3

Richards, Franklin D., 346

Richards, LeGrand, 737

Richards, Sarah Ellen, 727

Richards, Willard, 460, 594, 711, 720, 722

Rigdon, George, 469n1

Rigdon, Loammi, 562n2

Rigdon, Phebe, 469n1

Rigdon, Sidney: as scribe, 16, 229–32, 474; defends Church, 24, 491–92; degrees of glory revelation and, 24, 495–504; revelation for, 26; inerrancy and, 69; Literary Firm and, 71, 273; common consent and, 174; conversion of, 222, 224, 242; communal orders and, 249–52; settles in Jackson County, 274, 538n3, 540; Shaker missionary work and, 292–94; writes description of Zion, 314, 542; lives with John Johnson, 318; and conversion of Campbellites, 331–32; school of the prophets and, 358; ordained as counselor, 368; mental health of, 369–70; united orders and, 375; rebuked, 387; Kirtland Temple and, 392, 449n1; high council and, 434n2, 596–97; Bible revision and, 469; moves to Hiram, Ohio, 472; Book of Commandments and, 483, 484; code name for, 512; sitting in council and, 512; Jared Carter and, 515; called to high priesthood, 519; ordains Joseph to high priesthood, 524; receives reassurance for family, 525–27; as speaker, 526–27; dedicates Zion, 542; mission call of, 552; Missouri River accident and, 553–54; Edward Partridge and, 559, 563; persecution of, 560–63, 619n2; treasure hunting and, 605–8; taken prisoner, 619; incarcerated in Liberty Jail, 622n2; baptisms for the dead and, 669–70; presidential campaign and, 708n1

Riggs, Burr, 297

righteousness: persecution and, 409–10; priesthood power and, 622, 625

Ripley, Alanson, 663

rituals, 453–54, 654–55

Roberts, B. H.: on eternal laws, 117n1, 355; on receiving revelations, 146–47; on dates for revelations, 157n2; Whitmer home and, 192; on Light of Christ, 353; on intelligences, 381–82; Toronto incident and, 613–14; administers to Stanford Hinckley, 729

Robinson, George W., 515, 619

Robinson, Stephen E.: on restoration of priesthood, 109, 198, 199n2, 208; on receiving revelations, 154; on organization of Church, 211n1; on temple in New Jerusalem, 329n2; on "one mighty and strong," 343

Rockwell, Orrin Porter, 668–69

Roman Empire, 477

Rost, P. A., 348

Ryder, Simonds, 320, 492

Sabbath Day, 26, 547–50

sacrament, water and wine for, 175–77

sacrament meeting, 282, 716n2

sacrifices, of Twelve, 664n3

St. Ambrose, 671

Salem, Massachusetts, 605–9, 615–17

Salisbury, Wilkins J., 694n1

Salt Lake City, Utah, 719–23

salvation: knowledge and, xvi–xvii, 81n1, 700–701; baptism and, 11, 117–20, 178–82; revelations on, 30, 637–39; temporal and spiritual, 286; kingdom of God and, 476; baptisms for the dead and, 668n2; marriage and, 703

Sanka Coffee, 365n1
Satan: water and, 27; systemic injustice and, 61; plan of salvation and, 79; possesses Newel Knight, 165, 284–85; possesses Harvey Whitlock, 301; William W. Phelps sees, 553; discernment of, 674–78
school of the prophets, 357–58
Scone, John, 570
scripture(s): studying, with children, xv–xvii; context and, 39–43; studying, 40n3, 173–74; systemic injustice in, 61; revelation and, 114–15; Emma Smith and, 172; definition of, 488–89
sealing powers, 110, 458–59
Second Coming: signs preceding, 15, 18, 217–19, 276–80, 356; concerns on, 20; predictions on, 22, 425–27; gathering and, 235–36; remnant of Jacob and, 295; statement on, in D&C, 441n5; preparing for, 522–23, 558; disappointment over, 535–36; New Jerusalem and, 540–41; timing of, 573, 699–700
second endowment, 687
seers, 151–52, 205
seer stones, 46, 131, 144–47, 213–16
self-defense, 405
separation of church and state, 444
service, spiritual gifts and, 286
sexual sin, 262–63
Shakers, 292–95
Sharp, Thomas, 710
sheep and goats, parable of, 65n1
Sherman, Lyman, 22, 427–28
Shipps, Jan, 146n5, 480, 716–18
sick, healing, 167–68, 264–66
signs, seeking, 19, 315–16
sin: punishments for, 113–16; against Holy Ghost, 337, 686n1, 705; forsaking, 546
Sjodahl, Janne M., 435n1
Skinner, Andrew C., 117n1
slave rebellion, 279
slavery: Joseph Smith on, 51, 445; systemic injustice and, 60; Civil War revelation and, 346–47; W.W. Phelps speaks against, 396, 400; condemnation of, 411–12; Church views on, 442–43, 577
Slidell, John, 348

Smith, Albert Jesse, 728n1
Smith, Alfred Jason, 728n1
Smith, Alice, 728n1
Smith, Alvin, 454
Smith, Amelia, 727n2
Smith, Asael, 85
Smith, Bathsheba W., 652
Smith, Catherine, 694n1
Smith, Eden, 516–17
Smith, Elizabeth Bowman, 728n1
Smith, Emma Hale: revelation for, 13, 168–72; marriage of, 87–88; moves to Harmony, 125; Book of Mormon translation and, 147, 159; travels to Colesville, 166; Joseph Knight Sr. and, 175; disagreement with, 187; moves to Kirtland, 252–53; adopts twins, 277; Word of Wisdom and, 363; Reorganized Church of Jesus Christ of Latter Day Saints and, 447n2; Nauvoo House and, 644; plural marriage and, 681–82, 685n1
Smith, George A.: on false spirits, 283; Kirtland Temple and, 391, 447–48; on Lucinda Harris and Elizabeth Marsh, 461; on Jared Carter, 515; lays Far West Temple cornerstone, 587
Smith, Heber John, 728n1
Smith, Hyrum: mission call of, 11; counsel for, 13; revelation for, 27, 121, 162, 555–57; as witness, 101; Church building committee and, 387, 388; Kirtland Temple and, 391, 448; treasure hunting and, 605–8; taken prisoner, 619; incarcerated in Liberty Jail, 622n2; as Mason, 646; temple worship and, 654; called as patriarch, 655; plural marriage and, 682, 683; martyrdom of, 711
Smith, Hyrum M., 435n1, 507
Smith, Hyrum Mack, 728
Smith, Hyrum Mack Jr., 728n1
Smith, John, 663
Smith, John Schwartz, 728n1
Smith, Joseph: on knowledge, xvi–xvii, 700–701; as Church leader and prophet, 17, 23, 212, 267–69; Kirtland Temple visitation and, 23; on context and scripture study, 42; on parable of prodigal

Index

son, 42n5; radical Mormonism and, 48–53; methods of revelation for, 67–68; language limitations of, 70; weaknesses of, 74; birth of, 85; Manchester period and, 86–87; as worthy vessel, 91–92; endowment keys restored to, 106–8; relationship between Martin Harris and, 131n3; as seer and translator, 205; on organization of Church, 210–12; on murder, 261n2; healing of, 264–66; Saints commanded to uphold, 269; on false spirits, 297, 611; conflict between brethren and, 320; forgives Orson Hyde, 320–21n4; on Jesus Christ as Comforter, 353n1, 696n2; on God and eternal laws, 355n3; on spirits, 386n2; on Second Coming, 426–27; heals Lorenzo Young's son, 428–29; to defend Church, 491–92; on progression in spirit world, 503; code names for, 512; on Stephen Burnett, 516; as president of high priesthood, 523–25; receives reassurance for family, 525–27; as revelator, 526–27; visits Jackson County, 531–33; accused of adultery, 575; on prophets, 610; arrested in Far West, 627–29; on fulness of priesthood, 650; on baptisms for the dead, 672–73; on body of God, 695; on Zion and Second Coming, 699–700; on eternal laws, 701; on calling and election, 704, 705–6; on unpardonable sin, 704–5; eulogy to, 707–12; on African Americans, 732

Smith, Joseph F.: vision of spirit world, 32, 726–31; on "one mighty and strong," 341–42; on Spirit of God and Holy Ghost, 354n1; Aaronic Priesthood reorganization and, 438; on separation prior to resurrection, 730

Smith, Joseph Fielding: on restoration of priesthood, 198; on murder, 262; on Bible translation, 318n3; Word of Wisdom and, 366; on intelligences, 381, 382; on Elijah, 456; on progression in spirit world, 503; on priesthood and temple work, 650

Smith, Joseph F. Jr., 727n2

Smith, Joseph III, 447n2

Smith, Joseph Sr.: Manchester period and, 85–86; religious views of, 89–90; as witness, 101; revelation for, 121, 134–35; commanded to manage Williams farm, 312; generosity of, 371; sees Jesus Christ, 451n7; anointing of, 453; as patriarch, 732n1

Smith, Leonora, 728n1

Smith, Levira Annett Clark, 727

Smith, Lucy Mack: Manchester period and, 85–86; faith of, 89–90; on lost manuscript pages, 133; on Oliver Cowdery, 138; on Urim and Thummim, 145n1, 150n1, 159–60; on Book of Mormon witnesses, 194; on Edward Partridge, 230n4; on Sidney Rigdon, 369; on Kirtland Temple, 391–92; works to help support family, 667

Smith, Mary Fielding, 727

Smith, Mercy Josephine, 728–29

Smith, Rhoda Ann, 728n1

Smith, Robert, 728n1

Smith, Ruth, 728n1

Smith, Samuel H.: mission of, 11, 525; as witness, 101–2; revelation for, 121; Oliver Cowdery and, 138; baptism of, 162n1, 162n2; school of the prophets and, 357; Isaiah revelation and, 580

Smith, Sarah Ella, 728n1

Smith, Sarah Ellen Richards, 727

Smith, Sophronia, 694n1

Smith, William, 145n1, 145n3, 197n4

Smith, Zina, 728n1

Smoot, Reed, 48

Snow, Donald R., 502

Snow, Eliza R., 361, 449–50

Snow, Erastus, 608–9, 630

Snow, Lorenzo, 74, 450, 597–98, 645n2, 682

social injustice, 63–65

Solomon's Temple, 449

sons of Levi, 180–81

sons of perdition, 502, 503

Sorenson, John L., 538n1

"soup" theory of intelligence, 78n1, 382n3

Spencer, Orson, 734

spirit prison, 671–72

spirits: spirit children, 384; matter of, 386, 386n2, 705–6. *See also* false spirits

spiritual gifts, 18, 282–89

spirit world: vision of, 32, 726–31; death and, 81, 729; marriage and, 688–89; activities in, 696
Spring Hill, Missouri, 28
Stafford, John, 146n5
Stafford, Joshua, 146n5
Staker, Mark Lyman, 332, 546
stem of Jesse, 580
Stephens, Trent D., 225
stewardship. *See* consecration
stick of Ephraim, 177
stone, cut out of mountain, 476–77
storehouse, 508–13, 559
storm, protects Zion's Camp, 416–18
Stowell, Josiah, 87, 615
strong drinks, 364–65
study methods, 5–7
suffering, 621
Sweet, Northrup, 16, 226–28
swimming, missionaries and, 553–55
sword of Laban, 193–96
systemic injustice, 60–65

Talmage, James E., 337, 381, 503
Tanner, Nathan, 568
Tanner, N. Eldon, 365n1
Tate, George S., 729
Taylor, John: home of, 31; kingdom of God and, 54–55; school of the prophets and, 358; on alcohol use, 364; Quorum of the Seventy and, 439; lays Far West Temple cornerstone, 587; called to Twelve, 594; eulogy of, 707–12; Council of Fifty and, 708n2; after martyrdom, 720
tea, 365
telestial kingdom, 491, 500–501
temperance movement, 362–63
temple recommends, 657–58
temple(s): commandment to build, 328–29, 390–92, 537, 586–87; Solomon's Temple, 449; Far West Temple, 586–87, 656; Nauvoo Temple, 640–48; divine manifestations in, 645n2; Abrahamic covenant and, 653; prayer and, 654; rituals and, 654–55. *See also* endowment; Kirtland Temple
temple work: for the dead, 30, 180–82, 667–74; priesthood and, 109–10, 302–3,

649–52; restoration of keys for, 455–59; early Christians and, 648–49
tempting God, 160–61, 167–68, 315
Ten Commandments, 261–62
Ten Tribes, 457
terrestrial kingdom, 500
Tertullian, 699
Thayre, Ezra: mission call of, 16, 226–28, 312; criticism of, 19, 310, 311; French Farm and, 394
Thomas, Gospel of, 544n1
Thompson, Robert B., 180n3, 630
Three Witnesses, 90–91, 101, 193–200
tithing, 28, 253, 595–98
tobacco, 363, 364–65
Toronto incident, 613–15
transgression, as cause of persecution, 409–10. *See also* sin
translated beings, 141–42
translation: definition of, 12, 128, 139–40, 318n3; process for, 144–47, 213n1; Oliver Cowdery and, 147–48, 152–56; of Bible, 469, 474
translator, Joseph Smith as, 205, 212–13
treasure hunting, 87, 146n5, 605–12, 615–17
trials: warning of, 513; purpose of, 629
Trinity, 58, 206n3, 631n1, 695, 697
truth, 383–85
Turner, Jonathan B., 69n3
Turner, Nat, 279, 426

unanimity, 173–74, 434–37
Underhill, Samuel, 285–86, 363
Underwood, Grant, 338, 499
united orders: establishment of, 20, 374–75, 394–95; definition of, 273n2; common consent and, 422–25; consecration versus, 423n3; Sidney Rigdon and Newel K. Whitney form, 509; function of, 559n1. *See also* consecration
universal redemption, 504–5
universal revelation, 66–67, 212, 215–16n5
Urim and Thummim: context and, 41; revelation received through, 130–31; taken from Joseph Smith, 133; translation through, 144–47, 149–50; restored to

Index

Joseph Smith, 159–60; witnesses of, 193–96

Van Buren, Martin, 50, 641, 708n1
Van Wagoner, Richard S., 256, 294, 527
veil: seeing beyond, 485; help from beyond, 672–73
vineyard, parable of, 421
violence: renouncing, 22, 405–6, 572; against Mormons, 578, 618–19
vision(s): of celestial kingdom, 454; restoring priesthood keys, 455–59; of Satan on water, 553; Joseph Smith on, 611; of Twelve's sacrifices, 664n3

Wakefield, Joseph, 320, 491
Wall, William, 693–94n4
wars: Civil War, 20, 280, 345–49, 699; renouncing, 21, 398–406, 572; visions of, 351
Warsaw Signal (newspaper), 710
washing of feet, 338, 351, 357, 357n3
washings, 464
water: Satan and, 27; for sacrament, 175–77; missionary work and, 553–55
Waterloo, New York, 16
weaknesses: of Church leaders, 74–75; help for, 557
wealth: spiritual wealth, 163; Joseph Smith and, 167; as temptation, 260–61; equality in, 510–12
wedding feast, parable of, 544–46
Weeks, William, 642
Welch, John W., 97n1, 480
Wells, Seth Y., 369
Wentworth, John, 187n2
wheat and tares, parable of, 344–45
Whitlock, Harvey, 301, 478
Whitmer, Christian, 102, 483
Whitmer, David: revelation for, 14, 173–74, 191–93; mission call of, 15, 219–22; as witness, 90–91, 101, 193–96; disaffection of, 119n2; Urim and Thummim and, 150n1; on Book of Mormon, 159; travels to Colesville, 166; Joseph Knight Sr. and, 175; helps with Fayette move, 185–86; commandment to write to, 186n1; Quorum of the Twelve and, 196–200; high council and, 434n2; converts William McLellin, 478; Book of Commandments and, 483; excommunication of, 576, 576n3, 581, 594; Toronto incident and, 613, 615
Whitmer, Jacob, 102
Whitmer, John: revelation for, 14, 191–93; mission call of, 15, 219–22; called as Church Historian, 18, 289–90; Literary Firm and, 71, 273; as witness, 102; travels to Colesville, 166; Joseph Knight Sr. and, 175; on Church conference, 235; on consecration, 255, 320; on false revelations, 268; on false spirits, 283–84; responsibilities of, 340; letter from Joseph Smith to, 402–3; high council and, 434n2; Book of Commandments and, 482, 483, 490; commanded to keep history, 490; excommunication of, 576, 582
Whitmer, Nancy, 191
Whitmer, Peter, 14
Whitmer, Peter Jr.: mission call of, 15, 219–22; as witness, 102; revelation for, 191–93; Book of Commandments and, 483
Whitmer, Peter Sr., 186, 191–92, 483
Whitney, Elizabeth Ann Smith, 252n3
Whitney, Newel K.: home of, 17–18; store of, 19–21, 387–89; revelation for, 28; meets Joseph Smith, 252–53; called as bishop, 253, 274–75, 431–32; Joseph and Emma stay with, 277; Sidney Gilbert and, 306; fundraising efforts and, 314, 542; injury of, 325, 369; mission call of, 326–27; united orders and, 375; rebuked, 387; French Farm and, 393–94; sitting in council and, 512; on feast for poor, 546; bishop's storehouse and, 559n1; commanded to move to Far West, 589–92
widows, 27, 565
Widtsoe, John A.: on knowledge and progression, 355, 382n3; on Word of Wisdom, 367; on intelligences, 381, 382; on Garden of Eden, 601–4
Widtsoe, Leah D., 367
Wight, Lyman: conversion of, 222; sees Jesus Christ, 301; prophecies of, 304;

priesthood ordinations and, 330; on persecution in Missouri, 409; Zion's Camp and, 416; home of, 601n3; taken prisoner, 619; incarcerated in Liberty Jail, 622n2; on arrest of Joseph Smith, 627–29; arrest of, 635
Wilcox, Eber, 265
Wilkins, Catherine, 694n1
Williams, Frederick G.: on Lehi, 221n2, 225; conversion of, 224; Ezra Thayre and, 311; as scribe, 344; on high priest council, 352; school of the prophets and, 358; ordained as counselor, 368; united orders and, 374–75; rebuked, 387; on Kirtland Temple construction, 392; high council and, 434n2; called to high priesthood, 518; on Lamanites, 538n1; excommunication of, 594; on Church's financial difficulties, 607
Williams, Levi, 704
Winder, John R., 342
wine: for sacrament, 175–77; Word of Wisdom and, 364
Winter Quarters, Nebraska, 31, 721
witnesses: of Book of Mormon, 10, 90–91, 99–104; Martin Harris as, 136–37; revelation for, 193–96
women: to be supported by husbands, 27, 565; in nineteenth century, 172–73; temple ordinances and, 651–52
Wood, Wilford C., 605
Woodford, Robert, 210, 674, 681
Woodruff, Wilford: plural marriage and, 32; history of, 54; Kirtland Temple and, 452; on progression in spirit world, 502–3; on Sabbath day, 548; lays Far West Temple cornerstone, 587; called to Twelve, 594; temple recommends and, 657; baptisms for the dead and, 670; discernment of spirits and, 675; mission call of, 720; ends plural marriage, 724–26; vision of, 737
Word of Wisdom, 20, 176–77, 362–67, 657–58, 716n2
worldviews, 76–82, 383–85
World War I, 729
worship, purpose of, 380
worthy vessels, 12–14, 91–92

Wright, N. T., 76, 383
Yancey, William, 348
Young, Brigham, 733–34; temple cornerstone and, 28; missionary work and, 30, 664–66; on contextualization of scriptures, 39–40; on Bible, 114–15; sees Joseph in spirit, 143n3; organization of Church and, 198; communal orders and, 258; on temporal and spiritual salvation, 286; forgives Orson Hyde, 322n4; on section 87, 347; school of the prophets and, 358; Word of Wisdom and, 363, 366; united orders and, 375, 394–95, 424; on Thomas B. Marsh, 460, 461–62; on degrees of glory, 498; on progression in spirit world, 502; consecration and, 560; moves to Far West, 576; faith of, 582; lays Far West Temple cornerstone, 587; ordains Oliver Granger, 592n3; on Garden of Eden, 600n6; on accuracy of prophecies, 610–11; on testimony of leaders, 612; Committee on Removal and, 636; on priesthood and temple work, 650–51; appointed president of Twelve, 655; plural marriage and, 683, 726; performs sealing, 687n4; presidential campaign and, 708n1; Council of Fifty and, 708n2; revelation on exodus given to, 719–23; transfigured to look like Joseph Smith, 720; on African Americans, 733–34
Young, Joseph, 592n3
Young, Lorenzo Dow, 428
Young, William G., 687n4

Zarahemla, Iowa, 663
Zeezrom, 117n1
Zion: gathering in, 19; Jackson County as, 19, 531–33, 537–39; inheritance in, 20, 339–44; building, 21, 327, 522–23; location of, 26, 217; as early objective, 44; Joseph Smith and, 49–50; systemic injustice and, 61, 65; consecration and, 236; Second Coming and, 276–80, 558; Millennium and, 281; land purchases for, 291; temples in, 328–29; layout and plan for, 389–90; obedience and, 395–98, 420–21; location and definition of,

534–35, 588; disappointment over, 535–36; instructions for organizing, 539–46; love as characteristic of, 551; organizing, 560–63; failure of, 571; redeeming, 572; timing of, 573; Far West as, 585; temple symbolism and, 654n1

Zion's Camp: organization of, 22, 401; commandment to disband, 27, 570–73; Ezra Thayre and, 227n4; cholera epidemic and, 265–67; revelation on, 416–22; overview of, 567–69; failure of, 571

www.ingramcontent.com/pod-product-compliance
Lightning Source LLC
Chambersburg PA
CBHW060746230426
43667CB00010B/1456